ALL · IN · ONE

CISSP
Certification

EXAM GUIDE

ALL · IN · ONE

CISSP
Certification

EXAM GUIDE

Shon Harris

McGraw-Hill / Osborne

New York • Chicago • San Francisco • Lisbon
London • Madrid • Mexico City • Milan • New Delhi
San Juan • Seoul • Singapore • Sydney • Toronto

McGraw-Hill/Osborne
2600 Tenth Street
Berkeley, California 94710
U.S.A.

To arrange bulk purchase discounts for sales promotions, premiums, or fund-raisers, please contact **McGraw-Hill**/Osborne at the above address. For information on translations or book distributors outside the U.S.A., please see the International Contact Information page immediately following the index of this book.

CISSP All-in-One Certification Exam Guide

234567890 DOC DOC 0198765432

Book p/n 0-07-219354-9 and CD p/n 0-07-219355-7
parts of

ISBN 0-07-219353-0

Publisher
Brandon A. Nordin

Vice President & Associate Publisher
Scott Rogers

Acquisitions Editor
Michael Sprague

Senior Project Editor
Betsy Manini

Acquisitions Coordinator
Alexander Corona

Technical Editor
Christopher King

Full-Service Compositor
MacAllister Publishing Services, LLC

This book was composed with QuarkXpress™.

DEDICATION

May more people in this world have the integrity
and the gentle loving strength of **George Fairbairn**, my Grandpa.

Shon Harris, MCSE, CISSP, is a security consultant who provides security assessments and analysis, vulnerability testing, and solutions to a wide range of different businesses. She is a member of the Information Warfare unit in the Air Force, which performs military base assessments and 'red-teaming' activities during aggressor exercises.

Shon is a contributing writer to *Information Security Magazine* and *Windows 2000* magazine and a contributing author to *Hacker's Challenge: Test Your Incident Response Skills Using 20 Scenarios*, by Mike Schiffman (McGraw-Hill/Osborne, 2001). She also teaches networking and security classes at different local colleges. You can contact Shon at shonharris@hotmail.com.

BRIEF CONTENTS

CONTENTS

FOREWORD

Information security, in today's world, is somewhat of an oxymoron. As applications and systems hit the market at a rapid-fire pace, there is less time to assess them for security. We are quickly learning from experiences like *CodeRed* and *Nimda* that we need to look deeper, but where do we start? This is a good question with a multitude of answers, all of which lead back to educating our IT force in security awareness.

In 1999, McClure, Scambray, and Kurtz introduced the IT industry to the mind of a hacker with the book *Hacking Exposed* (McGraw-Hill, Osborne). They identified a trend that was overtaking the world and provided the first published bible of defense. The Computer Emergency Response Team (CERT) formed in 1988 and dealt with six reported incidents involving information security their first year; in the first three quarters of 2001, there were 85,334. We must act on that unbelievable statistic. Complacency is not an option; efficiency in education is the key. The IT industry is growing much faster than we can educate our people to maintain it. This leaves less time for the average IT specialist and security professional to "discover" new security practices and procedures and more time for hackers to learn how to get around them. We must provide our IT specialists with the tools required to maintain a secure information system without putting their company in debt with incident recovery costs and professional consultation fees. The only way we can do that is through documentation and education.

Only a handful of books exclusively outline good practices for network security. Of those books, none of them give a practical snapshot of how systems should be set up in order to efficiently and predictably balance risk with service. In the CERT's first 11 years of existence, no one provided a complete doctrine on how to design, implement, and maintain secure information systems. The lack of standardization for security professionals inspired the formation of the International Information Systems Security Certifications Consortium, Inc. (ISC)², home of the Certified Information Systems Security Professional (CISSP) certification. This is the first nonvendor specific security certification introduced to the IT industry and security world.

The need for standard guidelines on information security formed by many is much like teamwork versus individual effort. We can produce more results collectively than we can independently. We need to build a wall between our information and those that want to exploit it. Standardization and collaboration is the key to success. Without it, we are an unorganized force of chaos desperately grasping at our data as it flies by us into the wrong hands.

The CISSP All-In-One Study Guide you are about to read will bring you intimately close to information and network security. The author writes this book based on her broad range of experience in network and application security resulting from her work with the international banking industry and as a network aggressor for the Information Warfare group in the military. She has immeasurable passion for this industry. She will entertain you with her wit and beguile you with her knowledge. If your goal is to avoid becoming a CERT statistic, you have come to the right place.

Joseph Kowtko
Information Security Specialist—Network Engineering
Infrastructure Manager for the Financial Solutions Group Logistics
Getronics

ACKNOWLEDGMENTS

I would like to thank **Sam Tomaino** for attempting to explain to me many, many years ago how computers work. **Dan Ferguson** for never complaining about the bombardment of questions I continually fling his way and for fostering my never ceasing curiosity and quest of knowledge. And **Joe Kowtko** for the insight into the computing world and life in general that he continually provides me. Each one of these people has helped me write this book in more ways than they will ever know.

And most especially, I would like to thank my husband, **David Harris,** for his continual support and love. Without his steadfast confidence in me, I would not be able to accomplish half the things I have taken on in this lifetime.

INTRODUCTION

Computer, information, and physical security are becoming more important at an exponential rate since the tragedies of September 11, 2001. Over the last few years, the necessity for computer and information security has slowly been realized as Web sites are being defaced, denial-of-service attacks increase, credit card information being stolen, the increased sophistication of hacking tools that are openly available to the public, and the increased damage today's viruses and worms are causing.

Companies have had to spend millions of dollars to clean up the effects of these issues and millions of more dollars to secure their perimeter and internal networks with equipment, software, consultants, and education. But after September 11, 2001, the necessity and urgency for this type of security has taken on a new paradigm. It is slowly becoming apparent that governments, nations, and societies are vulnerable to many different types of attacks that can happen over the network wire and air waves. These societies depend heavily on all types of computing power and functionality that is mostly provided by the public and private sectors. This means that although the governments are responsible for protecting their citizens, they are slowly becoming apparent that the citizens and their businesses must become more secure to protect the nation as a whole.

This type of protection can really only *begin* through proper education and understanding and it must continue with a dedicated execution of this knowledge. This book is written to provide a foundation to the many different areas that make up effective security. We are all in a different time and place after September 11, for better or worse, and we all need to understand *all* of the threats and dangers we are vulnerable to and the steps that need to be taken to mitigate these vulnerabilities.

Reasons to Become a CISSP

In this chapter, you will learn the following information:

- The reasons to become a CISSP
- What the CISSP exam entails
- What the Common Body of Knowledge contains
- The history of $(ISC)^2$ and the CISSP exam
- Recertification requirements
- You will also be able to take a preassessment test to gauge your current computer and information security knowledge.

To properly study for the Certified Information Systems Security Professional (CISSP) exam, you must read a stack of books to ensure that you have studied all the necessary areas this test covers. You are required to have at least three years of experience in one of several domains of information security. This book is intended to combine the information from a large number of resources necessary for passing the CISSP exam into one resource. The exam covers ten domains and each domain is a full field of study that has several books and papers written on just that subject. This book attempts to extract the necessary information out of many different types of sources for each domain that is required to pass the CISSP exam, and works to serve as a reference that can be used long after you achieve the CISSP certification.

This book also is intended to welcome you to the exciting world of information security and start you on a new path toward obtaining your CISSP certification!

Why Become a CISSP?

Security is a hot issue in not only the security and technology field, but also in any organization that has computers hooked up to a network. Computer and information security used to be an obscure term known only by a few and the demand was not high because the risks were low and hacking was not a common event. However, today a majority of corporations and organizations are in a desperate search for talented and experienced security professionals to help them protect the resources that keep their companies alive and competitive. This certification identifies you as a security professional who has successfully met a predefined standard of knowledge and experience. Keeping this certificate current shows that you are one who is interested in keeping abreast of the current security technologies and events relevant to practicing information security.

The CISSP certification helps companies identify individuals who have the technical ability, knowledge, and experience to implement solid security practices, perform risk analysis, identify necessary countermeasures, and help the organization as a whole protect its facility, network, systems, and information. The CISSP certification also provides security professionals with the credential that acknowledges the skill set that they want to offer to employers. Today, a greater demand is put on security as an integral part of corporate success. This, in turn, increases the demand for highly skilled security professionals. The CISSP certification shows that a formalized organization recognizes an individual's technical and theoretical security expertise and distinguishes that individual from the rest.

Many times security is an essential part of being a good network administrator, programmer, or engineer. Many job descriptions that are not targeting specific security professionals mention security as an important concept for a potential candidate to understand and be able to implement to acquire the open position. Many organizations cannot afford a network staff and a security staff, but they understand that security has a very important place in many aspects of technology. Therefore, combining security knowledge with other technical knowledge can put you ahead of other individuals who do not possess this type of insight! There are many reasons to achieve a CISSP certification:

- Meet a growing demand and thrive in an exploding field.
- Expand your current knowledge of security concepts and practices.
- Bring security expertise to your current occupation.
- Become more marketable in this competitive workforce.

- Show a dedication to the security discipline.
- Increase salaries and different employment opportunities.

The CISSP Exam

The CISSP exam covers ten domains that make up the Common Body of Knowledge (CBK). This exam is commonly described as an inch deep and a mile wide, meaning that the questions are not necessarily very detailed in nature and do not require you to be a complete expert in each and every subject; however, the questions do require you to be familiar with many different subjects within the security arena.

The CISSP exam is made up of 250 multiple-choice questions and you are given up to six hours to complete it. These questions are chosen from a large question bank to ensure that the exams are as unique as possible for each person. Each question has four choices with only one right answer. Only 225 questions are scored; the remaining 25 questions are for research purposes only. These 25 questions are not distinguished from the questions that will be scored, so you will not know which questions are counted towards your overall grade. The passing score is 70 percent of the 225 questions. The exam is not product- or vendor-oriented; therefore, you will not have specific Windows NT or Unix questions asked of you, but you will be asked about the security models and methodologies used by these types of systems. As of this writing, the exam fee is $450.

To qualify to take the CISSP exam, you must have three years of direct work experience in one or more of the ten domains that make up the CBK. You are asked to supply the information that proves you indeed have this type of experience. This helps ensure that someone who achieves the certification has real-world experience to offer companies. There is nothing like a paper certification to bring down the value of the certification for everyone. Book knowledge is extremely important for theory, concepts, and understanding standards and regulations, but it will never take the place of real, hands-on experience.

What makes this exam challenging is that most individuals who work in the security field are not familiar with all ten domains. If a security professional is considered an expert in vulnerability testing or application security, she may not be familiar with physical security, cryptography, or security practices. Studying for this exam will stretch your boundaries of knowledge within the security field.

The exam questions address each of the following security domains that make up the CBK. These are shown in Table 1-1.

Table 1-1   Security Domains That Make Up the CBK

Domain	Description
Access Control Systems and Methodology	This domain examines mechanisms and methods used to enable administrators and managers to control what users can access, the extent of their capabilities after authentication and authorization, and the auditing and monitoring of these activities.
	Some of the topics covered include
	• Access control security models
	• Identification and authentication technologies and techniques
	• Access control administration
	• Data ownership
	• Attack methods
Telecommunications and Network Security	This domain examines internal, external, public, and private communication systems; networking structures; devices; protocols; and remote access and administration.
	Some of the topics covered include
	• OSI model and layers
	• Local area network (LAN), metropolitan area network (MAN), and wide area network (WAN) technologies
	• Internet, intranet, and extranet issues
	• Virtual private networks (VPNs), firewalls, routers, bridges, and repeaters
	• Network topologies and cabling
	• Attack methods
Security Management Practices	This domain examines the identification of company assets, the proper way to determine the necessary level of protection required, and what type of budget to develop for security implementations with the goal of reducing threats and monetary loss.
	Some of the topics covered include
	• Data classification
	• Policies, procedures, standards, and guidelines
	• Risk assessment and management
	• Personnel security, training, and awareness

Domain	Description
Application and Systems Development Security	This domain examines the security components with operating systems and applications and how to best develop and measure their effectiveness. This domain looks at software life cycles, change control, and application security.
	Some of the topics covered include
	• Data warehousing and data mining
	• Different development practices and their risks
	• System storage and processing components
	• System development life cycle
	• Malicious code
Cryptography	This domain examines methods and techniques for disguising data for protection purposes. This involves different cryptography techniques, approaches, and technologies.
	Some of the topics covered include
	• Symmetric versus asymmetric algorithms and uses
	• Public key infrastructure (PKI), Kerberos, and hashing functions
	• Encryption protocols and implementation
	• Attack methods
Security Architecture and Models	This domain examines concepts, principles, and standards for designing and implementing secure applications, operating systems, and systems. This covers international security measurement standards and their meaning for different types of platforms.
	Some of the topics covered include
	• Operating states, kernel functions, and memory mapping
	• Security models, architectures, and evaluations
	• Evaluation criteria — Trusted Computer Security Evaluation Criteria (TCSEC), Information Technology Security Evaluation Criteria (ITSEC), and Common Criteria
	• Common flaws in applications and systems
Operations Security	This domain examines controls over personnel, hardware, systems, and auditing and monitoring techniques. This also covers possible abuse channels and how to recognize and address them.
	Some of the topics covered include
	• Administrative responsibilities pertaining to personnel and job functions
	• Maintenance concepts of antivirus, training, auditing, and resource protection activities
	• Directive, preventative, detective, corrective, and recovery controls
	• Standards compliance and due care concepts

(continued)

Table 1-1   Security Domains That Make Up the CBK *(continued)*

Domain	Description
Business Continuity Planning and Disaster Recovery Planning	This domain examines the preservation of business activities when faced with disruptions or disasters. This involves the identification of real risks, proper risk assessment, and countermeasure implementation. Some of the topics covered include • Business resource identification and value assignment • Business impact analysis and prediction of possible losses • Unit priorities and crisis management • Plan development, implementation, and maintenance
Laws, Investigations, and Ethics	This domain examines computer crimes, laws, and regulations. This includes techniques in investigating a crime, evidence gathering, and handling procedures. It also covers how to develop and implement an incident-handling program. Some of the topics covered include • Laws, regulations, and crimes • Licensing and software piracy • Export and import laws and issues • Evidence types and admissibility into court • Incident handling
Physical Security	This domain examines threats, risks, and countermeasures to protect facilities, hardware, data, media, and personnel. This involves facility selection, authorized entry methods, and environmental and safety procedures. Some of the topics covered include • Restricted areas, authorization methods and controls • Motion detectors, sensors, and alarms • Intrusion detection • Fire detection, prevention, and suppression • Fencing, security guards, and security badge types

The International Information Systems Security Certification Consortium, or (ISC)², attempts to keep up with the changes in technology and methodologies brought to the security field by adding 100 to 150 new questions to the test question bank each year. These questions are based on current technologies, practices, approaches, and standards. So, for example, the CISSP exam given in 1998 did not have wireless security questions, but future exams will most likely contain wireless security topics because of its evolution and most recent importance to the technology industry.

Although the test is given only in English at this time, this does not mean it is exclusive to only certain countries or regions. The test is based on internationally accepted information security standards and practices, and the same English language version is given throughout the world. If you look at the (ISC)^2 Web site for test dates and locations, you will find that this Tuesday, a test may be offered in California and next Wednesday, the same test may be offered in Saudi Arabia. The test is offered in many states and countries for your testing preference.

In the event that you do not pass the exam, you can retake it as soon as you would like. (ISC)^2 used to restrict individuals to a waiting period before attempting the exam again, but this rule has been removed. Of course, it is better to take the time to properly study and go over the areas that you were weak in, but if you would like to give (ISC)^2 another $450 for the very next testing date, I am sure they will happily accept it.

CISSP—A Brief History

Computer security has suffered a history of confused perception and ill-defined professional objectives and purposes instead of a structured and disciplined profession.

In the mid-1980s, it was recognized that a certification program was needed to bring structure to the information security profession and provide ways of demonstrating competence and providing evidence of qualifications. This effort would help the credibility of the computer security profession as a whole and the individuals who make up the profession.

The Special Interest Group for Computer Security (SIG-CS) of the Data Processing Management Association (DPMA) brought several organizations that were interested in forming a security certification program together in November 1988. The organizations included the Information Systems Security Association (ISSA), the Canadian Information Processing Society (CIPS), the Computer Security Institute (CSI), Idaho State University, and several U.S. and Canadian government agencies. As a voluntary joint effort, these organizations developed the necessary components needed to offer a full-fledged security certification for interested professionals. The (ISC)^2 was formed in mid-1989 as a nonprofit corporation to develop a security certification program for information systems security practitioners. The certification was envisioned to measure professional competence and help companies in their selection of security professionals and personnel. The (ISC)^2 was established in North America, but has quickly gained international acceptance and offers training and testing capabilities all over the world.

Because security is a broad subject and can cover many different areas within the technology and business worlds, the group decided upon an information systems security CBK, which is made up of ten domains pertaining to every part of computer, network, and information security. In addition, because technology continues at a fast pace of change and evolution, staying current on security trends, technology, and business developments is a requirement to maintaining the CISSP certification. The group developed a Code of Ethics, test specifications, a draft study guide, an eight-day training seminar, and the exam itself.

How Do You Become a CISSP?

To become a CISSP, you must register for the exam at **www.isc2.org**. You will be asked to fill out your security work history to ensure that you have at least three years of experience in one of the ten domains that the test covers. You will also be asked to agree to follow the (ISC)² Code of Ethics and sign a form indicating that you understand these requirements and promise to abide by them. Then you send the (ISC)² a check for $450 and indicate when you would like to take the exam and at what location. The different testing sites and dates are listed at **www.isc2.org**.

Although three years of related experience is required, it can be experience that was accrued over time; thus, you do not need to have performed related security tasks for three years in a row. The (ISC)² accepts the following work history as valid experience to qualify individuals to take the test:

- Security investigator
- Security practitioner
- Information systems (IS) security-related work
- Security auditor
- Security consultant
- Security vendor
- Security instructor

Recertification Requirements

To renew your CISSP certification, you will not be required to retake exams, like Microsoft and Cisco require, but you do need to earn continuing professional education (CPE) credits. Maintaining a CISSP certification requires earning 120 CPE credits over a three-year recertification period. If you are not interested in earning the 120 credits, you can retake and pass the exam every three years to maintain your certification.

There are many types of activities that can qualify for CPE credits and they are broken down into two main sections: activities directly related to information security and educational activities that enhance a security professional's skill and knowledge.

Further Explanation of CPE Activities and Associated Credits

The following items can count as CPEs to keep your CISSP certification current:

- **Vendor training course** CISSPs can earn one CPE for each hour of attendance in a vendor training course, seminar, or presentation.

- **Security conference** CISSPs can earn one CPE for each hour of attendance at a security conference.

- **University or college security course** CISSPs can earn 11.5 CPEs per semester hour completed with a passing grade at an accredited college or university.

- **Publish a security article or book** CISSPs can earn 40 CPEs for publishing a security book or ten CPEs for publishing a security article. A maximum of 40 CPEs can be earned this way over a three-year period.

- **Provide security training** CISSPs can earn four CPEs per each hour spent per subject taught, lectured on, and presented. A maximum of 80 CPEs can be earned this way per year.

- **Serve on a board of a professional security organization** CISSPs can earn ten CPEs per year of service. A maximum of 20 CPEs can be earned in this way for service on more than one qualifying organization.

- **Self-study** CISSPs can earn CPEs for self-study activities. A maximum of 40 CPEs can be earned this way over a three-year period.

- **Read a security book** CISSPs can earn ten CPEs for reading an information security book. Only one book per year will be accepted.

- **Volunteer work** CISSPs can earn CPEs for volunteer work done on behalf of the $(ISC)^2$. The activities and credits earned are determined by the $(ISC)^2$.

- **Exceptions**   If a CISSP would like to offer a different type of activity used to gain CPEs, this must be submitted to the Recertification Committee via the $(ISC)^2$ for approval.

CISSPs have up to 120 days after the end of the certificate holder's three-year recertification cycle to complete the necessary requirements. Any CPEs exceeding the amount required that were achieved during the last six months of the recertification cycle are carried forward for credit towards the next cycle.

Along with providing the necessary level of CPEs, CISSPs are required to pay an $85 annual maintenance fee that is due 12 months after the exam is taken and each following year.

What Does This Book Cover?

This book covers everything you need to know to become an $(ISC)^2$-certified CISSP. It teaches you how and why corporations develop and implement policies, procedures, guidelines, and standards. It goes over network, application, and system vulnerabilities, what exploits them, and how to countermeasure these exploits. The book explains physical security, operational security, and why systems implement the security mechanisms that they do. It also reviews U.S. and international security criteria and evaluations that are performed on systems for security ratings, what these criteria mean, and why they are used. This book also explains the legal and liability issues that surround computer systems and the data that they hold, security crimes, forensics, and what should be done to properly prepare computer evidence for court.

This book is meant to be a study guide for the CISSP exam, but it is also meant to be used after you achieve your certification as an important and irreplaceable resource.

Tips for Taking the CISSP Exam

The test is 250 questions and you are given up to six hours to take it. Depending on the facility that hosts the test, you may not be allowed to bring in food or drinks, so plan ahead and eat a good breakfast full of protein for brainpower. Restroom breaks are usually limited to only allowing one person to leave at a time, so drinking 15 cups of coffee right before the exam might not be the best idea.

The questions are not long, which is good because the test has so many questions, but this also means you get less information about what they are really asking for. Make sure to read the question and the answers thoroughly instead of reading a few words and assuming you know what they are looking for right off the bat. Some of the answers can be subtly different from the others, so give yourself the time and patience to read through the question more than once. Like most tests, it is best to go through the questions and answers the ones that you know and come back to the ones that are causing you more difficulty. The CISSP exam is not computerized, so you will see a piece of paper with bubbles to fill in. I know you haven't seen those since the SAT, but they are back. The reason I bring this up is because if you scribble outside the lines, the machine that reads your answers may count a right question wrong. So I suggest that you go through each question and mark the right answer in the booklet with the questions, if the host allows this, and then go through the questions again and fill in the bubble only when you are sure of the answer. This causes less erasing and potential problems for the scoring machine.

When you are finished, take an extra two minutes to make sure you answered each question and that you did not accidentally fill in two bubbles for one question. Unfortunately, you will not receive the results of your test right away. They tell you that it can take up to six weeks, but the average is two to three weeks to receive your results in the mail. When you receive your results, you can find out if you passed before you even open the envelope because the address has your name and the credential "CISSP" following it if you passed. If you do not pass, this can be a frustrating ordeal, but know that some very smart and talented security professionals did not pass on their first try, mainly because the test covers so many broad topics.

If you passed the exam, the results sent to you will not contain your score; you will only know that you successfully passed. If you did not pass the exam, the results will have a breakdown of each domain, showing you where your weak areas are.

One of the most commonly heard complaints about this exam is the exam itself. The questions are not long winded, like many Microsoft tests, but at times it is difficult to decipher between two answers that seem to say the same thing. It has also been stated that the test seems to be a bit subjective. I do not say this to criticize the (ISC)^2 and the people who write the test, I only say it to you to help you better prepare for the test. This book covers all the necessary material for the test, but it also contains many questions and self-practice tests. Many of these questions are formatted in a way to better prepare you for what you will see on the test. For example, it might be easier to answer a technical question that asks for the exact mechanism used in Secure Sockets Layer (SSL) that protects against man-in-the-middle attacks than a question that asks you if an eight-foot perimeter fence provides low, medium, or high security. So make sure to read all the material in the book, but also pay close attention to the questions and their formats. Some questions can be missed, even if you know the subject quite well—it is part of learning how to take tests in general.

Familiarize yourself with industry standards and expand your technical knowledge and methodology outside the boundaries of what you use today. I cannot stress enough that just because you are the top dog in your particular field, it does not ensure that you are properly prepared for each and every domain this exam covers. Run through the assessment test in this chapter to gauge where you stand and be ready to read a lot of material you have not read before.

How to Use This Book

A lot of effort has gone into putting all the necessary information into this book; now it is up to you to put a lot of effort into extracting information out of the book. To best benefit from this book, you might want to use the following study method:

1. Study each chapter carefully and make sure you understand each concept presented. There are many concepts you need to fully understand and glossing over a couple here and there could be detrimental in the end.

2. Make sure to study and answer all of the questions at the end of the chapter and on the CD included with the book. If any of the questions confuse you, go back and study those sections again. Remember, some of the questions on the actual exam are a bit confusing because they do not seem straightforward. I have attempted to do the same on several questions to prepare you for this. So do not ignore the confusing questions thinking I do not know how to form questions well, but pay even closer attention to them because they are there for a very distinct purpose.

3. If you are not familiar with specific topics like firewalls, security laws, physical security, or protocol functionality, read other articles or books to give yourself a more in-depth perception and understanding about those subjects instead of only what you think you need to know to pass the CISSP exam.

4. After reading the book, study the questions and answers, and take the practice tests. Then review the (ISC)^2 study guide and make sure you are comfortable with each bullet item presented. If there are some items you are not comfortable with, revisit those chapters.

5. If you have taken other certification exams like Cisco, Novell, or Microsoft, you might be used to having to memorize details and configuration parameters, but remember this test is an inch deep and a mile wide, so make sure you understand the concepts of each of the subjects *before* trying to memorize the small, specific details.

References

www.isc2.org

www.gocsi.com/cissp.htm

www.cissps.com

www.cccure.org/

Questions

To get a better feel for your level of expertise and your current level of readiness for the CISSP exam, run through the following questions:

1. What is derived from a passphrase?
   a. Personal password
   b. Virtual password
   c. User ID
   d. Valid password

2. Which access control method is user-directed?
   a. Non-discretionary
   b. Mandatory
   c. Identity-based
   d. Discretionary

3. Which item is not part of a Kerberos authentication implementation?
   a. Message Authentication Code
   b. Ticket granting ticket
   c. Authentication service
   d. Users, programs, and services

4. If a company has a high turnover rate, which access control structure is best?
   a. Role-based
   b. Decentralized
   c. Rule-based
   d. Discretionary

5. In discretionary access control, who/what has delegation authority to grant access to data?
   a. User
   b. Security officer
   c. Security policy
   d. Owner

6. Remote access using a one-time password scheme is an example of which of the following?
   a. Something you have
   b. Something you know
   c. Something you are
   d. Two-factor authentication

7. What is a crossover error rate?
   a. Rating used to rank a biometric system
   b. The number of Type I errors
   c. The number of Type II errors
   d. The number reached when Type I errors exceed the number of Type II errors

8. What does a retina scan do?
   a. Examines the pattern, color, and shading of the area around the cornea
   b. Examines the patterns and records the similarities between an individual's eyes
   c. Examines the pattern of blood vessels at the back of the eye
   d. Examines the geometry of the eyeball

9. If you are using a synchronous token device, what does this mean?
   a. The device synchronizes with the authentication service by using internal time or events.
   b. The device synchronizes with the user's workstation to ensure that the credentials it sends to the authentication service are correct.
   c. The device synchronizes with the token to ensure that the timestamp is valid and correct.
   d. The device synchronizes by using a challenge-response method with the authentication service.

10. What is a clipping level?
    a. Threshold for an activity
    b. Size of control zone

c. Explicit rules of authorization

d. Physical security mechanism

11. Which intrusion detection system would monitor user and network behavior?

a. Statistical

b. Signature-based

c. Static IDS

d. Host-based

12. When should a Class C fire extinguisher be used instead of Class A?

a. When electrical equipment is on fire

b. When wood and paper is on fire

c. When a combustible liquid is on fire

d. When the fire is in an open area

13. How does Halon fight fires?

a. It reduces the fire's fuel intake.

b. It reduces the temperature of the area.

c. It disrupts the chemical reactions of a fire.

d. It reduces the oxygen in the area.

14. What is the optimal temperature for a room that performs data processing?

a. 70 to 74 degrees Fahrenheit

b. 65 to 70 degrees Fahrenheit

c. 70 to 75 degrees Fahrenheit

d. 60 to 65 degrees Fahrenheit

15. What is the definition of a power fault?

a. Prolonged loss of power

b. Momentary low voltage

c. Prolonged high voltage

d. Momentary power outage

16. Who has the primary responsibility of determining the classification level for information?

a. Functional manager

b. Senior management

c. Owner

d. User

17. Which best describes the purpose of the ALE calculation?
    a. Quantifies the security level of the environment
    b. Estimates the loss potential from a risk
    c. Quantifies the cost/benefit result
    d. Estimates the loss potential from a risk in a year span

18. How do you calculate residual risk?
    a. Threats × risks × asset value
    b. (Threats × asset value × vulnerability) × risks
    c. SLE × frequency = ALE
    d. (Threats × vulnerability × asset value) × control gap

19. What is the Delphi method?
    a. A way of calculating the cost/benefit ratio for safeguards
    b. A way of allowing individuals to express their opinions anonymously
    c. A way of allowing groups to discuss and collaborate on the best security approaches
    d. A way of performing a qualitative risk analysis

20. What are the necessary components of a smurf attack?
    a. Web server, attacker, and fragment offset
    b. Fragment offset, amplifying network, and victim
    c. Victim, amplifying network, and attacker
    d. DNS server, attacker, and Web server

21. In phone freaking, what is a red box?
    a. Voltage manipulation
    b. Replaying the noise coins make when dropping into a pay phone
    c. Using a hand-held device attached to a live phone wire to intercept calls
    d. Tone manipulation

22. What does the reference monitor do in an operating system?
    a. Intercepts subjects attempting to access objects
    b. Points virtual memory addresses to real memory addresses
    c. Houses and protects the security kernel
    d. Monitors privileged memory usage by applications

Answers

1. B.

2. D.

3. A.

4. A.

5. D.

6. A.

7. A.

8. C.

9. A.

10. A.

11. A.

12. A.

13. C.

14. A.

15. D.

16. C.

17. D.

18. D.

19. B.

20. C.

21. B.

22. A.

Security Trends

In this chapter, you will learn about the following items:

- Evolution of computing and how it relates to security
- Different areas that fall under the security umbrella
- Information warfare
- Recent security exploits
- A layered approach to security
- Politics that affect security

Security is a broad and fascinating topic because it covers so many different areas (physical, network, platform, and application), each with it own risks, threats, and solutions. When information security is discussed, it is usually about hackers and operating system vulnerabilities. Although these are big parts of security, they are only two components within a large sea of security issues. Hacking is thought about most because that is what is in the news and the headlines. Hacking is flashy and newsworthy, while not much coverage is given to all that is going on behind the scenes that pertains to corporations' global security issues and the Internet as a whole.

Security Trends

It is interesting to pick up different computer books and see that there is usually some type of history section in the beginning that sets the stage of what happened in the past and where society is today pertaining to computing and data processing. The interesting part is that the history dates start with the 1970s or so when other histories usually start in the B.C. time frame or in the 1800s or 1900s. A lot has happened in a short period of time, and computer security is just starting to reach its time in the limelight.

Twenty years ago the only computers were mainframes. They were few and far between and used for specialized tasks, usually running large batch jobs and complex computations. If users were connected to the mainframes, it was through dumb terminals that had limited functionality and were totally dependent on the mainframe for its operations and processing environment. This was a *closed environment* with little risk of security breaches or vulnerabilities being exploited. This does not mean that things were perfect, that security vulnerabilities did not exist, and that people were in a computing utopia. Instead, it meant there were a handful of guys working in a "glass house" who were the only ones who knew how to operate the computer, who configured it, and who decided who could access the mainframe and when.

In the days of mainframes, there were not Web sites describing the steps of how to break into a specific application or operating system. The network stacks and protocols being used were not as fully understood by such a vast amount of people as they are today. There were no point-and-click utilities that could overwhelm buffers or interrogate ports. This was a truly closed environment that only a select few understood. If networks were connected, it was done in a crude fashion for specific tasks, and corporations did not totally depend on data processing as they do today. The operating systems of that time had problems, software bugs, and vulnerabilities, but not many people were interested in taking advantage of them. Computer operators were at the command line and if they encountered a software problem, they usually just went in and manually changed the programming code. That was not that long ago, considering where we are today.

As companies became more dependent upon the computing power of the mainframes, the functionality of the systems grew and different applications were developed; it was clear that only giving employees small time slices of access to the mainframes was not as productive as it could be. Processing and computing power was brought closer to the employees, enabling them to run small jobs on their desk computers while the big jobs still took place within the "glass house." This trend continued and the individual computers became more independent and autonomous, only needing to access the mainframe for specific functionality.

As individual personal computers became more efficient, they continually took on more tasks and responsibilities. It was shown that several users accessing a mainframe was inefficient and that some major components needed to be more readily available to the users in order to perform their tasks in an efficient and effective way. This thinking brought along the birth of the client-server model. Although many of the individual personal computers had the processing power to compute their own calculations and perform their own logic operations, it did not make sense that each of the computers held information that was needed by all computers. Programs and data were centralized on servers with individual computers accessing them when necessary and accessing the mainframes less frequently, as shown in Figure 2-1.

As computing and processing was brought closer to the people, the individuals who used computers learned more about the technology. This knowledge was necessary to properly use the technology and for the technology to become actually useful. However, a majority of the good things in life have a darker side. Bringing technology down from the pedestal of the mainframe and into so many individuals' hands brought on a lot of issues that never had to be dealt with in the mainframe days. Now there were thousands of people not versed and experienced in computing that had much more

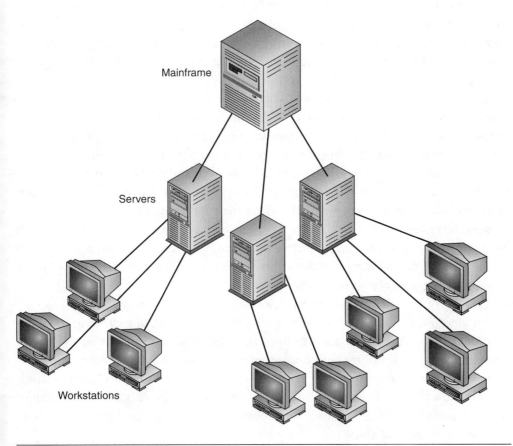

Figure 2-1   This figure shows the relationship among a mainframe, servers, and workstations.

access to important data and processes. Barriers and protection mechanisms were not put into place to protect employees and systems from others' mistakes, so important data got corrupted accidentally and individual mistakes affected many other systems instead of just their own.

Because so many more people were using systems, the software had to become more idiot-proof so that a larger audience of people could use the same platform. Computer operators in the mainframe days understood what the systems expected, knew how to format inputs, and properly read outputs. When this type of power was put on individuals' desktops, all imaginable and unimaginable inputs were used, which corrupted information and mangled operating systems.

Just like the understanding of the usefulness it would bring to put computing power in the employees' hands versus on one main computer, the comprehension arose that the company and these employees had to be protected from themselves and the data had to be protected from mishaps and mistakes. The employees needed layers of software between them and the operating system components and the data that they could destroy. These layers not only brought safety by taking individuals away from the core of the operating systems and files, but functionality continued to be inserted to make computers more useful to businesses and individuals.

Interesting symbiotic relationships grew as the computing world evolved among the technological advances of hardware, circuitry, processing power, and software. Once a breakthrough was made that enabled a computer to contain more memory and hard drive space, new software was right on its heels to use it and demand more. When software hit a wall because it was not supplied with the necessary registers and control units, the hardware industry was 'Johnny-on-the-spot' to develop and engineer the missing pieces to the equations. As the hardware end grew to provide a stable and rich platform for software, programmers developed software with the provided functionality and possibilities not even conceived a few years prior. It has been a wonderful game of leapfrog that does not seem to have any end in sight.

Lovely story, but what does it mean to security?

In the beginning, the issues associated with bringing computing closer to individuals brought along many mistakes, technological hurdles, and operational issues not encountered in the workforce before. Computers are tools; just like a knife can be a useful tool to cut meat and vegetables, it can also be a dangerous tool if it is in the hands of someone with malicious intent. The vast capabilities and functionality that computers have brought to society have also brought complex and troubling methods of destruction, fraud, and abuse.

Because computers are built on layers (hardware platform, chips, operating systems, network stacks, protocols, and applications), these complex issues have been interwoven throughout the stratum of computing environments. Plugging the holes, writing better software, and providing better perimeter security is often easier said than done because of the density of functionality within an infrastructure, interoperability issues, and the availability of the necessary functionality.

Over a short period of time, people and businesses have come to depend greatly upon computer technology in many different aspects of their lives. Computers run public utilities, military defense systems, financial institutions, medical equipment, and are heavily used in every possible business sector. Almost every company relies on data processing for one reason or another. This level of dependence and the extent of integration that technology has become in our lives have made security a much more necessary and essential discipline.

Computer security is not a game that will be completed in an instant. Security is a long run with a consistent and continual pace. It is not a short sprint and not for the nondedicated.

Different Areas of Security

Security has a wide base that touches on several different areas of life. The developers of the CISSP exam had the vision to understand this and demand that an individual who claims to be a security expert and wants to achieve this certification must also show that his expertise does not just lie in one area of security. Different areas of security affect each other. Physical security is interrelated with information security, database security lies on top of operating system security, operations security affects how computer systems are used, disaster recovery deals with systems in emergency situations, and almost every instance has some type of legal or liability issue tied to it. Technology, hardware, people, and procedures are woven together as a security fabric (Figure 2-2). When it is time to chase down a specific problem, several layers of unraveling may need to take place and the different pieces of the puzzle need to be understood so the best and most effective solution can be provided. Security is a wonderful and deep topic. The more stones that get lifted seem to find layers of possibilities that can be used for good or evil.

The next sections address some specific issues in security as it pertains to computers, information, and organizations. This is not an attempt to cover all relevant subjects, but to show specific instances to get an idea of the vastness of areas that security can touch. The information in these sections is not on the CISSP exam; thus, they do not need to be studied and memorized. They are provided to set the stage for the subjects covered in the following chapters.

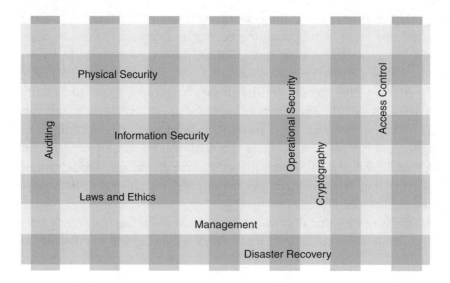

Figure 2-2 Technology, hardware, people, and procedures are woven together as a security fabric.

Informational Warfare

Computers and networks touch every facet of modern life. We are increasingly dependent on computer/network technology for communication, funds transfers, utility management, government services, military action, and maintaining confidential information. We use technology to provide energy, water supplies, emergency services, defense systems, electronic banking, and public health services. At the same time, this technology is being used in a form to disrupt communications and perform a variety of illegal activities. This technology is used to steal credit card numbers, perform fraudulent use of the telephone systems, illegally transmit trade secrets and intellectual property, deface Web sites for political reasons, disrupt communications, reveal critical national secrets and strategies, and even for extortion.

The term "informational warfare" covers many different activities that pertain to individuals, organizations, and nations. Governments have used informational warfare tactics to gather tactical information for years. Organizations have stolen trade secrets and plans of the competition's new products before they were released. Individuals have also used computers to steal money, gain personal financial information, and steal individual identity, deface Web sites, and cause destruction to raise attention to a particular cause.

Many of the hacking activities, viruses, and malware incidents that have been seen so far have been relatively benign. Most were carried out just to prove to the attacker that he is indeed clever enough to disrupt some businesses here and there, but not inflict the type of damage that is actually possible. Even though one of the recent worms released, called "The Naked Wife," actually deletes operating system files, it is only a lightweight. It is only a small step away from the more devastating destruction possible with worms and viruses. The developer of this worm is only getting self-satisfaction from the endeavor—the developer receives no money, trade secrets, political statements, or crucial military information. But the trend of joy-ride hacking is showing evidence of evolving into profit-driven activities. As the old saying goes, "Why did the thief rob the bank? Because that is where the money was kept." Why are thieves turning to computer attacks? Because that is where financial information and critical data is kept today.

Recent Evidence of the Evolution of Hacking

Several recent incidents indicate that not only is hacking activity on the rise, but that the sophistication of the attacks is advancing rapidly. Alarmingly, a majority of the attacks are using methods that have been understood for quite sometime and for which fixes are readily available. This proves that not enough network maintainers have kept up-to-date on security changes and installed the necessary patches or configurations.

It was discovered recently that a group of European hackers has been exploiting different computer vulnerabilities to steal over a million credit cards from U.S. computer systems associated with e-commerce and online banking depicted in Figure 2-3. The Federal Bureau of Investigation (FBI) and Secret Service have been working with the National Infrastructure Protection Center (NIPC) to investigate this series of hacker attacks. The attackers actually contact the financial institutions and use extortion means to increase the bounty of their deeds. They offer their 'security service' to patch the systems and if the institutions do not agree to pay for these security services, the attackers threaten more damage such as posting the customers' credit card numbers on Web sites available to the public. Many times this credit card information is sold to other organized crime groups.

The public only hears about the viruses, worms, and hacks that make the news. Many other types of attacks are underway, and they will only become more prevalent. The main reason the public is being continually informed of the recent European hackers is because they are affecting so many financial institutions and customers. The FBI and the Secret Service need the public to be aware and take the necessary steps to help stop this type of action.

There are many other financially motivated attacks. One involved a hacker who claimed to be 19 years old and from Russia. After he stole up to 300,000 card numbers from CD Universe customers in December 1999, he contacted the company, explained

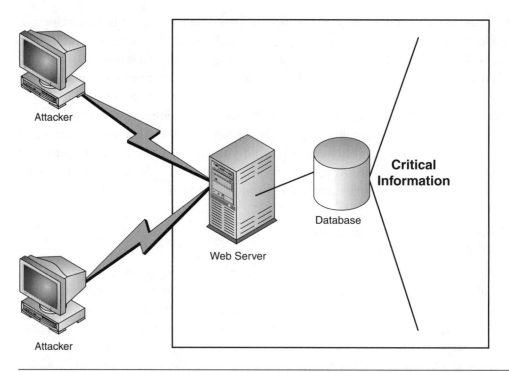

Figure 2-3   Attackers have been able to access critical information through Web servers.

his actions, and then asked for a $100,000 ransom. When this money was not paid to him, he released thousands of numbers to the Internet. Another Russian hacker stole more than 55,000 credit cards from CreditCards.com. Again, a $100,000 ransom was requested and after being ignored, 25,000 card numbers were posted on a Web site.

Bibliofind, an online bookseller service, realized attackers had been accessing customer credit card information every month between October 2000 and February 2001. The credit card information of over 98,000 customers was compromised.

Two hackers recently published a program that breaks the encryption mechanisms on older versions of IBM's e-commerce software. Using this tool and taking advantage of a server software flaw pertaining to address formatting, anyone can get the usernames and passwords of each and every account on a site using IBM's Net.Commerce and WebSphere Commerce Suite software. The hackers reported that they knew of over 330 Web sites vulnerable to this type of attack.

Egghead.com, Inc. in California had reports from some customers that their credit card number was stolen and one person reported having a debit charge to a Web site in Russia.

In September 2000, Western Union shut down its Web site for five days after hackers stole more than 15,000 customer credit card numbers. Microsoft itself was attacked and the source code of a new product could have easily been manipulated or stolen.

These examples represent only a small percentage of all the hacking activity that is going on. These attacks were identified and reported, but most are not. Many organizations do not report hacking activity because they are afraid of hurting their reputation, losing the faith of their customer base, and adversely affecting their shareholders and stock prices. Other attacks are not even realized or identified, and thus not reported. Computers and networks are great tools that have brought society much advancement, but like many other tools, they are also used for sinister gains.

How Are Nations Affected?

The art of war requires soldiers to outmaneuver the enemy and strike the enemy down if necessary.

In past wars, the enemy was usually easily detected. The enemy was driving a tank, bombing from an airplane, attacking from a submarine, or shooting intercontinental missiles. However, today the enemy is harder to find, some attacks are harder to track, and the objectives of the attacker are at times more nebulous. U.S. military intelligence has had to develop new methods of collecting information on potential foreign enemy movement, surveillance techniques, and proving guilt of criminal activities.

Although the U.S. military still trains the majority of soldiers how to shoot, fight in combat, and practice evasive maneuvers, a new soldier is being taught and molded. Because a majority of the military vehicles, weapons systems, and communication systems are controlled by technology, new soldiers need to know how to use these technological tools to achieve the same goals of the soldier of the past—win in war. Not only do today's soldiers need to know how to operate the new technology-driven weapon systems, but they also need to know how to defend these systems from attacks and possibly attack the enemy's defense systems. Figure 2-4 shows how attacks can come from many different sides.

Disrupting communication has always been an important tactic in war because it impedes proper planning and warnings of imminent attacks. Knocking out communication lines is one of the first steps in the recipe of a successful attack. Today, the military's communication is handled through computer-based systems, and the tools to disrupt communication of the enemy have changed.

The Central Intelligence Agency (CIA) reported to a U.S congressional committee that foreign nations include information warfare in their military arsenal and provide defensive and offensive attack methods. These nations are devising documentation, strategic plans, and tools to carry out informational warfare on other nations.

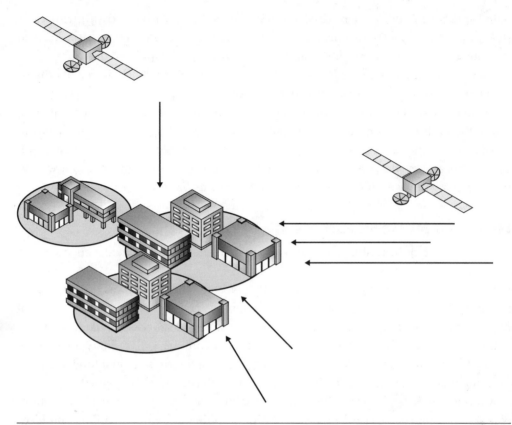

Figure 2-4 Information warfare tactics come in many different types of forms from different types of origins.

During the Gulf War, it was reported that hackers from the Netherlands penetrated 34 American military sites that supported Operation Desert Storm activities. They extracted information about the exact location of military troops, weapon details, and movement of American warships. It could have been a different war if Saddam Hussein had actually bought this information when it was offered to him, but he did not—he thought it was a trick.

It is reported that the Irish Republican Army stole telephone bills to determine the addresses of potential targets in their political attacks. Authorities seized a batch of computer disks in Belfast and were able to decrypt the information after months of effort. This information was most likely gained by successfully hacking into the telephone company's database.

A report declassified in May 1995 stated that prior to the August 1991 coup attempt in Russia, the KGB had been writing and developing viruses to be used to disrupt computer systems during times of war. Another report by the U.S. Defense Intelligence Agency indicated that Cuba had developed viruses to infect and damage U.S. civilian computers. There is no written proof that these viruses were released and actually caused damage, but there is no proof that they weren't either.

During the 1998 Kosovo air campaign, it has been reported that false messages were injected into Yugoslavia's computer-integrated air defense systems to point the weapons at false targets. It is clear that the military's use of computer-based tools and attacks is growing in sophistication and utilization.

Almost every task in an individual's day interrelates with a technology that is controlled or monitored by a computer-based system. Turning on the lights, paying a gas bill, flying on a plane for a business trip, talking on the telephone, and receiving medical treatments are all events that depend on large computer systems monitoring and providing the flow of service. Even sophisticated military defense systems rely on commercial power, communication, transportation, and monitoring capabilities, which are computer based. America's strength relies on its privately owned critical infrastructures and industries. These private sector infrastructures have already been victimized by computer attacks. A concerted attack on any of these key economic sectors or governmental services could have widespread ramifications. The U.S government has recognized this vulnerability and has started taking the necessary steps to evade these types of attacks and provide the necessary mechanisms to enable a quick and efficient recovery after an attack.

Enemy bullets used to come from guns. Now different types of bullets come from laptops and personal computers. The next war could target America's infrastructure with the new weapons—computer-generated attacks. Several factions of the U.S. military are developing more robust and skilled informational warfare units to act defensively and offensively in the best interest of the United States. There is a good reason. Future wars and power struggles may take place over computer lines instead of the more traditional battlefield.

How Are Companies Affected?

Many companies fail to understand how security implementations will help their bottom line: the gross margin. After all, doing business is done to make profit and if there is not a direct correlation for an item that ties in neatly to the linear cost and profit concept, that item is often pushed to the back of the bus. However, today many companies are finding out how security affects their bottom line in ways they never expected.

If a company suffers a security breach, the company will have to deal with a wide range of issues that it most likely is not prepared for. As described previously, several companies recently had their databases attacked and their customers' information compromised. Once customers find out that a company is not protecting their confidential and financial information properly, they will often take their business elsewhere. If the number of customers affected is in the range we have seen over the last year (10,000 to 300,000 credit cards stolen at a time), and if the company loses this many customers at one time, many businesses would go out of business. Of course, these events also affect the reputation of the company, their shareholders, and their stock prices. In addition, the customers can sue the company for damages, which would incur punitive damages and court fees. This would definitely impact the bottom line.

Companies have had trade secrets and intellectual property stolen by employees who have left the company to a competitor company. In these instances, unless the original company took the proper steps to protect this data and inform their employees that this action is wrong, the company has no legal leg to stand on. The company has to provide due diligence to protect their intellectual property from competitors inside and outside its company.

We are seeing more and more cases of companies firing employees for improper use of computer systems. However, if companies do not take the proper steps by having a comprehensive security policy in place and providing security awareness to the employees, the companies are often successfully sued for unfairly ending employment.

Another way a company can lose money and time is by their readiness to react to a situation. If a network does not have properly configured security mechanisms, the company's IT staff usually spends unnecessary time and resources putting out fires. In addition, when they are racing in a chaotic manner to find a solution, they may be creating more open doors into the network without realizing it. Without proper security planning, a lot of money, staff productivity, and time is wasted that they could be using for other tasks.

Many companies are covered by insurance in case of a natural disaster or a major security breach. However, to get a good insurance rate, companies must provide the necessary responsible and secure foundation and prove that they are doing all that they can to protect their own investments. In some cases, insurance providers refused to pay for a company's loss because the correct security measures were not in place. In cases where a company indeed did not provide a security policy, proper security mechanisms, and an updated disaster plan, the insurance company won the case in court and the company lost a lot more than just a court case.

Every business market is full of competition. If a company endures a security compromise that makes the press, which has been happening almost every month over the last year, they will have an even harder time attracting new business. A company wants to be in a position where all the customers come to them when another company suffers a security compromise, not the other way around.

The U.S. Government's Actions

One of the U.S. government's responsibilities is to protect American resources, people, and their way of life. One complex task the government has been faced with recently is protecting several critical infrastructures from computer-based attacks. Because computer technology is relatively young and changing rapidly, and because security has only come into real focus over the last four years, all these core structures contain their own vulnerabilities. If attackers disrupt these structures, the ramifications can be far reaching. For example, if attackers could bring down electrical grids forcing the government to concentrate on that crisis, they could then perform military action attacks from another side. This might sound like a John Grisham novel, but scenarios like this and many more need to be thought of, thought through, and defensive plans must be devised. One of the biggest threats we face is that terrorists or a hostile nation will attempt to inflict economic damage, disrupt business or productivity, and degrade our defense response by attacking the critical infrastructures.

On July 15, 1996, President Clinton approved the establishment of the President's Commission on Critical Infrastructure Protection (PCCIP). The responsibility of this commission was to investigate the types of attacks that were happening, extrapolate how attacks could evolve in the future, determine how they could affect the nation's computer infrastructures, and assess how vulnerable these structures were to such attacks at that time.

The returned report card was very sobering. The PCCIP published its report "Critical Foundations: Protecting America's Infrastructures" in 1997. The report outlined the current vulnerability level of critical U.S infrastructures pertaining to criminal activity, natural disasters, international terrorists, hackers, national intelligence, and information warfare. Long-standing security weaknesses were identified and reported, placing federal operations at serious risk. In response to this report, President Clinton signed two more orders, Presidential Decision Directives (PPD) 62 and 63, to improve the nation's defenses against terrorism, other computer-based attacks, and information warfare activities. The focus of these directives was to address cyberattacks at a national level.

The report recognized that many of the nation's critical infrastructures were privately owned and operated. This meant that there needed to be a marriage between these private organizations and government services to protect all of America's interests pertaining to these vulnerabilities.

It was obvious that the government and the private sector had to work together to properly and successfully fight this battle. There would be little benefit if the government services tried to provide this protection all by itself. In fact, it was recognized that these government departments could not provide this level of protection without the help and sharing of information with the public sector. A new National Coordinator within the Executive Office of the president was appointed to facilitate a partnership between the government and the private sector. The goal was for the government and the private sector to work together to strengthen the nation's defenses against cyberterrorism, theft, fraud, and other criminal activity. This produced the Critical Infrastructure Assurance Office (CIAO) under the Department of Commerce, Information Sharing and Analysis Centers (ISACs), and the NIPC under the sponsorship of the FBI.

ISAC provides a mechanism that enables information sharing among members of a particular industry sector. The information comes from public sector organizations and government agencies, and is shared by both. Sources of information can be authenticated or anonymous and the information can pertain to vulnerabilities, incidents, threats, and solutions. Submitted information is directed to the appropriate team members, who then investigate each submittal, quantify the seriousness of the vulnerability, and perform a trend analysis to identify the steps that might thwart this type of attack. The outcome is to enhance the security of individual organizations and the entire nation one industry sector at a time.

So What Does This Mean To Us?

Evidence and trend analysis show that people, businesses, and countries are becoming increasingly dependent on computer/network technology for communication, funds transfers, utility management, government services, military action, and maintaining confidential information. If any of these experienced a major disruption, millions of people could be affected. As our dependence grows, so should our protective measures.

Currently, the majority of computer attacks, hacks, and cracks are done for thrills and to measure one's skills, and only a small percentage of attacks are motivated by financial gain. It seems likely that this ratio will reverse in the future, and a majority of computer compromises and attacks will be for theft and fraud. At the same time, the laws will increase in severity so that computer joy riding will not be so joyful when one is caught snooping around or releasing a virus.

The U.S. military is quietly growing their informational warfare units. This growth is a response to the computer-related military actions that have already occurred and reflect an awareness of the need to plan for the future. Computer networks, communication systems, and resources are prime targets to reconfigure or destroy in the time of war or crisis, and good tools to use to watch other nations' movements and intentions during peacetime.

The antes are being raised, security issues are becoming more serious, and the effects are more detrimental. Take the necessary steps to protect yourself, your company, and your country.

Hacking and Attacking

There has been a definite and distinct evolution of hacking, cracking, and attacking. At one point of time, it was a compliment to be called a hacker or cracker because it indicated that the person took the time to learn things about computers that many others did not know and had the discipline and desire to find out what makes a computer tick. These types of people did not perform malicious acts, but were the ones called upon when really tough problems came about that left everyone else scratching their heads.

As computers became well-known tools used in many different environments, this definition started to change. The new hackers took on a profile of geeky young men (script kiddies) who would rather spend their time pinging computers all over the Internet instead of out looking for dates. Even this profile has evolved. Several girls and women have joined this once all-boy club and are just as knowledgeable and dangerous as the guys. Hacking and attacks are on the rise and the profile of an attacker is changing. However, the real change in the profile is that the serious attackers that are out for specific purposes with certain types of damage or fraud in mind.

Hacking and attacking is on the rise and the profile of an attacker is changing.

The dangerous attacker is the one that is willing to do his homework. This attacker will build a profile about the victim, find all the necessary information, and uncover many possible ways of getting into an environment before actually attempting it. The more an attacker knows about the environment, the more tools he has at his disposal. Attacks and hacks have been involved with information warfare, stealing money and credit cards, and defacing Web sites for political reasons. These are usually groups of determined and knowledgeable individuals that are hard to stop.

Another dangerous evolution pattern is the tools that are available to hackers these days. It used to take a certain skill set to be able to enter a computer through a port, reconfigure system files, find the hidden data, and get out without being noticed. However, today there are many tools with graphical user interface (GUI) front ends that only require a person to enter an IP address, or range, and hit the start button. Some of these tools provide a quiet mode, which means that the interrogations and exploit attempts will use methods and protocols that may not show up on intrusion detection systems or cause the user of that computer to recognize that something is going on with that particular system. However, this does not require a lot of knowledge on the attacker's part.

Security exploits and attacks are getting easier for the novice computer user.

The proliferation of tools on the Internet, Web sites, and books describing exactly how to exploit vulnerabilities, and the ease of use of these tools have greatly increased the hacker population. So some attacks that may require in-depth knowledge of protocol behaviors or skillful programming skills are now available to a wide range of people who have not necessarily ever heard of Transmission Control Protocol/Internet Protocol (TCP/IP).

As more vulnerabilities are uncovered every week, many more people are interested in trying the exploits out to quench their curiosity, provide bragging rights to other hackers, or because the person has distinct destructive goals to accomplish.

However, there is another side to hacking and attacking rarely discussed or understood. It can be looked at as doom and gloom and good versus evil, or it can be looked at as the computing society continually challenging itself to come up with better products, practices, and procedures. If hackers were not continually trying to break products, the products would not necessarily continue to evolve in the way that they have. Sure, products would continue to grow in functionality, but not necessarily in security.

So maybe instead of looking at hackers and attackers as selfish individuals out to cause harm and destruction, they can be looked at as the thorn in the side of the computing society that keeps it on its toes and ensures that the next product will provide great functionality, but in a secure manner.

Management

The changes that have had to happen and are going on now within management and security have been painful for many companies, as change can often be. This mainly has had to do with the attitude usually taken with technology and security in general. Management usually feels that it is the IT department's responsibility to choose the correct technologies, install them, and maintain them. Management has never really been pulled inside the realm of computers and the issues that surround them. This distance and attitude hurts many companies when it comes to dealing with security effectively.

Management has been responsible for hitting their numbers—whether it be profit margins, sales goals, productivity marks—or for managing people and projects. They have not had to think much about firewalls, hackers, and security breaches. However, this trend is fading and the new trend demands that management be much more involved in security and how it affects the company as a whole.

It is management's responsibility to set the tone for what type of role security will play in an organization. It is their responsibility to state what data is valuable and needs to be protected, who is responsible for protecting it and to what extent, what the acceptable actions are for employees, and what the consequences are for noncompliance. However, as of this writing, few corporations see these issues in this light and instead bounce security back into the laps of the IT staff. It is usually not that management is trying to dodge a bullet or skirt some type of responsibility. Instead, it is usually a misunderstanding and not fully comprehending what computer and information security entails.

Good security does not begin and end with erecting a firewall and installing antivirus software. Good security is planned, designed, implemented, maintained, and evolves. For security to be a good fit for a company, it has to be in line with the company's business goals and objectives. Management needs to understand security issues and how security affects the company and its customers, so that proper resources, time, and funding can be provided. Unfortunately, many times security is kept within the IT department, who can be overwhelmed with daily tasks and dealing with weekly disasters; thus, security is not done properly. In addition, when the IT department requests funds for security purposes, it often falls on deaf ears.

It is too much responsibility to put the full brunt of the security of a whole company in the IT department. It needs to be understood, supported, and funded from the top down. Management does not need to know the security mechanisms used, protocols in place, or configurations of components, but they do need to set the stage for everyone else to follow. Management should provide the framework and delegate who is to fill in the rest.

When a company is hacked and thousands of customers' credit cards are stolen, intellectual property is taken, or confidential information is leaked, it is the management staff that will be called to the carpet. They are the ones who will have to explain why due diligence was not practiced in protecting the company and its resources. These explanations may need to go to corporate offices, shareholders, judges, and to customers. So it should be management who truly understands how security works within the organization and should be calling the shots from the beginning.

Internet and Web Activities

The Internet started so that universities and government organizations could communicate in a more instantaneous manner. It not only provided a different communication path, but it opened the doors to possibilities, not only for mass communication, but also for a new and exciting mechanism that could provide layers of functionality and potential.

Communication on the Internet was mainly made up of nongraphical e-mail, news groups, and File Transfer Protocol (FTP) sites to exchange files. When HyperText Markup Language (HTML) came to life, people were able to make graphical representation of their concepts and ideas. These sites provided static pages with a small amount of capability to accept information from Internet users through forms and scripts. When it was realized that money could be made and the Internet was a new forum for advertising, sites became more abundant, Web pages more complex, more products and services were offered. Companies started integrating this new communication mechanism into their business model.

Another game of leapfrog began between telecommunication capabilities, Internet protocols, hardware platforms, and supporting applications. As HTML became more dynamic, Web server applications were developed to manage these pages and the back-end processes. This increased the need for more hard drive space, processing power, and memory accessible to the applications. Protocols evolved and matured to create more of a stable and meaningful experience on the Internet and enabled confidential information to stay secret and provided the necessary level of integrity for data being transmitted. Web servers became more powerful in processing as they offered more functionality to the users. As more sites connected to each other, the Internet brought along the World Wide Web.

The Web is actually a layer that operates on top of the Internet. The Internet provides the hardware, platforms, and communication mechanisms, whereas the Web provides the abundant software capabilities and functionality. Figure 2-5 illustrates this difference.

As companies brought their networks to the Internet and brought their services to the Web, they connected to the world in a different fashion. It is a great thing for a business to enable thousands or millions of people to view their product line, understand their business objectives, and learn about services offered. However, this also opens the doors to others who are interested in taking a peek under the covers, finding out more about the company's network topology and applications being used, accessing confidential information, and maybe causing some mayhem here and there in the process.

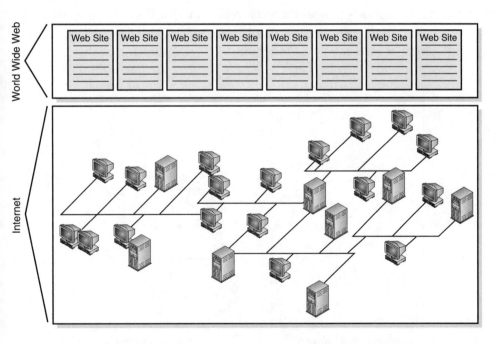

Figure 2-5 There is a difference between the Internet and the World Wide Web. The Web is a layer that exists on top of the Internet.

Offering services through the Internet is not the same as offering just another service to a customer base. It can be a powerful and useful move for a company, but if done haphazardly or in a manner that is not clearly thought out, implemented, and maintained, it could end up hurting a company or destroying it.

The software being used for a company to present a presence on the Web, the hardware configurations, and security measures that should be taken depend on the company, its infrastructure, and the type of data it needs to protect. In the beginning, a Web server was just another server on the Internet with a connection outside of the network. Static pages were used and no real information came from the Internet to the company through this channel. As forms and Common Gateway Interface (CGI) scripts were developed to accept customer information and the Internet as a whole became more used and well known, the Web servers were slowly moved to demilitarized zones (DMZs), or the perimeter networks (Figure 2-6). (Sadly, however, many Web servers today still live inside of networks, providing a lot of vulnerabilities to companies.)

As the Web servers and applications grew and moved from showing customers just the company's home page and services offered to providing complete catalogs of products and accepting orders via the Internet, databases had to be brought into the picture. Web servers and databases lived on the same system, or two systems within the DMZ, and provided information to the world and accepted information from the world. This setup worked until more customers were able to access back-end data (within the database) and corrupt it accidentally or intentionally. It was shown that there were not

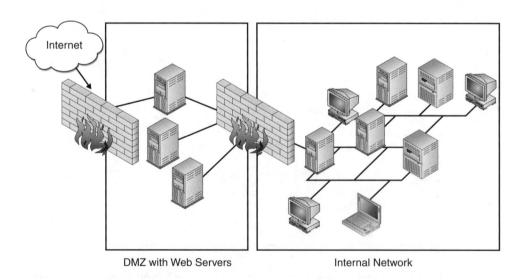

DMZ with Web Servers   Internal Network

Figure 2-6   Web servers were evidentially moved from the internal network to the DMZ.

enough layers and protection mechanisms between the users on the Internet and the data that was important to the company at hand.

This quickly brings us to where we are today. More and more companies are coming online and connecting their once closed (or semiclosed) environments to the Internet, which brings along a lot of threats and vulnerabilities and issues not dealt with before. If a company has static Web pages, their Web servers and back-end needs are not half as complicated as the companies that accept payments and offer services or hold confidential customer information via the Web. The companies that take credit card information, allow customers to view their bank account information, and offer products and services can work in a two-tier (Figure 2-7) or three-tier configuration.

Two-Tier Architecture

A two-tier architecture includes a line of Web servers that provide the customers with a Web-based interface and a back-end line of servers or databases that hold data and process the requests. The two tiers are either within a DMZ or the back-end database is protected by another firewall. Figure 2-8 shows a two-tier architecture.

This architecture is fine for some environments, but for companies that hold bank and/or credit card or sensitive information, a three-tier architecture is usually more appropriate. In the three-tier architecture, the first line is made up of a server farm that presents Web pages to customers and accepts requests. The farm is usually clustered and redundant to be able to handle a heavy load of connections and to be able to balance that load between servers.

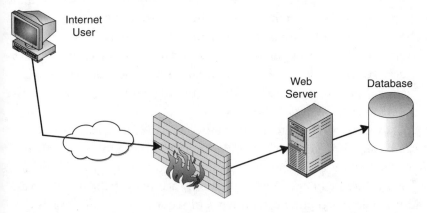

Figure 2-7 Attackers have easy access if databases are directly connected to Web servers with no protection mechanisms.

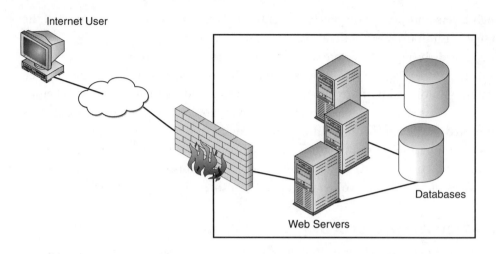

Internet User

Databases

Web Servers

Figure 2-8 A two-tier architecture consists of a server farm and back-end databases.

The back-end tier is basically the same as in the two-tier setup, which has database(s) or host systems. This is where sensitive customer information is held and maintained. The middle tier is new and provides the most interesting functionality. In many cases, this is where the business logic lives and the actual processing of data and requests happen. Figure 2-9 shows the three-tier architecture.

The middle tier is made up of application servers running some type of middleware, which communicates with the Web (public layer) and can be customized for proprietary purposes and needs, or acts basically as another layer of server farms with off-the-shelf products. This layer takes the heavy processing tasks off the front-line servers and provides a layer of protection between the users on the Internet and the sensitive data held in the databases. The middleware is usually made up of components built with object-oriented languages. The objects are the entities that work as binary black boxes by taking in a request, retrieving the necessary information from the back-end servers, processing the data, and presenting it back to the requesting entity. Figure 2-10 illustrates how a component works as a black box.

There are a lot of advantages to this architecture other than the previously mentioned issues. Security can be supplied in a more granular fashion if it is applied at different places in the tiers. The first firewall supports a particular security policy and provides the first line of defense. The first tier of Web servers only accepts specific requests, can authorize individuals before accepting certain types of requests, and can dictate who gets to make requests to the next tiers. The middle tier can provide security at the component level, which can be very detail-oriented and specific in nature. No requests

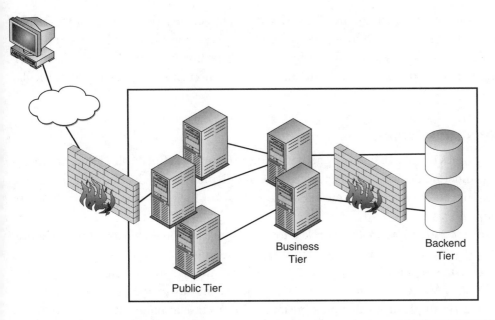

Figure 2-9   A three-tier architecture is made up of a front server farm, middle servers running middleware software, and back-end databases.

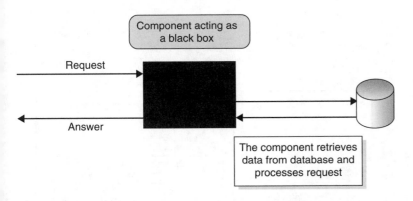

Figure 2-10   Components take requests and pass them on and process the answer.

should be made from the Internet directly to the back-end databases. Several middlemen should have to pass the request, each looking out for a specific security vulnerability and risk. The back-end databases are then acted upon on by the components in the middle tier, not the users themselves.

The second firewall should support a different security policy. If an attacker gets through the first firewall, it makes no sense for the second firewall to have the same configurations and settings that were just beat. This firewall should have different settings that are more restrictive to attempt to stop a successful intruder at that particular stage.

Database Roles

Many times databases will only accept requests from predefined roles to ensure that if an intruder made it all the way through the middlemen and to the place that holds the goods, it can only make a request if it is a member of the right group. This is shown in Figure 2-11.

All access attempts are first checked to make sure the requester is a member of a predefined and acceptable group. This means that individuals cannot make direct requests of the database, and it is highly unlikely that an attacker would know the necessary group she needs to be a member of and have the capability to add herself to this group. This is an example of another possible layer of protection available in a tiered approach of Web-based operations.

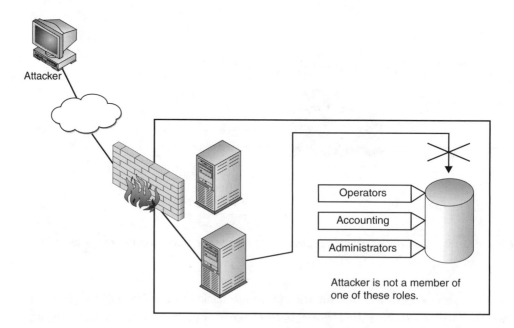

Figure 2-11 This database only accepts requests from members of the operators, accounting, and administrators roles.

These are architectural issues, which look at a broad view of things and how large components interact. However, security vulnerabilities usually take advantage of smaller components and issues that are easier to overlook. A great three-tier architecture can be setup with firewalls in the right places, Web servers, and databases providing their layers of functionality and security, but an attack can still take place at the protocol, component, or service level of an operating system or application. The types of attacks cover a wide range from denial of service (DoS) attacks, spoofing, masquerading, to buffer overflows and using an application's own functionality against itself. We will take a quick look at only one type of attack that has been used to steal millions of credit card numbers over the Internet.

Microsoft Data Access Components

Many companies use Microsoft Internet Information Services (IIS) for their Web server software. There are some specific vulnerabilities that give attackers access to data on the back-end servers in a privileged mode, which enables them to capture or modify information. These vulnerabilities have been known about for quite a while, but financial institutions are still falling victim to them because the IT staff is not properly installing the necessary security patches and making the corresponding configuration changes.

Microsoft Data Access Components (MDACs), which are used in IIS and Windows NT, have many different functions and services. One of the services, Remote Data Service, enables Web-based clients to issue structured query language (SQL) queries to remote resources using the Hypertext Transfer Protocol (HTTP). When Internet users make requests to the IIS server, the user executes the command at her browser and the msadcs.dll on the IIS server facilitates this request and employs the DataFlow Object. The DataFlow Object is the piece that enables requests to be sent and received to the back-end database.

The problem lies in the Microsoft's database engine because it enables embedded arguments to be passed within SQL query strings, as shown in Figure 2-12. This means attackers can embed commands within a request made to the database, which in turn can execute shell commands, tunnel open database connectivity (ODBC) requests to the back-end database, and access secured, nonpublished files. What makes this even more devastating is that IIS lets these ODBC commands run with system_local privileges.

In other words, the company could do a good job in setting up the right infrastructure, have the necessary firewalls configured, have the unnecessary ports and services disabled, and have the intrusion detection systems running, and still lose control of thousands or millions of credit card numbers to attackers. This is because there are several pieces to security. They all have their place, their importance, and their problems.

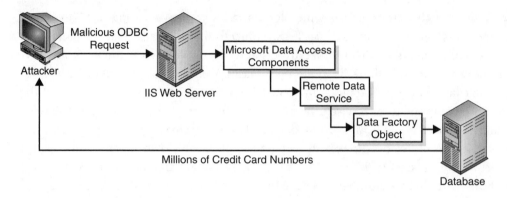

Figure 2-12 Weaknesses in the components of IIS running on Windows NT 4.0 enable attackers to access confidential information in back-end databases.

This example shows that vulnerabilities can lie at a code level that many network administrators and security professionals are not necessarily aware of. There are usually two main camps in the computer world: infrastructure individuals and programmers. Security vulnerabilities lie in each camp and affect each other; thus, it is better to have a full understanding of an environment and how security breaches can take place through infrastructure and code-based means.

So where do the vulnerabilities lie in Web-based activities?

- Incorrect configurations at the firewall

- Web servers that are not hardened, or locked down, and are open to attacks to the operating system or applications

- Middle-tier servers that do not provide the right combination and detailed security necessary to access back-end databases in a controlled manner

- Databases and back-end servers that accept requests from any source

- Databases and back-end servers that are not protected by another layer of firewalls

- Not running intrusion detection to watch for suspicious activity

- Routers that forward packets instead of routing them properly

- Enabling unnecessary protocols and services on computers

- Not keeping the computers patched and up-to-date

The list can go on for quite sometime, but one last item is important to touch on that is not approached as much as maybe it should be in security: application and programming security. Security is usually looked to in the light of firewalls, intrusion detection systems, and port scanners. However, the vulnerabilities that are exploited are within the code of the operating systems and applications. If these problems did not exist in the programming code in the first place, there would be nothing to exploit and no real reason to have firewalls and intrusion detection systems.

Programming has usually only been looked at in the light of providing more functionality to the user, not protecting the system it is installed upon or the data that it holds and processes. The security point of view has also not been as important as it is today. Attacks and exploits that are taking place were not even in the minds of the programmers while they were coding it a couple of years ago; thus, they most likely did not think of coding differently and testing for these specific weaknesses.

The real security problems companies are dealing with are embedded within the products they purchase and install. Only recently have vendors started to take these issues seriously and started to think how programming should be done differently. However, many times vendors are in a rush to get the product to the market and patch it later, so this may always be the crux of computer and information security. Proper techniques and extensive testing add a lot of expenses to developing a product, and most vendors are not willing to take on those extra expenses without seeing more profit in the end. It is really up to the consumer market to demand more secure products and pay for the products that have the necessary embedded protection mechanisms and methods. Until then, administrators will spend their days patching systems and applications and adjusting firewall and router configuration to try and thwart new vulnerabilities, continually updating intrusion detection signatures, and the rat race of trying to outrun hackers will continue.

A Layered Approach

Networks have advanced in possibilities, functionality, and complexity. Because vulnerabilities can take place at different layers of an infrastructure, it has been necessary for vendors, developers, administrators, and security professionals to understand these different layers and how each should be protected.

Many times we hear about a layered approach to security. We are supposed to implement different layers of protection to protect networks from different types of attacks. But what does a layered approach really mean? How do we know if we are applying a layered approach?

These are excellent questions that should be explored in-depth if we are serious about protecting our interior and exterior networks from all the possible security compromises and types of potential security breaches. Security is a complex subject because to protect an environment, one must truly understand the environment, the fixes that are to be applied, the differences between the numerous vendor applications and hardware variations, and how attacks are actually performed. The road to a secure environment is a windy one, with some bumps, sharp turns, and attacks that lunge out from the dark. However, the most important thing about this road to security is to understand the facets of the adventure and that the road never ends.

Security at Different Layers

When one talks of a layered approach, this can be an abstract and nebulous topic. Many times a layered approach means to implement solutions at different spectrums of the network. A layered approach presents layers of barriers an attacker must go through and compromise before getting to the sought after resource. Running antivirus software only on workstations is not a layered approach in battling viruses. Running antivirus software on each workstation, file server, mail server, and applying content filtering via a proxy server is considered a layered approach towards combating viruses. This is just one example.

How is file access protection provided in a layered approach? If an administrator puts all users in specific groups and dictates what those groups can and cannot do with the company's files, this is only one step in the layer. To properly protect file access, file and registry access control lists need to be configured to provide more granularity to users' and groups' file permissions. The system default user rights (in a Windows environment) need to be properly configured to give certain types of users certain types of rights. Physical security of the environment and of the computers needs to be considered and restraints applied where required. Users need to be placed into groups that have explicit permissions necessary to perform their duties and no more. A strict logon credential policy needs to be drafted and enforced, so not all users are logging in as the same user. Monitoring and auditing of file access and actions needs to be in place to identify any suspicious activity.

Sound like overkill? Not really. If an administrator made all users log in using different accounts, applied file and registry access lists, configured groups, and monitored audit logs without thinking about physical security, a user could use a floppy disk with a simple program to get around all other security barriers. All of these components must work in a synergistic manner, provide a blanket of security that individual security mechanisms could not fulfill on their own, and fill in all the gaps—even the smallest ones.

An Architectural View

Once we look at different types of vulnerabilities, attacks, and threats, we find that they exist at different layers within a network. This layered approach digs into more of the technology of an environment and the complexity of each of these technologies at each layer. This applies to the different protocols, applications, hardware, and security mechanisms that work at one or more of the seven layers in the OSI model. IP spoofing is an attack at the network layer, dictionary attacks happen at the application layer, traffic sniffing is at the data link and physical layer, and viruses enter through the application layer. If an organization just employs strict password rules and a firewall, this leaves many layers vulnerable to other types of attacks.

Many times organizations put too much faith in their new shiny firewalls, intrusion detection systems, or antivirus software. Once one or more of these solutions are implemented, there can be a false sense of security within the IT staff that travels up to management. It is more important to look at the flow of data in and out of a network and how the different applications and devices work together. This is an architectural view versus a device or application view.

In an architectural view, one must look at the data flow in and out of the environment, how this data is being authorized and monitored at different points, and how all the security solutions speak to each other in different situations. A network could either perform as a well-tuned orchestra or as several pieces that play wonderfully all by themselves but give you a headache when they are all brought into the same room. Each individual security component could be doing its job wonderfully by protecting its piece of the network, but when it is time to interrelate or to communicate its findings or status to another security component, the proverbial "security ball" may be getting dropped in the process.

Each environment is different because of the installed hardware, software, technologies, and configurations. However, the main differences between environments are the goals each is trying to achieve. A local area network (LAN) provides authentication, resources to its users, and an overall controlled inner atmosphere. A wide area network (WAN) provides connections between users and remote sites, protocol tunneling, and access control. An e-commerce arrangement provides a Web interface to Internet users, connection to data held on back-end servers, access control, and a different type of authentication than LANs and WANs. These different goals require different architectures, but can use the same basic security concepts.

Because there are different levels within an environment, as shown in Figure 2-13, different types of attacks can happen at these levels. The following is a small list of countermeasures, the layers they work at, and vulnerabilities to protect against.

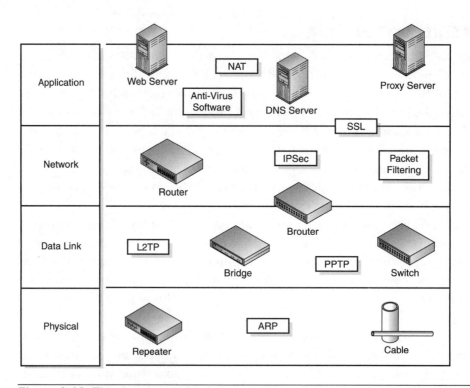

Figure 2-13 This shows a graphical representation of devices and protocols and where they appear within the OSI model.

- The firewall has packet filtering configured, which provides protection at the network layer. (This combats a range of attacks including IP spoofing and masquerading.)

- Proxy software configurations that protect at the application layer. (This combats a range of attacks including unauthorized access and packet spoofing.)

- Network address translation (NAT), which works at the network layer. (This hides LAN IP addresses and topology.)

- Shielded twisted pair (STP) wiring at the physical layer. (This helps protect against network eavesdropping and signal interference.)

- Network intrusion detection sensor monitors network traffic at the network level for known attack signatures. (This identifies known attacks and resets TCP connections if necessary.)

- The perimeter domain name server (DNS) contains only public records. This protection is at the application layer. (This protects private DNS records, network mapping, and individual computer information.)

- IPSec, which works at the network layer, is configured for virtual private network (VPN) connections into the perimeter network. (This protects against masquerading, data manipulating, and confidential information via encryption.)

- Web server configuration protects at the application layer by using different sites for public versus confidential information. (This protects from directory hopping and unauthorized access.)

- Only necessary services and ports enabled on all perimeter devices, which work at the network layer. (This reduces entry points into the network and denial of service attacks.)

- Mail server uses a store-and-forward method of messaging and runs antivirus software at the application layer. (This protects against viruses and denial of service attacks.)

- Secure Sockets Layer (SSL), which works at the session layer, is configured at the Web sites when customers need to access personal confidential information. (This provides confidentiality, data integrity, and protects against masquerading.)

- Network scanner runs a weekly probe on all perimeter network server ports at the data link and network layer to identify new vulnerabilities. (This protects from new vulnerabilities resulting from configuration changes or additional technology added.)

- A Web server, working at the application layer, using embedded cryptography within Extensible Markup Language (XML) code and Distributed Component Object Model (DCOM) security. (This provides confidentiality of information and restricts components from performing risky actions.)

- Web servers, working at the application and presentation layers, requiring valid digital signatures from each other for proper communication. (These protect against session hijacking and masquerading.)

This list shows a small percentage of the activity that happens at different points of the OSI model. If one or more of the devices or software had incorrect configurations or if the environment were missing one of these components, this could leave an open portal for an attacker into a beloved network.

A Layer Missed

Many environments do not contain all the devices and components in the previous example. The following example shows how employing several security mechanisms can seem to provide a fully secured environment, but can leave a small doorway of opportunity available for the clever attacker to take advantage of.

A firewall with packet filtering, a proxy server with content filtering, public and private DNS records clearly separated, SSL for Internet users, IPSec for VPN connections, public key infrastructure (PKI), and restricted service and port configuration may seem like a fortified environment, and a network administrator most likely implemented these mechanisms with the best intentions. However, one problem is that it is fortified only for a moment in time. Without a scanning device that probes the environment on a scheduled basis or an intrusion detection system that looks out for suspicious activity, the environment could be vulnerable even after the company has spent thousands of dollars to protect it. Technology continually changes, thus, so do networks and environments. The new application configurations, patches applied, or device installation brings change to the environment that could bring unpredictable consequences—not to mention the new ways hackers have found to circumvent the original security mechanisms.

Bringing the Layers Together

It is not always necessary to purchase the newest security solutions on the market, pay top dollar for the hardware solution versus the software solution, but it is necessary to be aware of where the risks can evolve and take the necessary steps to make sure all the basis are covered.

So when one hears of a layered approach to a problem, it means making sure all bases are covered on several different levels. In the computer and network world the complexity of the different levels can be a bit overwhelming at times. But the most important first step is to understand the environment that needs to be protected. Many times IT members come into an environment that was established years ago by another group of people. The environment is continually added onto; it is never stagnant. Usually, there is not an up-to-date network diagram because the daily tasks are time consuming, there is lack of useful documentation, and not one person who totally understands how the entire network works. This means when something goes wrong, 80 percent of the effort and time is spent in a chaotic confusing mad dash to a solution. It does not need to work this way, and there would be fewer security compromises if this scene were not so familiar.

Instead of looking at updating that old network diagram (or creating a first one) as a boring dreadful task, it could be approached as a fact-finding mission of crucial information. Instead of putting down the IT staff after a successful hacker attack, a change of attitude and practices can be employed. New software, patches, and devices should be clearly tested prior to implementation for any unforeseen events. An intrusion detection system should be established in potentially vulnerable segments of the network, if not all segments. Scheduled security scans should take place to seek out new vulnerabilities, not just when an audit is around the corner. In addition, security should be brought to the forefront of every network administrator's mind by keeping up-to-date on the recent security compromises, being aware of how changes to the network could open a door to clever attackers, and keeping those intrusion detection and antivirus signatures up-to-date.

Keeping up-to-date on network, software, configurations, and education can be overwhelming, but most of us in this line of work love to learn and these things make sure we will never stop.

Politics and Laws

As of this writing, it is rumored that a new cybersecurity czar might be appointed for the first time by the president of the United States. This is a strong message indicating that the government realizes the importance of security, both in the government and the private sectors. Governments all over the world have started to look at computers and the security issues that surround them more seriously over the last few years. Continual scuffle goes on about transboarder issues pertaining to cryptography, what can be encrypted, at what strength, and by whom. There are also boarder issues that come into play when an attack comes from another country that does not see that activity as illegal behavior. The legal system is meeting many unprecedented challenges when it comes to computer security.

As the Internet brings the world closer, it requires different governments to come to the table and agree upon different matters pertaining to computers, security, boundaries, and acceptable behavior.

One sign of countries attempting to get in step with each other is the acceptance of the Common Criteria. (Common Criteria is discussed at length in Chapter 5.) At one point, the United States had one specific way of evaluating and testing the security of a system or device. This was the Trusted Computer System Evaluation Criteria (TCSEC), which was based on the Orange Book. Europe had the Information Technology Security Evaluation Criteria (ITSEC). Canada and Britain developed their own criteria on how to determine if a system was declared safe and to what extent. The Common Criteria is an attempt to take the best of all of these methods and provide the world with one way of determining a product's security and protection level.

Other than different countries viewing computer security differently, another barrier to proper security is how laws deal with computer crimes. The courts have been running a continual game of catch up. The law cannot keep ahead or in step with technology, which is important if it is to regulate it and determine who is guilty and who is innocent in different situations. It is continually hard for a judge or jury to declare who is guilty in a computer crime because the whole playing field has changed. Prosecutors have a hard time of collecting usable evidence to present in court, and defense lawyers cannot fall back on precedent cases where similar acts took place.

In addition, these difficulties start with law enforcement who have a lack of personnel skilled in computer technology and computer forensics. If a person is accused of a cybercrime, law officers must search for evidence. But what do they search for? Most cops do not necessarily know how to dump data from memory into a file, find remnants of data after the criminal formatted the drive, or understand how computer crimes take place so they can look for the right clues. Law enforcement has to know how to remove evidence from computer systems and drives in a way that does not corrupt the data and is usable in court. They must gain much more computer knowledge and skills to be able to deal with computer crimes.

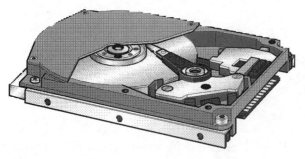

Law enforcement has to know how to remove evidence from computer systems and drives in a way that does not corrupt the data and is usable in court.

Computers are used in many different types of crimes and provide many different types of barriers that the law enforcement and courts are not used to dealing with. Data and communication may be encrypted and there are jurisdiction issues if a crime took place in Kansas but originated in Florida. Also, a lot of the communication is spoofed so the law enforcement must know how to track down criminals through binary, hexadecimal, and packet header means.

These barriers and issues help criminals who are computer savvy and if they do get caught, many of them are not prosecuted to the extent as if they had committed a crime that the courts were used to dealing with.

Tougher penalties need to be developed and enforced when it comes to computer crimes.

These are tough issues for the police force, FBI, CIA, and the judicial systems. However, with change comes growth. Laws are quickly being made and procedures being developed to effectively deal with computer crimes. Personnel is being increased to include people with technology skills, and computer training is a must in many parts of these organizations.

Education

Generally, if a person is considered a security specialist, this person has to have the interest and discipline to teach herself security issues, go to seminars and conferences all over the world, read stacks of books, and have a wide range of experience in different environments. There has not been a uniform standardized way of teaching security in vocational schools or universities. Some colleges offer some security classes in their CIS or MIS programs, and there are some schools that offer master or doctorates in computer security. However, they are few and far between.

Networking, programming, operating systems, and engineering are taught. Security can be sprinkled in as an elective or not even offered. This is because there has not been a high demand or need for this type of knowledge in the job market. However, computer and information security is gaining in importance, need, and demand. This has caused a handful of schools to offer security classes and possibly programs, but they will probably become more frequent and available as the job market demands more individuals with this skill set.

However, it is important that not only security courses and programs be offered, but that the networking, programming, and engineering classes have security integrated into them. Security should not be looked upon as an extra component or an option to be added on later. It should be interwoven into the code as a program is being developed, it should be an important piece of architecture and engineering, and it should be understood and practiced when networks are being built, added upon, and maintained. For security to be successful, it needs to be thought of in many different situations and cases.

Eduction is something the U.S. government has also recognized as an important step to protect its network infrastructure. It has setup criterion for schools to follow, which will, in turn, receive government grants and subsidiaries. If countries want to protect themselves and their resources from computer and cyberattacks, they must teach their people how to do this through education.

Summary

This chapter has touched on only a few of the exciting things that are happening within computer security and showed evidence of growth, evolution, and the inevitable change. It has been recognized for quite sometime that computers, data processing capabilities, and the Internet are extremely important tools for a vast array of reasons. It is only recently that securing these items has also been recognized as an important task.

This chapter was written to prepare you for the chapters to come. Some chapters, or items in the chapters might seem more interesting than other topics, but the CISSP certification was developed to ensure that you broaden your horizon when looking at and dealing with security issues. Information security would not be as effective if it was not provided with strong physical security; thus, it is important to know how each part works, how they overlap and integrate. No part of security would be totally effective if it was not enforced by regulations, laws, and liability responsibilities. The courts and law enforcement are having a larger involvement in many parts of computer security, and understanding these pieces can help you to best understand between what is acceptable, what is illegal, and how to deal with the issues that fall in between.

Each chapter ends with a section called "Quick Tips." This section provides a clear-cut bulleted list of items that outline what is important in the chapter for the CISSP exam. It does not outline all items within the chapter—only the items that are important for the exam. The same is true for the questions at the end of the chapter and on the accompanying CD-ROM. As stated before, these questions are presented in a way to prepare you for the exam. Each type of exam has its own way of asking questions. Novell and Microsoft give simulations and long-winded, scenario-based questions. Cisco gives shorted questions that get right to the point. (ISC)^2 asks short, somewhat vague questions. Knowing how the exam is structured will help in passing and accomplishing the CISSP certification.

Security Management Practices

3

In this chapter, you will learn about the following items:

- Security management responsibilities
- Three main security principles
- Difference between administrative, technical, and physical controls
- Risk management and risk analysis
- Data classification
- Security roles
- Personnel security issues

We hear about viruses causing millions of dollars in damages, hackers from other countries capturing credit card information from financial institutions, large corporation Web sites being defaced for political reasons, and clever hackers being caught and sent to jail. These are the more exciting and romantic pieces of computer security, but realistically these types of activities are not what the average corporation or security professional usually has to deal with when it comes to daily or monthly security tasks. Although viruses and hacking get all the headlines, security management is the core to a company's computer and information security.

Security Management

Security management includes risk management, security policies, and security education. These three core components serve as the foundation of a corporation's security program. The crux of security, and a security program, is to protect the company's assets. Risk management will identify these assets, discover the risks that threaten them, and estimate the possible damage and loss a company could endure if any of these risks become real. The results of the risk analysis help management to develop applicable security policies that provide direction for the security activities that will take place in the company and express the value that management places on the company's security program. Security education takes this information to each and every employee within the company so that everyone is properly informed and can more easily work towards the same security goals.

Security management has changed over the years because networked environments, computers, and the applications that hold information have changed. Information used to be held in mainframes, as mentioned in Chapter 2, and a more centralized network structure was in place. The mainframe and management consoles used to access and configure the mainframe were placed in a centralized area instead of the distributed approach we see today. Only certain people were allowed access and only a small set of people knew how the mainframe worked, which drastically reduced security risks. Users were able to access information on the mainframe through dumb terminals; they were called this because they had little or no logic built into them. This also drastically reduced the need for strict security controls to be put into place. However, the computing society did not stay in this type of architecture. Now most networks are filled with personal computers that have advanced logic and processing power, users know enough about the systems to be dangerous, and the information is not centralized within one "glass house." Instead, the information lives on servers, workstations, and other networks. Information passes over wires and airways at a rate that was not even conceived 10 to 15 years ago.

The Internet, extranets (business partner networks), and intranets not only make security much more complex, but they make security even more critical. The core network architecture has changed from being a stand-alone computing environment to a distributed computing environment that has increased exponentially with complexity. Although connecting a network to the Internet adds more functionality and services for the users and gives more visibility of the company to the Internet world, it opens the floodgates on potential security risks.

Today, a majority of organizations could not function if they lost their computers and computing capabilities. Computers have been integrated into the business and individual daily fabric and would cause great pain and disruption if they were suddenly unavailable. As networks and environments have changed, so has the need for security. Security is more than just a firewall and a router with an access list; these systems have to be managed and a big part of security is the actions of users and the procedures they follow. This brings us to security management practices, which focus on the continual protection of company assets.

Security Management Responsibilities

Okay, who is in charge and why?

In the world of security, management's functions involve determining objectives, scope, policies, priorities, standards, and strategies. A clear scope needs to be defined, and actual goals that are expected to be accomplished from a security program need to be determined before 100 people run off in different directions trying to secure the environment. Business objectives, security risks, user productivity, and functionality requirements and objectives need to be evaluated and steps need to be drawn out to ensure that all of these issues are accounted for and properly addressed. Many companies only look at the business and productivity elements of an equation and figure that information and computer security fall within the IT administrator's responsibilities. In these situations, management is not taking computer and information security seriously and it will most likely remain underdeveloped, unsupported, and unsuccessful. Security needs to be addressed at the highest levels of management. The IT administrator can consult on the subject, but the security of a company should not be laid in her lap.

Security management relies on the proper identification of a company's information assets, assigning values to these assets, developing, documenting, and implementing security policies, procedures, standards, and guidelines, which provides integrity, confidentiality, and availability. Different management tools are used to classify data and perform risk analysis and assessments. These tools identify threats and exposure rates and rank the severity of identified vulnerabilities so that effective countermeasures can be implemented to mitigate risk overall. Management's responsibility is to provide protection for the resources it is responsible for and the company it relies upon. These resources come in human, capital, hardware, and informational forms. Management must concern itself with recognizing the risks that can affect these resources and be assured that the necessary protective measures are put into effect.

The necessary resources, funding, and strategic representatives need to be available and ready to participate in the security program. Management must assign responsibility and the roles necessary to get the security program off the ground and keep it thriving and evolving as the environment changes. Management must also integrate the program into the current business environment and monitor its accomplishments. Management's support is one of the most important pieces of a security program. A simple nod and a wink will not provide the amount of support required.

Security Administration and Supporting Controls

If there is not a current security administration, one should be established by management, which is directly responsible for monitoring a majority of the facets of a security program. Depending on the organization, security needs, and size of the environment, the security administration can consist of one person or a group of individuals that work in a central or decentralized manner. A clear reporting structure, understanding of responsibilities, and monitoring are important to make sure that compromises do not slip in because of a lack of communication or understanding.

Information owners should dictate who can access resources and how much capacity users can possess pertaining to those resources. The security administration's job is to make sure this happens. Administrative, physical, and technical controls should be utilized to achieve the management's directives. *Administrative controls* include the development and publication of policies, standards, procedures, and guidelines, the screening of personnel, security awareness training, the monitoring of system activity, and change control procedures. *Technical controls* consist of logical access control mechanisms, password and resource management, identification and authentication methods, security devices, and configuration of the network. *Physical controls* entail controlling individual access into the facility and different departments, locking systems and removing unnecessary floppy or CD-ROM drives, protecting the perimeter of the facility, monitoring for intrusion, and environmental controls. Figure 3-1 illustrates how the administrative, technical, and physical controls work together to provide the necessary level of protection.

The *information owner* is usually a senior executive within the management group of the company. The information owner has the final corporate responsibility of data protection and would be the one held liable for any negligence when it comes to protecting the company's information assets. The person who holds this role is responsible for assigning a classification to the information and dictating how the information should be protected. If the information owner does not lay out the foundation of data protection and ensure that the directives are being enforced, this would violate the due care concept. (The due care concept is explained later in the chapter in the section "Implementation.")

Security administration brings a focal point to security and a hierarchical structure of responsibility. The security administration's job is to ensure that the management's directives are fulfilled when it comes to security, not to construct those directives in the first place. There should be a clear communication path between the security adminis-

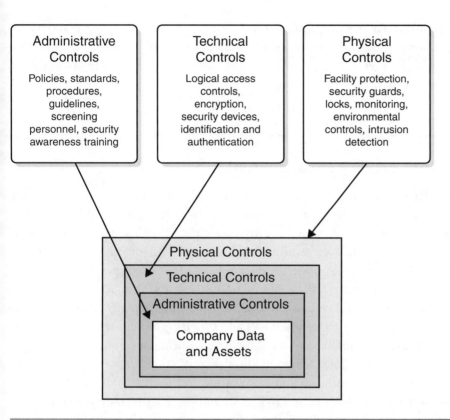

Administrative Controls	Technical Controls	Physical Controls
Policies, standards, procedures, guidelines, screening personnel, security awareness training	Logical access controls, encryption, security devices, identification and authentication	Facility protection, security guards, locks, monitoring, environmental controls, intrusion detection

Physical Controls

Technical Controls

Administrative Controls

Company Data and Assets

Figure 3-1   Administrative, technical, and physical controls work in a synergistic manner to protect a company's assets.

tration and senior management to ensure that the security program receives the proper support and that management makes decisions that it is responsible for. Too many times senior management is extremely disconnected from security issues and when a serious security breach takes place, they are the ones who have to explain the reasons to their business partners, shareholders, and the public. After this, they can become too involved. A healthy relationship between the security administration and senior management should be developed from the beginning and communication should easily flow in both directions.

Inadequate management can undermine the entire security effort in a company. This can happen because management does not fully understand the necessity of security, security is in competition with other management goals, it is viewed as expensive and unnecessary, or management applies lip service but no real action. Powerful and useful technologies, devices, software packages, procedures, and methodologies are available to provide the exact level of security required, but without proper security management and management support, it doesn't really matter.

Example of Security Management

Anyone who has been involved with a security rollout understands the conflicts between securing an environment and still allowing the necessary level of functionality so productivity is not affected. Many security projects start with proactive individuals who know the end result they are wanting to achieve and have lofty ideas of how quick and efficient their security rollout will be, only to hear all the users go up in arms when they find out what restrictions will be placed upon them and they scream about how they will not be able to fulfill certain parts of their job if this actually takes place. This usually causes the project to screech to a halt and *then* the proper assessments, evaluations, and planning are initialized to see how the environment can be slowly secured and how to ease users and tasks delicately into new restrictions or ways of doing business. This causes a lot of heartache and wastes time and money. Individuals who are responsible for security management activities should see that the understanding of the environment and proper planning happen *before* trying to kick off an implementation phase of a security program.

Fundamental Principles of Security

Now what are we trying to accomplish again?

There are several small and large objectives of a security program, but the main three principles in all programs are confidentiality, integrity, and availability. These are referred to as the *CIA triad*. The level of security required to accomplish these principles differs per company because their security goals and requirements may be different. All security controls, mechanisms, and safeguards are implemented to provide one or more of these principles and all risks, threats, and vulnerabilities are measured in their potential capability to compromise one or all of the CIA principles.

Confidentiality

Confidentiality provides the ability to ensure that the necessary level of secrecy is enforced at each junction of data processing and prevention of unauthorized disclosure. This level of confidentiality should prevail while data resides on systems and devices within the network, as it is transmitted, and once it reaches its destination.

Attackers can thwart confidentiality mechanisms by network monitoring, shoulder surfing, stealing password files, and social engineering. These topics will be addressed more in-depth in later chapters, but *shoulder surfing* is when a person looks over another person's shoulder and watches keystrokes or data as it appears on the screen. *Social engineering* is tricking another person into sharing confidential information by posing as an authorized individual to that information.

Users can intentionally or accidentally disclose sensitive information by not encrypting it before sending it to another person, falling prey to a social engineering attack, sharing a company's trade secrets, or not providing the extra care of protection of confidential information when processing it.

Confidentiality can be provided by encrypting data as it is stored and transmitted, network traffic padding, strict access control, data classification, and training personnel on the proper procedures.

Integrity

Integrity is upheld when the assurance of accuracy and reliability of information and systems is provided, and unauthorized modification of data is prevented. Hardware, software, and communication mechanisms must work in a concerted manner to maintain and process data correctly and move data to intended destinations without unexpected alteration. The systems and network should be protected from outside interference and contamination.

Environments that enforce and provide this attribute of security ensure that attackers or mistakes by users do not compromise the integrity of systems or data. When an attacker inserts a virus, logic bomb, or back door into a system, its integrity is compromised. This can, in turn, negatively affect the integrity of information held on the system by corruption, malicious modification, or replacing the data with incorrect data. Strict access controls, intrusion detection, and encryption can combat these attempts.

Users usually affect a system or its data's integrity by mistake, although internal users can also be up to malicious deeds. Users may accidentally delete configuration files because their hard drives are full and they don't remember ever using a boot.ini file. Or they can insert incorrect values into a data processing application that ends up charging a customer $300 instead of $3,000,000. Incorrectly modifying data kept in databases is another popular way of corrupting data by users that can have lasting effects.

Security should streamline the users' abilities and give them only certain choices and functionality so errors become less common and less devastating. System-critical files should be restricted from the users' view and access. Applications should provide mechanisms that check for valid and reasonable input values. Databases should let only authorized individuals modify data, and data in transit should be protected by encryption or other mechanisms.

Availability

The systems and networks should provide adequate capacity in order to perform in a predictable manner with the acceptable level of performance. It should be able to recover from disruptions in a secure and quick manner so productivity will not be negatively affected. Single points of failure should be avoided, backup measures should be taken, redundancy mechanisms should be in place when necessary, and the negative effects from environmental components should be prevented. Necessary protection mechanisms need to be in place to protect against inside and outside threats that could affect the availability and productivity of the network, systems, and information. *Availability* ensures the reliability and timely access to data and resources to authorized individuals.

System availability can be affected by device or software failure. Backup devices should be used and available to quickly replace critical systems, or employees should be skilled and available to make the necessary adjustments to bring the system back online. Environmental issues like heat, cold, humidity, static electricity, and contaminants can also affect system availability. These issues are addressed in detail in Chapter 6. Systems should be protected from these elements, properly grounded electrically, and closely monitored.

Denial of service (DoS) attacks are popular methods for hackers to disrupt a company's system availability and productivity. These attacks are mounted to reduce the ability of users to access system resources and information. To protect against these attacks, only the necessary services and ports should be available on systems, and intrusion detection should monitor the network traffic and host activities. Certain firewall and router configuration can also reduce the threat of DoS attacks and possibly stop them from occurring.

Critical Security Services

Integrity prevents unauthorized modification of systems and information.

Confidentiality prevents unauthorized disclosure of sensitive information.

Availability prevents disruption of service and productivity.

Integrity, confidentiality, and availability are critical principles of security. Understanding their meaning, how they are provided by different mechanisms, and how their absence can negatively affect an environment should be understood to best identify problems and provide proper solutions. Figure 3-2 illustrates the CIA triad.

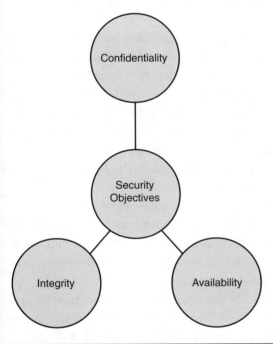

Figure 3-2 The CIA triad.

Security Definitions

Many times the words "threat," "vulnerability," "exposure," and "risk" are used to represent the same thing even though they have different meanings and relationships to each other. It is important to understand each word's definition, but more importantly, you should understand their association to each other.

A *vulnerability* is a software, hardware, or procedural weakness that may provide an attacker the open door he is looking for to enter a computer or network and have unauthorized access to resources within the environment. A vulnerability characterizes the absence or weakness of a safeguard that could be exploited. This vulnerability can be a service running on a server, unrestricted modem dial-in access, an open port on a firewall, a lax physical security so anyone can enter a server room, or nonenforced password management on servers and workstations.

A *threat* is any potential danger to information or systems. A threat agent could be an intruder accessing the network through a port on the firewall, a process accessing data in a way that violates that security policy, a tornado wiping out a facility, or an employee making an unintentional mistake that could expose confidential information or destroy a file's integrity.

A *risk* is the likelihood of a threat agent taking advantage of a vulnerability. A risk is the loss potential, or probability, that a threat will exploit a vulnerability. If a firewall has several ports open, there is a higher risk that an intruder will use one to access the network in an unauthorized method. If the users are not educated on processes and procedures, there is a higher risk that an employee will make an intentional or unintentional mistake that may destroy data. If an intrusion detection system is not implemented on a network, there is a higher risk that an attack will go unnoticed until it is too late. Reducing the vulnerabilities or the threat agents reduces the risk.

An *exposure* is an instance of being exposed to losses from a threat agent. A vulnerability can cause an organization to be exposed to possible damages. If password management is lax and password rules are not enforced, the company can be exposed to the possibility of having users' passwords captured and used in an unauthorized manner. If a company does not have its wiring inspected and does not put proactive fire prevention steps into place, it can expose itself to potentially devastating fires.

A *countermeasure*, or safeguard, mitigates the potential risk. A countermeasure is a software configuration, hardware, or procedure that eliminates a vulnerability or reduces the risk of a threat agent from being able to exploit a vulnerability. Countermeasures can be strong password management, a security guard, access control mechanisms within an operating system, the implementation of basic input/output system (BIOS) passwords, and security awareness training.

If a company has antivirus software only on the servers and the virus signatures are not kept up-to-date, this is a *vulnerability*. The company is vulnerable to virus attacks. The *threat* is a virus showing up in the environment and disrupting productivity. The likelihood of a virus showing up in the environment and causing damage is the *risk*. Because there is a possibility of losing or corrupting data from a virus attack, the company now has an *exposure*. The *countermeasures* in this situation are to update the signatures and install the antivirus software on all computers. The relationships between risks, vulnerabilities, and countermeasures are shown in Figure 3-3.

Applying the right countermeasure can eliminate the vulnerability and exposure and reduce the risk. The company cannot eliminate the threat, but it can protect itself and prevent this threat from exploiting vulnerabilities within the environment.

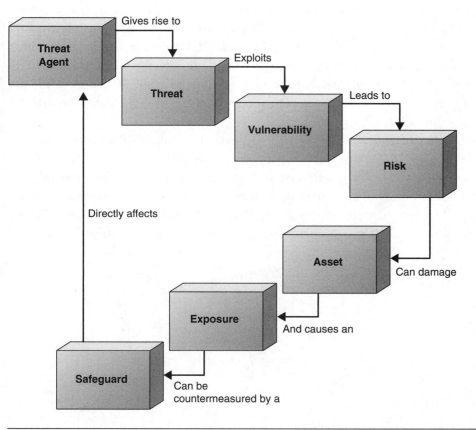

Figure 3-3 The relationships between the different security components

References

http://secinf.net/info/misc/handbook

http://csrc.ncsl.nist.gov

www.sans.org

www.cccure.org

The Top-Down Approach

When a house is built, the workers start with a blueprint of the structure, the foundation is poured, and the frame is erected. As the building of the house continues, the workers know what the end result is supposed to be, so they add the right materials, insert doors and windows in logical places, erect support beams, provide sturdy ceilings and floors, and add the plaster and carpet and smaller details until the house is complete. Then inspectors come in to ensure that the structure of the house and the components that were used to make it are acceptable. If this process did not start with a blueprint and a realized goal, the house could end up slanted with an unstable foundation with doors and windows that don't seem to shut properly. This house would not pass inspection; thus, a lot of time and money would have been wasted. Figure 3-4 illustrates this point.

The building of a house analogy can be applied to the building of a security program. When designing and/or implementing a security program, the functionality and end result expected need to be determined and realized. Many times companies just start locking down computers and installing firewalls without taking the time to understand the overall security requirements, goals, and assurance levels they expect from security as a whole within their environment. This process starts from the top with very broad

Figure 3-4 Without a solid blueprint (policy) and organized procedures, a security program could end up looking like this house.

ideas and terms (blueprint) and works its way down to detailed configuration settings and system parameters (windows and carpets). At each step, the overall security goals need to be kept in mind so that each added piece is sure to add more granularity to the intended goal and not splinter the main objectives by running in 15 different directions at once.

The security policy works as a blueprint for a company's security program and provides the necessary foundation to build upon. This policy needs to be taken seriously from the beginning and developed with the idea that it will continually be referenced to ensure that all security components stay in step and work to accomplish the same objectives. The next step is to develop and implement procedures, standards, and guidelines that support the security policy and identify the security components and methods that need to be put into place. Once these items are developed, the process increases with granularity by developing standards and configurations of the chosen security controls and methods.

If security starts with a solid foundation and develops over time with understood goals and objectives, a company does not need to make drastic changes midstream. The process can be methodical, requiring less time, funds, and resources, and provide a proper balance between functionality and protection. This is not the norm, but with your insight, maybe you can help companies approach security in a more controlled manner. You could provide the necessary vision and understanding of how security should be thought out, properly implemented, and should evolve in an organized manner instead of resulting in a giant heap of security products that are disjointed and full of flaws.

A security program should use a *top-down approach*, meaning that the initiation, support, and direction come from top management and work their way through middle management and then to staff members. In contrast, a *bottom-up approach* would be if the IT department tried to develop a security program without getting proper management support and direction. A bottom-up approach is usually less effective, not broad enough, and doomed to fail. A top-down approach makes sure that the people actually responsible for protecting the company's assets (senior management) are driving the program.

Organizational Security Model

An organizational security model is a framework made up of many entities, protection mechanisms, logical and physical components, procedures, and configurations that all work together in a synergistic way to provide a security level for an environment. Each model is different, but all models work in layers: one layer providing support for the layer above it and protection for the layer below it. The goal of a security model is assurance, which is the sum total of all security components within an environment that provide a level of confidence. Because a security model is a framework, companies are free to plug in different types of technologies, methods, and procedures to accomplish the necessary security assurance level in their environment. Figure 3-5 illustrates the pieces that can make up the security model.

Effective security requires a balanced approach and application of all security components and procedures. Some security components are technical (access control lists and encryption) and some are nontechnical (developing a security policy and enforcement of compliance), but each has an important place within the framework and if one is missing or incomplete, the whole framework can be affected.

A security model has different layers, but it also has different types of goals to accomplish in different time frames. You might have a goal for yourself today to brush your teeth, run three miles, finish the project you have been working on, and spend time with your kids. These are daily goals or *operational goals*. You might have mid-term goals to complete your master's degree, write a book, and get promoted. These take

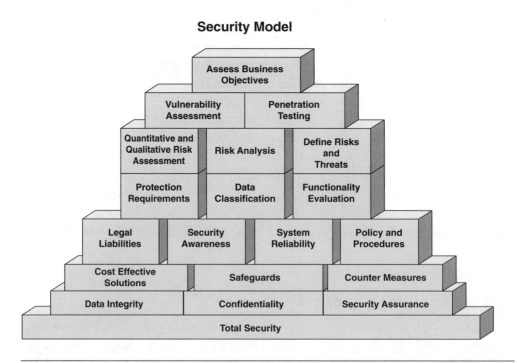

Figure 3-5 A comprehensive and effective security model has many integrated pieces.

more time and effort and are referred to as *tactical goals*. Your long-term goals may be to retire at age 55, save enough money to live comfortably, and to live on a houseboat. These goals are *strategic goals* because they look farther into the future.

The same thing happens in computer security planning. Daily goals, or operational goals, focus on productivity and task-oriented activities to ensure that the company's functionality happens in a smooth and predictable manner. Mid-term goals, or tactical goals, could be to integrate all workstations and resources into one domain so more central control can be achieved. A long-term goal, or strategic goal, may involve moving all the branches from dedicated communication lines to frame relay, implementing IPSec virtual private networks (VPNs) for all remote users instead of dial-up entry, and integrating wireless technology with the necessary security measures into the environment.

This approach to planning is called the *planning horizon*. A company cannot usually implement all changes at once, and some changes are larger than others. Many times certain changes cannot happen until other changes take place. If a company wants to implement its own certificate authority and wants to implement a full public key infrastructure (PKI) enterprise-wide, this cannot happen in a week if the company currently works in decentralized workgroups with no domain structure. So the operational goals are to keep production running smoothly and make small steps towards readying the environment for a domain structure. The tactical goal would be to put all workstations and resources into a domain structure, and centralize access control and authentication. The strategic goal is to have all workstations, servers, and devices within the enterprise use the PKI to provide authentication, encryption, and more secure communication channels.

Security works best if it's operational, tactical, and strategic goals are defined and work to support each other, which can be much harder than it sounds.

Business Requirements—Private Industry versus Military Organizations

The security model an organization chooses depends on its critical missions and business requirements. The private industry usually has much different missions and requirements than that of the military. The private industry thrives by beating the competition and this is done through marketing and sales, solid management decisions, understanding the target audience, and understanding the flow and ebb of the market. A private sector business is successful if its data is readily available, so processing order requests and fulfilling service orders can happen quickly and painlessly for the customer. The data also needs to be accurate to satisfy the customers' needs. Out of the three security services (confidentiality, integrity, and availability), data integrity and availability usually rank higher than confidentiality to most private sector businesses.

The military also thrives by beating their competition (other countries), which requires proper training, readiness, intelligence, and deployment. Although the private industry does need a degree of secrecy and ensured confidentiality, it does not play as of an important role as it does within a military organization. The military has more critical information that must not fall into the wrong hands; therefore, out of the three main security services, confidentiality is the most important to the military sector. In turn, this would cause a military installation to implement a more strict security model that emphasizes secrecy than a private sector organization.

Risk Management

Life is full of risk.

Risk is the possibility of something damaging happening; *risk management* is the process of identifying, assessing, and reducing this risk to an acceptable level and implementing the right mechanisms to maintain that level of risk. There is no such thing as a 100-percent secure environment. Every environment has vulnerabilities and risks to certain degrees. The real skill comes in identifying these risks, assessing the probability of them actually occurring and the damage they could cause, and then taking the right steps to reduce the overall level of risk in the environment.

Risks come in different forms to a company; they are not all computer related. When a company purchases another company, they are taking on a lot of risk in the hopes that this move will increase their market base and their productivity and profitability. If a company increases the product line that it sells, this can add overhead, increase the need for personnel and storage facilities, require more funding for different materials, and maybe increase insurance premiums and marketing campaigns. The risk is that this added overhead might not be matched in sales; thus, profitability will be reduced or not accomplished.

When we look at information security, there are several types of risk a corporation needs to be aware of and address properly. The following items touch on the major categories:

- **Physical damage** Fire, water, vandalism, power loss, and natural disasters
- **Human error** Accidental or intentional action or inaction that can disrupt productivity

- **Equipment malfunction**   Failure of systems and peripheral devices

- **Inside and outside attacks**   Hacking, cracking, and attacking

- **Misuse of data**   Sharing trade secrets, fraud, espionage, and theft

- **Loss of data**   Intentional or unintentional loss of information through destructive means

- **Application error**   Computation errors, input errors, and buffer overflows

The threats need to be identified, classified by category, and the actual magnitude of potential loss needs to be calculated. Real risk is hard to measure, but making priorities of the potential risks is attainable.

Risk Analysis

Risk analysis is a method of identifying risks and assessing the possible damage that could be caused in order to justify security safeguards. A risk is the probability of a threat agent exploiting a vulnerability and creating damage to a system or environment. Risk analysis is used to ensure that security is cost-effective, relevant, timely, and responsive to threats. Security can be quite complex, even for the well-versed security professionals, and it is easy to apply too much security, not enough security, the wrong security components, and spend too much money in the process without attaining the necessary objectives. Risk analysis helps companies prioritize their risks and shows them the amount of money that could be applied to protecting against those risks in a sensible manner.

A risk analysis has three main goals: identify risks, quantify the impact of potential threats, and provide an economic balance between the impact of the risk and the cost of the countermeasure. Risk analysis provides a *cost/benefit comparison* where the annualized cost of safeguards to protect against threats is compared with the expected cost of loss. A safeguard, in most cases, should not be implemented unless the annualized cost of loss exceeds the annualized cost of the safeguard itself. This means that if a facility is worth $100,000, it does not make sense to spend $150,000 trying to protect it.

A risk analysis helps integrate the security program objectives with the company's business objectives and requirements. The more the business and security objectives are in alignment, the more successful the two will be. The analysis also helps the company to draft a proper budget for a security program and the security components that make up that program. Once a company knows how much their assets are worth and the possible threats they are exposed to, the company can make intelligent decisions on how much money to spend on protecting those assets.

A risk analysis needs to be supported and directed by senior management if it is going to be successful. Management needs to define the purpose and scope of the analysis, a team needs to be appointed to carry out the assessment, and the necessary time and funds need to be available to conduct the analysis. It is essential for senior management to review the outcome of the risk assessment and analysis and act on its findings. What good is it to go through all the trouble of a risk assessment and not react to its findings? Surprisingly, this does happen.

Risk Analysis Team

Each organization has different departments. Each department has its own functionality, resources, tasks, and quirks. For the most effective risk analysis, a team needs to be built that includes individuals from many or all the departments to ensure that all the risks are identified and addressed. The team members can be management, application programmers, IT staff, auditors, systems integrators, and operational managers.

This is necessary because if the risk analysis team is only made up of individuals from the IT department, they may not understand the types of risks the accounting department faces with data integrity issues, or if their data files were wiped out in an accidental or intentional act, what this would mean to the company as a whole. The IT staff may not understand all the risks the employees in the warehouse would face if a natural disaster hit, what it would mean to their productivity and how it would affect the organization overall. Many times the risk analysis team is made up of members of different departments, and if that is not possible, the team should make sure to interview people in each department so all risks are fully understood and quantified.

Value of Information and Assets

If information does not have any value, then who cares about protecting it?

The value placed on information is relative to the parties involved, what work it took to develop this information, how much it costs to maintain it, what loss it would cause if it was lost or destroyed, and what benefit would be gained if another party obtained this information. Why should a company care? If a company does not know the value of the information it is trying to protect, they do not know how much money and time should be spent on protecting it. If you were in charge of making sure Russia does not know the encryption algorithms used when transmitting information to and from the U.S. spy satellites, you might use some more extreme and expensive security measures than if you were going to protect your peanut butter and banana sandwich recipe from your next-door neighbor. The value of the information supports security measure decisions.

Many of the following examples refer to assessing the value of *data* and protecting it, but this logic applies towards an organization's facility, systems, and resources. The value of the company's facility needs to be assessed, along with all printers, workstations, servers, peripheral devices, supplies, and resources. You do not know how much is in danger of being lost if you don't know what you have and what it is worth in the first place.

Costs That Make Up the Value

Information can have a quantitative and qualitative measure assigned to it, but this measurement needs to be derived. The actual cost of data is determined by the cost it takes to acquire, develop, and maintain it. The value is determined by the value it has to the owners, authorized users, and unauthorized users. Some information is important enough to a company to go through the steps of making it a trade secret or the company may choose to copyright specific logos and trademarks.

The value of an asset should reflect all identifiable costs that would arise if there were an actual impairment of the asset. If a server cost $4,000, this value should not be inputted as the value of the asset in a risk assessment. If the server went down, the cost of replacing it or repairing it, the loss of productivity, and the value of any data that may be corrupted or lost need to be accounted for to properly capture the amount the company would lose if the server were to fail for one reason or another.

The following issues should be considered when assigning value to information and assets:

- Cost to acquire or develop the asset
- Cost to maintain and protect the asset
- Value of the asset to owners and users
- Value of the asset to adversaries
- Value of intellectual property
- Price others are willing to pay for the asset
- Cost to replace the asset if lost
- Operational and productivity that is affected if the asset is unavailable
- Liability issues if the asset is compromised
- Usefulness of the asset

Understanding the value of information is the first step to understanding what security mechanisms should be put in place and what funds should go towards this protection. A very important question is how much it could cost the company to not protect the data.

Determining the value of an asset can fulfill several different types of requirements a company may be facing, including the following:

- The value of each asset is necessary to perform effective cost/benefit analysis.
- An asset's value supports the selection of specific countermeasures and helps in the safeguard selection decision-making process.
- The value of each asset is often required for insurance purposes.
- The value of each asset is necessary to understand what exactly is at risk.
- The value of each asset may be required to prevent negligence, conform to due care, and comply with legal and regulatory standards.

Identifying Threats

Okay, what should we be afraid of?

Earlier it was stated that the definition of a threat is the possibility that a threat agent may exploit a vulnerability to cause harm to a computer, network, or company. There are many types of threat agents that can take advantage of several types of vulnerabilities that can result in risks. Table 3-1 shows the relationship between some of these.

There are other types of threats that can happen within a computerized environment that are much harder to identify than those listed in Table 3-1. These have to do with application and user errors. If an application uses several complex equations to produce results, it can be difficult to discover and isolate if these equations are incorrect or if the application is using inputted data incorrectly. This can result in *illogical processing* and *cascading errors* as invalid results are passed on to another process. These types of problems lie within applications' code and are very hard to identify.

User errors, intentional or accidental, are easier to identify through the monitoring and auditing of user activities. Audits and reviews need to be conducted to uncover if employees are inputting values incorrectly into programs, misusing technology, or modifying data in an inappropriate manner.

Risks have *loss potential*, meaning that the company would lose something if a threat agent actually exploits a vulnerability. The loss can be corrupted data, destruction to systems and/or the facility, unauthorized disclosure of confidential information, and a reduction in employee productivity. When performing a risk analysis, the team also needs to look at *delayed loss* when assessing the damages that can occur from a risk. Delayed loss has negative effects on a company after a risk is initially exploited. The

Table 3-1 Relationship of Threat Agents, Vulnerabilities, and Risks

Threat Agents	Can Exploit This Vulnerability	Resulting in This Risk
Virus	Lack of antivirus software	Virus infection
Hacker	Powerful services running on a server	Unauthorized access to confidential information
Users	Misconfigured parameter in the operating system	System malfunction
Fire	Lack of fire extinguishers	Facility and computer damage, and possibly loss of life
Employee	Lax access control mechanisms	Damaging mission-critical information
Contractor	Lax access control mechanisms	Stealing trade secrets
Attacker	Poorly written application	Conducting a buffer overflow
Intruder	Lack of security guard	Breaking windows and stealing computers and devices
Employee	Lack of auditing	Altering data inputs and outputs from data processing applications
Attacker	Lack of stringent firewall settings	Conducting a denial of service attack

time period can be 15 minutes after the exploitation to years. Delayed loss issues can be reduced productivity over a period of time, reduced income to the company, lateness penalties accrued, extra expense to get the environment back to proper working conditions, and delayed collection of funds from customers.

For example, if a company's Web servers are attacked and brought offline, the immediate damage could be data corruption, the man hours necessary to bring the servers back online, and the replacement of any code or components that may be required. The company could lose productivity if it usually accepts orders and payments via its Web sites. If it takes a full day to get the Web servers fixed and back online, the company could lose a lot more sales and profits. If it takes a full week to get the Web servers fixed and back online, the company could lose enough sales and profits to not be able to pay other bills and expenses. This would be a delayed loss. If the company's customers lost confidence in them because of this activity, they could lose business for months or years. This is a more extreme case of delayed loss.

These types of issues bring complexity to being able to properly quantify losses that specific threats could cause, but they need to be taken into consideration to ensure that reality is represented in this type of analysis.

So up to now, we have management's support of the risk analysis, we constructed our team so that it represents different departments in the company, we placed a value on all the company's assets, and identified all the possible threats that could affect the assets. We have also taken into consideration all possible delayed losses the company may endure per asset per threat. The next step is to use qualitative or quantitative methods to calculate the actual risk the company faces.

Quantitative Approach

There are two types of approaches to risk analysis: *quantitative* and *qualitative*. Quantitative attempts to assign real numbers to the costs of countermeasures and the amount of damage that can take place. Quantitative also provides concrete probability percentages when determining the likelihood of threats and risks. Each element within the analysis (asset value, threat frequency, severity of vulnerability, impact damage, safeguard costs, safeguard effectiveness, uncertainty, and probability items) is quantified and entered into equations to determine total and residual risks. *Purely quantitative risk analysis is not possible because the method is attempting to quantify qualitative items.* If a severity level is high and a threat frequency is low, it is hard to assign corresponding numbers to these ratings and come up with a useful outcome.

Quantitative and qualitative approaches have their own pros and cons and each applies more appropriately to certain situations. The company, risk analysis team, and the tools they decide to use will determine which approach is best.

Analysis Inputs and Data Gathering

So where do we start?

After identifying the scope, goals, and team of a risk analysis, the next step is to gather the necessary data. This is the most time-consuming piece of an analysis and can prove to be the most difficult.

The necessary input for a quantitative analysis differs from a qualitative analysis because it deals with real numbers and percentages. The first step is to identify the following components that will make up the analysis.

- The assets that are to be protected should have values estimated and assigned.
- Each threat and corresponding risk needs to be identified.
- The loss potential of each risk needs to be estimated.

- An estimation of the possible frequency of the threat needs to be calculated.

- Remedial measures need to be recognized and recommended.

Once the data is gathered, it can be used in manual or automated methods to calculate the identified risks, their potential damages, and the amount of money that can be reasonably designated for the necessary countermeasures.

Automated Risk Analysis Methods

Collecting all the necessary data that needs to be plugged into risk analysis equations and properly interpreting the results can be overwhelming if done manually. There are several automated risk analysis tools on the market that can make this task much less painful and hopefully more accurate. The gathered data can be reused, greatly reducing the time required to perform subsequent analysis. They can also print out reports and comprehensive graphs to be presented to the management.

The objective of these tools is to reduce the manual effort of these tasks, perform calculations quickly, estimate future expected losses, and determine the effectiveness and benefits of the security countermeasures chosen. Most automatic risk analysis products port information into a database and are run several times with different parameters used to give a panoramic view of what the outcome will be if different risks come to bear. For example, after the tool has all the necessary information inputted, it can compute the potential outcome if a large fire took place, then rerun with different parameters to find out the potential losses if a virus damaged 40 percent of the data on the main file server, then rerun to find out how much the company would lose if an attacker stole all the customer credit card information held on three databases, and so on. Running through the different risk possibilities will give companies a more detailed understanding of which risks are more critical than others, and thus which ones to addressed first. Figure 3-6 shows an overly simple example of this process.

Steps of a Risk Analysis

There are many methods and equations that could be used when performing a quantitative risk analysis and many different variables that can be inserted into the process. We are going to go over the main steps that happen in every risk analysis and assessment.

1. Assign value to information and assets.
   a. What is the value of this asset to the company?
   b. How much does it cost to maintain it?
   c. How much does it make in profits for the company?
   d. How much would it be worth to the competition?

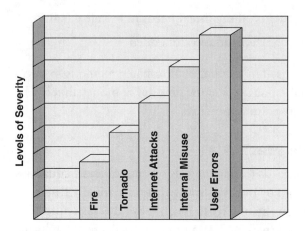

Figure 3-6 A simplistic example showing the severity of current threats versus the probability of them occurring

    e. How much would it cost to recreate or recover?

    f. How much did it cost to acquire or develop?

2. Estimate potential loss per risk.

    a. What physical damage can take place and how much would that cost?

    b. How much productivity can be lost and how much would that cost?

    c. What is the value lost if confidential information is disclosed?

    d. What is the cost of recovering from a virus attack?

    e. What is the cost of recovering from a hacker attack?

    f. How much would it cost if critical devices failed?

    g. Calculate the single loss expectancy (SLE) for each risk and scenario.

3. Perform a threat analysis.

    a. Gather information about the likelihood of each risk taking place from people in each department, past records, and official security resources that provide this type of data.

    b. Calculate the probability of occurrence for each risk identified.

    c. Calculate the annualized rate of occurrence, which is how many times each risk could happen in a year.

4. Derive the overall loss potential per risk.

    a. Combine potential loss and probability.

    b. Calculate the annualized loss expectancy (ALE) per risk by using the information calculated in the first three steps.

5. Choose remedial measures to counteract each risk.

6. Reduce, assign, or accept the risk.
   a. Risk reduction methods.
      i. Install security controls and components.
      ii. Improve procedures.
      iii. Alter environment.
      iv. Provide early detection methods to catch the risk as it's happening and reduce the possible damage it can cause.
      v. Produce a contingency plan of how business can continue if a specific risk takes place, reducing extending damages of the risk.
      vi. Erect barriers to the risk.
   b. Risk assignment.
      i. Buy insurance to transfer some or all of the risk.
   c. Risk acceptance.
      i. Live with the risks and spend no money towards protection.

Because we are stepping through a quantitative risk analysis, real numbers are used and calculations are necessary. *Single loss expectancy (SLE)* and *annualized loss expectancy (ALE)* were mentioned in the previous analysis steps. The SLE is a dollar amount that is assigned to a single event that represents the company's potential loss amount if a specific threat took place.

important on test

asset value × exposure factor (EF) = SLE

The *exposure factor* represents the percentage of loss a realized threat could have on a certain asset. So if a data warehouse has the asset value of $150,000 and if a fire took place, it is estimated that 25 percent of the warehouse would be damaged and the SLE would be $37,500. This figure is derived to be inserted into the ALE equation.

SLE × annualized rate of occurrence (ARO) = ALE

The *annualized rate of occurrence (ARO)* is the value that represents the estimated possibility of a specific threat taking place within in a one-year time frame. The range can be from 0.0 (never) to 1.0 (always) and anywhere in between. For example, if the probability of a flood taking place in Mesa, Arizona is once in 1,000 years, the ARO value is 0.001.

So if a fire taking place within a company's data warehouse facility can cause $37,500 in damages and the likelihood, or ARO, of a fire taking place has a ARO value of 0.1 (indicating once in ten years), then the ALE value is $3,750. ($37,500×0.1 = $3,750.)

The ALE value tells the company that if they want to put in controls or safeguards to prevent this type of damage from happening, they can sensibly spend $3,750 or less per year to provide the necessary level of protection. It is important to know the real possibility of a risk and how much damage, in monetary terms, that the threat can cause to know how much can be spent to try and protect from that threat in the first place. It would not make good business sense for the company to spend more than $3,750 per year to protect itself from this risk.

Risk Analysis Definitions

Exposure Factor (EF)   Percentage of asset loss caused by identified threat

Single Loss Expectancy (SLE)   Asset Value × Exposure Factor

Annualized Rate of Occurrence (ARO)   Estimated frequency a threat will occur within a year

Annualized Loss Expectancy (ALE)   Single Loss Expectancy × Annualized Rate of Occurrence

Great, now that we have all of these numbers, what do we do with them? Let's look at the example shown in Table 3-2.

Table 3-2 shows the outcome of a risk analysis. With this data, the company can make intelligent decisions on what risks need to be addressed first because of the sever-

Table 3-2   Breaking Down How SLE and ALE Values Are Used

Asset	Risk	Asset Value	Potential Loss (SLE)	Annualized Frequency	Annual Loss Expectancy (ALE)
Facility	Fire	$560,000	$230,000	.25	$57,500
Trade secret	Stolen	$43,500	$40,000	.75	$30,000
File server	Failed	$11,500	$11,500	.5	$5,750
Data	Virus	$8,900	$6,500	.8	$5,200
Customer credit card info	Stolen	$323,500	$300,000	.65	$195,000

ity of the risk, the likelihood of it happening, and how much could be lost if the risk did become real. The company now also knows how much money can be spent to protect against each risk, which will result in a good business decision instead of just buying protection here and there without a clear understanding of the big picture. Because the company has a risk of losing up to $5,200 if data is corrupted by virus infiltration, up to this amount of funds can be earmarked to go towards providing antivirus software and methods to ensure that a virus attack will not happen.

We have just explored the ways of performing risk analysis through quantitative means. This method tries to measure the loss in monetary values and assign numeric sums of each component within the analysis. A pure quantitative analysis is not achievable because it is impossible to assign the exact figures to each component and loss values. Although we can look at past events, do the best to assess the value of the assets, and contact agencies that provide frequency estimates of disasters happening in our area. We still cannot say for a fact that we have a 25 percent chance of a fire happening in a year and that it will cause exactly $57,500 in damage. In quantitative risk analysis, we do our best in providing all the correct information to the best of our knowledge and we will come close to the risk values, but we cannot predict the future and how much the future will cost us or the company.

Results of a Risk Analysis

The risk analysis team should have clearly defined goals and results that they are seeking. The following gives a short list of what generally is expected from the results of a risk analysis.

- Assigned monetary values assigned to assets
- Comprehensive list of all possible and significant threats
- Probability, or likelihood, of the occurrence rate of each threat
- Loss potential the company can endure per threat in a 12-month time span
- Recommended safeguards, countermeasures, and actions

Although this list looks small, there is usually an incredible amount of detail under each bullet item. This report will be presented and given to the senior management. They will be concerned with possible monetary losses and the necessary costs to mitigate these risks from taking place. Although the reports should be as detailed as possible, there should be executive abstracts for the senior management to quickly understand the overall findings of the analysis.

Qualitative Risk Analysis

Another method of risk analysis is qualitative, which does not assign numbers and monetary values to components and losses. Instead, qualitative methods walk through different scenarios of risk possibilities and rank the seriousness of the threats and the sensitivity of the assets. Qualitative analysis techniques include judgment, intuition, and experience. Examples of qualitative techniques are Delphi, brainstorming, storyboarding, focus groups, surveys, questionnaires, checklists, one-on-one meetings, and interviews. The risk analysis team will determine the best technique for the risks that need to be assessed and the culture of the company and individuals involved with the analysis.

The team that is performing the risk analysis gathers personnel who have experience and education on the risks being evaluated. When this group is presented with a scenario that describes a risk and loss potential, they will respond with their gut feeling on how the risk will actually carry out and what extent of damage may result.

A scenario is written for each major threat and each scenario should be approximately one page in length. The functional manager who is most familiar with this type of threat should review the scenario to ensure that it reflects how an actual threat would be carried out. Safeguards that would diminish the damage of this threat are then evaluated, and the scenario is played out for each safeguard. The exposure possibility and loss possibility can be ranked as high, medium, or low or on a scale of 1 to 5 or 1 to 10. Once the selected personnel rank the possibility of a threat happening, the loss potential, and the advantages of each safeguard, this information is compiled into a report and presented to management to help them make better decisions on how best to implement safeguards into the environment. The benefits of this type of analysis are the communication that has to happen between the team members to rank the risks, the identification of safeguard strengths and weaknesses, and the people who know these subjects the best provide their opinions to management.

Let's look at a *simple* example of a qualitative risk analysis:

The risk analysis team writes a one-page scenario explaining the threat of a hacker accessing confidential information held on the five file servers within the company and distributes it to a preselected team of five people (the IT manager, database administrator, application programmer, system operator, and operational manager.) The preselected team is given the sheet to rank the threat's severity, loss potential, and each safeguard's effectiveness with a rating of 1 to 5, 1 being the least severe, effective, or probable. Table 3-3 shows the results.

This data is complied and inserted into a report and presented to management. When management is presented with this information, they will see that their staff feels

Table 3-3   Example of a Qualitative Analysis

Threat = Hacker Accessing Confidential Information	Severity of Threat	Probability of Threat Taking Place	Potential Loss to the Company	Effectiveness of of Firewall	Effectiveness of Intrusion Detection System	Effectiveness of Honey Pot
IT manager	4	2	4	4	3	2
Database administrator	4	4	4	3	4	1
Application programmer	2	3	3	4	2	1
System operator	3	4	3	4	2	1
Operational manager	5	4	4	4	4	2
Results	3.6	3.4	3.6	3.8	3	1.4

that purchasing a firewall will protect the company from this threat more than purchasing an intrusion detection system, or setting up a honeypot machine.

This is the result of only one threat, and the management will view the severity of all threats, the probability, and the loss potential of each threat so that they know which threats cause the greatest risk and should be addressed first.

Delphi Technique

The Delphi technique is a group decision method and is used to ensure that each member of a group gives an honest opinion of what he or she thinks the result to a particular risk will be. This avoids a group of individuals feeling pressured to go along with others' thought processes and enables them to participate in an independent and anonymous way. Each member of the group writes down his or her opinion of a certain risk on a piece of paper and turns it into the team that is performing the analysis. The results are compiled and distributed to the group members who then write down their comments anonymously and return them back to the analysis group. The comments are compiled and redistributed for more comments until a consensus is formed. This method is used to obtain an agreement on cost, loss values, and probabilities of occurrence without individuals having to agree verbally.

Quantitative versus Qualitative

So which method should we use?

Each method has its advantages and disadvantages and Table 3-4 is a list of some of the differences between the two methods.

The risk analysis team, management, risk analysis tools, and culture of the company will dictate which approach, quantitative or qualitative, will be used. Management may feel very comfortable with their staff's opinion and just want the data gathered and presented. Another company with a different management might demand real numbers to be able to use with other business profit gain and loss numbers, expense forecasts, and market trends.

The goal of either method is to estimate a company's real risk and rank the severity of the risks so the correct countermeasures can be put into place using a practical budget.

Protection Mechanisms

Okay, so we know we are at risk, we know the probability of it happening, now what do we do?

The next step is to identify the current security mechanisms and evaluate their effectiveness.

Because a company has such a wide range of threats and not just computer viruses and attackers, each threat type needs to be addressed and planned for individually. Site location, fire protection, site construction, power loss, and equipment malfunctions are examined in detail in Chapter 6. Software malfunctions and applications considera-

Table 3-4 Quantitative versus Qualitative Characteristics

Attribute	Quantitative	Qualitative
Requires more complex calculations	x	
Degree of guesswork that is involved		x
Is easily automated	x	
Provides a cost/benefit analysis	x	
Uses independent and objective metrics	x	
Provides the opinions of the staff that knows the processes best		x
Shows clear-cut losses that can be accrued within one year's time	x	

tions are covered in Chapter 5. Telecommunication and networking issues are analyzed and presented in Chapter 7. Disaster recovery and business continuity are addressed in Chapter 9. All of these subjects have their own associated risks and planning requirements. The following section addresses identifying and choosing the right countermeasures for computer systems and gives the best attributes to look for and all the different cost scenarios that must be investigated when comparing different types of software countermeasures. The end product of the analysis of alternatives is to demonstrate why the selected alternative is the most advantageous to the company.

Countermeasure Selection

A security countermeasure, sometimes called a safeguard, must make good business sense. Good business sense means that it is cost-effective and that its benefit outweighs or equals its cost. This requires another type of analysis: a *cost/benefit analysis*.

A commonly used cost/benefit calculation for a given safeguard is

**(ALE before implementing safeguard) − (ALE after implementing safeguard) −
(annual cost of safeguard) = value of safeguard to the company**

For example, if the ALE of the threat of a hacker bringing down a Web server is $12,000 and after the suggested safeguard is implemented the ALE is now $3,000 and the annual cost of maintenance and operation of the safeguard is $650, then the value of this safeguard is $8,350 each year.

The cost of a countermeasure is more than just the amount that is filled out on the purchase order. The following items need to be considered and evaluated when deriving the full cost of a countermeasure:

- Product costs

- Design/planning costs

- Implementation costs

- Environment modifications

- Compatibility with other countermeasures

- Maintenance requirements

- Testing requirements

- Repair, replace, or update costs

- Operating/support costs

- Effects on productivity

A company can decide that to protect many of their resources and network traffic, an intrusion detection system (IDS) is warranted. So the company pays $5,500 for the software. Is that the total cost? Nope. This software should be tested in an environment that is segmented from production to uncover any unexpected activity. After this testing is complete and the IT group feels it is safe to insert into their production environment, they must install the monitor management software, the sensors, and properly direct the communication paths from the sensors to the manager console. Routers may need to be reconfigured to redirect traffic flow, and it needs to be ensured that users cannot access the IDS manager console. A database needs to be configured to hold all attack signatures, and simulations need to be run.

Anyone who has worked in an IT group knows that some adverse reaction almost always takes place in this type of scenario. The network performance can take an unacceptable hit after installing this product, users may no longer be able to access the Unix server for some mysterious reason, and the IDS vendor may not have explained that two more service patches are necessary for the whole thing to work correctly.

So the cost of this countermeasure is $5,500 for the product, $3,400 for the lab and testing time, $2,600 for the loss in user productivity once the product was introduced into production, $4,000 in labor for router reconfiguration, product installation, troubleshooting, and installation of the two service patches. So the real cost of this countermeasure is $15,500. If our total risk was calculated at $9,000, we went over budget when applying this countermeasure to the identified risk. Some of these costs could not be known about in the future, but an experienced risk analyst would account for these possibilities.

Functionality and Effectiveness of Countermeasures

Once you have a handle on the cost of the safeguard, you will then need to evaluate its functionality and effectiveness. When selecting a safeguard, some attributes are more favorable than others. Table 3-5 provides a list of attributes that should be considered *before* purchasing and committing to a security protection mechanism, or safeguard.

Table 3-5 Characteristics to Look For When Obtaining Safeguards

Characteristics	Description
Modular in nature	It can be installed or removed from an environment without adversely affecting other mechanisms.
Provides uniform protection	A security level is applied to all mechanisms it is designed to protect in a standardized method.

Characteristics	Description
Provides override functionality	An administrator can override the restriction if necessary.
Defaults to least privilege	When installed, it defaults to a lack of permissions and rights instead of installing with everyone having full control.
Independence of safeguard and the asset it is protecting	The safeguard can be used to protect different assets and different assets can be protected by different safeguards.
Flexibility and functionality	The more functionality the safeguard provides, the better. This functionality should come with flexibility, which enables you to choose different functions instead of all or none.
Clear distinction between user and administrator	A user should have less permissions when it comes to configuring or disabling the protection mechanism.
Minimum human intervention	When humans have to configure or modify controls, this opens the door to errors. The safeguard should be able to set itself up, pull the necessary information from the environment, and require the least amount of input from humans as possible.
Easily upgradeable	Software continues to evolve, and updates should be able to happen painlessly.
Auditing functionality	There should be a mechanism that is part of the safeguard that provides minimum or verbose auditing.
Minimizes dependence on other components	The safeguard should be flexible and not have strict requirements about the environment into which it will be installed.
Easily useable, acceptable, and tolerated by personnel	If the safeguards provide barriers to productivity or add extra steps to simple tasks, users will not tolerate it.
Must produce output in usable and understandable forms	Important information should be presented in forms easy for humans to understand and use for other tasks.
Must be able to reset safeguard	The mechanism should be able to be reset and return to original configurations and settings without affecting the system or asset it is protecting.
Testable	The safeguard should be able to be tested in different environments under different situations.
Does not introduce other compromises	The safeguard should not provide any covert channels or back doors.
System and user performance	System and user performance should not be greatly affected.
Proper alerting	A threshold should be able to be set as to when to alert personnel of a security breach and this type of alert should be acceptable.
Does not affect asset	The assets in the environment should not be adversely affected by safeguard.

Safeguards provide deterrence attributes if they are highly visible. This tells potential evildoers that adequate protection is in place and that they should move onto an easier target. Although the safeguard should be highly visible, the way that it works should not be attainable so the evildoers cannot attempt to modify the safeguard or know how to get around the reaches of the protection mechanism.

Putting It Together

So to perform a risk analysis, a company decides what asset needs to be protected and to what extent. It also indicates the amount of money that should go towards protecting specific assets. The functionality of the available safeguards needs to be evaluated and which ones would be most beneficial for the environment needs to be determined. Then the costs of the safeguards are appraised and compared. These steps and the resulting information enable management to make the most intelligent and informed decisions about selecting and purchasing countermeasures. Figure 3-7 illustrates these three steps.

Total Risk versus Residual Risk

The reason that a company implements countermeasures is to reduce their overall risk to an acceptable level. As stated earlier, no system or environment is 100-percent secure, which means there is always some risk left over to deal with. This is called *residual risk*. Many times after a countermeasure is installed, there is still some amount of risk, which is the residual risk.

Residual risk is different than *total risk*, which is when a company chooses not to implement any type of safeguard. The reason that this type of scenario takes place is

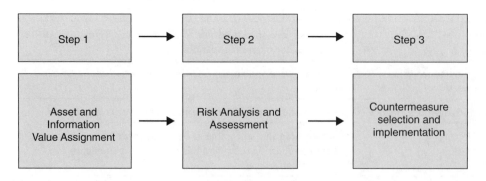

Figure 3-7   The main three steps in risk analysis and assessments

because of the cost/benefit analysis results. If there is a small likelihood that a company's Web servers can be compromised and the necessary safeguards to provide a higher level of protection cost more than the risk would cost in the first place, the company will choose not to implement the safeguard and is left with its total risk.

There is an important difference between total risk and residual risk and which type of risk a company is willing to accept.

threats × vulnerability × asset value = total risk

(threats × vulnerability × asset value) × controls gap = residual risk

During a risk assessment, the threats and vulnerabilities are identified. The possibility of these taking place is multiplied by the value of the assets that are at risk, which results in the total risk. Once the controls gap (countermeasures and safeguards) is factored in, the result is the residual risk. Implementing countermeasures is a way of mitigating risks. Because no company can remove all threats, this means there will always be some type of risk. The question is what level of risk the company is willing to accept.

Handling Risk

Now that we know about the risk, what do we do with it?

Once a company knows the amount of total and residual risk they are faced with, they must decide how to handle it. There are four basic ways of dealing with risk: transferring, rejecting, reducing, or accepting the risk.

There are many types of insurance available to companies when it comes to protecting its assets. If a company decides that the total or residual risk is too high to gamble with, they can purchase insurance, and this would *transfer the risk* to the insurance company.

If the company implements countermeasures, this will *reduce the risk*. If a company is in denial of its risk or ignores it, this is *rejecting risk*, which can be very dangerous and is unadvisable. The last approach is to *accept the risk*, which means the company understands the level of risk they are under and the cost of damage that is possible and they decide to just live with it. Many companies will accept risk when the cost/benefit ratio indicates that the cost of the countermeasure outweighs the cost of the risk. So the company will not implement the countermeasure and accept the risk.

References

www.securityauditor.net

www.all.net/journal/netsec/9703.html

Policies, Procedures, Standards, and Guidelines

Computers and the information that is processed on computers usually have a direct relationship with company's critical missions and objectives. Because of this level of importance, senior management should make protecting these items as their responsibility and provide the necessary support, funds, time, and resources to ensure that systems, networks, and information are protected in the most logical and cost-effective manner possible. A comprehensive management approach needs to be developed to accomplish these goals successfully.

For security to be ultimately successful in a business, it needs to start at the top level and be useful and functional at every single level within the organization. The senior management needs to define the scope of security, what needs to be protected, and to what extent. Management must understand the regulations, laws, and liability issues that they are responsible for when it comes to security and ensuring that the company as a whole fulfills the obligations of each of these. Senior management also needs to determine what is to be expected from employees and what the consequences of noncompliance will be. These decisions should be made by the individuals who will be held ultimately responsible if something goes wrong.

A security program contains all the pieces necessary to provide overall protection to a corporation and a long-term security strategy. A security program should have security policies, procedures, standards, guidelines, baselines, security awareness training, incident handling, and a compliance program. Human resources and the legal department need to be involved in the development and enforcement of some of these issues.

The language, level of detail, and formality of the policy, and supporting mechanisms should be examined. Security policies, standards, guidelines, and procedures must be developed in a realistic view to be most effective. Highly structured organizations will usually follow guidelines in a more uniformed way. Less structured organizations may need more explanation and emphasis to promote compliance. The more detailed the rules are, the easier it is to know when one has been violated. However, overly detailed documentation and rules can prove to be more of a burden than helpful. On the other hand, many times the more formal the rules, the easier they are to enforce. The business type, its culture, and goals need to be evaluated to make sure the right type of language is used when writing security documentation.

Security Policy

A *security policy* is a general statement produced by senior management (or a selected policy board or committee) to dictate what type of role security plays within the organization. A security policy can be an organizational policy, issue-specific policy, or system-specific policy. In an *organizational security policy*, management establishes how a security program will be set up, establishes the program's goals, assigns responsibilities, shows the strategic and tactical value of security, and outlines how enforcement should be carried out. This policy must address relative laws, regulations, and liability issues and how they are to be satisfied. The organizational security policy provides scope and direction for all future security activities within the organization. It also describes the amount of risk senior management is willing to accept.

Issue-specific policies address specific security issues that management feels need more detailed explanation and attention to make sure a comprehensive structure is built and all employees understand how they are to comply to these security issues. Organizations may choose to have an e-mail security policy that outlines what management can and cannot do with employees' e-mail messages and how employees can or cannot use different e-mail functionality and address-specific privacy issues. As an example, an e-mail policy might state that management can read any employee's e-mail messages that reside on the mail server, but not when they reside on the user's workstation. It might also state that employees cannot use e-mail to share confidential information, or used to pass inappropriate material, and may be subject to auditing of these actions. The employees should be made aware of these issues by signing a document, clicking Yes in a dialog box that explains these issues before they use their e-mail clients, or it can be presented as a banner when the users sign on to their computers. The policy provides direction and structure for the staff indicating what they can and cannot do, it informs the users of the expectations of their actions, and it provides liability protection in case an employee cries "fowl" for any reason dealing with e-mail use.

A *system-specific policy* presents the management's decisions that are closer to the actual computers, networks, applications, and data. This type of policy can provide an approved software list, which contains a list of applications that can be installed on individual workstations. This policy can describe how databases are to be protected, how computers are to be locked down, and how firewall, intrusion detection systems, and scanners are to be employed.

Types of Policies

Policies can fall into one of the following categories:

Regulatory   This policy is written to ensure that the organization is following standards set by a specific industry and is regulated by law. The policy type is detailed in nature and specific to a type of industry. This is used in financial institutions, health care facilities, and public utilities.

Advisory This policy is written to strongly suggest certain types of behaviors and activities which should take place within the organization. It also outlines possible ramifications for noncompliance activities to employees. This is used for handling medical information, financial transactions, and processing confidential information.

Informative This policy is written to inform employees of certain topics. It is not an enforceable policy, but one to teach individuals about specific issues relevant to the company. It could explain how the company interacts with partners, the company's goals and mission, and a general reporting structure in different situations.

Policies are written in broad and overview terms to cover many subjects in a general fashion. Much more granularity is needed to develop the ways and methods that need to happen to actually support the policy, and this happens with the use of procedures, standards, and guidelines. The policy provides the foundation. The procedures, and standards, and guidelines provide the security framework. And the necessary security components, implementations, and mechanisms are used to fill in the framework and to provide a full security program and secure infrastructure.

Further information and sample policies are in the appendices.

Standards

Some things you just gotta do.

Organizational security *standards* specify how hardware and software products are to be used. They provide a means to ensure that specific technologies, applications, parameters, and procedures are carried out in a uniform way across the organization. It may be an organizational standard that requires all employees to have their company identification badges on their person at all times, or that unknown individuals are to be challenged about their identity and purpose, or that confidential information has to be encrypted. These rules are usually *compulsory* within a company, and if they are going to be successful, they need to be enforced.

As stated in an earlier section, there is a difference between tactical and strategic goals. A strategic goal can be viewed as the ultimate end point and the tactical goals are the steps to achieve it. As shown in Figure 3-8, standards, guidelines, and procedures

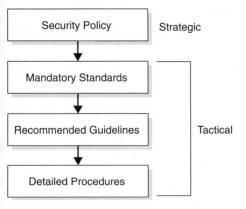

Figure 3-8 Policy establishes the strategic plans, and the lower elements provide the tactical support.

are the tactical goals used to achieve and support the directives in the security policy, which is considered the strategic goal.

Baselines

Baselines provide the minimum level of security necessary throughout the organization. A consistent baseline needs to be established before the security architecture can be properly developed. Standards are usually developed from baselines and baselines are sometimes considered the abstraction of standards.

Most of the time, baselines are platform-unique security implementations that are necessary to provide the required level of protection. For example, a company may require all workstations in the company to have at least a C2 security clearance. The baseline security level would be C2 and supporting procedures would provide step-by-step instructions on how the operating system and components have to be installed to achieve this specific security level.

The baseline is a *minimum* level of security and other business requirements may require specific systems to contain mechanisms that provide an even higher level of protection.

Guidelines

Guidelines are recommendation actions and operational guides to users, IT staff, operations staff, and others when a specific standard does not apply. They deal with the methodologies of securing computers and their software. There are always gray areas in life and guidelines can be used as a reference during those times. Whereas standards are specific mandatory activities, guidelines are general approaches that provide the necessary flexibility for unforeseen circumstances.

A policy might state that access to confidential data must be audited. A supporting guideline could further explain that audits should contain sufficient information to allow reconciliation with prior reviews. Supporting procedures would explain the necessary steps to configure, implement, and maintain this type of auditing.

Procedures

Procedures are detailed step-by-step actions to achieve a certain task. The steps can apply to users, IT staff, operations staff, security members, and others who may need to install or configure a computer component. Many organizations have written procedures on how operating systems are to be installed, how security mechanisms are to be configured, how to configure access control lists, set up new user accounts, assign computer privileges, auditing, material destruction, incident reporting, and much more.

Procedures are looked at as the lowest level in the policy chain because they are closest to the computers and provide detailed steps for configuration and installation issues. They provide the steps to actually implement the statements in the policies, standards, and guidelines.

Modular Elements

Standards, guidelines, and baselines should not be in one large document. Each has a specific purpose and a different audience. A document describing how to be in compliance with a specific regulation may go to the management staff, whereas a detailed procedure on how to properly secure a specific operating system is directed towards an IT member.

Being separate and modular in nature helps for proper distribution and updating when it is necessary.

Procedures spell out how the policy, standards, and guidelines will actually be implemented in an operating environment. If a policy states that all individuals who access confidential information must be properly authenticated, the supporting procedures will explain the steps for this to happen by defining the access criteria for authorization, how access control mechanisms are implemented and configured, and how access activities are audited. If a standard states that backups should be performed, then the procedures will define the detailed steps necessary to perform the backup, timelines of backups, storage of backup media, and so on. Procedures should be detailed enough to be able to be understood and used by a diverse group of individuals.

Security procedures, standards, measures, practices, and policies cover a number of different subject areas. Table 3-6 describes some of the subject areas affected.

To tie these items together, let's walk through an example:

A corporation's security policy states that confidential information should be properly protected. This states the issue in very broad and vague terms. A supporting standard mandates that all customer information held in databases must be encrypted with the Data Encryption System (DES) algorithm while it is stored and only transmitted using IPSec encryption technologies. The standard indicates what type of protection is required and another level of granularity and explanation is provided. The supporting procedures explain exactly how to implement the DES and IPSec technologies, and guidelines could cover how to handle cases when data is accidentally decrypted,

Table 3-6   Areas That Policies, Standards, Guidelines, and Procedures Cover

Subject Area	Examples
Accountability controls	Audit trails, reviewing audit logs, automation of auditing and necessary configurations, and storage of audit information
Physical and environmental controls	Intrusion detection system installation, configuration, and monitoring; cooling system, maintenance, and monitoring
Administration controls	Separation of duties, performing background checks, supervision, and rotation of duties
Access controls	Identification and authentication mechanisms; biometric installation, configuration, and calibration; smart card creation, use, and destruction
Cryptography	When to use it, which encryption technology to use, installation, and configurations
Business continuity planning (BCP) controls	Who is on the BCP team, when drills take place, what is to be documented, and what off-site facility is to be used
Computer operations	How operating systems are to be installed and configured, how applications are to be installed, how to secure workstations, and how to replace hard drives
Incident handling	What defines a security incident, who should the report go to, what should be in the report, and what is done with a report once it is turned in

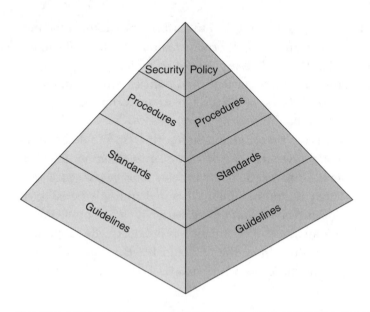

Figure 3-9   Security policies, procedures, standards, and guidelines work together.

corrupted, or compromised during transmission. As shown in Figure 3-9, all of these work together to provide a company with a security structure.

Implementation

Unfortunately, many times security policies, standards, procedures, baselines, and guidelines are written because an auditor instructed a company to document these items, but they live at the bottom of a file cabinet and are not shared, explained, or used. To be useful, they need to be put to use. No one is going to follow the rules if people don't know that the rules exist. Security policies and the items that support them not only have to be developed, but they also have to be implemented.

To be effective, employees need to know about security issues within these documents; therefore, they need visibility. Awareness training, manuals, presentations, newsletters, and legal banners can achieve this visibility. It needs to be clear that the directives came from senior management and the full management staff supports these policies. Employees need to understand what is expected of them in their actions, behavior, accountability, and performance.

Due Care and Due Diligence

Due care and due diligence are terms that are used throughout this book. A company practices due care by developing security policies, procedures, and standards. Due care shows that a company has taken responsibility for the activities that take place within the corporation and has taken the necessary steps to help protect the company, its resources, and employees from possible risks. Due diligence is practiced by activities that make sure that the protection mechanisms are continually maintained and operational. If a company does not practice due care and due diligence pertaining to the security of its assets, it can be legally charged with negligence and held accountable for any ramifications of that negligence.

Implementing security policies and the items that support them shows *due diligence* by the company and its management staff. Informing employees of what is expected of them and the consequences of noncompliance can come down to a liability issue. If a company fires an employee because he was downloading pornographic material to the company's computer, the employee can take the company to court and win if the employee can prove that he was not properly informed of what was considered acceptable and unacceptable use of company property and what the consequences were. Security awareness and training are covered in later sections, but understand that companies that do not supply these to their employees are not practicing due care and due diligence.

References

www.ncsa.uiuc.edu/People/ncsairst/Policy.html

www.security.kirion.net/securitypolicy/

www.sans.org/newlook/resources/policies/policies.htm

www.baselinesoft.com

www.information-security-policies-and-standards.com

Data Classification

Earlier in this chapter, the importance of recognizing what information is critical to a company and assigning a value to it was touched upon. The rationale behind assigning a value to data is to be able to gauge the amount of funds and resources that should go towards protecting it because not all data has the same value to a company. After the exercise of identifying important information, it should then be properly classified. A company has a lot of different information that is created and maintained. The reason to classify data is to organize it according to its sensitivity to loss or disclosure. Once data is segmented according to its sensitivity level, then the company can decide upon what security controls are necessary to protect different types of data. This ensures that information assets receive the appropriate level of protection and classifications indicate the priority of that security protection. The primary purpose of data classification is to indicate the level of confidentiality, integrity, and availability that is required for each type of information.

Data classification helps to ensure that the data is protected in the most cost-effective manner. There are security costs in overhead, maintenance, and funds and it is important to endure these costs for the information that actually requires this type of protection. Going back to our very sophisticated example of spies and peanut butter and banana sandwich, if a company was in charge of protecting spy files, it would classify this data as top secret and apply complex and highly technical security controls and procedures to ensure that it is not accessed in an unauthorized method and disclosed. On the other hand, the sandwich recipe would have a lower classification and you might protect it by not talking about it.

Each sensitivity classification should have separate handling requirements and procedures pertaining to how that data is accessed, used, and destroyed. For example, in a corporation, confidential information may be only accessed by senior management and a select few throughout the company. To access the information, it may require two or more people to enter their access codes, the auditing could be very detailed and monitored daily, and paper copies of the information may be kept in a vault. To properly erase this data, degaussing may be required or media physically destroyed. Other information in this company may be classified as sensitive and a slightly larger group of people can view it. Access control on the information classified as sensitive may require only one set of credentials: auditing happens but is only reviewed weekly, paper copies are kept in locked file cabinets, and the data can be deleted using regular measures when it is time to do so. Then the rest of the information is marked public and all employees can access it and no special auditing or destruction methods are required.

Private Business versus Military Classifications

Earlier we touched on how organizations choose different security models. It depends upon the type of organization, its goals, and objectives. Military organizations are more concerned about not disclosing confidential information than most private sector businesses. Private sector businesses are usually more concerned with the integrity and availability of data than most military organizations. This comes into play in data classification also.

To properly implement data classifications a company must first decide upon the sensitivity schemes they are going to use. One company can choose to use only confidential and public, while another company can choose to use top secret, secret, confidential, sensitive, and unclassified. Table 3-7 explains the types of classifications available. Note that some classifications are used for commercial businesses, whereas others are military classifications.

Table 3-7 Commercial Business and Military Data Classifications

Classification	Definition	Example	Organization That Would Use This
Sensitive	• Requires special precautions to ensure the integrity of the data by protecting it from unauthorized modification or deletion. • Requires higher than normal assurance of accuracy and completeness.	• Financial information • Details of projects • Profit earnings and forecasts	Commercial business
Confidential	• For use within the company only. • Data that is exempt from disclosure under the Freedom of Information Act or other laws and regulations. • Unauthorized discloser could seriously affect a company.	• Trade secrets • Health care information • Programming code • Information that keeps a company competitive	Commercial business and military
Private	• Personal information for use within a company. • Unauthorized disclosure could adversely affect personnel.	• Work history • Human resource information • Medical information	Commercial business

(continued)

Table 3-7 Commercial Business and Military Data Classifications *(continued)*

Classification	Definition	Example	Organization That Would Use This
Proprietary	• If disclosed, it could reduce competitive edge.	• Recipe to soft drink or other trade secret • Technical specifications of a product	Commercial business
Public	• All data that does not fit into previous classes. • Disclosure is not welcome, but it would not cause an adverse impact to company or personnel.	• How many people are working on a specific project • Upcoming projects	Commercial business
Secret	• If disclosed, it could cause serious damage to national security.	• Deployment plans for troops • Nuclear bomb placement	Military
Top secret	• If disclosed, it could cause grave damage to national security.	• Blueprints of new wartime weapons • Spy satellite information • Espionage data	Military
Sensitive but unclassified (SBU)	• Minor secret. • If disclosed, it could cause serious damage.	• Medical data • Answers to test scores	Military
Unclassified	• Data is not sensitive or classified.	• Computer manual and warranty information • Recruiting information	Military

The following shows the levels of sensitivity from the highest to the lowest for commercial business:

- Confidential
- Private
- Sensitive
- Public

The following shows the levels of sensitivity from the highest to the lowest for the military:

- Top secret
- Secret
- Confidential
- Sensitive but unclassified
- Unclassified

Once the scheme is decided upon, the company needs to develop the criteria they are going to use to decide what information goes into which classification. The following list shows some criteria parameters that an organization may use to determine the sensitivity of data:

- Usefulness of data
- Value of data
- Age of data
- The level of damage that could be caused if the data was disclosed
- The level of damage that could be caused if the data was modified or corrupted
- Laws, regulations, or liability responsibility about protecting the data
- Effects the data has on national security
- Who should be accessing this data?
- Who should be maintaining this data?
- Where should this data be kept?
- Who should be able to reproduce this data?
- What data would require labels and special marking?

So now that we have the sensitivity scheme chosen and all data is classified, which was determined by the criteria it met, the next step is to specify how each classification should be dealt with. Provisions for access control, identification, and labeling needs to be specified along with how data in specific classifications is stored, maintained, transmitted, and destroyed. Auditing, monitoring, and compliance issues need to be ironed out also. Each classification requires a different degree of security and therefore different requirements from each of the mentioned items.

Data Classification Procedures

1. Identify data custodian who will be responsible for maintaining data and its security level.

2. Specify the criteria that will determine how data is classified.

3. The data owner must indicate the classification of the data she is responsible for.

4. Indicate the security controls that are required for each classification level.

5. Document any exceptions to the previous classification issues.

6. Indicate the methods that can be used to transfer custody of the information to a different data owner.

7. Indicate termination procedures for declassifying the data.

8. Integrate these issues into the security awareness program so that all employees understand how to handle data at different classification levels.

Reference

www.sans.org/infosecFAQ/securitybasics/class.htm

Layers of Responsibility

Senior management and other levels of management understand the vision of the company, the business goals, and objectives. The next layer down is the functional management, who understands how their individual departments work, what roles individuals play within the company, and how security affects their department directly. The next layers are operational managers and staff. This layer is closer to the actual operations of the company and knows detailed information about the technical and procedural requirements, the systems, and how they are used. This layer understands how security mechanisms integrate into systems, how to configure them, and how they affect daily productivity. Each layer has a different insight into what type of role security plays within an organization. Each layer should have input into the best security practices, procedures, and chosen controls to ensure that the security level that is agreed upon provides the necessary level of protection without negatively affecting the company's productivity.

Although each layer is important to the overall security of an organization, there are specific roles that must be clearly defined. These roles are the data owner, data custodian, and user.

Data Owner

The *data owner* is usually a member of senior management and is ultimately responsible for the protection and use of the data. The data owner falls within the bounds of the due care responsibilities and will be held responsible for any negligent acts that result in the corruption or disclosure of the data. The data owner decides upon the classification of the data he is responsible for and alters these classifications if the business needs arise. The data owner will delegate the responsibility of the day-to-day maintenance of the data, which is the responsibility of the data custodian.

Data Custodian

The *data custodian* is given the responsibility of the maintenance and protection of the data. This role is usually filled by the IT department, usually by the network administrator, and the duties include performing regular backups of the data, implementing security mechanisms, periodically validating the integrity of the data, restoring data from backup media, and fulfilling the requirements specified in the company's security policy, standards, and guidelines that pertain to information security and data protection.

User

The *user* is considered any individual who routinely uses the data for work-related tasks. The user must have the necessary level of access to the data to perform the duties within her position and is responsible for following operational security procedures to ensure the data's confidentiality, integrity, and availability to others.

Poor security management causes a majority of security problems. Different levels of management have different layers of security responsibility. A senior-level committee should be established to ensure that security issues receive appropriate and proper attention by senior officials. A Chief Information Officer (CIO) should work with senior management to define strategic security procedures and support business managers in defining their information and security needs. Business managers have the primary responsibility for determining the level of protection needed for information system resources; therefore, they should be intimately involved with the selection of security safeguards. A security administrator's tasks are many, but include creating new system user accounts, implementing new security software, testing security patches and components, and issuing new passwords. They should not have to actually *approve* new system user accounts, this is a responsibility of the business managers.

Security Roles Within an Organization

Senior manager   Ultimately responsible for security of the organization and the protection of its assets

Security professional   Functionally responsible for security and carries out senior manager's directives

Data owner   Determines data classification of information within the organization

Data custodian   Maintains data in ways to preserve and protect its confidentiality, integrity, and availability

User   Uses data for data-processing tasks

Auditor   Examines security practices and mechanisms within the organization

A decision maker is not the proper role for the information security specialists in protecting system resources. They may have the technical knowledge of how security mechanisms should be implemented and configured, but they should not be put into a position of deciding how the company approaches security and what security measures should be implemented. Too many times companies handle security at the security administrator level. In these situations, security is not viewed in broad enough terms, proper risk analysis is usually not performed, senior management is not fully aware of the risks the company faces, not enough funds are available for security, and when a security breach takes place, there is not an efficient way of dealing with it. As stated previously, security should work in a top-down fashion to be ultimately successful.

A company's security is not only tied to the type of firewall installed and the timeliness of security patches being applied. A company is an environment that is filled with different resources, activities, people, and practices. The security of the environment needs to be approached in a holistic way with each part of security addressed in a serious and responsible manner. The following sections describe compartments of security not usually thought about when one thinks about securing a company's environment.

Personnel

There are many facets of personnel responsibilities that fall under management's umbrella, and several of these have a direct correlation to the overall security of the environment.

Although society has evolved to be extremely dependent upon technology in the work area, people are still the key ingredient to a successful company. Within security, they are often the weakest link. Either accidentally through mistakes or lack of training or intentionally through fraud and malicious intent, personnel cause more security issues than hacker attacks, outside espionage, or equipment failure. Although the future actions of individuals cannot be predicted, it is possible to minimize the risks by providing preventive measures by hiring the most qualified individuals, performing background checks, employing detailed job descriptions, providing necessary training, enforcing strict access control, and terminating individuals in a way that protects all parties involved.

Structure

If a company wants to have effective employee safety, a certain structure needs to be put into place by management and actually followed. This structure includes job descriptions, clear definitions of responsibilities, lines of authority, and acceptable reprimands for specific activities. A clear-cut structure takes the mystery out of who does what and how things are handled in different situations.

There are several items that can be put into place to reduce the possibilities of fraud, sabotage, misuse of information, theft, and other security compromises. *Separation of duties* makes sure that one individual cannot complete a risky task by herself. In the movies when a submarine captain launches a nuclear torpedo, which is necessary to blow up the enemy and save civilization as we know it, it usually requires three codes to be entered into the launching mechanism by three different senior crewmembers. This is an example of separation of duties and it makes sure that the captain cannot complete such an important and terrifying task all by himself.

In an organization that practices separation of duties, collusion is required to take place for different types of security compromises. *Collusion* means that more than one person would need to work together to cause some type of destruction or fraud and this drastically reduces its probability.

In a software development environment, there should be clear distinctions between programmers, test beds, libraries, operations, and production. Programmers should be able to work on their code and test it as needed. Once the programmer is finished with her tasks, she turns the code over to quality assurance who run their own tests in another environment that mirrors the production environment. Once the code passes all the necessary tests, it should be stored in a software library. When it is necessary for the code to go into production, it moves from the library to the production environment. Code should not go from the programmer directly to production without testing and checking it into the library. The test environment should be clearly differentiated from the production environment to ensure that untested code does not accidentally go into production. And the programmer should not 'tinker' with the software once it is in production. These clear-cut methods make sure that no steps are skipped in the development phase of software and that changes are not made in unstructured and dangerous ways.

Hiring Practices

Depending on the position that needs to be filled, a level of screening should be practiced to ensure that the company hires the right individual for the right job. Skills should be tested and evaluated, and the caliber and character of the individual should be examined. Joe might be the best programmer in the state, but if someone looked into his past and found out that he hacked up his wife with a knife, the hiring manager might not be so eager to bring Joe into the organization.

Nondisclosure agreements need to be developed and signed by new employees to protect the company if and when this employee leaves for one reason or another. Any conflicts of interests need to be addressed, and there should be different agreements and precautions taken with temporary and contract employees.

References should be checked, military records reviewed, education verified, and if necessary, a drug test should be administered. Many times, important personal behaviors can be concealed and that is why hiring practices now include scenario questions, personality tests, and observations of the individual versus just looking at a person's work history. When a person is hired, he is bringing in his business skills and whatever other baggage he carries. A company can reduce their heartache pertaining to personnel by first conducting useful and carefully carried out hiring practices.

Operations

A management structure must be in place to make sure everyone has someone to report to and the responsibility for another person's actions is spread equally and intelligently. Consequences for noncompliance or unacceptable behavior must be communicated before an event takes place. Proper supervisory skills need to be acquired and used to ensure that operations go smoothly and any out-of-the-ordinary activities can be taken care of before they get out of control.

Job rotation is an important part of keeping operations a healthy and productive part of the company. No one person should stay in one position for a long period of time because it can end up giving too much control of a segment of the business to this one individual. Such total control could result in fraud, data modification, and misuse of information. Employees in sensitive areas should be forced to take their vacations. This would require other individuals to fulfill their positions and any fraudulent errors or activities can be detected.

Termination

Because terminations can happen for a variety of different reasons and people will provide different reactions, companies should have a specific set of procedures that happen with each and every termination. The employee must leave the facility immediately under the supervision of a manager or security guard, the employee must surrender any identification badges, keys, complete an exit interview, return company supplies, and that user's accounts and passwords should be disabled or changed immediately. It seems harsh and cold when this actually takes place, but too many companies have been hurt by vengeful employees that have lashed out at the company when their positions were revoked for one reason or another.

Security Awareness

The management's directives pertaining to security is captured in the security policy, and the standards, procedures, and guidelines are developed to support these directives. However, this will not be effective if no one knows about these items and how the company expects them to be implemented. For computer security to be successful and effective, senior management on down to the rest of the staff need to be fully aware of the importance of computer and information security. All employees should understand the underlying significance of security and the specific security-related requirements expected of them.

The controls and procedures of a security program should reflect the nature of the data being processed. A company that sells baseball cards would not need the level of structured controls and security procedures that may be required of a company that develops heat-seeking missiles. These different types of companies would also have very different cultures. For a security awareness program to be effective, these considerations must be understood and the program should be developed in a fashion that makes sense per environment.

For an organization to achieve the desired results of their security program, they must communicate the what, how, and why of security to their employees. It should be comprehensive, tailored for specific groups, and organization-wide. The goal is that each employee understands the importance of security to the company as a whole and to each individual. Expected responsibilities and acceptable behaviors need to be clarified, and noncompliance repercussions that could range from a warning to dismissal need to be explained before being invoked.

Different Types of Security Training

There are usually at least three different audiences for a security awareness program: management, staff, and technical employees. Each type of awareness training needs to be geared towards the individual audience to ensure that each group understands its particular responsibilities, liabilities, and expectations. If a technical security training were given to the senior management, their eyes would glaze over as soon as protocols and firewalls were mentioned. On the flip side, if legal ramifications, company liability issues pertaining to protecting data, and shareholder's expectations were discussed with the IT group, they would quickly start a game of hangman or tic-tac-toe with their neighbors.

Management would benefit the most from a short, focused security awareness orientation that discussed corporate assets, financial gains and losses pertaining to security, how stock prices can be negatively affected by compromises, possible threats and their outcomes, and an explanation of how it needs to be integrated into the environment in the same way as other business policies and strictly enforced. The management group must lead the rest of the company in support for security; thus, they must gain the right mind-set of its importance.

Mid-management could be addressed as a different audience, if the organization is large. This group would benefit from more detailed explanations of the policies, procedures, standards, and guidelines and how they map to individual departments that this level of management is responsible for. They should be shown how critical their support is for their specific departments and their level of responsibility for ensuring that employees practice safe computing standards. They should also be shown how the consequences of noncompliance by individuals that report to them can affect the company as a whole and how they, as managers, may have to answer for such indiscretions.

The technical department(s) must receive a different presentation that aligns more to their daily tasks. They should receive a more in-depth training to discuss technical configurations, indications of different types of security compromises so they can be properly recognized, and incident handling procedures.

Each group needs to know whom it should report suspicious activity to and how they are expected to handle these situations. Employees should not try to combat an attack or fraud by themselves. Each employee should be told to report it to upper management, and upper management should determine how the situation is to be handled.

Staff members need to understand why security is important to the company and important to them individually. The more that it can be shown how individuals can be negatively affected by insecure activities, the more they will be willing to participate. This presentation should have many examples of acceptable and unacceptable activities. Examples of these activities include questioning an unknown individual in a restricted portion of the facility, proper Internet use, expected use of e-mail capabilities, not removing company-owned material, and intellectual property issues. The employees should fully understand what is expected of them and what could happen if they do not follow these guidelines. It is usually best to have each employee sign a document indicating that he has heard and understands all the security topics discussed and he understands the ramifications of noncompliance. This enforces the importance to the employee and also provides evidence down the road if the employee claims that he was never told about these expectations.

Security training should happen periodically and continually. We learn mostly by repetition, and this training should take place at least once a year. The goal is to not only get individuals to understand how security works in their environment, but to also get individuals to understand *why*.

References

www.cissps.com

www.cccure.org

Summary

Security management embodies the administrative and procedural activities necessary to support and protect information and computer security companywide. It includes development and enforcement of security policies and their supporting mechanisms: procedures, standards, baselines, and guidelines. It encompasses risk management, security awareness, and proper countermeasure selection and implementation. Personnel (hiring, terminating, training, and management structure) and operational (job rotation and separation of duties) activities must also be conducted properly to ensure a secure environment. The management must understand the legal and ethical responsibilities it is required to respect and uphold. Figure 3-10 illustrates the necessary pieces for an effective and efficient security program.

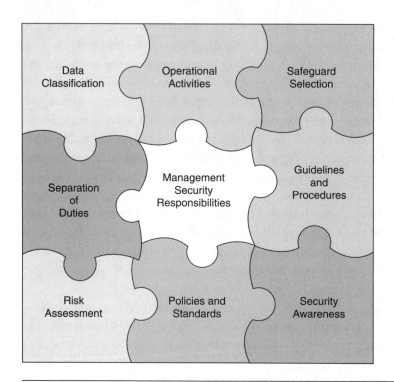

Figure 3-10 Necessary pieces that fit together to form effective and efficient security.

Security is a business issue and should be treated as such. It needs to be properly integrated into the company's overall business goals and objectives because of the importance and dependence upon its resources, assets, information, and employees. More and more corporations are finding out the price that has to be paid when security is not given the proper attention, support, and funds. This is a wonderful world to live in, but bad things can happen. The ones who realize this notion not only survive, but they also thrive.

Quick Tips

- A vulnerability is the absence or weakness of a safeguard that could be exploited.
- A threat is any potential danger to a computer, network, or data.
- A risk is the probability of a threat agent exploiting a vulnerability and the loss potential from that action.

- Reducing vulnerabilities and/or threat agents reduces the risk.

- An exposure is an instance of being exposed to losses from a threat.

- A countermeasure, also called a safeguard, mitigates the potential risk.

- A countermeasure can be an application, software configuration, hardware, or procedure.

- Security management has become more important over the years because networks have evolved from centralized environments to distributed environments.

- The objectives of security are to provide confidentiality, integrity, and availability of data and resources.

- Strategic planning is long-term, tactical planning is mid-term, and operational planning is day-to-day.

- Security components can be technical (firewalls, encryption, and access control lists) or nontechnical (security policy, procedures, and compliance enforcement).

- Assurance is the confidence that a computer system meets its security requirements.

- Security management should work from the top down, from senior management down to the staff.

- The security model a company chooses depends on the type of business, its critical missions, and objectives.

- Risk management is the process of reducing risk to an acceptable level and maintaining that level.

- Risk can be transferred, rejected, reduced, or accepted.

- An example of risk transference is when a company buys insurance.

- A way of reducing risk is to improve security procedures and/or implementing safeguards.

- If a company is rejecting risk, it is choosing to ignore it, which can be dangerous.

- Threats $\times$ vulnerability $\times$ asset value = total risk

- (Threats $\times$ vulnerability $\times$ asset value) $\times$ controls gap = residual risk

- The main goals of risk analysis are the following: identify risks, quantify the impact of potential threats, and provide an economic balance between the impact of the risk and the cost of the safeguards.

- A risk analysis is a tool used to identify the degree of risk a company is under and estimate the proper budget that should be formed to reduce and mitigate this risk.

- A quantitative risk analysis attempts to assign monetary values to components within the analysis.

- A purely quantitative risk analysis is not possible because it is trying to quantify qualitative items.

- When determining the value of information, the following issues need to be considered: the cost to acquire and develop data; the cost to maintain and protect data; the value of the data to owners, users, and adversaries; the cost of replacement if lost; the price others are willing to pay for the data; and the usefulness of the data.

- There are automated risk analysis tools that reduce the amount of manual work involved. They estimate future expected losses and calculate the benefits of different security measures.

- Single loss expectancy is the amount that would be lost if a specific threat agent exploited a vulnerability.

- Annualized loss expectancy = single loss expectancy × frequency per year

- Qualitative risk analysis uses judgment and intuition instead of numbers.

- Qualitative risk analysis uses scenarios that walk through risks and have the people with the experience and education on such matters rate the probability, potential loss, and severity of each risk.

- The Delphi technique is a group decision method where each member can vote anonymously.

- When choosing the right safeguard to reduce a specific risk, the cost, functionality, and effectiveness need to be evaluated and a cost/benefit analysis needs to be performed.

- Safeguards should be highly visible, but their mechanisms should be hidden.

- A security policy is a statement by management dictating the role security plays in the organization.

- Procedures are detailed step-by-step actions that should be followed to achieve a certain task.

- A standard specifies how hardware and software are to be used and are compulsory in nature.

- Baseline provides a minimum level of security acceptable for an environment.

- Guidelines are recommendations and general approaches that provide advice and flexibility.

- Data is classified to assign priorities to data and ensure that the appropriate level of protection is provided.

- The military is more concerned about confidentiality of data, whereas commercial businesses are usually more concerned with data integrity and availability.

- Data owners specify the classification of data, and it is management's responsibility to protect that data.

- The objective of every loss prevention program is to reduce losses to a predefined level of tolerance.

- Security has functional requirements, which define the expected behavior from a product or system, and assurance requirements, which establish confidence of the implemented products or systems overall.

- Risk management mitigates risks by defining and controlling threats and vulnerabilities.

- The security program should be integrated with the business objectives and goals.

- Management needs to define the scope and purpose of security management, provide support, appoint a security team, delegate responsibility, and review the team's findings.

- The security team should be individuals from different departments within the organization and not just technical personnel.

- A risk analysis can take a lot of time from different people within the company. The process of a risk analysis needs to be understood prior to starting the analysis.

- A risk can have delayed loss and/or delayed damages, meaning that losses can be experienced over a period of time or damages can be experienced at a later date.

- A qualitative rating would be expressed in high, medium, or low or on a scale of 1 to 5 or 1 to 10. A quantitative result would be expressed in dollar amounts and percentages.

- Safeguards should default to least privilege, have fail-safe defaults, and override capabilities.

- Safeguards should be imposed uniformly so everyone has the same restrictions and functionality.

- For security purposes, information should be categorized on the basis of confidentiality, integrity, and availability.

- A key element during the initial security planning process is to define reporting relationships.

Questions

Please remember that these questions are formatted and asked in a certain way for a reason. The questions and answers may seem odd or vague, but this is what you will see on the actual CISSP test.

1. Who has the primary responsibility of determining the classification level for information?
   a. Functional manager
   b. Senior management
   c. Owner
   d. User

2. Which group causes the most risk of fraud and computer compromises?
   a. Employees
   b. Hackers
   c. Attackers
   d. Contractors

3. If different user groups with different security access levels need to access the same information, which of the following actions should management take?
   a. Decrease the security level on the information to ensure accessibility and usability of the information.
   b. Require specific approval each time an individual needs to access the information.
   c. Increase the security controls on the information.
   d. Increase the classification label on the information.

4. What does management need to consider when classifying data?
   a. Type of employees, contractors, and customers who will be accessing the data.
   b. Confidentiality, integrity, and availability.
   c. First assess the risk level and implement the correct countermeasures.
   d. The access controls that will be protecting the data.

5. Who is ultimately responsible for making sure data is classified and protected?
   a. Data owners
   b. Users
   c. Administrators
   d. Management

6. What is a procedure?
   a. Rules on how software and hardware must be used within the environment
   b. Step-by-step directions on how to accomplish a task
   c. Guidelines on how to approach security situations that are not covered by standards
   d. Compulsory actions

7. Which factor is the most important item when it comes to ensuring that security is successful in an organization?
   a. Senior management support
   b. Effective controls and implementation methods
   c. Updated and relevant security policies and procedures
   d. Security awareness by all employees

8. When is it acceptable to not take action on an identified risk?
   a. Never — good security addresses and reduces all risks.
   b. When political issues prevent this type of risk from being addressed.
   c. When the necessary countermeasure is complex.
   d. When the cost of the countermeasure outweighs the value of the asset.

9. What are security policies?
   a. Step-by-step directions on how to accomplish security tasks
   b. General guidelines to use to accomplish a specific security level
   c. Broad, high-level statements from the management
   d. Detailed documents explaining how security incidents should be handled

10. Which is the most valuable technique when determining if a specific security control should be implemented?
    a. Risk analysis
    b. Cost/benefit analysis
    c. ALE results
    d. Identifying the vulnerabilities and threats causing the risk

11. Which best describes the purpose of the ALE calculation?
    a. Quantifies the security level of the environment
    b. Estimates the loss possible for a risk
    c. Quantifies the cost/benefit result
    d. Estimates the loss potential of a risk in a year span

12. Tactical planning is:
    a. Mid-term
    b. Long-term
    c. Day-to-day
    d. Six months

13. What is the definition of a security exposure?
    a. An instance of being exposed to losses from a threat
    b. Any potential danger to information or systems
    c. An information security absence or weakness
    d. A lost potential of a threat

14. An effective security program requires a balanced application of:
    a. Technical and nontechnical methods
    b. Countermeasures and safeguards
    c. Physical security and technical controls
    d. Procedural security and encryption

15. A security function defines the expected behavior from a security mechanism and assurance defines:
    a. The controls the security mechanism will enforce
    b. The data classification after the security mechanism has been implemented
    c. The confidence of the security the mechanism is providing
    d. Cost/benefit relationship

16. Which statement is true when looking at security objectives in the private business sector versus the military sector?
    a. Only the military has true security.
    b. Businesses usually care more about data integrity and availability, whereas the military is more concerned with confidentiality.
    c. The military requires higher levels of security because the risks are so much higher.
    d. The business sector usually cares most about data availability and confidentiality, whereas the military is most concerned about integrity.

17. How do you calculate residual risk?
    a. Threats × risks × asset value
    b. (Treats × asset value × vulnerability) × risks
    c. SLE × frequency = ALE
    d. (Threats × vulnerability × asset value) × control gap

18. Which of the following is not a purpose of doing a risk analysis?
    a. Delegate responsibility.
    b. Quantify impact of potential threats.
    c. Identify risks.
    d. Define the balance between the impact of a risk and the cost of the necessary countermeasure.

19. How does a risk analysis show management how much money to spend per security measure?
    a. It shows management how much could be lost if the security measure is not implemented.
    b. It calculates the frequency of the risk times the cost/benefit ratio of the ALE.
    c. It shows management how much money could be saved if the security program was implemented.
    d. It provides the qualitative severity of the security measure.

20. Which of the following is not a management role in the process of implementing and maintaining security?
    a. Support.
    b. Perform risk analysis.
    c. Define purpose and scope.
    d. Delegate responsibility.

21. Why should the team that is going to perform and review the risk analysis information be made up of people in different departments?
    a. To make sure the process is fair and that no one is left out.
    b. They shouldn't—it should be a small group brought in from outside the organization because otherwise the analysis is biased and unusable.
    c. Because people in different departments understand the risks of that department and it ensures that the data going into the analysis is as close to reality as possible.
    d. Because the people in the different departments are the ones causing the risks, so they should be the ones held accountable.

22. Which best describes quantitative risk analysis?
    a. Scenario-based analysis to research different security threats
    b. A method used to apply severity levels to potential loss, probability of loss, and risks

    c. A method that assigns monetary values to components in the risk assessment

    d. A method that assigns percentages to losses, probabilities, risks, and safe-guards

23. Why is a quantitative risk analysis not possible?

    a. It is possible, which is why it is used.

    b. It assigns severity levels. Thus, it is hard to translate into monetary values.

    c. It is dealing with purely quantitative elements.

    d. Quantitative measures must be applied to qualitative elements.

24. If there are automated tools for risk analysis, why does it take so much time to complete?

    a. A lot of data has to be gathered to be inputted into the automated tool.

    b. Management has to approve it and then a team has to be built.

    c. Risk analysis cannot be automated because of the nature of the assessment.

    d. Many people have to agree on the same data.

Answers

1. C.	7. A.	13. A.	19. A.
2. A.	8. D.	14. A.	20. B.
3. C.	9. C.	15. C.	21. C.
4. B.	10. B.	16. B.	22. C.
5. D.	11. D.	17. D.	23. D.
6. B.	12. A.	18. A.	24. A.

CHAPTER 4

Access Control

In this chapter, you will learn about the following items:

- Identification methods and technologies
- Biometrics
- Authentication methods, models, and technologies
- Discretionary, mandatory, and nondiscretionary access control
- Accountability, monitoring, and auditing practices
- Emanation security and technologies
- Possible threats to access control practices and technologies

A cornerstone in the foundation of information security is controlling how resources are accessed so they can be protected from unauthorized modification or disclosure. The controls that enforce access control can be hardware or software tools, which are technical, physical, or administrative in nature.

Access Control

Access controls are security features that control how users and systems communicate and interact with other systems and resources. They protect the systems and resources from unauthorized access and usually determine the level of authorization after an authentication procedure has successfully completed. Although we usually think of a user as the entity that requires access to a network resource or information, there are many other types of entities that require access to other network entities and resources that are subject to access control. It is important to understand the definition of a subject and an object when working in the context of access control.

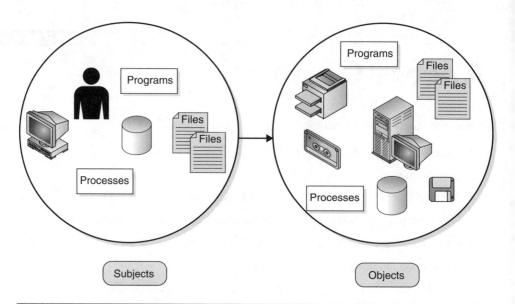

Figure 4-1   Subjects are active entities that access objects; objects are passive entities.

Access is the flow of information between a subject and an object. A *subject* is an active entity that requests access to an object or the data within an object. A subject can be a user, program, or process that accesses information to accomplish a task. When a program accesses a file, the program is the subject and the file is the object. An *object* is a passive entity that contains information. An object can be a computer, database, file, computer program, directory, or field contained in a table within a database. When you look up information in a database, you are the active subject and the database is the passive object. Figure 4-1 illustrates subjects and objects.

Access control is a broad term that covers several different types of mechanisms that enforce access control features on computer systems, networks, and information. It is extremely important because it is one of the first lines of defense used to fight against unauthorized access to systems and network resources. When a user is prompted with a username and password to be able to use a computer, this is access control. Once the user logs in and later attempts to access a file, that file can have a list of users and groups that have the right to access it. If the user is not on this list, the user is denied. This is another form of access control. The users' permissions and rights are based on the identity, clearance, and/or group membership. Access controls give organizations the ability of controlling, restricting, monitoring, and protecting resource availability, integrity, and confidentiality. Figure 4-2 shows the three main attributes of security.

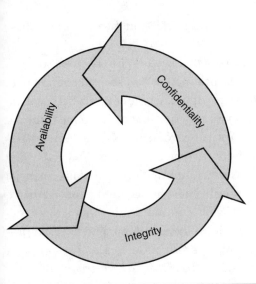

Figure 4-2   The three main attributes of security are confidentiality, integrity, and availability.

Security Principles

The three main security principles for any type of security control are confidentiality, integrity, and availability. These issues were touched upon in Chapter 3 and will be a running theme throughout this book because each core subject of each chapter approaches these principles in a unique way. In Chapter 3, security management procedures include identifying threats that can negatively affect the confidentiality, integrity, and availability of the company's assets and finding cost-effective countermeasures that will protect them. This chapter looks at the ways that the three principles can be affected and protected through access control methodologies and technologies.

Confidentiality

Confidentiality is the assurance that information is not disclosed to unauthorized individuals, programs, or processes. Some information is more sensitive than other information and requires a higher level of confidentiality. Control mechanisms need to be in place to dictate who can access data and what the person can do with it once it has been accessed. These activities need to be controlled, audited, and monitored. Some types of information that would be considered confidential are health records, financial account information, criminal records, source code, trade secrets, and military tactical plans. Some security mechanisms that would provide confidentiality are encryption, logical and physical access controls, transmission protocols, database views, and controlled traffic flow.

It is important for a company to identify the data that needs to be classified so it can ensure that a top priority of security protects this information and keeps it confidential. If this information is not singled out, too much time and money can be spent on implementing the same amount of security levels for critical and mundane information. It may be necessary to configure virtual private networks (VPNs) between organizations with the IPSec encryption protocol to encrypt all messages passed when communicating about trade secrets, sharing customer information, or making financial transactions. This takes a certain amount of hardware, man hours, funds, and overhead. The same security precautions are not necessary when communicating that today's special in the cafeteria is liver and onions with a roll on the side. So the first step in protecting data's confidentiality is identifying which information is sensitive, to what degree, and then implementing security mechanisms to protect it properly.

Integrity

Information must be accurate, complete, and protected from unauthorized modification. When a security mechanism provides *integrity*, it will protect data from being altered in an unauthorized fashion, and if some type of illegitimate modification does occur, the security mechanism must alert the user or discard the message altogether. One example is when a user sends a request to her online bank account to pay her $24.56 water utility bill. This user needs to be sure that the integrity of that transaction was not altered during transmission, so the user does not end up paying the utility company $240.56 instead. Integrity of data is very important. What if a confidential e-mail was sent from the secretary of state to the president and was intercepted and altered without a security mechanism in place that disallows this or alerts the president that this message has been altered? Instead of receiving a message reading, "We would love for you and your wife to stop by for drinks tonight," the message could be altered to say, "We have just bombed Libya." Big difference.

Availability

Information, systems, and resources need to be available to users in a timely manner so productivity will not be affected. Most information needs to be accessible and available for users when it is requested so they can carry out tasks and fulfill their responsibilities. Accessing information does not seem that important until it is inaccessible. Administrators experience this when a file server goes offline or a highly used database is out of service for one reason or another. Fault tolerance and recovery mechanisms are put into place to ensure the continuity of the *availability* of resources. User productivity can be greatly affected if requested data is not readily available.

Information has different attributes like accuracy, relevance, timeliness, privacy, and security. It may be extremely important for a stockbroker to have information that is accurate and timely, so he can buy and sell stocks at the right times at the right prices. The stockbroker does not necessarily care about the privacy of this information, but that it is readily available. A soft drink company that depends on its soda pop recipe would care about the privacy of this trade secret and the security mechanisms in place need to ensure this secrecy.

Different security mechanisms can supply different degrees of confidentiality, integrity, and availability. The environment, the classification of the data that is to be protected, and the security goals need to be evaluated to ensure that the proper security mechanisms are bought and put into place. Many corporations have wasted a lot of time and money not following these steps and instead buying the new "gee-wiz" product that recently hit the market.

Identification, Authentication, Authorization, and Accountability

For a user to be able to access a resource, it must be determined if this individual is who he claims to be, if he has the necessary credentials, and if he has been given the necessary rights or privileges to perform the actions he is requesting. Once these steps are completed successfully, the user can access and use network resources; however, it is necessary to track the user's activities and enforce accountability for his actions. *Identification* describes a method of ensuring that a subject (user, program, or process) is the entity it claims to be. Identification can be verified through the use of a credential like a username, personal identification number (PIN), smart card, digital signature, account number, or an anatomical attribute. To be properly *authenticated*, the subject is usually required to provide a second piece to the credential set; this piece could be a password, passphrase, cryptographic key, or token. These two credential items are compared to what information has been previously stored for this subject. If these credentials match the stored information, the subject is authenticated. But we are not done yet. Once the subject provides its credentials and is properly identified, the system it is trying to access needs to determine if this subject has been given the necessary rights and privileges to carry out the requested actions. The system will look at some type of access control matrix or compare security labels to verify that this subject can indeed access the requested resource and perform the actions he is attempting. If the subject can access the resource, the subject has just been *authorized*. Although identification, authentication, and authorization have close and complementary definitions, they each have distinct functions that fulfill a specific requirement in the process of access control. A user may be properly identified and authenticated to the network, but he may not have the authorization to access the files on the file server. On the other hand, a user may be authorized to access the files on the file server, but until she is properly identified and authenticated, those resources are out of reach. Figure 4-3 illustrates the three steps that must happen for a subject to access an object.

The subject needs to be held accountable for the actions taken within a system or domain. The only way to ensure accountability is if the subject is uniquely identified and the subject's actions are recorded.

Logical access controls are tools used for identification, authentication, authorization, and accountability. They are software components that enforce access control measures for systems, programs, processes, and information. The logical access controls can be embedded within operating systems, applications, add-on security packages, or within database and telecommunication management systems. It can be challenging to get all access controls synchronized without producing overlaps of functionality and ensuring that all vulnerabilities are covered; however, if it were easy, security professionals would not be getting the big bucks!

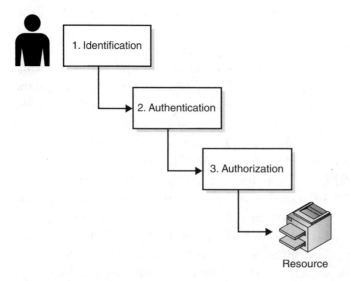

Figure 4-3   There are three steps that must happen for a subject to access an object: identification, authentication, and authorization.

Identification

Now, who are you again?

If resources are valuable, they need to be protected and accessible to only intended individuals.

An individual's identity needs to be verified during the authentication process. Authentication usually contains a two-step process: entering public information (a username, employee number, account number, department ID, or biometric feature) and then entering private information (a static password, smart token, cognitive password, one-time password, PIN, digital signature, smart card, or memory card). Entering public information is the identification step and entering private information is the authentication step of the two-step process. Each technique used for identification and authentication has its pros and cons. Each should be properly evaluated to determine the right mechanism for the right environment.

Biometrics

Biometrics verifies an individual's identity by a unique personal attribute, which is one of the most effective and accurate methods of verifying identification. Biometrics is a very sophisticated technology; thus, it is much more expensive than the other types of identity verification processes. A system scans an attribute of a person and compares it to a record that was created in an earlier enrollment process. Because this system inspects the grooves of a person's fingerprint, the pattern of someone's retina, or pitches of someone's voice, it has to be extremely sensitive. The system must perform accurate and repeatable measurements of anatomical or physiological characteristics. This type of sensitivity can easily cause false positives or false negatives. The system must be calibrated so these false positives and false negatives have a low occurrence, and the results are as accurate as possible.

Biometrics can use several different types of physiological attributes of a person.

When a biometric system rejects an authorized individual, it is called a *Type I error*. When the system accepts impostors who should be rejected, it is called a *Type II error*. The goal is to obtain low numbers for each type of error. When comparing different biometric systems, many different variables are used, but the most important variable is the *crossover error rate (CER)*. This rating is stated in a percentage and represents the point at which the false rejection rate equals the false acceptance rate. This rating is the most important measurement when determining the system's accuracy. A biometric system that delivers a CER of 3 will be more accurate than a system that delivers a CER of 4.

Biometrics is the most expensive method of verifying a person's identity and it faces other barriers to becoming widely acceptable. These include user acceptance, enrollment time frame, and throughput. Many times people are reluctant to let a machine read the pattern of their retina or scan the geometry of their hand. This lack of enthusiasm has slowed down the widespread use of biometric systems within our society. The enrollment phase requires an action to be performed several times to capture a clear and indistinguishable reference record; people are not particularly fond of expending this time and energy when they are used to just picking a password instead and quickly typing it into their console. When a person attempts to be identified by a biometric system, sometimes the system will request an action to be completed several times. If the system was unable to get a clear reading of an iris scan or could not capture a full voice verification print, the individual may have to repeat the action. This causes low throughput, stretches the individual's patience, and reduces acceptability.

There are many types of biometric systems that examine different personal characteristics. With each type of system, the individual must go through an enrollment process, which captures the biometric data and stores it in a reference file. This reference file is used later when the person attempts to be authenticated. The following is an overview of the different types of biometric systems and the physiological characteristics they examine.

Fingerprint   Fingerprints are made up of ridge endings and bifurcations exhibited by the friction ridges and other detailed characteristics that are called *minutiae*. It is the distinctiveness of these minutiae that gives each individual a unique fingerprint. An individual places his finger on a device that reads the details of the fingerprint and compares this to a reference file. If the two match, the individual's identity has been verified.

NOTE   Finger-Scan Technology: Fingerprint systems store the full fingerprint, which is actually a lot of information that takes up hard drive space and makes it harder for quick comparisons when a user is attempting to get authenticated. The finger-scan technology extracts specific features from the fingerprint and stores just that information, which takes up less hard drive space and allows for quicker database lookups and comparisons.

Palm Scan   The palm holds a wealth of information, and has many aspects that are used to identify an individual. The palm has creases, ridges, and grooves throughout it that are unique to a specific person. The palm scan also includes the fingerprints of each finger. An individual places his hand on the biometric device, which scans and captures this information. This information is compared to a reference file and the identity is either verified or rejected.

Hand Geometry   The shape of a person's hand (the length and width of the hand and fingers) measures hand geometry. This trait differs significantly between people and is used in some biometric systems to verify identity. A person places her hand on a device that has grooves for each finger. The system compares the geometry of each finger, and the hand as a whole, to the information in a reference file to verify that person's identity.

Retina Scan   A system that reads a person's retina scans the blood-vessel pattern of the retina on the backside of the eyeball. This pattern has shown to be extremely unique between people. A camera is used to project a beam inside the eye and capture the pattern and compare it to a reference file recorded previously.

Iris Scan   The iris is the colored portion of the eye that surrounds the pupil. The iris has unique patterns, rifts, colors, rings, coronas, and furrows. The uniqueness of each of these characteristics within the iris is captured by a camera and compared with the information gathered during the enrollment phase.

NOTE   Iris Scan Potential Problem: When using an iris pattern biometric system, the optical unit must be positioned so that the sun does not shine into the aperture, so when implemented it must be properly placed in a building.

Signature Dynamics   When a person signs a signature, usually it is done in the same manner and speed each time. Signing a signature produces electrical signals that can be captured by a biometric system. The physical motions performed when someone is signing a document create these electrical signals. The signals provide unique characteristics that can be used to distinguish one individual from another. There is more information within signature dynamics versus a static signature, so there are more variables to verify when confirming an individual's identity and more assurance that this person is who he claims to be.

Keyboard Dynamics   Signature dynamics is a method that captures the electrical signals when a person signs a name, and keyboard dynamics capture electrical signals when a person types a certain phrase. As a person types a specified phrase, the biometric system captures the speed and motions of this action. Each individual has a certain style and speed, which translate into unique signals. This type of authentication is more effective than typing in a password because a password is easily obtainable. It is much harder to repeat a person's typing style than it is to acquire a password.

Voice Print   There are many subtle distinguishing differences in people's speech sounds and patterns. A biometric system that is programmed to capture this voice print and compare it to the information captured in a reference file can differentiate one individual from another. During the enrollment process, an individual is asked to say several different words. Later when this individual needs to be authenticated, the biometric system jumbles these words and presents them to the individual. The individual then repeats the sequence of words given. This is used as a deterrent so others will not attempt to record the session and play it back in hopes of obtaining unauthorized access.

Facial Scan   A system that scans a person's face takes many attributes and characteristics into account. People have different bone structures, nose ridges, eye widths, forehead sizes, and chin shapes. These are all captured during a facial scan and compared to an earlier captured scan held within a reference record. If the information is a match, the person is positively identified.

Hand Topology   Hand geometry looks at the size and width of an individual's hand and fingers. During a hand topology scan, a side-view picture of the hand is captured. Hand topology looks at the different peaks and valleys of the hand, along with its overall shape and curvature. When an individual wants to be authenticated, a hand is placed on the system, and a camera is off to one side of it. The camera snaps a picture of the hand from a different view and angle than that of systems that target hand geometry, and thus captures different data.

Order of Effectiveness

Each biometric method has a degree of overall effectiveness when compared to the other available biometric methods. Effectiveness is rated by the CER rating. The following lists the most effective (lowest CER) to the least effective (highest CER):

- Palm scan
- Hand geometry
- Iris scan
- Retina pattern
- Fingerprint
- Voice verification
- Facial recognition
- Signature dynamics
- Keystroke dynamics

Order of Acceptance

Each biometric method has a level of acceptance by society as a whole. This is a degree of comfort for a person when a scan needs to be performed. The following lists the most accepted methods to the least accepted:

- Iris scan
- Keystroke dynamics
- Signature dynamics
- Voice verification
- Facial recognition
- Fingerprint
- Palm scan
- Hand geometry
- Retina pattern

You may be surprised that the iris scan is the highest acceptable and that the retina pattern is the lowest when they seem so similar. This is because for an iris scan to take place, a person only needs to glance at a camera that could be placed above a door. The retina pattern scan requires an individual to place her eye up to a device, and may require a puff of air to be blown into the eye.

References

http://biometrics.cse.msu.edu/

http://webusers.anet-stl.com/~wrogers/biometrics

www.engr.sjsu.edu/biometrics

Authentication

Once a person has been identified, she must be authenticated, which means she must prove she is who she says she is. There are three general types of authentication: something a person knows, something a person has, and something a person is. Something a person knows can be a password, PIN, mother's maiden name, or a combination to a lock. Authenticating a person by something that she knows is usually the least expensive to implement. The downside to this method is that another person may gain this knowledge and gain unauthorized access to a system. Something a person has can be a key, swipe card, access card, or badge. This method is mainly common for accessing facilities. A downside to this method is that the item can be lost or stolen, which could result in unauthorized access. Something a person is becomes a bit more interesting, which is biometrics. Biometrics is used for identification in physical controls and for authentication purposes in technical controls.

Out of the something a person knows, has, or is, *strong authentication* contains two out of these three methods. Using a biometric system by itself does not provide strong authentication because it is only providing one out of the three methods. Biometrics supplies what a person is, not what a person knows or has. For a strong authentication process to be in place, a biometric system needs to be coupled with a mechanism that checks for one of these other two methods. Many times a PIN number is typed into a keypad before the biometric scan is performed. This satisfies the "what the person knows" category. Conversely, the person could be required to swipe a magnetic card through a reader prior to the biometric scan. This would satisfy the "what the person has" category. Whatever identification system is used, for strong authentication to be in process, it must include two out of the three categories.

The following sections explain the different types of authentication methods commonly used in networked environments.

Passwords

User identification coupled with a password is the most common form of system identification and authorization mechanism. A password is a protected string of characters
that is used to authenticate an individual. As stated previously, authentication factors
are based on what a person knows, has, or is. A password is based on something the
user knows.

Password Management *What is my password to get to my most sacred, top-secret,
important information? Answer: Password.*

  Although passwords are the most commonly used authentication mechanisms, they
are also considered one of the weakest security mechanisms available. Why? Users usually choose passwords that are easily guessed (spouse's name, birth date, or dog's
name), tell others their passwords, and many times write the passwords down on a
sticky note and leave it under the keyboard. To most users, security is usually not the
most important or interesting part of using their computers—except when someone
hacks into their computer and steals confidential information. Then security is all
the rage.

  This is where password management steps in. If passwords are properly generated,
updated, and kept secret, then passwords can provide effective security. Password generators can be used to create passwords for users. This ensures that a user will not be using
"Bob" or "Spot" for a password, but if the generator spits out "kdjasijew284802h," the
user will surely scribble it down on a piece of paper and safely stick it to the monitor,
which defeats the whole purpose. If a password generator is going to be used, the tools
should create pronounceable nonwords to help users remember them and not be too
complicated to cause the user to write them down.

  If the users can choose their own passwords, then the operating system should
enforce certain password requirements. The operating system can require that a password contain a certain number of characters, unrelated to the user ID, include special
characters, include upper- and lowercase letters, and is not easily guessed. The operating system can keep track of the passwords a specific user generates to ensure that no
passwords are reused. The users should also be forced to change their passwords periodically. All of these factors make it harder for an attacker to guess or obtain passwords
within the environment.

  If an attacker is after a password, there are a few techniques she can try such as electronic monitoring, accessing the password file, brute force attacks, dictionary attacks,
and social engineering. *Electronic monitoring* is an activity that listens to network traffic
and can capture information, especially when a user is entering a password. The password can be copied and reused by the attacker at another time. Accessing the password

file is done, usually, on the authentication server. The password file contains many users' passwords, and if compromised, can cause a lot of damage. This file should be protected with access control mechanisms and one-way encryption. Brute force attacks are performed with tools that cycle through many possible character, number, and symbol combinations to guess a password. Dictionary attacks have files of thousands of words that are used to compare to the user's password until a match is found.

There are techniques that can be implemented to provide another layer of security for passwords and their use. After each successful logon, a message can be presented to a user indicating the date and time of the last successful logon, the location of this logon, and if there were any unsuccessful logon attempts. This alerts the user if suspicious activity has been going on, and if anyone has attempted to log on using his credentials. An administrator can set operating parameters that allow a certain number of failed logon attempts to happen before a user is locked out; this is also referred to as a *clipping level*. The user can be locked out for five minutes or a full day after the threshold (or clipping level) has been exceeded. It depends on the how the administrator configures this mechanism. An audit trail can also be used to track password usage, and successful and unsuccessful logon attempts. This audit information should include the date, time, user ID, and workstation the user logged in from.

A password's lifetime should be short but practical. The shorter the lifetime of a password, the more assurance that the password will not be guessed by an intruder; however, if the lifetime is too short, it causes unnecessary management overhead and causes the users to forget which password is active. A balance between protection and practicality needs to be decided upon and enforced.

As with many things in life, education is the key. Password requirements, protection, and generation should be addressed in security awareness programs so users understand what is expected of them, why they should protect their passwords, and how passwords can be stolen. Users should be an extension to a security team, not the opposition.

Reference

www.hill.com/library/archives/password.shtml

Password Checkers   Several organizations test user-chosen passwords using tools that perform a dictionary attack to detect the weak passwords. This helps the environment as a whole to be less susceptible to dictionary, or exhaustive attacks, that are used to discover users' passwords. Many times the same tools used to attempt to crack a password are used by a network administrator to make sure the password is strong enough and by the attacker in an attempt to discover a user's password. Most security tools have this dual nature. They are used by security professionals and IT staff to test for vulnerabilities within their environment in the hopes of uncovering them and fixing them before an attacker finds the vulnerabilities and an attacker uses the same tools to uncover vulnerabilities to exploit before the security professional can fix them. It is the never-ending cat-and-mouse race.

So if a tool is called a password checker, it is a tool used by a security professional to test the strength of a password. If a tool is called a password cracker, it is usually used by a hacker; however, most of the time, they are one in the same tool.

Password Generators Some operating systems or third-party products include password generators that produce users' passwords instead of allowing them to choose the passwords themselves. The generator should produce random but pronounceable passwords.

Password Aging Many systems enable administrators to set expiration dates for passwords, forcing users to change them at regular intervals. The system may also keep a list of the last five to ten passwords and not let the users revert back to already used passwords.

Limit Login Attempts A threshold can be set to allow only a certain number of unsuccessful login attempts. After the threshold is met, the user's account can be locked for a period of time or indefinitely, which requires an administrator to manually unlock the account. This protects against dictionary and exhaustive attacks that continually apply credentials until the right combination of username and password is discovered.

Cognitive Passwords

What is your mother's name? Answer: Shucks, I don't remember. I have it written down somewhere.

Cognitive passwords are fact- or opinion-based information used to verify an individual's identity. A user is enrolled by answering several questions based on her life experiences. Passwords can be hard for people to remember, but that same person will not likely forget her mother's maiden name or the school she graduated from. After the enrollment process, the user can answer the questions asked of her to be authenticated instead of having to remember a password. This authentication process is best for a service the user does not use on a daily basis because it takes longer than other authentication mechanisms. This can work well for help-desk services. The user can be authenticated via cognitive means. This way the person at the help desk can be sure he is talking to the right person, and the user in need of help does not need to remember a password that may be used once every three months.

One-time Passwords

How many times is a one-time password good for? Answer: One, brainiac.

A *one-time password* is also called a dynamic password. It is used when a user needs to authenticate himself. After the password is used, it is no longer valid; thus, if a hacker obtained this password, it could not be reused. This type of authentication mechanism is used in environments that require a higher level of security than static passwords provide. There are two general types of one-time passwords: synchronous and asynchronous. Each type is generated by a token device that is used to communicate with an authentication service on a server or workstation. The following sections explain these concepts.

Token Device

The *token device*, or password generator, is usually a hand-held device that has a LCD display and keypad. This device is a separate piece of hardware than the computer the user is attempting to access. The token device and authentication service need to be synchronized, or use the same challenge-response scheme, to be able to authenticate a user. The token device presents the user with a list of characters to be entered as a password when logging into a computer. Only the token device and authentication service knows the meaning of these characters. Because the two are synchronized, the token device will present the exact password the authentication service is expecting. This password is a one-time password, also called a token, and is no longer valid after initial use.

Synchronous   A *synchronous token device* synchronizes with the authentication service by using time or an event as the core piece of the authentication process. If the synchronization is *time based*, the token device and the authentication service must hold the exact same time within their internal clocks. The time value on the token device is encrypted with a secret key and displayed to the user. The user enters this value and a user ID into the computer, which then passes it to the server running the authentication service. The authentication service decrypts this value and compares it to the value that it expected. If the two match, the user is authenticated and allowed to use the computer and resources.

If the token device and authentication service use *event-synchronization*, then the user may need to initiate the logon sequence on the computer and push a button on the token device. This causes the token device and the authentication service to advance to the next authentication value. This value is encrypted by the token device and displayed to the user. The user enters this value along with a user ID to be authenticated. In either time- or event-based synchronization, the token device and authentication service must share the same secret key used for encryption and decryption.

Asynchronous A token device that is using an *asynchronous token*-generating method uses a challenge-response scheme to communicate with the authentication service. In this situation, the computer the user is attempting to log onto displays a challenge value to the user. The user types this value into the hand-held token device. The token device returns a value to the user, who then types this new value and an ID into the computer. The authentication service will be expecting a particular value and if the user types in this value, she is authenticated, as shown in Figure 4-4. As with the synchronous systems, this type of asynchronous method creates a one-time password, which is sometimes called a token.

 NOTE Asynchronous and Synchronous Token Device: The actual implementation and process that these devices follow can differ between different vendors. What is important to know is that asynchronous is based on challenge-response mechanisms and synchronous is based on time- or event-driven mechanisms.

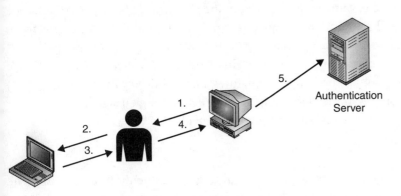

1. Challenge Value displayed on workstation.
2. User enters challenge value and PIN into token device.
3. Token device presents a different value to the user.
4. User enters new value into the workstation.
5. Value sent to authentication service on server.
6. Authentication service is expecting a specific value.
7. User is authenticated and allowed access to workstation.

Figure 4-4 Authentication using a token device includes a workstation, token device, and authentication service.

Both token systems can fall prey to masquerading if a user shares his identification information (ID or username) that is entered along with the one-time password. The token device can also have battery failure or other malfunctions that would stand in the way of a successful authentication. However, this type of system is not vulnerable to electronic eavesdropping, sniffing, or password guessing. It presents strong authentication because it is using two factors—a username, or ID, and a password and the user must have access to the token device.

References

www.rsasecurity.com/products/securid/authenticators.html

www.networkcomputing.com/1018/1018f1.html

Cryptographic Keys

Another way to prove one's identity is to present a private key or a digital signature. A private key or digital signature would be used in place of using a password. Passwords are the weakest form of authentication and can be easily sniffed as they travel over a network. Private keys and digital signatures are forms of authentication used in environments that require higher security protection than what is provided by passwords.

A private key is a secret value that should be in the possession of one person, and one person only. A digital signature uses a private key to encrypt a hash value. The act of encrypting this hash value with a private key is called *digitally signing* a message.

A public key can be available to anyone; this is why it is called a public key. We explore private keys, public keys, digital signatures, and public key infrastructure (PKI) in Chapter 8, but for now, understand that a private key and digital signatures are other mechanisms that can be used to authenticate an individual.

Passphrase

A *passphrase* takes the place of a password during an authentication process. The passphrase is a sequence of characters that is longer than a password, and thus is called a phrase. The user enters this phrase into an application and the application transforms the value into a *virtual password*. If a user wants to authenticate to an application, like Pretty Good Privacy (PGP), he types in a passphrase, let's say "StickWithMeKidAnd YouWillWearDiamonds." The application converts this phrase into a virtual password that is used for the actual authentication. The user usually generates the passphrase just like when a user creates a password the first time he logs onto a computer. A passphrase is more secure than a password because it is longer, and thus harder to obtain by an attacker. In many cases the user is more likely to remember a passphrase than a password.

Memory Cards

The main difference between memory cards and smart cards is the processing power. A *memory card* holds information, but does not *process* information. A *smart card* has the necessary hardware and logic to actually process information. A memory card holds a user's authentication information, so this user only needs to type in a user ID or PIN, present the memory card, and if the two match and are approved by an authentication service, the user is successfully authenticated. An example of a memory card is a swipe card that must be used for an individual to be able to enter a building. The user enters a PIN and swipes the memory card through a card reader. If this is the correct combination, the reader flashes green and the individual can open the door and enter the building. Another example is the ATM card. If Buffy wants to withdrawal $40 from her checking account, she needs to enter the correct PIN and slide the ATM card (or memory card) through the reader.

Memory cards can be used with computers, but they require a reader to process the information. The reader adds cost to the process, especially when one is needed per computer, and the overhead of PIN and card generation adds additional cost and effort to the whole authentication process. A memory card provides a more secure authentication method than using a password because the attacker would need to obtain the card and know the correct PIN. Administrators and management need to weigh the costs and benefits of a memory token-based card implementation to determine if it is the right authentication mechanism for their environment.

Smart Card

A *smart card* has the capability of processing information because it has a microprocessor and integrated circuits incorporated into the card itself. Memory cards do not have this type of hardware and lack this type of functionality. A smart card also provides a two-factor authentication method because the user has to enter a user ID or PIN to unlock the smart token. This means the user must provide something she knows (PIN) and something she has (smart card).

To authenticate using a smart card, the user inserts the card into the card reader and enters a PIN. The reader performs a one-way transformation on the PIN and stores it in the memory of the card reader. The reader then performs the same one-way transformation on the information on the smart card and compares the two values. If the values match, the reader authenticates the user to the computer she is attempting to access. The authentication to the computer can be in the form of a one-time password, use of a challenge-response value, or by providing the user's private key if it is used within a PKI environment. Any of these methods cause the card to mutually authenticate to the authentication service. This means there are two authentication processes going on during this operation: the user authenticates to the card by providing the correct PIN, and then the card authenticates the user the authentication service.

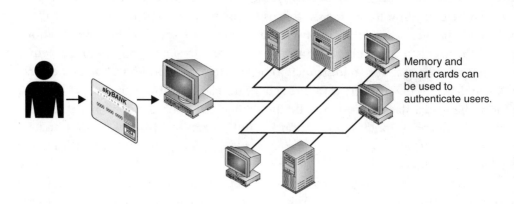

Memory and smart cards can be used to authenticate users.

The information held within the memory of a smart card is not readable until the correct PIN is entered. This fact and the complexity of the smart token make these cards resistant to reverse-engineering and tampering methods. So if George loses his smart card he uses to authenticate to the domain at work, the person who finds the card would need to know his PIN to be able to do any real damage.

The downfalls to using a smart card is the extra cost of the readers and the overhead of PIN and card generation, as with memory cards. The smart cards themselves are more expensive than memory cards because of the extra integrated circuits and microprocessor.

References

www.javaworld.com/javaworld/jw-12-1997/jw-12-javadev.html

www.scia.org/

Authorization

Now that I know who you are, let's see if I will let you do what you want.

The difference between authentication and authorization can prove to be a little confusing at first. Although these two concepts are quite different, they require a synergic relationship to accomplish the task of allowing a user to access a resource. Authentication is the process of proving that an individual holds the identity that he claims to hold. A system may know who you are, but will it allow you to carry out the actions you are requesting? That piece is authorization.

Authorization is a core component of every operating system, but applications, security add-on packages, and resources themselves can also provide this functionality. Once Marge is authenticated through the authentication server, she requests to view a spreadsheet that lives on a file server. When she finds this spreadsheet and double-clicks on the icon, she sees an hourglass instead of a mouse pointer. At this stage, the file server is seeing if Marge has the rights and permissions to view the requested spreadsheet. It also checks to see if Marge can modify, delete, move, or copy the file. Once the file server searches through an access matrix and finds that Marge does indeed have the necessary rights to view this file, the file opens up on Marge's desktop. The decision of whether to allow Marge to see this file or not was based on access criteria. Access criteria is the crux of authentication.

Access Criteria

You can perform that action only because we like you, and you wear a funny hat.

We have gone over the basics when it comes to access control. This subject can get very granular in its level of detail when it comes to dictating what a subject can or cannot do to an object or resource. This is a good thing because network administrators and security professionals want to have as much control over the resources they have been put in charge of protecting, and a fine level of detail enables them to give out just the precise level of access to individuals. It would be frustrating if access control permissions were based only on full control or no access. These choices are very limiting, and an administrator would end up giving everyone full control, which would provide no protection. Instead, there are different ways of limiting access to resources and if they are understood and used properly, they can give just the right level of access desired.

Granting access rights to subjects should be based on the level of trust a company has in a subject and the subject's need to know. Just because a company completely trusts Joyce with their files and resources does not mean she fulfills the need-to-know criteria to access the company's tax returns and profit margins. If Maynard fulfills the need-to-know criteria to access employees' work histories, it does not mean that the company trusts him to access all of the company's other files. These issues need to be identified and integrated into the access criteria. The different access criteria can be broken up into roles, groups, location, time, and transaction types. *Roles* can be an efficient way to assign rights to a type of user who performs a certain task. This role is based on a job assignment or function. If there is a position within a company for a person to audit transactions and audit logs, that role would only need a read function to those types of files. This role would not need full control, modify, or delete privileges.

Groups are another effective way of assigning access control rights. If several users require the same type of access to information and resources, it is easier to manage if they were all put into a group and then rights and permissions were assigned to that group instead of to each and every individual within the group. If a specific printer was only available to the accounting group, when a user attempts to print to it, the group membership of the user will be checked to see if she is indeed in the accounting group. This is one way that access control is enforced through a logical access control mechanism.

Physical or logical location can also be used to restrict access to resources. Some files may only be available to users who can log on interactively to a computer. This means the user must be physically at the computer and enter the credentials locally versus logging in remotely from another computer. This restriction is implemented on several server configurations to restrict unauthorized individuals from being able to get in and reconfigure the server remotely.

Logical location restrictions are usually done through network address restrictions. If a network administrator wants to ensure that status requests of an intrusion detection management console are only accepted from a certain section of the network, this can be configured within the software and any requests originating outside of this section would be rejected. An administrator who configures a domain name server (DNS) to only allow zone transfers to a specific IP address is another example of a logical location access control restriction.

Time of day or days during the week is another access control mechanism that can be used. If a security professional wants to ensure that no one is accessing payroll files between the hours of 8 P.M. and 4 A.M., this is a configuration that can be implemented to ensure that access at these times are restricted. If the same security professional wants to ensure that no bank account transactions happen during days that the bank is not open, she can indicate in the logical access control mechanism that this type of action is prohibited on Sundays.

Transaction type restrictions can be used to control what data is accessed during certain types of functions and what commands are carried out on the data. An online banking program may allow a customer to view his account balance, but may not allow the customer to transfer data until he has a certain security level or access right. A bank teller may be able to cash checks up to $2,000, but would need a supervisor's access code to retrieve more funds for a customer. A database administrator may be able to build a database for the human resource department, but may not be able to read certain confidential files within that database. These are all examples of transaction-type restrictions to control access to data and resources.

Default to No Access

If you're unsure, just say no.

Access control mechanisms should default to no access to provide the necessary level of security and ensure that no security holes go unnoticed. There is a wide range of access levels that are available to assign to individuals and groups, depending on the application and/or operating system. A user can have read, change, delete, full control, or no access permissions. When it is said that security mechanisms should default to no access, it means that if nothing has been specifically configured for an individual or the group she belongs to, then that user should not be able to access that resource. If access is not explicitly allowed, then it should be implicitly denied. Security is all about being safe, and this is the safest approach to practice when we are dealing with access control methods and mechanisms.

This is how most access control lists (ACLs) work on routers and packet-filtering firewalls. In Figure 4-5, it is shown that traffic from subnet A is allowed to access subnet B,

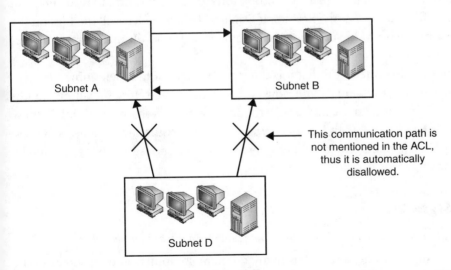

Access Control List

Subnet A can access Subnet B.
Subnet D cannot access Subnet A.
Subnet B can access Subnet A.

Subnet A

Subnet B

This communication path is
not mentioned in the ACL,
thus it is automatically
disallowed.

Subnet D

Figure 4-5   What is not explicitly allowed should be disallowed.

traffic from subnet D is not allowed to access subnet A, and subnet B is allowed talk to subnet A. So all other traffic not listed here is not allowed by default. If subnet D wants to talk to subnet B, this will not happen because it is not explicitly indicated in the router's ACL.

Need to Know

If you need to know, I will tell you. If you don't have a need to know, leave me alone.

The *need-to-know* principle is similar to the least-privilege principle. Administrators only want users to have the necessary rights and permissions they need to fulfill the obligations of their jobs within the company. Giving any more rights to a user just asks for headaches and the possibility of that user abusing the permissions assigned to him. An administrator wants to give a user the least amount of privileges she can, but just enough for that user to be productive when carrying out tasks. The management will decide what a user needs to know, or what access rights are necessary, and the administrator will configure the access control mechanisms to allow this user to access the information he needs to know, but only at the access level that is required, and thus least privileged.

For example, if management has decided that Dan the copy boy needs to know where the files are that he needs to copy and how to print them, this fulfills Dan's need-to-know criteria. Now an administrator can give Dan full control of all the files he needs to copy, but that would not be practicing the least-privilege principle. The administrator should restrict Dan's rights and permissions to only allow him to read and print the necessary files, and no more. Besides, if Dan accidentally deletes all the files on the whole file server, whom do you think management will hold ultimately responsible? Yep, the administrator.

It is important to understand that it is the management's job to determine the security requirements of individuals and how access is authorized. It is the administrator and IT staff that configure the access control and security mechanisms to fulfill these requirements, but it is not their job to determine security requirements of users. If there is a security breach, management will ultimately be held responsible, so they should be the ones making these decisions in the first place.

Single Sign-On

I only want to have to remember one username and one password for everything!

Many times employees need to access many different computers and resources in the course of a day to complete their tasks. This requires the employees to remember multiple user IDs and passwords for these different computers. In a utopia, a user would only need to enter one user ID and one password to be able to access all resources in all the networks this user is works in. In the real world, this is hard to implement and hard to control.

Because of the proliferation of client/server technologies, networks have migrated from centrally controlled networks to heterogeneous, distributed environments. The propagation of open systems and the increased diversity of applications, platforms, and operating systems have caused the end user to have to remember several user IDs and passwords just to be able to access and use the different resources within his own network. Although the different IDs and passwords are supposed to provide a greater level of security, they often end up compromising security and causing more effort and overhead for the staff that manages and maintains the network.

As any network staff member or administrator can attest to, too much time is devoted to resetting passwords for users who have forgotten them. More than one employee's productivity is affected when forgotten passwords have to be reassigned. The network staff member who has to reset the password could be working on other tasks, and the user who forgot the password cannot complete his task until the network staff member is finished resetting the password. Many help-desk employees report that a majority of their time is spent on users forgetting their passwords. System administrators have to manage multiple user accounts on different platforms, which all need to be coordinated in a manner that maintains the integrity of the security policy. At times the complexity can be overwhelming which results in poor access control management and the generation of many security vulnerabilities because the user IDs and passwords are usually written down and posted on the side of the monitor or underneath the user's keyboard. This fact defeats the purpose of using passwords in the first place. So a lot of time is spent on multiple passwords, and in the end, they do not provide us with more security.

The increased cost of managing a diverse environment, security concerns, and user habits has brought about the idea of *single sign-on* capabilities. These capabilities would allow a user to enter credentials one time and be able to access all resources in primary and secondary network domains. This reduces the amount of time users spend authenticating to resources and it gives the administrator the ability to streamline user accounts and have better control over access rights. It improves security by reducing the probability of users writing down passwords and reduces the administrator's time spent on adding and removing user accounts and modifying access permissions. In the event that an administrator needs to disable or suspend a specific account, it can be done uniformly instead of having to alter configurations on each and every platform.

So that is our utopia: Log on once and you are good to go. So what busts this bubble? Mainly interoperability issues. For single sign-on to actually work, every platform, application, and resource needs to accept the same type of credentials, in the same format, and interpret their meanings the same. When Steve logs onto his NT 4.0 workstation and gets authenticated by a mixed-mode Windows 2000 domain controller, it needs to authenticate him to the resources he needs to access on the Apple computer, the Unix server running VisionFS, the mainframe host server, the MICR print server, and the Windows 98 computer in the secondary domain that has the plotter connected to it. Nice idea, until reality hits.

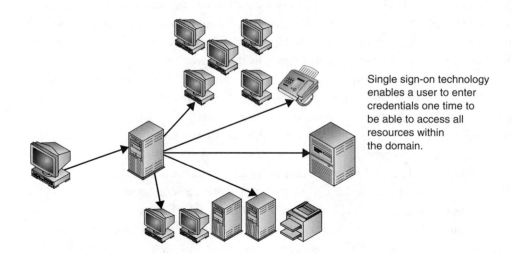

Single sign-on technology enables a user to enter credentials one time to be able to access all resources within the domain.

There is also a security issue to consider in a single sign-on environment; once an individual is in, he is in. If an attacker was able to break into the network by hijacking or creating an account, she would now have access to basically every resource within the environment.

There are different types of a single sign-on implementation. Each has its own advantages and disadvantages, shortcomings, and quality features. It is rare to see a real single sign-on environment, but instead, you will see a cluster of computers and resources that accept the same credentials, whereas other resources still require more work on the administrator or the user side to access. The most popular methods of single sign-on are described in the next sections.

References

http://developer.netscape.com/docs/manuals/security/SSO/contents.htm

www.opengroup.org/security/sso/

Scripting The more simplistic single sign-on systems are written with batch files and scripts that contain each user's ID, password, and logon commands necessary for each platform. When a user requests access to a resource, a script will run in the background and perform the same commands and tasks that the user would have to perform to properly authenticate to this resource. The scripts can use a macro language that replays user keystrokes or provides commands that work within a shell. Although this is easier on the user, it demands much more work on the administrator and his staff. The scripts have to be written, and if a user changes his user ID or password, the script needs to be updated also. Because these scripts contain credentials, they must be stored in a protected area and the transmission of the scripts must be dealt with carefully. As platforms are upgraded and changed, this requires the scripts to follow the same suit to ensure the proper interface between the user's computer, script, and resource.

Kerberos

Sam, there is a three-headed dog in front of the server!

Kerberos is the name of a three-headed dog that guards the entrance to the underworld in Greek mythology. This is a great name for a security system that provides authentication and message protection. Kerberos is an authentication protocol and was designed in the mid-1980s as part of MIT's Project Athena. Products supporting Kerberos are becoming more frequent, so this one might be a keeper.

Three headed-dog Kerberos
(Greek myth)
protects the gates of the underworld.

Kerberos is an example of a single sign-on system for distributed environments, and is a de facto standard for heterogeneous networks. Kerberos incorporates a wide range of security technologies, which gives companies much more flexibility and scalability when needing to provide an encompassing security architecture. However, this open architecture also invites interoperability issues. When a vendor has a lot of freedom to customize a product, it usually means that no two vendors will customize in the same fashion. This brings interoperability and incompatibility issues.

Kerberos uses symmetric key cryptography and provides end-to-end security, meaning that information being passed between a user and a service is protected without the need of an intermediate component. Although it allows the use of passwords for authentication, it was designed specifically to eliminate the need for transmitting passwords over the network. Most Kerberos implementations work with cryptography keys and shared secret keys instead of passwords.

Main Components in Kerberos   The *Key Distribution Center (KDC)* is the most important component within a Kerberos environment. The KDC holds all users' and services' cryptographic keys. It provides authentication services, as well as key distribution functionality. The clients and services trust the integrity of the KDC, and this trust is the foundation of Kerberos security.

The KDC provides security services to entities referred to as *principals*. These principals can be users, applications, or services. The KDC and each principal share a secret key. (A secret key is a cryptographic key used to encrypt and decrypt data.) When the KDC and a principal share a secret key, this means the KDC uses the secret key to encrypt data, sends it to the principal, and the principal uses the secret key to decrypt and process the data. Because the KDC and the principal are the only ones sharing this specific secret key, their communication is protected from eavesdropping or network sniffing. The KDC has a database that contains identity information on all principals within its realm and a secret key it shares with each and every principal.

A *ticket* is generated by the KDC and given to a principal when that principal, let's say a user, needs to authenticate to another principal, let's say a print server. The ticket enables one principal to authenticate to another principal. So if Emily needs to use the print server, she needs to prove to the print server she is who she claims to be and that she is authorized to use the printing service. So Emily requests a ticket from the KDC. The KDC gives Emily the ticket, and in turn, Emily passes this ticket onto the print server. If the printer server approves of this ticket, Emily is allowed to use the print service.

A KDC provides security services for a set of components and principals. This set is called a *realm* in Kerberos. The KDC is the trusted authentication server for all users, applications, and services within a realm. One KDC can be responsible for one realm or several realms. Realms are used to allow an administrator to logically group resources and users.

So far we have principals (users and services) that authenticate to a KDC. The KDC has a database filled with information about each and every principal within its realm. The KDC holds and delivers cryptographic keys and tickets. Tickets are used for principals to authenticate to each other. So how does this work?

Kerberos Authentication Process   The user and the KDC share a secret key; the service and the KDC share a different secret key. The user and the service do not share a secret key in the beginning. So the user trusts the KDC because they share a secret key, they can encrypt and decrypt data they pass between each other, and thus have a protected communication path. The same is true for the service and the KDC. Once the user authenticates to the service, they too will share a secret key that will enable them to encrypt and decrypt the information they need to pass to each other. This is how Kerberos provides data transmission protection.

What are the exact steps you ask? Hold onto your hat, here we go!

1. Emily needs to print a very important "Happy Birthday" sign for her cousin Katie.

2. The Kerberos client software on Emily's computer prompts her for a user ID. Emily enters her user ID, and the client software sends the ID to the KDC along with the name of the print service Emily has requested.

3. The authentication service (AS), which is part of the KDC, receives this request and verifies that Emily and the print service are in its database. If both are in the database, the KDC provides a session key for Emily and the print service to use. One instance of the session key is encrypted with the service's secret key, and the another instance of the session key is encrypted with Emily's secret key. This ensures that this session key came from the KDC, because only the KDC shares the secret key with a principal.

4. The KDC generates a service ticket that holds both instances of the session key, and it is sent back to the client software on Emily's computer. The client software prompts Emily for a password. Once she types the password in, the client converts it into the key that is necessary to decrypt the session key within the ticket. If Emily did not type in the right password, the client could not generate the correct key to decrypt the ticket, which means Emily could not authenticate and use the print service. However, Emily is a bright lass, and she remembers her password.

5. The client software on Emily's computer decrypts her portion of the ticket, which gives her a copy of the session key and sends the ticket onto the print service to

authenticate Emily. The print service has the necessary secret key to decrypt the ticket, so the print service now also has a copy of the session key.

6. So the client software decrypted a session key for Emily and the print service decrypted the ticket and has a copy of the same session key. Emily is now authenticated to the print service and they can use this session key to encrypt and decrypt messages they send to each other.

7. Emily can now print Katie's birthday banner, and *you* can sit back and have a glass of water.

So the user, Emily, asks the KDC to give her a ticket to present to the print service. This ticket will authenticate her to the print service and enables her to use this service. The KDC verifies that it knows about Emily and the print service, and sends Emily the ticket. Emily then sends the ticket to the print service, and she is now allowed to print to her heart's desire. Figure 4-6 provides a simplistic view of this process.

The AS is the part of the KDC that authenticates a principal and the Ticket Granting Service (TGS) is the part of the KDC that makes the tickets and hands them out to the principals. Make sure to understand that a session key is different than a secret key. A secret key is shared between the KDC and a principal. A session key is shared between two principals. This is a very basic view of how Kerberos works. There are types of secu-

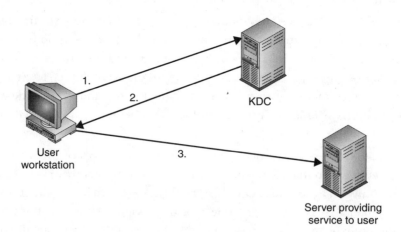

1. User requests access to service running on a different server.
2. KDC authenticates user and sends a ticket to be used between the user and the service on the server.
3. User's workstation sends ticket to service to authenticate and use the requested service.

Figure 4-6   The user needs to receive a ticket from the KDC before being able to use requested resource.

rity technologies that can be plugged into a Kerberos framework, with many different parameters and configurations.

So why are we talking about Kerberos? Because it is one example of a single sign-on system. The user enters a user ID and password one time and one time only. The tickets have time limits on them that administrators can configure. Many times the lifetime of a ticket is eight hours, so when the user comes in the next day, he will have to present his credentials again.

Weaknesses of Kerberos   Kerberos provides confidentiality and integrity of data by the use of its cryptographic keys and encryption processes. It does not protect a computer or service's availability, which is another security service. The following lists some of the potential weaknesses of Kerberos:

- The KDC is a single point of failure. If the KDC goes down, no one can access needed resources, so in many instances users cannot work.

- The AS on the KDC must be able to handle the number of requests it receives in a timely manner.

- Secret keys are temporarily stored on the users' workstations, which means it is possible for an intruder to obtain this cryptographic key.

- Session keys are decrypted and reside on the users' workstations, either in a cache or in a key table. Again, an intruder can capture this key.

- Kerberos is vulnerable to password guessing. The KDC does not know if a dictionary attack is taking place.

- Network traffic is not protected by Kerberos.

- When a user changes his password, it changes the secret key. So when a user changes his password, the KDC database needs to be updated.

References

www.ietf.org/html.charters/cat-charter.html

www.nrl.navy.mil/CCS/people/kenh/kerberos-faq.html

www.mit.edu/afs/athena.mit.edu/astaff/project/kerberos/www/papers.html

SESAME   The Secure European System for Applications in a Multivendor Environment (SESAME) project is another type of single sign-on technology that was developed in the hopes of addressing some of the weaknesses in Kerberos.

SESAME uses public key cryptography for the distribution of secret keys, which reduces key management overhead. Like Kerberos, SESAME uses a ticket for authorization, which is called a *Privilege Attribute Certificate*. SESAME adds more access control features than Kerberos, has scalability of public key systems, and is easier to manage.

SESAME is vulnerable to password guessing, as is Kerberos.

References

www.cosic.esat.kuleuven.ac.be/sesame/html/sesame_what.html

www.cosic.esat.kuleuven.ac.be/sesame/html/sesame_links.html

Thin Clients   Diskless computers, sometimes called dumb terminals or thin clients, cannot store information because of their lack of an operating system and necessary resources. This type of technology forces users to log onto the network just to be able to use the computer. When the user starts the computer, it runs a short list of instructions and then points itself to a server that will actually download the operating system to the terminal. This enforces a strict type of access control because the computer cannot do anything on its own until it authenticates to the server, and then the server gives the computer its operating system, profile, and functionality. Thin client technology provides another type of single sign-on access for users.

Types of Single Sign-On Methods

- **Scripts**   Files containing user credentials for different resource types
- **Kerberos**   Authentication protocol that uses a centralized authentication server, the KDC
- **SESAME**   An access control technology developed in Europe
- **Thin clients**   Dumb terminals authenticating to a server

Access Control Models

An *access control model* is a framework that dictates how subjects access objects. It uses access control technologies and security mechanisms to enforce the rules and objectives of the model. There are three main types of access control models: discretionary, mandatory, and nondiscretionary (also called role-based). Each model type uses different methods to control how subjects access objects and has its own merits and limitations. The business and security goals of an organization will help prescribe what access control model should be used, along with the culture of the company and the habits of conducting business. Some models are used exclusively and sometimes they are combined to be able to accomplish the necessary level of security an environment requires. The following sections explain these models, their supporting technologies, and when they should be implemented.

Discretionary

If a user creates a file, he is the owner of that file. Ownership might also be granted to a specific individual. For example, a manager for a certain department might be made the owner of the files and resources within her domain. An identifier for this user is placed in the file header. A system that uses *discretionary access control (DAC)* enables the owner of the resource to specify what subjects can access specific resources. This model is called discretionary because the control of access is based on the discretion of the owner.

In a DAC model, access is restricted based on the authorization granted to the users. This means that subjects are allowed to specify what type of access can occur to the objects they own. If an organization is using a DAC model, the network administrator can allow resource owners control of who has access to their files. The most common implementation of DAC is through ACLs, which are dictated by owners, set by the network administrator, and enforced by the operating system. This does not lend itself to a centrally controlled environment and can make a user's ability to access information dynamic versus the more static role of mandatory access control (MAC).

It is through the discretionary model that Sam can share his D: drive to David, so David can copy all of Sam's MP3s. Sam can also block access to his D: drive from his manager so his manager does not know that Sam is wasting valuable time and resources by downloading MP3s from Napster.

References

http://security.isu.edu/isl/dac.html

http://security.tsu.ru/info/rainbow/tg03.htm

Mandatory

In a *mandatory access control (MAC)* model, users and data owners do not have as much freedom to determine who can access their files. Data owners can allow others to have access to their files, but it is the operating system that will make the final decision and can override the data owner's wishes. This model is much more structured and strict and is based on a security label system. Users are given a security clearance (secret, top secret, confidential, and so on) and data is classified (secret, top secret, confidential, and so on). The classification is stored in the security labels of the resources. The classification label specifies the level of trust a user must have to be able to access the file. When the system makes a decision about fulfilling a request to access an object, it is based on the clearance of the subject and the classification of the object. The rules of how subjects access data are made by management, configured by the administrator, enforced by the operating system, and supported by security technologies.

Security labels are attached to all objects; thus, every file, directory, and device has its own security label with its classification information.

A user may have a security clearance of secret and the data that he requests may have a security label of top secret. In this case, the user will be denied because his clearance is not equivalent to or superior to the classification of the object. This type of model is used in environments where information classification and confidentiality is of utmost importance—like a military institution.

References

http://research-istw.saic.com/cace/overview.html

http://csrc.nist.gov/publications/nistpubs/800-7/node36.html#
SECTION05161000000000000000

Sensitivity Labels

When MAC is being used, every subject and object must have a sensitivity label also called a security label. It contains a classification and different categories. The classification indicates the sensitivity level and the categories indicate which objects take on that classification. Figure 4-7 illustrates a sensitivity label.

The classifications follow a hierarchical structure, one level being more trusted than another. However, the categories do not follow a hierarchical scheme, because they represent different areas of information within a system. The categories can correspond to departments (accounting, payroll, or sales), projects (Big Blue, CBFSecurity, or CRM), or management levels. In a military environment, the classifications would be top secret, secret, confidential, and unclassifed. Each classification is more trusted than the one below it. A commercial organization might use confidential, proprietary, corpo-

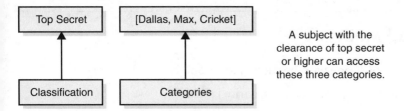

A subject with the
clearance of top secret
or higher can access
these three categories.

Figure 4-7 A sensitivity label is made up of a classification and categories.

rate, and sensitive. The definition of the classification is up to the organization and should make sense for the environment they are used in.

NOTE In MAC implementations, the system makes the access decisions by comparing the security labels of the subject and object. In DAC, the owner of the file can make access decisions.

Reference

http://csrc.nist.gov/publications/nistpubs/800-7/node37.html#
SECTION05162000000000000000

Role-Based

A *role-based access control (RBAC)* model, also called *nondiscretionary access control*, uses a centrally administered set of controls to determine how subjects and objects interact. This type of model allows access to resources based on the role the user holds within the company. Administrators put users into roles and then assign access rights to those roles. If Terry was assigned the task of backing up data, the administrator would put him into a backup operator role and assign the necessary permissions to the role, not directly to Terry.

NOTE Introducing roles also introduces the difference between rights being assigned explicitly and implicitly. If rights and permissions are assigned explicitly, it indicates that they are assigned to a specific individual. If they are assigned implicitly, it indicates that they are assigned to a role or group.

Access Control Models

- **DAC**   Data owners decide who has access to resources.
- **MAC**   Access decisions are based on security labels.
- **RBAC**   Access decisions are based on subject's role.

Roles and groups are different, although they serve a similar purpose. They both work as containers for users to be put into. A company may have an auditors group, which contains several different users. These users can be part of other groups and usually have their own individual rights and permissions assigned to them also. So if Diane is part of the auditors group, she can access files and resources assigned to this group, but as a user, she also has permissions that give her certain other access rights. If a company uses roles, any user assigned to that role only has the rights of that role. This provides tighter control. For example, if John was assigned to the contractor role, he could only access resources that are granted to this role; he will not usually have any of his own individual rights or permissions. Figure 4-8 shows the concept of roles.

A RBAC model is the best system for companies that have high turnovers. If John, who is mapped to the contractor role, leaves the company, then Chrissy can be easily mapped to this role. This way the administrator does not need to continually change the individual's permissions that fulfill a specific role in the company; he only needs to create a role (contractor), assign permissions to this role, and map the new user to this role.

Organizations usually set up a hierarchical structure of groups and roles and assign each employee to the corresponding container. If Stacy is in charge of ordering brooms, she is the BroomMaster, and this is the account she uses to access information within the network. When she moves onto bigger and better things, the next person who is in charge of ordering brooms uses this same account. The RBAC model can use *role-based access* (determined by the role the user has within the company), *task-based access* (determined by the task assigned to this user), or a *lattice-based access* (determined by the sensitivity level assigned to the role).

Lattice-based access control provides an upper bound and lower bound of access capabilities for every subject and object relationship. For example, if the BroomMaster role were assigned a clearance level of confidential, the upper bound of access would be confidential, while the lower bound would be public. Figure 4-9 shows lattice-based access control. The subject can access all objects in this range of classification.

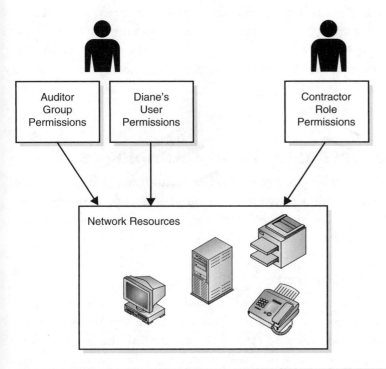

Figure 4-8 Individuals assigned to roles usually only have the permissions of that role.

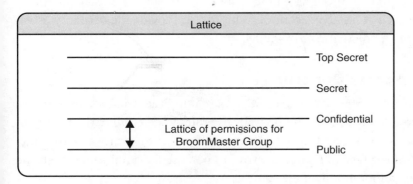

Figure 4-9 Lattice provides upper and lower bounds of permissions for a subject.

Lattice-based control is a way of setting boundaries on what a subject can and cannot access. If the user in the BroomMaster role attempts to access a file that has the classification of top secret, she would receive a message indicating she did not possess the necessary rights to access this file. This is because this file is not within the user's latticed-based boundaries.

Access Control Techniques and Technologies

Once an organization determines what type of access control model is going to be used, the technologies and techniques need to be identified and refined to support the model. The following sections describe the different access controls and technologies available to support different access control models.

Role-Based Access Control

Access rights can be based on the tasks and responsibilities that individuals need to accomplish to fulfill the obligations of their positions in the company. The administrator is tasked with assigning individuals to roles that correlate with the positions they hold within the company. RBAC can be used with discretionary and mandatory access control models. In DAC models, administrators can develop roles and owners can decide if these roles can have access to their resources. In a MAC model, roles can be developed and sensitivity labels assigned to those roles indicating its security level. So role-based access can be enforced as a model, meaning it would be used enterprise-wide, or it can be used as an access control technique to provide the necessary access level schemes within a different type of model.

Rule-Based Access Control

Rule-based access control is based on specific rules that indicate what can and cannot happen to an object. Many routers and firewalls use rules to determine which types of packets and requests are allowed into a network and which ones are rejected. Rule-based access control is a type of mandatory control because the administrator sets the rules and the users cannot modify these controls.

Restricted Interfaces

Constrained user interfaces restrict users' access abilities by not allowing them to request certain functions, information, or have access to specific system resources.

There are three major types of restricted interfaces: menus and shells, database views, and physically constrained interfaces.

When menu and shell restrictions are used, the users are only given the options of the commands they can execute. If an administrator only wants users to be able to run and exit one program, these are the only choices that would be available on the menu. This limits the user's functionality. A shell is a type of virtual environment within a system. If restricted shells were used, the shell would contain only the commands the administrator wants the users to be able to execute.

Many times a database administrator will configure a database so users cannot see fields that he wants to keep secret. *Database views* are mechanisms used for restricting user access to data that is contained in databases. If the database administrator wants managers to be able to view their employees' work records, but not their salary information, then the salary fields would not be available to these types of users. Similarly, when payroll employees looks at the same database, they will be able to view the salary information, but not the work history information. This example is illustrated in Figure 4-10.

Physically constraining a user interface can be implemented by only providing certain keys on a keypad or touch buttons on a screen. We see this when we get money from the ATM machine. This device has a type of operating system that can accept all kinds of commands and configuration changes, but we are physically constrained from being able to carry out these functions. We are presented with buttons that only enable us to withdrawal, view our balance, or deposit funds. Period.

Harris, D	$45,000	8am-5pm
Torkelson, T	$60,000	6pm-2am
Kowtko, J	$45,000	8am-5pm
Swenson, J	$65,000	6pm-2am

Payroll Database View

Harris, D	Work History	8am-5pm
Torkelson, T	Work History	6pm-2am
Kowtko, J	Work History	8am-5pm
Swenson, J	Work History	6pm-2am

Manager Database View

Figure 4-10   Different database views

Access Control Matrix

An *access control matrix* is a table of subjects and objects indicating what actions individual subjects can take upon individual objects. Matrices are data structures that programmers implement as table lookups that will be used and enforced by the operating system. Table 4-1 provides an example of an access control matrix.

This type of access control is usually an attribute of DAC models and the access rights can be assigned directly to the subjects (capabilities) or to the objects (ACLs).

Capability Tables

A *capability table* specifies the access rights a certain subject possesses pertaining to specific objects. A capability table is different than an ACL because the subject is bound to the capability table, whereas the object is bound to the ACL.

The capability corresponds to the subject's row in the access control matrix. In Table 4-1, Diane's capabilities are File1: read and execute; File2: read and write; File3: no access. This outlines what Diane is capable of doing to each resource. An example of a capability-based system is Kerberos. In this environment, the user is given a ticket, which is his capability table. This ticket is bound to the user and dictates what objects that user can access and to what extent. The access control is based on this ticket, or capability table, not on an ACL bound to the object. Figure 4-11 shows the difference between a capability table and an ACL.

Access Control Lists

Access control lists (ACLs) are used in several operating systems, applications, and router configurations. They are lists of subjects that are authorized to access a specific object and they define what level of authorization is granted. Authorization can be specified to an individual, role, or group.

Table 4-1 Access Control Matrix

Users	File1	File2	File3
Diane	Read and execute	Read and write	No access
Katie	Read and write	Write and execute	No access
Chrissy	Read, write, and execute	Read	Read
John	Read and execute	Read	Read, write, and execute

Capabilities Table

Plotter—Print
Printer1—Print
Printer2—No Access
Accountng.xls—Full control
Accounting.doc—Read, Write
Payroll.xls—No Access
Clipart—Full Control

Access Control Lists

Tom Harris—Print
Joni Swenson—Full Control
Maynard Harris—No Access
Evelyn Seaton—Print
Iqqi Hammond—Full Control
David Arnold—Print

Figure 4-11   A capability table is bound to a subject, whereas an access control list is bound to an object.

Table 4-2   The ACL for File1

User	
Diane	Read and execute
Katie	Read and write
Chrissy	Read, write, and execute
John	Read and execute

ACLs map values from the access control matrix to the object. Whereas a capability corresponds to a row in the access control matrix, the ACL corresponds to a column of the matrix. The ACL for File1 in Table 4-1 is shown in Table 4-2.

Content-Dependent Access Control

Just like the name sounds, access to objects is determined by the content within the object. This is used many times in databases and the type of Web-based material a firewall allows. Our earlier example pertaining to database views showed how *content-dependent access control* can work. If the table within the database contains information about employee salaries, the managers were not allowed to view it, but they could view information about an employee's work history. The content of the database fields dictates which users can see specific information within the database tables.

Access Control Techniques

Access controls techniques are used to support the access control models.

- **Role-based** Access to objects is based on subject's role.
- **Rule-based** Rules outline how subjects can access objects.
- **Restricted interfaces** Limits the user's environment within the system, thus limiting access to objects.
- **Access control matrix** Table of subjects and objects outlining their access relationships.
- **Capability table** Bound to a subject and indicates what objects that subject can access.
- **ACL** Bound to object and indicates what subjects can access it.
- **Content-based access** Access decision based on data, not solely on subject identity.

Access Control Administration

Once an organization develops a security policy, supporting procedures, standards, and guidelines (described in Chapter 3), the decision of the type of access control model must be decided upon: DAC, MAC, or role-based models. Once the model is chosen, the different access control technologies and techniques need to be selected and implemented: access control matrices, restricted interface, content-dependent, and rule- or role-based controls.

If the environment does not require a high level of security, the choices are usually discretionary and role-based. The discretionary model gives data owners the ability to allow other users to access their resources, so that choice should be made with full knowledge of what it entails. If the organization has a high turnover rate, the role-based model is more appropriate. If the environment requires a higher security level and it is desired that only the administrator grants access control, then a MAC model is the best choice.

So now what is there to work out? How the access control model will be administered. Access control administration comes in three basic flavors: centralized, decentralized, and a hybrid of the two. Each should be understood so that the proper method is chosen and implemented to achieve the level of protection required.

Centralized

I control who accesses what. Answer: So what.

A *centralized access control administration* method is basically what it sounds like. One entity (department or individual) is responsible for granting all users access to resources. The management determines how users and resources should interact, and this entity configures the mechanisms that enforce access control, process any changes needed to a user's access control profile, disable access when necessary, and completely remove these rights when a user is terminated, leaves the company, or moves into a different position. This type of administration provides a consistent and uniform method of controlling users' access rights. It can supply strict control over data because only one entity (department or individual) has the necessary rights to change access control profiles and permissions. Although this provides for a more consistent and reliable environment, it can be a slow one because all changes must be processed by one entity.

The following sections show some examples of centralized access control technologies.

RADIUS

Remote Authentication Dial-in User Service (RADIUS) is an authentication protocol that authenticates and authorizes users usually dial-up users. A network may have a modem pool dedicated for remote users to dial into, which is connected to access servers. The access server requests the remote user's login credentials and passes them back to a RADIUS server, which houses a database of usernames and passwords, or other authenticating information. The remote user is a client to the access server and the access server is a client to the RADIUS server.

The access server may be at the same location of the requested network or it may be at the Internet Service Provider (ISP) that the remote user connects to obtain Internet access. Figure 4-12 shows how RADIUS implementations can be configured.

TACACS

Terminal Access Controller Access Control System (TACACS) has a very funny name. Not funny ha-ha, but funny huh? Anyway, TACACS has been through three generations: TACACS, Extended TACACS (XTACACS), and TACACS+. TACACS combines its authentication and authorization processes, XTACACS separates authentication, authorization, and accounting processes, and TACACS+ is XTACACS with extended two-factor user authentication.

TACACS is a client/server protocol that provides the same type of functionality as RADIUS. A remote user can dial into a location that has a TACACS client, most likely

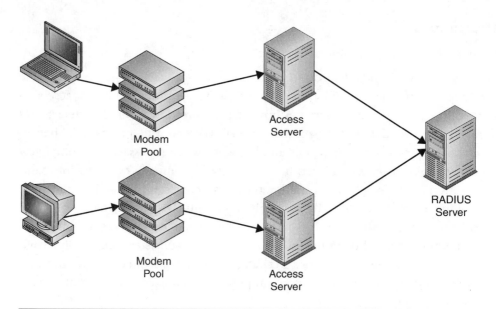

Figure 4-12 RADIUS is one way of administrating access control centrally.

an ISP. The client (or access server) prompts the user for credentials, and the client passes these credentials onto the TACACS server. The TACACS server verifies the credentials and authenticates the user to now be able to use resources within the network. TACACS+ enables credentials to take the form of username and passwords, Kerberos, or can use dynamic passwords through security tokens.

TACACS+ and RADIUS provide the same functionality, but RADIUS is an actual Internet standard. Figure 4-13 shows how RADIUS and TACACS work.

Decentralized and Distributed Access Administration

A *decentralized administration* method gives control of access to the people closer to the resources—thus, the people who better understand who should and should not have access to certain files, data, and resources. Many times it is the functional manager who assigns access control rights to employees. The reason an organization would use a decentralized model is because the managers usually have better judgment of which users should be able to access different resources, and there is no business requirement that dictates that strict control through a centralized body is necessary.

Changes can happen faster through this type of administration because not just one entity is making changes for the whole organization. However, there is a possibility that

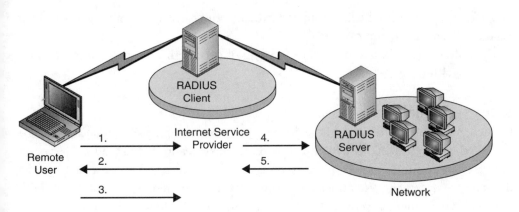

1. User initiates PPP authentication with ISP.
2. RADIUS client prompts user for credentials.
3. User supplies credentials.
4. RADIUS client sends credentials to RADIUS server.
5. RADIUS server responds with Accept, Reject, or Challenge.
6. If authentication is successful, RADIUS client allows access to network.

Figure 4-13   The RADIUS or TACACS client could reside at an ISP.

conflicts of interest could arise that may not benefit the organization. Because there is not one entity controlling access as a whole, different managers and departments can practice security and access control in different ways. This does not provide uniformity and fairness across the organizations. One manager could be too busy with daily tasks and decide that it is easier to let everyone have full control over all the systems in the department, whereas another department may practice more strict and detail-oriented method of control by only giving employees the level of permissions needed to fulfill their tasks.

Also, certain controls can overlap; thus, actions are not properly proscribed or restricted. If Mike is part of the accounting group and has been recently under suspicion for altering personnel account information, the accounting manager may restrict his access to these files to read. However, the accounting manager does not realize that Mike still has full control access under the network group he is also a member of. This type of administration does not provide methods for consistent control like a central-ized method would. Another issue that comes up with decentralized administration is when Sean is fired for looking at girly pictures on his computer, all the groups Sean is a member of may not disable his account once Sean is fired. So the company could still give access to Sean once he is terminated, which could cause the company heartache if Sean is a disgruntled employee.

The following sections show some examples of decentralized access control administration techniques.

Security Domain

In the context of decentralized access control management, a *security domain* can be described as a realm of trust. Within this domain, or realm of trust, all subjects and objects share common security policies, procedures, and rules and they are managed by the same management system. Each security domain is different because different policies and management govern it. A security domain can dictate what actions a program can perform, the objects and resources it can interact with, and the boundaries that restrict it from working with other security domains. (The security domain used in this context is similar but different than how Microsoft uses the concept of a network domain. Please do not get the two confused.) Figure 4-14 shows two different security domains.

A security domain defines the objects a subject can access. For example, a program can have access control parameters that restrict it to being able to work with only certain memory segments, files, and processes as shown in Figure 4-15. Access control mechanisms are used to define and enforce these restrictions. This means this subject (the program) has a security domain (boundaries to work within) of specific objects. This principle of separation protects resources and controls how access activities are performed.

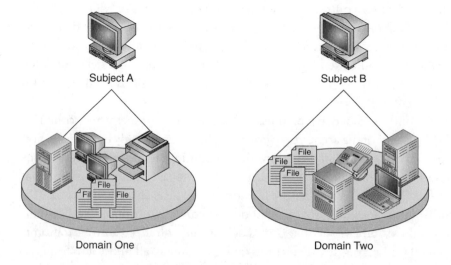

Subject A   Subject B

Domain One   Domain Two

Figure 4-14   Each subject can have a different security domain.

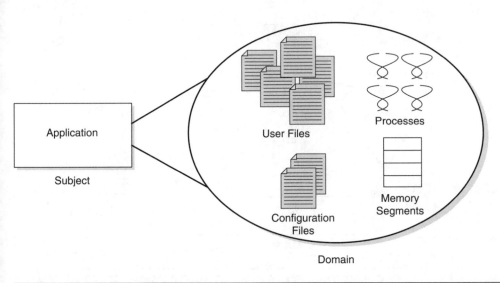

Figure 4-15   A subject can only interact with objects in its own domain.

Security domains can be implemented in hierarchical structures and relationships. A higher-privileged subject can have access to high and low domains, while lower-privileged subjects can access only lower-classed domains. This is a separation mechanism that controls resource access capabilities and activities.

Security domains are used within operating systems and applications to ensure that rogue activities do not accidentally damage important system files or processes. A subject with a higher level of trust may be able to access memory segments and configuration files that are restricted from a lower-level subject. A subject with a lower level of trust should only have access to resources that it can be trusted to use in a proper and predictable manner. For example, the kernel of an operating system is highly trusted. The subjects that work within the kernel have access to objects in a high security domain (like restricted memory segments and system files) and also have access to objects in a low security domain (like user files). This concept is illustrated in Figure 4-16.

This protection is done through segmenting memory spaces and addresses. An application may have the right to only access information in a lower-privileged memory space, whereas the operating system processes might have the right to access information in all memory spaces. This ensures that a poorly written application will not damage core operating system operations and disrupt the activities of the system as a whole. We will revisit this concept in Chapter 5, but for now understand that a security domain is a type of decentralized access control technology.

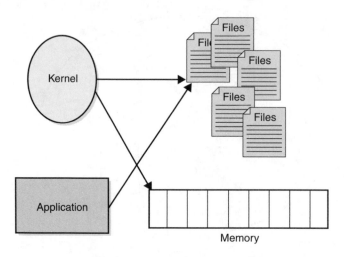

Figure 4-16 Entities that are more trusted by the system can access more objects and system resources than entities that are not as highly trusted.

A security domain can also be described as the resources available to a user. A user may be able to use the printer, access certain files, and use a plotter. If this is all the user can access, this is the extent of his domain. If each user's domain is not monitored and controlled by a specific individual (administrator) or a group, then this is an example of decentralized access control administration. This is the confusing part between a network domain and a security domain. We naturally think of a network domain as a centralized administration control because a network administrator is dictating what resources users can access. A security domain is all the objects a subject can access, which may or may not be granted by an administrator.

Hybrid

A *hybrid administration* is a combination of the centralized and decentralized access control administration methods, but I bet you already guessed that. Many times when an organization employs this type of control, the central administration is used for the sensitive types of access (domain logon, system file access, and database access) and the users can determine who can access the individual files they have created. Many times users are required to log into a network domain so that they can access network resources. This type of access is controlled centrally by the network administrator. When users create files and share them, they can dictate who can and cannot access them, which is a type of decentralized access control. This gives the users more control and functionality, but it does not provide a strictly secure and controlled environment.

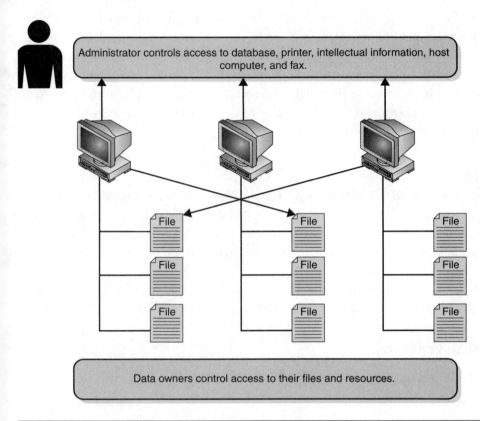

Administrator controls access to database, printer, intellectual information, host computer, and fax.

File

File

File

File

File

File

File

File

File

Data owners control access to their files and resources.

Figure 4-17   Hybrid access control administration

Figure 4-17 shows a hybrid model where the administrator can control which subjects can access specific objects within the environment and data owners can control which subjects can access the resources they are responsible for.

Access Control Methods

Access controls can be implemented at various layers of a network and individual systems. Some controls are core components of operating systems, or embedded into hardware, and some security controls require third-party add-on packages. Although different controls provide different functionality, they all work together to keep the bad guys out, the good guys in, and to provide the necessary quality of protection.

Most companies do not want people to be able to walk arbitrarily into their building, sit down at an employee's computer, and access network resources. Companies also don't want every employee to be able to access all information within the company: for example, human resource records, payroll information, and trade secrets. Companies want to have some assurance that employees who can access confidential information will have some restrictions put upon them so a disgruntled employee does not have the ability to delete financial statements, tax information, and top secret data that would put the company at risk. There are several types of access controls that prevent these things from happening.

Access Control Layers

There are three broad categories of access control: administrative, logical, and physical. Each category has different access control mechanisms that work within a hierarchal layer and many can be carried out manually or automatically. All of these access control mechanisms should work in concert with each other to protect an infrastructure and its data.

Each category of access control has several components that fall within it. The following list shows these components and the category they belong to.

Administrative

- Policies and procedures
- Personnel controls
- Supervisory structure
- Security awareness training
- Testing

Physical Controls

- Network segregation
- Perimeter security
- Computer controls
- Work area separation
- Data backups
- Cabling

Technical Controls

- System access

- Network architecture

- Network access

- Encryption and protocols

- Control zone

- Auditing

The following sections quickly explain each of these components and how they relate to access control.

Administrative Controls

Senior management must decide how security will play a role in their organization. They must determine the security goals and objectives within the organization. These directives will dictate how all the supporting mechanisms will fall into place. Basically, senior management provides the skeleton of a security infrastructure and then appoints the proper entities to fill in the rest.

The first piece to building a security foundation within an organization is a security policy. It is management's responsibility to construct a security policy and delegate the development of the supporting procedures, standards, and guidelines, indicate which personnel controls should be used, and how testing should be carried out to ensure that all pieces fulfill the company's security goals. These items are described as *administrative controls* and work at the top layer of a hierarchical access control model. (Administrative controls are examined in detail in Chapter 3, but are shown here briefly to show the relationship to logical and physical controls pertaining to access control.)

Policy and Procedures

Now what's our overall plan?

A *security policy* is a high-level plan stating management's intent pertaining to how security should be practiced within an organization, what actions are acceptable, and what level of risk the company is willing to accept. This policy is derived from the laws, regulations, and business objectives that shape and restrict the company. The security policy provides direction for each employee and department pertaining to how security should be implemented and followed, and the repercussions for noncompliance.

Procedures, guidelines, and standards provide the details that support the company's security policy.

The way that the company carries out and enforces access control is derived from its security policy. Senior management will decide if DAC, MAC, or RBAC access methodology should be used and if it should be administered via centralization or decentralization methods. They make the decisions and the IT department usually carries them out.

Personnel Controls

Personnel controls indicate how employees are expected to interact with security mechanisms and noncompliance issues pertaining to these expectations. These controls indicate what security actions should be taken when an employee is terminated, suspended, moved into another department, or promoted. Specific procedures need to be developed for each situation and many times the human resource and legal departments are involved with making these decisions.

The separation of duties and rotation of duties are also personnel controls that need to be dictated by management. The *separation of duties* should be enforced so not one individual can carry out a critical task alone that could prove to be detrimental to the company. A bank teller who needed to get supervisory approval to cash checks over $3,000 would be an example of separation of duties. For a security breach to occur, it would require *collusion*, which means that more than one person would need to commit fraud and this effort would need to happen in a concerted effort. This drastically reduces the chances of security breaches and fraud.

Rotation of duties means that people know how to fulfill the obligations of more than one position. In many companies, there is just that one person who knows how to work the big important machine that keeps the company in business. If this person gets hit by a bus or finds a better job, the company's productivity can drop while it is frantically training the new person. If there were a practice of rotation of duties within this company, so much would not be riding on just one individual.

If an individual attempts to commit fraud within his position, it would be easier to detect by another individual who knows what tasks should be performed in that position and how they should be performed. The rotation of duties acts as a safeguard against fraud and it provides cross training and supplies trained backup personnel.

Supervisory Structure

Management must construct a management and supervisory structure. Each employee has a superior to report to, and that superior in return is responsible for that employee's actions. This forces management staff members to be responsible for employees and take a vested interest in their actions. If an employee is caught hacking into a server that holds customer credit card information, that employee and her supervisor will be called to the carpet. This is an administrative control that aids in fighting fraud and enforcing proper access control.

Security Awareness Training

How do you know they know what they are supposed to know?

In many organizations, management has a hard time spending money and allocating resources to items that do not seem to affect their bottom line: profitability. This is why training is usually pushed to the back of the bus, but as computer security becomes more and more of an issue to companies, security awareness training is not viewed as a waste of time.

A company's security depends upon technology and people, and people are usually the weakest link and cause the most security breaches and compromises. If users understand how to properly access resources, why access controls are in place, and the ramifications for not using these access controls properly, a company can reduce many of the types of security incidents that take place.

Testing

All security controls and mechanisms need to be tested on a periodic basis to ensure they properly support the security policy, goals, and objectives set for them. This testing can be a drill to test the reaction of a physical attack or disruption of the network, a penetration test of the firewalls and perimeter network to uncover vulnerabilities, a query to employees to gauge their knowledge, or a review of the procedures and standards to make sure they still align to business and/or technologies changes that have been implemented. Because change is constant and environments continually evolve, security procedures and practices should be continually tested to ensure that they align with the management's expectations and stay up-to-date with each addition to the infrastructure. It is management's responsibility to make sure these tests take place.

Physical Controls

We will go much further into physical security in Chapter 6, but it is important to understand that there are physical controls that must support and work with administrative and logical controls to supply the right degree of access control. Physical controls range from verifying individuals identities prior to entering a facility, erecting fences around the exterior of the facility, making sure server rooms and wiring closets are locked and protected from environmental elements (humidity, heat, and cold), and allowing only certain individuals to access work areas that contain confidential information. The following items explain some physical controls, but these and more physical mechanisms are explored in Chapter 6.

Network Segregation

Network segregation can be carried out through physical and logical means. A network might be physically designed to have all AS400 computers and databases in a certain area. This area can have doors with security swipe cards that allow only individuals who have a specific clearance to access this section and these computers. Another section of the network can contain Web servers, routers, and switches, and yet another network portion has employee workstations. Each area would have the necessary physical controls to ensure that only the right individuals would have access into and out of those sections. A simple example of network segregation is shown in Figure 4-18.

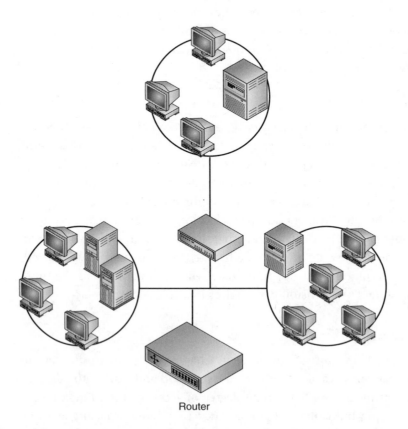

Router

Figure 4-18 Network segmentation allows the network administrator to better control the environment.

Perimeter Security

How perimeter security is implemented depends on the company and the security requirements of that environment. One environment may require employees to be authorized by a security guard by showing a security badge that contains picture identification before being allowed to enter a section. Another environment may require no authentication process and let anyone and everyone into different sections. Perimeter security can also encompass closed-circuit TVs that scan the parking lots and waiting areas, fences surrounding a building, lighting of walkways and parking areas, motion detectors, sensors, alarms, and the location and visual appearance of a building. These are examples of perimeter security mechanisms that provide physical access control by providing protection for individuals, facilities, and the components within facilities.

Computer Controls

Each computer can have physical controls installed and configured. These types of controls could be locks on the cover so the internal parts of a computer cannot be stolen, the removal of the floppy and CD-ROM drives to prevent copying of confidential information, or implementing a protection device that reduces the electrical emissions to thwart attempts of gathering information through airwaves.

Work Area Separation

Some environments might dictate that only particular individuals can access certain sections of the facility. Research companies might not want office personnel to be able to enter laboratories in fear of disrupting experiments or having access to test data. Most network administrators only allow network staff in the server rooms and wiring closets to reduce the possibilities of errors or sabotage attempts. In financial institutions, only certain employees can enter the vaults or other restricted areas. These are examples of work area separation and they are physical controls that are used to support access control and the overall security policy of the company.

Data Backups

Backing up data is a physical control to ensure access to information in case of an emergency or a disruption of the network or a system. When a network administrator of a bank backs up that day's transaction records, account histories, and financial information, it is stored on a type of physical media (tape, drive, or CD-ROM) and usually kept in a fireproof safe or copied and transported to an off-site facility. This provides physical protection of this data and a way to recover this information in case the original data is lost.

Cabling

There are different types of cabling that can be used to carry information throughout a network. Some cable types have sheaths that protect the data from being affected by electrical interference of other devices that emit electrical signals. Some types of cable have protection material around each individual wire to ensure that there is no cross talk between the different wires. All cables need to be routed throughout the facility in a manner that is not in people's way or that could be exposed to any danger of being cut, burnt, crimped, or eavesdropped upon. (Please refer to Chapter 6 for more in-depth information.)

Logical Controls

Logical controls, also called technical controls, are the hardware and software tools used to restrict subjects' access to objects. They are core components of operating systems, add-on security packages, applications, network hardware devices, protocols, and access control matrixes. These controls work at different layers within a network or system and need to maintain a synergistic relationship to ensure that there is no unauthorized access to resources and that the resources' confidentiality, integrity, and availability is guaranteed. Technical controls protect the integrity and availability of resources by limiting the number of subjects that can access them and protect the confidentiality by preventing disclosure to unauthorized subjects. The following sections explain how some technical controls work and where they are implemented within an environment.

System Access

Different types of controls and security mechanisms control how a computer is accessed. If an organization is using a MAC architecture, the clearance of a user is identified and compared to the resource's classification level to verify that this user can access the requested object. If an organization is using a DAC architecture, the operating system checks to see if a user has been granted permission to access this resource. The sensitivity of data, clearance level of users, and users' rights and permissions are used as logical controls to control access to a resource.

There are many types of technical controls that enable a user to access a system and the resources within that system. This can be a username and password combination, Kerberos implementation, biometrics, public key technology, RADIUS, TACACS, or being authenticated using a smart card through a reader connected to a system. These technologies verify that the user is who he says he is by different types of authentication methods. Once a user is properly authenticated, then he can be authorized and allowed access to network resources. These technologies are addressed in further detail in future chapters, but for now understand that system access is a type of technical control that can enforce access control objectives.

Network Architecture

The architecture of a network can be constructed and enforced through several logical controls to provide segregation and protection of an environment. Networks can be segregated by walls and location, which are types of physical segregation. There is also a way of segregating a network logically. This consists of IP address ranges, subnets, and controlling the communication flow between the segments. Many times it is important to control how one segment of a network communicates with another segment.

Figure 4-19 is an example of how an organization may segregate its network and determine how network segments can communicate. This example shows how the

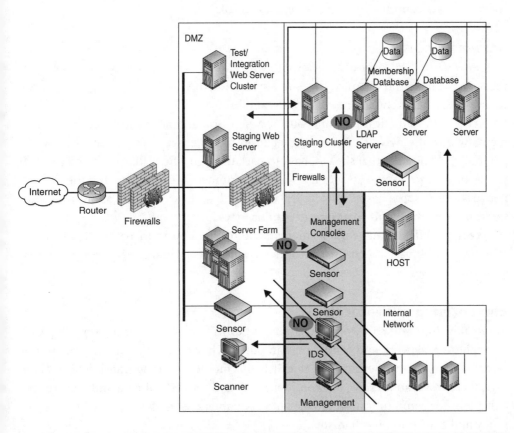

Figure 4-19   Logical network segmentation controls how different network segments communicate.

organization does not want the internal network and the demilitarized zone (DMZ) to have open and nonrestricted communication paths. There is usually no reason for internal users to have direct access to the systems in the DMZ and cutting off this type of communication reduces the possibilities of internal attacks on those systems. Also, if an attack came from the Internet and successfully compromised a system on the DMZ, it is important that the attacker could not easily access the internal network, which this type of logical segregation protects against.

This example also shows how the management segment can communicate with all other network segments, but those segments cannot communicate in return. This is because the management consoles that control the firewalls and intrusion systems reside in the management segment and there is no reason that users, other than the administrator, should have access to these computers.

A network can be segregated physically and logically. This type of segregation and restriction is accomplished through logical controls.

Network Access

Systems have logical controls that dictate who can and cannot access them and what those individuals can do once they are authenticated. This is also true for networks. Routers, switches, network interface cards, and bridges all work as technical controls to enforce access restriction into and out of a network, and access to the different segments within the network. If an attacker from the Internet wants to get to a specific computer, chances are that she will have to hack through a firewall, router, and a switch just to be able to start an attack on a specific computer that resides within the internal network. Each device has its own logical controls that make decisions about what entities can access them and what type of actions they can carry out.

Access to different network segments should be granular in nature. Routers and switches can be used to ensure that only certain types of traffic get through to each segment.

Encryption and Protocols

Encryption and protocols work as technical controls to protect information as it passes throughout a network and resides on computers. They ensure that the information is received by the correct entity, and that it is not modified during transmission. These logical controls can preserve the confidentiality and integrity of data and enforce specific paths for communication to take place. (Chapter 8 is totally dedicated to cryptography and encryption mechanisms.)

Control Zone

A *control zone* is a technical and physical control. It is a specific area that surrounds and protects network devices that emit electrical signals. These electrical signals can travel a certain distance and can be contained by a specially made material, which is used to construct the control zone. Some companies use this material in their walls of the building to zone off areas that have computers that deal with top-secret information and it is used to resist penetration attempts and disallow sensitive information to "escape" through the airwaves. We will address how information can be captured from emitted electrical waves in the "Emanation Security" section of this chapter, but for now understand that a control zone is used as a technical and physical control to ensure that confidential information is contained and works to hinder intruders for accessing information through the airwaves. Figure 4-20 depicts a control zone.

Auditing

Auditing tools are technical controls that track activity within a network, on a network device, or on a specific computer. Even though auditing is not an activity that will deny

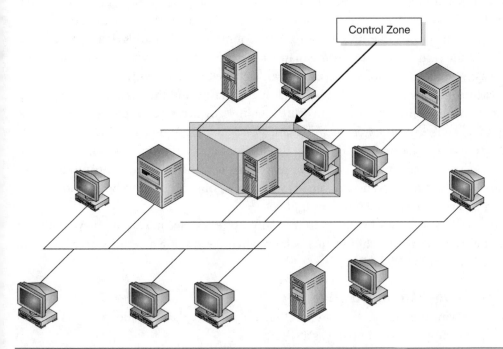

Figure 4-20 Companies can implement control zones, which control the amount of radiation and electrical signals that are emitted from sections of the facility.

an entity access to a network or computer, it will track activities so a network administrator can understand the types of access that took place, identify a security breach, or warn the administrator of suspicious activity. This information can be used to point out weaknesses of other technical controls and help the administrator understand where changes need to be made to preserve the necessary security level within the environment.

NOTE Many of the subjects touched on in these sections will be fully addressed and explained in later chapters. What is important to understand is that there are administrative, technical, and physical controls that work towards providing access control, and you should know several examples of each for the exam.

Access Control Types

Previously, it was stated that access control types (administrative, physical, and technical) work at different levels, but different levels of what? They work together at different levels within their own categories. A security guard is a type of control used to scare off evildoers and ensure that only authorized personnel enter a building. If an intruder gets around the security guard in some manner, he could be faced with motion detectors, locks on doors, and alarms. These layers are depicted in Figure 4-21.

Each control works at a different level of granularity, but they can also perform different functionality. The different functionalities of access controls are *preventative, detective, corrective, deterrent, recovery,* and *compensating*. When looking at a security structure of an environment, it is most productive to use a preventative model and then use detective, recovery, and corrective mechanisms to help support this model. Basically, you want to stop any trouble before it starts, but you need to be able to quickly react and combat trouble if it does find you.

The following control types (administrative, physical, technical) are preventative in nature. These are important to understand when developing a security access control model and for the CISSP Exam.

Preventive—Administrative

The following are the *soft* mechanisms that are put into place to enforce access control and protection for the company as a whole:

- Policies and procedures
- Effective hiring practices

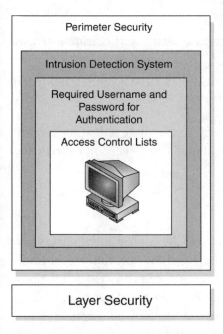

Figure 4-21   Security should be implemented in layers, which provides several barriers to attackers.

- Pre-employment background checks
- Controlled termination processes
- Data classification and labeling
- Security awareness

Preventive—Physical

The following can physically restrict access to a facility, specific work areas, or computer systems:

- Biometrics, badges, and swipe cards
- Guards, dogs, motion detectors, CCTV,
- Fences, locks, man-traps, and alarms

Preventive—Technical

The following are logical controls that are part of operating systems, third-party application add-ons, or hardware units:

- Passwords, biometrics, smart cards

- Encryption, protocols, call-back systems, database views, and constrained user interface

- Antivirus software, ACLs, firewalls, routers, intrusion detection system (IDS), and clipping levels

Many of these also serve as detective controls because they have a dual function of trying to stop security breaches from happening and then can be used to collect clues after a security breach takes place.

Table 4-3 shows how these different categories of access control mechanisms perform different types of functionality. The table is used to show how different controls can provide one or more security attributes, but does not necessarily cover all the possibilities. For example, a fence can provide preventative and deterrent measures by making it harder for intruders to access a facility, but it could also be a compensating control. If a company cannot afford a security guard, it might erect a fence to act as the compensating physical control. There are good arguments of each control being able to meet more requirements than what is listed in the table. Table 4-3 is only an example to show the relationship between the different controls and the security attributes they could provide.

There are several types of security mechanisms and they all need to work together. The complexity of the controls and of the environment they are in can cause the controls to contradict each other or leave gaps in security. This can introduce unforeseen holes in the company's protection that are not fully understood by the implementers. Very strict technical access controls can be in place and all the necessary administrative controls up to snuff, but if any person is allowed to physically access each and every system in the facility, then there are clear security dangers present within the environment. Together these controls should work in harmony to provide a healthy, safe, and productive environment.

Accountability

Auditing capabilities ensure that users are accountable for their actions, verify that the security policies are enforced, work as a deterrent to improper actions, and are used as investigation tools. There are several reasons why network administrators and security professionals want to make sure accountability mechanisms are in place and configured properly: to be able to track bad deeds back to individuals, detect intrusions, reconstruct

Table 4-3 Services that Security Controls Provide

Type of Control / Category of Control	Preventative	Detective	Corrective	Deterrent	Recovery	Compensation
	Controls used to deter and avoid undesirable events from taking place	Controls used to identify undesirable events that have occurred	Controls used to correct undesirable events that have occurred	Controls used to discourage security violations	Controls used to restore resources and capabilities	Controls used to provide alternatives to other controls
Physical						
Fences	×		×		×	
Locks	×		×		×	
Badge system	×		×			
Security guard	×	×	×		×	
Biometric system	×	×	×			
Mantrap doors	×		×		×	
Lighting	×		×		×	
Motion detectors		×				
Closed-circuit TVs	×	×	×			
Alarms	×	×	×		×	
Backups		×		×	×	
Administrative						
Security policy	×		×			
Monitoring and supervising	×	×		×		×

(continued)

Table 4-3 Services that Security Controls Provide *(continued)*

Type of Control	Preventative	Detective	Corrective	Deterrent	Recovery	Compensation
	Controls used to deter and avoid undesirable events from taking place	Controls used to identify undesirable events that have occurred	Controls used to correct undesirable events that have occurred	Controls used to discourage security violations	Controls used to restore resources and capabilities	Controls used to provide alternatives to other controls
Category of Control						
Administrative						
Separation of duties	×			×		
Job rotation	×	×				
Information classification	×					
Personnel procedures	×	×		×		×
Investigations		×				
Testing	×					
Security awareness training	×	×				
Technical						
ACLs	×					
Routers	×					
Encryption	×			×		
Audit logs		×				
IDS	×	×	×	×		
Antivirus software	×	×	×		×	
Firewalls	×	×		×		
Smart cards	×					
Dial-up call-back systems	×					
Alarms and alerts		×				

events and system conditions, provide legal recourse material, and produce problem reports. Audit documentation and log files hold a mountain of information—the trick is usually deciphering it and presenting it in a useful and understandable format.

Accountability is tracked through recording user, system, and application activities. This recording is done through auditing functions and mechanisms within an operating system or security application. Audit trails contain information about operating system activities, application events, and user actions. They can be used to verify the health of a system by checking out performance information or certain types of errors and conditions. After a system crashes, many times a network administrator will review audit logs to try and piece together the status of the system and attempt to understand what events could have attributed to the disruption.

An administrator configures what actions and events are to be audited and logged. If it were a high security environment, the administrator would configure more activities to be captured and the threshold of those activities to be more sensitive. The events can be reviewed to identify where breaches of security occurred and if the security policy had been violated. If the environment does not require such level of security, the events analyzed would be fewer with having less demanding thresholds.

Items and actions to be audited can become an endless list. A security professional should be able to assess an environment and its security goals, know what actions should be audited and what is to be done with that information after it is captured, without wasting too much disk space, CPU power, and staff time. The following gives a broad overview of the items and actions that can be audited and logged:

- **System-level events**
  - Monitor system performance
  - Logon attempts (successful and unsuccessful)
  - Logon ID
  - Date and time of each logon attempt
  - Lockouts of users and terminals
  - Use of administration utilities
  - Devices used
  - Functions performed
  - Requests to alter configuration files
- **Application-level events**
  - Error messages
  - Files opened and closed

- Modifications of files
- Security violations within application
- **User-level events**
  - Identification and authentication attempts
  - Files, services, and resources used
  - Commands initiated
  - Capture security violations

The threshold (clipping level) and parameters for each of these items needs to be configured. For example, an administrator can audit each logon attempt or just each failed logon attempt. System performance can look only at the amount of memory used within an eight-hour period, or the memory, CPU, and hard drive space used within an hour.

IDSs continually scan audit logs for suspicious activity and if an intrusion or harmful event takes place, audit logs are usually kept to be used later to prove guilt and prosecute if necessary. If severe security events take place, many times the IDS will alert the administrator or staff member so proper actions can take place to end the destructive activity that is taking place. If a dangerous virus is identified, administrators may take the mail server offline. If an attacker is accessing confidential information within the database, this computer may be temporarily disconnected from the network or Internet. If an attack is in progress, the administrator may want to watch the actions taking place so she can track down the intruder. IDSs can watch for this type of activity during real time and/or scan audit logs and watch for specific patterns or behaviors.

Review of Audit Information

It does no good to collect it if you don't look at it.

Audit trails can be reviewed manually or through an automated means, either way as long as they are reviewed and interpreted. If an organization reviews audit trails manually, there needs to be a rhyme and reason to how they are viewed, when, and why. Usually audit logs are very popular items right after a security breach, unexplained system action, or system disruption. An administrator or staff member rapidly tries to piece together the activities that led up to the event. This type of audit review is event-oriented. Audit trails can also be viewed periodically to watch for unusual behavior of users or systems, and to help understand the healthy baseline of a system. Then there is a real-time audit analysis, or near real-time, that uses a batch function to review audit information as it is created. Administrators should have a scheduled task of reviewing audit data. The audit material usually needs to be parsed and saved to another location for a certain time period. This information should be stated in the company's security policy and procedures.

Reviewing audit information manually can be overwhelming, so there are specific applications, audit trail analysis tools, developed to reduce the volume of audit logs to review and improve the efficiency of manually review procedures. A majority of the time audit logs contain information that is unnecessary or unneeded, so these tools parse out only specific events and present them in a useful and usable format. There are three main types of audit trail analysis tools: audit reduction, variance-detection, and attack signature-detection.

An *audit reduction* does just what it sounds like—reduces the amount of information within an audit log. This tool discards mundane task information and records system performance, security, and user functionality information that can be useful to a security professional or administrator. A *variance-detection* tool can monitor computer and resource usage trends and detect variations. If an employee works from 8 A.M. to 5 P.M., which is the normal time his computer is used and resources are accessed, and recently this computer has been used at 2 A.M. and at times on the weekend, the analysis tool can capture this information and alert the administrator of unusual activity. If an *attack signature-detection* tool is used, the application will have a database of information that has been known to indicate specific attacks. This type of tool will parse audit logs in search for certain patterns. If a pattern matches a pattern, or signature, held within its database, the tool indicates that an attack is in progress.

Keystroke Monitoring

Keystroke monitoring is a type of auditing that can review and record keystrokes entered by a user during an active session. The person using this type of monitoring can either view the characters as they are typed, or have the characters written to an audit log to be reviewed at a later time. This type of auditing is usually done only for special cases and only for a specific amount of time, because the amount of information captured can be overwhelming. If a security professional or administrator is suspicious of an individual and his or her activities, this type of monitoring may be invoked.

A hacker can also do this type of activity. If an attacker can successfully install a Trojan horse on a computer, it can install an application that will capture data as it is typed into the keyboard. Most of the time these programs are most interested in user credentials and can alert the attacker when credentials have been successfully captured.

Keystroke monitoring captures every keystroke.

There are privacy issues with this type of monitoring and administrators could be subject to criminal and civil liabilities if it is done without proper notification and authorization. As of this writing, there have been no known court cases pertaining to keystroke monitoring and thus no legal precedent has been set. If a company wants to be able to use this type of auditing, it should be stated in the security policy, addressed in security awareness training, and a banner notice should be presented to the user warning that the activities at that computer may be monitored in this fashion. These steps should be taken to protect the company from violating an individual's privacy, and it informs the users where their privacy boundaries start and stop pertaining to computer use.

Protecting Audit Data and Log Information

If an intruder breaks into your house, the intruder will do his best to cover his tracks, not leave fingerprints or any other clues that can be used to tie him to the criminal activity. The same is true in computer fraud and illegal activity. The intruder will work to cover his tracks. Many times attackers delete audit logs, or data within the log, which is called *scrubbing*, that hold this incriminating information. Deleting this information can cause the administrator to not be alerted or aware of the security breach, and can destroy valuable data. So audit logs and information should be protected by strict access control.

Only certain individuals, the administrator and security personnel should be able to view, modify, and delete audit trail information. No other individuals should be able to view this data, much less modify or delete it. The integrity of the data can be ensured with the use of digital signatures and strong access controls. Its confidentiality can be protected with encryption and access controls, if necessary, and the information can be stored on *write-once media* (CD-ROM) to prevent losing or modification of the data. Unauthorized access attempts to audit logs should be captured and reported.

Audit logs may be used in a trial to prove an individual's guilt, demonstrate how an attack was carried out, or to corroborate a story. The integrity and confidentiality of these logs will be under scrutiny; thus, proper steps need to be taken to ensure that the confidentiality and integrity of the audit information is not compromised in any way.

References

www.ietf.org/html.charters/aaa-charter.html

http://directory.google.com/Top/Computers/Security/Authentication

http://csrc.nist.gov/publications/nistpubs/800-7/node2.html

Access Control Practices

Least amount of doors open allows the least amount of flies in.

We have gone over how users are identified, authenticated, authorized, and auditing their actions. These are necessary parts of a healthy and safe network environment, but you also want to take steps to ensure there are no unnecessary open doors and that the environment stays at the same security level you have worked so hard to achieve. This means you need to implement good access control practices. Not keeping up on daily or monthly tasks usually causes the most vulnerabilities in an environment. It is hard to put out all the network fires, fight the political battles, fulfill all the users' needs, and still keep up with small maintenance tasks. However, many companies have found that not keeping up on these small maintenance tasks caused them the greatest heartache of all.

The following is a small list of tasks that need to be accomplished on a weekly or monthly basis to ensure that security stays at a satisfactory level:

- Deny access to systems by undefined users or anonymous accounts.
- Limit and monitor the usage of administrator and other powerful accounts.
- Suspend or delay access capability after a specific number of unsuccessful logon attempts.
- Remove obsolete user accounts as soon as they leave the company.

- Suspend inactive accounts after 30 to 60 days.

- Enforce strict access criteria.

- Enforce the need-to-know and least-privilege practices.

- Disable unneeded system features, services, and ports.

- Replace default password settings on accounts.

- Limit and monitor global access rules.

- Logon IDs need to be nondescriptive of job function.

- Remove redundant resource rules from accounts and group memberships.

- Remove redundant user IDs, accounts, and role-based accounts from resource access lists.

- Enforce password rotation.

- Enforce password requirements (length, contents, lifetime, distribution, storage, and transmission).

- Audit system and user events and actions and review reports periodically.

- Protect audit logs.

Unauthorized Disclosure of Information

There are several ways that information can become available to others for whom it was not intended, which can bring about unfavorable results. Sometimes this is done intentionally, but it can be done unintentionally also. Information can be disclosed unintentionally when one falls prey to attacks that specialize in this. These attacks are social engineering, covert channels, malicious code, and electrical airwave sniffing. Information can be disclosed accidentally through object reuse methods, which is explained in the next section.

Object Reuse

Can I borrow this floppy? Answer: Let me destroy it first.

Object reuse issues pertain to reassigning media to a subject that contained one or more objects. Huh? This means before someone uses a hard drive, floppy disk, or tape it should be cleared of any residual information that was on it previously. This ensures that information not intended for this individual does not get to him or her accidentally. Many times floppy disks are exchanged without much thought in a work environment. What if a supervisor lent a floppy to an employee without erasing it and it contained confidential employee performance reports and salary raises forecasted for the next year? This could prove to be a bad decision and maybe turn into a morale issue if the information was passed around. Formatting a disk or deleting files only removes the pointers to the files; it does not remove the actual files. This information will still be on the disk and available until the operating system needs that space and then over-writes those files. So for media that holds confidential information, more extreme methods should be taken to ensure the files are actually gone, not just their pointers.

Sometimes evildoers will actually configure a sector on a hard drive so that it is marked as bad and unusable to an operating system, but this sector is actually fine and may hold malicious data. The operating system will not write information to this sector because it thinks it is corrupted. This is a form of *data hiding*. This is one reason that extreme measures need to be taken when erasing confidential information from media.

Sensitive data should be classified (secret, top secret, confidential, unclassified, and so on). The flow of this data should be understood and tracked, and how it is stored and accessed is also something that should be strictly controlled and audited. However, it does not end there; before allowing one subject to use media that was previously used, it should be erased, degaussed, or formatted. If media holds sensitive information and cannot be purged, there should be steps on how to properly destroy it so that there is no way for others to obtain this information. The most effective way of ensuring that confidential information is not disclosed in an unauthorized manner is to physically destroy the media.

Emanation Security

Quick, cover your computer and your head in tinfoil!

All electronic devices emit electrical radiation, as shown in Figure 4-22. This radiation can hold important information, and if an attacker bought the right equipment and positioned himself in the right place, the attacker could capture this information from the airwaves and listen to data transmissions as if he had a tap directly on the network wire.

Figure 4-22 All electrical devices emit electrical signals.

There have been several incidents of intruders purchasing inexpensive equipment and intercepting electrical emissions as they radiated from a computer. This equipment can reproduce data streams and display the data on the intruder's monitor. This can enable intruders to learn of covert operations, find out military strategies, and uncover and exploit confidential information. This is not just stuff found in spy novels; it really happens so the proper countermeasures have been devised.

TEMPEST

TEMPEST is the study and control of spurious electrical signals that are emitted by electrical equipment. There is special shielding that equipment uses to suppress or mask the signals as they are radiated from devices. TEMPEST equipment is implemented to prevent intruders from picking up information through the airwaves with listening devices. There are specific standards that this type of equipment must meet to be rated as providing TEMPEST shielding protection. TEMPEST refers to standardized technology that suppresses signal emanations with shielding material. It is an actual standard, and vendors who manufacture this type of equipment must be certified to this standard.

There are allowable limits of levels of emissions that can radiate and still be considered safe. The approved products must ensure that only this level of emissions is allowed to escape the area. This type of protection is usually only needed in military institutions, although other highly secured environments do utilize this type of safeguard.

Many military organizations are concerned with stray radio frequencies emitted by computers and other electronic equipment because an attacker may be able to pick them up, reconstruct them, and give away some secrets that were meant to stay secret.

TEMPEST technology is complex, cumbersome, and expensive, and therefore only used in highly sensitive areas that really need this high level of protection.

Two alternatives to TEMPEST are using white noise or a zone concept, explained next.

NOTE TEMPEST is the name of a program, and now a standard, that was developed in the late 1950s by the U.S. government. It was developed to deal with electrical and electromagnetic radiation emitted from electrical equipment, mainly computers. The selling of this type of equipment is under constant scrutiny and usually used by U.S. intelligence, military, government, and law enforcement agencies.

White Noise

Some implementations used to combat intruders from extracting information from electrical transmissions use white noise. *White noise* is a uniform spectrum of random electrical signals. It is distributed over the full spectrum so that the bandwidth is constant and an intruder is not able to decipher real information from random noise, or random information.

Zones

Another alternative to using TEMPEST equipment is to use the zone concept, which was addressed earlier in this chapter. Some environments use material in their facility walls to contain electrical signals to prevent intruders from being able to access information that is emitted via electrical signals from network devices. This control zone creates a type of security perimeter and is constructed to protect against unauthorized access to data or compromise of sensitive information.

Access Control Monitoring

Access control monitoring is a method of keeping track of who attempts to access specific network resources. It is an important detective mechanism and there are different technologies that can fulfill this need.

Intrusion Detection

Intrusion detection systems (IDS) are used to monitor a network or individual computers. There are two main types of IDS: *network-based*, which monitors a network or a segment of the network, and *host-based*, which monitors a particular system.

IDS can be configured to watch for attacks, parse audit logs, alert an administrator as attacks are happening, protect system files, expose a hacker's techniques, illustrate which vulnerabilities need to be addressed, and possibly help to track down individual hackers.

Host-based IDS can be installed on individual workstations and/or servers and watch for inappropriate or anomalous activity and insider attacks. Host-based IDSs are usually used to make sure users do not accidentally delete system files, reconfigure important settings, or put the system at risk any other way. Network-based IDSs monitor network traffic and uncover possible attacks or suspicious activities. This is usually done by anomaly detection and pattern detection.

Knowledge- or Signature-Based
Intrusion Detection

Knowledge is accumulated about specific attacks and how they are carried out. Models of how the attacks are carried out are developed and called *signatures*. Each identified attack has a signature, which is used to detect an attack in progress or if one has occurred within the network. Any action that is not recognized as an attack is considered acceptable. The effectiveness of this type of protection depends on the regularity of updating the software with new signatures, or known attacks. This type of IDS is weak against new types of attacks because it can only recognize the ones that have been previously identified.

Behavior-Based or Statistical Intrusion Detection

This type of software observes and detects deviation from expected behavior of users and systems. A reference model of normal behavior is compiled and future activities are compared against. This type of IDS can use *expert system* technology, which attempts to think like a human expert and provide the same type of reasoning. It can detect real-time anomalies by detecting deviations from sequential rules, and it can review audit log files to detect suspicious activity that has already taken place.

For an IDS to be able to perform real-time anomaly detection, it uses a *time-based induction machine (TIM)*. This is a virtual machine that tracks and builds behavior profiles for system usage, network traffic, and user activities. The profile is made up of sequences of events to be used to try and determine when something out of the ordinary happens.

The behavior-based, or statistical, IDS can detect new, unforeseen vulnerabilities, but it can also cause many false alarms.

Once an attack is discovered, there are several things that can take place, and this is up to the capabilities of the IDS and the policy that has been assigned to it. The IDS can send an alert to a console to tell the right individuals that an attack is being carried out, it can send an e-mail to the individual who has been delegated to respond to such activities, it can kill the connection of the detected attack, or reconfigure a router or firewall to try and stop any further similar attacks.

IDS Sensors

Network-based IDSs use sensors for monitoring purposes. A sensor is placed on the network segment it is responsible for monitoring. This sensor works as an agent and sends data back to a monitoring console for further analysis. The monitoring console monitors all sensors and compares the data that they send back to a database of known attack signatures.

These are the components that enable network-based intrusion-detection to actually work. Sensor placement is a critical part of configuring an effective IDS. An organization can place a sensor outside of the firewall to detect attacks and inside the firewall, (in the perimeter network) to detect actual intrusions. Sensors should also be placed in

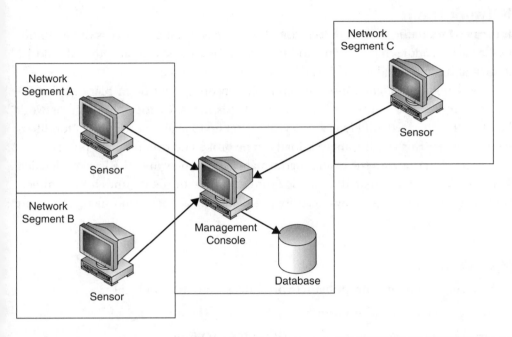

Figure 4-23 Sensors need to be placed in each network segment that is to be monitored by the IDS.

highly sensitive areas, on networks with many transient employees, and extranets. Figure 4-23 shows the importance of placed sensors in each network.

There are five basic components of intrusion detection:

- **Sensors** Detects events and sends this data to the monitoring software
- **Central monitoring software** Accepts data from all sensors on the network and analyzes it
- **Analysis of event reports** Might offer a recommendation for counteracting the event
- **Database components** Determines if an IP address or an attack has been seen before. This is trend analysis.
- **Response boxes** This component can take information for the previous three components and respond to the event.

Network Traffic

If the network traffic volume exceeds the IDS system's threshold, attacks can go unnoticed. Each vendor's IDS system product has its own threshold, and that should be known and understood before it is purchased and configured.

In very high-traffic environments, multiple sensors should be in place so that no packet can pass without being investigated. If it is necessary for optimizing network bandwidth and speed, different sensors can be set up to analyze each packet for different signatures. This way the analysis load can be broken up over different points.

A network IDS affects the overall performance of the network. The level of detailed scrutiny the IDS is configured to provide for network traffic determines how hard performance will be hit. As always, security is a balancing act between functionality and security.

References

www.robertgraham.com/pubs/network-intrusion-detection.html

www.gocsi.com/intrusion.htm

www.sans.org/newlook/resources/IDFAQ/ID_FAQ.htm

Honeypot

A *honeypot* is a computer set up as a sacrificial lamb on the network. The system is not locked down and has open ports and services enabled. This is to entice a would-be attacker to this computer instead of attacking authentic computers on a network. The honeypot contains no real company information, and thus will not be at risk if and when it is attacked.

This enables the administrator to know when certain types of attacks are happening and allows the administrator to fortify the environment and perhaps track down the attacker. The longer the hacker stays at the honeypot, the more will be disclosed about her techniques.

It is important to draw a line between *enticement* and *entrapment* when implementing a honeypot system. There are legal and liability issues around each. If the system only had open ports and services an attacker might want to take advantage of, this would be an example of enticement. If the system had a Web page indicating that the user can download files, and once the user does this the administrator charges this user with hacking, it would be entrapment. Entrapment is illegal and cannot be used when charging an individual with hacking or unauthorized activity.

References

http://project.honeynet.org

www.sans.org/newlook/resources/IDFAQ/honeypot3.htm

Network Sniffers

A packet or network *sniffer* is a type of wiretap device that plugs into a network for the purpose of eavesdropping on network traffic. The traffic that is being transferred over a network medium is in binary (actually electrical signals that represent binary code), so the sniffer has to have a protocol analysis capability to recognize the different protocols passing over the network.

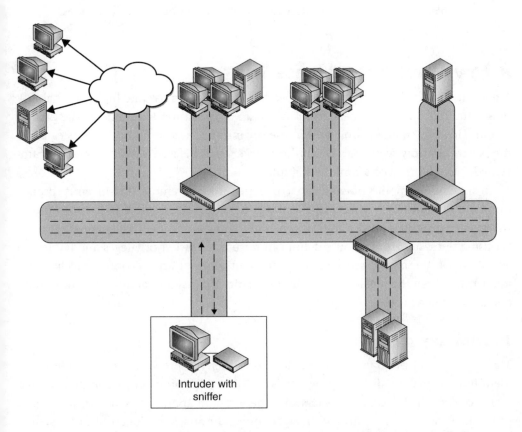

Figure 4-24   Sniffers are used to capture data as it travels throughout the network.

The sniffer has a network adapter that works in promiscuous mode and a driver that captures the data. This data can be overwhelming so it must be properly filtered. The filtered data is stored in a buffer and this information is displayed. Many sniffers allow the data to be modified and retransmitted over the network. This is how some types of spoofing and man-in-the-middle attacks are carried out. Figure 4-24 illustrates a sniffer connected to a network.

Network sniffers are used by the people in the white hats (administrators and security professionals) usually to try and track down a recent problem with the network. But the guys in the black hats (attackers and evildoers) can use them to learn about what type of data is passed over a specific network segment and to modify data in an unauthorized manner.

For security purposes, network cable should not be out in the open because this would enable an attacker to tap into the network and monitor traffic. Network sniffers are great tools, but like most tools, they can be used for good and evil agendas.

A Few Threats to Access Control

A majority of security professionals know that there is more risk and higher probability of an attacker causing mayhem from within an organization than outside the organization. However, many people within the organizations do not know this because in the paper they only see stories about the attackers that defaced a Web server or circumvented a firewall to access confidential information.

An attacker from the outside can come in through remote dial-in entry points, through firewalls and Web servers, physically break in, or exploit a partner communication path (extranet, vendor connection, and so on). An insider has legitimate reasons for using the system and resources, but can misuse his or her privileges and launch an actual attack. We have discussed many different types of access control mechanisms that work to keep the outsiders outside and restrict the insiders' abilities to a minimum and audit their actions.

Dictionary Attack

There are several programs that enable an attacker (or proactive administrators) to identify user credentials. The program is fed lists (dictionaries) of commonly used words or combinations of characters, and the program applies these values to a logon prompt. Once the right combination is identified, the attacker is logged into the system and authenticated. Because many systems have thresholds that dictate how many login attempts are acceptable, the same type of activity can happen to a captured password file. The program encrypts the combination of characters and compares them to the encrypted entries in the password file. If a match is found, the program has uncovered a password.

The dictionaries come with the programs and extra dictionaries can be found on several sites on the Internet.

Countermeasure

- Do not allow passwords to be sent in clear text.
- Encrypt the passwords with encryption algorithms or hashing functions.
- Employ one-time password tokens.
- Use hard-to-guess passwords.
- Rotate passwords on a frequent basis.
- Employ IDS to detect this type of suspicious behavior.
- Use dictionary attacks to find weak passwords chosen by users.
- Use special characters, numbers, and upper- and lowercase letters within the password.
- Protect password files.

Brute Force Attack

There are several types of *brute force attacks*, but overall it is an attack that continually tries different inputs to achieve a predefined goal. In password guessing, an attacker will try different variations of characters to try and derive the correct combination. If a dictionary tool has found that a user's password starts with Dallas, then the brute force tool will try Dallas1, Dallas01, Dallas#1, and so on until a successful login credential is uncovered.

These attacks are also used in *wardialing* efforts. A long list of phone numbers are inserted into a wardialing program in hopes of finding a modem that can be exploited to gain unauthorized access. A program is used to go through many phone numbers and weed out the numbers that are used for voice calls and fax machine services. The attacker usually ends up with a handful of numbers he can now try to exploit and gain access into a system or network.

So a brute force attack perpetuates a specific activity with different input parameters until the goal is achieved.

Countermeasure

For phone brute force attacks, auditing and monitoring of this type of activity should be in place to uncover patterns that could indicate a wardialing attack.

- Perform brute force attacks to find weaknesses.
- Make sure only necessary phone numbers are made public.
- Provide stringent access control methods that would make brute force attacks less successful.
- Monitor and audit for such activity.
- Employ an IDS to watch for suspicious activity.
- Set lockout thresholds.

Spoofing at Login

A program that presents a fake login screen can be presented by an attacker, which tricks the user to attempt to log in. The user is asked for a username and password, which is stored for the attacker to access at a later time. The user does not know this is not his usual login screen because they look exactly the same. A fake error message can appear, indicating that the user mistyped his credentials. At this point, the fake login program exits and hands control over to the operating system, which prompts the user for a username and password. The user assumes he mistyped his information and doesn't give it a second thought, but an attacker now knows the user's credentials.

Countermeasure

The system can be configured to display the number of failed login attempts that could indicate to the user what just happened. If the first login attempt seemed to have failed, but was really the attacker's program, and it was not reported at the second attempt and the user could get suspicious as to what just took place.

A guaranteed *trusted path* can be provided. A trusted path tells the user that he is communicating directly to the operating system instead of a fake, spoofing program. Windows NT uses a sequence of CTRL-ALT-DEL to invoke the operating system's login screen. (However, some sneaking fake programs can set themselves to be called by this combination of keys also.)

Reference

www.sans.org/infosecFAQ/hackers/hackers_list.htm

Summary

Access controls are security features that are usually one of the first lines of protection. They are used to dictate how subjects access objects and resources, and their main goal is to protect the resources from unauthorized access. These controls can be administrative, physical, or technical in nature and can supply preventative, detective, and corrective services.

Access control defines how users and subjects should be identified, authenticated, and authorized. These issues are carried out differently in different access control models and technologies, and it is up to the organization to determine which best fits their business and security needs.

Quick Tips

- Access is a flow of information between a subject and an object.
- A subject is an active entity that requests access to an object, which is a passive entity.
- A subject can be a user, program, or process.
- Confidentiality is the assurance that information is not disclosed to unauthorized subjects.
- Security mechanisms that provide confidentiality are encryption, logical and physical access control, transmission protocols, database views, and controlled traffic flow.
- There are three main access control models: discretionary, mandatory, and nondiscretionary.
- Discretionary access control (DAC) enables data owners to dictate what subjects have access to the files and resources they own.
- Mandatory access control (MAC) uses a security label system. Users have clearances and resources have security labels that contain data classifications. MAC compares these two attributes to determine access control capabilities.
- Nondiscretionary access control uses a role-based method to determine access rights and permissions.
- Lattice-based access provides an upper and lower bound of access control rights.
- Role-based access control is based on the user's role and responsibilities within the company.

- There are three main types of restricted interface measurements: menus and shells, database views, and physically constrained interfaces.

- Access control lists are bound to objects and indicate what subjects can use them.

- A capability table is bound to a subject and lists what objects it can access.

- There are three main ways of administrating access control: centralized, decentralized, and a hybrid of both.

- Centralized administration examples are RADIUS and TACACS.

- A decentralized administration example is a security domain.

- There are three main categories of access control: administrative, logical, and physical.

- Examples of administrative controls are security policy, personnel controls, supervisory structure, security awareness training, and testing.

- Examples of physical controls are network segregation, perimeter security, computer controls, work area separation, data backups, and cable.

- Examples of technical controls are system access, architecture of a network, network access, encryption and protocols, control zone, and auditing.

- Access control mechanisms provide one or more of the following functionalities: preventive, detective, corrective, deterrent, recovery, or compensating.

- For a subject to be able to access a resource, it must be identified, authenticated, authorized, and should be held accountable for its actions.

- Authentication can be accomplished by biometrics, a password, passphrase, cognitive password, one-time password, and token.

- A Type I error in biometrics means the system rejected an authorized individual and a Type II error means an imposter was authenticated.

- A memory card cannot process information, but a smart card can.

- Access controls should default to no access.

- Least-privilege and need-to-know principles limit users' rights to only what is needed to perform tasks of their job.

- Single sign-on only requires a user to be authenticated to the network one time.

- Single sign-on can be accomplished through scripting, Kerberos, SESAME, and thin clients.

- In Kerberos, a user receives a ticket from the KDC to be able to access a service.

- Thin clients or dumb terminals, must receive their operating systems from another source.

- Types of access control attacks include denial of service, spoofing, dictionary, brute force, and wardialing.

- Accountability is usually performed through audits.

- Audits can track user activities, application and system events.

- Keystroke monitoring is a type of auditing that tracks each keystroke made by a user.

- Audit logs should be protected and reviewed.

- Object reuse can unintentionally disclose information.

- Just removing pointers to files is not always enough protection for proper object reuse.

- Information can be obtained via electrical signals in airwaves. The ways to combat this type of intrusion is: TEMPEST, white noise, and zone control.

- User authentication is accomplished by what someone knows, is, or has.

- One-time passwords can use synchronous or asynchronous token methods.

- Strong authentication requires two of the three user authentication attributes (what someone knows, is, or has).

- Kerberos does not protect computers or servers; it authenticates principals and provides a secure communication channel to be established.

- Kerberos addresses privacy and integrity but not availability.

- The following are weaknesses of Kerberos: KDC is a single point of failure, it is susceptible to password guessing, session keys are vulnerable, AS needs to always be available, secret keys are on workstations temporarily, and there must be management of secret keys.

- Users must be authorized explicitly or implicitly.

- Access control monitoring happens through intrusion detection systems (IDSs).

- IDS can be statistical (monitors behavior), signature-based (watches for known attacks), or adaptive to anomaly detection.

- Degaussing is safeguard against disclosure of confidential information because it returns media back to its original state.

Questions

Please remember that these questions are formatted and asked in a certain way for a reason. The questions and answers may seem odd or vague, but this is what you will see on the actual CISSP test.

1. Which of the following statements correctly describes biometric methods?
   a. They are the least expensive and most secure.
   b. They are the most expensive and least secure.
   c. They are the least expensive and least secure.
   d. They are the most expensive and most secure.

2. What is derived from a passphrase?
   a. Personal password
   b. Virtual password
   c. User ID
   d. Valid password

3. Which of the following statements correctly describes passwords?
   a. They are the least expensive and most secure.
   b. They are the most expensive and least secure.
   c. They are the least expensive and least secure.
   d. They are the most expensive and most secure.

4. What is the reason for enforcing the separation of duties?
   a. No one person can complete all the steps in a critical activity.
   b. Induce an atmosphere for collusion.
   c. Increase dependability upon individuals.
   d. Make critical tasks easier to accomplish.

5. Which of the following is not a logical access control?
   a. Encryption
   b. Network architecture
   c. ID badge
   d. Access control matrix

6. An access control model should work mainly in a _____ manner.
   a. Detective
   b. Recovery
   c. Corrective
   d. Preventive

7. Which access control policy is enforced when an environment uses groups?
    a. Rule-based
    b. Role-based
    c. Identity-based
    d. Mandatory

8. How is a challenge-response protocol utilized with token implementations?
    a. They are not; cryptography is used.
    b. A computer generates a challenge, and the smart token generates a response based on the challenge.
    c. The token challenges the user for a username and password.
    d. The token challenges the user's password against a database of stored credentials.

9. Which access control method is user-directed?
    a. Nondiscretionary
    b. Mandatory
    c. Identity-based
    d. Discretionary

10. Which provides the best authentication?
    a. What a person knows
    b. What a person is
    c. What a person has
    d. What a person has and knows

11. Which item is not part of a Kerberos authentication implementation?
    a. Message Authentication Code
    b. Ticket granting ticket
    c. Authentication service
    d. Users, programs, and services

12. Which implements access control matrices?
    a. Mandatory
    b. Centralized
    c. Decentralized
    d. Discretionary

13. What does authentication mean?
    a. Registering a user
    b. Identifying a user
    c. Validating a user
    d. Authorizing a user

14. If a company has a high turnover rate, which access control structure is best?
    a. Role-based
    b. Decentralized
    c. Rule-based
    d. Discretionary

15. A password is mainly used for what function?
    a. Identity
    b. Registration
    c. Authentication
    d. Authorization

16. The process of mutual authentication involves _____.
    a. A user authenticating to a system and the system authenticating to the user
    b. A user authenticating to two systems at the same time
    c. A user authenticating to a server and then to a process
    d. A user authenticating, receiving a ticket, and then authenticating to a service

17. Reviewing audit logs is an example of which security function?
    a. Preventive
    b. Detective
    c. Deterrence
    d. Corrective

18. In discretionary access control security, who has delegation authority to grant access to data?
    a. User
    b. Security office
    c. Security policy
    d. Owner

19. Which could be considered a single point of failure risk within a single sign-on implementation?
    a. Authentication server
    b. User's workstation
    c. Logon credentials
    d. RADIUS

20. What role does biometrics play in access control?
    a. Authorization
    b. Authenticity
    c. Authentication
    d. Accountability

21. What determines if an organization is going to operate under a discretionary, mandatory, or nondiscretionary access control model?
    a. Administrator
    b. Security policy
    c. Culture
    d. Security levels

Answers

1. D.	7. B.	13. C.	19. A.
2. B.	8. B.	14. A.	20. C.
3. C.	9. D.	15. C.	21. B.
4. A.	10. D.	16. A.	
5. C.	11. A.	17. B.	
6. D.	12. D.	18. D.	

CHAPTER 5

Security Models and Architecture

In this chapter, you will learn about the following topics:

- Computer architecture and the items that fall within it
- Trusted computing base and security mechanisms
- Components within an operating system
- Different security models used in software development
- Security criterion and ratings
- Certification and accreditation processes

Computer and information security covers many areas within an enterprise. Each area has security vulnerabilities and corresponding countermeasures that raise the security level and provide better protection. Not understanding the different areas and security levels of network devices, operating systems, hardware, protocols, and applications can cause security vulnerabilities that can affect the environment as a whole.

Two fundamental concepts in computer and information security are the security model, which outlines how security is to be implemented, and the architecture of a computer system, which is the framework and structure of a system.

A security policy outlines how data is accessed, what level of security is required, and what actions should be taken when these requirements are not met. The policy is usually a high-level document explaining the expectations from a computer system, device, or environment. A *security model* is a statement that outlines the requirements necessary to properly support a certain security policy. If a security policy dictates that all users must be identified, authenticated, and authorized before accessing network resources, the security model might lay out an access control matrix that should be constructed so that it fulfills this security policy. If a security policy states that no one from a lower security level should be able to view or modify information at a higher security level, the supporting security model will outline the necessary logic that needs to be implemented to ensure that under no circumstances can a lower-level subject access a higher-level object in an unauthorized manner. A security model provides a deeper explanation of how a computer operating system should be developed to properly support a specific security policy.

Security Models and Architecture

Computer security can be a slippery term because it means different things to different people. There are many aspects of a system that can be secured, and security can happen at different levels and to different degrees. We have stated in previous chapters that computer security is made up of the following main attributes:

- **Confidentiality**   Prevention of unauthorized disclosure of data
- **Integrity**   Prevention of unauthorized modification of data
- **Availability**   Prevention of loss of access to resources and data

From here these main attributes branch off into more granular security attributes like authenticity, accountability, nonrepudiation, and dependability. How does a company know which of these it needs, to what degree they are needed, and if the operating systems and applications they use actually provide these features and protection? These questions get much more complex as one looks deeper into the questions and systems themselves. Companies are not just concerned about e-mail messages being encrypted as they pass through the Internet. They are also concerned about the confidential data stored in their databases, the security of their Web farms that are connected directly to the Internet, the integrity of data entry values going into applications that process business-oriented information, the internal users sharing trade secrets, the external attackers bringing down servers and affecting productivity, viruses spreading, the internal consistency of data warehouses, and much more. These issues not only affect productivity and profitability, but also raise legal and liability issues with securing data. Companies, and the management that run them, can be held accountable if many of the previously mentioned issues go wrong. So it is, or at least it should be, very important for companies to know what security they need and how to be properly assured that the protection is actually being provided by the products they purchase.

Many of these security issues must be thought through before and during the design and architectural period of a product. Security is best if it is built into the foundation of operating systems and applications and not added on as an afterthought. Once security is integrated as an important part of the design, it has to be engineered, implemented, tested, audited, evaluated, certified, and accredited. The security that a product provides has to be rated on the confidentiality, integrity, and availability it claims. Consumers then use these ratings to determine if specific products provide the level of security they require. This is a long road, with many different entities involved with different responsibilities. This chapter takes you from the steps necessary before actually developing an operating system, to how these systems are evaluated and rated by government and other agencies, and what these ratings actually mean.

However, before we dive into these concepts, it is important to understand how the basic elements of a computer system work. These elements are the pieces that make up the computer's architecture.

Computer Architecture

Put the processor over there by the plant, the memory by the window, and the secondary storage upstairs.

Computer architecture encompasses all the parts of a computer system necessary for it to function, including the operating system, memory chips, circuits, hard drive, security components, buses, and networking components. The interrelationships and internal working of all of these parts can be quite complex, and making them work together in a secure fashion is comprised of complicated methods and mechanisms. Thank goodness for the smart people who figured this stuff out! Now it is up to us to learn how they did it and why.

The more one understands about how these different pieces work and process data, the more one understands how different vulnerabilities actually occur and how the different countermeasures work to impede and hinder vulnerabilities from being introduced, found, and exploited.

Central Processing Unit

Hey, when is it my turn to use the CPU? Answer: When the control unit says it's your turn.

The *central processing unit (CPU)* is a microprocessor that contains a control unit, an *arithmetic logic unit (ALU)*, and primary storage, which is a type of memory. The *control unit* manages and synchronizes the system while an application is being executed. It determines what application instructions get processed and in what time slice.

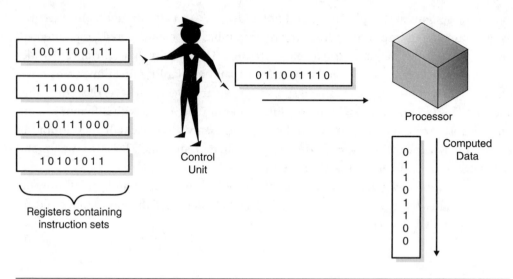

Figure 5-1 The control unit works as a traffic cop, indicating when instructions are sent to the processor.

It controls when instructions are executed and this execution enables applications to process data. The control unit does not actually process the data; it is like the traffic cop telling traffic when to stop and start again, as shown in Figure 5-1.

The chips within the CPU cover only a couple of square inches, but contain over a million transistors. All operations within the CPU are performed by electrical signals at different voltages in different combinations, and each transistor holds this voltage, which represents 0's and 1's to the computer. The CPU contains registers that point to memory locations that contain the next instructions to be executed and enables the CPU to keep status information of the data that needs to be processed. The ALU performs mathematical functions and logical operations on data. The ALU can be thought of as the brain of the CPU and the CPU as the brain of the computer.

Software holds its instructions and data in memory. When action needs to take place on the data, the instructions and data are passed to the CPU portion of the system, as shown in Figure 5-2. The CPU components handle the flow of instructions from the operating system and applications. The data that needs to be processed is passed into the instruction registers. When the control unit indicates that the CPU can process them, they are passed to the CPU for actual processing, number crunching, and data manipulation. The results are sent back to the computer's memory so the software can use this processed data to continue its tasks.

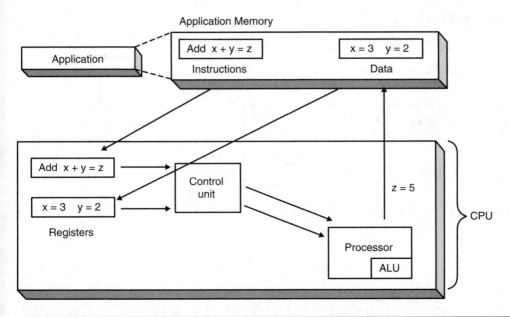

Figure 5-2 Instructions and data are passed to the CPU for processing.

Instructions and data are held in the ***primary storage unit*** until needed by the CPU. The software instructions are first ported into the CPU because these instructions indicate what actually needs to happen to the data. The primary storage is not a permanent storage area, but a temporary memory area to hold instructions that are to be interpreted by the CPU and used for data processing.

The data being processed is entered into the CPU in blocks at a time. If the software instructions do not properly set the boundaries for how much data can come in as a block (for example, 64 bits at a time), extra data can slip in and be executed. This is how ***buffer overflows*** work. If a buffer overflow takes place, it is due to the operating system or application software instructions that is processing the data, not the computer system itself. If extra data slips in, it can be executed in a privileged mode and cause disruption to the instruction execution of the CPU. This can result in the computer system freezing, rebooting, or data corruption. Buffer overflows can be corrected by well-written programs that verify how much data is to be inputted into the CPU at a time.

A CPU's time and processing power has to be shared between many tasks. Software and system interrupts are used to make sure that all data is processed in a timely manner and priorities are used to ensure that critical tasks are performed before less important tasks. As instructions and data are processed, they are moved back to the system's

Data Processing

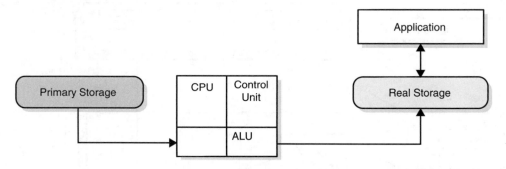

Figure 5-3 Primary storage is used to hold instructions for the CPU and real storage is used by applications.

memory spaces, called *real storage*, and new instructions and data are moved into the instruction transistors awaiting processing time from the CPU. Figure 5-3 illustrates primary storage and real storage. (In this context, storage refers to memory areas, not storage devices as in hard drives and CD-ROMs.)

Memory

The operating system instructions, applications, and data are held in memory, but so are the basic input/output system (BIOS), device controller instructions, and firmware. They do not all reside in the same memory location or even the same type of memory. The different types of memory, what they are used for, and how each is accessed can get a bit confusing because the CPU deals with several different types for different reasons.

The following sections quickly outline the different types of memory within a computer system.

Random access memory (RAM) is a type of temporary storage facility where data can be held and altered. It is used for read/write activities by the operating system and applications. It is described as *volatile* because if the computer's power supply is terminated, then all information within this type of memory is erased. There are different types of RAM, but the most well-known types are dynamic and static RAM. *Static RAM* lives up to its name, because when it stores data, it stays there without the need of being continually refreshed. *Dynamic RAM*, on the other hand, requires that the data held within it be periodically refreshed because the data dissipates and decays.

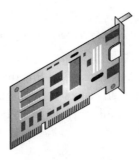

Read-only memory (ROM) is a *nonvolatile* storage facility, meaning that when a computer is turned off, the data is still held within the memory chips. For the most part, when data is inserted into ROM memory chips, it cannot be altered. The software that is stored within ROM is called *firmware*.

Erasable and programmable read-only memory (EPROM) can be modified, deleted, or upgraded. EPROM holds data that can be electrically erased or written to.

References

www.howstuffworks.com/ram.htm

www.softpanorama.org/Internals/index.shtml

Cache Memory

I am going to need this later, so I will just stick it into cache for now.

Cache memory is a part of RAM that is used for high-speed writing and reading activities. It holds instructions and data from primary storage and is accessed when application instructions and data are being executed. When the system assumes that it will need to access specific information many times throughout its processing activities, it will store it in cache memory so that it is easily and quickly accessible. Data being retrieved from cache can be accessed much quicker than if it was stored in real memory; thus, it affects the overall speed of the computer system.

An analogy is how the brain stores information that is used often. If one of Marge's primary functions at her job is ordering parts and telling vendors the company's address, this information is held within a portion of her brain that is easily and quickly accessible for Marge when she needs it. This information is held in a type of cache. If Marge was asked to remember her third grade teacher's name, this information would not necessarily be held in cache memory, but in a more long-term storage facility within her noggin.

Memory Mapping

Okay, here is your memory, here is my memory, and here is Bob's memory. No one use each other's memory!

Because there are different types of memory holding different types of data, a computer system does not want to let every user, process, and application access all types of memory anytime they want to. Access to memory needs to be controlled to ensure that data does not get corrupted. This type of control takes place through memory mapping and addressing.

The CPU is one of the most trusted components within a system, and therefore it can access memory directly. It uses physical addresses instead of pointers to memory segments. The CPU has physical wires connecting it to the memory chips within the computer. Because there are physical wires connecting the two types of components, physical addresses are used to represent the intersection between the wire and the transistor on a memory chip. Software does not use physical addresses; instead, it uses virtual or logical memory. Accessing memory indirectly provides an access control layer between the software and the memory, which is done for protection and efficiency. Figure 5-4 illustrates how the CPU can access memory directly using physical addresses and how software must use memory indirectly through a memory mapper.

Let's look at an analogy. You would like to talk to Mr. Marshall about possibly buying some acreage in Iowa. You don't know Mr. Marshall personally, and you do not want to give out your physical address and have him show up at your doorstep. Instead, you would like to use a more abstract and controlled way of communicating, so you give Mr. Marshall your phone number so you can talk about the land and you can make a determination if you want to meet Mr. Marshall in person. The same type of thing happens in computers. When a computer runs software, it does not want to expose itself unnecessarily to software written by good and bad programmers. Computers enable software to use memory indirectly using index tables and pointers, instead of giving them the right to access the memory directly. Only the system itself can access memory directly and programs can access the memory indirectly, but it is the same memory storage. This is one way the computer system protects itself.

When a program attempts to access memory, its access rights are verified and then instructions and commands are carried out in a way to ensure that badly written code does not affect other programs or the system itself. Applications, and their processes, can only access the memory allocated to them, as shown in Figure 5-5. This type of memory architecture provides protection and efficiency.

If programs accessed data held in memory directly, each program would have to wait until the prior program is done before it could access and process data. Mapped mem-

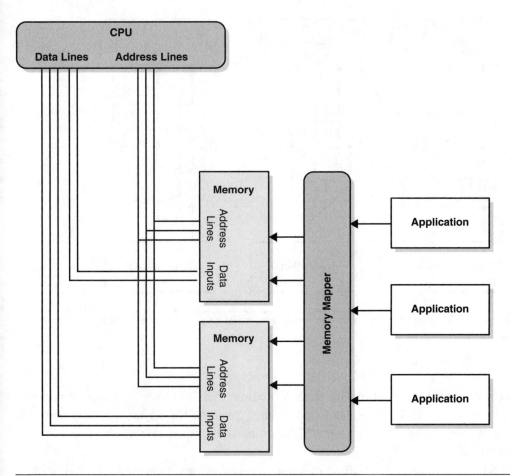

Figure 5-4   The CPU and applications access memory differently.

ory enables different programs to access the data and perform their own separate functions on it in a more economical and resourceful manner.

Secondary storage is considered nonvolatile storage media, which can be the computer's hard drive, floppy disks, or CD-ROM.

When RAM and secondary storage are combined, the result is *virtual storage*. The system uses hard drive space to extend RAM memory space capability. The hard drive space that is used to extend the RAM memory capabilities is incremented in pages. When a system fills up its volatile memory space, it will write data from memory onto the hard drive. When a program or user requests access to this data, it is brought from the hard drive back into memory. This process is called *paging.* Accessing data that is

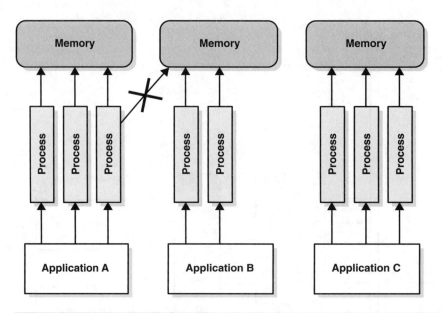

Figure 5-5 Applications, and the processes they use, only access their own memory segments.

kept in pages on the hard drive takes more time than accessing data kept in memory because actual disk access has to take place; however, the payoff is that it seems as though the system can hold an incredible amount of information in memory, as shown in Figure 5-6.

Sadly, the names of all these different types of storage make these concepts more confusing than necessary, so let's quickly review what we have:

- **Primary storage**   Main memory directly accessed by the CPU

- **Secondary storage**   Nonvolatile storage (floppy disk, CD-ROM disk, and hard drive)

- **Real storage**   Memory allocation for programs

- **Virtual storage**   RAM and secondary storage used together

CPU Modes and Protection Rings

If I am corrupted, very bad things can happen. Answer: Then you need to go into Ring 0.

If an operating system is going to be stable, it must be able to protect itself from its users and their applications. This requires the capability to distinguish between operations

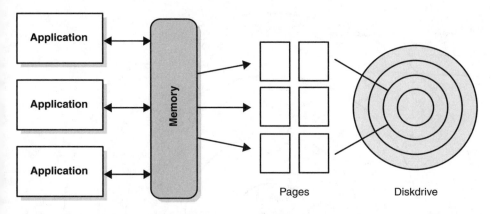

Figure 5-6   Systems send data from memory to the hard drive in units of pages to enable memory to reach gigabyte sizes.

performed on behalf of the operating system itself and operations performed on behalf of the users. This can be complex because the operating system software can be accessing memory segments, sending instructions to the CPU for processing, accessing secondary storage devices, and each user application (e-mail client, antivirus, Web browser, word processor, personal firewall, and so on) can be attempting the same types of activities at the same time. The operating system must keep track of all of these events and ensure that not one of them violates the security policy.

The operating system has several protection mechanisms to ensure that processes do not negatively affect each other or the critical components of the system itself. One has already been mentioned: memory segment. Another security mechanism that the system uses is *protection rings*. These rings provide strict boundaries and definitions on what the processes that work within each ring can access and what commands they can successfully execute. The processes that operate within the inner rings have more privileges than the processes operating in the outer rings. This is because the inner rings only permit the most trusted components and processes to operate within them. Although operating systems can vary in the number of protection rings, processes that execute within the inner rings are usually referred to as existing in a *privileged,* or supervisor, mode and the processes working in the outer rings are said to exist in a *user mode.*

Operating system components operate in a ring that gives them the most access to memory locations, peripheral devices, system drivers, and sensitive configuration parameters. Because this ring provides much more dangerous access to critical resources, it is the most protected. Applications usually operate in ring 3, which limits the type of memory, peripheral device, and driver access activity, and is controlled through the

General Protection fault occurs when ring3 → ring0

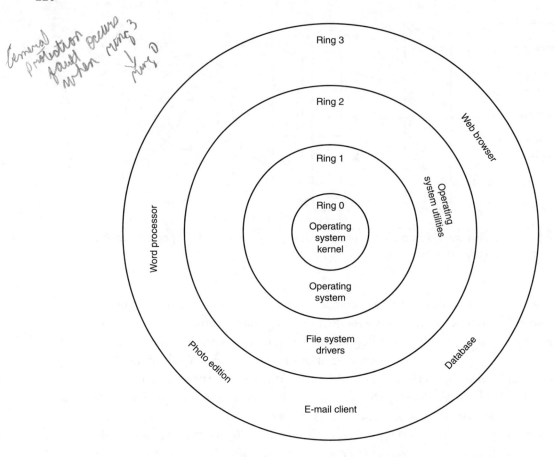

Figure 5-7   More trusted processes operate within lower-numbered rings.

operating system functions or system calls. The different rings are illustrated in Figure 5-7. The type of commands and instructions that are sent to the CPU from applications in the outer rings are more restrictive in nature. If an application tries to send instructions to the CPU that fall outside of its permission level, the CPU treats this violation as an exception and shows a General Protection Fault, a panic, or exception error and attempts to shut down the offending application.

Protection rings support the integrity, availability, and confidentiality requirements of multitasking operating systems. Many systems use four protection rings:

- **Ring 0**   Operating system kernel
- **Ring 1**   Remaining parts of the operating system

- **Ring 2**   I/O drivers and utilities

- **Ring 3**   Applications and programs

These protection rings provide an intermediate layer between subjects and objects, and are used for access control when a subject tries to access an object. The ring determines the access level to sensitive system resources. The lower the number, the greater the amount of privilege that is given to the process that runs within that ring. Each subject and object is assigned a number (0 through 3) depending on the level of trust the operating system assigns it. A subject in ring 3 cannot directly access an object in ring 1, but subjects in ring 1 can directly access an object in ring 3. Entities can only access objects within their own ring and outer rings, as shown in Figure 5-8. When an application needs access to components in rings that it is not allowed to directly access, it makes a request of the operating system to perform the necessary tasks. This is handled through system calls, where the operating system executes instructions not allowed in user mode.

When the operating system executes instructions for processes in rings 0 and 1, it operates in system mode, or privileged mode. When the operating system executes

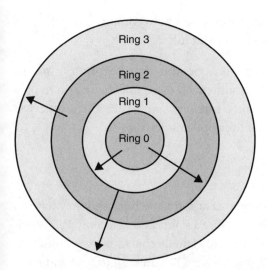

Ring 0—Operating system kernel
Ring 1—Remaining parts of the operating system
Ring 2— I/O drivers and utilities
Ring 3 —Applications and programs

Figure 5-8   Processes in inner rings can directly access processes in outer modes but not vice versa.

instructions for applications and processes in ring 3, it operates in user mode. User mode provides a much more restrictive environment for the application to work in, which in turn protects the system from misbehaving programs.

Operating States

If I am waiting for instructions, am I in the state of Wyoming? Answer: No, you are in ready state.

The operating system can operate in system or user mode depending on what process made a request to execute instructions, but there are also different *operating states* in which the system can exist. The following outlines the four possible states a system can operate in:

- **Ready state**   An application is ready to resume processing.

- **Supervisory state**   The system is executing a system, or highly privileged, routine.

- **Problem state**   The system is executing an application. (*A problem state sounds as if there is something wrong, but it means that the system is working on a problem, or task, presented by the application.*)

- **Wait state**   An application is waiting for a specific event to complete, like the user finishing typing in characters or waiting for a print job to finish.

These protection rings, operational modes, and operating states work together to ensure a secure and predictable operating environment. They enable the system to protect itself and work to protect the confidentiality, integrity, and availability of the system, information that is being processed, and the applications installed.

Multithreading, Multitasking, and Multiprocessing

Computers run different applications and programs at the same time and they have to share resources and play nice with each other to ensure a stable and safe computing environment. Some memory, data files, and variables are actually shared between different applications. It is critical that more than one process does not attempt to read and write to these items at the same time. The operating system is the master program that prevents this type of action from taking place and ensures that programs do not corrupt each other's data held in memory. The operating system works with the CPU to provide time slicing and interrupts to ensure that processes are provided with adequate access to the CPU. This also ensures that critical system functions are not negatively affected by rogue applications.

Process versus Thread

A *process* is a program in execution that works in its own address space and can only communicate with other processes in a controlled manner handled by the operating system. A *thread* represents a piece of code that is executed within a process, as shown in Figure 5-9.

When an application runs on a computer, it thinks it is the only program running and it does not necessarily know that it is sharing resources with several other types of programs, applications, and processes. This simplifies the issues that programmers need to be concerned about when writing an application. Because the application thinks it is the only one executing, it needs to be presented with an environment that reflects this type of reality. This is done through virtual machines and virtual memory. The operating system creates a virtual environment (virtual machine) for the application to work in and allots it a segment of virtual memory, as shown in Figure 5-10. Another application could have its own virtual machine and virtual address segment and the two would not know that each other even existed. This way the two applications do not interact with each other's data in memory or step on each other's toes while being executed by the CPU. It is a very orchestrated, controlled, and timed event-oriented atmosphere. An analogy is two people with two different offices. George has his office, computer, file cabinet, closet, and window. Marge has an office with the same materials. If George and Marge had to use the same computer, file cabinet, and closet, they could easily move each other's items around, accidentally delete each other's files, or wear each other's coat home. However, because they each have their own office and components, these events will not take place.

PROCESS

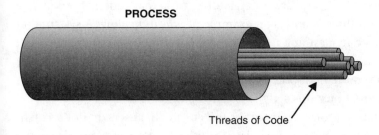

Threads of Code

Figure 5-9 Threads are pieces of a process.

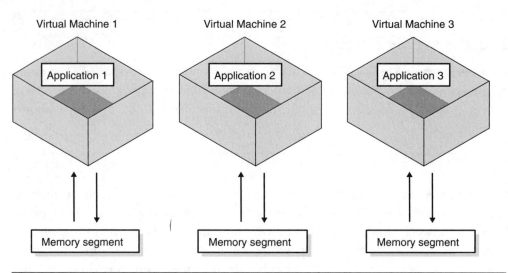

Figure 5-10   Virtual machines only access their allotted memory segments.

process addms
= to control unit

The granularity of this type of separation and protection becomes very detailed within a computer system. A process is used to request resource access, carry out data manipulation activities, and is the mechanism used to enable applications and the operating system to communicate. A process is like a phone call. If an application wants to print a form, it calls (or communicates via a process) the operating system, which calls the printer driver, and the printer driver calls the printer. These processes can only communicate in a way that has been previously approved by the operating system and outlined in the security model. The application cannot make a direct call to the printer driver because it does not operate in a privileged ring; thus, it does not have the necessary type of authority. The security architecture of the operating system dictates this type of communication authority.

One application can make several calls at one time. It can ask to print a form, accept a fax, display data to the monitor, and ask for an address from that address book. These different calls use different threads and is an example of *multithreading*. A system that can process more than one request at a time is capable of multithreading. If the CPU can process more than one process, or task, at one time, it is considered a *multitasking* system. If a computer has more than one CPU (also called processor), it can use them in parallel to execute instructions; this activity is called *multiprocessing*.

An operating system has to protect its integrity and ensure that users do not accidentally or intentionally access someone else's data. Multitasking systems interleave the execution of processes belonging to different users, which adds complexity to protecting itself and users' data. The operating system uses logical separation between users' data, which takes place in file and memory management.

Input/Output Device Management

When a user chooses to print a document, or a word processor displays a file previously stored, or if a user saves files to a Zip drive, these requests are going from the application the user is working in, through the operating system, and to the device requested. The operating system uses a device driver to communicate to a device controller, which is an electrical component with its own software used to provide a communication path that enables the device and operating system to exchange data. The operating system sends commands to the device controller's registers and the controller then writes data to the peripheral device or extracts data to be processed by the CPU, depending on the given commands. This communication happens through specific communication channels dedicated just for these types of functions. Once the device controller retrieves the requested information, it is stored in main memory for the operating system, application, and CPU to perform their necessary functions.

It is important that the devices and computer resources are properly accessed and released. Different operating systems handle accessing devices and resources differently. For example, Windows NT is considered a more stable and safer data processing environment than Windows 9x because applications cannot make direct requests to hardware devices. Windows NT and Windows 2000 have a much more controlled method of accessing devices than Windows 9x. This helps to protect the system from badly written code that does not properly request and release resources. This level of protection helps to ensure the resources' integrity and availability.

Proper input/output management is a core component of operating systems. When a request for a resource (memory allocation, printer, secondary storage devices, disk space) is made, certain data structures are built and processes are dedicated for this action to take place. Once the action takes place (a document is printed, a file is saved, or data is retrieved from the drive), the program, or operating system, needs to tear down these built structures and release the resources back into a pool to be available for other programs and processes. If this does not happen properly, a *deadlock* situation can occur or a computer may not have enough resources to process other requests (result of a denial-of-service attack). A deadlock situation can happen with peripheral devices, memory, database, or file access. If Sean accesses a database and his process never properly releases the necessary resources back to the system, when Debbie attempts to perform the same action, a deadlock situation can occur and Sean, Debbie, and the system that contains the database can be negatively affected. This has a direct correlation to a main security principle: availability.

Different operating systems have different methods of dealing with resource requests and releases and solving deadlock situations. In some systems, if a requested process is unavailable for a certain period of time, some operating systems will kill that process. This action releases the process from the application that had committed it, releases the supporting system resources necessary to commit this resource, and restarts the process so it is 'clean' and available to be used by other applications. Other operating systems might require a program to request all of the resources it needs *before* it actually starts executing instructions or requires a program to release its currently committed resources before being able to acquire more. Input/output management is a core responsibility of the operating system, along with memory management, CPU tasks, and file system management.

Tying It Together

Each of the earlier sections has complete books written on them because of their complexity and importance to the computing world. Each topic also relates to a part of security. An operating system is a complex beast that performs many complicated tasks in order to provide a useful and secure work environment for a user. It must recognize each process and program that is running, make access decisions, support system calls, protect memory segments, validate requested commands, properly process instructions, and ensure that none of these activities introduce vulnerabilities that can violate the security policy of the system. It does this by enforcing protection rings, mapping memory, implementing virtual machines, working in different states, and assigning trust levels to each and every process. These are integral parts of the security model for the operating system.

System Architecture

Designing a system from ground zero is a complicated task and has many intricate and abstract goals that have to be achieved through mathematics, programming code, and implementation. There are fundamental design decisions that need to be made when constructing a system. Security is only one of the goals of a system, but it is the goal security professionals are most concerned about.

Confidentiality, integrity, and availability can be enforced at different places within an enterprise. For example, a company may store customer credit card information in a database that many users can access. This information, obviously, requires protection to ensure that it is not accessed or modified in an unauthorized manner. We start with general questions and gradually drill down into the details. Where should this protection be placed? Should there be access controls that screen users when they log in and assign them their rights at that point dictating what data they can and cannot access? Should the data files holding the credit card information be protected at the file system level? Should protection be provided by restricting users' operations and activities? Or should there be a combination of all of these? The first and most general questions are where should the protection take place: at the user's end, where the data is stored, or by restricting user activities within the environment? These are illustrated in Figure 5-11.

Once these general questions have been answered, the placement of the mechanisms needs to be addressed. Security mechanisms can be placed at the hardware, kernel, operating system, services, or program layers. At which layer(s) should security mechanisms be implemented? If protection is implemented at the hardware layer, the protection mechanisms will be more simplistic, provide broad and a general type of protection, and focus on protecting data. As we ascend up the layers, more complexity is added, and functionality becomes more specific and granular. The top layer holds the most complexity because it is directed towards providing the user with a vast amount of functionality and options. Functionality and complexity of security increases as it approaches the layers that are closer to the user. The increased complexity lowers the assurance levels of the security mechanisms. This is shown in Figure 5-12.

The more complex a security mechanism becomes, the less assurance it provides. This is because the complexity of the mechanism demands more technical understanding from the individuals who install, test, maintain, and use it. The more complex the tools, the more chances there are for errors, and therefore increased chances for security compromises. The more complex the security mechanism, the harder it is to fully test it under all possible conditions. However, on the other hand, simplistic mechanisms cannot provide the desired richness of functionality and options, although they are easier to install, maintain, use, and test. So the trade-offs between functionality and assurance

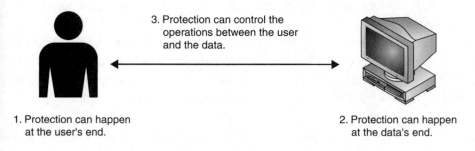

1. Protection can happen at the user's end.
2. Protection can happen at the data's end.
3. Protection can control the operations between the user and the data.

Figure 5-11   Security can take place at three main areas.

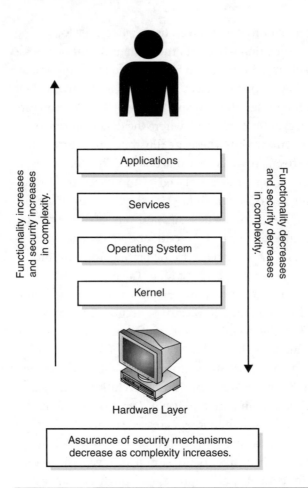

Figure 5-12 caption components:

Applications

Services

Operating System

Kernel

Hardware Layer

Functionality increases and security increases in complexity.

Functionality decreases and security decreases in complexity.

Assurance of security mechanisms decrease as complexity increases.

Figure 5-12 As functionality increases, complexity increases and the assurance of security decreases.

need to be fully understood to make the right security mechanism choices when designing a system.

Once the designers have an idea of what the security mechanisms should focus on (users, operations, or data), what layer(s) the mechanisms should be placed at (hardware, kernel, operating system, services, or program), and the complexity of each mechanism, they need to be built and integrated in a way to have a proper relationship with other parts of the system.

The first step is to decide what system mechanisms need to be trusted and specify how these entities can interact in a secure manner. Although it might seem that you would want to trust all the components within the system, this would cause too much overhead, complexity, and performance bottlenecks. For a mechanism to be trusted, it means that it protects itself and the data it is processing, it performs in predictable and secure manners, and it does not adversely affect other trusted or untrusted mechanisms. In return, these trusted components have access to more privileged services, have direct access to memory, usually have higher priority when requesting CPU processing time, and have more control over system resources. So the trusted subjects and objects need to be identified and distinguished from the untrusted ones and placed into defined subsets.

Defined Subset of Subjects and Objects

As stated previously, not all components need to be trusted and therefore do not fall under the *trusted computing base (TCB)*. The TCB is defined as the total combination of protection mechanisms within a computer system. The TCB includes hardware, software, and firmware. These are part of the TCB because the system is sure that these components will enforce the security policy and not violate it.

The components that do fall under the TCB need to be identified and their accepted capabilities defined. For example, a system that has a lower trust level rating may permit all authenticated users to access and modify all files on the computer. This subset of subjects and objects is large and the relationship between them is loose and relaxed. A system with a much higher trust level rating may permit only two subjects to access all files on a computer system, and only one of those subjects can actually modify all the files. This subset is much smaller and the rules being enforced are more stringent and detailed.

Again, it depends upon what type of system the developers are aiming at building. If developers want to develop a system with an Orange Book security rating of D (very low), then what makes up the TCB or not is not much of an issue because the system will not be expected to provide a very high level of security. However, if the developers want to develop a system with an Orange Book rating of B2 or B1 (much higher than rating D), then they will need to specify what makes up the TCB, enforce strict rules that dictate how subjects and objects interact, and ensure that these items are identified, authenticated, and audited because these are the components that will be scrutinized, tested, and evaluated before a rating of B2 or B1 can be given. (The *Orange Book* and its ratings are addressed in the section "The Orange Book" later in the chapter.)

Trusted Computing Base

The term "trusted computing base (TCB)" originated from the Orange Book and does not address the level of security a system provides, but the level of trust. This is done because no computer system can be totally secure and the types of attacks and vulnerabilities change and evolve over time and with enough time and resources, most attacks can become successful. However, if a system meets a certain criteria, it is then looked upon as providing a certain level of trust.

The TCB does not just address operating systems because a computer system is not made up of only an operating system. The TCB addresses hardware, software, components, and firmware because each can affect the computer's environment in a negative and positive manner and each has a responsibility of supporting and enforcing the security policy of that particular system. Some components and mechanisms have direct responsibilities in supporting the security policy like firmware that will not let a user boot a computer from a floppy disk or the memory manager that will not let users overwrite other users' data. Then there are components that do not enforce the security policy, but must behave properly and not violate the trust of a system. The types of violations a component could cause against the system's security policy could be an application that attempts to make a direct call to a piece of hardware instead of using the proper calls through the operating system, a program that attempts to read data outside of its approved memory space, or a piece of software that does not properly release resources after use.

Not every part of a system needs to be trusted and a part of evaluating the trust level of a system is to identify the architecture, security services, and assurance mechanisms that make up the TCB. It must be shown how the TCB is protected from accidental or intentional tampering and compromising activity. For systems to achieve a higher trust level, they must meet well-defined TCB requirements and the details of their operational states, developing stages, testing procedures, and documentation will be reviewed with more granularity than systems that are attempting to achieve a lower trust rating.

By using specific security criteria, trust can be built into a system, evaluated, and certified. This approach can provide a measurement system for customers to use when comparing one system to another. It also gives vendors guidelines on what expectations are put upon their systems and provides a common security rating so when one group talks about a C2 rating, everyone else is on the same page and understands what these terms mean.

The Orange Book defines a trusted system as hardware and software that utilize measures to protect the integrity of unclassified or classified data for a range of users without violating access rights and the security policy. It looks at all protection mechanisms within a system to enforce the security policy and provide an environment that will behave in a manner expected of it. This means that each layer of the system must trust the underlying layer to perform the expected functions, provide the expected functionality, and operate in an expected manner under many different situations. When the operating system makes calls to hardware, it is anticipating data to be returned in a specific data format and to behave in a consistent and predictable manner. Applications that run on top of the operating system expect to be able to make certain system calls and receive the required data in return and to be able to operate in a reliable and dependable environment. Users expect the hardware, operating system, and applications to perform in particular fashions and provide a certain level of functionality. For all of these actions to behave in such predicable manners, the requirements of a system must be addressed in the planning stages of production, not afterwards.

Security Perimeter

Now, whom do we trust? Answer: Anyone inside the security perimeter.

As we stated, not every component and resource falls within the TCB, so some resources fall outside of this imaginary boundary referred to as the *security perimeter*. For the system to stay in a secure and trusted state when a component within the TCB needs to communicate with a component outside of the TCB, precise communication standards must be developed to ensure that this type of communication cannot bring on unexpected security compromises. This type of communication is handled and controlled through interfaces.

For example, a resource that is within the boundary of the TCB, or security perimeter, must not pass confidential information to resources outside the TCB. The resource within the TCB must also be careful about the commands and information it accepts from less-trusted resources. These limitations and restrictions are built into the interfaces that permit this type of communication to take place and are the mechanisms that enforce the security perimeter, as shown in Figure 5-13. Communication between trusted components and untrusted components needs to be controlled to ensure that confidential information does not flow in an unintended way.

Reference Monitor and Security Kernel

So up to now, our developers have accomplished many things in developing their system. They have defined where the security mechanisms will be located (hardware, kernel, operating system, services, or program), they have defined the objects that are within the TCB and how those components interact with each other, the security perimeter that separates the trusted components and the untrusted components has been delineated, and they have developed proper interfaces for these entities to communicate securely. Now they need to develop and implement a mechanism that ensures that the subjects that access objects have been given the necessary permissions

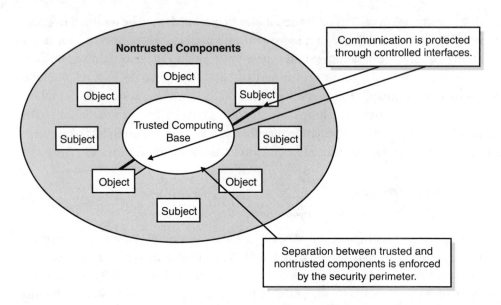

Nontrusted Components

Object

Object

Subject

Subject

Trusted Computing Base

Subject

Object

Object

Subject

Communication is protected through controlled interfaces.

Separation between trusted and nontrusted components is enforced by the security perimeter.

Figure 5-13 Interfaces control the communication between trusted and untrusted process.

to do so. This means the developers need to develop and implement a reference monitor and security kernel.

The *reference monitor* is an abstract machine, which mediates all access subjects have to objects to ensure that the subjects have the necessary access rights and to protect the objects from unauthorized access and destructive modification. For a system to achieve a higher level of trust, it must enforce subjects (programs, users, or processes) to be fully authorized prior to accessing an object (file, program, or resource). It must be made certain that the subject has been granted access privileges prior to letting the subject use the requested object. The reference monitor is an access control concept, not an actual physical component. The *security kernel* is made up of mechanisms that fall under the TCB and implements and enforces the reference monitor concept. The security kernel is made up of hardware, firmware, and software components that mediate all access and functions between subjects and objects. The security kernel is the core of the TCB and is the most commonly used approach to building trusted computing systems. There are three main requirements of the security kernel:

- It must provide isolation for the processes carrying out the reference monitor concept and they must be tamperproof.

- The reference monitor must be invoked for every access attempt and must be impossible to circumvent. Thus, the reference monitor must be implemented in a complete and foolproof way.

- It must be small enough to be able to be tested and verified in a complete and comprehensive manner.

These are the requirements of the reference monitor; therefore, they are the requirements of the components that provide and enforce the reference monitor concept—the security kernel.

These issues work in the abstract, but are implemented in the physical world of hardware devices and software code. The assurance that the components are enforcing the abstract idea of the reference monitor is proved through testing and functionality.

 NOTE The reference monitor is a concept where an abstract machine mediates all accesses to objects by subjects. The security kernel is the hardware, firmware, and software of a TCB that implements this concept. The TCB is the totality of protection mechanisms within a computer system that work together to enforce a security policy. The TCB contains the security kernel and all other security protection mechanisms.

Figure 5-14 provides a quick analogy to show you the relationship between the components that make up the kernel, the kernel itself, and the reference monitor concept. Individuals make up a society. The individuals can represent the components and the society can represent the kernel. For a society to have a certain standard of living, it needs to react in specific ways, which is why we have laws. The laws represent the reference monitor which enforces proper activity. Each individual is expected to stay within the bounds of the laws and act in specific ways so society as a whole is not adversely affected and the standard of living is not threatened. The components within a system must stay within the bounds of the reference monitor's laws so that they will not adversely affect other components and threaten the security of the system.

References

www.kernel.org/pub/linux/libs/security/Orange-Linux/refs/Orange/
   OrangeI-II-6.html

http://citeseer.nj.nec.com/299300.html

www.ccert.edu.cn/documents/fcvol1.pdf

www.cs.cornell.edu/html/cs513-sp99/NL05.html

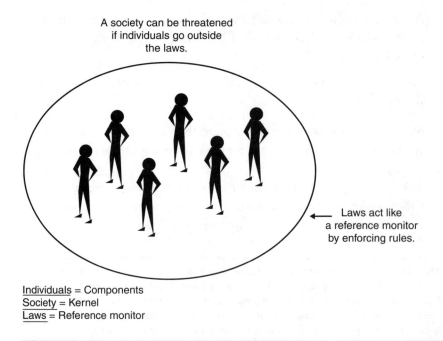

A society can be threatened
if individuals go outside
the laws.

Laws act like
a reference monitor
by enforcing rules.

Individuals = Components
Society = Kernel
Laws = Reference monitor

Figure 5-14 Components, like people, need to say inside the bounds of the rules.

Domains

Okay, here are all the marbles you can play with. We will call that your domain of resources.

In Chapter 4, a *domain* was defined as a set of objects that a subject is able to access. This domain can be all the resources a user can access, all the files available to a program, the memory segments available to a process, or the services and processes available to an application. A subject needs to be able to access and use objects (resources) to perform tasks, and the domain defines which objects are available to the subject and which objects are untouchable and therefore unusable by the subject.

These domains have to be identified, separated, and strictly enforced. An operating system may work in a privileged mode and a user mode. The reason to even use these two different modes is to define two different domains. The privileged mode has a much larger domain to work with (or more resources to access); thus, it can provide much more functionality. When an operating system works in privileged mode, it can physically access memory modules, transfer data from an unprotected domain to a protected domain, and can directly access and communicate with hardware devices. An application that functions in user mode cannot access memory directly and has a more limited amount of resources available to it. Only a certain segment of memory is available to this application and it must be accessed in an indirect and controlled fashion. The application can copy files only within its own domain and cannot access hardware directly.

A program that resides in a privileged domain needs to be able to execute its instructions and process its data with the assurance that programs in a different domain cannot negatively affect its environment. This is referred to as an *execution domain*. Because programs in a privileged domain have access to sensitive resources, the environment needs to be protected from rogue program code or unexpected activities resulting from programs in other domains. Some systems may only have distinct user and privilege areas, whereas other systems may have complex architectures that contain up to ten security domains.

A security domain has a direct correlation to the protection ring that a subject or object is assigned to. The lower the protection ring number, the higher the privilege and the larger the security domain. This concept is depicted in Figure 5-15.

Resource Isolation

To properly enforce access control, auditing, and determining what subjects and objects reside in this domain or that domain, each resource has to be clearly separated from another. This modularity requirement enables each subject and object to be identified uniquely, permissions and rights to be assigned independently, accountability to be enforceable, and intricate and minute activities to be tracked precisely. The subjects, objects, and protection controls need to be clearly isolated from each other and the isolation methods and enforcement are a requirement of the architecture of a system and its security model.

Processes are also resources that need to be isolated and this is usually done through distinct address allocation. Virtual memory (explained in the section "Multithreading, Multitasking, and Multiprocessing" earlier in the chapter) techniques are used to make sure different processes have their own memory addresses to use and do not access each other's memory. If a process has a particular memory range allocated to it, then it does not know that there is other memory in the system. The process works happily in the memory allocated and does not stomp on another process' data in another segment of memory.

Systems of a higher trust level may need to implement *hardware segmentation* of the virtual memory used by different processes. This means that memory is separated physically instead of just logically. This adds another layer of protection to ensure that a lower-privileged process does not access and modify a higher-level process' memory space.

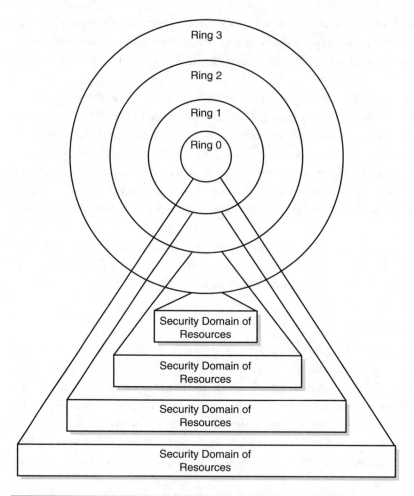

Figure 5-15 The higher the level of trust, the larger the number of available resources.

Security Policy

So we have stated that the TCB contains components that directly enforce the security policy, but what is a security policy?

A *security policy* is a set of rules, practices, and procedures dictating how sensitive information is managed, protected, and distributed. A security policy is a document that expresses exactly what the security level should be by setting the goals of what the security mechanisms are to accomplish. This is an important element that has a major role in defining the design of the system. The security policy is a foundation for the specifications of a system and provides the baseline for evaluating a system. In Chapter 3, security policies were examined in depth, but those policies were directed towards the company itself. The security policies being addressed here are for operating systems and applications. The different policies are similar but have different targets: an organization versus an individual computer system.

A system provides trust by fulfilling and enforcing the security policy and typically deals with the relationships between subjects and objects. The policy must indicate what subjects can access individual objects, and what actions are acceptable and unacceptable. The definition of what trust means is derived from a framework and the security policy works as this framework for computing systems.

For a system to provide an acceptable level of trust, it must be based on an architecture that provides the capabilities to protect itself from untrusted processes, intentional or accidental compromises, and attacks at different layers of the system. A majority of the trust ratings require a defined subset of subjects and objects, explicit domains, and the isolation of resources so their access can be controlled and activity performed on them can be audited.

Let's regroup. We know that a system's trust is defined by a set of criteria. When a system is tested against this set of criteria, a rating is assigned to the system and this rating is used by customers, vendors, and the computing society as a whole. The criteria will determine if the security policy is being properly supported and enforced. The security policy lays out the rules and practices pertaining to how a system will manage, protect, and distribute sensitive information. The reference monitor is a concept that says all subjects must have proper authority to access objects and is implemented by the security kernel. The security kernel is made of all the resources that supervise system activity in accordance with the system's security policy and is part of the operating system that controls access to system resources. For this to work correctly, the individual resources need to be isolated from each other and domains need to be defined to dictate what objects are available to subjects.

Security policies that prevent information from flowing from a high security level to a lower security level are called *multilevel security policies*. These types of policies permit a subject to access an object only if the subject's security level is higher than or equal to the object's classification.

As we said, these are abstract ideas that will be manifested into physical hardware components, firmware, software code, and activities through designing, building, and implementing a system. These ideas are like abstract goals and dreams we would like to accomplish, which are accomplished by our physical hard work and items that we produce.

Least Privilege

Once resources and processes are isolated properly, *least privilege* needs to be enforced. This means that a resource, or process, has no more privileges than necessary to be able to fulfill its functions. Only resources and processes that *need* to carry out critical system functions should be allowed to and other less-privileged processes should call upon the more privileged processes to carry out these types of activities when necessary. This type of indirect activity protects the system from poorly written or misbehaving code. Processes should possess a level of privilege only as long as they really need it. If a process needs to have its status increased so it can interact directly with sensitive information, as soon as its tasks are complete, the process's status should be dropped to a lower privilege to ensure that another mechanism cannot use it to adversely affect the system. Only processes needing complete system privileges are located in the kernel; other less-privileged processes call upon them to process sensitive or delicate operations.

References

www.cs.cornell.edu/html/cs513-sp99/NL03.html

www.iwar.org.uk/comsec/resources/standards/rainbow/NCSC-TG-028.htm

www.kernel.org/pub/linux/libs/security/Orange-Linux/refs/Orange/OrangeI-II-2.html

Layering, Data Hiding, and Abstraction

Systems that meet certain trust levels must supply mechanisms that force processes to work in layers, which means certain functionality takes place in different layers of a system. This requires a structured and hierarchical architecture that has the basic functionality taking place at lower layers and more complex functions at the higher layers. *Layering* further separates processes and resources and adds modularity to the system. The different layers can communicate, but only through detailed interfaces that uphold the security integrity of the system. In some instances, it is required that processes in different layers do not communicate; therefore, they are not supplied with interfaces to interact with each other. This process is called *data hiding* in that the data in one layer is hidden because the subjects in another layer do not even know the data exists; thus, it is hidden. If a subject in one layer has no interface to be able to communicate with data at another layer, this data is hidden from that subject.

Objects can be grouped into sets called classes. When a class of objects is assigned specific permissions and acceptable activities are defined, it is called *abstraction*. This makes management of different objects easier because classes can be dealt with instead of each and every individual object. When a class is defined, all the objects within that class are assigned an abstract data type, which is a precise definition of the format the object will accept data and the format it will present its processed data to other objects and subjects. This provides a predictable way of communicating and helps prevent authorized entities from modifying the data within an object in an inappropriate way. For example, when one object passes a registry value to another object, it is done in a predefined manner and the receiving object will not accept values outside of these predefined boundaries. If the receiving object is expecting a binary value, it will not accept a hexadecimal value in its place. This type of restriction is defined in the object's abstract data type.

Layering, data hiding, and abstraction are all methods to protect subjects, objects, and the data within the objects. These concepts are foundational pieces to a security model.

Security Models

An important concept in the design and analysis of secure systems is the security model, because it incorporates the security policy that should be enforced in the system. A model is a symbolic representation of a policy. It maps the desires of the policy makers into a set of rules that are to be followed by a computer system.

We have continually mentioned the security policy and its importance, but it is an abstract term that represents the objectives and goals a system must meet and accomplish to be deemed secure and acceptable. How do we get from an abstract security policy to an administrator being able to uncheck a box on the graphical user interface (GUI) to disallow David from accessing configuration files on his system? There are many complex steps in between that take place during the system's development.

Analogy of the Relationship Between a Security Policy and a Security Model

If someone tells you to live a healthy and responsible life, this is very broad, vague, and abstract notion. So when you ask this person how this is accomplished, they outline the things you should and should not do (do not harm others, do not lie, eat your vegetables, and brush your teeth). The security policy provides the abstract goals and the security model provides the do's and don'ts necessary to fulfill these goals.

A security model maps the abstract goals of the policy to information system terms by specifying explicit data structures and techniques necessary to enforce the security policy. A security model is usually represented in mathematics and analytical ideas, which is then mapped to system specifications, and then developed by programmers through programming code. So we have a policy that encompasses security goals like each subject must be authorized to access each object. The security model takes this requirement and provides the necessary mathematical formulas, relationships, and structure to be followed to accomplish this goal. From here, specifications are developed per operating system type (Unix, Windows, or Macintosh), and individual vendors can decide how they are going to implement mechanisms that meet these necessary specifications.

So in a very general and simplistic example, if a security policy states that subjects need to be authorized to access objects, the security model would provide the mathematical relationships and formulas explaining how x can access y only through outlined specific methods. Specifications are then developed to provide a bridge to what this means in a computing environment and how it maps to components and mechanisms that need to be coded and developed. The developers then write the program code to produce the mechanisms that provide a way for a system to use access control lists and give administrators some degree of control. This mechanism presents the network administrator with a GUI representation, like check boxes, to choose which subjects can access what objects, to be able to set this configuration within the operating system. This is an extremely rudimentary example because security models can be very complex, but it is used to demonstrate the relationship between the security policy and the security model.

Some security models enforce rules to protect confidentiality, Bell-LaPadula, and some models enforce rules to protect integrity, Biba. Formal security models, such as Bell-LaPadula, are used to provide high assurance in security and informal models, such as Clark-Wilson, are used more as a framework to describe how security policies should be expressed and executed.

A security policy outlines goals with no idea of how they would be accomplished and a model is a framework that gives the policy form and solves security problems for particular situations. Several security models have been developed to enforce security policies and the following sections provide overviews of each model.

State Machine Models

No matter what state I am in, I am always trustworthy.

In *state machine models*, to verify the security of a system, the state is used, which means all current permissions and all current instances of subjects accessing objects must be captured. Maintaining the state of a system deals with each subject's association with objects. If the subjects can only access objects by means that are concurrent with the security policy, then the system is secure. State machines have provided a basis for important security models. A state of a system is a snapshot of a system in one moment of time. There are many activities that can alter this state, which is referred to as a *state transitions*. The developers of a state machine model need to look at all the different state transitions that are possible and assess if a system starts up in a secure state, can any of these events put the system into an insecure state? If all of the activities that are allowed to happen in the system do not compromise the system and put it into an insecure state, then the system executes a secure state machine model.

So a system that has employed a state machine model will be in a secure state in each and every instance of its existence. It will boot up into a secure state, execute commands and transactions securely, and will allow subjects to access resources only in secure states.

Bell-LaPadula Model

In the 1970s, the U.S. military used time-sharing mainframe systems and was concerned about the security of these systems and leakage of classified information. The *Bell-LaPadula model* was developed to address these concerns. Its development was funded by the government to provide a framework for computer systems that would be used to store and process sensitive information. The model's main goal is to prevent secret information from being accessed in an unauthorized manner.

A system that employs the Bell-LaPadula model is called a multilevel security system because users with different clearances use the systems, and the systems process data with different classifications. Government and commercial organizations use different data classification schemes. The government uses top secret, secret, unclassified, and so on, whereas commercial organizations usually classify their data as confidential, proprietary, and public. The level at which information is classified determines the handling procedures that should be used. These classifications together form a *lattice*, which is an upper bound and lower bound of authorized access. A subject that has top secret clearance can access top secret, secret, and unclassified data. Top secret is the upper bound and unclassified is the lower bound. Mandatory access control is based on a lattice of security labels.

The Bell-LaPadula model is a state machine model enforcing the confidentiality aspects of access control. An access control matrix and security levels are used to determine if subjects can access different objects. The subject's clearance is compared to the object's classification; if the clearance is higher or equal to the object's classification, then the subject can access the object without violating the security policy.

The model uses subjects, objects, access operations (read, write, and read/write), and security levels. Subjects and objects can reside at different security levels and have relationships and rules dictating the acceptable activities between them. If properly implemented and enforced, this model has been mathematically proven to prevent data from a higher security level from flowing to a lower security level. It is an *information flow security model* also, which means that information does not flow to an object of lesser or noncomparable classification.

There are two main rules used and enforced in the Bell-LaPadula model: the simple security rule and the *-property rule. The *simple security rule* states that a subject at a given security level cannot read data that resides at a higher security level. The **-property* rule states that a subject in a given security level cannot write information to a lower security level. The simple security rule is referred to as the "no read up" rule and the*-property is referred to the as "no write down" rule, as shown in Figure 5-16. The simple security and *-property rules indicate what states the system can go into.

The state of a system changes as different operations take place. The Bell-LaPadula model defines a secure state, meaning a secure computing environment and the allowed actions which are security-preserving operations. This means that the model provides a secure state and only permits operations that will keep the system within a secure state and not let it enter into an insecure state. So if 100 people access 2,000 objects in a day using this one system, this system is put through a lot of work and several complex activities have to take place. However, at the end of the day, the system is

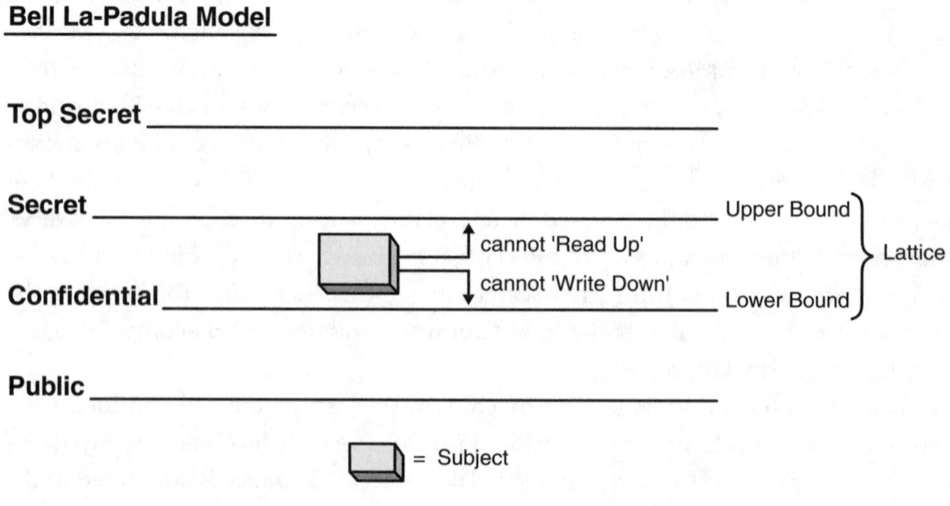

Bell La-Padula Model

Figure 5-16 In the Bell-LaPadula model, each subject has a lattice of rights.

just as secure as it was in the beginning of the day. This is definition of the Basic Security Theorem used in computer science.

NOTE   The definition of the Basic Security Theorem is that if a system initializes in a security state and all state transitions are secure, then every subsequent state will be secure no matter what inputs occur.

where used ?

An important thing to note is that the Bell-LaPadula model was developed to make sure secrets stay secret; thus, it provides confidentiality. This model does not address integrity of the data the system maintains—only who can and cannot access the data.

So What Does This Mean and Why?

Subjects and objects are assigned labels. The subject's label is a clearance label (top secret, secret, confidential, and so on) and the object's label is a classification label (top secret, secret, confidential, and so on). When a subject attempts to access an object, the system compares the subject's clearance label and the object's classification label and looks at an access control matrix to see if this is a legal and secure activity. So let's say it is a perfectly fine activity and the subject is given access to the object. Now if the subject's clearance label is top secret and the object's classification label is secret, the subject cannot write to this object, because of the *-property rule. This makes sure that subjects cannot accidentally or intentionally share confidential information by writing to an object at a lower security level. If a busy and clumsy general in the army opens up a briefing letter that will go to all clerks at all bases all around the world and he attempts to write that the United States is attacking Cuba, the Bell-LaPadula model will come into action and not permit this general to write this information to this type of file because his clearance is higher than that of the memo.

Likewise, if a nosey clerk tried to read a memo that was available only to generals and above, the Bell-LaPadula model would stop this activity also. The clerk's clearance is lower than that of the object, the memo, and this violates the simple security rule of the model. It is all about keeping secrets secret.

The following lists some criticism towards the Bell-LaPadula model:

- It deals only with confidentiality and does not address integrity.

- It does not address management of access control, because there is no mechanism to modify access rights.   *I thought models were abstract, so they should not describe any access rights*

- The model does not prevent or address covert channels.   *?*

- The model does not address file sharing used in more modern systems.   *a communication path that enables a process to transmit a message in a way that violates the system security policy.*

Biba

The *Biba model* was developed after the Bell-LaPadula model. It uses a state machine model and is very similar to the Bell-LaPadula model. Biba addresses the integrity of data being threatened when subjects at lower security levels are able to write to objects at higher security levels and when subjects can read data at lower levels. If implemented and enforced properly, the Biba model prevents data from any *integrity* level from flowing to a higher integrity level. Biba has two main rules to provide this type of protection. The first rule, referred to as "no write up," states that a subject cannot write data to an object at a higher *integrity* level. The second rule, referred to as "no read down," states that a subject cannot read data from a lower integrity level. This second rule might sound a little goofy, but it is protecting the subject and data at a higher integrity level from being corrupted by data in a lower integrity level. An analogy would be if you were writing an article for the *New York Times* about the security trends over the last year, the amount of money businesses lost, and the cost/benefit ratio of implementing firewalls, intrusion detection systems, and scanners. You do not want to get your data and numbers for any old Web site without knowing how those figures were calculated and the sources of the information. Your article (data at a higher integrity level) can be compromised if mixed with unfounded information from a bad source (data at a lower integrity level).

Bell-LaPadula versus Biba

The Bell-LaPadula model is used to provide confidentiality. The Biba model is used to provide integrity. The Bell-LaPadula and Biba models are informational flow models because they are most concerned about data flowing from one security level to another.

When first learning about the Bell-LaPadula and Biba model, they seem very similar, and the reasons for their differences may bring about some confusion. The Bell-LaPadula model was written for the government and the government is very paranoid about the leakage of their secret information. So in their model a user cannot write to a lower level because that user might let out some secrets. Similarly, a user at a lower level cannot read anything at a higher level because that user might learn some secrets. However, not everyone is so worried about confidentiality and has such big, important secrets to protect. The commercial industry is more concerned about the integrity of its data. An accounting firm is more worried about keeping their numbers straight and making sure decimal points are not dropped in a process carried out by an application or extra zeros are not added. The accounting firm is more concerned about the integrity of this data and is usually under little threat of someone trying to steal these numbers, so they would employ the Biba model. Of course, the accounting firm does not look for the name Biba on the back of a product or has to ensure if it is in the design of their operating system. It is something that was decided upon and implemented when the system was being developed and the different security ratings are what consumers use to determine if a system is right for them. So even if the accountants are using a system using the Biba model, they would not know and we're not going to tell them.

Clark-Wilson Model

The *Clark-Wilson model* was developed after Biba and takes some different approaches to protecting the integrity of information by focusing on preventing authorized users from making unauthorized modification of data, fraud, and errors within commercial applications.

As stated earlier, military institutions are usually more concerned about confidentiality and the commercial sector is usually more concerned with the integrity of the data they process. In the Clark-Wilson model, users cannot access and manipulate objects directly, but must access the object through a program. This provides another layer of protection between the user and the object and further restricts the type of actions that can take place on that object, thus protecting the integrity of the object.

Let's say Emily is a user of a system that has been built around the Clark-Wilson model. She is restricted to only being allowed to use three programs. She cannot access files directly, but must open and manipulate files through one of these three programs. The programs have their own set of restrictions dictating what actions they can and cannot perform on objects. This streamlines the way objects are protected and reduces the methods that could cause the data to be corrupted or changed in an undesirable manner.

This model also uses *separation of duties*, which divides an operation into different parts and requires different users to perform each part. This prevents authorized users from making unauthorized modifications to data, which again protects its integrity. Auditing is also required in this model to track the information coming in from the outside of the system.

So the Clark-Wilson model prevents authorized users from making modifications by requiring them to go through programs to modify objects. It also prevents authorized users from making improper modifications by enforcing separation of duties, and maintains an audit log for external transactions.

Information Flow Model

Now, which way is the information flowing in this system? Answer: Not to you.

Bell-LaPadula model is concerned about information that can flow from a high security level to a low security level. The Biba model is concerned about information that can flow from a high integrity level to a low integrity level. Both of these use an *information flow model*. Information flow models can deal with any kind of information flow, not only the direction of the flow. This type of model looks at insecure informational flow that can happen at the same level and between objects along with the flow between different levels. When the information flow model is used, a system is secure if there is no illegal information flow permitted.

Basically, information can flow from one security level to another or from one object to another in the same security level until a restricted operation is attempted. In most systems, once a restricted operation is attempted, the system looks at an access control matrix to see if this action has been specifically permitted for this specific subject or object.

Noninterference Model

Multilevel security properties can be expressed in other ways, one being *noninterference*. This concept is implemented to ensure that any actions that take place at a higher security level do not affect, or interfere, with actions that take place at a lower level. This type of model does not concern itself with the flow of data, but with what a subject knows about the state of the system. So if an entity at a higher security level performs an action, it cannot change the state for the entity at the lower level.

If a lower-level entity was aware of a certain activity that took place by an entity at a higher level and the state of system changed for this lower-level entity, the entity might be able to deduce too much information about the activities of the higher state, which in turn is a way of leaking information.

Users at a lower security level should not be aware of the commands executed by users at a higher level and should not be affected by those commands in any way.

Security Models

- **Bell-LaPadula model** Protects the confidentiality of the information within a system.

  - **Simple security rule** Subject cannot read data at a higher security level (no read up).

  - ***-property rule** Subject cannot write data to an object at a lower security level (no write down).

- **Biba model** Protects the integrity of the information within a system.

  - **Simple integrity axiom** A subject cannot read data at a lower integrity level (no read down).

  - *** integrity axiom** A subject cannot modify an object in a higher integrity level (no write up).

- **Clark-Wilson model** Prevents authorized users from making unauthorized modification to data.

  - Subjects can only access objects through authorized programs.

  - Separation of duties is enforced.

  - Auditing is required.

- **Information flow model** Information is restricted in its flow to only go to and from approved security levels.

- **Noninterference model** Commands and activities performed at one security level should not be seen or affect subjects or objects at a different security level.

References

www.cccure.org/Documents/HISM/087-089.html

http://all.net/books/ip/Chap3-3.html

http://infoeng.ee.ic.ac.uk/~malikz/surprise2001/spc99e/article1/

www.wi-inf.uni-essen.de/~ifs/summerschool/

Security Modes of Operation

A system can operate at different types of modes depending on the sensitivity of the data being processed, the clearance level of the users, and what those users are authorized to do. The *mode of operation* describes the security conditions under which the system actually functions. There are four modes of operations a system can function under and the following sections describes each one.

Dedicated Security Mode

A system is operating in a *dedicated security mode* if all users have the clearance or authorization and need-to-know to *all* data processed within the system. All users have been given formal access approval for *all* information on the system and have signed nondisclosure agreements pertaining to this information. The system can handle a single classification level of information.

Many military systems were designed in the past to handle only one level of security, which worked in dedicated security mode. This required everyone who used the system to have the highest level of clearance required by any and all data on the system. If a system held top secret data, only users with this clearance could use the system. Now many military systems work with multiple security levels, which is done by compartmentalizing the data. These types of systems can support users with high and low clearances simultaneously.

System-High Security Mode

A system is operating in *system-high security mode* when all users have a security clearance or authorization to access the information but not necessarily a need-to-know for all the information processed on the system. So the difference between the dedicated security mode and the system-high security mode is that in the dedicated security mode, all users have a need-to-know pertaining to *all* data on the system; in system-high security mode, all users have a need-to-know pertaining to *some* of the data.

This mode also requires all users to have the highest level of clearance required by any and all data on the system. However, just because a user has the necessary security level to access an object, the user could be restricted via the access control matrix because they do not have a need-to-know pertaining to that specific object.

Compartmented Security Mode

A system is operating in *compartmented security mode* when all users have the clearance to access all the information processed by the system, but might not have the need-to-know and formal access approval. In compartmented security mode, users are restricted to being able to access some information because they do not need to access it to perform the functions of their jobs and they have not been given formal approval to access this data. In this mode, users can access a segment, or compartment, of data only.

The objective is to ensure that the minimum possible number of people learn of information at each level. Compartments are security levels (top secret, secret, and so on) with limited number of subjects cleared to access data at each level. *Compartmented mode workstations (CMW)* enable users to process multiple compartments of data at the same time, if they have the necessary clearance.

Multilevel Security Mode

A system is operating in *multilevel security mode* when it permits two or more classification levels of information to be processed at the same time when all the users do not have the clearance or formal approval to access all the information being processed by the system.

The Bell-LaPadula model is an example of a multilevel security model because it handles multiple information classifications at a number of different security levels within one system.

References

www.tpub.com/ans/51.htm

http://security.isu.edu/isl/atcse385.html

www.cs.nps.navy.mil/curricula/tracks/security/notes/chap02_17.html

http://security.tsu.ru/info/rainbow/std003.htm

http://chacs.nrl.navy.mil/publications/CHACS/1997/jifi_web/node24.html

www.dss.mil/isec/ch8nispom/toc.htm

Trust and Assurance

We discussed the TCB concept in the section "Trusted Computing Base" and explained that no system is really secure because with enough resources almost any system can be compromised in one way or another; however, systems can provide levels of trust. The trust level tells the customer how much he can expect out of this system, what level of security it will provide, and the *assurance* that the system will act in a correct and predictable manner in each and every computing situation.

The TCB is made up of all the protection mechanisms within a system (software, hardware, firmware). All of these mechanisms need to work in an orchestrated way to enforce all the requirements of a security policy. When evaluated, these mechanisms are tested, their designs are inspected, the supporting documentation is reviewed and evaluated. How the system is developed, maintained, and even delivered to the customer are all under review when the trust for a system is being gauged. All of these different evaluation components are put through an evaluation process to assign the correct level of trust and assurance. Customers then use this assignment, or rating, to determine which system best fits their security needs.

Assurance and trust are similar in nature, but slightly different when we are looking at rating computer systems. A trusted system means that all protection mechanisms work together to process sensitive data for many types of uses and still keeps the same secure computing environment. Assurance looks at the same issues but with more depth and detail. Systems that provide higher levels of trust mean that their designs were thoroughly inspected, the development stages were reviewed, the technical specifications and test plans were evaluated, and the system was tested extensively. You can buy a car and you can trust it, but you have a much deeper sense of assurance of that trust if you know how it was built, what it was built with, who built it, what tests it was put through, and how it performed in many different situations.

In the Orange Book, which we will address shortly, the lower security level ratings look at a system's performance and testing results to produce a security rating, but the higher security level ratings look more at the system design, specifications, development procedures, supporting documentation, and the testing results. The protection mechanisms in the higher security level systems are not much different than those in the lower security level systems, but the way they were designed and built is under much more scrutiny. With this extra scrutiny comes higher levels of assurance of the trust that can be put into a system.

Systems Evaluation Methods

A *security evaluation* examines the security-relevant parts of a system, meaning the TCB, access control mechanisms, reference monitor, kernel, protection mechanisms. The relationship and interaction between these components are also evaluated. There are different methods of evaluating and assigning security and trust levels to systems. The reason that there is more than one type of security evaluation process is that the methods and ideologies have evolved over time and because various parts of the world look at computer security differently and rate some aspects of security higher than others.

Each method will be explained and then at the end of the section they will be compared to each other to show the differences and strengths, and look at where security evaluation methods are heading.

The Orange Book

The U.S. Department of Defense developed the *Trusted Computer System Evaluation Criteria (TCSEC)*, which is used to evaluate operating systems, applications, and systems. This evaluation criteria is published in a book with an orange cover, which is called appropriately the *Orange Book*. (We like to keep things simple in security!) Customers use the security rating that the criteria presents so they have a metric to use when comparing different systems. It also provides direction for manufactures so they know what specifications to build to, and provides a one-stop evaluation process so customers do not need to have individual components within the systems evaluated.

The Orange Book evaluates products to assess if they contain the security properties they claim and evaluate if the product is appropriate for a specific application or function. The Orange Book looks at the functionality, effectiveness, and assurance of a system during its evaluation and it uses classes that were devised to address typical patterns of security requirements.

TCSEC provides a graded classification of systems that is divided into hierarchical divisions of security levels:

A Verified protection

B Mandatory protection

C Discretionary protection

D Minimal security

The classification A represents the highest level of security and D represents the lowest level of security.

Each division can have one or more numbered classes and each has a corresponding set of requirements that must be met for a system to achieve that particular rating. The classes with higher numbers indicate a greater degree of trust and security. So B2 would offer more trust than B1, and C2 would offer more trust than C1.

The criteria includes four main topics: security policy, accountability, assurance, and documentation, but these actually break down into seven different areas:

- **Security policy** The policy must be explicit and well defined and enforced by the mechanisms within the system.

- **Identification**   Individual subjects must be uniquely identified.

- **Labels**   Access control labels must be associated properly with objects.

- **Documentation**   This includes the test, design, specification documents, user guides, and manuals.

- **Accountability**   Audit data must be captured and protected to enforce accountability.

- **Life cycle assurance**   Software, hardware, and firmware must be able to be tested individually to ensure that each enforces the security policy in an effective manner throughout its lifetime.

- **Continuous protection**   The security mechanisms and the system as a whole must perform predictably and acceptably in different situations continuously.

These categories are evaluated independently, but the rating that is assigned at the end does not specify these different objectives individually. The rating is a sum total of these items.

Each division and class incorporates the requirements of the ones below it. This means that C2 must meet its criteria requirements and all of C1 requirements, and B3 has its requirements to fulfill along with those of C1, C2, B1, and B2. Each division or class ups the ante on security requirements and is expected to fulfill the requirements of all the classes and divisions below it.

When a vendor submits a product for evaluation, the product is submitted to the National Computer Security Center (NCSC). The process of evaluation is called the Trusted Products Evaluation Program (TPEP) and successfully evaluated products are placed on the Evaluated Product List (EPL) with their corresponding rating. When consumers are interested in certain products and systems, they can check the EPLs to find out the security level that are assigned to these products.

Division D—Minimal Protection

There is only one class in this division and it is reserved for systems that have been evaluated but fail to meet the criteria and requirements of the higher divisions.

Division C—Discretionary Protection

C1

Discretionary Security Protection   Discretionary access control is based on individuals and/or groups. It requires a separation of users and information, and identification and authentication of individual entities. Some type of access control is necessary so users can ensure that their data will not be accessed and corrupted by others. The system architecture must supply a protected execution domain so privileged system processes are not adversely affected by lower-privileged processes. There must be specific ways of validating the system's operational integrity. The documentation requirements include design documentation, which shows the way the system was built to include protection mechanisms, test documentation (test plan and results), a facility manual so companies know how to install and configure the system's correctly, and user manuals.

The environment that would require this rating would be where users are processing information at the same sensitivity level; thus, strict access control and auditing measures are not required. It would be a trusted environment with low security concerns.

C2

Controlled Access Protection   Users need to be identified individually to provide more precise access control and auditing functionality. Logical access control mechanisms are used to enforce authentication and the uniqueness of each individual's identification. Security-relevant events are audited and these records must be protected from unauthorized modification. The architecture must provide resource, or object, isolation so proper protection can be applied to the resource and that actions taken upon it can be properly audited. The *object reuse* concept must also be invoked, meaning that any medium holding data must not contain any remnants of information after it is released for another subject to use. If a subject uses a segment of memory, that memory space must not hold any information after the subject is done using it. The same is true for storage media, objects being populated, temporary files being created —all data must be efficiently erased once the subject is done with that medium.

This class requires a more granular method of providing access control. The system must enforce strict logon procedures and provide decision-making capabilities when subjects request access to objects. A C2 system cannot guarantee that it will not be compromised, but it supplies a level of protection that would make compromising attempts harder to accomplish.

The environment that would require systems with a C2 rating would be one that contains users that are trusted, but a certain level of accountability is required. C2, overall, is regarded to be the most reasonable class for commercial applications, but the level of protection is still weak.

Division B—Mandatory Protection

Mandatory access control is enforced by the use of security labels. The architecture is based on the Bell-LaPadula security model and evidence of reference monitor enforcement must be available.

B1

Labeled Security   Each data object must contain a classification label and each subject must have a clearance label. When a subject attempts to access an object, the system must compare the subject and object's security labels to ensure the requested actions are acceptable. Data leaving the system must also contain an accurate security label. The security policy is based on an informal statement and the design specifications are reviewed and verified.

It is intended for environments that require systems to handle classified data.

 NOTE   Security labels are not required until security rating B; thus, C2 does not require security labels but B1 does.

B2

Structured Protection   The security policy is clearly defined and documented and the system design and implementation is subjected to more thorough review and testing procedures. This class requires more stringent authentication mechanisms and well-defined interfaces between layers. Subjects and devices require labels, and the system must not allow covert channels. A trusted path for logon and authentication processes must be in place, which means there are no trapdoors. There is a separation of operator and administration functions within the system to provide more trusted and protected operational functionality. Distinct address spaces must be provided to isolate processes, and a covert channel analysis is conducted. This class adds assurance by adding requirements to the design of the system.

The environment that would require B2 systems could process sensitive data that requires a higher degree of security. This environment would require systems that are relatively resistant to penetration and compromise.

(A trusted path means that the user can be sure that he is talking to a genuine copy of the operating system.)

B3

Security Domains   In this class, more granularity is provided in each protection mechanism and the programming code that is not necessary to support the security policy is excluded. The design and implementation should not provide too much complexity because as the complexity of a system increases, the ability of the individuals who need to test, maintain, and configure it reduces; thus, the overall security can be threatened. The reference monitor components must be small enough to test properly and be tamperproof. The security administrator role is clearly defined and the system must be able to recover from failures without its security level being compromised. When the system starts up and loads its operating system and components, it must be done in an initial secure state to ensure that any weakness of the system cannot be taken advantage of in this slice of time.

An environment that requires B3 systems is a highly secured environment that processes very sensitive information. It requires systems that are highly resistant to penetration.

Division A—Verified Protection

Formal methods are used to ensure all subjects and objects are controlled with the necessary discretionary and mandatory access controls. The design, development, implementation, and documentation are looked at in a formal and detailed way. The security mechanisms between B3 and A1 are not very different, but the way that the system was designed and developed is evaluated in a much more structured and stringent procedure.

A1

Verified Design   The architecture and protection features are not much different than systems that achieve a B3 rating, but the assurance of an A1 system is higher than a B3 system because the formality in the way the system was designed, the way the specifications were developed, and the level of detail in the verification techniques. Formal techniques are used to prove the equivalence between the TCB specifications and the security policy model. More stringent change configuration is put in place with the development of an A1 system and the overall design can be verified. In many cases, even the way that the system is delivered to the customer is under scrutiny to ensure that there is no way of compromising the system before it reaches its destination.

An environment that would require A1 systems is the most secure of secured environments. This environment deals with top secret information and cannot adequately trust anyone using the systems without strict authentication, restrictions, and auditing.

 NOTE TCSEC addresses confidentiality, but not integrity. Functionality of the security mechanisms and the assurance of those mechanisms are not evaluated separately, but combined and rated as a whole.

References

www.boran.com/security/tcsec.html

http://williamstallings.com/Extras/Security-Notes/lectures/trusted.html

www.jos.org/doc/security/ob_index.html

Rainbow Series

Why are there so many colors in the rainbow? Answer: Because there are so many security topics in the computing world that needed names.

The Orange Book mainly addresses government and military requirements and expectations from their computer systems. Many people within the security field have pointed out several deficiencies of the Orange Book particularly when it is being applied to systems that are to be used in commercial areas instead of government organizations. The following summarizes a majority of the troubling issues security practitioners have expressed about the use of the Orange Book:

- The Orange Book looks specifically at the operating system and not other issues like networking, databases, and so on.

- The Orange Book focuses mainly on one attribute of security, confidentiality, and not at integrity, availability, and authenticity.

- The Orange Book works with government classifications and not the protection classifications that commercial industries use.

- The Orange Book has a relatively small number of ratings, which means many different aspects of security are not evaluated and rated.

The Orange Book places great emphasis on controlling which users can access a system and virtually ignores controlling what those users do with the information once they are authorized. Authorized users can, and usually do, cause more damage to data than outside attackers. Commercial organizations have expressed more concern about the integrity of their data while the military organizations stress that their top concern is confidentiality. Because of these different goals, the Orange Book is a better evaluation tool for government and military systems.

Because the Orange Book focuses on the operating system, many other areas of security were left out. The Orange Book provides a broad framework for building and evaluating trusted systems, but it leaves many questions about topics other than just an operating system unanswered. So more books were written to extend the coverage of the Orange Book into other areas of security. These books provide detailed information and interpretations of certain Orange Book requirements and describe the evaluation processes. These books are collectively called the *Rainbow Series* because each book has a different color cover.

For an explanation of each book and its usage, please refer to the following references.

References

www.radium.ncsc.mil/tpep/library/rainbow

http://csrc.ncsl.nist.gov/secpubs/rainbow/

www.fas.org/irp/nsa/rainbow.htm

http://secinf.net/rainbowe.html

Red Book

The Orange Book addresses single-system security, but networks are a combination of systems and the network needs to be secure without having to fully trust each and every system connected to it. The *Trusted Network Interpretation (TNI)*, also called the *Red Book* because of the color of its cover, addresses security evaluation topics for networks and network components. It addresses isolated local area networks and wide area internetwork systems.

Like the Orange Book, the Red Book does not supply specific details about how to implement security mechanisms; instead, it provides a framework for securing different types of networks. A network has a security policy, architecture, and design, as does an operating system, and subjects accessing objects on the network need to be controlled, monitored, and audited. In a network, the subject could be a workstation and an object could be a network service on a server.

The Red Book rates confidentiality and integrity of data and operations that happen within a network and the network products. Data and labels need to be protected from unauthorized modification and the integrity of information as it is transferred needs to be ensured. The source and destination mechanisms used for messages are evaluated and tested to ensure that modification is not allowed.

Encryption and protocols are components that provide a lot of the security within a network, and the Red Book measures their functionality, strength, and assurance.

The following is a brief overview of the security items addressed in the Red Book:

- Communication integrity

  - **Authentication**   Protects against masquerading and playback attacks. Mechanisms include digital signatures, encryption, timestamp, and passwords.

  - **Message integrity**   Protects protocol header, routing information, and the packet payload from being modified. Mechanisms include message authentication and encryption.

  - **Nonrepudiation**   Ensures that a sender cannot deny sending a message. Mechanisms include encryption, digital signatures, and notary.

- Denial of service prevention

  - **Continuity of operations**   Ensures that network is available even if attacked. Mechanisms include fault tolerant and redundant systems and the capability to reconfigure network parameters in case of an emergency.

  - **Network management**   Monitors network performance and identifies attacks and failures. Mechanisms include components that enable network administrators to monitor and restrict resource access.

- Compromise protection

  - **Data confidentiality**   Protects data from being accessed in an unauthorized method during transmission. Mechanisms include access controls, encryption, and physical protection of cables.

  - **Traffic flow confidentiality**   Ensures that unauthorized entities are not aware of routing information or frequency of communication via traffic analysis. Mechanisms include padding messages, sending noise, or false messages.

  - **Selective routing**   Routes messages in a way to avoid specific threats. Mechanisms include network configuration and routing tables.

Assurance is derived from a theory of how things should work and then compared to how they actually perform. Assurance is also derived by testing configurations in many different scenarios, evaluating engineering practices, and validating and verifying security claims. The Red Book ratings available are the following:

- None
- C1—Minimum
- C2—Fair
- B2—Good

TCSEC was introduced in 1985 and retired in December 2000. It was the first methodical and logical set of standards developed to secure computer systems. It was greatly influential in several counties who based their evaluation standards off the TCSEC guidelines. TCSEC was finally replaced with the Common Criteria.

Information Technology Security Evaluation Criteria

The *Information Technology Security Evaluation Criteria (ITSEC)* was the first attempt of establishing a single standard for evaluating security attributes of computer systems by many European countries. ITSEC is only used in Europe, not internationally. The United States looked to the Orange Book and Rainbow Series, and Europe employed the ITSEC to evaluate and rate computer systems. (Actually, today everyone is migrating to the Common Criteria explained in the next section.)

There are two main attributes of a system when it is evaluated under ITSEC or TCSEC: functionality and assurance. When the functionality of a system is being evaluated the services that are provided to the users (access control mechanisms, auditing, authentication, and so on) are examined and measured. System functionality can be very diverse in nature because systems are developed differently just to provide different functionality to users. Nonetheless, when functionality is evaluated, it is tested to see if the system delivers what it says it delivers. Assurance, on the other hand, is more abstract and harder to test. Assurance is the degree of confidence in a security component, and its effectiveness and capability to perform consistently. Assurance is generally tested by examining development practices, documentation, configuration management, and testing mechanisms.

It is possible for two systems that provide the same functionality to have very different assurance levels. This is because of the underlying mechanisms providing the functionality, and the way it was developed, engineered, and implemented. ITSEC actually separates these two attributes and rates them separately, whereas TCSEC clumps them together and assigns them one rating (D through A1).

When we look back at our example of two systems that provide the same functionality but have very different assurance levels, using the TCSEC approach will make this individual factor hard to distinguish. Under the ITSEC approach, the functionality is rated separately from the assurance. In the ITSEC criteria, classes F1 to F10 rate the functionality of the system, whereas E0 to E6 rate the assurance of a system.

So the fundamental difference between ITSEC and TCSEC is that TCSEC bundles functionality and assurance, whereas ITSEC evaluates these two attributes separately.

The following is a general mapping of the two evaluation schemes to show you their relationship to each other:

ITSEC	TCSEC
E0	= D
F1 + E	= C1
F2 + E2	= C2
F3 + E3	= B1
F4 + E4	= B2
F5 + E5	= B3
F5 + E6	= A1
F6	= Systems the provide high integrity
F7	= Systems that provide high availability
F8	= Systems that provide data integrity during communication
F9	= Systems that provide high confidentiality (like cryptographic devices)
F10	= Networks with high demands on confidentiality and integrity

As you can see, a majority of the ITSEC ratings can be mapped to the Orange Book ratings, but then ITSEC took a step farther and added F6 through F10 for specific needs consumers might have that the Orange Book does not address.

ITSEC is a criteria for both security products and security systems and refers to both as the target of evaluation (TOE). So if you are reading literature discussing the ITSEC rating of a product and it states that the TOE has a rating of F1 and E5, you know that the TOE is the product that was evaluated and that it has a low functionality rating and a high assurance rating.

References

www.cesg.gov.uk/assurance/iacs/itsec/index.htm

www.cordis.lu/infosec/src/crit.htm

www.iwar.org.uk/comsec/resources/standards/itsec.htm

Common Criteria

*"The TCSEC is too hard, the ITSEC is too soft, but the Common Criteria is just right,"
said the little bear.*

The Orange and Red Book provided evaluation schemes that were too rigid and ITSEC attempted to provide a more flexible approach by separating the functionality and assurance attributes and considering the evaluation of entire security systems. However, this flexibility added complexity because evaluators could mix and match functionality and assurance ratings, which ended up in too many classifications to keep straight. Because we are a species that continues to try to get it right, the next attempt for an effective and usable evaluation criteria was the *Common Criteria*.

In 1990, the International Organization for Standardization (ISO) identified the need of international standard evaluation criteria to be used globally. The Common Criteria project started in 1993 when several organizations came together to combine and align existing and emerging evaluation criteria (TCSEC, ITSEC, Canadian Trusted Computer Product Evaluation Criteria (CTCPEC), and the Federal Criteria). It was developed through a collaboration among national security standards organizations within the United States, Canada, France, Germany, the United Kingdom, and the Netherlands.

The benefit of having a worldwide recognized and accepted criteria helps consumers by reducing the complexity of the ratings and eliminating the need to understand the definition and meaning of different ratings within different evaluation schemes. This also helps manufacturers because now they can build to one specific set of requirements if they want to sell their products internationally, instead of having to meet several different ratings with varying rules and requirements.

The Orange Book evaluated all systems by how they compared to the Bell-LaPadula model. The Common Criteria provides more flexibility by evaluating a product against a protection profile, which is structured to address specific security problems. So while the Orange Book said, "Everyone march this direction in this form using this path," the Common Criteria says, "Okay, what are the threats we are facing today and what are the best ways of battling them?"

An evaluation is carried out on a product and is assigned an *evaluation assurance level (EAL)*. The thoroughness and stringent testing increases in detailed-oriented tasks as the levels increase. The Common Criteria has seven assurance levels. The ranges go from EAL1, where functionality testing takes place, to EAL7, where thorough testing is performed and the system design is verified.

The Common Criteria uses *protection profiles* to evaluate products. The protection profile contains the set of security requirements, their meaning and reasoning, and the corresponding EAL rating. The profile describes the environmental assumptions, the objectives, and functional and assurance level expectations. Each relevant threat is listed along with how it is to be controlled by specific objectives. It also justifies the assurance level and requirements for the strength of each protection mechanism.

The protection profile provides a means for a consumer, or others, to identify specific security needs; this is the security problem that is to be conquered. The profile goes on to provide the necessary goals and protection mechanisms to achieve the necessary level of security and a list of the things that can go wrong during this type of system development. This list is used by the engineers who develop the system and the same list is used by the evaluators to make sure the engineers dotted every *i* and crossed every *t*.

The Common Criteria was developed to stick to evaluation classes but also to retain some degree of flexibility. Protection profiles were developed to describe the functionality, assurance, description, and rationale of its findings.

Like other evaluation criteria before it, Common Criteria works to answer two basic and general questions about products being evaluated: what does it do (functionality), and how sure are you of that (assurance)? This system sets up a framework for consumers to be able to clearly specify their security issues and problems and developers to specify their security solution to those problems and evaluators to unequivocally determine what the product actually accomplishes.

A protection profile contains the following five sections:

- **Descriptive elements**   Name of profile and a description of the security problem that was to be solved.

- **Rationale**   Justification of the profile and a more detailed description of the protection problem to be solved. The environment, usage assumptions, and threats are illustrated along with guidance on the0 security policies that can be supported by products and systems that conform to this profile.

- **Functional requirements**   A protection boundary is established, meaning that threats or compromises that were within this boundary could be countered. The product or system must provide the boundary established in this section.

- **Development assurance requirements** The development phases from design to implementation have specific requirements established that the product or system must meet.

- **Evaluation assurance requirements** Establishes the type and intensity of the evaluation.

The evaluation process is just one leg of determining the security of a product or system. Once a product or system achieves a specific rating, it only applies to that particular version and only to certain configurations of that product or system. So if a company buys a firewall product because it has a high security rating, it doesn't mean the next version of that software automatically inherits that rating. The next version will need to go though its own evaluation review. If this same company buys the firewall product and installs it with configurations not recommended, the level of security they were hoping to achieve can easily go down the drain. So all of this rating stuff is a formalized method of a system being evaluated in a lab. When the product is implemented into a real environment, other factors than just its rating need to be addressed and assessed to ensure that it is properly protecting resources and the environment.

References

http://csrc.nist.gov/cc

www.commoncriteria.org/

www.rycombe.com/cc.htm

Certification versus Accreditation

We have gone through the different types of evaluation criteria a system can be appraised against to receive a specific rating. This is a very formalized process and the evaluated system or product will then be placed on an EPL indicating what rating it achieved. Consumers can check this listing and compare the different products and systems to see how they rank against each other in the property of security. However, once a consumer buys this product and sets it up in his environment, it does not guarantee security because security is made up of system administration, physical security, installation, and configuration mechanisms within the environment, and other security issues. To fairly say a system is secure, all of these items need to be taken into account. The rating is just one piece in the puzzle of security.

Certification

Certification is the technical evaluation of the security components and their compliance for the purpose of accreditation. A certification process can use safeguard evaluation, risk analysis, verification, testing, and auditing techniques to assess the appropriateness of a specific system, which processes a certain classification level of information within a particular environment. For example, if Dan were the security officer for a company that just purchased new systems to be used to process their confidential data, he would like to know if these systems are appropriate for these tasks and if they are going to provide the necessary level of protection. He could pay a company that specializes in these matters to perform the necessary procedures to certify the systems. The company will perform tests on the software configurations, hardware, firmware, design, implementation, system procedures, and the physical, and communication controls. The certification will indicate the good, bad, and the ugly about the security protection level and the mechanisms that support it within these systems and how they work within the given environment. If the outcome of this process looks good to Dan, he will take it to his management to start the accreditation process.

Accreditation

Accreditation is the formal acceptance of the adequacy of a system's overall security by the management. The certification information is presented to management, or the responsible body, and it is up to the management to ask questions, review the reports and findings, and decide upon the acceptance of the safeguards and if any corrective action needs to take place. Once satisfied with the system's overall security as it is presented, management makes a formal accreditation statement. By doing this, management is stating that it understands the level of protection the system will provide in its current environment and understands the security risks associated with installing this system.

So certification is the process of assessing the security mechanisms and controls and evaluating their effectiveness. Accreditation is management's official acceptance of the information in the certification process findings.

Because software, systems, and environments continually change and evolve, the certification and accreditation should also continue to take place. Any major addition of software, change to the system, or modification of the environment should initiate a new certification and accreditation cycle.

Open versus Closed Systems

Computer systems can be developed to integrate easily with other systems and products (open systems) or can be developed to be more proprietary and work with only a subset of other systems and products (closed systems). The following sections describe the difference between these approaches.

Open Systems

I want to be able to work and play well with others.

Systems that are described as *open* have an architecture that has published specifications, which enables third-party vendors to develop add-on components and devices. This type of architecture provides interoperability between products by different vendors of different operating systems, applications, and hardware devices. This interoperability is provided by all the vendors involved who follow specific standards and provide interfaces that enable each system to easily communicate with other systems and allow add-ons to hook into the system easily.

A majority of the systems in use today are open systems. The reason that an administrator can have Windows NT 4.0, Windows 2000, Macintosh, and Unix computers on the same network communicating easily is because these platforms are open. If a vendor creates a closed system, they are restricting their sales to proprietary environments instead of to the whole world.

Closed Systems

I only want to work and play with you and him.

Systems that are referred to as *closed* use an architecture that does not follow industry's standards. Interoperability and standard interfaces are not employed to enable easy communication between different types of systems and add-on features. Closed systems are proprietary, meaning that the system can only communicate with like systems.

A closed architecture provides more security to the system because it does not have as many doorways in, and it operates in a more secluded environment than open environments. Because a closed system is proprietary, there are not as many tools to thwart the security mechanisms and not as many people who understand its design, language, and security weaknesses to exploit. However, more security brings less functionality. A majority of the systems today are built with open architecture to enable them to work with other types of systems, easily share information, and take advantage of the functionality that third-party add-ons bring. However, this opens the doors to more hacks, cracks, and attacks. You can't have your cake and eat it too.

A Few Threats to Security Models and Architectures

Now that we have talked about how everything is suppose to work, let's take a quick look at some of the things that can go wrong when designing a system.

Software almost always has bugs and vulnerabilities because the rich functionality demanded by users brings about deep complexity, which usually opens the doors to problems in the computer world. Also, vulnerabilities are always around because attackers continually find ways of using system operations and functionality in a negative and destructive way. Just like there will always be cops and robbers, there will always be attackers and security professionals. It is a game of trying to outwit each other and seeing who will put the necessary effort into winning the game.

Covert Channels

example

A *covert channel* is a way for an entity to receive information in an unauthorized manner. It is an information flow that is not controlled by a security mechanism. This type of information path is usually not used for communication; thus, the system does not properly protect this path because the developers never envisioned information being passed this way. For an entity to receive information in this manner violates the security policy of the system.

There are two types of covert channels: timing and storage. In a *covert timing channel*, one process relays information to another by modulating its use of system resources. The modulation of system resources can be accessing the hard drive, using excessive CPU cycles, or head placement on a hard drive track. A *covert storage channel* is when a process writes data to a storage location and another process directly, or indirectly, reads it. The problem occurs when the processes are at different security levels, and therefore not supposed to be sharing sensitive data.

is this a good example

A real world example of a covert channel is when a computer is infected by a Trojan horse. The firewall protecting the environment could allow only HTTP traffic through port 80. The firewall allows this type of communication because it expects it to be used only for Web access by the users behind the firewall. But if the Trojan horse uses this communication path as a way to communicate to the attacker that planted it, this is a covert channel because it is using a communication path in a way that was unintended and that violates the security policy.

Countermeasures

Because all operating systems have some type of covert channels, it is not always feasible to attempt to get rid of them all. The amount of acceptable covert channels usually depends on the security rating of a system. A system that has a B2 rating has less convert channels than a C1 system. There is not much a user can do to countermeasure these channels; instead, they are addressed when constructing and developing a system.

In the Orange Book, covert channels in operating systems are not addressed until the security level B2 and above because these are the systems that would be holding data sensitive enough for others to go through all the necessary trouble to access data in this fashion.

Other types of covert channels can happen within an environment, as in the example of the Trojan horse using HTTP as a communication channel.

- It is unlikely that intrusion detection systems will detect this type of attack within an operating system, but it always worth a try.

- A network and host intrusion detection system can be more successful in identifying covert channels within the network.

- Auditing should be enabled to try and detect a covert channel use pattern, although it can be hard to detect within an operating system or product. Auditing for covert channel violations within the network could be much more successful.

Back Doors

In the programming world, *back doors* are also called *maintenance hooks*. They are instructions within software that only the developer knows about and can invoke. It is placed in the software for easy maintenance and provides the capability of adding features without having to reinstall the software. It also allows the developer to view and edit the code without having to go through regular access controls. During the development phase of the software, these can be very useful, but if they are not removed before going into production, they can cause major security issues.

The back door is usually initiated by a random sequence of keys that provides access into the software without having to go through normal access control and security checks and mechanisms.

An application that has a maintenance hook enables the developer to execute specific commands by using a specific sequence of keys. Once this is done successfully, the developer is inside the application looking directly at the code. She might do this to watch specific problem areas within the code, check variable population, export more code into the program, or fix problems that she sees that are taking place. Although this sounds nice and healthy, if an attacker finds out about this maintenance hook, more sinister actions may be taken. So all back doors need to be removed from software before it goes into production.

Backdoor (handwritten margin note)

Countermeasures

Because back doors are inserted by programmers, they are the ones who usually take them out before the programs and systems go into production. Code reviews, and unit and integration testing should always be looking out for back doors in case the programmer overlooked extracting them. Because back doors are within the code of an application or system, there is not much a user can do to prevent their presence, but when a vendor finds out that a back door exists in their product, they usually develop and release a patch to reduce this vulnerability. The following lists some preventative measures against back doors:

- A host intrusion detection system can be used to watch for an attacker using a back door into the system.
- File system permissions can be set to try and protect configuration files and sensitive information from being modified.
- Strict access control can be added to prevent access to the system in the first place.
- File system encryption can be used to protect sensitive information.
- Auditing should be in place to detect any type of back door use.

Timing Issues

Specific attacks can take place on a system that take advantage of the way a system processes requests and performs tasks. A timing attack, or *asynchronous attack*, deals with the timing difference of the sequences of steps a system uses to complete a task. For example, if a system uses an autoexec.bat file, the system first goes through a boot process and it will check to see if an autoexec.bat file exists on the system. If one does not exist, it will continue with its bootup procedures, but if it does exist, it will open the file and process it line by line. There is a timing difference of when the system checks to see if an autoexec.bat file exists and actually accesses and opens the file. A *time-of-check versus time-of-use (TOC/TOU)* attack could replace the autoexec.bat with a different autoexec.bat that compromises the system before the system actually initiates it.

now?, (handwritten margin note)

TOC/TOU attacks are also called race conditions where an attacker attempts to gain privilege by racing the system or program to a resource. This flaw can be created when the system, or application, splits up the operations of verifying credentials and providing access to a resource.

Countermeasures

It would take a dedicated attacker with great precision to perform this type of attack, but it is possible and has been done. The following can be used to protect against this type of attack:

- A host intrusion detection system can be used to watch for this type of suspicious *detective* behavior.

- File system permissions and encryption can be set to protect sensitive files.

- Strict access control measures can be used to prevent an intruder from accessing the system in the first place.

- Auditing should be in place to catch patterns or indications of TOC/TOU attacks.

Buffer Overflows

Buffer overflows happen when programs do not check the length of data that is inputted into a program and then processed by the CPU. The programmer can set the value of a required input to be 80 characters, but does not ensure that only up to 80 are actually inputted from a user or another program. If more than 80 characters are entered, this extra data overflows and is executed by the CPU's execution stack. This extra data can launch another program or set of code that was devised to perform disruptive behavior in the system. This is sometimes referred to as "smashing the stack." A buffer overflow is usually aimed at systems that let the overrun software be executed with privileged rights, meaning the software executes in a more privileged mode and has access to more system resources.

Countermeasures

The first and best countermeasure to buffer overflows is proper programming and good coding practices. There are also several types of tools available to help prevent buffer overflows. Some tools monitor dynamic-link library (DLL) usage and some tools provide a wrapper around the kernel that monitors calls and watches for known buffer overflow attacks.

There is not much a user can do to prevent buffer overflows because they are part of the program code, but when vendors discover these issues, they develop and distribute patches to reduce this type of vulnerability. The following can be used to protect against buffer overflows:

- A host intrusion detection system can be used to watch for this type of suspicious behavior.

- File system permissions and encryption can be set to protect sensitive files.

- Strict access control measures can be used to prevent an intruder from accessing the system in the first place.

- Auditing should be in place to catch patterns or indications of buffer overflow attacks.

Summary

The architecture of a computer system is very important and covers many different types of topics. The system has to make sure that memory is properly segregated and protected, ensure that only authorized subjects access objects, ensure that untrusted processes cannot perform activities that would put other processes at risk, control the flow of information, and define a domain of resources for each subject. It also must ensure that if the computer experiences any type of disruption, it will not result in an unsecure state. Many of these issues are dealt with in the system's security policy and the security model is built to support the requirements of the security policy.

Once the security policy, architecture, and model have been developed, the computer operating system, or product, must be built, tested, evaluated, and rated. Evaluation is done by comparing the system to predefined criteria. The rating that is assigned to the system depends on how it fulfills the requirements in the criteria. Customers use this rating to understand what they are really buying and how much they can trust this new product. Once the customer buys the product, it must be tested within their own environment to make sure it meets their company's needs, which takes place through certification and accreditation.

Quick Tips

- A system can have the exact same hardware, software, and applications, but provide different levels of protection because of the different security policies and security models that the systems were built upon.

- A CPU contains a control unit, which controls the timing of the execution of application instructions, an ALU, which performs mathematical functions and logical operations, and primary storage, which is where data is temporarily held before being processed by the CPU.

- Most systems use protection rings. The more privileged processes run in the lower ring numbers and have access to all or most of the system resources. Applications run in higher numbered rings and have access to a smaller amount of resources.

- Operating system processes are executed in system mode and applications are executed in user mode.

- Applications are given a segment of memory called real storage to hold data and instructions.

- Secondary storage is nonvolatile and can be a hard drive, CD-ROM, floppy drive, tape backup, or a Zip drive.

- Virtual storage combines RAM and secondary storage so the system seems to have a large bank of memory.

- A deadlock situation occurs when two processes are trying to access the same resource at the same time or if a process commits a resource and does not release it.

- Security mechanisms can focus on different issues, work at different layers, and vary in complexity.

- The more complex a security mechanism, the less amount of assurance it can provide.

- Not all system components fall under the TCB; only those that enforce the security policy directly and need to be. These components are within the security perimeter.

- Components that make up the TCB are hardware, software, security components, and firmware because they all provide some type of security protection.

- A security perimeter is an imaginary boundary that has trusted components within it (those that make up the TCB) and untrusted components on the outside of the boundary.

- The reference monitor is an abstract machine that ensures that all subjects have the necessary access rights before accessing objects.

- The security kernel is the mechanism that actually enforces the rules of the reference monitor.

- The security kernel must isolate processes carrying out the reference monitor concept, must be tamperproof, must invoke the reference monitor for each access attempt, and must be small enough to test properly.

- A security domain is all the objects available to a subject.

- Processes need to be isolated, which can be done through segmented memory addressing.

- A security policy is a set of rules that dictate how sensitive data is to be managed, protected, and distributed. It provides the security goals that the system must accomplish.

- The level of security a system provides depends on how well it enforces the security policy.

- A multilevel security system processes data at different classifications (security levels), and users with different clearances (security levels) can use the system.

- Processes should be assigned least privilege so they have just enough system privileges to fulfill their tasks and no more.

- Some systems provide functionality at different layers of the system, which is called layering. This separates the processes and provides more protection for them individually.

- Data hiding is when the processes at different layers do not know about each other, and therefore do not know about data at different layers. This provides more protection for the data.

- When a class of objects is assigned permissions, it is called abstraction.

- A security model maps the abstract goals of a security policy to computer system terms and concepts. It gives the security policy structure and provides a framework for the system.

- The Bell-LaPadula model deals only with confidentiality and the Biba and Clark-Wilson models deal with data integrity.

- A state machine model deals with the different states a system can enter. If a system starts in a secure state and all activities that take place in the system are secure, the system will never end up in an insecure state.

- A lattice provides an upper bound and a lower bound of authorized access.

- An information flow security model does not permit data to flow to an object in an insecure manner.

- The Bell-LaPadula model has a simple security rule, which means that a subject cannot read data from a higher level (no read up). The *-property rule means that a subject cannot write to an object at a lower level (no write down).

- The Biba model does not let subjects write to objects at a higher level (no write up) and it does not let subjects read data at a lower level (no read down). This is done to protect the integrity of the data.

- The Bell-LaPadula model is used mainly in military systems and the Biba and Clark-Wilson models are used in the commercial sector.

- The Clark-Wilson model enforces subjects accessing objects through approved programs, separation of duties, and auditing.

- If a system is working in a dedicated security mode, then the system only deals with one level of data classification and all users must have this level of clearance to be able to use the system.

- Compartmented and multilevel security modes enable the system to process data classified at different classification levels.

- Trust means that a system uses all of its protection mechanisms properly to process sensitive data for many types of users. Assurance is the level of confidence you have in this trust and that the protection mechanisms behave properly in all circumstances continuously.

- The lower ratings in the different evaluation criteria review the performance of a system and its testing results, and the higher ratings look at this information and the system design, development procedures, and documentation.

- The Orange Book, also called Trusted Computer System Evaluation Criteria (TCSEC), was developed to evaluate systems built to be used mainly by the military.

- In the Orange Book, D classification means a system provides minimal security and is used for systems that were evaluated but failed to meet the criteria of higher divisions.

- In the Orange Book, the C division deals with discretionary protection (need-to-know) and division B deals with mandatory protection (security labels).

- In the Orange Book, the A division means the system's design and level of protection is verifiable and provides the highest level of security and trust.

- In the Orange Book, C2 requires object reuse protection and auditing.

- In the Orange Book, B1 is the first rating that requires security labels.

- In the Orange Book, B2 requires all subjects and devices to have security labels, there must be a trusted path and covert channel analysis, and separate administrator functionality is provided.

- In the Orange Book, B3 requires security notifications to be sent, the security administration role is defined, and the system must recover without compromising the security of the system.

- The Orange Book deals mainly with operating systems, so a range of books were written to cover many other topics in security; these books are called the Rainbow Series.

- The Red Book, or Trusted Network Interpretation (TNI), provides guidelines for networks and network components.

- The Information Technology Security Evaluation Criteria (ITSEC) was an attempt by European countries to develop and use one set of evaluation criteria instead of several.

- The ITSEC evaluates the assurance and functionality of a system separately, whereas the TCSEC combines the two into one rating.

- The Common Criteria was developed to provide a globally recognized evaluation criteria and is in use today. It combined sections of the TCSEC, ITSEC, CTCPEC, and the Federal Criteria.

- The Common Criteria uses protection profiles and ratings from EAL1 to EAL7.

- Certification is the technical evaluation of a system and its security components. Accreditation is management's formal approval and acceptance of the security provided by a system.

- An open system provides better interoperability with other systems and products, but a lower security level. A closed system works within a proprietary environment, which lowers its interoperability and functionality possibilities, but provides higher security.

- A covert channel is a communication path that transfers data in a way that violates the security policy. There are two types: timing and storage covert channels.

- A covert timing channel enables a process to relay information to another process by modulating its use of system resources.

- A covert storage channel enables a process to write data to a storage medium so another process can read it.

- A back door, also called a maintenance hook, is developed to let a programmer into the application quickly for maintenance or adding functionality. This should be removed before the application goes into production or it can cause a serious security risk.

- An execution domain is where instructions are executed by the CPU. The operating system's instructions are executed in a privileged mode and application's instructions are executed in user mode.

- Process isolation ensures that multiple processes can run concurrently and the processes will not interfere with each other or affect each other's memory segments.

- The only processes that need complete system privileges are located in the system's kernel.

- A single state machine processes data of a single security level. A multistate machine processes data at two or more security levels without risk of compromising the system's security.

- Abstract data types define the acceptable activities involving objects and the data format the objects can receive and process. This helps prevent authorized users from modifying the data by inappropriate methods.

- Strong typing indicates that there is strong enforcement of abstract data types.

- TOC/TOU stands for time-of-check versus time-of-use. This is a class of asynchronous attacks.

- The Biba model is based on a hierarchical lattice of integrity levels.

- The Biba model addresses the first goal of integrity, which is to prevent unauthorized users from making modifications.

- The Clark-Wilson model addresses all three integrity goals: prevent unauthorized users from making modifications, prevent authorized users from making improper modifications, and maintain internal and external consistency through auditing.

- In the Clark-Wilson model, users can only access and manipulate objects through programs. It uses access triple, which is subject-program-object.

- ITSEC was developed for European countries. It was not an international evaluation criterion.

Questions

Please remember that these questions are formatted and asked in a certain way for a reason. The questions and answers may seem odd or vague, but this is what you will see on the actual CISSP test.

1. Which of the following is an example of a lattice-based access control model?
    a. Clark-Wilson model
    b. Bell-LaPadula model
    c. Separation of duties model
    d. Security policy model

2. What flaw creates buffer overflows?
    a. Application executing in privileged mode
    b. Inadequate memory segmentation
    c. Inadequate protection ring use
    d. Insufficient parameter checking

3. The operating system performs all except which of the following tasks?
   a. Memory allocation
   b. Input and output tasks
   c. Resource allocation
   d. User access to database views

4. If an operating system allows sequential use of an object without refreshing it, what security issue can arise?
   a. Disclosure of residual data
   b. Unauthorized access to privileged processes
   c. Data leakage through covert channels
   d. Compromising the execution domain

5. What is the final step in authorizing a system for use in an environment?
   a. Certification
   b. Security evaluation and rating
   c. Accreditation
   d. Verification

6. What feature enables code to be executed without the usual security checks?
   a. Covert channel
   b. Maintenance hook
   c. Timing channel
   d. Ready state

7. If a component fails, a security system should be designed to do which of the following?
   a. Change to a protected execution domain
   b. Change to a problem state
   c. Change to a more secure state
   d. Release all data held in volatile memory

8. What advantage does firmware have over software?
   a. It is difficult to modify without physical access.
   b. It requires a smaller memory segment.
   c. It does not need to enforce the security policy.
   d. It is easier to reprogram.

9. Which is the first level that requires classification labeling of data?
   a. B3
   b. B2

    c. B1

    d. C2

10. Which of the following best describes a reference monitor?

    a. A software component that monitors activity and writes security events to an audit log

    b. A software component that determines if a user is authorized to perform a requested operation

    c. A software component that isolates processes and separates privilege and user modes

    d. A software component that works in the center protection ring and provides interfaces between trusted and untrusted objects

11. The Information Technology Security Evaluation Criteria was developed for which of the following?

    a. International use

    b. U.S. use

    c. European use

    d. Global use

12. A security kernel contains which of the following?

    a. Software, hardware, and firmware

    b. Software, hardware, and system design

    c. Security policy, protection mechanisms, and software

    d. Security policy, protection mechanisms, and system design

13. What characteristic of a trusted process does not allow users unrestricted access to sensitive data?

    a. *-property rule

    b. Simple security rule

    c. Need-to-know

    d. TCB

14. The Orange Book states that the trusted computing base should uniquely identify each user for accountability purposes and _____.

    a. Require the user to perform object reuse operations.

    b. Associate this identity with all auditable actions taken by that individual.

    c. Associate this identity with all processes the user initiates.

    d. Require that only that user have access to his specific audit information.

15. The trusted computing base controls which of the following?
    a. All trusted processes and software components
    b. All trusted security policies and implementation mechanisms
    c. All trusted software and design mechanisms
    d. All trusted software and hardware components

16. What is the imaginary boundary that separates components that maintain security from components that are not security related?
    a. Reference monitor
    b. Security kernel
    c. Security perimeter
    d. Security policy

17. Which model deals only with confidentiality?
    a. Bell-LaPadula
    b. Clark-Wilson
    c. Biba
    d. Reference monitor

Answers

1. B.	6. B.	11. C.	16. C.
2. D.	7. C.	12. A.	17. A.
3. D.	8. A.	13. C.	
4. A.	9. C.	14. B.	
5. C.	10. B.	15. D.	

Physical Security

In this chapter, you will learn about the following items:

- Administrative, technical, and physical controls pertaining to physical security
- Facility location, construction, and management
- Physical security risks, threats, and countermeasures
- Electrical issues and countermeasures
- Fire prevention, detection, and suppression
- Authenticating individuals and intrusion detection

Security is very important to companies and their infrastructures, and physical security is no exception. Physical security encompasses a different set of threats, vulnerabilities, and risks than the other types of security that have been addressed so far. Physical security mechanisms include site design and layout, environmental components, emergency response readiness, training, access control, intrusion detection, and power and fire protection. Physical security mechanisms protect people, data, equipment, systems, and the facility itself.

Physical Security

Physical security of computers and their resources in the 1960s and 1970s was not as much of a challenging task as it is today, because computers were mostly mainframes locked away in server rooms with a handful of people who knew what to do with them. Today, there is a computer on almost every desk in every company, devices and resources are spread throughout the environment, larger companies have several wiring closets and server rooms, and remote and mobile users take computers and resources out of the facility. Properly protecting these computer systems and devices has become an overwhelming burden to many companies.

Internal theft, fraud, sabotage, and accidents are raising costs for many companies because environments are becoming more complex and dynamic. Most companies have experienced memory or processors being stolen from workstations and some have had computers and laptops taken. The companies may have resorted to security guards, closed-circuit TVs (CCTVs), and mounted cameras, requiring users to sign out materials, and requiring their staff to have a higher awareness of these risks. Contract and temporary workers may have special access badges and are only allowed in certain areas if they are escorted. More strict access control may be implemented with individual access badges and motion detectors, and infrared systems may be installed. These are only some of the items that fall within the physical security boundaries and if any one of these does not provide the necessary protection level, then it can be the weak link that causes security breaches.

Physical security is accomplished through proper facility construction, fire and water damage protection, anti-theft mechanisms, intrusion detection systems, and security procedures that are adhered to and enforced. The components that achieve this type of security are physical, technical, and administrative control mechanisms.

Security needs to protect people and hardware. Security should enhance productivity by providing a secure and predictable environment. It enables employees to focus on their tasks at hand and the evildoers will know to move onto a more vulnerable and easy target. This is the hope anyway.

Physical security has a different set of vulnerabilities than computer and information security. These vulnerabilities have more to do with physical destruction, intruders, environmental issues, and employees misusing their privileges and causing unexpected damage to data or systems. When security professionals are looking at *computer* security, they are thinking about how someone can enter an environment in an unauthorized manner through a port or modem. When they are looking at *physical* security, they are concerned with how people can physically enter an environment, how environmental issues affect the systems, or what type of intrusion detection system is best for a particular facility. Figure 6-1 illustrates the difference between computer and physical security. Each type of security has its own issues to be aware of and countermeasures to implement, but the more a security professional knows about all areas of security, the more beneficial it is because she can understand how all the pieces interrelate and depend upon one another.

Hacker   Intruder

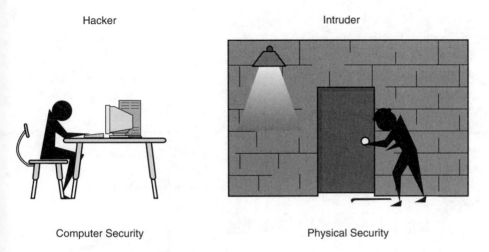

Computer Security   Physical Security

Figure 6-1   Whereas computer security involves attackers, crackers, and hackers, physical security involves intruders, vandals, and thieves.

Planning Process

Okay, so what are we doing?

The environment that must be protected includes all personnel, equipment, data, communication devices, power supply, and wiring. The necessary level of protection depends on the value of the data, the computer systems, and the company assets within the facility. The value of these items can be determined by a *critical-path* analysis, which lists each piece of the infrastructure and what is necessary to keep those pieces healthy and operational. This analysis also outlines the paths data takes when passing through a network. Data can go from remote users to servers, from servers to workstations, from workstations to mainframes, and from mainframes to other mainframes. It is important to understand these paths and the possible threats that can disrupt them.

The critical-path analysis lists all pieces of an environment and how they interact and how they are interdependent. Diagrams should be developed to show the devices and their place and relevance to a facility. This diagram should include power, data, water, and sewer lines. Air conditioners, generators, and storm drains may also be included to provide a full description and understanding. Figure 6-2 shows a simplistic example of this type of diagram.

The critical path is defined as the path that is critical for business functionality. The critical path should be shown in detail with all supporting mechanisms. Redundant

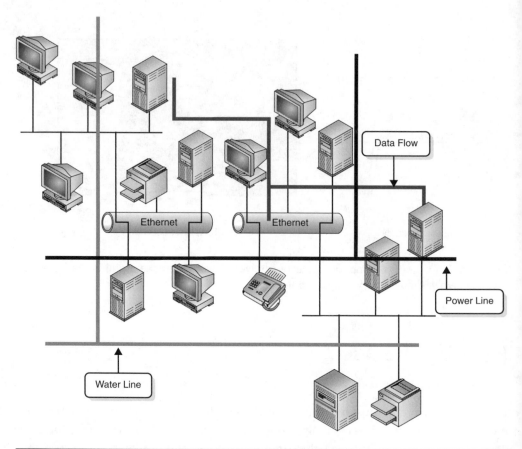

Figure 6-2 A diagram showing that power, water, sewer lines, and the flow of critical data is a necessary reference

paths should be shown and there should be at least one redundant path for every critical path.

Physical Security Controls

There are several types of control that fall under the physical security umbrella. Here is a list of some of those controls:

- Administrative controls
    - Facility selection or construction

- Facility management
- Personnel controls
- Training
- Emergency response and procedures
- Technical controls
  - Access controls
  - Intrusion detection
  - Alarms
  - Monitoring (CCTV)
  - Heating, ventilation, and air conditioning (HVAC)
  - Power supply
  - Fire detection and suppression
  - Backups
- Physical controls
  - Fencing
  - Locks
  - Lighting
  - Facility construction materials

Facilities Management

The physical facility is usually the building that houses employees, equipment, data, and network components. Facility management responsibilities start before the building is built, by choosing the right location, materials, and supporting systems. Many times in a company, a facilities manager is hired to be totally responsible for all facets of the building and this individual interfaces with the systems administrator and management staff to ensure that all overlapping issues are agreed upon and properly protected.

Physical Attributes of the Facility

Katie states, "I can't see the building, Dusty." Dusty replies, "That is the whole idea."

When a company decides to erect a building, there are several things that go into consideration prior to pouring the first batch of cement. Of course, land prices, customer population, and marketing strategies are reviewed, but as security professionals we are more interested in the confidence and protection a specific location can provide. Some organizations that deal with top secret or confidential information make their facilities unnoticeable so they do not attract attention of would-be attackers. The building can be hard to see from the surrounding roads, the company signs and logos are small and not easily noticed, and the markings on the buildings do not give away any information that pertains to what is going on inside that building. It is a type of city or urban camouflage that makes it harder for the enemy to seek them out.

Issues with Selecting a Facility Site

When selecting a location for a facility, some of the following items are critical to the decision making process:

- Visibility
  - Surrounding terrain
  - Building markings and signs
  - Types of neighbors
  - High or low population in the area
- Surrounding area and external entities
  - Crime rate
  - Proximity to police, medical, and fire stations
  - Possible hazards from surrounding area
- Accessibility
  - Road access
  - Excessive traffic
  - Proximity to airports, train stations, and highways

- Natural disasters

  - Likelihood of floods, tornadoes, earthquakes, or hurricanes

  - Hazardous terrain (mudslide, falling rock from mountains, or excessive snow or rainfall)

Some buildings are put into areas that are surrounded by hills or mountains to help prevent eavesdropping of electrical signals emitting from the facility's equipment. Other facilities are built underground or right into the side of a mountain for conceal-ment and disguise in the natural environment, and protection from radar tools and spying activities.

Location selection also means identifying other types of risks related to specific areas. These issues deal with natural disaster possibilities, crime rates, surrounding neighbors, and proximity to airports and railways. If a company is considering the pos-sibility of building a facility in Kansas, then tornado insurance will certainly have to be built into cost and maintenance equations. If the company is also looking at erecting a building in a low-income area, although the land prices will most likely be cheap, there will be a need for higher physical and perimeter security levels, which bring along costs and overhead.

An inspection of the facility should be done to reveal the vulnerabilities and the extent of those vulnerabilities. The value of property within the facility and the value of the facility itself need to be ascertained to determine the proper budget that should be allotted for physical security.

Construction

We need a little more than glue, tape, and a stapler.

Physical construction materials and structure composition need to be evaluated for their protective characteristics, appraised for their utility, and their cost and benefits need to be calculated. Different building materials provide different levels of fire pro-tection and combustibility, which correlate with their fire ratings. The type of construc-tion material used (wood, concrete, or steel) needs to be combined with what the building is going to be used for when making structural decisions. If an area is going to be used to store documents and old equipment, it has far different needs and legal requirements than if this area will be used for employees to work in every day of the week.

The *load* (how much weight that can be held) of a building's walls, floors, and ceilings needs to be estimated and projected to ensure that the building will not collapse in different situations. The walls, ceilings, and floors must contain the necessary materials to supply the necessary fire rating and sometimes equally important protection against water damage. The windows (interior and exterior) may need to provide ultraviolet (UV) protection, may be required to be shatterproof, or may need to be translucent or opaque depending on the placement of the window and the contents of the building. The doors (exterior and interior) may need to have *directional opening*, have equal fire rating as the surrounding walls, disallow forcible entries, contain emergency egress (markings), and depending on placement, may require monitoring and attached alarms. In most buildings, raised floors are used to hide and protect wires and pipes, but in turn these floors need to be electrically grounded because they are raised.

Building codes regulate all of these issues, but there are still many options within each category. The right options should accomplish the company's security and functionality needs and still be cost effective.

When designing and building a facility, the following are major items that need to be addressed from a physical security point of view:

Walls

Combustibility material (wood, steel, concrete)

Fire rating

Reinforcements for secured areas

Doors

Combustibility material (wood, pressed board, aluminum)

Fire rating

Resistance to forcible entry

Emergency marking

Placement

Alarms

Directional opening

Electric door locks may need to revert to disabled state if a power outage occurs for safe evacuation.

Type of glass—if necessary, this may need to be shatterproof or bulletproof.

Ceilings

Combustibility material (wood, steel, concrete)

Fire rating

Load and weight bearing rating

Drop ceiling considerations

Windows

Translucent or opaque requirements

Shatterproof

Alarms

Placement

Accessibility (intruders can break in and access facility)

Flooring

Load and weight bearing rating

Combustibility material (wood, steel, concrete)

Fire rating

Raised flooring (electrical grounding)

Nonconducting surface and material

Heating and Air Conditioning

Positive air pressure

Protected intake vents

Dedicated power lines

Emergency switch-off valves and switches

Placement

Power Supplies

Backup and alternate power supplies

Clean power source

Dedicated feeders to required areas

Placement and access to distribution panels and circuit breakers

Water and Gas Lines

Shutoff valves

Positive flow (material should flow out of building, not in)

Placement

Fire Detection and Suppression

Placement of sensors and detectors

Placement of sprinklers

Type of detectors and sprinklers

A security professional may be involved with the planning phase of building a facility and each of these items comes into play when constructing a secure building and environment. These topics will be explained in further detail throughout this chapter.

Facility Components

There are many components that make up a facility that must be looked at from a security point of view. *Internal partitions* are used to create barriers between one area and another. These partitions can be used to segment a network, separate work areas, and provide protected areas for sensitive systems and devices. Many buildings have hung ceilings, meaning the interior partitions may not extend above the ceiling; therefore, an intruder can lift a ceiling panel and climb over the partition. This example of intrusion is shown in Figure 6-3. In many situations, this would not require forced entry, specialized tools, or much effort. These types of internal partitions should not be solely relied upon for providing protection for sensitive areas.

Surfaces that can conduct electricity, even static electricity, should be avoided in places where sensitive electrical devices are being used. Carpet may be acceptable in employee work areas, but it should not be used in server rooms or wiring closets.

Data centers usually hold expensive equipment and the company's critical data; therefore, its protection should be thought out before implementation. Data centers should not be located on the top floors of buildings in case of a fire or in the basements in case of floods. Data centers should usually be located at the core of a building to provide protection from natural disasters or bombs and provide easier access to emergency crewmembers if necessary. They should be in semisecluded areas to limit its accessibility and not right next to the cafeteria or other areas where employees gather.

External entities may need to be considered also. A company should evaluate how close the facility would be to a police station, fire station, and medical facilities. Many

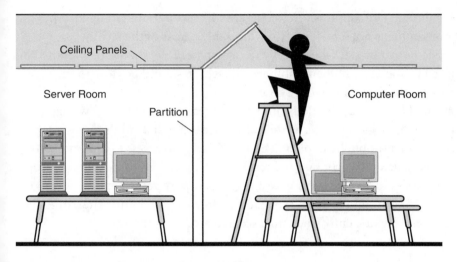

Figure 6-3   An intruder can lift ceiling panels and enter a secured area with little effort.

times, the close proximity of these entities raises the real estate value of properties, but for a good reason. If a chemical company that manufactures highly explosive materials needs to build a new facility, it may make good business sense to put it in a location that is quickly and easily accessible to the nearest fire station. If another company that builds and sells expensive electronic devices is expanding and needs to move operations into another facility, police reaction time may be looked at when choosing one area over another. Each of these issues, police station, fire station, and medical facility proximity, can also reduce insurance rates, and must be looked at carefully.

Computer and Equipment Rooms

In the past it was usually necessary to have personnel within the computer rooms for proper maintenance and operations. Today most servers, routers, bridges, mainframes, and other equipment that are housed in computer rooms are controlled remotely. This enables computers to live in rooms that have fewer people milling around and spilling coffee. Because the computer rooms no longer have personnel sitting and working in them for long periods of time, the rooms can be constructed in an efficient manner for equipment instead of people.

Computer rooms do not usually need to provide comfort and operational needs for people; they have become smaller and expensive fire suppression systems may no longer be required. In the past Halon fire suppression was the most popular way of protecting personnel that worked inside computer rooms. These systems are expensive to install and maintain. Fire suppression systems are still necessary, but different types can be used if human life is not a major factor within these areas of the facility.

Smaller systems can be stacked vertically to save space. They should be mounted on racks or placed inside of equipment cabinets. The wiring should be close to the equipment to save on cable costs and reduce confusion.

The location of these areas should be in the core areas of a facility near wiring distribution centers. Only one access door should be necessary and no through access to other unsecured area should be in place. There should be no access to these areas from public areas like stairways, corridors, and restrooms. This helps ensure that the people who are by the doors to secured areas have a specific purpose versus on their way to the restroom or standing around in a common area talking with others drinking coffee. Figure 6-4 illustrates only one entry way into a secured area.

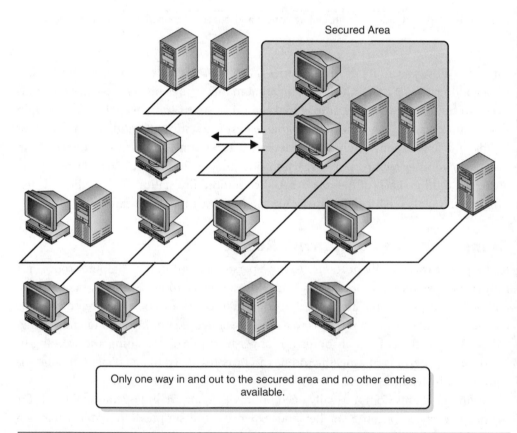

Only one way in and out to the secured area and no other entries available.

Figure 6-4   A secured area should have one entry that is properly controlled.

Physical Security Risks

Okay, so what are we supposed to be afraid of?

The main risks that physical security components combat are theft, interruptions to services, physical damage, compromised system integrity, and unauthorized disclosure of information.

Physical theft usually results in stolen computer equipment or other devices. Real loss is determined by the cost to replace the stolen items plus the cost to restore the lost data. Many times companies will just perform an inventory of their hardware and provide value estimates that are plugged into risk analysis to determine what the cost to the company would be if the equipment was stolen or destroyed. However, the information held within the equipment can be much more valuable than the equipment itself, and proper recovery mechanisms and procedures also need to be plugged into the risk assessment for a more realistic and fair assessment.

Interruptions of services can be the loss of computer services, power resources, water supply, and telecommunication services. These scenarios have to be evaluated and recovery plans developed. This was painfully obvious to many companies in California that experienced brownouts and blackouts during the times the state was running low on power resources and supply. These items bring up issues that need to be addressed in business continuity and disaster recovery planning, but it also brings up issues for physical security concerns. If a company loses power supply, they could also lose their electrical security systems and computerized intrusion detection systems. This could provide an intruder with easy access; thus, a backup generator or backup procedures need to be thought of, thought through, and funds properly allocated before being faced with this type of situation.

Depending on a company's reliance upon telecommunication services, backup options may need to be put into place to ensure redundancy or communication circuits that can be activated on an as-needed basis. If a company provides a call center for a large software manufacturer, their profitability could be threatened if their telephone connection suddenly went down for a period of time. Stockbrokers need to be in touch with many other entities via their network, the Internet, and through telephone communication lines. If a company of stockbrokers lost communication abilities, their profits and their clients could be severely affected. Other companies may not have such a dependency on telecommunication services, but this risk needs to be evaluated, informed decisions need to be made, and backup alternatives need to be available.

The loss of computer services is mainly addressed in Chapter 7 with backup and redundant array of inexpensive disk (RAID) protection mechanisms, and redundancy issues are addressed in Chapter 9 as it pertains to business continuity and disaster recovery. Physical security looks more at providing protection for the computers themselves and the facility they reside in. The magnitude of loss from physical damage depends on the cost of repair or replacement, the cost of replacing data, and the costs arising from service interruptions it causes.

Physical security countermeasures also protect against unauthorized disclosure of information and loss of system integrity and availability. Information can be disclosed to unauthorized individuals in many ways. Network traffic can be sniffed, electrical signals can be extracted from airwaves, and hardware or media can be stolen or modified. Physical security plays a role in each of these types of security vulnerabilities and risks.

Physical Security Component Selection Process

David exclaims, "I spent $30,000 to protect this floppy disk that is worth 50 cents." Doug replies, "You're not too bright, are ya son?"

All protection mechanisms must be cost beneficial to companies and physical security components are no different. If a company spends $500,000 yearly for protection of an operation that is worth $120,000, new risk assessment tools and methods need to be looked at as well as a new operator of those tools. A security mechanism that is cost beneficial means that the reduction in potential loss is significantly greater than the cost of implementing the mechanism in the first place and its lifetime maintenance. This realization needs to come from precise and detailed fact gathering, risk analysis and assessment, and a proper review of all available mechanisms that can provide the same type of protection—not necessarily the new gee-wiz gadget on the market.

There are some musts in life, like paying taxes, dying, and obeying one's wife. In selecting physical security components, there are some 'musts' and some 'shoulds' that need to be clearly understood so the most informed and intelligent decisions can be made.

Security Musts

A majority of companies are obliged by law to obey certain safety requirements. A building can contain only a certain number of individuals, must have stairs instead of just elevators, must have properly working fire alarms and smoke detectors, must have exit signs illuminated and easily visible, and the fire exit doors cannot not be blocked and must have panic bars located on them to enable people to evacuate during emergencies. These options must be implemented and are required by law, no matter how much they cost a company.

These regulations vary depending on the geographic location, the type of business, or if facilities are used for office buildings, storage facilities, or assembly lines. These issues get very detailed with safety codes, federal and state regulations, and building codes. It is out of the scope of this book to go into these issues, but the following items must be looked at very seriously: the costs, overhead, and the inherited vulnerabilities and risks.

Security Shoulds

There are protection procedures that should be put into place to help protect the company from devastating activities and their results. Many times these protection procedures use security components that are already part of the environment, and therefore, require no extra budget efforts or relinquishing of funds. These procedures include: backing up critical data, configuring security components that are already part of the operating systems and hardware instead of purchasing items that provide the same functionality, watching for suspicious activity of employees, logically and physically segmenting a network, and having the security guard walk around departments instead of staying in just one area. These all add another layer of protection without a lot of extra effort or money.

If there are security protection mechanisms that require a low cost but the benefit is material, then these mechanisms should be implemented. Locks are inexpensive prevention tools, but can protect a facility and its contents from theft and destruction. Providing chains to an outside gate might cause would-be looters to move onto another victim. A guard shack with no real guard could deter individuals who were out to loiter, inflict property damage, or try their hand at graffiti to a building or facility. The cost of upkeep for these security mechanisms is minimal, but the benefits could be significant thus, they should be implemented.

Backups

Backing up data seems like a hassle except for the day when the network goes down, data gets lost or corrupted, and users and management are screaming. Then proper backups are better than sliced bread.

Performing continual and consistent backups is done with prevention in mind, because one cannot predict when something is going to go wrong and to what extent. As with many other pieces to security, when the cost of recovery outweighs the cost of the protective mechanism, it always makes good sense to implement the protective mechanism.

Not every piece of data needs to be backed up, so it is important to identify the data that is critical, important, and mundane. This is the process of establishing priorities pertaining to different types of data, applications, and programming code. If one tries to save everything, most likely nothing will be saved properly. It is important to establish priorities of what needs to be backed up and in the case of an emergency what needs to be restored prior to other items. The programs that enable different facilities to communicate and access data on host systems, and applications that protect and process business-critical information should be brought online and assurance of their functionality should be in place before worrying about word processors and programs to make birthday cards. Proper utilization of priorities will provide for realistic scheduling, provide assurance in that the critical jobs are done on time, and the costs will be kept reasonable.

More than just data needs to be backed up and in place in the time of need. Hardware, electrical supplies, and personnel are all necessary pieces to a successful and smooth running data processing environment.

Hardware

Many companies implement alternate sites to help in the recovery process after a disaster. It is unlikely that two sites will be affected by the same disaster; thus, the measure seems prudent. The farther the two sites are from each other, the greater the safety factor, but the increase in cost of transporting people, equipment, and data is also greater. If a secondary site must be used, there is an initial cost of getting the site up and running and getting the right people in the right place. However, if operations need to take place at the secondary site for a month and it is over 100 miles away, the cost of providing living areas and travel expenses for employees is a cost that needs to be considered. (Alternate sites will be addressed fully in Chapter 9, but for now understand that it is an example of backing up necessary hardware.)

Other than major disasters taking place, providing redundancy hardware is important for the smaller emergencies that can take place. If a particular file server provides critically needed services to the company 24 hours a day, 7 days a week, it is usually mirrored or RAID capabilities are put into place to protect the data. But what about the hardware itself? If there is physical damage to a system, having the necessary files is not useful if there is not a healthy system to install them to. *Service level agreements (SLAs)* with hardware vendors need to be kept up-to-date to ensure that their service level provides the necessary level of protection. If the vendor promises to repair a product within three days and the business could lose massive profits if the product is down for three hours, then this is not a realistic protection mechanism.

Each device has a *mean time between failure (MTBF)* and a *mean time to repair (MTTR)*. The MTBF estimate is used to determine the expected lifetime of a device or when an element within that device is expected to give out. The MTTR value is used to estimate the amount of time between repairs. These estimates can be used to calculate the risk of utility failure, and evaluate other devices that may have better MTBF or MTTR values. If a company depends greatly on a specific cooling device for their server room that contains over 200 servers, they may have one or two backup devices in case the primary one in use fails. Or they may send one of their network staff members to training on how to repair this device to help ensure a lower MTTR value. Figure 6-5 shows an example of MTBF and MTTR values.

Redundant hardware can be an expensive way to provide protection in case of a failure or emergency, but the possible adversary effects and those costs need to be weighed and compared to the cost of having an extra router ready to be put to work if the original router fails. A cost analysis of vendor service level agreements, possibly obtaining redundant hardware, the MTTR and MTBF values, and the cost expectancy of critical hardware needs to be done to make the most useful decisions.

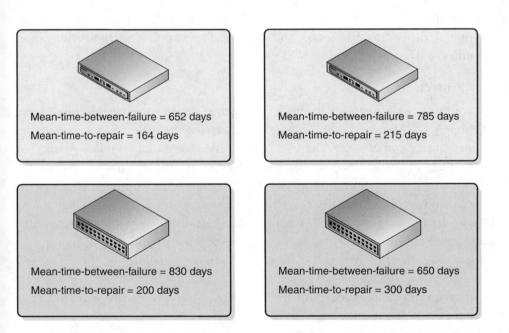

Mean-time-between-failure = 652 days
Mean-time-to-repair = 164 days

Mean-time-between-failure = 785 days
Mean-time-to-repair = 215 days

Mean-time-between-failure = 830 days
Mean-time-to-repair = 200 days

Mean-time-between-failure = 650 days
Mean-time-to-repair = 300 days

Figure 6-5 When comparing different vendor products, the MTBF and MTTR values should be evaluated.

Power Supply

We don't need no stinkin' power supply. Just rub these two sticks together.

Because computing has become so necessary and depended upon in the corporate world, power failure is a much more devastating event than it was 10 to 15 years ago. Thus, the need for good plans to fall back on is more crucial to provide the assurance that a business will not be drastically affected by storms, high winds, hardware failure, lightning, or other causes that can stop or disrupt power supplies.

There are several types of power backup capabilities and choosing the right one should be done after the total cost of anticipated downtime and its effects are calculated. This information can be gathered from past records and other businesses in the same area on the same power grid. Dividing the annual expenditures by the annual standard hours of use derives the total cost per hour for backup power.

There are large and small issues that can cause power failure or fluctuations. The effects manifest in variations of frequency, amplitude, and voltage that can last a millisecond to days. A company can pay to have two different supplies of power to reduce their risks, but this approach is can be extremely costly. Another less expensive mechanism is to have generators in place. Some generators have sensors to detect power failure and will start automatically. Thresholds can be calibrated to best serve an environment, depending on the type and size of the generator, it might provide power for minutes or days.

Power Protection

There are three main methods to protecting against power problems: uninterrupted power supply (UPS), power line conditioners, and backup sources. UPS uses batteries that range in size and capacity. The UPS can be online or standby. *Online systems* use AC line voltage to charge a bank of batteries. When in use, the UPS has an inverter that changes the DC output from the batteries into the required AC form and regulates the voltage as it powers computer devices. This conversion process is shown in Figure 6-6.

Standby UPS devices stay inactive until a power line fails. The system has sensors that detect a power failure and the load is switched to the battery bank.

Backup power supplies are necessary when there is a power failure and the outage will last longer than a UPS can last. Backup supplies can be a line from another electrical substation or from a motor generator and can be used to supply main power or charge the batteries in a UPS system.

Critical systems that need protection from interrupted power supplies need to be identified and how long secondary power would be needed and how much power is

On-Line UPS

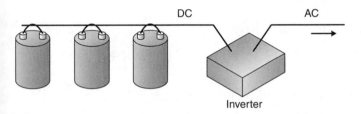

DC   AC

Inverter

Figure 6-6   A UPS device converts DC current from its batteries to usable AC by using an inverter.

required per device needs to be estimated. Some UPSs provide just enough power to allow systems to shut down cleanly, whereas some will allow the systems to run for a longer period of time. It needs to be determined if systems should have enough power supply to be shut down in a proper manner or if they actually need to be up and running to keep critical operations available.

Just having a generator in the closet should not give a company the warm fuzzy feeling of security. The alternate power source should be tested on a periodic basis to make sure it works and to the extent expected. It is never good to get all the way to an emergency state to find out that the generator does not work or someone forgot to buy the gas necessary to keep the thing running.

Electrical Issues

Electric power is very important to all of us. It enables us to be productive and functional in many different ways, but if not installed, monitored, and respected properly, it can bring us great harm.

Power needs to be provided in the appropriate levels and with the appropriate quality. There are two main types of power sources: primary and alternate. A *primary power source* is what is used to provide day-to-day operations, and an *alternate power source* is used in the event of some type of failure of the primary power source. The primary power source has at least one dedicated feeder from a utility station or power grid. An alternate power supply provides backup functionality to a primary power source and can take the form of a UPS, generator, or batteries.

Electrical Power Definitions

- **Ground**   The pathway to the earth to enable excessive voltage to dissipate
- **Noise**   Electromagnetic or frequency interference that disrupts the power flow and can cause fluctuations
- **Transient noise**   Short duration of power line disruption
- **Clean power**   Power that does not fluctuate

When clean power is being used, it means that the power supply contains no interferences or voltage fluctuation. The types of interference (or *line noise*) possible are from *electromagnetic interference (EMI)* or *radio frequency interference (RFI)* and transient noise, which is disturbance to the flow of electric power while it travels across a power line, as shown in Figure 6-7. EMI is created by the difference between three wires: hot, neutral, and ground. Lightning and electrical motors can induce EMI. RFI is created by components of an electrical system. Electrical cables and fluorescent lighting usually cause RFI.

Interference interrupts the flow of an electrical current and fluctuations can actually deliver a different level of voltage than what was expected. Each can be damaging to

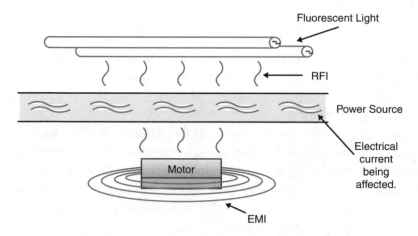

Figure 6-7   RMI and EMI can cause line noise on power lines.

devices and people. The following explains the different type of voltage fluctuations that are possible with electrical power:

- Power excess
  - **Spike** Momentary high voltage
  - **Surge** Prolonged high voltage
- Power loss
  - **Fault** Momentary power out
  - **Blackout** Prolonged loss of power
- Power degradation
  - **Sag** Momentary low voltage
  - **Brownout** Prolonged power supply that is below normal voltage

Surge Surges can cause a lot of damage very quickly. A *surge* is one of the most common power problems and is controlled with surge protectors. These protectors use a device, called a metal oxide varistor, which moves the excessive voltage to ground when a surge is experienced.

Blackout Instead of a low amount of voltage available over a power line, a *blackout* is when the voltage drops to zero. This can be caused by lightning, a car taking out a power line, storms, or when a utility switches generators. It can last for seconds or days. This is the point when a backup power source is required.

Brownout When power companies are experiencing high demand, they will frequently reduce the voltage in a grid, which is referred to as a *brownout*. Constant-voltage transformers can be used to regulate this fluctuation of power. It can take different ranges of voltage and only release the expected 120 volts to customers.

Noise *Noise* on a power line takes place when electrical interference is superimposed onto the power line itself. The noise usually results from a local source such as transformers, lightning, fluorescent lighting, and signals from televisions and radio stations. Frequency ranges overlay, which can affect electrical device operations. Noise suppression circuitry is usually part of other power line conditioners like surge protectors.

Many times lightning produces voltage spikes on communication and power lines, which can destroy equipment or alter data that is being transmitted. When generators are switched on because power loads have increased, they too can cause voltage spikes that can be harmful and disruptive. Storms and intense cold or heat can also put a heavier load on generators that can cause a drop in voltage line. Each of these instances is an example of normal behaviors of environments and how the power voltage is affected that can eventually adversely affect equipment, communication, or the transmission of data.

Because these and other occurrences are far from rare, there should be mechanisms in place to detect unwanted power fluctuations to protect the integrity of the data processing environment. *Voltage regulators* and *line conditioners* can be used to ensure a clean and smooth distribution of power and uninterruptible power supplies should always be handy in case of power failure.

Many data centers are constructed in a manner that takes power sensitivity equipment into consideration. Because surges, sags, brownouts, blackouts, and voltage spikes frequently cause data corruption, the centers are built to provide a high level of protection from these issues. Other types of environments are usually not built with these things in mind and do not provide this level of protection. Offices usually have different types of devices connected and plugged into the same outlets. Outlet strips are plugged into outlet strips, which are connected to extension cords. This causes more line noise and reduction of voltage to each device. Figure 6-8 depicts an environment that can cause line noise, voltage problems, and possibly a fire hazard.

Figure 6-8 This configuration can cause a lot of line noise and a fire hazard.

Offices that experience these types of issues may need voltage regulators and line conditions to maintain a clean power supply. All devices must be grounded properly for safety reasons. Two-prong outlets should be replaced with three-prong outlets to provide proper grounding. Vacuum cleaners and other devices should not be plugged into outlets used by computers and computing devices.

Preventative Measures and Good Practices

When dealing with electrical power issues, the following items can help protect devices and the environment:

- Every device should have a surge protector to protect from voltage fluctuations.
- Shutting down devices in an orderly fashion helps avoid data loss or damaging devices due to voltage changes.
- Do not have devices or media around powerful magnetic lines, energized conductors, or circuits that could create magnetic fields.
- Power line monitors should be employed to detect frequency and voltage amplitude changes.
- Regulators should be used to keep voltage steady and power clean. Regulators may also filter out line noise.
- Connections need to be grounded from the device to the earth.
- Protection from magnetic induction should be provided through shielded lines.
- UPS or generators should be available for backup power supply.
- Shield long cable runs.
- Avoid fluorescent lights if possible.
- Use three-prong connections and adapters if using two-prong cables.
- Connect all systems to the same power line if possible (this reduces noise and provides a common ground).
- Do not plug outlet strips and extension cords into each other.

Personnel

Job rotation has been explained in other chapters, so we will only touch on the subject and show how it pertains to providing a type of backup. A company can have a stack of redundant hardware, more than enough power sources, and off-site facilities, but if there are not the right people in place to make these things work, it could be a waste of time and money.

Many companies have that one person who knows too much. Knowledgeable people are wonderful and necessary, but that knowledge needs to be spread around. Resignations, vacations, illnesses, promotions, or the proverbial "getting hit by a bus" brings these issues into the light for companies, and they usually find they are not prepared to deal with them properly.

It is usually too expensive to have more than one person on payroll to perform a certain job, but cross training can help when the employees need to take time off or move on. Personnel should also be periodically retrained in manual tasks that have been automated to make sure that if the automated process fails, the company will not take such a big hit.

The following sections list other personnel controls that affect the physical security of an environment.

Pre-employment Screening

Check references, other employment, and education

Character evaluation and response to different scenario questions

Background investigation if needed

Drug test if needed

Employee Maintenance

Periodic reviews

Reevaluating security clearances

Supervisor updates and recommendations

Job rotation

Separation of duties

Post-employment

Friendly termination

Exit interview

Escorted removal from facility

Locking computer accounts

Obtaining company property

Changing passwords

These are procedures that should be thought out before hiring or terminating employees and should be practiced for each and every employee. This will help to ensure that the right individuals are selected, employee actions are always known and reviewed, and that termination processes reduce possible damage to the company and its assets.

Environmental Issues

Improper environmental controls or unsupervised environment utilities can cause damage to services, hardware, and lives. Services can be interrupted that can cause unpredicted and unfortunate results. Power, heating, ventilation, air conditioning, and air quality controls can be complex and contain many variables. They all need to be operating properly and be monitored regularly.

During facility construction, it must be made certain that water, steam, and gas lines have proper shutoff valves, shown in Figure 6-9, and *positive drains*, which means their

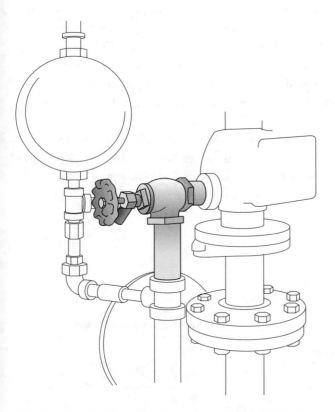

Figure 6-9   Water, steam, and gas lines should have emergency shutoff valves.

contents flow out instead of in. If there is ever a break in a main water pipe, the water flow must be able to be turned off. In case of a surrounding flood, a company wants to ensure that material cannot travel up through the water pipes and into their water supply or facility. If there is presence of fire within a building, gas lines need to be able to be terminated. Facility, operating, and security personnel should know where these valves are and there should be strict procedures to follow in case of these types of emergencies. This will help reduce the possible devastation of a disaster as a whole.

Most electronic equipment must operate in a climate-controlled atmosphere. Although it is important to keep the atmosphere at a good working temperature, it is important to understand that it is the components within the equipment that will suffer the most from overheating. Many times internal computer fans are not cleaned or are blocked, which overheats the internal components of a computer. When devices are overheated, the components can expand and contract, which causes components to change their electronic characteristics, reducing their effectiveness or damaging the system overall.

Maintaining appropriate temperature and humidity levels is important in any facility, especially facilities with computer systems. Both can cause damaging effects to computers and electrical devices. High humidity can cause corrosion and low humidity can cause excessive static electricity. This static electricity can short out devices, cause the loss in information, or provide amusing entertainment for unsuspecting employees. Relative humidity between 45 and 60 percent is acceptable for areas that are processing data.

Lower temperatures can cause mechanisms to slow or stop, and higher temperatures can cause devices to use too much fan power and eventually shut down. The temperature of an area containing computing devices should fall into the range of 70 and 74 degrees Fahrenheit. Table 6-1 lists different components and damaging temperature levels.

Table 6-1   Components Affected by Specific Temperatures

Material or Component	Damaging Temperature
Computer systems and peripheral devices	175°F
Magnetic storage devices	100°F
Paper products	350°F

Preventative Steps Against Static Electricity

- Use anti-static flooring in data processing areas.

- Ensure proper humidity.

- Have proper grounding of building and outlets.

- Don't have carpeting in data centers or have static-free carpets if necessary.

- Wear anti-static bands when working inside of computer systems.

In dryer climates, or during the winter, the air contains less moisture, which can cause static electricity when two dissimilar objects touch each other. This electricity usually travels through the body and produces a spark from a person's finger that can release several thousand volts. This can be more damaging that one would think. Usually the charge is released on a system casing, but if it were released directly to an internal component, the outcome could be worse. This is why people who work on the internal parts of a computer usually wear anti-static armbands to reduce this from happening.

In more humid climates, or during the summer, more humidity is in the air, which can also affect components. Particles of silver can begin to move away from connectors onto copper circuits, which cement the connectors into their sockets. This can adversely affect the electrical efficiency of the connection. A *hygrometer* is usually used to monitor humidity. It can be manually read or an automatic alarm can be set up to go off if the humidity passes a set threshold.

Ventilation

Air ventilation has several requirements to aid in providing a safe and comfortable environment. A closed-loop recirculating air conditioning system should be installed to maintain air quality. Positive pressurization and ventilation should also be implemented to control contamination. *Positive pressurization* means that when an employee opens a door, the air goes out and outside air does not come in. If a facility were on fire, you would want the smoke to go out the doors instead of being pushed back in when people were fleeing? Figure 6-10 illustrates positive pressurization during a fire.

Figure 6-10 Positive pressurization causes smoke to go out the doors instead of being sucked back into the environment.

Contaminants need to be understood by how they enter an environment, the damage they could cause, and the steps to ensure that a facility is protected from dangerous substances or high levels of average contaminants. Airborne material and particle concentrations must be monitored for inappropriate levels. Dust can impact a device's functionality by clogging up the fan that is supposed to be cooling it. Excessive concentrations of certain gases can accelerate corrosion and cause performance issues or failure of electronic devices. Although most disk drives are hermetically sealed, other storage devices can be affected by airborne contaminants. Air quality devices and ventilation systems deal with these issues.

Fire Prevention, Detection, and Suppression

We can either try to prevent fires or have one really expensive weenie-roast.

The subject of physical security would not be complete without a discussion about fire safety. There are national and local standards that must be met pertaining to fire prevention, detection, and suppression methods. *Fire prevention* comes from training employees how to react properly when faced with a fire, supplying the right equipment and ensuring that it is in working order, making sure there is an easily reachable water supply, and storing combustible elements in the proper manner.

Fire detection response systems come in many different forms. There are the red manual pull boxes we have seen on many walls in many buildings. An example of a red manual pull box is shown in Figure 6-11. There are also automatic detectors that have sensors that react when they detect the presence of a fire. The automatic system can be a sprinkler system or a Halon discharge system. Automatic sprinkler systems are widely used and highly effective in protecting buildings and their contents. When deciding upon the type of fire suppression systems to install, many factors need to be evaluated including an estimate of the occurrence rate of a possible fire, the amount of damage that can result, and the types of systems to choose from.

Fire protection consists of early smoke detection and shutting down systems until the source of the heat is eliminated so combustion does not occur. If necessary, an automated system should shut down all the systems. A warning signal should first sound and an override button available to postpone the shutdown process if the problem is under control and danger has passed.

Types of Fire Detection

Fires present a very dangerous security threat because they can damage hardware, data, and risk human life. Smoke, high temperatures, and corrosive gases from a fire can cause devastating results; thus, it is important to evaluate the fire safety measurements of a building and the different sections within it.

Figure 6-11   The red manual pull box is one example of a fire detection response system.

A fire begins because something ignited it. Ignition sources can be failure of an electrical device, improper storage of combustible materials, carelessly discarded cigarettes, malfunctioning heating device, and arson. A fire needs fuel and oxygen to continue to burn and grow; the more fuel per square meter, the more intense the fire will become. A facility should be built, maintained, and operated in a way to minimize the accumulation of fuels that can feed fires.

There are three classes (A, B, and C) of fire that are possible. It is important to know the difference between the types of fire so you know how to properly distinguish them. Fire extinguishers have markings indicating what type of fire they should be used on. The markings indicate what types of chemicals are within the canisters and what types of fires they have been approved to be used on. Figure 6-12 depicts a portable extinguisher. Portable extinguishers are usually filled with carbon dioxide (CO_2) or soda acid and should be located within 50 feet of any electrical equipment and located near exits. The extinguishers should be marked clearly, with an unobstructed view. They should be easily reachable and operational by employees, and inspected quarterly.

A lot of systems are made of components that do not support combustion, but will melt or char if overheated. Most computer circuits use only two to five volts of direct

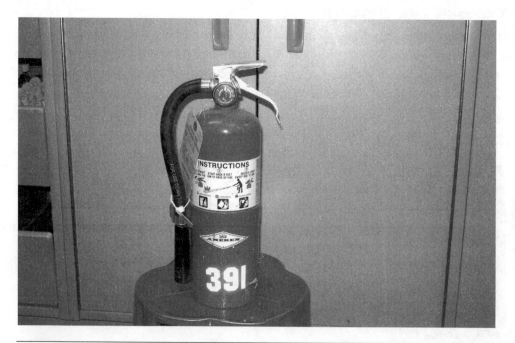

Figure 6-12 Portable extinguishers are marked indicating what type of fire they should be used on.

current, which usually cannot start a fire. Fuses are put into place so that devices will shut down if overheating occurs. In the event that a fire does happen in a computer room, it will most likely be an electrical fire caused by overheating of wire insulation or overheating components igniting surrounding plastics. There is usually prolonged smoke before combustion actually takes place.

Fire Detectors

There are several types of fire detectors, each working in a different way with different goals. All of them sense thermal combustion and respond to incremental changes in temperature. The detector can be activated by heat, smoke, flame, or combustion particles.

Smoke Activated   Smoke-activated detectors are good for early warning devices. They can be used to sound a warning alarm before the water sprinklers turn on. A *photoelectric device*, also referred to as an optical detector, detects the change in the electrical current when there is a variation in light intensity. The detector produces a beam of light across a protected area and if the beam is obstructed, the alarm assumes it is smoke and sounds. Figure 6-13 illustrates how a photoelectric device works. Another type of photoelectric device samples the surrounding air by drawing air into a pipe. If the light source is obscured, the alarm will sound.

Heat Activated   Heat-activated detectors can either alarm when a predefined temperature is reached or it can detect an increase in temperature that exceeds a predefined rate, or a combination of both. *Rate-of-rise temperature sensors*, shown in Figure 6-14, usually provide a quicker warning than *fixed-temperature sensors* because they are more sensitive, but they can also cause more false alarms. The sensors can either be spaced uniformly throughout a facility or a line type of installation can be implemented, which is operated by a heat-sensitive cable.

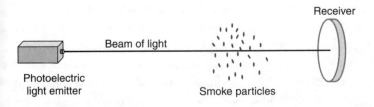

Figure 6-13   A photoelectric device uses a light emitter and receiver. If there is an obstruction between the emitter and receiver, an alarm will sound.

Figure 6-14 Once a predefined temperature is reached, this sprinkler head begins to release water into the area.

Flame Activated A flame-activated sensing device either senses the pulsations of a flame or senses the infrared energy that is associated with flames and combustion.

Flame-activated devices are much more expensive than other types of fire detectors and are usually only used in special cases when high-valued equipment needs to be protected. These devices can respond quicker than other detectors, release an extinguishing agent, and sound an alarm.

Automatic Dial-up Alarm This type of system is configured to call the local fire station, and possibly the police station, to report a detected fire. The system plays a prerecorded message giving the necessary information so the officials can properly prepare and arrive at the right location. Many times this system is combined with one of the previously mentioned detection systems and adds another layer of functionality.

It is not enough to have these fire and smoke detectors installed in a facility; they must be installed in the right places. Detectors should be on and above suspended ceilings, because smoke usually gathers there first before entering other spaces. Detectors should be installed below raised floors because many types of wires live there that could start an electrical fire. No one would know about the fire until it broke through the floor if a detector were not below the raised floor to protect this area also. Detectors should also be located in enclosures and air ducts because smoke can gather in these

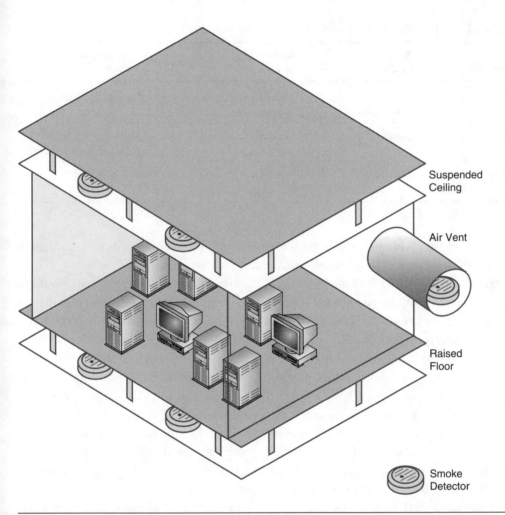

Figure 6-15 Smoke detectors should be located above suspended ceilings, below raised floors, and in air vents.

areas before entering other spaces. It is important that people are alerted about a fire as quickly as possible so the damage may be reduced, fire suppression activities may start quicker, and lives may be saved. Figure 6-15 illustrates the proper placement of smoke detectors.

Fire Suppression

It is important to know the types of fires that can take place and what should be done to properly suppress them. Each fire type has a rating that indicates what materials are

Table 6-2   Three Types of Fire and Their Suppression Methods

Fire Class	Type of Fire	Elements of Fire	Suppression Method
A	Common combustibles	Wood products, paper, and laminates	Water or soda acid
B	Liquid	Petroleum products and coolants	Gas (Halon), CO_2, or soda acid
C	Electrical	Electrical equipment and wires	Gas (Halon) or CO_2

actually on fire. Table 6-2 shows the three types of fire and their suppression methods that should be known by all employees.

There are several ways of suppressing a fire, and certain precautions that should be taken. In many buildings, there are suppression agents located in different areas that are designed to initiate after a specific trigger has been set off. Each agent has a zone of coverage, meaning an area that the agent is responsible for. If a fire ignites within a certain zone, it is the responsibility of that suppression agent to initiate and suppress that fire. There are different types of suppression agents: some use water, Halon, or CO_2. If an agent uses CO_2, it should have a delay mechanism within it. The delay mechanism would make sure that the agent does not start applying CO_2 to the area until after an audible alarm has sounded and people have been given time to evacuate. CO_2 is a colorless, odorless substance that is potentially lethal because it removes oxygen from the air. Gas masks do not provide protection against CO_2; thus, this type of fire suppression mechanism is best used in unattended facilities and areas.

A fire needs fuel, oxygen, and high temperatures. Table 6-3 shows how different suppression substances interfere with these elements of fire.

Table 6-3   How Different Substances Interfere with Elements of Fire

Combustion Elements	Suppression Methods	How Suppression Works
Fuel	CO_2 and soda acid	Removes fuel and oxygen
Oxygen	CO_2 and soda acid	Removes fuel and oxygen
Temperature	Water	Reduces temperature
Chemical Combustion	Gas—Halon or Halon substitute	Interferes with the chemical reactions between elements

Once a smoke detector is activated, an automatic fire suppression system should kick in. Older systems used CO_2, which extinguishes fires but can suffocate people. Halon was later used, which is harmless to people, in small quantities, but affects the ozone. Halon is no longer manufactured as of January 1, 1994 by an international agreement.

Production of Halon has been stopped since 1994 because it has ozone-depleting substances within it. The most effective replacement of Halon is FM-200, which is similar to Halon, but does not negatively affect the ozone.

Halon

Halon is a gas that was used to suppress fires because it interferes with the chemical combustion of the elements within a fire. It mixes quickly with the air and does not cause harm to computer systems and other data processing devices; therefore, it was used mainly in data centers and server rooms.

It was found that Halon has chemicals that deplete the ozone and concentrations greater than 10 percent were dangerous to people. If Halon was used on extremely hot fires, it degraded into toxic chemicals, and was even more dangerous to humans.

This caused Halon to be federally restricted and no companies are allowed to purchase and install new Halon extinguishers. Companies that still have Halon systems have been asked to replace them with nontoxic extinguishers.

The following lists EPA-approved replacements for Halon:

- FM-200
- NAF-S-III
- CEA-410
- FE-13
- Water
- Inergen
- Argon
- Argonite

Companies that have Halon extinguishers do not have to replace them by law, but the extinguishers cannot be refilled. So companies that have Halon extinguishers do not have to have them replaced right away, but when the extinguisher's lifetime runs out, they should be substituted with FM-200 extinguishers, or other EPA-approved chemicals.

Another fire suppression issue is the HVAC system. The HVAC system should be connected to the fire alarm and suppression system so that it properly shuts down if a fire is identified. A fire needs oxygen and this type of system can feed oxygen to the fire. Plus, the HVAC can spread deadly smoke into all areas of the building. Many fire systems will configure the HVAC to stop working if a fire alarm is triggered.

Water Sprinklers

Water sprinklers can be simpler and less expensive than Halon and FM-200 systems, but can initiate unnecessarily, which can cause water damage. If an electrical fire is in process, the water can increase the intensity of the fire, causing greater damage. So, a company needs to take great care in deciding which is best for them.

Sensors should be in place to shut down electrical power before water sprinklers activate. Each sprinkler head should activate individually to avoid wide-area damage and there should be shutoff valves so the water supply can be stopped if necessary.

There are four main types of sprinkler systems available: wet pipe, dry pipe, preaction, and deluge.

Wet Pipe   *Wet pipe systems* always contain water in the pipes and are usually discharged by temperature control level sensors. When the temperature meets a predefined temperature, a link melts, which releases the water. These systems are very common and considered the most reliable. One disadvantage of wet pipes is that the water in the pipes may freeze, either breaking the pipes or providing less than acceptable results in the event of a fire. Also, if there is a nozzle or pipe break, it can cause extensive water damage. These types of systems are also called *closed head systems*.

Dry Pipe   In *dry pipe systems*, the water is not actually held in the pipes, but is held back by a valve until a specific temperature is reached. There is a time delay between the predefined temperature being met and the release of water. This can be a good thing because it provides time for someone to shut down the system in case of a false alarm, but it also does not react as quickly as wet pipe systems do, meaning it may permit more damage to take place before taking action.

Water is not allowed into the pipes that feed the sprinklers until that actual fire alarm is sounded. First a heat or smoke sensor is activated, then the water fills the pipes leading to the sprinklers, the fire alarm sounds, the electrical power supply is disconnected, and water is now allowed to flow from the sprinklers. These pipes are best used in colder climates because the pipes will not freeze. Figure 6-16 depicts a dry pipe system.

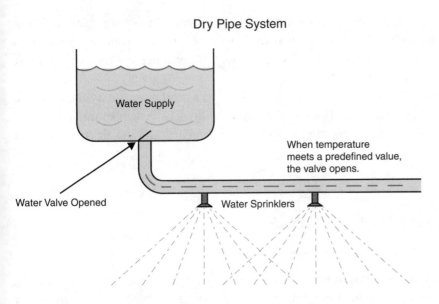

Dry Pipe System

Water Supply

When temperature
meets a predefined value,
the valve opens.

Water Valve Opened

Water Sprinklers

Figure 6-16   Dry pipe systems do not hold water in the pipes, but release it once a specific temperature is reached.

Preaction   *Preaction systems* combine the use of wet and dry pipe systems. Water is not held in the pipes and is only released into the pipes once a predefined temperature is met. Once this temperature is met, the pipes are filled with water, but it does not release right away. A link has to melt before the water is released from the sprinkler head itself. The purpose of combining these two techniques is to be able to react quicker to false alarms or to small fires that can be handled by other means. If a small fire starts and can be put out by a hand-held extinguisher, this would be better than destroying a lot of electrical equipment from water damage. These systems are usually chosen for equipment that is costly and when the company wants to prevent water damage.

Deluge   A *deluge system* is the same as a dry pipe system except the sprinkler head is open. In a dry pipe system the sprinkler head is closed and must open to allow water to escape. In the deluge systems, the heads are open to allow a larger volume of water to be released in a shorter period of time. Because the water being released is in such large volumes, these types of systems are usually not used in data processing environments.

A dry pipe system is used to protect against water damage and from false fire alarms. In addition, when a facility is in a location where freezing temperatures and broken pipes are an issue, a dry pipe system can be useful because the pipes are not full of water. The pipes are full of air until an alarm is activated and then water is released into the pipes. In wet pipe systems, the pipes are always full of water and can easily rupture in freezing temperatures.

All sensors and smoke detectors are usually tied to a central security system. The system can cover a specific area, floor, or the entire facility. The system should send a signal to the local fire station alerting them of the emergency, and the air circulation for that area should be shut down.

Administrative Controls

Okay, a disaster hit. Who do we blame?

Ultimately, management is responsible for everything that happens within a company, with little exception. Good management must have the foresight to look into the future and understand that some things may go not go as planned, situations will arise that need special handling, and employees might be faced with emergency situations. It is management's responsibility to practice due diligence and think through many types of scenarios, develop procedures and responses that should take place when these situations arise, and plan for backup and contingency activities to ensure the health of the company and the safety of the people. Disaster recovery and business continuity are covered in Chapter 9. The following sections touch on some of the same issues, but show how they relate to physical security.

Emergency Response and Reactions

During the development of disaster and business continuity planning, different disaster scenarios are played out, situations are examined, and circumstances are thought through. Physical security issues play a huge role in these exercises and if and when the real thing hits. There are administrative controls that need to be put in place to ensure that when a disaster hits, people are ready to react properly. These administrative controls are: evacuation procedures, system shutdown procedures, fire suppression techniques, proper ways of dealing with bomb threats and civil unrest, and what to do if specific utilities fail.

Evacuation plans need to be developed and procedures of shutting down systems in emergency situations need to be formed. During the development of a business continuity plan, systems that hold important information will be identified. During an emergency situation, they should be treated differently than regular workstations. Precautions need to be taken to ensure that the systems are brought down as delicately as possible to protect from the loss of data, or prevent the interruption of some other important service.

Emergency Response and Procedures

- Evacuation Procedures

- System shutdown

- Training and drills

- Integration with disaster plans

- Easily accessible documented procedures for different types of emergencies

- Periodic equipment tests

Redundant utilities may need be put in place to provide the necessary coverage and assurance of continued power supply in case of an electronic power failure. The cost of a UPS depends on the electrical load it can support, the length of time it can support this load, and the speed with which it assumes the load when the primary source fails. If long-term power supply is required, an on-site generator may be needed. The type and cost of the required generator depends upon the load that would be transferred to it and the size of the on-site fuel supply.

Emergency procedures need to be in place to deal with fires, bomb threats, hurricanes, tornadoes, and civil unrest. The ranking of these types of risks are done during a disaster and business continuity plan development exercise as discussed in Chapter 9. When a disaster happens, certain people must take on specific responsibilities and carry out tasks expected of them. The delegation of these duties also happens during the business continuity-planning phase, periodic training, exercises, and drills. These activities should take place to enforce the requirements of these duties. It is management's responsibility to ensure that employees are trained on disaster recovery and business continuity procedures. All procedures should be documented and that documentation should be readily accessible. There should be periodic inspections to review the documentation, procedures, and individual's knowledge of what is expected of him. A company and its environment continually changes, and therefore so does its threats and vulnerabilities. A recovery plan should be a living document that is continually reviewed, updated, and practiced.

...meter Security

...first line of defense deals with perimeter control to prevent unauthorized access to ...e facility. This defense works in two main modes: security practices during operation and security during the time the facility is closed.

When the facility is closed, all doors should be locked with monitoring mechanisms in strategic positions to alert others of suspicious activity. When the facility is in operation, security gets more complicated because authorized individuals need to be distinguished from unauthorized individuals.

Perimeter security deals with access control, surveillance monitoring, intrusion detection, and corrective actions. The following sections describe the elements that make up these categories.

Facility Access Control

Access control needs to be enforced through physical and technical components when it comes to physical security. Access controls protect facilities, computers, and people. In some situations, the objectives of physical access controls and the protection of people's lives may come into conflict. In these situations, a person's life always takes precedence. Many physical security controls make entry into and out of a facility hard, if not impossible. However, special consideration needs to be taken when this could affect lives. A physical security control that is used to ensure that the bad guys do not get in needs allow the good guys to get out in the situation of a fire or a similar type of emergency.

Physical access controls use mechanisms to identify individuals who are attempting to enter a facility, area, or system. It makes sure that the right individuals get in and the wrong individuals stay out and provides an audit trail of these actions. Personnel within sensitive areas can be one of the best security controls a company has because they can personally detect suspicious behavior; however, they need to be trained on what activity is considered suspicious and how reporting of such activities should take place.

Before the proper protection mechanisms can be put into place, a detailed analysis needs to be done on which data is sensitive and needs protection, which individuals should be allowed into what areas, which workspaces and systems are considered critical to the company's mission, and how the data and work flow happens within the facility. Access control points will be identified and classified as external, main, and secondary entrances. Personnel will be expected to enter and exit through a specific entry, deliveries may be expected to come to a different entry, and sensitive areas will be identified. Figure 6-17 illustrates the different types of access points into a facility. These

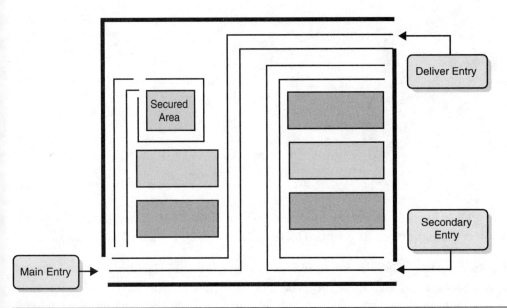

Figure 6-17   Access points should be identified, marked, and monitored properly.

important first steps help outline what needs to be protected, so the next step is how it is protected.

Locks

Locks and keys are the most inexpensive access control mechanisms. Locks are considered deterrents to semiserious intruders and delaying devices to serious intruders. The longer it takes to break or pick a lock, the longer a security guard or police officer has to arrive on the scene if the intruder has been detected. Almost any type of a door can be equipped with a lock, but keys can be easily lost and duplicated, and locks can be picked or broken. If a company depends solely on a lock-and-key mechanism for protection, an individual who has the key can come and go as he likes without control and he can remove items from the premises without detection. Locks should be used as part of the protection scheme, but not solely used as the protection scheme.

Locks vary in functionality. Padlocks can be used on chained fences, preset locks are usually used on doors, and programmable locks (require a combination to unlock) are used on pushbutton doors or vaults. Locks come in all types and sizes. It is important to have the right type of lock so that it provides the correct level of protection.

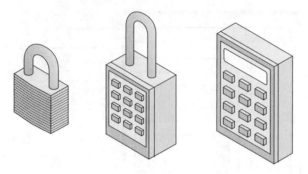

Preset Locks   *Preset locks* are locks usually used on doors. They can be a key-and-knob combination, mortise, or rim locks with latches and deadbolts as needed.

Cipher Locks   *Cipher locks*, also known as programmable locks, use keypads to control access into an area or facility. The lock can require a specific combination to be entered into the keypad, or a swipe card, or a combination. The costs are more than traditional locks, but combinations can be changed, specific combinations locked out, and personnel who are in trouble or duress can enter a specific code that will open the door and initiate a remote alarm at the same time. Thus, cipher locks can provide a much higher level of security and control of who can access a facility more than traditional locks.

The following are some options available on many cipher locks that improve the performance of access control and provide for increased security levels:

- **Door delay**   If a door is held open for a long period of time, an alarm will trigger to alert personnel of suspicious activity.

- **Key-override**   A specific combination can be programmed to be used in emergency situations to override usual procedures or for supervisory overrides.

- **Master-keying**   This option enables supervisory personnel to change access codes and other features of the cipher lock.

- **Hostage alarm**   If an individual is in duress and/or held hostage, there can be a combination he or she enters to communicate this situation to the guard station and/or police station.

If a door is accompanied by a cipher lock, it should have a corresponding visibility shield so that a bystander cannot see the combination as it is keyed in. Automated cipher locks must have a backup battery system and be set to unlock during a power failure so personnel are not trapped inside during an emergency.

Device Locks   Unfortunately, hardware has a tendency to walk away from facilities; therefore, device locks are sometimes necessary to thwart these attempts. Cable locks consist of a vinyl-coated steel cable-enabling computers and peripherals to be anchored to desks, chairs, and other stationary components. A cable lock is shown in Figure 6-18 and Figure 6-19 illustrates how to lock and secure a computer. There is a wide range of device locks created to protect the different types of devices used in an environment.

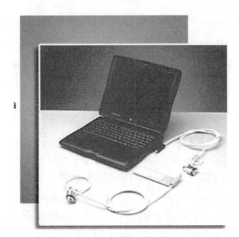

Figure 6-18   FMJ/PAD.LOCK's notebook security cable kit secures a notebook by enabling the user to attach the device to a stationary component within an area.

Figure 6-19   FMJ/PAD.LOCK's Full Metal Jacket© protects a tower computer by providing a "steel cage" for it.

The following describe some of the different types of device locks available and their capabilities:

- **Switch controls**   Covers on/off power switches.
- **Slot locks**   A bracket is mounted in a spare expansion slot and a steel cable is used to secure the system to a stationary component.
- **Port controls**   Blocking access to disk drives or unused serial or parallel ports.
- **Peripheral switch control**   Secures a keyboard by inserting an on/off switch between the system unit and the keyboard input slot.
- **Cable traps**   Prevents the removal of input/output devices by passing their cables through a lockable unit.

Personnel Access Controls

Proper identification needs to take place to verify if the person attempting to access a facility or area should actually be allowed in. Identification can happen through identifying an anatomical attribute (biometric system), smart or memory cards (swipe cards), personal recognition by a security guard and presenting a photo ID, using a key, or providing a card and entering a password or PIN.

A common problem with controlling authorized access into a facility or area is called *piggybacking*. This occurs when an individual gains unauthorized access by using someone else's legitimate credentials or access rights. Usually an individual just follows another person closely through a door without providing any credentials. The best preventive measure against this type of a problem is a security guard and employee education on good security practices.

If a company is employing a card badge reader, there are several different types of systems to choose from. The magnetic card can contain a magnetic strip, containing authorization information, a magnetic dot, embedded wire (resists tampering), or a proximity card, which means it does not need to be swiped through a reader, but a camera above a door can read the card as the individual approaches it. The following sections describe these items in further detail.

Magnetic Cards

Individuals have cards that have embedded magnetic strips that contain access information. The reader can just look for simple access information within the magnetic strip or it can be connected to a more sophisticated system that scans the information, makes more complex access decisions, and logs badge ID and access time.

If the card is a memory card, then the reader will just pull information from it and make an access decision. If the card is a smart card, the individual may be required to enter a PIN or password, which the reader compares against the information held within the card. (Memory and smart cards are covered in Chapter 4.)

Wireless Proximity Readers

Unlike a swipe card implementation, a wireless proximity reader does not require the individual to insert a card into the reader. The reader can sense the card when it is within a certain distance and makes access decisions. The two main types of proximity readers are user activated and system sensing.

User Activated When this type of reader is used, the proximity card transmits a sequence of values to the reader. The reader is expecting a specific sequence and if what is sent to it matches this preset value, then the individual is given access.

System Sensing In this type of system, the system-sensing proximity card will recognize the presence of the coded device within a specific area. A system-sensing access control system is a device that does not require the individual to enter any sequence or perform any action. Figure 6-20 shows how the reader can process the card and send the credentials to an authentication server, which will make the access decision.

There are three main types of system sensing cards and the differences among them are based on the way that power is generated.

- **Transponders** The card and reader has a receiver, transmitter, and battery. The reader sends signals to the card to request information. The card sends the reader an access code. These transponder devices contain a radio receiver and transmitter, a storage place for the access code, control logic, and a battery.

- **Passive devices** The card is considered passive because it does not have any power source of its own, but uses power from the reader. If it is a passive device, the card can sense the electromagnetic field, which is transmitted by the reader. When an individual is already in a secure area and is approaching a door to leave the sensitive area to a less sensitive area, the reader will detect the presence of this card and go ahead and unlock the door for the person.

- **Field-powered devices** The card and reader contain a transmitter and active electronics. The card has its own power supply and does not need to rely on the reader's power supply.

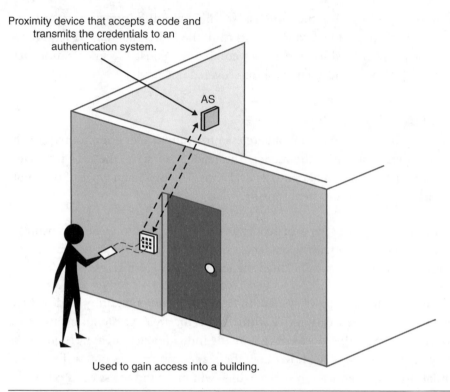

Proximity device that accepts a code and
transmits the credentials to an
authentication system.

AS

Used to gain access into a building.

Figure 6-20 A card communicates with a proximity reader to provide access.

External Boundary Protection Mechanisms

Let's build a fort and let only the people who know the secret handshake inside!

There are several types of protection mechanisms and controls that can be put into place to protect a company's facility. They can deter would-be intruders, detect intruders and unusual activities, and can provide ways of dealing with these issues when they arise. The different mechanisms and controls are examined in the following sections.

Fencing

Fencing is quite an effective physical barrier because it works as a preventative and deterrent mechanism. Fencing can provide crowd control and helps control access to entrances and access to facilities. However, fencing can be costly and unacceptably unsightly. Many companies plant bushes or trees in front of the fence that surrounds their building for aesthetics and as possible attempts to make the building less noticeable.

Fences come in varying heights and each height provides a different level of security:

- Fences three to four feet high only deter casual trespassers.

- Fences six to seven feet high are considered too high to climb easily.

- Fences eight feet high with strands of barbed wire at the top mean you are serious about protecting your property. This will deter the more determined intruder.

Critical areas should have fences at least eight feet in height to provide the proper level of protection.

Lighting

Lighting should be used to discourage intruders and provide safety for personnel, entrances, parking areas, and critical sections. Lighting is a physical control that provides preventative and deterrent protection. A company practices due diligence when it supplies the correct type of lighting for areas that could be considered dangerous. For example, if an employee was attacked in the company's parking lot, that employee could sue the company for not providing the proper security measures. If the company did not take the necessary steps to ensure a safe environment for its employees, it could be found negligent and may lose a court case. The National Institute of Standards and Technology (NIST) standard pertaining to perimeter protection states that critical areas should be illuminated eight feet high and two feet out. (It is referred to as two-feet candles that reach eight feet in height.)

There are several types of lights a company can choose to implement: searchlights, streetlights, floodlights, and fresnel units, which contain small lenses that can be focused.

Surveillance Devices

Usually installing fences and installing lights does not provide the necessary level of protection a company needs to protect its facility, equipment, and employees. Areas need to be under surveillance so that improper actions are noticed and taken care of before damage occurs. Surveillance can happen through visual detection of problems or technology devices that use sophisticated means of detecting abnormal behavior or unwanted conditions. Three main surveillance categories are security guards, dogs, and visual recording devices.

Patrol Force and Guards   One of the best security mechanisms is a security guard and/or a patrol force to monitor a facility's grounds. This type of security control is more flexible than other security mechanisms, provides good response to suspicious activities, and works as a great deterrent. However, it can be a costly endeavor, which requires a salary, benefits, and time off. People are usually limited in their reliability. Screening and bonding is an important part of selecting a security guard, but this only provides a certain level of assurance.

Intrusion detection systems and physical protection measures ultimately require human intervention. Security guards can be at a fixed post or a patrolling entity that covers specific areas. Different organizations will have different needs from security guards. They may be required to check individual credentials and enforce filling out a sign-in log, they may be responsible for monitoring intrusion systems and expected to respond to alarms, they may need to issue and recover visitor badges, respond to fire alarms, enforce rules established by the company within the building, and control what materials can come into or out of the environment. The guard may need to verify that doors, windows, safes, and vaults are secured; report identified safety hazards; enforce restrictions of sensitive areas; and escort individuals throughout facilities.

The security guard should have clear and decisive tasks he is expected to fulfill. The guard should be fully trained on the activities he is expected to perform and on the responses expected from him in different situations. The guard should have a central control point to check into, two-way radios to ensure proper communication, and necessary access into the areas he is responsible to protect.

The best security has a combination of security mechanisms and does not depend on just one component of security. A security guard should be accompanied by other surveillance and detecting mechanisms.

Dogs   Dogs have proven to be highly useful in detecting intruders and other unwanted conditions. Their hearing and sight capabilities outperform humans and their intelligence and loyalty can be used as protection measures.

The best security dogs go through intense training so that they have a wide range of commands to respond to and capabilities they can perform. Dogs can be trained to hold an intruder at bay until security personnel arrive or chase an intruder and attack. Some dogs are trained to recognize smoke so that they could alert others of an ongoing fire.

Of course, dogs cannot always know the difference between an authorized person versus an unauthorized person, so if someone goes into work after hours, she can have more on her hands than expected. Dogs can provide a good supplement security mechanism, or a company can ask the security guard to bare his teeth at the sight of an unknown individual instead. Whatever works.

Visual Recording Devices   Because surveillance is based on sensory perception, surveillance devices usually work in conjunction with guards to extend their capabilities and range of perception.

Cameras can be used to take still photographic pictures, which are stored for later viewing or a company can choose to use *closed-circuit TVs (CCTVs)*. A CCTV enables a guard to monitor many different areas at once from a centralized location.

Critical areas may need another level of protection to ensure that these areas are indeed vacant during off-hours or downtimes. The technical controls used to provide this type of protection are CCTV systems and light beam systems. CCTVs enable one person to view and monitor a large area, but require that person to sit and watch the display. This is a very boring task, which puts the night security guard right to sleep; therefore, a CCTV should be used in combination with another type of intrusion detection system. If this other type of detection system sounds an alarm, then the guard can view the CCTV to assess the situation.

Detecting

Surveillance techniques are used to watch for unusual behaviors, whereas detecting devices are used to sense changes that take place in an environment. Both are monitoring methods, but use different devices and approaches. The following sections address the types of technologies that can be used to detect the presence of an intruder. An example of a type of perimeter scanning device is shown in Figure 6-21.

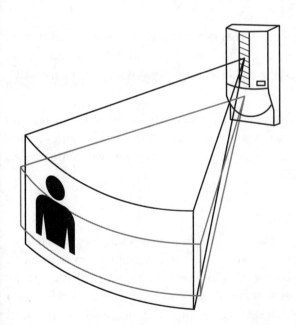

Figure 6-21   Different perimeter scanning devices work by covering a specific area.

Proximity Detection System A proximity detector, or capacitance detector, emits a measurable magnetic field while in use. The detectors monitor this electrical field and an alarm sounds if the field is disrupted. These devices are usually used to protect specific objects (artwork, cabinets, or a safe) versus protecting a whole room or area.

Photoelectric or Photometric System This type of system detects the change in the level of light within an area, and thus must be used in windowless rooms. These systems work like photoelectric smoke detectors, which emit a beam and the beam is expected to hit the receiver. If this beam of light is disrupted, an alarm sounds. The beams emitted by the photoelectric cell are cross-sectional and can be invisible or visible beams. If they are visible, they may be able to be stepped over or gone under, as seen in many suspense movies.

Wave Pattern The different wave pattern motion detectors range in the frequency of waves that they detect. The different ranges are microwave, ultrasonic, and low frequency. All of these devices generate a wave pattern that is sent over a sensitive area and reflected back to a receiver. If the patterns are returned undisturbed, then the device does nothing. If the patterns return altered, then an alarm sounds.

Passive Infrared System This type of system identifies the changes of heat waves with an area it is configured to protect. If the particles within the air rise, it could be an indication of the presence of an intruder.

Acoustical-Seismic Detection System This type of system is sensitive to sounds and vibrations and detects the changes in the noise level of an area it is placed within. These devices do not emit any waves; they only listen for sounds within an area, and are considered passive devices.

The type of motion detector, its power capacity, and configurations will dictate the number needed to cover a sensitive area. Also the size and shape of the room and the items within the room may cause barriers; therefore, more detectors would be needed to provide the necessary level of coverage.

Intrusion Detection Systems

Intrusion detection systems, or burglar alarms, are used to detect unauthorized entries and alert a responsible entity to respond. These systems can monitor entries, doors, windows, devices, or removable coverings of equipment. Many work with magnetic contacts or vibration-detection devices that are sensitive to certain types of changes in the environment. When a change is detected, an alarm is sounded either in the local area, or in both the local area and to a remote police or guard station.

The most popular types of intrusion detection systems in use today are the electro-mechanical types that detect a change or break in a circuit. The electrical circuits can be strips of foil embedded or connected to windows. If the window breaks, the foil strip breaks, which sounds an alarm. Vibration detectors can detect movement on walls, screens, ceilings, and floors when the fine wires embedded within the structure are broken. Magnetic contact switches can be installed on windows and doors. If the contacts are broken because the window or door is opened, an alarm will sound.

What is the difference among a proximity detector, seismic detector, vibration detector, and intrusion detector? Vibration and seismic detectors both sense vibration or movement and interprets this as a physical attack and sound an alarm. A proximity detector can sense an object or individual entering a protected area and perceives that as an attack and sounds an alarm. An intrusion detection system is configured to detect an individual or an object crossing a line or entering an area, and then initiates an alarm.

Motion detectors, light beams, and vibration sensors are expensive to install and monitor. If an alarm is sounded, it requires a human response. They are prone to activating alarms in situations that do not include intruders or any penetration attempts. These detection devices can be penetrated and are not expected to provide all necessary security of a facility.

Fire, intrusion-type, and motion detectors do not usually exist separately, but are part of an alarm system. All alarm systems require constant electrical power, and many times the ways intruders try to get around the systems is by eliminating their electrical source. The system has to be sensitive to tampering and sound an alarm if tampering is detected. The alarms need to have a direct current power source and emergency backup power sources.

Doorways

Entry doors into a facility, or specific areas, should be able to resist forced entry attempts. When determining which type of door to purchase and implement, the level of security required and the level of risk that will be accepted needs to be weighed. Reinforced strike plates and doorframes may be required as well as tamper-resistant hinges, shatterproof vision plates, and alarms that are trigged during forced entry.

If possible, all doors to storage rooms, service areas, equipment rooms, and secured areas should look alike so that the secured areas do not call attention to themselves. Each door should be self-closing and should not contain a hold-open feature. It is preferable to have a sensor built into the doorframe to indicate when a door did not close or has been open for an extended period of time.

Stationary and revolving doors can be used as physical access control mechanisms. They are used in mantraps and *turnstiles* so that unauthorized individuals entering a facility cannot get out if it is activated. *Mantraps* protect physical access by routing

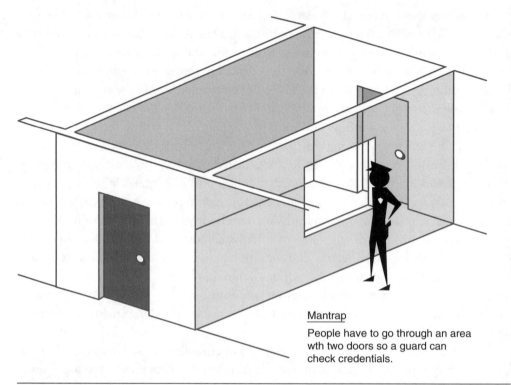

Mantrap

People have to go through an area
wth two doors so a guard can
check credentials.

Figure 6-22 Mantraps are used in highly secured areas and enable security guards to activate and restrain an individual in a closed area if necessary.

personnel past a security guard and through a double-door area where the individuals are subject to further identification and authentication. Figure 6-22 illustrates the function of mantraps.

Doorways with automatic locks can be configured to be fail-soft or fail-safe. A *fail-soft* setting means that if there were a power disruption, which would affect the automated locking system, the doors would default to being unlocked. A *fail-safe* configuration means that a door would default to being locked if there were any problems with the power. A company needs to decide which is best for its needs.

Auditing Physical Access

Physical access control systems can use software and auditing features to produce audit trails pertaining to access attempts. The following information should be logged and reviewed:

- Date and time of access attempt
- Entry point in which access was attempted
- User ID used when access was attempted
- Unsuccessful access attempts, especially if during unauthorized hours
- Modifications to access rights and privileges

As with audit logs produced by computers, access logs provide no use unless someone actually reviews them. A security guard may be required to review these logs, but a security professional or a facility manager should also review these logs periodically. It is important that management knows where entry points into the facility exist and who attempts to use them.

Audit and access logs are detective, not preventative. They are used to piece together a situation after the fact instead of attempting to prevent an access attempt in the first place.

Summary

Our distributed networks have put much more responsibility on the individual user, network personnel, and administrative procedures and controls than in the old mainframe days. Physical security is not carried out just with the night guard that carries around a big flashlight. Now security, if extremely technical, comes in all forms, and raises many liability and legal issues. Natural disasters, fires, floods, intruders, vandals, environmental issues, construction materials, and power supplies are all things in life that need to be planned for and dealt with.

Physical security is not often thought about when people think of security, but there are real threats and risks that need to be addressed and planned for. Who cares if a hacker can get through an open port on the Web server if the building is burning down?

References

http://nces.ed.gov/pubs98/safetech/chapter5.html

http://netsecurity.about.com/library/weekly/aa020501a.htm

http://security.org/dial-80/links.htm

www.eb-datacenters.com/tech/sec1198.html

www.itl.nist.gov/fipspubs/0-toc.htm

Quick Tips

- Physical security is the first line of defense against environmental risks and unpredictable human behavior.

- The value of property within the facility and the value of the facility itself needs to be ascertained to determine the proper budget that should be allotted for physical security.

- Automated environmental controls help minimize the resulting damage and speed of the recovery process. Manual controls can be time-consuming, error-prone, and require constant attention.

- Physical construction materials and structure composition need to be evaluated for their protective characteristics, appraised for their utility, and their cost and benefits need to be calculated.

- Some physical security controls may conflict with the safety of people. These issues need to be addressed and human life is always more important than protecting a facility or the devices it contains.

- When looking at locations for a facility, local crime natural disaster possibilities, and distance to hospitals, police and fire stations, airports, and railroads need to be considered.

- HVAC should maintain the appropriate temperature and humidity levels, provide closed-loop recalculating air conditioning, and positive pressurization and ventilation.

- Optimal temperature for systems and operators is 70 to 74 degrees Fahrenheit.

- Devices have mean time between failure (MTBF) and mean time to repair (MTTR). These values should be used to determine the total cost of repair and maintenance of the device and required actions necessary to provide uninterrupted service.

- Relative humidity should be around 45 to 60 percent for data processing. High humidity can cause corrosion and low humidity can cause static electricity.

- Dust and other air contaminants may adversely affect computer hardware, and therefore should be kept to acceptable levels.

- Administrative controls include drills and exercises of emergency procedures, simulation testing, documentation, inspections and reports, prescreening of employees, post-employment procedures, delegation of responsibility and rotation of duties, and security awareness training.

- Emergency procedure documentation should be readily available and periodically reviewed and updated.

- Access control badges can contain magnetic strips, embedded wire, a magnetic dot, or be proximity badges that do not need to be physically inserted into a reader.

- Proximity identification devices can be user activated (meaning action needs to be done by a user) or system sensing (meaning no action needs to be done by the user).

- A transponder is a proximity identification device that does not require action by the user. The reader transmits signals to the device and the device responds with an access code.

- Exterior fencing can be costly and ugly, but can provide crowd control and helps control access to the facility.

- Interior partitions may not go all the way up to the ceiling; therefore, an intruder can remove a ceiling tile and climb over the partition into a critical portion of the facility.

- Critical areas should be illuminated up to eight feet high and two feet in length.

- Physical access controls restrict the entry and exit of personnel.

- Intrusion detection devices can be motion detectors, CCTVs, vibration sensors, and/or light beams.

- Intrusion detection devices can be penetrated, are expensive to install and monitor, require human response, and are subject to false alarms.

- CCTV enables one person to monitor a large area, but should be coupled with alerting functions to ensure proper response takes place.

- Security guards are expensive but provide flexibility in response to security breaches and can deter intruders from attempting an attack.

- A cipher lock uses keypad access control and is programmable.

- Company property should be marked as such and security guards should be trained on how to identify when these items leave the facility in an improper manner.

- Media should be protected from destruction, modification, theft, unauthorized copying, and disclosure.

- Floors, ceilings, and walls need to be able to hold the necessary load and provide the required fire rating.

- Water, steam, and gas lines need to have shutoff valves and positive drains (substance flows out instead of in).

- The threats in physical security are interruption to services, theft, physical damage, unauthorized disclosure, and loss of system integrity.

- Primary power source is what is used in day-to-day operations and alternate power source is a backup in case the primary source fails.

- Power spike is momentary high voltage, power surge is prolonged high voltage, power fault is a momentary power out, power blackout is a prolonged loss of power, a power sag is a momentary low voltage, and a power brownout is a prolong power supply that is below normal voltage.

- Power companies usually plan and implement brownouts when they are experiencing high demand.

- Power noise is a disturbance of power to a device and can be caused by electromagnetic interference (EMI) or radio frequency interference (RFI).

- EMI can be caused by lightning, motors, and the current difference between wires. RFI can be caused by electrical system mechanisms, fluorescent lighting, and electrical cables.

- Power transient noise is the disturbance imposed on a power line, which causes electrical interference.

- Power regulators condition the line to keep voltage steady and clean.

- UPS cost factors are the size of the electrical load it can support, the speed it can assume the load when the primary source fails, and the time it can support the load.

- Shielded lines protect from electrical and magnetic induction, which causes interference to the power voltage.

- Perimeter protection is used to provide deterrence of trespassing and to enable people to enter a facility through a few controlled entrances.

- Fire detectors should be located on and above suspended ceilings, below raised floors, and in air ducts.

- There are three fire classes: A = common combustibles (suppress with soda acid or water), B = liquids (suppress with Halon, soda acid, or CO_2), and C = electrical (suppress with Halon or CO_2).

- A fire needs high temperatures, oxygen, and fuel, so to suppress it, one or more of those items needs to be reduced or eliminated.

- Gases, like Halon and FM-200 and other Halon substitutes, interfere with the chemical reaction of a fire.

- HVAC should be turned off before activation of a fire suppressant to ensure that it stays in the needed area and smoke is not distributed to different areas of the facility.

- Portable fire extinguishers should be located within 50 feet of electrical equipment and should be inspected quarterly.

- CO_2 is a colorless, odorless, and potentially lethal substance because it removes the oxygen from the air to suppress fires.

- Piggybacking, when unauthorized access is achieved to a facility via another individual's legitimate access, is a common concern with physical security.

- Halon is no longer available because it depletes the ozone. FM-200 or other similar substances are used instead of Halon.

- Proximity systems (motion detectors, vibration sensors, and light beams) require human response, can cause false alarms, and depend on a constant power supply, so these protection systems should be backed up by other types of security systems.

- Dry pipes systems reduce the accidental discharge of water because the water does not enter the pipes until an automatic fire sensor indicates that there is an actual fire.

- In locations with freezing temperatures where broken pipes cause problems, dry pipes should be used.

- A preaction pipe sounds an alarm and delays water release. A wet pipe releases water at a set temperature and does not delay water release.

Questions

Please remember that these questions are formatted and asked in a certain way for a reason. The questions and answers may seem odd or vague, but this is what you will see on the actual CISSP test.

1. What is the first step that should be done when a fire has been detected?
   a. Turn off the HVAC system and activate fire door releases.
   b. Determine which type of fire it is.
   c. Advise individuals within the building to leave.
   d. Activate fire suppression system.

2. Which of the following items does not provide physical protection?
   a. Smart card
   b. Token
   c. Biometric device
   d. Single sign-on system

3. When should a Class C fire extinguisher be used instead of a Class A?
   a. When electrical equipment is on fire
   b. When wood and paper is on fire
   c. When a combustible liquid is on fire
   d. When the fire is in an open area

4. Which is not a preventative physical security control?
   a. Fences
   b. Locks
   c. Security guard
   d. Access and audit log

5. How does Halon fight fires?
   a. It reduces the fires fuel intake.
   b. It reduces the temperature of the area and cools the fire out.
   c. It disrupts the chemical reactions of a fire.
   d. It reduces the oxygen in the area.

6. What is a mantrap?
   a. An trusted security domain
   b. A logical access control mechanism
   c. A double-door facility used for physical access control
   d. A fire suppression device

7. What is true about a transponder?
   a. It is a card that can be read without sliding it through a card reader.
   b. It is a passive proximity device.
   c. It is a card that a user swipes through a card reader to gain access to a facility.
   d. It exchanges tokens with an authentication server.

8. When is a security guard the best choice for a physical access control mechanism?
   a. When discriminating judgment is required
   b. When intrusion detection is required
   c. When the security budget is low
   d. When access controls are in place

9. Critical areas should have illumination of _____.
   a. Three-feet candles and eight feet in height
   b. Two-feet candles and eight feet in height
   c. Three-feet candles and six feet in height
   d. Two-feet candles and six feet in height

10. What is a common problem with vibration-detection devices used for perimeter security?
    a. They can be defeated by emitting the right electrical signals in the protected area.
    b. The power source is easily disabled.
    c. They cause false alarms by things that do not cause a threat to the environment.
    d. They interfere with computing devices.

11. What is the optimal temperature for a room that contains systems that perform data processing?
    a. 70 to 74 degrees Fahrenheit
    b. 65 to 70 degrees Fahrenheit
    c. 70 to 75 degrees Fahrenheit
    d. 60 to 65 degrees Fahrenheit

12. What is the relative humidity for an area to conduct safe data processing?
    a. 30 to 40 percent
    b. 50 to 60 percent
    c. 50 to 55 percent
    d. 40 to 60 percent

13. What are the problems from humidity in an area with electrical devices?
    a. High humidity causes excess electricity and low humidity causes corrosion.
    b. High humidity causes corrosion and low humidity causes static electricity.
    c. High humidity causes power fluctuations and low humidity causes static electricity.
    d. High humidity causes corrosion and low humidity causes power fluctuations.

14. What does positive pressurization pertaining to ventilation mean?
    a. When a door opens, the air comes in.
    b. When a fire takes place, the power supply is disabled.
    c. When a fire takes place, the smoke is diverted to one room.
    d. When a door opens, the air goes out.

15. When deciding on a location to build a facility, which item is not as important as the rest?
    a. Possibility of natural disasters
    b. Crime rate
    c. Proximity to library
    d. Proximity to fire station

16. Which is not an administrative control pertaining to emergency procedures?
    a. Intrusion detection systems
    b. Awareness and training
    c. Drills and inspections
    d. Delegation of duties

17. If an access control has a fail-soft characteristic and not a fail-safe characteristic, what does that mean?
    a. It defaults to no access.
    b. It defaults to being unlocked.
    c. It defaults to being locked.
    d. It defaults to sounding a remote alarm instead of a local alarm.

18. Which of the following is not a type of card badge that is processed by a reader?
    a. Biometric cards
    b. Proximity cards
    c. Cards with embedded wire
    d. Cards with magnetic dots

19. What are the two general types of wireless proximity identification devices?
    a. Biometric devices and access control devices
    b. Swipe card devices and passive devices
    c. Preset code devices and wireless devices
    d. User-activated devices and system sensing devices

20. Which type of device uses radio waves to communicate with an individual's access control badge?
    a. Biometric device
    b. User-activated proximity device
    c. Fail-safe device
    d. Transponder

21. Which item is not an intrusion detection mechanism?
    a. Vibration sensor
    b. CCTV
    c. Fresnel unit
    d. Motion detector

22. Which is not a downfall to installing intrusion detection and monitoring systems?
    a. Expensive to install
    b. Cannot be penetrated
    c. Requires human response
    d. Subject to false alarms

23. What is a cipher lock?
    a. A lock that uses cryptographic keys
    b. A lock that uses a type of key that cannot be reproduced
    c. A lock that uses a token and perimeter reader
    d. A lock that uses a keypad

24. If a cipher lock has a door delay option, what does that mean?
    a. After a door is open for a specific period of time, the alarm goes off.
    b. It can only be opened during emergency situations.
    c. It has a hostage alarm capability.
    d. It has supervisory override capability.

25. What reason has not added to the increased user responsibility pertaining to computer and information security?
    a. We have moved from a central administration model to a distributed network.
    b. Information has decreased in value.
    c. A network can be spread across different facilities, states, or countries, which makes it harder to enforce strict security.
    d. Network devices have taken on a lot of forms, such as palmpilots, personal computers, and remote dial-in devices.

26. Water and gas lines should have shutoff values and positive drains. What is a positive drain?
    a. Water does not go into the drain until a fire has been detected.
    b. This characteristic ensures that the pipe is unbreakable.
    c. Water, or gas, flows out instead of in.
    d. Water, or gas, flows in instead of out.

Answers

1. C.	8. A.	15. C.	22. B.
2. D.	9. B.	16. A.	23. D.
3. A.	10. C.	17. B.	24. A.
4. D.	11. A.	18. A.	25. B.
5. C.	12. D.	19. D.	26. C.
6. C.	13. B.	20. D.	
7. A.	14. D.	21. C.	

Telecommunications and Networking Security

In this chapter, you will learn about the following items:

- OSI model
- TCP/IP and many other protocols
- LAN, WAN, and MAN technologies
- Cabling and data transmission types
- Network devices and services
- Intranets and extranets
- Telecommunication protocols and devices
- Remote access methods and technologies
- Resource availability
- Wireless technologies

Telecommunications and networking contain many different mechanisms, devices, software, and protocols that are interrelated and integrated. Networking is one of the more complex topics in the computer field mainly because there are so many things involved. A network administrator, or engineer, must know how to configure networking software, protocols, devices, deal with interoperability issues, install, configure, and interface with telecommunication software and devices, and have a strong ability to troubleshoot. A security professional must understand these issues and have the ability to look into and understand these same topics a few levels deeper to fully understand where vulnerabilities can arise within networks. This can be an overwhelming and challenging task. However, if you are someone who enjoys challenges and appreciates the intricacies of technology, then this may be more fun than work.

To truly secure something, you must understand it. A security professional cannot advise others on how to secure an environment if he does not truly understand it in the first place. Securing an application that contains a buffer overflow means that the person understands what a buffer overflow is, what the outcome of exploiting it is, how to properly identify a buffer overflow, and possibly how to properly write program code to remove this weakness from the program. Securing a network architecture means that the person understands the different networking platforms involved, network devices, and how data flows through a network. This person must know how many different protocols work, their purposes, their interactions with other protocols, how the protocols can provide exploitable vulnerabilities, and know how to choose and implement the appropriate types of protocols in a given environment. The security professional must also understand the different types of firewalls, routers, switches, and bridges and when one is more appropriate than the other, where they are to be placed, their interactions with other devices, and the degree of security each provides.

The reason there are so many different types of devices, protocols, and security mechanisms within an environment is because of the different functionality they provide, but they also provide a layered approach to security. Layers within security are important so that if an attacker is able to bypass one layer, there is another layer standing in the way protecting the internal network. Many networks have routers, firewalls, intrusion detection systems (IDSs), antivirus software, and more. Each specializes in a certain piece of security, but they all should work in concert to provide a layered approach to security.

There is a lot involved with networking and telecommunications, but that is what makes it the most fun for those who truly enjoy these fields. However, many times complexity is the enemy of security. It is important to understand the components within an environment and their relationship to other components that make up the environment as a whole. This chapter addresses many of the telecommunication and networking aspects that are in many networks.

Telecommunications and Network Security

Telecommunication is the electrical transmission of data between systems whether it is through analog, digital, or wireless transmission types. The data can flow across copper wires, fiber, or airwaves, which may be a network cable within a company's infrastructure, the telephone company's public-switched telephone network (PSTN), or a service provider's fiber cables, switches, and routers. There are definitive lines drawn between the media used for transmission, technologies, protocols, and whose equipment is being used. However, the definitive lines get blurry when one follows how data that is created on a user's workstation flows through a complex path of Ethernet cables, to a router that divides the company's network and the rest of the world, through the ATM switch provided by the service provider, to the many switches the packets transverse throughout the ATM cloud, onto another company's network, through their router, and to another user's workstation within seconds. Each piece is interesting, but when they all integrate and work together, it is awesome.

Telecommunications usually refers to telephone systems, service providers, and carrier services. Most telecommunication systems are regulated by governments and international organizations. In the United States, telecommunication systems are regulated by the Federal Communications Commission (FCC), which affects voice and data transmissions. Globally, there are organizations that develop policies, recommend standards, and work together to provide standardization and the capability of proper interactions between different technologies.

The main standards organizations are the International Telecommunication Union (ITU) and the International Standards Organization (ISO). Their models and standards have shaped our technology today and these issues are addressed throughout this chapter.

NOTE Do not get overwhelmed with the size of this chapter and the amount of information within it. This chapter, as well as the others, attempts to teach you the concepts and meanings behind the definitions and answers you will need for the CISSP exam. This book is not intended to give you one-liners to remember for the exam, but teaches you the meaning behind the answers. The "Quick Tips" section at the end of the chapter and the questions help you zero in on the most important concepts for the exam itself.

Open System Interconnect Model

The Open System Interconnect (OSI) is a worldwide federation that works to provide international standards. In the early 1980s, it worked to develop a protocol set that would be used by all vendors throughout the world. This movement was fueled with the hopes of ensuring that all vendor products and technologies could communicate and interact across country and technical boundaries. The actual protocol set did not catch on as a standard, but the model of this protocol set was adopted and is used as an abstract framework that most applications and protocols adhere to.

Protocol

A protocol is a standard set of rules that determine how systems will communicate across networks. Two different systems can communicate and understand each other because they use the same protocols in spite of their differences. It is the same when two people communicate and can understand each other because they are using the same language.

Many people think that the OSI model arrived at the beginning of the computing age as we know it and helped shape and provide direction for many if not all technologies. However, this is not true. It was only developed in the 1980s, introduced in 1984, and the basics of the Internet had already been developed and implemented and the basic Internet protocols had been in use for many years. The Transmission Control Protocol/Internet Protocol [TCP/IP] protocol suite and Unix systems actually have their own models that are often used today when examining and understanding networking issues. Figure 7-1 shows the differences between the OSI and TCP/IP networking models. In this chapter, we will focus more on the OSI model.

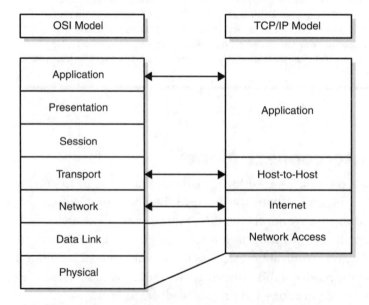

Figure 7-1 The OSI and TCP/IP networking models

The OSI model does provide important guidelines that are used by vendors, engineers, developers, and others. The model segments the networking tasks, processes, and services into different layers. Each layer has its own responsibilities when it comes to how two computers communicate over a network. Each layer has certain functionalities and the services and protocols that work within that layer fulfill them.

The OSI model's goal is to help others develop products that will work within an open network architecture. In an open network architecture, no one vendor owns it, it is not proprietary, and it can easily integrate different technologies and vendor implementations of those technologies. Vendors have used the OSI as a jumping board and developed their own networking frameworks. These vendors used the OSI model as a blueprint and developed their own protocols and interfaces to produce different or overlapping functionality than other vendors. However, because these vendors use the OSI model as their starting place, integration of different vendor products is an easier task and the interoperability issues are less burdensome than if the vendors developed their own networking framework from scratch.

Although computers communicate in a physical sense (electronic signals are passed from one computer over a wire to the other computer), they also communicate through logical channels. Each protocol at a specific OSI layer communicates with a protocol that operates at the same OSI layer on another computer. This happens through *encapsulation*. A message is constructed at the application layer and then passed down through the protocol's stack. Each layer adds its own information to the message; thus, the message grows in size as it goes down the protocol stack. The message is then sent to the destination computer and the encapsulation is reversed by taking the message apart through the same steps as the source computer that encapsulated it. At the data link layer, only the information pertaining to it is extracted and the message is sent up to the next layer. Then at the network layer, only the network layer data is stripped and processed and the message is again passed up to the next layer. This is how computers communicate logically. Each layer adds its own information to the packet and then each layer at the destination computer only takes information that pertains to it. The information stripped off at the destination computer informs it how to properly interpret and process the packet. Data encapsulation is shown in Figure 7-2.

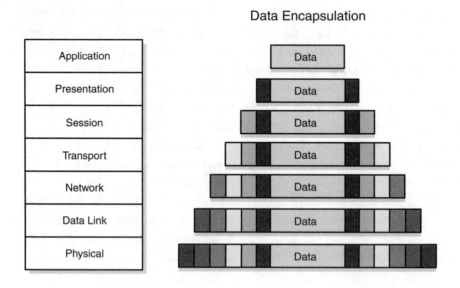

Figure 7-2 Each OSI layer adds its own information to the data packet.

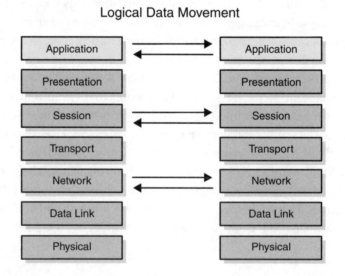

Each layer has specific responsibilities and control functions it performs, and data format syntaxes it expects. The benefit of modularizing these layers, and the functionality within each layer, is that different technologies, protocols, and services can interact with each other and provide the proper interfaces to enable communications. This means that a computer can use an application developed by Adobe, a transport protocol developed by Cisco, and a data link protocol developed by 3COM to construct and send a message over the network. The protocols, technologies, and computers that operate within the OSI layer are considered **open systems**. Open systems are capable of communicating with other open systems because they implement international standard protocols.

OSI Model

| Application |
| Presentation |
| Session |
| Transport |
| Network |
| Data Link |
| Physical |

Understanding the functionalities that take place at each OSI layer and the corresponding protocols that work at those layers helps you to understand the overall communication process between computers. Once this is understood, a more detailed look at each protocol will show the full range of options each protocol provides and the security weaknesses embedded into each of those options.

Application Layer

Hand me your information. I will take it from here.

The *application layer*, layer 7, works closest to the user and provides file transmissions, message exchanges, terminal sessions, and much more. This layer does not include the actual applications, but includes the protocols that support the applications. When an application needs to send data over the network, it passes instructions and the data to the protocols that support it at the application layer. This layer processes and properly formats the data and passes it down to the next layer within the OSI model. This

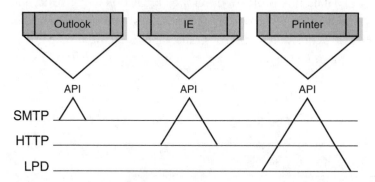

Application Layer

Figure 7-3 Applications send requests to an API, which is the doorway to the supporting protocol.

happens until the data that the application layer constructed contains the essential information from each layer necessary to transmit data over the network. The data is then put on the network cable and is routed until it arrives at the destination computer.

Some examples of the protocols working at this layer are the Simple Mail Transfer Protocol (SMTP), Hypertext Transfer Protocol (HTTP), Line Printer Daemon (LPD), File Transfer Protocol (FTP), World Wide Web (WWW), Telnet, and Trivial File Transfer Protocol (TFTP). Figure 7-3 shows how applications communicate to the underlying protocols through application program interfaces (API). If a user makes a request to send an e-mail through her e-mail client Outlook, the e-mail client sends this information to SMTP. SMTP will add its information to the user's information and pass it down to the presentation layer.

Presentation Layer

You will now be transformed into something that everyone can understand.

The *presentation layer*, layer 6, receives information from the application layer protocols and puts it into a format that all computers following the OSI model can understand. This layer provides a common means of representing data in a structure that can be properly processed by the end system. This means that when a user constructs a word document and sends it out to several people, it does not matter if the receiving computer is a Macintosh, Windows 98, Windows NT 3.51, or Unix computer; each of these computers will be able to receive this file, and understand and present it to its user as a word document. It is the data representation processing that is done at the presentation layer that enables this to take place. For example, when a Windows 98 computer receives a file from another computer system, there is information within the file's header explaining what type of file it is. The Windows 98 operating system has a list of file types it understands and a table describing what program should be used to open and manipulate each of these file types. The sender could create a word file in Office Word 2000 and the receiver only has StarOffice. The receiver can open this file because the presentation layer on the sender's system converted it to American Standard Code for Information Interchange (ASCII) and the receiver's computer knows that it opens these types of files with its word processor, StarOffice. The presentation layer is not concerned with the meaning of data, but with the syntax and format of that data. It works as a translator, which translates the format an application is using to a standard format used for passing messages over a network. If a user uses a Corel application to save a graphic, the presentation layer would convert the graphic into a Tagged Image File Format (TIFF), Graphic Interchange Format (GIF), or Joint Photographic Experts Group (JPEG) format. This way if the user sends this graphic to another user who does not have the Corel application, the user's operating system can still present the graphic because it has been saved into a standard format. Figure 7-4 shows how the presentation layer can convert a file into different standard file types.

This layer also handles data compression and encryption. If a program at the application layer requests a certain file to be compressed and encrypted before being transferred over the network, the presentation layer is the place where this functionality is actually carried out.

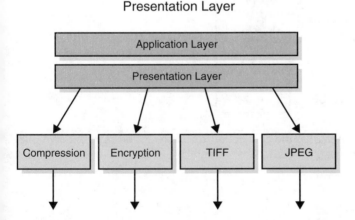

Figure 7-4   The presentation layer receives data from the application layer and puts it into a standard format.

Session Layer

When two computers need to communicate, or transfer information, a connection session needs to be set up between them. The *session layer*, layer 5, is responsible for establishing a connection between the two computers, maintaining it during the transferring of data, and controlling the release of this connection. A good analogy for the functionality within this layer is a telephone conversation. When Kandy wants to call a friend, she uses the telephone. The telephone circuitry sets up the connection over the telephone lines, maintains that communication path, and when Kandy hangs up, it releases all the resources it was using to keep that connection open.

Similar to how telephone circuitry works, the session layer works in three phases: connection establishment, data transfer, and connection release. It provides session restart and recovery if necessary and provides the overall maintenance of the session end to end. When the conversation is over, this path is broken down and all parameters are set back to their original settings. This process is known as dialog management. Figure 7-5 depicts the three phases of a session. Some protocols that work at this layer are Secure Sockets Layer (SSL), Network File System (NFS), Structured Query Language (SQL), and Remote Procedure Call (RPC).

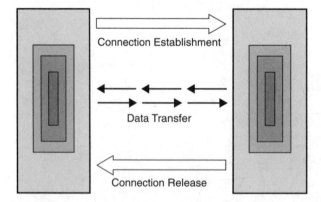

Session Layer

Connection Establishment

Data Transfer

Connection Release

Figure 7-5 The session layer sets up the connection, maintains it, and tears it down once communication is completed.

The session layer enables communication between two computers to happen in three different modes:

- **Simplex** Communication takes place in one direction.

- **Half-duplex** Communication takes place in both directions, but only one system can send information at a time.

- **Full-duplex** Communication takes place in both directions and both systems can send information at the same time.

Transport Layer

How do I know if I lose a piece of the message? Answer: The transport layer will fix it for you.

When two computers are going to communicate, they must first agree on how much information each computer will send at a time, how to verify the integrity of the data once it is received, and how to determine if a packet was lost along the way. The two computers agree on these parameters through a handshaking process at the *transport layer*, layer 4. The agreement on these issues before transferring data helps provide more reliable data transfer, error detection and correction, flow control, and it optimizes the network services needed to perform these tasks. The transport layer provides end-to-end data transport services and establishes the logical connection between two communicating computers.

The transport layer receives data from many different applications and assembles the data into a stream so that it can be properly transmitted over the network. If data needs to be multiplexed, it happens at this layer. The protocols that work at this layer are TCP, User Datagram Protocol (UDP), and Sequenced Packet Exchange (SPX). Information is passed down from different entities at higher layers to the transport layer, which must assemble the information into a stream, as shown in Figure 7-6.

Network Layer

There are many roads that lead to Rome.

The main responsibility of the **network layer** is to insert information into the packet's header so that it can be properly routed. In a network, there can be many routes to one destination. The protocols at the network layer must determine the best path for the

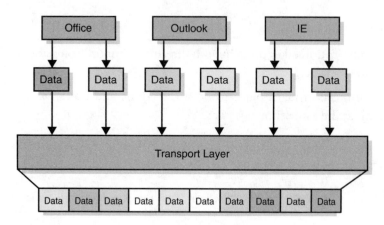

Figure 7-6 TCP formats data from applications into a stream to be prepared for transmission.

packet to take. Routing protocols build and maintain their routing tables at this layer. These tables are maps of the network, and when a packet needs to be sent from computer A to computer M, the protocols check the network table, add the necessary information to the packet's header, and send it on its way.

The protocols that work at this layer do not ensure the delivery of the packets. They depend on the protocols at the transport layer to catch any problems and resend packets if necessary. IP is the main protocol working at the network layer, although other routing protocols work there also. The other protocols are the Internet Control Message Protocol (ICMP), Routing Information Protocol (RIP), Open Shortest Path First (OSPF), Border Gateway Protocol (BGP), and Internet Group Management Protocol (IGMP). Figure 7-7 shows that there are many routes a packet can take and it is the network layer that enters routing information into the header to help get the packet to its destination

Data Link Layer

Can you translate that message into bits for me? That is all I really understand.

As we continue down the protocol stack, we are getting closer and closer to the actual network wire all this data will travel over. The outer format of the data packet changes

Network Layer

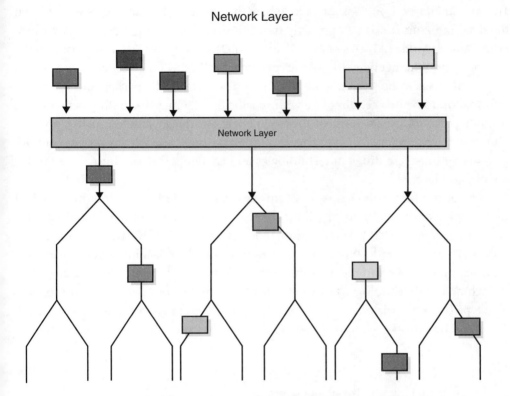

Figure 7-7 The network layer decides on the most efficient path for each packet to take.

slightly at each layer, and it comes to a point where it needs to be translated into local area network (LAN) or wide area network (WAN) technology binary format for proper line transmission. This happens at the *data link layer*.

NOTE APSTNDP: To remember all the layers within the OSI model in the correct order, memorize "All People Seem To Need Data Processing."

There are different LAN and WAN technologies that use different protocols, network interface cards (NICs), cables, and transmission methods. These different technologies have different data format structures and they interpret electricity voltages differently.

The *data link layer*, layer 2, is the place where the operating system knows what format the data frame must be in to properly transmit over Token Ring, Ethernet, Asynchronous Transfer Mode (ATM), or Fiber Distributed Data Interface (FDDI) networks. If the network is an Ethernet network, all the computers will expect the header to be a certain length, the flags to be positioned in a certain place within the packet, and the trailer information to be in a certain place with specific fields. On a Token Ring network, the computers would expect most of these parameters to be in different places and the frames to have different formats. The data link layer is responsible for proper communication within these different technologies and changing the data into 1s and 0s for the physical layer.

Some of the protocols that work at this layer are the Serial Line Internet Protocol (SLIP), Point-to-Point Protocol (PPP), Reverse Address Resolution Protocol (RARP), Layer 2 Forwarding (L2F), Layer 2 Tunneling Protocol (L2TP), FDDI, and Integrated Services Digital Network (ISDN). Figure 7-8 shows how the data link layer converts the information into bits and the physical layer converts those bits into electrical signals.

Each network technology (Ethernet, Token Ring, and so on) defines the compatible wire type (coaxial, twisted pair, or fiber) that is required to enable network communication. Each network technology also has defined electronic signaling and bit patterns.

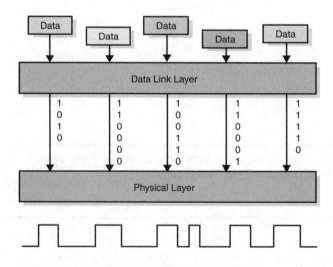

Data Link and Physical Layers

Figure 7-8   The data link layer converts the data into bits for the physical layer.

This means that a signal with the voltage of 0.5 volts on one technology may represent a 0 and within another technology 0.5 volts may represent a 1. The data link protocol specifies the proper bit patterns and the physical layer translates this information into electrical encoding and electricity state transitions. Network cards bridge the data link and physical layers. Information is passed down through the first six layers and hits the network card driver at the data link layer. Depending on the network technology being used (Ethernet, Token Ring, FDDI, and so on), the network card driver will encode the bits at the data link layer that are then turned into electricity states at the physical layer, and then placed onto the wire for transmission.

Physical Layer

Everything ends up as electrical signals anyway.

The *physical layer*, layer 1, converts bits into voltage for transmission. Signals and voltage schemes have different meanings for different LAN and WAN technologies. If a user sends data through his dial-up software and out his modem onto a telephone line, the data format, electrical signals, and control functionality would be much different than if that user sent data through the NIC and onto a unshielded twisted pair (UTP) wire. The mechanisms that control this data going onto the telephone line, or the UTP wire, work at the physical layer. This layer controls synchronization, data rates, controlling line noise, and medium access.

Functions and Protocols in the OSI Model

Application

File transfer, virtual terminals, network management, and fulfilling networking requests of applications

- **Protocols That Work at This Layer**
  - File Transfer Protocol (FTP)
  - Simple Network Management Protocol (SNMP)
  - Simple Mail Transfer Protocol (SMTP)
  - Trivial File Transfer Protocol (TFTP)
  - World Wide Web (WWW)

Presentation

Translation into standard formats, data compression and decompression, data encryption and decryption

- **Presentation Layer Standards**
  - American Standard Code for Information Interchange (ASCII)
  - Extended Binary-Coded Decimal Interchange Mode (EBCDIC)
  - Tagged Image File Format (TIFF)
  - Joint Photographic Experts Group (JPEG)
  - Motion Picture Experts Group (MPEG)
  - Musical Instrument Digital Interface (MIDI)

Session

Set up connection between computers, maintain dialog, negotiate, establish, maintain, and tear down the communication channel with another computer

- **Protocols That Work at This Layer**
  - Secure Sockets Layer (SSL)
  - Network File System (NFS)
  - Structured Query Language (SQL)
  - Remote Procedure Call (RPC)

Transport

End-to-end transmission, segmentation into a data stream, integrity checking, multiplexing, flow control, and sequencing

- **Protocols That Work at This Layer**
  - Transmission Control Protocol (TCP)
  - User Datagram Protocol (UDP)
  - Sequenced Packet Exchange (SPX)

Network

Internetworking service, routing, addressing

- **Protocols That Work at This Layer**
  - Internet Protocol (IP)
  - Internet Control Message Protocol (ICMP)
  - Routing Information Protocol (RIP)
  - Open Shortest Path First (OSPF)

Data Link

Converts into LAN or WAN frames for transmission, converts message into bits, and defines how a computer accesses a network

- **Protocols That Work at This Layer**
  - Address Resolution Protocol (ARP)
  - Point-to-Point Protocol (PPP)
  - Serial Line Internet Protocol (SLIP)

Physical

Converts bits into electrical signals and controls physical aspects of the data

- **Standard Interfaces at This Layer**
  - High-Speed Serial Interface (HSSI)
  - X.21
  - EIA/TIA-232 and EIA/TIA-449

Tying the Layers Together

All of these different layers work together to form the OSI model, which is used as a framework for many different products and many types of vendors. Different types of devices and protocols work at different parts of this seven-layer model. Whereas computers can interpret and process data at each of the seven layers, routers can only understand information up to the network layer. This is because a router's main function is to route packets and it does not need to know about any further information within the packet. A router will peel back the header information until it reaches the network layer data. This is where the routing information and IP address information is located. The

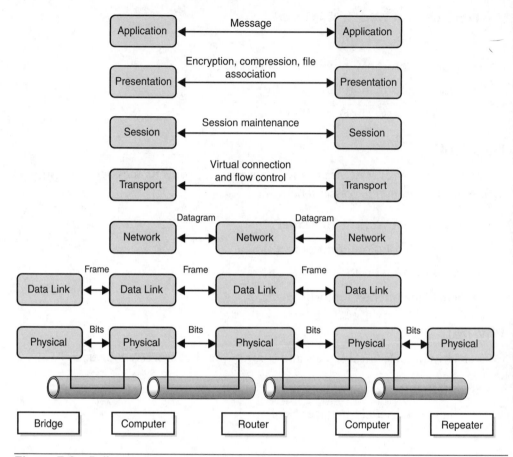

Figure 7-9 Different devices understand different layers within the OSI model.

router looks at this information to make its decisions on where the packet should be sent next. Bridges understand only up to the data link layer and repeaters only understand data at the physical layer. Figure 7-9 shows what level of the OSI model each type of device understands.

References

www.iso.chwww.salford.ac.uk/iti/books/osi/osi.html

www.wizard.com/users/baker/public_html/NetTutor.html

www.protocols.com

http://directory.google.com/Top/Computers/Internet/Protocols

TCP/IP

Transmission Control Protocol/Internet Protocol (TCP/IP) is a suite of protocols that govern the way that data travels from one device to another. There are two main components, TCP and IP protocols, although there are other protocols that make up this suite. IP is a network layer protocol and provides datagram routing services. IP's main task is to support internetwork addressing and packet forwarding and routing. It is a connectionless protocol that envelopes data passed to it from the transport layer. The IP protocol addresses the datagram with the source and destination IP addresses. The protocols within the TCP/IP suite work together to break the data passed down from the application layer into pieces that can be moved along a network. They work with other protocols to transmit the data to the destination computer and then to reassemble the data back into a form that the application layer can understand and process.

There are two main protocols that work at the transport layer: TCP and UDP. *TCP* is a reliable and *connection-oriented protocol*, which means that it ensures that packets are delivered to the destination computer. If a packet is lost during transmission, TCP has the capability to resend it. TCP also supports packet sequencing (to ensure each and every packet was received), flow and congestion control, and error detection and correction. *UDP*, on the other hand, is a *best-effort* and *connectionless-oriented protocol*. It does not have packet sequencing, flow and congestion control, and the destination does not acknowledge every packet it receives.

IP

The Internet Protocol (IP) is a connectionless protocol that provides an envelope and address for each package of data. It is the mechanism that enables the network to read IP addresses and implement proper routing functions.

The data, IP, and network relationship can be compared to the relationship of a letter and the postal system. The message is the letter, which is enveloped and addressed by IP, and the network and its services enable the message to be sent from its origin to its destination, like the postal system.

Data = Letter

IP = Addressed Envelope

Network = Postal System

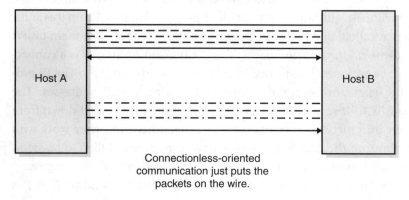

Connection-oriented communication
performs handshaking, sets up a virtual
circuit, and verifies that each packet
reaches its destination.

Host A

Host B

Connectionless-oriented
communication just puts the
packets on the wire.

Figure 7-10   Connection-oriented versus connectionless-oriented protocol functionality

TCP is referred to as a connection-oriented protocol because handshaking takes place between the two systems that want to communicate before any data is actually sent. Once the handshaking completes successfully, a virtual circuit is set up between the two systems. The UDP protocol is considered connectionless because it does not go through these steps. Instead, UDP sends out messages without first contacting the destination computer and does not know if the packets were received properly or dropped. Figure 7-10 shows the difference between a connection-oriented and a connectionless-oriented protocol.

UDP and TCP sit together on the transport layer and developers have a choice of which to choose when they are coding applications. Many times TCP is the transport protocol of choice because it provides reliability and ensures that the packets are delivered. For example, SMTP is used to transmit e-mail messages and uses TCP because it needs to make sure that the data is delivered. TCP provides a full-duplex, reliable communication mechanism, and if any packets are lost or damaged, they are resent; however, TCP requires a lot of system overhead. If the programmer knows that if the data that is being sent gets dropped and it is not detrimental to the application, then UDP may be the protocol of choice because it is quicker and requires fewer resources. An example of using UDP instead of TCP is when a server sends out status information to all listening nodes on the network. A node will not be negatively affected if, by some chance, it did not receive this status information because it will be repeated every 30 minutes.

TCP Handshake

Every proper dialog begins with a polite handshake.

TCP has to set up a virtual connection between two hosts before any data is sent. This means that the two hosts must agree on certain parameters, data flow, and options. These issues are negotiated during the handshaking phase, as shown in Figure 7-11.

The host that initiates communication sends a synchronous (SYN) packet to the receiver. The receiver acknowledges this request by sending a SYN/ACK packet. This packet translates into "I have received your request and am ready to communicate with you." The sending host acknowledges this with an acknowledgment (ACK) packet, which translates into "I received your acknowledgment. Let's start transmitting our data." This completes the handshaking phase, a virtual connection is set up, and actual data can now be passed.

UDP and TCP are transport protocols that applications use to get their data across a network. They both use ports to communicate with upper OSI layers and to keep track of different conversations that take place at the same time. The ports are also the mechanism used to identify how other computers access services. When a TCP or UDP message is formed, there is a source and destination port within the header information along with the source and destination address; this makes up a socket. This is how packets know where to go, by the address, and how to communicate with the right service on the other computer, by the port number. The IP address acts as the doorway to a computer, and the port acts as the doorway to the service. To properly communicate, the packet needs to know these different doors. Figure 7-12 shows how packets communicate with different applications and services, which is through ports.

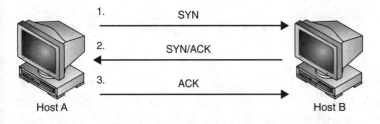

Figure 7-11 TCP three-way handshake

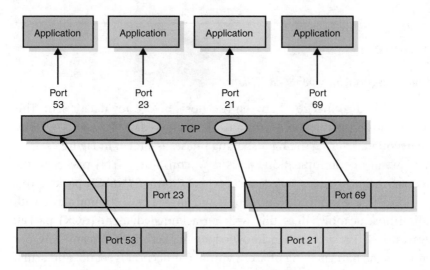

Figure 7-12 It is through a port that the packet can communicate with upper-layer applications and services.

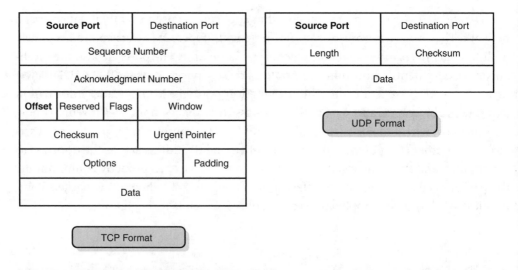

Figure 7-13 TCP carries a lot more information within its segment format because it offers more services than UDP.

The difference between TCP and UDP can also be seen in the differences in their message format. Because TCP offers more services than UDP, it must contain much more information within its packet format, as shown in Figure 7-13. Table 7-1 lists the major differences between the TCP and UDP.

Table 7-1 Major Differences Between the TCP and UDP

Service	TCP	UDP
Reliability	Ensures that packets reach their destinations, returns ACKs when a packet is received, and is a reliable protocol	Does not return ACKs and does not guarantee that a packet will reach its destination, and is an unreliable protocol
Connection	Connection-oriented, thus it performs handshaking and develops a virtual connection with destination computer	Connectionless-oriented, thus it does no handshaking and does not set up a virtual connection
Packet sequencing	Uses sequence numbers within packets to make sure that each packet within a message is received	Does not use sequence numbers
Congestion controls	The destination computer can tell the source if it is overwhelmed and to slow the transmission rate.	The destination computer does not communicate back to the source computer about flow control.
Usage	Used when reliable delivery is required as in e-mail and domain name service (DNS) requests	Used when reliable delivery is not required as in streaming video and status broadcasts
Speed and overhead	Uses a considerable amount of resources and is slower than UDP	Uses fewer resources and is faster than TCP

Data Structures

What's in a name?

As stated earlier, the message is usually formed at the application layer and sent down through the protocol stack. Each protocol at each layer adds its own information to the message and passes it down to the next level. As the message is passed down the stack, it actually goes through a sort of evolution and each stage has a specific name that indicates what is taking place. Within the IP protocol suite, when an application formats data to be transmitted over the network, it is called a *message*. The message is sent to the transport layer where TCP does its magic on the data. The bundle of data is now a *segment*. The segment is sent to the network layer. The network layer adds routing and addressing, and now the bundle is called a *datagram*. The network layer passes it off to the data link layer, which frames the datagram with a header and a trailer, and now it is a *frame*. Figure 7-14 illustrates these stages.

Sometimes when an author talks about a datagram, he is specifying the stage the data is in. If the literature is describing routers, which work at the network layer, he

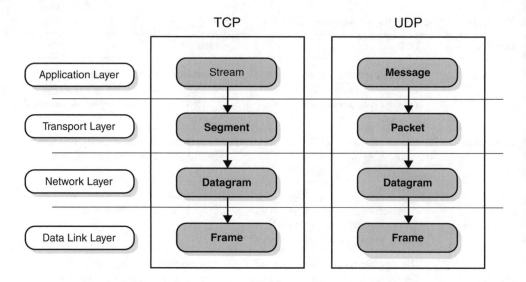

Figure 7-14 The data goes through its own evolutionary stages as it passes through different layers within the OSI model.

might use the word datagram because the data at this level has routing and addressing information attached. If an author is describing network traffic and flow control, she might use the word frame because all data actually ends up in the frame format before it is put on the network wire. However, sometimes authors refer to all data packages as packets and call it a day.

So what is important to understand is the different steps a data package goes through when it goes up and down the protocol stack and that just because an author refers to data as a packet, it does not mean that he is necessarily indicating the data structure.

IP Addressing

Take a right at the router, and a left at the access server. I live at 10.10.2.3.

Each node on a network must have a unique IP address. Today, *IP version 4 (IPv4)* is the version most in use, compared to *IP version 6 (IPv6)*. IPv6 was created because IPv4 addresses are so high in demand that their supply started running out. (IPv6 also has many security features built into it that are not part of IPv4.).

IPv4 uses 32 bits for its address, and IPv6 uses 128 bits; thus, it provides more possible addresses. Each address has a host and network portion of the address and the addresses are grouped into classes and then into subnets. The subnet mask of the address differentiates the different groups of addresses that define the different subnets of a network.

Although each node has an IP address, people usually refer to their hostnames instead of IP numbers. Hostnames, like **www.isc2.org**, are easier to remember than 10.13.84.4. However, the use of these two nomenclatures requires mapping between the hostnames and IP addresses, because the computer only really understands the numbering scheme. This process is addressed in the "DNS" section.

Networking

We really need to connect all these resources together.

The three main reasons to have a network in the first place are to be able to communicate between computers, share resources, and to provide central administration. Most users on a network will need to use the same type of resources such as printers, file servers, plotters, fax machines, Internet connections, and so on. Why not just string all the computers together and have these resources available to all? Great idea, and we shall call it networking!

Networking has had amazing advances in just a short period of time. In the beginning of the computer age, mainframes were the name of the game. They were isolated powerhouses and many had dumb terminals hanging off them. However, this was not true networking. In the late 1960s and early 1970s, some technical researchers came up with ways of connecting all the mainframes and Unix systems to enable them to communicate. This marked the Internet's baby steps.

Microcomputers evolved and were used in many offices and work areas. Slowly dumb terminals got a little smarter and more powerful and users needed to share office resources. And bam, Ethernet was developed, which allowed for true networking. There was no turning back after this.

 NOTE Identification and authentication is a large part of networking, which is covered extensively in Chapter 4. However, it is important to note that node authentication, by itself, should not be used to establish trustworthiness of a user within the network. Within a distributed network, knowing whom to trust is a major security issue.

References

http://grouper.ieee.org/groups/

www.lantronix.com/learning/wp/index.html

LAN Media Access Technologies

A *LAN* is a network that provides shared communication and resources in a relatively small area. What defines a LAN, as compared to a WAN, looks more at the physical medium, encapsulation protocols, and functionality. For example, a LAN could use 10Base-T cabling, IPX/SPX encapsulation protocols, and could enable users to communicate who are in the same local building. A WAN, on the other hand, could use fiber-optic cabling, L2TP encapsulation protocol, and could enable users from one building to communicate with other users in another building in another state. Most of the differences between these different technologies take place at the data link layer.

The definition of *local* in LAN is the limitation of the shared medium, the number of devices and computers that can be connected to it, transmission rates, cable types, and devices used. If a network administrator develops a very large LAN that should really be multiple LANs, there could be too much traffic, which would cause a big performance hit or the cabling could be too long so that attenuation (signal loss) becomes a factor. In environments where the network segments are too large, routers, bridges, and switches may be overwhelmed, and administration of this network could get hairy and complex, which opens the doors for errors and security holes. The network administrator should follow the specifications of the technology he is using and once he has maxed out these numbers, he should consider implementing two LANs instead of one large LAN.

Question

A LAN is said to cover a relatively small area. When is a LAN no longer a LAN?

Answer: When two distinct LANs are connected by a router, the result is an internetwork, not a larger LAN. Each distinct LAN has its own addressing scheme, broadcasts, and communication mechanisms. If these two LANs are connected by a different data link layer technology, like frame relay or X.25, then we are looking at a WAN.

LANs are defined by their physical topologies, data link layer technologies, protocols, and devices used. The following sections go over these topics and how they interrelate to each other.

References

www.wizard.com/users/baker/public_html/NetTutor.html

http://grouper.ieee.org/groups/802

http://web66.coled.umn.edu/Construction

Ethernet

Ethernet is a LAN sharing technology that enables several devices to communicate on the same network. Ethernet usually uses a bus or star topology. If a bus topology is used, then all devices connect to one cable. If a star topology is used, then each device is connected to a cable that is connected to a centralized hub. Ethernet was developed in the 1970s and commercially available in 1980 and became the IEEE 802.3 standard.

Ethernet has seen quite an evolution in its short history from purely coaxial cable installation that worked at 10 Mbps to mostly Category 5 twisted-pair cable that works at 100 Mbps, 1,000 Mbps, and Gbps speeds.

Ethernet is defined by the following characteristics:

- Shared media (all devices must take turns using the same media and detect collisions)

- Uses broadcast and collision domains

- Uses carrier sense multiple access with collision detection (CSMA/CD) access method

- Supports full-duplex on twisted-pair implementations

- Can use coaxial or twisted-pair media

- Defined by standard 802.3

Ethernet deals with how computers share a common network, how they deal with collisions, data integrity, communication mechanisms, and transmission controls. These are the common characteristics of Ethernet, but Ethernet does vary in the type of cabling schemes and transfer rates it can supply. There are several types of Ethernet implementations, which are listed in Appendix E, but the following sections discuss 10Base2, 10Base5, and 10Base-T, which are common implementations.

10Base2, ThinNet, is a common Ethernet implementation that uses coaxial cable, which is thin, flexible, and easy to work with. It has a maximum cable length of 185 meters, provides 10-Mbps transmission rates, and requires British Naval Connectors (BNCs) to network devices. Figure 7-15 shows a simple 10Base2 Ethernet implementation.

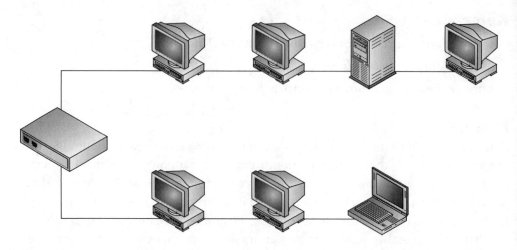

Figure 7-15 10Base2 is a coaxial cable Ethernet implementation that provides 10-Mbps transmission.

10Base5, ThickNet, uses a thicker coaxial cable, which is not as flexible as ThinNet and harder to work with. However, ThickNet can have longer cable segments than Thin-Net and is often used as network backbones. ThickNet is more resistant to electrical interference than ThinNet and is usually preferred when stringing wire through electrically noisy environments that contain heavy machinery and magnetic fields. ThickNet also requires BNCs because it uses coaxial cables.

10Base-T uses twisted-pair copper wiring instead of coaxial cabling. Twisted-pair wiring uses one wire for transmitting data and the other for receiving data. 10Base-T is usually implemented in a star topology, which provides easy network configuration. In a star topology, all systems are connected to hubs and these hubs can be in a flat or hierarchical configuration. The different types of Ethernet are shown in Table 7-2.

Table 7-2 Types of Ethernet

Ethernet Type	Cabling Type	Speed
10Base2, ThinNet	Coaxial	10 Mbps
10Base5, ThickNet	Coaxial	10 Mbps
10Base-T	UTP	10 Mbps
100Base-TX, Fast Ethernet	UTP	100 Mbps
1000Base-T, Gigabit Ethernet	UTP	1,000 Mbps

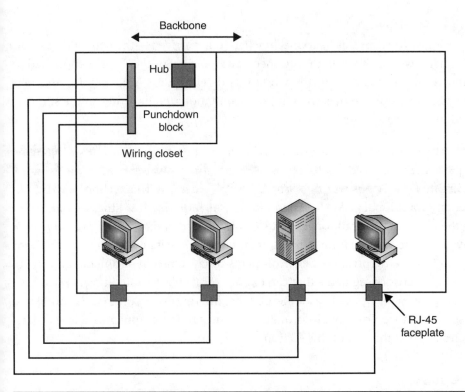

Figure 7-16   Ethernet hosts connect to a punchdown block within the wiring closet, which is connected to the backbone via a hub.

10Base-T networks have RJ-45 connector faceplates that the computer connects to. The wires usually run behind a wall, and connect the faceplate to a punchdown block within a wiring closet. Many times the punchdown block is connected to a 10Base-T hub that serves as a doorway to the network's backbone cable or to a central switch. This type of configuration is shown in Figure 7-16.

Question

Why does my NIC have two input connectors that are shaped differently?

Answer: Most NICs provide support for 10Base2 and 10Base-T. The round connector is used for 10Base2, which is the BNC, used for coaxial wiring. The connector that looks like a phone connector supports 10Base-T, which is twisted-pair wiring. (10Base2, 10Base5, and 10Base-T specifications are explained further in Appendix E.)

Ethernet in Overdrive

Not surprisingly, 10 Mbps was heaven-sent when it first arrived to the networking scene, but soon many were demanding more speed and power. So, the smart people had to gather into small rooms and hit the white boards with ideas, calculations, and new technologies. The results of these meetings, computations, engineering, and testing are addressed in the next section.

Fast Ethernet   *Fast Ethernet* is regular Ethernet, but running at 100 Mbps over twisted-pair wiring instead of 10 Mbps. Around the same time that Fast Ethernet arrived, another 100 Mbps was developed: 100-VG-AnyLAN. This technology did not use Ethernet's traditional CSMA/CD and did not catch on like Fast Ethernet did.

Fast Ethernet uses the traditional CSMA/CD (*explained in the "CSMA" section later in the chapter*) and the original frame format of Ethernet. These issues are the main reasons it is used in many enterprise LAN environments today. One environment can run 10- and 100-Mbps network segments that can communicate via 10/100 hubs or switches.

There are four main types of Fast Ethernet; the differences pertain to the cabling and transmission distance. For more information on these, refer to Appendix E and the reference sites given at the end of this section.

References

www.iol.unh.edu/consortiums/fe/

http://alumni.caltech.edu/~dank/fe

www.ots.utexas.edu/ethernet/100mbps.html

Token Ring

Like Ethernet, *Token Ring* is a LAN technology that enables the communication and sharing of networking resources. The Token Ring topology was originally developed by IBM and holds the IEEE 802.5 standard. It uses a *token-passing* technology with a star-configured topology. The ring part of the name pertains to how the signals travel, which is in a logical ring. Each computer is connected to a central hub, called a *Multistation Access Unit (MAU)*. So, physically the topology can be a star, but the signals and transmissions are passed in a ring.

At first Token Ring technology had the capability of transmitting data at 4 Mbps and later it was improved to transmit at 16 Mbps. When a frame is put on the wire, each computer will look at it to see if the frame is addressed to it. If the frame does not have that specific computer's address, the computer will put it back on the wire, properly amplify the message, and pass it to the next computer on the ring.

Token Ring has a couple of mechanisms that deal with problems that can occur on this type of a network. The *active monitor* mechanism removes frames that are continually circulating on the network. This can happen if a computer locks up or is taken offline for one reason or another and cannot properly receive a token destined to it. Another mechanism this type of network uses is *beaconing*. If a computer detects a problem with the network, it sends a beacon frame. This frame generates a failure domain, which is between the computer that issued the beacon and its neighbor downstream. The computers and devices within this failure domain will attempt to reconfigure certain settings to try and work around the detected fault. Figure 7-17 depicts a Token Ring network that is in a physical ring.

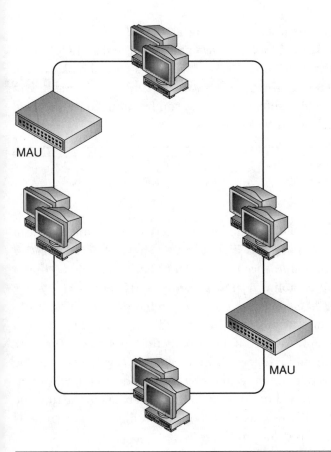

Figure 7-17   Token Ring network

Token Ring networks were popular in the 1980s and 1990s and although some are still around, Ethernet has become much more popular and taken over the LAN networking market.

References

www.8025.org

www.faqs.org/faqs/LANs/token-ring-faq

www.techfest.com/networking/lan/token.htm

Question

Where do the differences between Ethernet, Token Ring, and FDDI lie?

Answer: These technologies are data link layer technologies. The data link layer is actually made up of a Medium Access Control (MAC) layer and a Logical Link Control (LLC) layer. These different technologies live at the MAC layer and have to interface to the LLC layer. These LAN technologies differ in how they communicate to the protocol stack and what type of functionalities they can provide.

FDDI

Fiber Distributed Data Interface (FDDI) technology was developed by the American National Standards Institute (ANSI) and is a high-speed token-passing media access topology. FDDI has a data transmission speed of 100 Mbps and is usually used as a backbone network using fiber-optic cabling. FDDI also provides fault tolerance by providing a second counterrotating fiber ring. The primary ring has data traveling clockwise and is used for regular data transmission. The second ring transmits data in a counterclockwise fashion and is only invoked if the primary ring goes down. There are sensors watching the primary ring and if it goes down, these sensors will invoke a ring wrap so that the data will be diverted to the second ring. Each node on the FDDI network has relays, which are connected to both rings, so if there is a break in the ring, the two rings can be joined. When FDDI is used as a backbone network, it usually connects several different types of networks, as shown in Figure 7-18.

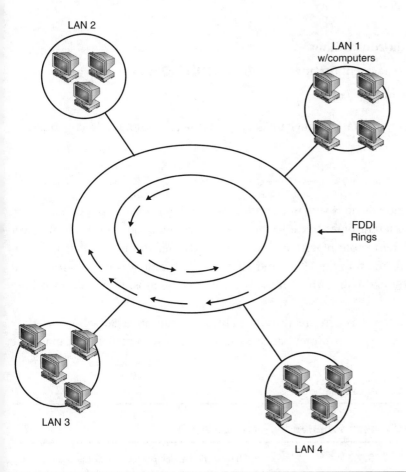

Figure 7-18 FDDI rings can be used as backbones to connect different LAN networks.

Before Fast Ethernet and Gigabit Ethernet hit the market, FDDI was used mainly as campus and service provider backbones. Because FDDI can be used for a distance up to 100 kilometers, it was often used in metropolitan area networks (MANs). The benefit of FDDI is that it can work over long distances and at high speeds with minimal interferences. It enables several tokens to be present on the ring at the same time, causing more communication to take place simultaneously and provides predictable delays, which helps connected networks and devices know what to expect and when.

FDDI has a version that can work over UTP cabling: Copper Distributed Data Interface (CDDI). Whereas FDDI would be used more as a backbone, CDDI can be used within a LAN environment connecting systems.

References

www.iol.unh.edu/consortiums

www.cicese.mx/~aarmenta/frames/redes/fddi/FDDIFAQ.html

www.nswc.navy.mil/ITT/x3t12

Table 7-3 sums up the important characteristics of the technologies described in this section.

Cabling

Network cabling and wiring is very important when setting up a network or extending an existing one. Different types of cables need to be used with specific data link layer technologies. Different cable types have varying speeds, maximum lengths, and connectivity issues with NICs. In the 1970s and 1980s coaxial cable was the way to go, but in the late 1980s twisted-pair wiring hit the scene and is the most popular networking cable used today.

Electrical signals travel as currents through cables and can be negatively affected by many things within the environment such as motors, fluorescent lighting, magnetic

Table 7-3 LAN Media Access Methods

LAN Media Access Method	IEEE Standard	Characteristics
Ethernet	802.3	• Shared media—all devices must take turns using the same media and detect collisions. • Uses broadcast and collision domains • Uses CSMA/CD access method • Can use coaxial or twisted-pair media • Transmission speeds of 10 Mbps–1 Gbps
Token Ring	802.5	• All devices connect to a central MAU. • Token-passing media access method • Transmission speeds of 4–16 Mbps • Uses an active monitor and beaconing
FDDI	802.8	• Token-passing media access method • Dual counterrotating ring for fault tolerance • Transmission speeds of 100 Mbps over fiber-optic cable • Operates over long distance at high speeds, and is therefore used as backbones • CDDI works over UTP.

forces, and other electrical devices. These items can corrupt the data as it travels through the cable. This is the reason that there are cable standards that indicate cable type, shielding, transmission rates, and cable distances.

Cabling has bandwidth and data rate values associated with it. Although these two terms are related, they are indeed different. The **bandwidth** of a cable indicates the highest frequency range that it uses; for instance, 10Base-T uses 10 MHz and 100Base-TX uses 80 MHz. This is different than the actual amount of data that can be pushed through a cable. The **data rate** is the actual data throughput of a cable after compression and encoding have been used. 10Base-T has a data rate of 10 Mbps and 100Base-TX has a data rate of 100 Mbps. So, the bandwidth can be thought of as the size of the pipe and the data rate is the actual amount of data going through that pipe.

Coaxial Cable

Coaxial cabling has a copper core that is surrounded by a shielding layer and grounding wire, as shown in Figure 7-19. This is all encased within a protective outer jacket. Coaxial cable is more resistant to electromagnetic interference (EMI), provides a higher bandwidth, and longer cable lengths can be used when compared to twisted-pair cabling. So, why is twisted pair more popular? Twisted-pair cabling is cheaper, easier to work with, and the move to switched environments that provide hierarchical wiring schemes has overcome the cable length issue of twisted-pair cables.

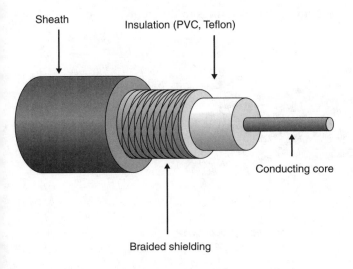

Figure 7-19   Coaxial cable

The two main types of coaxial cable used within LAN environments are the 50-ohm cable (used for digital signaling) and 75-ohm cable (used for high-speed digital signaling and analog signaling). The coaxial cable types are 10Base2 (ThinNet) and 10Base5 (ThickNet). Coaxial can transmit using a *baseband* method, where the cable carries only one channel, or a *broadband* method, where the cable carries several channels.

Twisted-Pair Cable

This cable is kind of flimsy. Why do we use it? Answer: It's cheap and easy to work with.

Twisted-pair cabling has insulated copper wires that are surrounded by an outer protective jacket. If the cable has an outer foil shielding, it is referred to as *shielded twisted pair (STP)*, which is added protection from radio frequency interference. Another type of twisted-pair cabling does not have this extra outer shielding and is called *unshielded twisted pair (UTP)*.

The cable contains copper wires that twist around each other, as shown in Figure 7-20. This twisting of the wires protects the signals they carry from radio frequency and electromagnetic interference, and crosstalk. Each wire forms a balanced circuit because the voltage in each pair uses the same amplitude, just with opposite phases. The tighter the twisting of the wires, the more resistant the cable is to interference and attenuation. UTP has different categories of cabling that have different characteristics. The difference in the category ratings is based on how tightly wound the cables are.

The twisting of the wires, the type of insulation used, the quality of the conductive material, and the shielding of the wire determine the rate that data can be transmitted. These components are used to assign different ratings to different types of UTP cables.

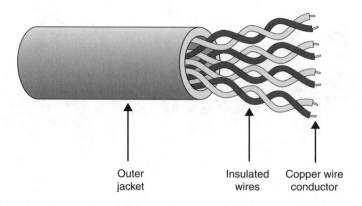

Outer jacket   Insulated wires   Copper wire conductor

Figure 7-20 Twisted-pair cabling uses copper wires.

Table 7-4   UTP Cable Ratings

UTP Category	Characteristic	Usage
Category 1	Voice-grade telephone cable	Not recommended for network use, but modems can communicate over it
Category 2	Data transmission up to 4 Mbps	Used in mainframe and minicomputer terminal connections, but not recommended for high-speed networking
Category 3	10 Mbps for Ethernet and 4 Mbps for Token Ring	Used in 10Base-T network installations
Category 4	16 Mbps	Used usually in Token Ring networks
Category 5	100 Mbps for 100Base-TX and FDDI networks; has high twisting, and thus low crosstalk	Used in 100Base-TX, FDDI, and ATM installations; most widely used for new network installations
Category 6	155 Mbps	Used in new network installations requiring high-speed transmission
Category 7	1 Gbps	Used in new network installations requiring higher-speed transmission

Some types are more suitable and effective for specific uses and environments. Table 7-4 lists the cable ratings.

Copper cabling has been around for many years; it is inexpensive and well understood. A majority of the telephone systems today use copper cabling with the rating of voice grade. Twisted-pair wiring is the preferred network cabling, but it also has its drawbacks. Copper actually resists the flow of electrons, which causes a signal to degrade after it has traveled a certain distance. This is why cable lengths are recommended for copper cables and if they are not abided by, a network could experience signal loss and corruption. Copper also radiates energy, which means that information can be monitored and captured by intruders. UTP is the least secure networking cable compared to coaxial and fiber. If a company requires higher speed, higher security, and cables to have longer runs than what is allowed in copper cabling, then fiber optic may be a better choice.

Fiber-Optic Cabling

"Hey Bill, I can't tap into this fiber cable." Bill replies, "Exactly."

Twisted-pair and coaxial cabling use copper wires as their data transmission media, but fiber-optic cables use a type of glass. The glass carries light waves, which represent the data that is being transmitted. The glass core is surrounded by a protective cladding and is all encased within an outer jacket.

Because of the use of glass, fiber-optic cabling has higher transmission speeds that can travel over longer distances and is not affected by attenuation and EMI when compared to cabling that uses copper. It does not radiate signals like UTP cabling and is very hard to tap into; therefore, fiber-optic cabling is much more secure than UTP, STP, or coaxial.

Fiber optic sounds like the way to go, so why even bother with UTP, STP, and coaxial? Fiber-optic cabling is extremely expensive and very hard to work with. Fiber-optic cabling is usually used in backbone networks and environments that require high data transfer rates. Most networks use UTP and connect to a backbone that uses fiber.

Cabling Problems

Cables are extremely important within networks and when they have problems, the whole network could experience problems. This section addresses some of the more common cabling issues many networks experience.

Noise

Noise on a line is usually caused by surrounding devices or characteristics of the environment that the wiring is in. This noise can be caused by motors, computers, copy machines, florescent lighting, and microwave ovens. This background noise can combine with the data being transmitted over the cable and distort the signal, as shown in Figure 7-21. The more noise that interacts with the cable, the more likely it is that the

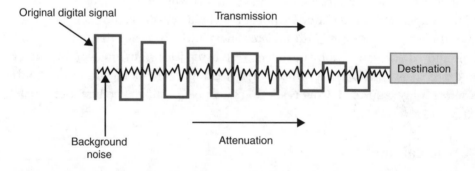

Figure 7-21 Background noise can merge with an electronic signal and alter the signal's integrity.

receiving end will not receive the data in the form that was originally transmitted. (These issues and line conditioners are discussed in Chapter 6.)

Attenuation

Attenuation is the loss of signal strength as it travels. The longer a cable is, the more attenuation will be introduced and the signal that is carrying data will deteriorate. Suggested cable run lengths are part of standards because once data travels over a certain distance, the restriction of electron flow aggregates and destroys the integrity of the signal.

The effects of attenuation increase with higher frequencies; thus, 100Base-TX at 80 MHz has a higher attenuation rate than 10Base-T at 10 MHz. This means that cables used to transmit data at higher frequencies should have shorter cable runs to ensure that attenuation does not become an issue.

Attenuation can also be caused by cable breaks and cable malfunctions. This is why cables should be tested. If a cable is suspected of attenuation problems, cable testers can inject signals into the cable and read the results at the end of the cable. The effects of attenuation are illustrated in Figure 7-22.

Crosstalk

UTP is susceptible to *crosstalk*, which is when electrical signals of one wire spill over to another wire. When the different electrical signals mix, their integrity lessens and there is a higher chance of data corruption. UTP is much more vulnerable to this than STP or coaxial because it does not have extra layers of shielding to help protect against it.

As stated earlier, the two wire pairs within twisted-pair cables form a balanced circuit because they both have the same amplitude, just with different phases. Crosstalk and background noise can throw off this balance and the wire can actually start to act like an antenna, which means it will be more susceptible to picking up other noises in the environment.

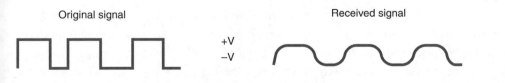

Figure 7-22   Attenuation weakens a signal.

Fire Rating of Cables

This cable smells funny when it's on fire.

Just as buildings must meet certain fire codes, so must certain wiring schemes. A lot of companies string their network wires in drop ceilings, the space between the ceiling and the next floor. This enables the cables to be out of sight and not likely to be tripped over. However, when wires are strung in places like this, they are more likely to catch on fire without anyone knowing about it. Some burning cables produce hazardous gases that would spread throughout the building very quickly. Network cabling that is placed in this type of area, called *plenum space*, must meet a specific fire rating to ensure that it will not produce and release harmful chemicals in case of a fire.

Nonplenum cables usually have a polyvinyl chloride (PVC) jacket covering, whereas plenum-rated cables have jacket covers made of fluoropolymers. When setting up a network or extending an existing network, it is important to know which wire types are required in which situation.

There are several things to consider when choosing cabling for a network. The cabling needs to fit the needs of the company and network pertaining to cost, ease of handling, possible signal interference, distance of cable run, necessary speed of transmission, security, and fire rating.

Cables should be installed in unexposed areas so that they are not easily tripped over, damaged, or eavesdropped upon. The cables should be strung behind walls and in the protected spaces between the ceiling and next floor. In some situations, wires are encapsulated within *pressurized conduits*, so that if there is an attempt to access a wire, the pressure of the conduit will change and sound an alarm or send a message to the administrator.

In the cases where heavy machinery or other devices that conduct electromagnetic fields are used, STP or fiber-optic cabling should be installed. If security is a top priority to a company, then fiber-optic cabling should be used.

Types of Transmission

Data transmission can happen in different ways (analog or digital), use different controlling schemes (synchronous or asynchronous), and can use only one channel over a wire (as in baseband), or use several different channels over one wire (as in broadband). These different transmission types and their characteristics are described in the next sections.

Analog and Digital

Analog transmission signals are continuously varying electromagnetic waves that can be carried over air, water, twisted-pair, coaxial, or fiber-optic cable. Through a process of modulation, this analog signal is combined with a carrier signal of a specific frequency. The modulation of a signal differs in amplitude (height of the signal) and frequency (number of waves in a defined period of time), as shown in Figure 7-23. This means that data (the analog signal) is put on the back of a carrier signal. It is the different carrying signals that provide many different radio stations, frequency ranges, and communication channels. Each radio station is given a certain carrier signal to use for its transmission. This is how there can be three different country stations on three different radio channels.

Computers use digital signals when moving data from one component to another within the computer itself. When this computer is connected to a telephone line via a dial-up connection, a modem (modulate/demodulate) must transform this digital data into an analog signal because this is what is expected and used on the telephone lines. The modem actually modulates the digital data onto an analog signal. Once the data reaches the destination computer, it must be transformed back into a digital state so that the destination computer can understand it. *Digital signals* represent binary digits as electrical pulses. Each individual pulse is a signal element and represents either a 1

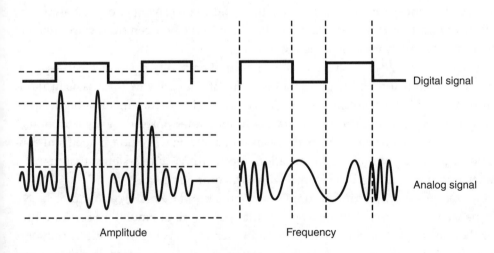

Figure 7-23 Analog signals are measured in amplitude and frequency, whereas digital signals represent binary digits as electrical pulses.

or a 0. Bandwidth refers to the number of electrical pulses that can be transmitted over a link within a second and these electrical pulses carry individual bits.

Digital signals are more reliable over a long distance and provide a clear cut and efficient signaling method because the voltage is either on (1) or not on (0), compared to interpreting the waves of an analog signal. Digital signals can easily be extracted from noise and retransmitted. It is harder to extract analog signals from background noise because the amplitudes and frequency slowly lose form. Digital systems are superior to analog systems in that they can transport more calls and data transmissions on the same line at higher quality over longer distances.

Communication used to be mainly transmitted via analog signals, but today, most communication is digitized. Telephone companies digitize telephone calls and many corporate telephone systems are digitized. Other than radio waves used by radio stations, ham radios, and the like, the only communication that is still analog is the copper wiring that goes from a residential house to the telephone company's central office.

Asynchronous and Synchronous

It's all in the timing.

Two devices can communicate through asynchronous or synchronous means; it depends on the type of communication and if the two systems are synchronized in any way.

Asynchronous communication is used when the two devices are not synchronized in any way. The sender can send data at anytime and the receiving end must always be ready. In contrast, *synchronous communication* takes place between two devices that are synchronized, usually via a clocking mechanism.

Usually when two devices have a large amount of data to transfer, they will use synchronous transmission and with a small amount of data, they will use asynchronous transmission. This does not mean one device can decide, "Huh, this is a big heap of data. I better send it the through my synchronous route instead of asynchronous." Instead, systems that usually transfer large amounts of data will be developed and configured with synchronous communication mechanisms and systems that transfer smaller amounts of data are developed with asynchronous means.

One example of asynchronous communication takes place between a terminal and a terminal server. If a user is using a system that has terminal emulation software running, then she has the desktop that the terminal server wants her to have. She only sees the desktop on her computer and all processing actually takes place on the terminal server. This means that every mouse click, keystroke, and command she initiates actually travels over the networking cable to the terminal server and the terminal server performs the actions that correspond with these commands. The results are transmitted back to the user's desktop so that it seems her computer did the work, when in fact it was done on the terminal server, which could be on another floor or another location altogether. This type of technology usually transmits a small amount of data at a time; thus, it uses asynchronous data transmission.

Modems also use asynchronous data transmission. Because the data can travel at anytime and be any length, there must be a stop and start delimitinator to tell the receiving end when to start processing a request and when to stop. Each character, which is really just a string of 1s and 0s, has a start-of-character bit and a stop bit before and after the character. This produces a lot of overhead and extra bits, but is necessary in asynchronous communications.

Synchronous communication, on the other hand, transfers data as a stream of bits instead of data framed in start and stop bits. The synchronization can happen with both systems using the same clocking mechanism or a signal can be encoded into the data stream to let the receiver synchronize with the sender of the message. This synchronization needs to take place before the first message is sent. The sending system can transmit a digital clock pulse to the receiving system, which translates into, "We will start here and work in this type of synchronization scheme."

Broadband and Baseband

How many channels can you shove into this one wire?

Baseband is a transmission method that is accomplished by applying direct current to a cable. The signals, or currents, hold binary information. Higher voltage usually represents the binary value of 1, or a lower, voltage represents the binary value of 0.

Baseband uses the full cable for its transmission, whereas *broadband* usually divides the cable into channels so that different types of data can be transmitted at the same time. Baseband permits only one signal to be transmitted at a time, whereas broadband carries several signals over different channels. For example, the coaxial cable TV (CATV) system is a broadband technology that delivers multiple television channels over the same cable. This system also provides home users Internet access, but this data is transmitted at a different frequency spectrum than the TV channels. Ethernet is a baseband network that transmits only one signal at time.

Broadband encompasses many different types of technologies, but one general rule is that it provides data transmissions higher than 56 to 128 Kbps, which is what the standard telephone line provides. Broadband communications provide channels for data transmission and can be used by many different users. The types of broadband communication systems available today are leased lines (T1, T3), ISDN, ATM, Digital Subscriber Line (DSL), broadband wireless, and CATV.

LAN Transmission Methods

Sometimes a packet needs to go to only one workstation, a set of workstations, or to all workstations on a particular subnet. If a packet needs to go from the source computer to one particular system, then a *unicast* transmission method is used. If the packet needs to go to a specific group of systems, then the sending system uses the *multicast* method. If a system wants all computers on its subnet to receive a message, it will use the *broadcast* method.

Unicast is pretty simple because it has a source and destination address. The data goes from point A to Z, it is a one-to-one transmission, and everyone is happy. Multicast is a bit different in that it is a one-to-many transmission. Multicasting enables one computer to send data to a selective group of computers. A good example is tuning into a radio station on a computer. Some computers have software that enables the user to determine if she wants to listen to country western, pop, Christian, or head-banging rock. Once the user selects one of these, the software must tell the NIC driver to not only pick up packets addressed to its specific IP address, but also pick up packets that contain a specific multicast address.

The difference between broadcast and multicast is that in a broadcast, one-to-all transmission, everyone gets the data and in multicast, only a few who have chosen to receive the data actually get it. So, how does a server three states away multicast to one particular computer on a specific network and no other networks in between? Good question, glad you asked. The user who elects to receive a multicast actually has to tell her local router that she wants to get frames with this particular multicast address passed her way. The local router must tell the router upstream and this process continues so that each router between the source and destination know where to pass this multicast data. This makes sure the user can get her head-banging rock music and other networks are not bothered with this extra data. (The user does not actually need to tell her local router anything; the software on her computer will pass along the information and it is passed off and handled through a routing protocol.)

IP multicast protocols use a class D address, which is a special address designed especially for multicasting. It can be used to send out information, multimedia data, and even real-time video and voice clips.

Reference

www.cisco.com/univercd/cc/td/doc/cisintwk/ito_doc/ipmulti.htm

Transmission Definitions

- *Digital signals* represent binary digits as electrical pulses.

- *Analog signals* are continuous signals that vary by amplification and frequency.

- *Asynchronous communication* transfers data sequentially, uses start and stop bits, and communicating devices must communicate at the same speed.

- *Synchronous communication* is high-speed transmission controlled by electronic clock timing signals.

- *Baseband transmission* uses the full bandwidth for only one channel and has a low data transfer rate.

- *Broadband transmission* divides the bandwidth into many channels, enabling different types of data to be transmitted, and provides a high data transfer rate.

- *Unicast transmission* is when a packet is sent from one source computer to one destination computer.

- *Multicast transmission* is when a packet is sent from one source computer to several specific computers.

- *Broadcast transmission* is when a packet is sent from one source computer to all computers on a certain network segment.

Network Topology

Okay, so where is everything?

The actual physical arrangement of computers and devices is called a *network topology*. Topology refers to the manner in which a network is physically connected and shows the layout of resources and systems. There is a difference between the physical network topology and the logical topology. A network can be configured as a physical star, but work logically as a ring, as we saw in the "Token Ring" section.

How nodes are supposed to interact, the protocols used, types of applications that can be available, the reliability, expandability, physical layout of a facility, existing wiring, and the technologies implemented will dictate the best type of topology to install. The wrong topology, or combination of topologies, can negatively affect the network's performance, productivity, and growth possibilities.

This section describes the basic types of network topologies, but most networks are much more complex and can merge different types of topologies.

Ring Topology

A *ring topology* has a series of devices connected by unidirectional transmission links. These links form a closed loop and do not connect to a central system as in a star topology. In a physical ring formation, each node is dependent upon the preceding nodes. In very simple networks, if one system failed, all other systems could fail because of this interdependence. Today most networks have redundancy in place or other mechanisms that will protect a whole network from being affected by one workstation, but one disadvantage of using a ring topology is that this possibility exists.

A ring formation can be used in LAN, MAN, and WAN networks. A ring backbone is a high-speed network that connects many slower-speed networks. This is usually an FDDI ring, which has connections at different drops for different networks. Figure 7-24 illustrates an FDDI ring topology.

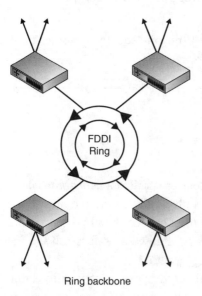

Ring backbone

Figure 7-24   A ring topology forms a closed-loop connection.

Bus Topology

In a simple *bus topology*, a single cable runs the entire length of the network. Nodes are attached to the network through drop points on this cable. Data communications transmit the length of the medium and each packet transmitted is looked at by all nodes. Each node decides to accept, process, or ignore the packet.

There are two main types of bus topologies: linear and tree topologies. The *linear bus* topology has a single cable with nodes attached and each message is either ignored or accepted by each node. A *tree topology* has branches from the single cable, and each branch can contain many nodes.

In simple implementations of a bus topology, if one workstation fails, other systems can be negatively affected because of the degree of interdependence. In addition, because all nodes are connected to one main cable, the cable itself becomes a potential single point of failure. Traditionally, Ethernet uses bus topologies.

Star Topology

In a *star topology*, all nodes connect to a central hub, or switch. Each node has a dedicated link to the central hub.

The central hub needs to provide enough throughput not to be a detrimental bottleneck for the network as a whole. Because a central hub is required, it is a potential single point of failure and redundancy may need to be put into place. Hubs can be configured in flat or hierarchical implementations so that larger organizations can use them.

When one workstation fails on a star topology, it does not affect other systems as in a ring topology. In a star topology, each system is not as dependent upon others as it is dependent upon the central connection hub. This topology generally requires less cabling than other types of topologies. Because less cabling is in use, there is a lower chance of cut cables and detecting cable problems is an easier task.

Not many networks use true linear bus and ring topologies anymore within LAN environments. A ring topology can be used for a backbone network, but most LANs are constructed in a star topology because it enables the network to be more resilient and not as affected if an individual node experiences a problem. Remember, there is a difference between media access methods and the physical topology. Even though a network is a Token Ring or Ethernet, this only describes how each node accesses the media and deals with traffic. Although Token Ring is usually thought of as a ring and Ethernet is considered a bus implementation, this only describes how they work logically. They can be easily implemented physically as a star, and they usually are.

Mesh Topology

A *mesh topology* is when all systems and resources are connected to each other in a way that does not follow the uniformity of the previous topologies, as shown in Figure 7-25. It is a network of interconnected routers and switches that provide multiple paths to all the nodes on the network. This provides a greater degree of complexity and redundancy. A full mesh topology has every node connected to every other node, which provides a great degree of redundancy. A partial mesh topology does not have every node connected to each other and may be used to connect full mesh networks. The Internet is an example of a partial mesh topology.

A summary of the different network topologies and their important characteristics is provided in Table 7-5.

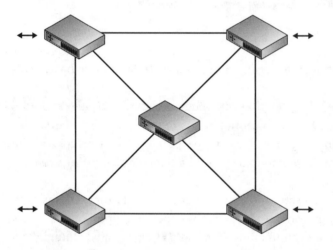

Figure 7-25 A mesh topology has each node connected to all other nodes, which provides for redundant paths.

Table 7-5 Summary of Network Topologies

Topology Type	Characteristics	Problems	Technologies
Bus	This uses a linear, single cable for all computers attached. All traffic travels the full cable and is received by all other computers.	If one station experiences a problem, it can negatively affect all other computers on the same cable.	Ethernet

Topology Type	Characteristics	Problems	Technologies
Ring	All computers are connected by an unidirectional transmission link and the cable is in a closed loop.	If one station experiences a problem, it can negatively affect all other computers on the same ring.	Token Ring and FDDI
Star	All computers are connected to a central device, which provides more resilience for the network.	The central device is a single point of failure.	Logical bus (Ethernet) and ring topologies (Token Ring) can run over a physical star.
Tree	This is a bus topology that does not have one linear cable, but branches of cables.		Ethernet
Mesh	Computers are connected to each other, which provides redundancy.	This requires more expense in cabling and extra effort to track down cable faults.	The Internet is an example of this type of network.

LAN Media Access Technologies

The physical topology of a network is the lower layer or foundation of a network. It determines what type of media will be used and how the media will be connected between different systems. Media access technologies deal with how these systems communicate over this media and are usually represented in protocols and interfaces. LAN access technologies set up the rules of how computers will communicate on a network, how errors are handled, what physical medium is to be used, the maximum transmission unit (MTU) size of frames, and much more. These rules enable all computers and devices to communicate, recover from problems, and enable the users to be productive in accomplishing their network tasks. Each participating entity needs to know how to properly communicate so that all other systems will understand the transmissions, instructions, and requests. This is taken care of by the LAN media access technology. (An MTU is a parameter that indicates how much data a frame can carry on a specific network. Different types of networks can require a different size MTU, which is why frames are fragmented.)

Token Passing

All right, who has the magic token? I need to talk!

A *token* is a 24-bit control frame used to control which computers communicate at what intervals. The token is passed from computer to computer and only the computer that has the token can actually put frames onto the wire. The token grants a computer the right to communicate. The token contains data to be transmitted and routing information. When a system has data that it needs to transmit, it has to wait to receive the token. The computer then connects its message to the token and puts it on the wire. Each computer checks this message to see if it is addressed to it until the destination computer receives the message. The destination computer makes a copy of the message and sets a bit to tell the source computer that it did indeed get its message. Once this gets back to the source computer, it will remove the frames from the network. The designation computer makes a copy of the message, but only the originator of the message can remove the message from the token.

If a computer that receives the frame does not have a message to transmit, it sends the token to the next computer on the network. An empty token has a header, data field, and trailer, but a token that has an actual message has a new header, destination address, source address, routing information, and a new trailer indicating the destination system.

This type of network access method is used by Token Ring, and FDDI topologies. Token-passing methods do not cause collisions because only one computer can communicate at a time. Token passing is the access method defined in the 802.5 networking standard.

CSMA

Ethernet protocols define how nodes are to communicate, recover from errors, and how they are to access the shared network cable. Ethernet uses CSMA as an access method to the network cable. There are a couple of different flavors of CSMA: CSMA/CD and CSMA/CA. A transmission is called a *carrier*, so if a computer is transmitting frames, this computer is performing a carrier activity. When computers use the *carrier sense multiple access with collision detection (CSMA/CD)* protocols, they monitor the transmission activity, or carrier activity, on the wire so that they can determine when would be the best time to transmit data. Each node monitors the wire continuously and waits until the wire is free to transmit its data. An analogy is when there are several people gathered in a group talking here and there about this and that. If a person wants to talk, she will usually listen to the current conversation and once it is ended she can then proceed to tell her story. If she does not wait for the first person to stop talking, then there are two people speaking at the same time and the people around them may not be able to fully understand what each is trying to say.

When using the CSMA/CD access method, computers listen for the absence of a carrier tone on the cable, which indicates that no one else is transmitting data. If two computers sense this absence and transmit data at the same time, contention and a collision can take place. *Contention* means that the nodes have to compete for the same shared medium. A *collision* happens when two or more frames collide, which most likely corrupts both frames. If a computer puts frames on the wire and its frames collide with another computer's frames, it will abort its transmission and alert all other stations that a collision just took place. All stations will execute a random collision timer to force a delay before they attempt to transmit data. This random collision timer is called the *back-off algorithm*. CSMA/CD is the access method used in the 802.3 Ethernet networking standard. (Contention is usually reduced by dividing a network with bridges or switches.)

When a receiving system receives a message, it will send an acknowledgment indicating that this delivery happened successfully. If the sending system does not receive this acknowledgment, it will assume that the packet did not arrive and will retransmit the data.

Carrier sense multiple access with collision avoidance (CSMA/CA) is an access method where each computer signals its intent to transmit data before it actually does so. This tells all other computers on the network not to transmit data right now or there is a possibility of a collision. This approach is called collision avoidance because the computers listen before they transmit data versus just detecting when a collision actually happened.

Carrier-Sensing and Token-Passing Access Methods

Overall, carrier-sensing access methods are faster than token-passing access methods, but they do have the problem of collisions. A network segment with many devices can cause too many collisions and slow down the speed of the network. Token-passing technologies do not have the problems with collisions, but do not perform at the speed of carrier-sensing technologies.

Reference

www.frick-cpa.com/netess/Net_MAC.asp

Collision Domains

As indicated earlier, a collision happens on Ethernet networks when two computers transmit data at the same time. Other computers on the network detect this collision because the overlapping signals of the collision increase the voltage of the signal above a specific threshold. The more devices there are on a contention-based network, the more likely collisions are, which increases network latency. A *collision domain* is a group of computers that are contending, or competing, for the same shared communication medium.

An unacceptable amount of collisions can be caused by a highly populated network, a damaged cable or connector, too many repeaters, or cables that exceed the recommended length. If a cable is longer than what is recommended by the Ethernet specification, then two computers on opposite ends of the cable may transmit data at the same time. The problem is that because they are so far away from each other, they may both transmit data, listen to ensure that a collision did not occur, determine that a collision did not occur, and go merrily along with their business. If the cable is too long, the computers may not listen long enough for evidence of a collision. If the destination computers received these corrupted frames, they then have to send a request to the source system to retransmit the message, causing more traffic.

These types of problems are dealt with mainly by implementing collision domains. An Ethernet network has broadcast and collision domains. One subnet will be on the same broadcast and collision domain if it is not separated by routers or bridges. If the same subnet is divided by bridges, the bridges can enable the broadcast traffic to pass between the different parts of a subnet, but not the collision, as shown in Figure 7-26. This is how collision domains are formed. Isolating collision domains reduces the amount of collisions that will take place on a network and increases its overall performance.

Another benefit of restricting and controlling broadcast and collision domains is that it makes it harder for an intruder to sniff the network and obtain useful information as he transverses the network. A useful tactic for attackers is to install a Trojan horse that sets up a network sniffer on the compromised computer. The sniffer is usually configured to look for a specific type of information, like usernames and passwords. If broadcast and collision domains are in effect, the compromised system will only have access to the broadcast and collision traffic within its specific subnet or collision domain. The compromised system will not be able to listen to traffic on other broadcast and collision domains and this can greatly reduce the amount of traffic and information available to an attacker.

Reference

www.transition.com/learning/whitepapers/colldom_wp.htm

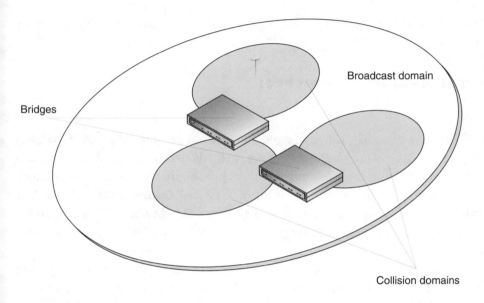

Figure 7-26   Collision domains within one broadcast domain

Polling

Hi. Do you have anything you would like to say?

In an environment where **polling** is used, some systems are configured to be primary stations and others are secondary stations. At predefined intervals, the primary station will ask the secondary station if it has anything to transmit. This is the only time a secondary station can communicate.

Polling is a method of monitoring multiple devices and controlling network access transmission. If polling is used to monitor devices, then the primary device will communicate with each secondary device in an interval to check its status. The primary device will then log the response it receives and move onto the next device. If polling is used for network access, then the primary station will ask each device if it has something to communicate to another device. Network access transmission polling is used mainly with mainframe environments.

Protocols

Some protocols, UDP, TCP, and IP, have been addressed in earlier sections. Networks are made up of many different types of protocols that provide an array of different functionality. Several of the most widely used protocols are discussed in the following sections.

Address Resolution Protocol

This IP does me no good! I need a MAC!

On a TCP/IP network, each computer and network device requires a unique IP address and also a unique physical hardware address. Each NIC has a unique physical address that is programmed into the read-only memory chips on the card by the manufacture. The physical address is also referred to as the *Media Access Control (MAC)* address. The network layer works with and understands IP addresses and the data link layer works with and understands physical addresses. So, how do these two types of addresses work together?

When data comes from the application level, it goes to the transport layer for sequence numbers, session establishment, and fragmentation. The data is then passed to the network layer, where routing information is added to the packet and the source and destination IP addresses are attached to the data bundle. Then it goes to the data link layer, which must find the MAC address and add it to the header portion of the frame. When a frame hits the wire, it only knows what MAC address it is heading towards. At this lower layer of the OSI model, the mechanisms do not even understand IP addresses. So, if a computer cannot resolve the IP address passed down from the network layer to the corresponding MAC address, it cannot communicate with the requested computer.

 NOTE   A MAC address is unique because the first 24 bits represent the manu-facturer code and the last 24 bits represent the unique serial number assigned by the manufacturer.

MAC and IP addresses must be properly mapped so that they can be correctly resolved. This happens through the *Address Resolution Protocol (ARP)*. When the data link layer receives a frame, the network layer has already attached the destination IP address to it, but the data link layer cannot understand the IP address and invokes the ARP for help. ARP broadcasts a frame requesting the MAC address that corresponds with the destination IP address. Each computer on the subnet receives this broadcast frame and all but the computer that has the requested IP address ignore it. The computer that has the destination IP address responds with its MAC address. Now ARP knows what hardware address corresponds with that specific IP address. The data link layer takes the frame and adds the hardware address to it and passes it onto the physical layer, which enables the frame to hit the wire and go to the destination computer. ARP maps the hardware address and associated IP address and stores it in its table for a predefined amount of time. This caching is done so that when another frame destined for the same IP address needs to hit the wire, ARP does not need to broadcast its request again; it just looks in its table for this information.

Sometimes attackers alter a system's ARP table so that it contains incorrect information, which is called *ARP table poisoning*. The goal of this type of attack is for the attacker to receive packets that were intended for another computer. This is a type of *masquerading* attack. If computer A has an IP address of 10.19.34.3 and a MAC address of *x* and computer B has this mapping in its ARP table, an attacker can alter the ARP table to indicate that IP address 10.19.34.3 is mapped to MAC address *y* (the attacker's MAC address), so that any packets computer B tries to send to computer A actually go to the attacker's computer.

References

www.erg.abdn.ac.uk/users/gorry/course/inet-pages/arp.html

www.freesoft.org/CIE/Topics/61.htm

Reverse Address Resolution Protocol

There are a few different ways for a computer to receive its IP addresses when it first boots up. If it has a statically assigned address, then nothing needs to happen. If a computer depends upon a Dynamic Host Configuration Protocol (DHCP) server to assign it the right IP address, it will boot up and make a request to the DHCP server. The DHCP server will assign the IP address and everyone is happy and healthy. But what if the environment has diskless workstations, meaning they have no operating system?

Diskless workstations have just enough code to know how to boot up, broadcast for an IP address, and have a pointer to the server that holds its operating system. The diskless workstation knows its hardware address, so it broadcasts this information so that a server can assign it the correct IP address. As with ARP, *Reverse Address Resolution Protocol (RARP)* frames go to all systems on the subnet, but only the RARP server responds. Once the RARP server receives this request, it looks in its table to see which IP address matches the broadcasted hardware address. The server then sends a message back to the requesting computer that contains its IP address. The system now has an IP address and can function on the network.

ARP and RARP

ARP knows the IP address and broadcasts to find the matching hardware address, the MAC address. RARP knows the hardware address and broadcasts to find the IP address.

The *Boot Protocol (BOOTP)* was created after RARP to enhance the functionality that RARP provides for diskless workstations. BOOTP can receive the computer's IP address from the BOOTP server, the name server address for future name resolutions, and the gateway address from the BOOTP server. BOOTP usually provides more functionality to diskless workstations than RARP.

Internet Control Message Protocol

The *Internet Control Message Protocol (ICMP)* is basically IP's messenger boy. ICMP delivers messages, reports errors, replies to certain requests, reports routing information, and is used to test connectivity and troubleshoot problems on IP networks. ICMP is a protocol within the TCP/IP suite.

The most commonly understood use of ICMP is the ping utility. When a person wants to test the connectivity to another system, he may ping it, which sends out ICMP ECHO frames. When this user sees replies on his screen from the ping utility, these are really ICMP REPLY frames that are responding to the ECHO frames. If a reply is not returned within a predefined time period, the ping utility sends more ECHO frames. If there is still no reply, then ping indicates that the host is unreachable.

ICMP also indicates when there are problems with a specific route on the network and tells computers and devices about better routes to take based on the health and congestion of the different pathways. Routers use ICMP to send messages in response to datagrams that could not be delivered. The router selects the proper ICMP response, wraps it into an IP frame, and sends it back to the requesting host indicating there were problems with the transmission request.

References

www.ee.siue.edu/~rwalden/networking/icmpmess.html

www.ncmag.com/2001_03/ICMP/

Networking Devices

There are several types of devices used in LANs, MANs, and WANs to provide intercommunication between computers and networks. The differences of these devices pertain to their functionality, capabilities, intelligence, and network placement.

Repeaters

A *repeater* provides the simplest type of connectivity because it only repeats and amplifies electrical signals between cable segments. A repeater extends a network because it receives data from one cable segment and transmits it onto another segment.

Repeaters work at the physical layer and are add-on devices for extending a network connection over a greater distance. The device amplifies signals because signals become weaker the farther they have to travel, which is known as attenuation.

Repeaters are also known as line conditioners because some of them can actually clean up the signals. If a repeater is converting analog into digital signals, it will provide a clean digital signal. However, if a repeater is amplifying analog signals, it will also amplify any noise or distortion that is present in the signal, so the distortion is also amplified.

Bridges

A *bridge* is a LAN device used to connect different LAN segments. It works at the data link layer, and therefore works with MAC addresses. A repeater does not work with addresses; it just forwards on all signals it receives. When a frame comes to a bridge, the bridge will determine if the MAC address is on the local network segment or not. If the MAC address is not on the local segment, the bridge will forward it onto the next network segment.

A bridge is used to divide overburdened networks into smaller segments to ensure better use of bandwidth and traffic control. A bridge amplifies the electrical signal like a repeater, but it has more intelligence and is used to extend a LAN and enable the administrator to filter frames so that she can control what frames go where. One issue that has to be watched carefully with bridges is ***broadcast storms***. Because bridges forward all traffic, they forward all broadcast packets. This can overwhelm the network and result in a broadcast storm, which degrades the network bandwidth and performance.

There are three main types of bridges: local, remote link, and translation. A *local bridge* connects two or more LAN segments within a local area, which is usually a building. A *remote bridge* can connect two or more LAN segment over a wide area network by using telecommunications. A remote bridge is equipped with telecommunication ports, which enable it to connect two or more LANs that are separated by a long distance and can be brought together via telephone lines. A *translation bridge* is needed if the two LANs being connected are different types and use different standards and protocols. The usual type of connection would be between a Token Ring network and an Ethernet network. The frames on each network type are different sizes, the fields contain different protocol information, and the different networks transmit at different speeds. If a regular bridge were put into place, Ethernet frames would go to the Token Ring network and vice versa and no one would be able to understand messages that came from the other network segment. A translation bridge does what its name says— it will translate between the two network types.

The following items outline the functions of a bridge:

- Segment a large network into smaller, more controllable pieces.
- Use filtering based on MAC addresses.
- Join different types of network links while retaining the same broadcast domain.
- Isolate collision domains within the same broadcast domain.
- Bridging can take place locally within a LAN or remote bridging can connect two distant LANs.
- Some bridges translate between protocol types.

Question

What is the difference between two LANs connected via bridges versus being connected via routers?

Answer: If two LANs are connected with a bridge, the LAN has been extended because they are both in the same broadcast domain. A router can be configured to not forward broadcast information, so if two LANs are connected with a router, it is considered an internetwork. An *internetwork* is a group of networks connected in a way that enables any node on any network to communicate to any other node. The Internet is an example of an internetwork.

NOTE   Routers versus Bridges: Routers work at the network layer and filter frames based on IP addresses. Bridges work at the data link layer and filter frames based on MAC addresses.

Routers will not, usually, pass broadcast information. Bridges will pass broadcast information.

Forwarding Tables

You go that way. And you, you go this way!

A bridge must know how to get a frame to its destination, meaning it must know which port the frame must be sent to and where the destination host is located. Years ago network administrators had to type in route paths into bridges so that the bridges had static paths indicating where to pass frames that were headed for different destinations. This was a tedious task and prone to errors. Today bridges use *transparent bridging* or *source routing*.

If transparent bridging is used, a bridge starts to learn about the network's environment as soon as it is powered on and as the network changes. It does this by examining frames and making entries into its forwarding tables. When a bridge receives a frame from a new source computer, the bridge will associate this new source address and the port it arrived on. It does this for all computers that send frames on the network. Eventually, the bridge knows each address of each computer on the different network segments and which port they are connected to. If the bridge gets a request to send a frame onto a destination that is not in its forwarding table, then it sends out a query frame on each network segment except for the source segment. The destination host is the only one that replies to this query. The bridge updates its table with this computer address and which port it is connected to and forwards on the frame.

Many bridges use the Spanning Tree Algorithm (STA), which adds more intelligence to the bridge. The STA ensures that frames do not circle networks forever, provides redundant paths in case a bridge goes down, assigns unique identifiers to each bridge, assigns priority values to these different bridges, and calculates path costs. This creates much more efficient frame forwarding processes by each bridge. The STA also enables an administrator to indicate that she wants traffic to travel certain paths instead of others.

If *source routing* is used, instead of transparent bridging, then the packets themselves have the necessary information within them to tell the bridge where they should go. The packets hold the forwarding information so that they can find their way to their destination themselves without bridges and routers dictating their paths. If the computer wants to dictate its forwarding information instead of depending on a bridge, how does it know the right route to the destination computer? The source computer sends out explorer packets that arrive at the destination computer. These packets contain the route information it had to take to get to the destination, including what bridges it had to pass through. The destination computer then sends these packets back to the source computer and the source computer strips out the routing information, inserts it into the packets, and sends them onto the first bridge.

References

www.ietf.org/html.charters/bridge-charter.html

www.erg.abdn.ac.uk/users/gorry/course/lan-pages/bridge.html

Routers

We are going up the chain of the OSI layers when discussing devices. Repeaters work at the physical layer, bridges work at the data link layer, and routers work at the network layer. As we go up one layer at a time, each device has more intelligence and functionality. This is because each device can look deeper into the frame. A repeater just looks at the electrical signal. The bridge can look at the MAC address within the header. The router can peel back the first header information and look farther into the frame and find out the IP address and other routing information. The farther a device can look into a frame, the more decisions it can make based on the information within the frame. We will see later that gateways can look all the way to the core of the frame, which is the data that the user sent in the first place and not just addresses and routing information.

Routers are layer 3, or network layer, devices that are used to connect similar or different networks. (This means they can connect two Ethernet LANs or an Ethernet LAN to a Token Ring LAN.) A router is a device that has two or more interfaces and a routing table so that it knows how to get packets to their destination. It can filter traffic based on access control lists (ACL), and fragments packets when necessary. Because routers have more network level knowledge, they can perform higher-level functions like calculating the shortest and most economical path between the sending and receiving hosts.

Routers discover information about routes and changes that take place in a network through its routing protocols (RIP, BGP, and OSPF). These protocols tell routers if a link has gone down, if a route is congested and if another route is more economical, they update router route tables, and indicate if a router is having problems or has gone down.

A bridge uses the same network address for all of its ports, but a router assigns a new address per port, which enables it to connect more network together.

The router may be a stand-alone device or a computer running a networking operating system that is dual homed. When packets arrive at one of the interfaces, the router compares those packets to its ACLs. This list indicates what packets are allowed in and what packets are denied. Access decisions are based on source and destination IP address, protocol type, and destination port. An administrator may block all packets coming from the 10.10.12.0 network, any FTP requests, or any packets headed towards a specific port on a specific host. This type of control is provided by the ACLs, which the administrator must program and update as necessary.

So, what actually happens inside the router when it receives a packet? Let's follow the steps:

1. A frame is received on one of the interfaces of a router. The router strips off the header information to be able to view the routing data.

2. The router retrieves the destination IP network address from the datagram; it does not care about the host portion of the IP address.

3. The router looks at its routing table to see which port matches the requested destination IP network address.

4. If the router does not have information in its table about the destination address, it sends out an ICMP error message to the sending computer indicating that the message could not reach its destination.

5. If the router does have a route in its routing table for this destination, it decrements the Time to Live (TTL) value and sees if the MTU is different for the destination network. If the destination network requires a smaller MTU, the router fragments the datagram.

6. The router changes header information in the frame so the frame can go to the next correct router, or if the destination computer is on a connecting network, the changes made enable the frame to go right to the destination computer.

7. The router then sends the frame to its output queue for the necessary interface.

Table 7-6 Main Differences Between Bridges and Routers

Bridge	Router
Reads header information, but does not alter it	Creates a new header for each frame
Builds forwarding tables based on MAC addresses	Builds routing tables based on IP addresses
Uses the same network address for all ports	Assigns a different network address per port
Filters traffic based on MAC addresses	Filters traffic based on IP addresses
Forwards broadcast packets	Does not forward broadcast packets
Forwards traffic if destination address is unknown to the bridge	Does not forward traffic that contains a destination address unknown to the router

Table 7-6 provides a quick review of the differences between routers and bridges.

So when is it best to use a repeater, bridge, or router? A repeater is used if an administrator needs to expand a network and amplify signals so that they do not weaken on longer cables. However, a repeater will forward collision and broadcast information because it does not have the intelligence to decipher between different types of traffic. Bridges work at the data link layer and have a bit more intelligence than a repeater. Bridges can do simple filtering and they separate collision domains, not broadcast domains. A bridge should be used when an administrator wants to divide a network into segments to reduce traffic congestion and excessive collisions. A router splits up a network into different collision domains and different broadcast domains. A router gives more of a clear-cut division between network segments than repeaters or bridges. A router should be used if an administrator wants to have more defined control of where the traffic goes because there is more sophisticated filtering in routers, and when used to segment a network, the result is more controllable sections.

A router is used when an administrator wants to divide a network along the lines of departments, workgroups, or other business-oriented divisions. A bridge divides segments based more on the traffic type and load.

Routing

Routing is a packet-forwarding process that takes place on internetworks. When a computer needs to send a packet, the sending computer needs to know if the destination computer is local or on a remote network, which is indicated by the network portion of its IP address. If the destination computer is on the same local network segment, the sending computer sends the packet to that computer. If the destination computer is on a remote network, the sending computer must send the packet to its default gateway, a router, that will forward the packet to the right network. How the router(s) forwards packets from the source to the destination computer is referred to as routing.

Routing is actually performed by protocols and algorithms within the router. The routers use these to determine the next hop that will get the frame closer to its destination, but are not responsible for knowing and mapping out the complete path to the destination computer. The router just needs to get the packet to the destination computer or to the next router closer to the target network.

Originally, tables were built statically, meaning the administrator had to type in each and every route that different frames could take. Static routing is still used in smaller networks, but the larger the network, the more overwhelming static routing will become. Dynamic routing was developed, which means that a dynamic routing protocol discovers routes and makes the necessary changes to the routing tables. If routes go down or become congested, the protocol will update the table with the new information instead of requiring the administrator to manually alter the table.

Routing environments are based on different autonomous systems (ASs). An AS is a specific network that is managed by a specific authority and implements its own internal routing. An AS is a routing domain, meaning it uses its own address scheme and internal routing protocols. Figure 7-27 shows two different ASs and how they connect and communicate.

The Internet is a large collection of many different ASs. The lines between these ASs are drawn by the individual service providers and carrier networks, not the individual corporate networks on their own. The different ASs are connected to each other through routers and routing protocols. Routing takes place within an AS through internal routing protocols like OSPF and RIP. The ASs communicate to each other through exterior routing protocols like BGP.

Any traffic that needs to leave an AS heads towards that AS's border router. The boarder router provides a gateway to the world for a specific network. Any data coming into the AS comes to the same boarder router and the traffic is routed internally as required. The different AS networks share routing information so that the Internet works more efficiently.

References

www.cisco.com/univercd/cc/td/doc/cisintwk/ito_doc/routing.htm

www.ietf.org/html.charters/wg-dir.html

http://directory.google.com/Top/Computers/Internet/Routers_and_Routing

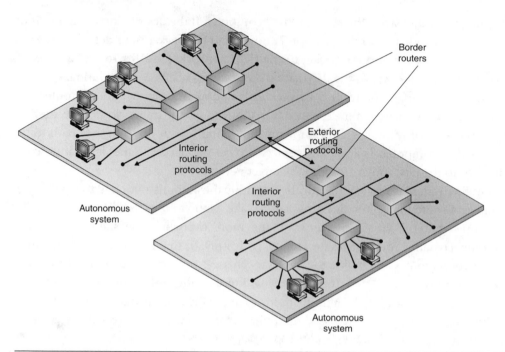

Figure 7-27 Autonomous systems

Switches

Switches actually combine the functionality of a repeater and the functionality of a bridge. A switch amplifies the electrical signal, like a repeater, and has the built-in circuitry and intelligence of a bridge. It is a multiport connection device that provides connections for individual computers or other hubs and switches. Any device connected to one port can communicate with a device connected to another port with its own virtual private link. How is this different than how devices communicate using a bridge or a repeater? When a frame comes to a repeater, it sends it out through all of its ports. When a frame comes to a bridge, the bridge sends it to the port that the destination network segment is connected to. When a frame comes to a switch, it sends the frame directly to the destination computer; thus, there is a reduction of traffic. Figure 7-28 illustrates a network configuration that has computers directly connected to their corresponding switches.

On Ethernet networks, computers have to compete for the same shared network medium. Each computer must listen for activity on the network and transmit its data when it thinks the coast is clear. This contention and the resulting collisions cause traffic delays and use up precious bandwidth. When switches are used, contention and col-

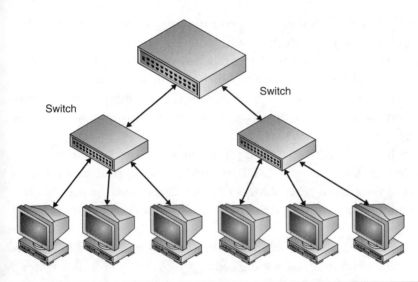

Figure 7-28   Switches enable devices to communicate with each other with their own virtual link.

lisions are not issues, which results in more efficient use of the network's bandwidth and decreased latency. Switches reduce or remove the sharing of the network medium and the problems that come with it.

A switch is a multiport bridging device and each port provides dedicated bandwidth to the device attached to it. A port is bridged to another port so that the two devices have an end-to-end private link. The switch employs full-duplex linking so that one wire pair is used for sending and another pair is used for receiving. This ensures that the two connected devices do not contend for the connection between them.

Basic switches work at the data link layer and forward traffic based on MAC addresses. However, today there are layer 3 switches and layer 4 switches, which have more enhanced functionality than layer 2 switches. These higher-level switches have routing functionality, packet inspection, traffic prioritization, and quality of service (QoS) functionality. These switches are referred to as *multilayered switches* because they combine data link layer and network layer functionality.

Multilayered switches use hardware-based processing power, which enables them to look deeper within the packet, make more decisions based on the information found within the packet, and then provide routing and traffic management tasks. Usually this amount of work creates a lot of overhead and traffic delay, but multilayered switches perform these activities within an application-specific integrated circuit (ASIC). This means that most of the functions the switch performs are done at the hardware and chip level versus the software level, which is a much quicker method.

Many enterprises today use a switched network where computers are connected to dedicated ports on Ethernet switches, Gigabit Ethernet switches, ATM switches, and more. This evolution of switches, added services, and the capability to incorporate repeater, bridge, and router functionality have made switches an important part of today's networking world.

Because security has to do with controlling who can access specific resources, the more intelligent devices can make more detail-oriented decisions; thus, they can provide a higher level of protection. When devices can look deeper into the packets, they have more information to make access decisions, which provides more granular access control.

As stated before, switching makes it harder for intruders to sniff and monitor network traffic because there is not broadcast and collision information continually traveling throughout the network. So, switches provide a security service that the other devices cannot. Virtual LANs (VLANs) are also an important part of switching networks because they enable administrators to have more control over their environment and they can isolate users and groups into logical and manageable entities. VLANs are described in the next section.

References

www.enterasys.com/products/whitepapers

www.cisco.com/univercd/cc/td/doc/cisintwk/idg4/nd2012.htm

VLAN

Virtual LANs (VLANs) enable administrators to logically separate and group users based on resource requirements, security, or business needs instead of the standard physical location of the users. When using repeaters, bridges, and routers, users are grouped in a manner that is dictated by their physical location. Figure 7-29 shows how computers that are physically located next to each other can be grouped into different VLANs. Administrators can form these groups based on the user's and company's needs instead of the physical location of systems and resources.

An administrator may want to place all users in the marketing department in the same VLAN network so that they all receive the same broadcast messages and can access the same types of resources. This could get tricky if a few of the users are in another building or another floor, but VLANs provide the administrator with this type of flexibility. VLANs also enable an administrator to apply different security policies to differ-

These three VLANs span across four different buildings. The computers and users are grouped logically instead of physically.

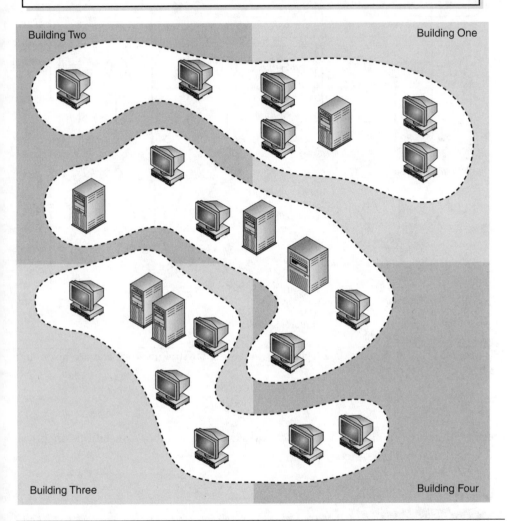

Figure 7-29 VLANs enable administrators to put users into logical networks.

ent logical groups. This way if tighter security is required for the payroll department, the administrator can develop a policy, add all payroll users to a specific VLAN, and apply the security policy only to the payroll VLAN.

A VLAN exists on top of the physical network, as shown in Figure 7-30. If workstation P1 wants to communicate with workstation D1, the message has to be routed

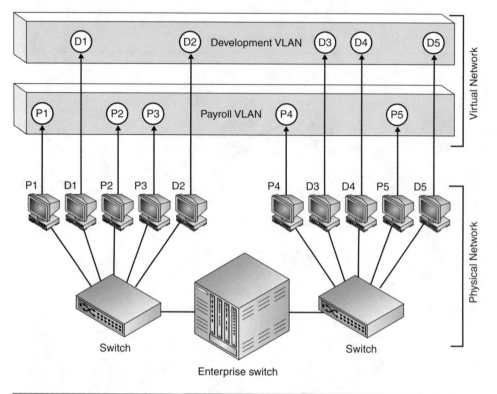

Figure 7-30 VLANs exist on a higher level than the physical network and are not bound to it.

because they are on different logical networks even though the workstations are physically right next to each other.

Brouters

A *brouter* is a hybrid device that combines the functionality of a bridge and a router. A brouter can bridge multiple protocols and can route packets on some of those protocols. When a router receives a packet and it cannot determine its proper address using the protocol information available, it drops the packet. A brouter first tries to route the packet using this same information and if it is unsuccessful, it attempts to bridge the packet using the MAC address.

Gateways

A *gateway* is a general term for software running on a device that connects two different environments and acts as a translator for them or somehow restricts their interactions. Usually a gateway is needed when one environment speaks a different language, meaning it uses a certain protocol that the other environment does not understand. The gateway can translate IPX protocol packets to IP packets, accept mail from one type of mail server and format it so another type of mail server can accept and understand it, or connect and translate different data link technologies like FDDI to Ethernet.

Gateways almost always work at the application layer because they need to see a majority of the information within a frame and not just the address and routing information that a router or bridge requires. Gateways perform much more complex tasks than these types of connection devices. However, some people refer to routers as gateways when they connect two unlike networks (Token Ring and Ethernet) because the router has to translate between the data link technologies. Figure 7-31 shows how a network access server (NAS) functions as a gateway between telecommunication and network connections.

When networks connect to a backbone, there can be a gateway that translates the different technologies and frame formats used on the backbone network versus the connecting LAN. If a bridge was set up between an FDDI backbone and an Ethernet LAN, the computers on the LAN would not understand the FDDI protocols and frame

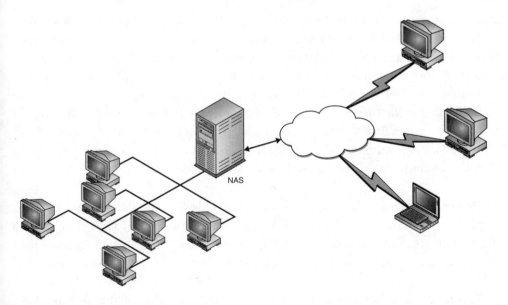

Figure 7-31 There are several types of gateways; an NAS is one example.

formats. In this case, a LAN gateway would be needed to translate the different protocols used between the different networks.

A very popular type of a gateway is an electronic mail gateway. There are several different e-mail vendors who have their own syntax, message format, and ways of dealing with message transmission. If David writes an e-mail message and his corporate network uses sendmail and the message is headed to Dan, whose corporate network uses Microsoft Exchange, a mail gateway is required. The mail gateway will usually convert the message into a standard that all mail servers understand, X.400, and pass it onto Dan's mail server.

Another example of a gateway is a voice and media gateway. Recently, there has been a drive to combine voice and data networks. This provides for a lot of efficiency because the same media can be used for both types of data transfers. However, voice is a streaming technology, whereas data is usually transferred in packets. So, this shared media eventually has to communicate with two different types of networks: the telephone company's PSTN and routers that will take the packet-based data off to the Internet. This means a gateway must take the combined voice and data information, separate it, and put it into a form that each of the following networks can understand.

Table 7-7 shows the different devices covered in the last sections and points out their important characteristics.

PBX

Telephone companies use switching technologies for transmitting phone calls to where they need to go. The telephone company's central office houses the switches that connect towns, cities, and metropolitan areas to larger optical rings. When Dusty makes a phone call from his house, the call first hits his local central office and the switch within that office decides if it is a local or long-distance call and where it needs to go from there. A *Private Branch Exchange (PBX)* is a telephone switch that is located on a company's property. This switch performs some of the same switching tasks that take place at the telephone company's central office. This PBX has a dedicated connection to its local telephone company's central office, where more intelligent switching takes place.

A PBX can interface with several different types of devices and provides a number of different telephone services. The data is multiplexed onto a dedicated line connected to the telephone company's central office. Figure 7-32 shows how different types of data can be placed on one line at the PBX and sent to the telephone company's switching facility.

PBXs use digital switching devices that can control analog and digital signals. Older PBXs may only support analog devices, but most have been moving quickly to digital.

Table 7-7   Comparision Between the Different Devices and Their Functionality

Device	OSI Layer	Functionality
Repeater	Physical layer	Amplifies signal and extends networks
Bridge	Data link layer	Forwards packets and filters based on MAC addresses; forwards broadcast traffic, but not collision traffic.
Router	Network layer	Separates and connects LANs creating inter-networks; routers filter based on IP addresses.
Brouter	Data link and network layers	A hybrid device that combines the functionality of a bridge and a router. A brouter can bridge multiple protocols and can route packets on some of those protocols.
Switch	Data link layer More intelligent switches work at the network layer	Provides a private virtual link between communicating devices, allows for VLANs, reduces traffic, and impedes network sniffing.
Gateway	Application layer (although different types of gateways can work at other layers)	Connects different types of networks, performs protocol and format translations.

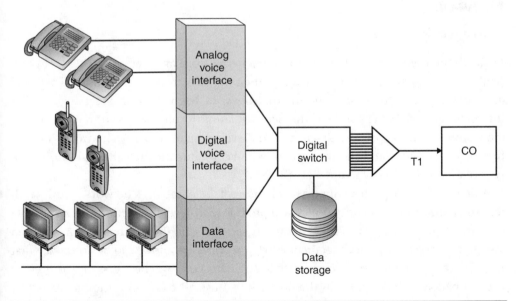

Figure 7-32   A PBX combines different types of data onto the same lines.

This move to digital systems and signals has reduced a number of the PBX and telephone security vulnerabilities that used to be available. However, that in no way means that PBX fraud does not take place today. Many companies have modems hanging off their PBX to enable the vendor to dial-in and perform maintenance to the system. The modem should actually only be activated when there is a problem that requires the vendor to dial in, and then it should be disabled.

Also, many PBX systems have default system manager passwords that are hardly ever changed. These passwords are set by default; therefore, if 100 companies purchased and implemented 100 PBX systems from the PBX vendor ABC and they do not reset the password, a phreaker who knows this default password now has access to 100 PBX systems. Once a phreaker breaks into a PBX system, she can cause mayhem by rerouting calls, reconfiguring switches, or configuring the system to provide her and her friends with free long-distance calls. This type of fraud happens more than most companies know because many companies do not closely watch their phone bills.

PBX systems are also vulnerable to brute force attacks, where phreakers use scripts and dictionaries to guess the necessary credentials to gain access to the system. There have also been cases where phreakers listened to people's voice messages and changed their voice mail messages. So when people call to leave Bob a message, they might not hear his usual boring message, but a new message that is screaming obscenities and insults.

Firewalls

Stop! Who goes there?

Firewalls are used to restrict access to one network from another network. Most companies have firewalls to restrict access into their network from Internet users. They may also have firewalls to restrict one internal network segment from accessing another internal segment. For example, if the network administrator wants to make sure that employees cannot access the Research and Development network, she would place a firewall between this and all other networks and configure the firewall to allow only the type of access she deems acceptable.

A firewall is a device that supports and enforces the company's network security policy. An organizational security policy will provide high-level instructions on acceptable and unacceptable actions as they pertain to security. The firewall has a more defined and granular security policy that dictates what services are allowed to be accessed, what IP addresses and ranges are to be restricted, and what ports can be accessed. The firewall is described as a choke point in the network because all communication should flow through it and this is where traffic is inspected and restricted.

A firewall is actually a type of gateway that can be a router, server, authentication server, or specialized hardware device. It monitors packets coming into and out of the network it is protecting. It filters out the packets that do not meet the requirements of the security policy. It can discard these packets, repackage them, or redirect them depending upon the firewall configuration and security policy. Packets are filtered based on their source and destination addresses and ports by service, packet type, protocol type, header information, sequence bits, and much more. Vendors have different functionality and different parameters they can use for identification and access restriction.

Many times companies set up firewalls to construct a *demilitarized zone (DMZ)*, which is a network segment that is located between the protected and the unprotected networks. This provides a buffer zone between the dangerous Internet and the goodies within the internal network that the company is trying to protect. As shown in Figure 7-33, usually two firewalls are installed to form the DMZ. The DMZ usually contains Web, mail, and DNS servers, which must be hardened down because they would be the first in line for attacks. Many DMZs also have an intrusion detection system (IDS) sensor that listens for malicious and suspicious behavior.

There are actually many different types of firewalls because different environments have different requirements and security goals. Actually, firewalls have gone through an evolution of their own and have grown in sophistication and functionality. The following sections describe the different types of firewalls.

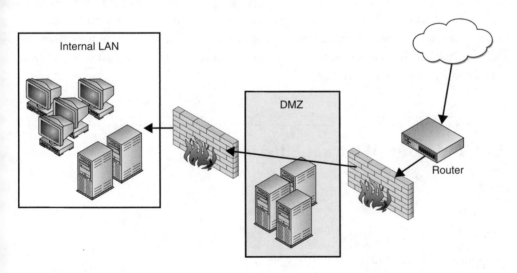

Figure 7-33   At least two firewalls are usually used to construct a DMZ.

Packet Filtering

I don't like this packet. Oh, but I like this packet. I don't like this packet. This other packet is okay.

Packet filtering is a security method of controlling what data can flow into and from a network. Packet filtering takes place by using ACLs, which are developed and applied to a device. ACLs are just lines of text, called rules, that the device will apply to each packet that it receives. The lines of text give specific information pertaining to what packets can be accepted and what packets are denied. For instance, an ACL can have one line that states that any packets coming from the IP range 172.168.0.0 must be denied. Another line may indicate that no packets using the Telnet service will be allowed to enter the network and another line may indicate that no traffic is to be allowed through port 443. Then it can have a line indicating that all traffic on port 80 is acceptable and that it should be routed to a specific IP address, which is the Web server. Each time the device receives a packet, it compares the information in the packet's header to each line in the ACL. If the packet indicates that it is using Telnet or requests to make a connection to port 443, it is discarded. If the packet header information indicates that it wants to communicate through port 80 using HTTP over TCP, then the packet is accepted and redirected to the Web server.

This filtering is based on network layer information, which means that the device cannot look too far into the packet itself. It can only make decisions based on header information, which is limited. Most routers use ACLs to act as a type of firewall and to carry out routing decisions, but they do not provide the level of protection other types of firewalls, which look deeper into the packet, provide. Because packet filtering only looks at the header information, it is not application-dependent like many proxy firewalls are. Packet-filtering firewalls also do not keep track of the state of a connection, which takes place in a stateful firewall.

Pros and Cons of Packet Filtering

Pros

Scalable

Provides high performance

Application independent

Cons

Does not look into the packet past the header information

Low security relative to other options

Does not keep track of the state of a connection

Used in first-generation firewalls

Stateful Packet Filtering

When packet filtering is used, a packet arrives at the router, and the router runs through its ACLs to see if this packet should be allowed or denied. If the packet is allowed, it is passed onto the destination host, or another router, and the router forgets it ever received this packet in the first place. This is different than stateful filtering, which remembers and keeps track of what packets went where until that particular connection is closed.

Stateful packet filtering is like a nosey neighbor who gets into people's business and conversations. She keeps track of who said what and when. This can be annoying until your house is broken into. Then you and the cops will want to talk to the nosey neighbor because she knows everything that is going on in the neighborhood and would be the most likely one to know if something unusual happened. A stateful filtering router is nosier than a regular filtering device, because it keeps track of what computers say to each other. This requires the firewall to maintain a state table, which is like a score sheet of who said what to whom.

Stateful firewalls also make decisions on what packets to allow or disallow, but their functionality goes a step farther. For example, a regular packet-filtering device may deny any UDP packets requesting service on port 25 and a stateful packet-filtering device may have the rule to only allow UDP packets through if they are responses to outgoing requests. Basically, the stateful firewall will only allow packets in that its internal hosts requested. So if Mitchell sends a request to a computer on a different network, this request will be logged in the firewall's state table. The table will indicate that Mitchell's computer made a request and there should be packets coming back to Mitchell. When the computer on the Internet responds to Mitchell, these packets will be compared to data in the state table at the firewall. Because the state table does have information about a previous request for these packets, the firewall allows the packets to pass through. If, on the other hand, Mitchell did not make any requests and packets were coming in from the Internet to him, the firewall will see that there was no previous request for this information and then look at its ACLs to see if these packets are allowed to come in.

Stateful Inspection Characteristics

- The firewall maintains a state table that tracks each and every communication channel.

- Frames are analyzed at all communication layers.

- It provides a high degree of security and does not introduce the performance hit that proxy firewalls introduce.

- It is scalable and transparent to users.

- It provides data for tracking connectionless protocols like UDP and RPC.

- The state and context of the data within the packets are stored and updated continuously.

- It is used in third-generation firewall applications.

So regular packet filtering compares incoming packets to rules defined in its ACLs. When stateful packet filtering receives a packet, it first looks in its state table to see if a connection has already been established and if this data was requested. If there is no previous connection and the state table holds no information about the packet, the packet is compared to the device's ACLs. If the ACL allows this type of traffic, the packet is allowed to access the network. If that type of traffic is not allowed, the packet is dropped.

Although this provides an extra step of protection, it also adds more complexity because this device must now keep a dynamic state table and remember connections. This has opened the door to many types of denial of service (DoS) attacks. There are several types of attacks that are aimed at flooding the state table with bogus information. The state table is a resource like a system's hard drive space, memory, and CPU. When the state table is stuffed full of bogus information, it can either freeze the device or cause it to reboot. Also if this firewall has to be rebooted for some reason, it loses its information on all recent connections; thus, it will deny legitimate packets.

Proxy Firewalls

Meet my proxy. He will be our middleman.

A *proxy* is a middleman. If someone needed to give a box and a message to the president of the United States, this person could not just walk up to him and give him these items. The person would have to go through a middleman who would accept the box and message and thoroughly go through the box to ensure that nothing dangerous was inside. This is what a proxy firewall does—it accepts messages either entering or leaving a network, inspects it for malicious information, and when it decides things are okay, it passes the data onto the destination computer.

A proxy stands between a trusted and untrusted network and actually makes the connection, each way, on behalf of the source. So if a user on the Internet requests to send data to a computer on the internal, protected network, the proxy will get this request and look it over for suspicious information. The request does not automatically go to the destination computer—instead, the proxy firewall impersonates the internal destination computer and accepts the request on behave of the computer it is protecting. If the proxy decides the packet is safe, it sends it onto the destination computer. When the destination computer replies, the reply goes back to the proxy server, which repackages the packet to contain the source address of the proxy server, not the host system on the internal network. What is important is that a proxy firewall breaks the communication channel. There is no direct connection to internal computers.

This type of firewall makes a copy of each accepted packet before transmitting it. It repackages the packet to hide the packet's true origin. If an attacker attempts to scan or probe a company's network, he will only receive information that has been intercepted and repackaged by proxy server. The returned packets will only have the IP address of the firewall, and the information released will be sparse, thus the internal network is protected and hidden.

Proxy Firewall Pros and Cons

Pros

Looks at the information within a packet all the way up to the application layer

Provides better security than packet filtering

Is aware of the protocols, services, and commands being used

Cons

Limited to what applications it can support

Degrades traffic performance

Poor scalability

Breaks client/server model, which is good for security but at times bad for functionality

---

The proxy firewall is the only machine that talks to the outside world. This ensures that no computer has direct access to internal computers. This also means that the proxy server is the only computer that needs a valid IP address. The rest of the computers on the internal network can use private (non-routable IP addresses on the Internet) addresses, because no computers on the outside will see their addresses anyway.

Many times proxy servers are used when a company is using a *dual-homed firewall*. A dual-homed firewall has two interfaces: one facing the external network and the other facing the internal network. This is different than a computer that has forwarding enabled, which just lets packets pass through its interfaces with no access control enforced. A dual-homed firewall has two NICs and has packet forwarding turned off. Packet forwarding is turned off for security reasons. If forwarding were enabled, the computer would not apply the necessary ACLs, rules, or other restrictions necessary of a firewall. Instead, a dual-homed firewall requires a higher level of intelligence to tell it what packets should go where and what types of packets are acceptable. This is where the proxy comes in. When a packet comes to the external NIC from the untrusted network on a dual-homed firewall, the computer does not know what to do with it, so it passes it up to the proxy software. The proxy software inspects the packet to make sure that it is legitimate. Then the proxy software makes a connection with the destination computer on the internal network and passes on the packet. When the internal computer replies, the packet goes to the internal interface on the dual-homed firewall and is passed up to the proxy software. The proxy inspects the packet and slaps on a different header and passes the packet out the external NIC that is connected to the external network.

Dual-Homed Host Firewalls

- Single computer with separate network cards connected to each network.
- Used to divide an internal trusted network from an external untrusted network.

- Must disable computer's forwarding functionality so the two networks are truly segregated.

- Usually used with proxy software.

- Users can easily and accidentally enable packet forwarding, which causes a security breach in the firewall.

The proxy firewall is an important part to a dual-homed firewall and the dual-homed firewall is an important part of a proxy firewall. If the proxy firewall were on a computer that had packet forwarding enabled, the packets would never be passed up to the proxy server software. If the dual-homed firewall did not have a proxy server, it would not know what to do with the packets it receives.

There are two types of proxies: application and circuit proxies, which are described next.

Application- and Circuit-Level Proxies   Proxies have been described generally as middlemen between untrusted external hosts and trusted internal hosts. However, there are more specifics when looking at the two different types of proxy firewalls available.

Application-level proxies inspect the entire packet and make access decisions based on the actual content of the packet. They understand different services and protocols and the commands that are used within them. An application-level proxy can distinguish between an FTP GET command and an FTP PUT command and make access decisions based on this granular level of information, where packet-filtering firewalls can only allow or deny FTP requests as a whole, not the commands used within the FTP protocol.

An application-level proxy works for one service or protocol. A computer can have many different types of services and protocols (FTP, NTP, SMTP, Telnet, and so on)— thus, there must be one application-level proxy per service.

A *circuit-level proxy* creates a circuit between the client computer and the server. It does not understand or care about the higher-level issues that an application-level proxy deals with. It knows the source and destination addresses and makes access decisions based on this information.

Providing application-level proxy services can be much trickier than it appears. The proxy must totally understand how specific protocols work, what commands are legitimate, and be aware of what applications use these protocols and services. This is a lot to know and look at during the transmission of data. If the application-level proxy firewall does not understand a certain protocol or service, it cannot protect this type of communication. This is when a circuit-level proxy can come into play because it does not deal with such complex issues. An advantage of a circuit-level proxy is that it can handle a wider variety of protocols and services than an application-level proxy, but the downfall is that the circuit-level proxy cannot provide the degree of granular control that an application-level proxy can. Life is just full of compromises.

A circuit-level proxy works similar to a packet filter in that it knows the source and destination addresses and sends packets on their way. It looks at the data within the packet header versus the data within the payload of the packet. It does not know if the contents within the packet are actually safe or not.

So an application-level proxy is dedicated to a particular protocol or service. There must be one proxy per protocol and service because one proxy could not properly interpret all the commands of all the protocols coming its way. A circuit-level proxy works at a lower layer of the OSI model and does not require one proxy per protocol because it is not looking at such detailed information.

Application- versus Circuit-Level Proxy Firewall Characteristics

Application-Level Proxy Firewall

Transfers a copy of each approved packet from one network to another network

Different proxy required for each service allowed

Hides network information from potential attackers

Hides internal computer information and address

Provides more intricate control than circuit-level proxy firewalls

Reduces network performance

Circuit-Level Proxy Firewall

Provides a circuit between the source and destination computers

Does not require a proxy for each and every service

Does not provide the detailed control that an application-level proxy firewall provides

Provides security for a wider range of protocols

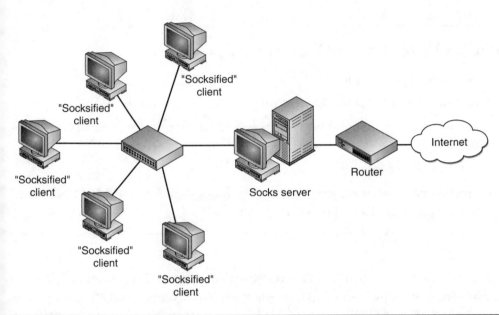

Figure 7-34   The SOCKS server usually sits behind a router and each SOCKS client must have SOCKS software installed.

SOCKS is an example of a circuit-level proxy gateway that provides a secure channel between two TCP/IP computers. When a SOCKS-enabled client sends a request to access a computer on the Internet, this request actually goes to the network's SOCKS proxy server, as shown in Figure 7-34, which inspects the packets for malicious information and checks its policy rules to see if this type of connection is allowed. If the packet is acceptable and this type of connection is allowed, the SOCKS server sends the message to the destination computer on the Internet. When the computer on the Internet responds, it sends its packets to the SOCKS server, which again inspects the data and then passes it onto the client computer.

The SOCKS server can screen, filter, audit, log, and control data flowing in and out of a protected network. SOCKS also provides accounting, management, auditing, and security functionality. Because of its popularity, many applications and protocols have been configured to work with SOCKS in a manner that takes less configuration on the administrator's part.

SOCKS Proxy Server Characteristics

- Circuit-level proxy server
- Requires clients to be SOCKS-ified with SOCKS client software
- Mainly used for outbound Internet access and virtual private network (VPN) functionality
- Can be resource-intensive
- Provides authentication and encryption features similar to other VPN protocols, but not considered a traditional VPN protocol

Because SOCKS is a circuit-level proxy, it does not provide detailed protocol-specific control. The SOCKS product includes the SOCKS server software, which runs on Unix servers, a SOCKS client library, SOCKS-ified versions of several applications and protocols, and SOCKS wrappers for certain utilities like traceroute and ping.

Firewall Architecture

*Firewalls are great, but where do we **put** them?*

Firewalls can be placed in different areas of a network for different reasons. They can protect an internal network from an external network and act as a choke point for all traffic. A firewall can be used to segment network sections and enforce access controls between different subnets. Firewalls can also be used to construct a DMZ to provide a buffer zone between the internal network and the external network.

Bastion Host   The *bastion host* can be thought of as the foundation for the firewall software to operate upon. It is *the* machine that will be accessed by any and all entities trying to access or leave the network. A bastion host is a highly exposed device because it is the frontline in a network's security and its existence is known on the Internet. This means that the device must be extremely locked down, no unnecessary services running, unused subsystems must be disabled, vulnerabilities must be patched, unused user accounts must be disabled, and ports that are not needed must be closed. These measures are necessary because if this system becomes compromised, then the network has just lost its main defender. Once the firewall is broken or disabled, there is not much standing in the way between the evildoers on the Internet and the vulnerable systems on the internal network.

A bastion host can support packet filtering, proxy, and hybrid firewall applications. A bastion host is not specific to a specific type of operating system, firewall, or hardware— it is just the locked down system that houses the firewall.

Screened Host

A *screened host*, many times, is a bastion host firewall that communicates directly with a border router and the internal network. Figure 7-35 shows this type of architecture.

Traffic that comes in from the Internet is first filtered via packet filtering on the outer router. The traffic that makes it past this phase is then sent to the screened-host firewall (bastion host system), which applies more rules to the traffic and drops the denied packets. After this phase, the traffic finally moves to the internal destination hosts. The screened host (the firewall) is the only device that receives traffic directly from the router. No traffic goes from the Internet, through the router, and to the internal network. The screened host is always part of this equation.

If the bastion host has an application-level proxy gateway installed, then there is protection at the network layer, by the router, and protection at the application level, by the proxy. This provides a higher degree of security. For an attacker to be successful, she would have to compromise two systems.

What does the word "screening" mean in this context? As shown in Figure 7-35, the router is a screening router and the firewall is the screened host. This just means that there is a layer of protection for the firewall. A screened host is different than a screened subnet, which is described next.

Screened Subnet

A *screened-subnet* architecture adds another layer of security upon the screened-host architecture. In this environment, the bastion host, housing the firewall, is sandwiched between two routers. The external router is just like what is shown in Figure 7-35. It applies packet filtering to data entering the network and ports the traffic to the bastion host. However, instead of the bastion host then redirecting the traffic directly to the internal network, there is an interior router that also filters the traffic.

This provides another layer of security because in an environment that has only a screened host, if an attacker successfully breaks through the firewall, there is nothing in her way to prevent her from having full access to the internal network. In an environment that is using a screened subnet, there is another router that the attacker would have to successfully hack through. This is a layered approach to security and many times the more layers, the better the protection. Figure 7-36 shows a simple example of a screened subnet.

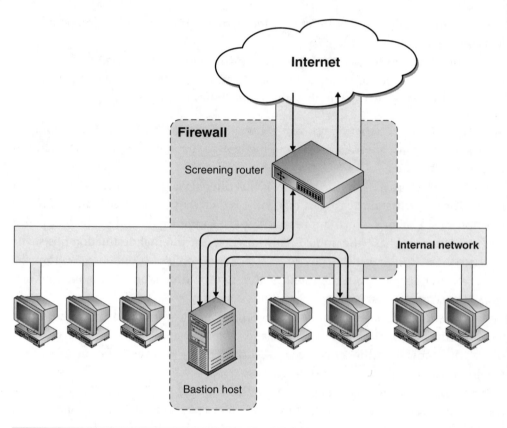

Figure 7-35 A screened host

These examples are very simple in nature. Although they are used, many times more complex networks and DMZs are implemented. Figures 7-37 and 7-38 show some other possible architectures of screened subnets and their configurations.

The screened subnet approach provides more protection than a stand-alone firewall or a screened-host firewall because there are three devices that are working together and three devices that must be compromised before an attacker can get access to the internal network. This architecture also sets up a DMZ between the two routers. The DMZ functions as a small network isolated between the trusted internal and untrusted external networks and provides a buffer zone. The internal users usually have limited access to the servers within this area. Many times Web, mail, and other public servers are placed within the DMZ. Although this provides the highest security, it also brings along the most complexity. Configuration and maintenance can prove harder in this setup

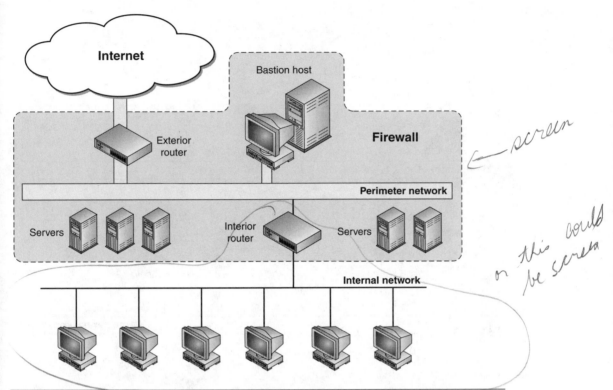

Figure 7-36 When using a screened subnet, the firewall is sandwiched between two routers.

and when new services need to be allowed, three systems may need to be reconfigured instead of just one.

The complexity and configuration of the DMZ, perimeter network, and screened hosts and subnets are dictated by the security policy. The required level of security, and the services that need to be available to internal and external users should be clearly outlined in the policy.

Tables 7-8 and 7-9 list the important concepts and characteristics of the devices and architectures discussed in the previous sections.

Shoulds of Firewalls   The default action of any firewall should be to implicitly deny any packets not explicitly allowed. This means if there is not a rule that says that the packet can be accepted, then that packet should be denied, no questions asked. Any packets entering the network that have a source address of an internal host should be

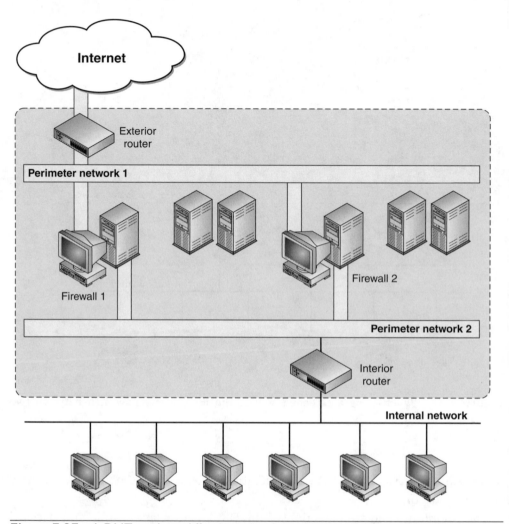

Figure 7-37 A DMZ can have different networks within it and different firewalls that filter for different vulnerabilities.

denied. This is a popular attacking trick called *masquerading* or *spoofing*. The attacker modifies a packet header to have the source address of a host inside the network that she wants to attack. This packet is spoofed and illegitimate. There is no reason that a packet coming from the Internet should have an internal source network address, so the firewall should deny it. The same is true for outbound traffic. No traffic should be allowed to leave a network that does not have an internal source address. This means

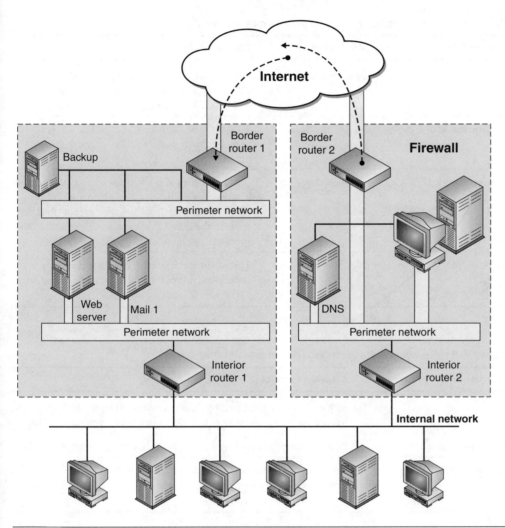

Figure 7-38 Some architectures have separate DMZs with different server types on each.

that someone, or some program, on the internal network is spoofing traffic. This is how zombies work, which are the agents used in distributed DoS attacks. If packets are leaving a network with different source addresses, these packets are spoofed and the network is most likely being used as an accomplice in a distributed DoS attack.

When security is a top priority for a company, their firewalls should reassemble fragmented packets before sending them onto their destination. There are several types of

Table 7-8 Difference Between the Different Types of Firewalls

Firewall Type	OSI Layer	Characteristics
Packet filtering	Network layer	Routers using ACLs dictate acceptable access to a network. This looks at destination and source addresses, ports, and services requested.
Application-level proxy	Application layer	This looks deep into packets and makes granular access control decisions. It requires one proxy per service.
Circuit-level proxy	Network layer	This looks only at the header packet information. It protects a wider range of protocols and services than application-level proxies, but does not provide the detailed level of control available to application-level proxies.
Stateful	Network layer	This keeps track of each conversation using a state table. It looks at the state and context of packets.

Table 7-9 Firewall Architecture Characteristics

Architecture Type	Characteristics
Dual homed	Single computer with two NICs, one connected to the trusted internal network and one connected to the untrusted external network.
Screened host	Router filters (screens) traffic before it is passed to the firewall.
Screened subnet	External router filters (screens) traffic before it enters the DMZ. Traffic headed towards the internal network then goes through a firewall and another router.

attacks where the hackers alter the packets and make them seem to be something they are not. When a fragmented packet comes to a firewall, the firewall is only seeing part of the picture. It will make its best guess on if this piece of a packet is malicious or not. Because the fragments only contain a part of the packet, the firewall is making a decision without having all the facts. Once all fragments are allowed through to a host computer, they can be reassembled and actually be malicious and cause a lot of damage. In environments that require higher security, the firewall should accept each fragment, assemble them, and make an access decision based on the whole packet, not just parts of it. The drawback is that firewalls that do reassemble packet fragments before allow-

How much delay

ing them to go on to their destination computer cause traffic delay and more overhead. It is up to the network administrator and company to decide if this configuration is necessary and if the added traffic delay is acceptable.

Many companies choose to deny packets entering their network that contain source routing information. Source routing means that the packet decides how it is to get to its destination, not the routers in between the source and destination computer. Source routing is a way of moving a packet throughout a network in a predetermined path. The sending computer must know about the topology of the network and know how to properly route data. This is easier for the routers and connection mechanisms in between because they do not need to make any decisions on how to route the packet— however, it can also cause a security risk. When a router receives a packet that contains source routing information, it figures the packet knows what needs to be done and passes it on. In some cases, not all filters may be applied to the packet and a network administrator may want packets to only be routed through a certain path and not the route that a particular packet dictates. To make sure none of this happens, many firewalls are configured to check for source routing information within the packet and deny it if it is present.

Unfortunately, once many companies erect a firewall, they have a false sense of security. Firewalls are only one piece of the puzzle, and security has a lot of pieces. The following list addresses some of the disadvantages of firewalls:

- Security is concentrated in one spot versus a distributed approach that secures many different places within the network.

- Firewalls present a potential bottleneck to the flow of traffic.

- Firewalls restrict desirable services that users may want to use. (This is a disadvantage to the users, but an advantage to the security professional.)

- Most firewalls do not protect from viruses being downloaded or passed through e-mail.

- Firewalls provide little protection against the inside attacker.

- Firewalls do not protect the modems that are used for remote connectivity.

Many firewalls also perform authentication so that the identity of the user or process requesting connections or services can be known. Authenticating users and processes give the firewalls added information to make better decisions on allowing or denying specific packets. A network administrator may want to allow remote access to the FTP server only to valid company users. So when remote users request access to the FTP server, the firewall can see if the user is authorized to use this functionality. Today

Remote Authentication Dial-in User Service (RADIUS) is a popular way of authenticating users and processes, which is also used in dial-up network access and by ISPs.

The role of the firewall is becoming more and more complex as they evolve and take on more functionality and responsibility. At times, this complexity works against the network administrator and security professional because there is a lot to understand and properly implement. Without understanding the different types of firewalls and architectures available, many more security holes can be introduced, which lays out the welcome mat for attackers.

Honeypot

Hey, here is a vulnerable system to attack!

A *honeypot* system is a computer that sits in the DMZ in hopes to lure attackers to it instead of actual production computers. To make a honeypot system lure attackers, administrators may enable services and ports that are popular to exploit for attackers. However, care needs to be taken to ensure that this box is isolated in a way so that when it is attacked, the hacker is not successful at accessing other computers on the network. Some honeypot systems have services emulated, meaning the actual service is not running but software that acts like those services are available.

In Chapter 10, honeypot systems are talked about in the context of enticement versus entrapment. A legal honeypot can entice attackers to access the computer and attempt to hack into it, but it cannot entrap them. The example given in Chapter 10 shows how having a banner on one system indicating that there are free MP3s to download on the honeypot system is entrapment because this is setting up the user to access the honeypot for reasons that are different than the intent to harm. If there are services running, ports open, and banners available for viewing, this will be quite enough to entice, not entrap, attackers.

Some network administrators just want to keep the attackers away from their other systems and set up honeypots as decoys. Other administrators want to go after those who hurt them. These administrators would keep detailed logs, enable auditing, and perform different degrees of forensics in the hopes of turning the attackers over to the authorities for prosecution.

Network Segregation and Isolation

This topic was covered in Chapter 6, but network segregation and isolation is a very important piece that interrelates with the topics in this chapter. It is important to segregate networks and subnets from each other. This usually means implementing routers that do not pass on broadcast and collision domain information. Many networks today use Ethernet technology, which continually broadcasts information. This information can be very useful to inside and outside attackers. Because data is so freely broadcasted in these environments, it is important to make sure that networks that house sensitive information are properly segmented from other network sections.

The architecture of a network should be clearly thought out, fully documented, and tested. A network administrator may not want everyone to be able to talk directly to a mainframe that holds critical information. This traffic should be ported through one channel and filtered by a router. An administrator may not want everyone on the network to be able to access the administrator's subnet, which holds the management consoles for all the routers, IDS systems, logging servers, and auditing systems. The computers within this subnet need to talk to different systems throughout the network, but there is really no good reason that regular users should be able to freely access this subnet. So this subnet needs to be isolated by ACLs enforced by surrounding routers and properly segregated.

Also, it is one thing to document what one thinks the architecture of a network is, but just because it is on paper, does not make it true. If the network schematic indicates that no one from subnet A can contact subnet B because of router ACLs, this needs to be tested and penetration attacks should be launched to see if this is indeed true.

Networking Services

So far we have touched on protocols, technologies, topologies, and devices that can be used within a LAN environment. These are not strictly used in only LAN environments, but are used in MAN and WAN infrastructures also. The purpose of splitting these sections into LAN and WAN segments is to provide a clear-cut understanding of the difference between the different networking concepts.

As stated earlier in this chapter, a network is set up to enable users to communicate with each other, create central administration, and share resources. The resources usually come in the form of networking services, and the following sections address many of the most used services in most LAN environments.

Network Operating Systems

A *network operating system (NOS)* is designed to control network resource access and provide the necessary services to enable a computer to interact with the surrounding network. An NOS is different than a single-user operating system. A NOS is built to work in a client/server model. This model enables resources, files, and applications to be centralized and all users access them on servers versus having individual copies of those resources on each and every workstation.

A NOS also has built-in authentication mechanisms, which are necessary for a network environment and auditing functionality. Single-user operating systems do not enforce strong authentication. Anyone who has worked on Windows 95 or 98 knows that you can just press the OK button when it requests a username and password. These operating systems do not require authentication. However, anyone who has worked on Windows NT and Windows 2000 systems knows that these systems will not let you just push the OK button. If you do not know the correct username and password, you're not playing.

Single-user operating systems can work in a peer-to-peer environment, meaning a type of workgroup, and implement resource and file sharing. However, a peer-to-peer environment does not provide the level of security, centralized management, and access control necessary in most environments. Single-user operating systems also do not have the powerful directory services that NOS systems provide. This is an important piece of most networks today.

The following is a short list of many of the services NOS systems provide that most single-user systems do not:

- Directory services

- Internetworking, routing, and WAN support

- Support for remote dial-up users

- Clustering functionality

- Strong authentication, authorization, access control, and auditing

- File and printing services including backup and replication services

- Management and administration tools for remote clients

- Software distribution, and software and hardware inventory functionality

- Fault tolerance capabilities

When a user of a computer running an NOS needs to access a resource on the network, the NOS software uses a redirector, which points the computer to the actual requested resource. Many times this redirector functionality works at a lower layer of processing than the higher-level requesting application. The application, usually, does not realize that the resource is not on the local computer. This reduces a lot of confusion and extra work for the programmers of the applications compared to if they had to figure out how to track down network resources themselves.

References

http://compnetworking.about.com/compute/compnetworking/cs/networknos

www.nwfusion.com/netresources/nos.html

http://directory.google.com/Top/Computers/Software/Operating_Systems

DNS

The *domain name service (DNS)* is a method of resolving hostnames to IP addresses. When the Internet was made up of about 100 computers, instead of over 1 million, a list used to be kept that mapped everyone's hostname to their IP address. This list was kept on an FTP server so everyone could access it. It did not take long for the task of maintaining this list to become overwhelming and the computing community looked to automate it.

A hierarchical system for domain names was developed and in 1992 the National Science Foundation (NSF) awarded Network Solutions, Inc. (NSI) with the contract to manage and maintain domain names and the registration process of those names. NSI handled the name registration and a hostname resolution directory of DNS servers. It also maintained the authoritative database of the Internet, which is the root DNS server. This authoritative root DNS server contained 13 files, one for each of the top-level domain servers.

Up until 1999, the Internet Assigned Numbers Authority (IANA) maintained and coordinated the allocation of IP addresses. Large ISPs would apply to the registries for blocks of these IP addresses and allocate the blocks to smaller ISPs or individual users. However, after 1999 the Internet Corporation for Assigned Names and Numbers (ICANN) took over the responsibilities of IP address block allocation, DNS management, and root server system management. NSI still maintains the authoritative root database.

Wonderful, we have had a history lesson. But how does DNS work and what is its place in a network?

When a user types in a Uniform Resource Locator (URL) in his Web browser, it is made up of words or letters that are in a sequence that makes sense to that user, such as **www.ISC2.org**. However, these words are only for humans—computers do not really understand these words. Computers work with IP addresses. So after the user enters this URL and presses ENTER, behind the scenes his computer is actually being directed to a DNS server that will resolve this URL, or hostname, into an IP address the computer understands. Once the hostname has been resolved to an IP address, then the computer knows how to get to the Web server holding the requested Web page.

Many companies have their own DNS server to resolve their internal hostnames. These companies usually also use the DNS servers at their ISPs to resolve hostnames on the Internet. An internal DNS server can be used to resolve hostnames on the entire network, but usually there is more than one DNS server so that the load can be split up and there is redundancy and fault tolerance in place.

Networks are split up into *zones*. One zone may contain all hostnames for the marketing and accounting departments and another zone may contain administration, research, and the legal departments. The DNS server that holds the files for one of these zones is said to be the *authoritative* name server for that particular zone. A zone may contain one or more domains and the DNS server holding those host records is the authoritative name server for those domain(s).

The zone files contain records that map hostnames to IP addresses, which are referred to as *resource records*. When a user's computer needs to resolve a hostname to an IP address, it looks to its TCP/IP settings to find its DNS server. The computer then sends a request, containing the hostname, to the DNS server for resolution. The DNS server looks at its resource records and finds the record with this particular hostname, retrieves the address, and replies to the computer with the corresponding IP address.

It is recommended that there be a *primary* and *secondary DNS* server for each zone. The primary contains the actual resource records for a zone and the secondary contains copies of those records. Users can use the secondary DNS server to resolve names, which takes a load off of the primary server. If the primary server goes down for any reason or is taken offline, users can still use the secondary for name resolution. Having a primary and secondary DNS provides fault tolerance and redundancy to ensure that users can continue to work if something happens to one of these servers.

Internet DNS and Domains

Networks on the Internet are connected in a hierarchical structure, as are the different DNS servers, as shown in Figure 7-39. While performing routing tasks, if a router does not know the necessary path to the requested destination, then that router passes the packet up to a router above it. The router above it knows about all the routers underneath it. This router has a broader view of the routing that takes place on the Internet and has a better chance of getting the packet to the correct destination. This holds true with DNS servers also. If one DNS server does not know which DNS server holds the necessary resource record to resolve a hostname, it can pass the request up to a DNS server above it.

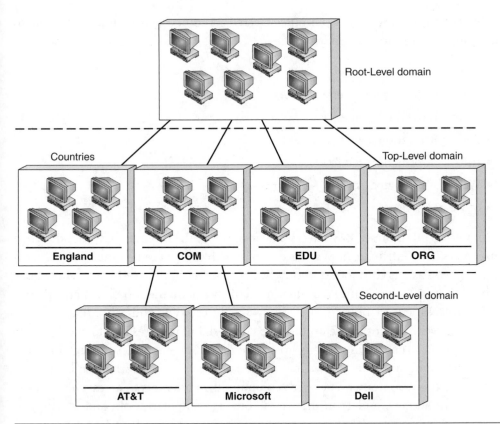

Figure 7-39   The DNS naming hierarchy is similar to the network and routing hierarchy on the Internet.

The naming scheme of the Internet resembles an inverted tree with the root server at the top. Lower branches of this tree are divided into top-level domains with second-level domains under it. The most common top-level domains are

- **COM**   Commercial
- **EDU**   Education
- **MIL**   U.S. military organization
- **INT**   International treaty organization
- **GOV**   Government
- **ORG**   Organizational
- **NET**   Networks

The International Ad Hoc Committee created seven new generic top-level domains that companies can register under:

- **Firm**   Business or firm
- **Arts**   Cultural and entertainment
- **Nom**   Individual nomenclature
- **Rec**   Recreational entertainment
- **Info**   Information services
- **Web**   Web-related entities
- **Store**   Merchants

So how do all of these DNS servers play together in the Internet playground? When a user types in a URL in the hopes of accessing a Web site that sells computer books, his computer will ask its corporate authoritative DNS server if it can resolve this hostname to an IP address. Because this Web site is most likely not on the corporate network, this particular DNS server will not usually know the necessary IP address of that Web site. The DNS server does not just reject the user's request, but it passes it onto another DNS on the Internet. The request for this hostname resolution continues through different DNS servers until one does know what the IP address is. This information is reported back to the user's computer. The user's computer then attempts to access the Web site using the IP address, and soon the user is buying computer books and is happy as a clam.

DNS server and hostname resolution is extremely important in corporate networking and Internet use. Without it, users would have to remember and type in the IP address for each Web site instead of the name. That would be a mess.

References

http://web-wise-wizard.com/internet-web-www/internet-dns-explained-tutorial.html

http://216.167.114.240/articles/3956/

http://dc.qut.edu.au/itb535/pracs/itb535_dns.htm

Directory Services

A *directory service* has a hierarchical database of users, computers, printers, resources, and attributes of each. The directory is mainly used for lookup operations, which enable users to track down resources and other users. Most directory service databases are built on the X.500 model and use Lightweight Directory Access Protocol (LDAP) to access the directory database.

Many times directory services are compared to telephone white and yellow pages because if you want to know how to contact someone, you can easily look though the white pages and find the necessary contact information. The same is true about directory services, although usually they contain much more than just phone numbers. (Actually, DNS is a type of directory service.)

The directory itself uses classes of objects and subclasses of those objects to provide organization to the directory repository, which is usually a database. Then policies can be applied to these objects in a central administration method. The entities within objects can be users, their location, and peripheral information, resources, profiles, electronic commerce information, network services, and much more. The administrator can then develop access control, security, and auditing policies that dictate who can access these objects, how the objects can be accessed, and audit each of these actions. Policies can also be developed and applied to control bandwidth management, firewall filtering, VPN access, and QoS.

Many times different directories are developed and maintained. These different directories can be based on business or security needs, have different security policies, access control, and profiles applied to them. When there is more than one directory, they need a way to communicate to each other, which takes place through *metadirectories*. *Metadata* is data about data. In the case of directories, metadirectories hold top-level information about the directory itself, which enables a user in one directory to quickly locate the object he is looking for in a totally different directory.

Each directory follows a specific schema, like regular databases. The schema is what provides structure to the directory repository and defines how objects and their relationships are to be represented. Each directory service vendor has a baseline schema that enables administrators to define their own objects and corresponding attributes. However like many other types of products, there are interoperability issues between vendors' schemas so that they cannot easily communicate with each other. If one company buys another company and their networks need to be merged and directory services combined, this can turn into a tricky and hairy project.

Directory services offer rich services to users, administrators, and networks as a whole. They enable administrators to maintain and control all resources and users within an environment. The directory database acts as a holding place for almost all of the network's important information and enables users to easily and quickly track down needed services or resources. Two examples of directory services are Microsoft's Active Directory and Novell Directory Services (NDS). These are based on the X.500 model but do not easily communicate with each other.

There are many services that are made available to users within a network, which is a big reason to construct a network in the first place. This section described NOS, DNS, and directory services, but a network offers much more. Many offer print services that enable many users to share local and remote printers and print servers. The administrators have centralized network management services that let them view the network as a whole from one graphical application, add and delete users, troubleshoot network issues, audit activities, add and remove services, control remote user access, and much more. Some networks have terminal emulation services, which enable users to have a lower-powered workstation that only sees the desktop. The operating system actually sits on a server somewhere else and does all the processor-intense activities.

Networks and networking are one of the most interesting, confusing, and rewarding constructs of today's computing world. However, the complexity causes many errors, security holes, and vulnerabilities. This is just what potential attackers are counting on. The more one knows and understands about networking and how each component works with other components, the more efficiently security mechanisms can be applied and a higher level of protection can be provided.

References

www.ietf.org/html.charters/ldapext-charter.html

www.ietf.org/html.charters/policy-charter.html

Intranets and Extranets

We kind of trust you, but not really. We're going to put you on the extranet.

Web technologies and their uses have exploded with functionality, capability, and popularity. Companies set up internal Web sites for centralized business information like employee phone numbers, policies, events, news, and operations instructions. Many companies have also implemented Web-based terminals that enable employees to perform their daily tasks, access centralized databases, make transactions, collaborate on projects, access global calendars, use videoconferencing tools and whiteboard applications, and obtain often used technical or marketing data. Web-based clients are different than workstations that log into a network and have their own desktop. Web-based clients limit a user's abilities to access the computer's system files, resources, hard drive space, access back-end systems, and more. The Web-based client can be configured to provide a graphical user interface (GUI) with only the buttons, fields, and pages necessary for the users to perform their tasks. This gives all users a standard universal interface with similar capabilities.

When a company uses Internet- or Web-based technologies inside their networks, they are using an *intranet*. The company has Web servers, client machines using Web browsers, and uses the TCP/IP protocol suite. The Web pages are written in Hypertext Markup Language (HTML) or Extensible Markup Language (XML) and are accessed via HTTP.

Another common element of intranets is that they usually use private IP addresses instead of publicly registered addresses. These addresses are free for any company to use and provide a degree of safety because they cannot be routed on the Internet. The following section lists current private IP addresses.

Private IP Addresses

- **10.0.0.0** Class A network

- **172.16.0.0–172.31.255.255** 16 contiguous class B networks

- **192.168.0.0–192.168.255.255** 256 contiguous class C networks

Using Web-based technology has many pluses. It has been around for quite some time, it is easy to implement, there are no major interoperability issues, and with just a click on a link, a user can be taken to the location of the requested resource. Web technologies are not platform-dependent, meaning all Web sites and pages may be maintained on a Unix server, while all different flavors of client workstations can access them. They only need a Web browser.

An *extranet* extends outside the bounds of the company' network to enable two or more companies to share common information and resources. Business partners commonly set up extranets for business-to-business communication to take place. One business may post orders to the other business via the extranet, work on projects together, share marketing information, allow employees to communicate and work collaboratively on issues, and share catalogs, pricing structures, or upcoming event information. Many times trading partners use Electronic Data Interchange (EDI), which provides structure and organization to electronic documents, orders, invoices, purchase orders, and a data flow. EDI has evolved into Web-based technologies to provide easy access and easier methods of communication.

For many businesses, an extranet can provide a weakness or hole in their security if not implemented and maintained properly. Properly configured firewalls need to be in place to control who comes in and out of the extranet communication channels.

Extranets used to be based mainly on dedicated links, which are harder for attackers to infiltrate, but today many extranets are set up over the Internet, which requires properly configured VPNs and security policies.

References

www.intranetroadmap.com

www.cio.com/forums/intranet

www.intranetjournal.com

Network Address Translation

I have one address I would like to share with everyone!

When computers need to communicate to each other, they need to use the same type of addressing scheme so everyone understands how to find and talk to one another. The Internet uses the IP address scheme and any computers or networks that want to communicate with other users on the network must conform to this scheme; otherwise that computer will sit in a virtual room with only itself to talk to.

However, IP addresses have become scarce (until the full adoption of IPv6) and expensive. So some smart people came up with *network address translation (NAT)*, which enables a network that does not follow the Internet's addressing scheme to still have the capability to communicate over the Internet.

Private IP addresses were discussed in an earlier section. These addresses can be used within the boundaries of a company, but cannot be used on the Internet because they will not be properly routed. NAT enables a company to use these private addresses and still be able to communicate transparently with computers on the Internet.

NAT is a gateway between a network and the Internet, or another network, that performs transparent routing and address translation. Because IP addresses were depleting fast, IPv6 was developed, which was intended to be the long-term fix to the address shortage problem. NAT was developed as the short-term fix to enable more and more companies to participate on the Internet. However, to date, IPv6 is extremely slow in acceptance and implementation and NAT has caught on like wildfire. Many firewall vendors have implemented NAT into their products and it is found that NAT actually provides a great security benefit. When attackers want to hack a network they first do what they can to learn all about the network, its topology, services, and addresses. Attackers cannot easily find out a company's addresses scheme and its topology when NAT is in place because NAT acts like a large nightclub bouncer by standing in front of the network and hiding the true IP scheme. Because private IP addresses are not used on the Internet, attackers cannot find out the actual address a particular computer is using.

NAT hides internal addresses by centralizing them on one router and any frames that leave that network only have the source address of that router, not the actual computer that sends the message. So when a message comes from an internal computer with the address of 10.10.10.2, the message is stopped at the device running NAT software, which happens to have the IP address of 1.2.3.4. NAT changes the header of the message from the internal address, 10.10.10.2, to the valid IP address of the NAT device, 1.2.3.4. (Yes, I know 1.2.3.4 isn't valid, but I think you get the concept.) When a computer on the Internet replies to this message, it replies to the address 1.2.3.4. The NAT device changes the header on this reply message to 10.10.10.2 and puts it on the wire for the internal user to receive.

In some cases, the NAT has a pool of IP addresses to work with, which are used to translate between internal and external addresses. A company needs to have enough addresses to ensure that communication is not negatively affected. If a company has only four IP addresses and they are all used when another computer wants to communicate to the outside world, the last user has to wait until one of the addresses in the pool is freed up.

Most NAT implementations are stateful, meaning they keep track of a communication between the internal host and an external host until that session is ended. The NAT device needs to remember the internal IP address and port to send the reply messages back. This stateful characteristic is similar to stateful firewalls, but NAT does not perform scans on the incoming packets looking for malicious characteristics. Instead, NAT is a service usually performed on proxy servers within a company's DMZ.

Although NAT was developed to provide a quick fix for the depleting IP address problem, it has actually put the problem off for quite some time. The more companies that implement private address schemes, the less the addresses become scarce. This has been very helpful to NAT and the vendors that implement this technology, but it has put the acceptance and implementation of IPv6 much farther down the road.

References

http://safety.net/nattech.html

www.tcpipprimer.com/nat.cfm

www.homenethelp.com/web/explain/about-NAT.asp

Metropolitan Area Network

A *metropolitan area network (MAN)* is usually a backbone that connects businesses to WANs, the Internet, and other businesses. A majority of today's MANs are *Synchronous Optical Network (SONET)* or FDDI rings provided by the telephone companies. These rings cover a large area and businesses can connect to the rings via T1, fractional T1s, and T3 lines. Figure 7-40 illustrates two companies connected via SONET ring and the devices usually necessary to make this type of communication possible. This is one example of a MAN, although in reality there are usually several businesses connected to one ring.

FDDI technology was discussed earlier in the chapter and now we will quickly go over SONET. SONET is actually a standard for telecommunication transmissions over fiber-optic cables. Carriers and telephone companies have deployed SONET networks worldwide, and if they follow the SONET standards properly, the different networks can communicate with little difficulty.

SONET is self-healing, meaning that if there is a break in one of its lines due to an earthquake or some other type of disaster, it can use a backup redundant ring to ensure that transmission continues. All SONET lines and rings are fully redundant. The redundant line is waiting in the wings in case anything happens to the primary ring or line.

SONET networks can transmit voice and data over optical networks. Many times slower-speed SONET networks feed into larger, faster SONET networks. This enables businesses in different cities and regions to communicate.

References

www.iec.org/tutorials/index.html

www.techfest.com/networking/wan.html

www.cisco.com/warp/public/cc/pd/rt/1200/tech/posdh_wp.htm

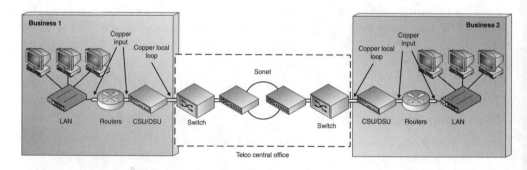

Figure 7-40 A MAN covers a large area and enables businesses to connect to each other, the Internet, or other WAN connections.

Wide Area Network

LAN technologies provide communication capabilities over a small geographic area, whereas *Wide Area Network (WAN)* technologies are used when communication needs to travel over a larger geographical area. LAN technologies encompass how a computer puts its data onto a network cable, the rules and protocols of how that data is formatted and transmitted, how errors are handled, and how the destination computer picks this data up from the cable. When a computer on one network needs to communicate with a network on the other side of the country or in a different country altogether, then WAN technologies kick in.

The network must have some avenue to other networks, which is most likely a router that communicates with the company's service provider's routers or telephone company facilities. Just like there are several types of technologies within the LAN arena, there are also several types within the WAN arena. This section touches on many of these technologies.

Telecommunications Evolution

On the eighth day God created the telephone.

Telephone systems have been around for about 100 years and they started as copper-based analog systems. Central switching offices connected individual telephones by hand (a human operator) and then by electronic switching equipment. Once two telephones were connected, they had an end-to-end connection, or an end-to-end circuit. Multiple phone calls were divided up and placed on the same wire, which is called multiplexing. *Multiplexing* is a method of combining multiple channels of data over a single transmission path. The transmission is so fast and efficient that the receiving ends do not realize they are sharing a line with many other entities. They think they have the line all to themselves.

In the mid-1960s digital phone systems emerged with a T1 trunk, which carried 24 voice communication calls over two pairs of copper wires. This provided a 1.544-Mbps transmission rate, which brought quicker service, but also the capability to put more multiplexed calls onto one wire. When calls take place between switching offices, say local phone calls, they are multiplexed on T1 lines. When a longer distance call needs to take place, the calls coming in on the T1 lines are multiplexed onto T3 lines, which can carry up to 28 T1 lines. This is shown in Figure 7-41.

The next entity to join the telecommunication party was fiber optics, which enabled even more calls to be multiplexed onto one trunk over longer distances. Then came optical carrier technologies, SONET, which transmitted digitized voice signals in packets. SONET is a standard for telecommunication transmission over fiber-optic cables. This

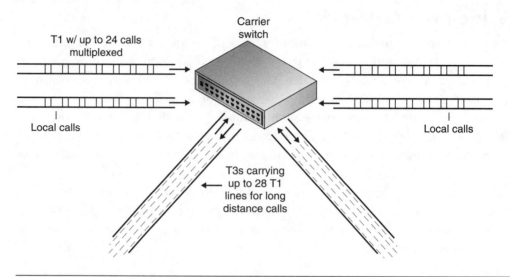

Figure 7-41 Local calls were multiplexed onto T1 lines and longer distance calls were moved from T1 lines to T3 multiplexed lines.

standard defines how data is to be framed, outlines access methods, and outlines necessary parameters for transporting digital information over optical systems. Telecommunication carriers used this technology for lower-speed optical links to be multiplexed into higher-speed links similar to how lower-speed LANs connect to higher-speed WAN links today. Figure 7-42 shows an example of SONET rings connected together.

Figure 7-42 shows how telecommunication carriers can provide telephone and Internet access to companies and individuals in large areas. The SONET standard gives all world carriers the capability to interconnect.

The next evolutionary step in telecommunication's history is ATM. ATM encapsulates data in fixed cells and can be used to deliver data over the SONET network. Many times the analogy of a highway and cars is used to easily describe the SONET and ATM relationship. SONET is the highway that provides the foundation, or network, for the cars, ATM packets, to travel on.

ATM is a high-speed network technology that is used in LAN and WAN implementations by carriers, ISPs, and telephone companies. ATM uses a fixed cell size instead of the variable frame size used by earlier technologies. This fixed size provides better performance and a reduced overhead for error handling. (More information on ATM technology is provided in the "WAN Technologies" section.)

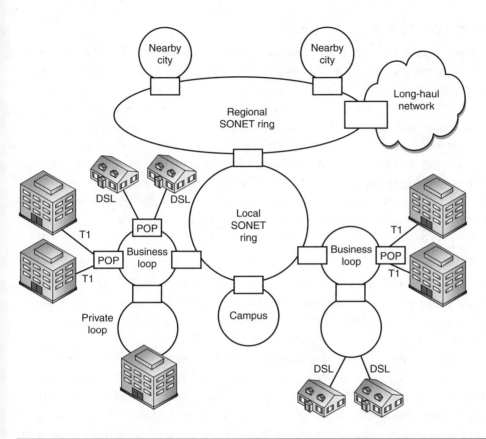

Figure 7-42 SONET technology enables several optical communication loops to communicate.

Here is a quick snapshot of telecommunication history:

- Copper lines carrying purely analog signals
- T1 lines that carry up to 24 conversations
- T3 lines that carry up to 28 T1 lines
- Fiber optics and the SONET network
- ATM over SONET

This was only a quick glimpse at an amazing, complex giant referred to as telecommunications. There are many more technologies being developed and implemented to increase the amount of data that can be efficiently delivered in a short period of time.

Dedicated Links

A *dedicated link* is also called a leased line or point-to-point link. It is one single link that is pre-established for the purposes of WAN communications between two destinations. It is dedicated, meaning that only the destination points can communicate with each other. This link is not shared by any other entities at any time. This was the main way companies communicated in the past because there were not as many choices as there are today. A dedicated link is good for two locations that will communicate often and require fast transmission and a specific bandwidth, but it is expensive compared to other possible technologies that enable several companies to share the same bandwidth and also share the cost. This does not mean that dedicated lines are not in use—; they definitely are used, but there are just many other options now.

T-carriers

T-carriers are dedicated lines that can carry voice and data information over trunk lines. The most commonly used T-carriers are T1 lines that provide up to 1.544 Mbps and T3 lines that provide up to 45 Mbps. They are both digital circuits that multiplex several individual channels into a higher-speed channel.

These lines perform multiplex functionality through time-division multiplexing (TDM). What does this multiplexing stuff really mean? Let's take a T1 line, which can multiplex up to 24 channels. If a company has a PBX connected to a T1 line, which in turn connects to the telephone company switching office, then 24 calls can be chopped up and placed on the T1 line and transferred to the switching office. If this company did not use a T1 line, they would have to have 24 individual twisted pairs of wire to handle this many calls.

As shown in Figure 7-43, data is inputted into these 24 channels and transmitted. Each channel gets to insert up to 8 bits into its established time slot. Twenty-four of

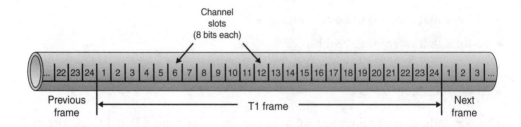

Figure 7-43 Multiplexing is a way of taking several different phone calls, or data transmissions, and putting them on the same wire.

these 8-bit time slots make up a T1 frame. That does not sound like very much information, but 8,000 frames are built per second. Because it is so quick, the receiving end does not notice a delay and does not know that it is sharing its connection and bandwidth with up to 23 other devices.

Originally, T1 and T3 lines were used by the carrier companies, but they have been replaced mainly with optical lines. Now T1 and T3 lines feed data into these powerful and super fast optical lines. The T1 and T3 lines are leased to companies and ISPs that need high-capacity transmission capability. Sometimes T1 channels are split up between different companies who do not really need the full bandwidth of 1.544 Mbps. These are called *fractional* T lines.

As mentioned earlier, dedicated lines have their drawbacks. They are expensive and inflexible. If a company moves to another location, a T1 line cannot easy follow them. It is expensive because companies have to pay for a dedicated connection with a lot bandwidth even when they do not use the bandwidth. Not many companies require this level of bandwidth 24 hours a day. Instead, they may have data to send out here and there but not continuously.

The cost of a dedicated line is determined by the distance to the destination. If a T1 line is run from one building to another building two miles away, it will be much cheaper than a T1 that covers 50 miles or a full state.

References

www.bell-labs.com/technology/common/t1carrier.html

www.dcbnet.com/notes/9611t1.html

www.everythingt1.com

S/WAN

Secure WAN (S/WAN) was originally an initiative of RSA Security, who worked with many firewall and protocol vendors in the efforts to build secure firewall-to-firewall connections through the Internet. S/WAN is based on VPNs that are created with IPSec. IPSec is the newest and most secure tunneling protocol because it provides hard-to-break encryption, the option of encrypting the header information and not just the payload data, and it incorporates authentication based off of the public-key technology.

One other advantage of using IPSec in S/WAN devices is that it will ensure that all firewalls are using the same protocol. This will help battle the ongoing interoperability issues when different firewall, or VPN, vendors use their own proprietary protocols that other vendors cannot understand. IPSec is an integrated part of IPv6 and an add-on option for IPv4. It performs authentication via the IP address and the use of certificates instead of user authentication that usually requires a username and password.

There is an open-source version of S/WAN that provides VPN services in Linux environments. It provides secure gateways and VPN connections and is called FreeS/WAN.

References

www.freeswan.org

www.rsasecurity.com

WAN Technologies

WAN technologies, I am sure you have guessed, are used to enable networks to communicate over long distances. There are different WAN technologies available to companies today and the information that is used to make the decision pertaining to which is the most appropriate usually includes functionality, bandwidth demands, service level agreements, required equipment, cost, and what is available from their service providers. The following sections go over some of the WAN technologies available today.

CSU/DSU

A *Channel Service Unit/Data Service Unit (CSU/DSU)* is required when digital equipment will be used to connect a LAN network to a WAN network. This connection can take place with T1 and T3 lines, as shown in Figure 7-44. This is necessary because the

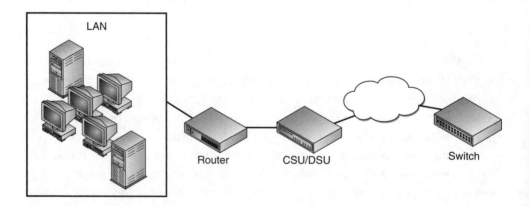

Figure 7-44 A CSU/DSU is required for digital equipment to be able to properly communicate with telephone lines.

signals and frames are so different between the LAN equipment and the WAN equipment used by service providers.

The DSU device converts digital signals from routers, bridges, and multiplexers into signals that can be transmitted over the telephone company's digital lines. The DSU device is the device that ensures that the voltage levels are correct and that information is not lost during the conversion. The CSU is the unit that connects the network directly to the telephone company's line. The CSU/DSU is not always a separate device and can be part of a networking device.

The CSU/DSU provides a digital interface for Data Terminal Equipment (DTE), like terminals, multiplexers, or routers and an interface to the Data Circuit-Terminating Equipment (DCE) device, like a carrier's switch. The CSU/DSU basically works as a translator and at times a line conditioner.

Switching

Dedicated links have one single path to transverse; thus, there is no complexity when it comes to determining how to get packets to different destinations. There are only two points of reference and a packet leaves one and heads towards the other. It gets much more complicated when thousands of networks are connected to each other and many times this is where switching comes in.

There are two main types of switching: circuit switching and packet switching. *Circuit switching* sets up a virtual connection that acts like a dedicated link between two systems. ISDN is an example of circuit switching, which is shown in Figure 7-45.

When the source system makes a connection with the destination system, they set up a communication channel. If the two systems are local to each other, then fewer devices need to be involved with setting up this channel. The farther the two systems are from each other, the more the devices are required to be involved with setting up the channel and connecting the two systems.

An example of a circuit-switching system is daily telephone use. When one person calls another, the same type of dedicated communication link is set up. Once the connection is made, the devices that are supporting that communication channel do not dynamically move the call through different devices, which is what takes place in a packet-switching environment. The channel remains configured at the original devices until the call, or connection, is done and torn down.

Packet switching, on the other hand, will not set up a dedicated link and packets from one call can pass through a number of different individual devices, instead of all of them following one another through the same devices. Some examples of packet-switching technologies and networks are the Internet, X.25, and frame relay. The infrastructure that

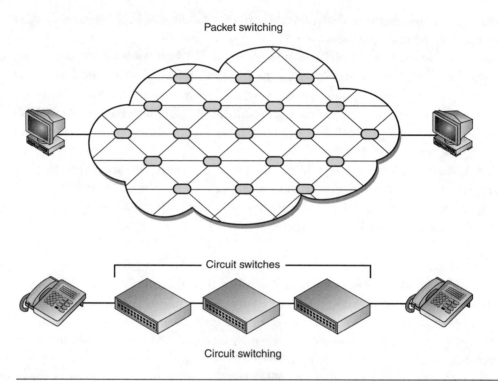

Packet switching

Circuit switches

Circuit switching

Figure 7-45 Circuit switching provides one road for a communication path, whereas packet switching provides many different possible roads.

supports these methods is made up of routers and switches of different types. They provide multiple paths to the same destinations, which provide a high degree of redundancy.

In a packet-switched network, the data is broken up into packets containing sequence numbers. These packets will go through different devices and their path can be dynamically altered by a router or switch that determines that there is a better route for a specific packet to take. Once the packets are received at the destination computer, all the packets are reassembled sequentially and interpreted.

Because the path a packet will take on a packet-switching environment is not set in stone, there could be variable delays when compared to a circuit-switching technology. This is okay because packet-switching networks usually carry data rather than voice. Because voice connections clearly detect these types of delays, in many situations a circuit-switching network is more appropriate for voice connections. Voice calls usually provide a steady stream of information, whereas a data connection is burstier in nature. When you talk on the phone, the conversation keeps a certain rhythm. You and your friend do not talk extremely fast and then take a few minutes in between conversations to fill the void with complete silence. However, this is usually how a data connection works. A lot of data is sent from one end to the other at one time and then there is dead time until it is time to resend more data.

Circuit versus Packet Switching

Circuit Switching

Connection-oriented virtual links.

Traffic travels in a predictable and constant manner.

Fixed delays.

Usually carries voice-oriented data.

Packet Switching

Packets can use many different dynamic paths to get to the same destination.

Supports traffic that is bursty.

Variable delays.

Usually carries data-oriented information.

References

www.bell-labs.com/technology/packet

www.rad.com/networks/1998/packet/ps.htm

Frame Relay

Why are there so many paths to choose from?

For a long time, many companies used dedicated links to communicate with other companies. This means that company A has a pipeline to company B that provides a certain bandwidth 24 hours a day and is not used by any other entities. This is great because only the two companies can use it and a certain level of bandwidth is always available, but it is expensive and most companies did not use the full bandwidth each and every hour that this link was available. Thus, the companies spent a lot of money for a service that they do not use all the time. Frame relay is one type of technology that companies have turned to instead of using dedicated lines.

Frame relay is a WAN protocol that operates at the data link layer. It is a MAN and WAN solution that uses packet-switching technology, which enables multiple companies and networks to share the same WAN media. Whereas direct point-to-point links have a cost based on the distance between the end points, frame relay has a cost that is based on the amount of bandwidth used. Because several companies and networks use the same media and devices (routers and switches), the cost can be greatly reduced per company compared to dedicated links.

If a company knows that it will usually require *x* amount of bandwidth each day, it can pay a certain fee to make sure this amount of bandwidth will always be available to it. If another company knows that it will not have a high bandwidth requirement, it can pay a lower fee that does not guarantee the higher bandwidth allocation. This second company will have the higher bandwidth available to them anyway until that link gets busy, and then the bandwidth level will reduce. (Companies that pay more to ensure that a higher level of bandwidth will always be available to them pay a *committed information rate [CIR]*).

There are two main types of equipment used in frame relay connections: Data Terminal Equipment (DTE) and Data Circuit-Terminating Equipment (DCE). The DTE is usually a customer-owned device, like a router or switch that provides connectivity between the company's own network and the frame relay network. DCE is the service provider's, or phone company's, device that does the actual data transmission and switching in the frame relay cloud. So the DTE is a company's ramp way onto the frame relay network and the DCE devices are the ones that actually do the work within the frame relay cloud.

The frame relay cloud is the collection of DCEs that provide switching and data communication functionality. There are several different service providers that provide this type of service and some providers use other provider's equipment and it can all get very confusing because there are so many different routes a packet can take. It is called a cloud to differentiate it from other types of networks and because when a packet hits this cloud, users do not usually know the route that their frames will take. The frames will either be sent through permanent or switched virtual circuits that are defined within the DCE, or carrier switches.

Frame relay is an any-to-any service that is shared by many users. As stated earlier, this is good because the monthly costs are much lower than those of dedicated leased lines. Because it is shared, if one subscriber is not using his bandwidth, it is available to others to use. On the other hand, when traffic levels increase, the available bandwidth

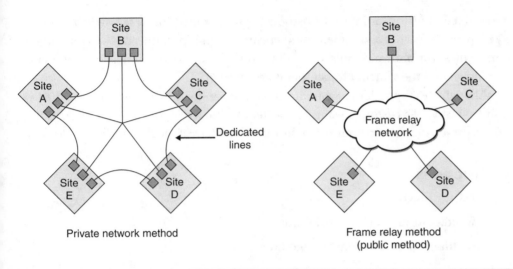

Private network method

Frame relay method
(public method)

Figure 7-46 A private network connection requires several expensive dedicated links. Frame relay enables users to share public resources.

is shared. This is why there is a committed rate for the subscribers who want to ensure that a certain bandwidth is always available to them.

Figure 7-46 shows the difference between five sites being connected via dedicated lines versus five sites connecting through the frame relay cloud. The first solution requires many dedicated lines that are very expensive and not very flexible. The second solution is cheaper and provides companies much more flexibility.

Virtual Circuits

Frame relay forwards frames across virtual circuits. These circuits can be permanent, meaning that they are programmed in advance or the circuits are switched, meaning that the circuit is quickly built when it is needed and torn down when it is no longer needed. The *permanent virtual circuit (PVC)* works like a private line for a customer with an agreed-upon bandwidth availability. When a customer decides to pay for the committed rate, a PVC is programmed for that customer to ensure that he will always receive a certain amount of bandwidth.

Unlike PVCs, *switched virtual circuits (SVCs)* require steps similar to a dial-up and connection procedure. This is because a permanent path is set up for PVC frames and when SVCs are used, a circuit needs to be built. It is similar to setting up a phone call over the public network. During the setup procedure, the required bandwidth is requested, the destination computer is contacted and must accept the call, a path is determined, and forwarding information is programmed into each switch along the SVC's path. SVCs are good for teleconferencing, temporary connections to remote sites, data replication, and voice calls. Once the connection is no longer needed, the circuit is torn down and the switches forget that it ever existed.

Although a PVC provides a guaranteed level of bandwidth, it does not have the flexibility of a SVC. If a customer wants to use her PVC for a temporary connection, as mentioned earlier, the customer must call the carrier and have it set up, which can take hours.

References

www.frforum.com

www.rad.com/networks/tutorial.htm

www.alliancedatacom.com/framerelay.asp

X.25

X.25 is an older WAN protocol that defines how devices and networks establish and maintain connections. Like frame relay, X.25 is a switching technology that uses carrier switches to provide connectivity for many different networks. It also provides an any-to-any connection, meaning that many users use the same service simultaneously. Subscribers are charged on the amount of bandwidth they use instead of a flat fee as in dedicated links.

Data is divided into 128 bytes and encapsulated in High-level Data Link Control (HDLC) frames. The frames are then addressed, and forwarded across the carrier switches. Much of this sounds the same as frame relay, and it is, but frame relay is much more advanced and efficient when compared to X.25. This is because the X.25 protocol was developed and released in the 1970s. During this time, many of the devices that were connected to networks were dumb terminals, the networks did not have built-in functionality and fault tolerance, and the Internet overall was not as foundationally stable and resistant to errors as it is today. When these characteristics were not part of the Internet, X.25 was required to compensate for these deficiencies and provide many layers of error checking, error correcting, and fault tolerance. This made the protocol fat, which was required back then, but today it clogs down the system and provides a lower performance rate than frame relay or ATM.

References

www.blackbox.nl/techweb/protocol/x25.htm

www.patton/com/patton/fridayfax/article23.html

ATM

Asynchronous Transfer Mode (ATM) is another switching technology, but instead of being a packet-switching method, it uses a cell-switching method. ATM is a high-speed networking technology used for LAN, WAN, and service provider connections. Like frame relay, it is a connection-oriented switching technology. IP is an example of a connectionless-oriented switching technology. Within the TCP/IP protocol suite, IP is connectionless and TCP is connection-oriented. This means that IP segments can be quickly and easily routed and switched without each router or switch in between having to worry about if the data actually made it to its destination. That is TCP's job. The protocol TCP works at the source and destination ends to ensure that data was properly transmitted and resends data that ran into some types of problems. When using ATM or frame relay, the devices in between the source and destination have to be more conscious of data and whether it gets to where it needs to go, unlike when purely IP is being used.

ATM is a cell-switching technology versus a packet-switching technology. This means that data is segmented into fixed size cells, 53 bytes, instead of variable-size packets. This provides for more efficient and faster use of the communication paths. ATM sets up virtual circuits, which act like dedicated paths between the source and destination. These virtual circuits can guarantee bandwidth and QoS, unlike IP. For these reasons, ATM is a good carrier for voice and video transmission, because it promises a bandwidth level and a dedicated path. ATM enables companies to replace individual voice and data lines and combine them into one.

ATM technology is used by carriers and service providers and makes up part of the core technology of the Internet, but this technology can also be used for a company's private use in backbones and connections to the service provider's networks.

Traditionally, companies used dedicated lines, usually T-carrier lines, to connect to the public networks. However, companies have also moved to implementing an ATM switch onto their network, which connects them to the carrier infrastructure. Because the fee is based on bandwidth used instead of a continual connection, it can be much cheaper. Some companies have replaced their Fast Ethernet and FDDI backbones with ATM. When ATMs are used as private backbones, the companies have ATM switches that take the Ethernet, or whatever data link technology that is being used, and frame and convert them into the 53-byte, ATM cells.

ATM supports different interfaces to provide this type of flexibility and different use. A DSU device is used to connect a LAN to the public ATM network. This architecture is used when a company's network is connected to the ATM network via router or bridge. The DSU device is necessary to make sure that the digital signals are converted to a signal type the ATM network can understand. Other private LANs may have ATM switches as part of their environment.

Like frame relay, ATM can set up PVCs, which are preprogrammed into the switches along that particular communication path and SVCs, which are set up at the time they are required and torn back down when they are done being used.

References

www.scan-technologies.com/tutorials/ATM%20Tutorial.htm

www.atmforum.com

SMDS

Switched Multimegabit Data Service (SMDS) is a high-speed packet-switched technology used to enable customers to extend their LANs across MANs and WANs. When a company has an office in one state that needs to communicate with an office in a different state, the two LANs can use this packet-switching protocol to communicate across the already established public network. This protocol is connectionless and can provide bandwidth on demand.

SDLC

Synchronous Data Link Control (SDLC) protocol is based on networks that use dedicated, leased lines with permanent physical connections. It is used mainly for communication to IBM hosts within a Systems Network Architecture (SNA). It was developed by IBM in the 1970s. It is a bit-oriented, synchronous protocol that has been evolved into other communication protocols such as HDLC, Link Access Procedure (LAP), and Link Access Procedure-Balanced (LAPB).

SDLC was developed to enable mainframes to communicate with remote locations. The environments that use SDLC usually have primary systems that control secondary stations' communication. SDLC provides the polling media access technology, which is the mechanism that enables secondary stations to communicate on the network. Figure 7-47 shows the primary and secondary stations on a SDLC network

HDLC

High-level Data Link Control (HDLC) protocol is also a bit-oriented link layer protocol used for transmission over synchronous lines. HDLC is an extension of SDLC, which is mainly used in SNA environments. HDLC provides high throughput because is supports full-duplex transmissions and is used in point-to-point and multipoint connections.

Like SDLC, HDLC works with primary stations that contact secondary stations to establish data transmission. Vendors have developed their own parameters within their

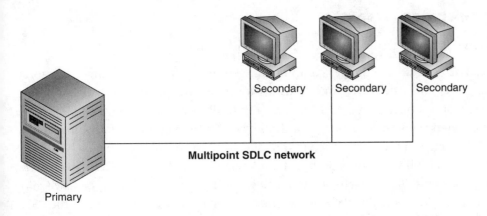

Figure 7-47   SDLC is used mainly in mainframe environments within a SNA network.

version of HDLC, which has ended up with interoperability issues between different vendor HDLC implementations.

References

www.ftp.uni-erlangen.de/pub/other/Documents/ISO/asynch-HDLC

www.rad.com/networks/1994/hdlc/hdlc/html

www.erg/abdn.ac.uk/users/gorry/course/dl-pages/hdlc.html

HSSI

High-Speed Serial Interface (HSSI) is an interface used to connect multiplexers and routers to high-speed communication services like ATM and frame relay. It supports speeds up to 52 Mbps as in T3 WAN connections, which are usually integrated with router and multiplex devices to provide serial interfaces to the WAN.

These interfaces define the electrical and physical interfaces to be used by DTE/DCE devices; thus, it works at the physical layer. The interface was developed by Cisco and T3plus Networking.

References

www.cisco.com/univercd/cc/td/doc/cisintwk/ito_doc/hssi.htm

http://cio.cisco.com/warp/public/459/8.html

Multiservice Access

Let's see how many services we can shove onto this one cable.

Multiservice access technologies combine different types of communication categories (data, voice, and video) over one transmission line. This provides for higher performance, reduced operational costs, and greater flexibility, integration, and control for the customers. This advancement in technology is clearing up the usually blurred division lines between the Internet service providers and the telephone carriers.

The regular phone system is based on a circuit-switched voice-centric network, referred to as public-switched telephone network (PSTN). PSTN uses circuit switching instead of packet switching. When a phone call is made, the call is placed at the PSTN interface, which is the user's telephone. This PSTN is connected to the telephone company's local loop via copper wiring. Once the signals for this phone call gets to the telephone company's central office (the end of the local loop), they are now part of the telephone company's circuit-switching world. A connection is made between the source and the destination and as long as the call is in session, the data flows through the same switches.

When a phone call is made, the connection has to be set up, signaling has to be controlled, and the session must be torn down. This takes place through the Signaling System 7 protocol. When Voice over IP (VoIP) is used, its signals can use these same networks and its protocols must be properly transmitted so the devices involved can understand this different signaling scheme.

This PSTN network is being replaced by data-centric, packet-oriented networks that can support voice, data, and video. The new VoIP networks use different switches, protocols, and communication links. This means that the VoIP has to go through a tricky transition stage that enables the old systems and infrastructures to communicate with the new systems until the old is dead and gone.

High-quality compression is used with VoIP technology and the identification numbers (phone numbers) are IP addresses. This technology gets around some of the barriers that are present in the PSTN today. The interface devices (telephones) have embedded functions and logic that make it more difficult to implement different types of services that the network as a whole can support. In VoIP, the interface to the network can be a computer, server, PBX, and much more that runs a telephone application. This provides for much more flexibility when it comes to adding new services. This gives a lot more control and intelligence to the interfacing devices.

Because this is a packet-oriented switching technology, there are possible latency delays that can occur. This manifests as longer delays within a conversation and lets the conversation seem to get out of synch a bit. When someone using VoIP for a phone call experiences these types of lags in the conversation, it is because the packets holding the other person's voice message got queued somewhere within the network and is on its way. This is referred to as *jittering*, but there are protocols being developed to help smooth out these issues and provide a more continuous telephone call experience.

H.323

The ITU-T Recommendations cover a wide variety of multimedia communication services. H.323 is part of this family of recommendations, but is also a standard that deals with video, real-time audio, and data packet-based transmissions where multiple users can be involved with the data exchange. An H.323 environment has terminals, which can be telephones or computers with telephony software, gateways that connect this environment to the public telephone network, multipoint control units, and gatekeepers that manage calls and functionality.

Like any type of gateway, H.323 gateways connect different types of systems and devices and provide the necessary translation functionality. The H.323 terminals are connected to these gateways and the gateways are connected to the PSTN. These gateways translate protocols used on the circuit-based telephone network and the packet-based VoIP network. These gateways also translate the circuits into packets and packets into circuits as required.

The technology is only a few years old, but it is catching on fast and the new devices and protocols are being implemented and used. Today it is necessary to also implement the gateways that enable the new technology to communicate with the old, but soon the old telephone network may be a thing of the past and all communication may take place over packets instead of circuits.

The newer technology looks to provide transmission mechanisms that will involve much more than just voice. Although we have gone over mainly VoIP, there are other technologies that support the combination of voice and data over the same network such as voice over ATM, and voice over frame relay. ATM and frame relay are connection-oriented protocols and IP is connectionless. This means that frame relay and ATM provide better QoS and less jittering and latency.

So the best of both worlds is to combine IP over ATM or frame relay. This allows for packet-oriented communication over a connection-oriented network that will provide an end-to-end connection. IP is at the network layer and is media independent—this means that it can run over different data link layer protocols and technologies.

Traditionally, a company has a PBX, which is a switch between the company and the PSTN. The company usually has the PBX on their premises and there are T1 or T3 lines connecting the PBX to the telephone company's central office, which houses switches that act as ramps onto the PSTN. When WAN technologies are used instead of accessing

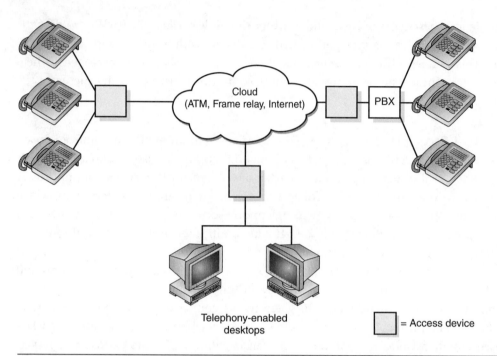

Figure 7-48   Regular telephone calls connect phones to the PSTN. Voice over WAN technologies connect calls to the Internet cloud.

the PSTN through the central office switches, the data is transmitted over the frame relay, or ATM, cloud. An example of this configuration is shown in Figure 7-48.

Because frame relay and ATM utilize PVCs and SVCs, they both have the capability of using SVCs for telephone calls. Remember that PVCs are used when a company wants to ensure that it will always have a certain bandwidth available to it. When a company pays for this guaranteed bandwidth, they are paying for the switches and routers to be programmed to control their connection and for that connection to be maintained. SVCs, on the other hand, are set up on demand and are temporary in nature. They are perfect for making telephone calls or transmitting video during videoconferencing.

We have covered several WAN technologies in these last sections. Table 7-10 provides a snapshot of the important characteristics for each.

Table 7-10   The Characteristics of Discussed WAN Technologies

WAN Technologies	Characteristics
Dedicated lines	• Dedicated, leased line that connect two locations • Expensive compared to other WAN options • Secure because only two locations are using the same media
Frame relay	• High-performance WAN protocol that uses packet-switching technology, which works over public networks • Shared media between companies • Uses SVCs and PVCs • Fee based on used bandwidth
X.25	• First packet-switching network developed to work over public networks • Shared media between companies • Lower speed than frame relay because of its extra overhead • International standard and used more in countries other than the United States
SMDS	• High-speed switching technology to be used over public network
ATM	• High-bandwidth switching and multiplexing technology that has a low delay • Uses 53-byte fixed-size cells • Uses PVCs and SVCs • Very fast because of the low overhead
SDLC	• Enables mainframes to communicate with remote offices • Provides polling mechanism to allow primary and secondary stations to communicate
HDLC	• A data encapsulation method for synchronous serial links • Point-to-point and multipoint communication
HSSI	• DTE/DCE interface to enable high-speed communication over WAN links
VoIP	• Combines voice and data over the same IP network media and protocol • Reduces costs of implementing and maintaining two different networks

References—VoIP

www.cisco.com/univercd/cc/td/doc/product/access/acs_mod/cis3600/
voice/4936vqsg.htm

www.ietf.org/html.charters/iptel-charter.html

References—Voice over Frame Relay

www.frforum.com

www.Mot.com/networking/frame-relay

References—Voice over ATM

www.Atmforum.com/atmforum/specs/approved.html

www.iec.org/tutorials/vtoa/index.html

Remote Access

I need to talk to you, but I am way over here!

Remote access covers several technologies that enable remote and home users to connect to networks, which will grant them access to network resources that help them to perform their necessary tasks. Most of the time these users must first gain access to the Internet through an ISP, which will then set up a connection to the destination network.

For many corporations, remote access is a necessity because it enables users to obtain up-to-date information, can reduce networking costs by using the Internet as the access media instead of expensive dedicated lines, and extends the workplace for employees to their homes or on the road.

Remote access can streamline access to resources and information through Internet and intranet connections and provides a competitive advantage by letting partners, suppliers, and customers have closely controlled links. The most common types of remote connectivity methods used are VPNs, dial-up connections, ISDN, cable modems, DSL connections, and wireless technologies.

Dial-Up and RAS

Remote access is usually gained by connecting to a network access server (NAS). The NAS acts as a gateway and an end point to a PPP session. Then NAS provides authentication and authorization and usually controls a bank of modems.

If the network is using Microsoft Windows platforms, then the users may be dialing into a Remote Access Service (RAS) server, which performs authentication by comparing the provided credentials with the database of credentials it maintains. Another type of access server used in remote access situations is RADIUS, which is covered in Chapter 4. There are several configurations an administrator can set to dictate what actions will take place when a remote user attempts to connect to the NAS. Usually a request for a username and password takes place and the NAS may hang up the call in order to call the user back at a predefined phone number. This is a security activity that is used to try and ensure that only authenticated users are given access to the network and it reverses the long-distance charges back to the company. Even if an attacker finds out the logon credentials necessary to gain remote access, it is unlikely that the attacker will also be at the predefined phone number. However, this security measure can be compromised if someone implements call forwarding.

Remote access methods are a highly targeted item when it comes to trying to find an entry point into a network. This is because many companies have a stack of modems to provide remote access to their network and somehow think that their firewall magically protects all access to their network. So when a company has a false sense of security because they have implemented a firewall but has not implemented any (or strong) access control over the modem pool, the attackers can easily walk into a network without ever having to bother with the firewall.

Wardialing is a process used by many attackers to identify remote access modems. There are specially written tools that programmatically dial a large bank of phone numbers that is fed to them. The tools log valid data connections (modems used for data transmission) and attempt to identify the system on the other end of the phone line. Some of these tools have the option of performing a dictionary attack, which attempts many possible username and password combinations in the hopes of being authorized and allowed to access the network. Wardialing enables an attacker to find all the modems that provide remote access into a network. Once she finds a modem, she will attempt to access the network through this entry point. If there are modems within an infrastructure, they are usually much easier to compromise than a firewall.

Many times companies have hanging modems off of workstations here or there without even knowing about it. Employees may install them or the IT staff may install them and then forget about them. This is why it is important for companies to perform wardialing on their own network to make sure there are no modems attached that they do not know about.

ISDN

Integrated Services Digital Network (ISDN) is a communication protocol provided by telephone companies. This protocol and the necessary equipment enable data, voice, and other types of traffic to travel over a medium in a digital manner that was previously only used for voice calls. The telephone companies actually went all digital many years ago, except for the local loop. The local loop consists of the copper wires that connect houses and businesses to their carrier provider's central offices. These central offices contain the telephone company's switching equipment and are where the analog to digital transformation takes place. However, the local loop was always analog, and was therefore slower. ISDN was developed to replace the aging telephone analog systems, but has yet to catch on to the level that was expected.

ISDN

ISDN breaks the telephone line into different channels and transmits data in a digital form versus the old analog method. There are three ISDN implementations:

- **Basic Rate Interface (BRI) ISDN** This implementation operates over existing copper lines in the local loop and provides digital voice and data channels. This implementation uses two B channels and one D channel with a combined bandwidth of 144 Kbps. This is used usually for home subscribers.

- **Primary Rate Interface (PRI) ISDN** This implementation has up to 23 B channels and 1 D channel, at 64 Kbps. The total bandwidth is equivalent to a T1, which is 1.544 Mbps. This would be more suitable for a company that requires a higher amount of bandwidth.

- **Broadband-ISDN (BISDN)** This implementation can handle many different types of services at the same time and is mainly used within telecommunication carrier backbones. When BISND is used within a backbone, ATM is used to encapsulate data at the data link layer into cells and these cells travel over a SONET network.

ISDN uses the same wires and transmission media used by analog dial-up technologies, but works in a digital fashion. If a computer uses a modem to communicate with an ISP, it converts its data from digital to analog to be transmitted over the phone line. If that same computer was configured and had the necessary equipment to utilize

ISDN, it would not need to convert the data from digital to analog, but would keep it in a digital form. This, of course, means that the receiving end would also require the necessary equipment to properly receive and interpret this type of communication. Communicating in a purely digital form provides higher bit rates that can be sent more economically.

ISDN is a set of telecommunication services that can be used over public and private telecommunication networks. It provides a digital point-to-point circuit-switched medium and establishes a circuit between the two communicating devices. An ISDN connection can be used for anything a modem can be used for, but it provides more functionality and higher bandwidth. This switched digital service can provide bandwidth on an as-needed basis and can be used for LAN-to-LAN on-demand connectivity instead of using an expensive dedicated link.

As stated in an earlier section, analog uses a full channel for communication, but ISDN can break this channel up into multiple channels to provide full-duplex communication and a higher level of control and error handling. ISDN provides two basic home and business services: Basic Rate Interface (BRI) and Primary Rate Interface (PRI). BRI has two B channels that enable data to be transferred and one D channel that provides for call setup, network management, error control, caller ID, and more. The bandwidth available with BRI is 144 Kbps, whereas the top modems can only provide 56 Kbps.

The D channel provides for a quicker call setup and process of making a connection. An ISDN connection may only require a two to five second setup connection time, whereas a modem may require a 45- to 90-second time frame. This D channel provides for out-of-band communication between the local loop equipment and the user's terminal. It is out of band because the control data is not mixed in with the user communication data. This makes it harder for a would-be defrauder to send bogus instructions back to the service provider's equipment in the hopes of causing a denial of service, obtaining services not paid for, or some other type of destructive behavior.

DSL

Digital Subscriber Line (DSL) is another type of high-speed connection technology used to access the Internet. It can provide 6 to 30 times higher bandwidth speeds than ISDN and analog technologies. It uses existing phone lines and provides a 24-hour connection to the Internet. This does indeed sound better than sliced bread, but only certain people can get this service because they have to have a service provider that provides this service and they have to be within a 2.5-mile radius of the service provider's equipment. As the distance between a residence and the central office increases, the transmission rates for DSL decreases.

DSL is a broadband technology that can provide up to 52-Mbps transmission speed without the need of replacing the carrier's copper wire. The end user and the carrier's equipment do need to be upgraded for DSL though, and this is why many companies and residents cannot use this service at this time. The user and carrier must have DSL modems that use the same modulation techniques.

DSL actually has several different types of services. The services can be symmetric, which means that traffic flows at the same speed upstream and downstream, or asymmetric where the downstream speed is much higher than upstream. In most situations, an asymmetric connection is fine for residence users because they usually download items from the Web much more than they upload data.

References

www.paradyne.com/sourcebook_offer.

www.dsllife.com

www.nwfusion.com/netresources/dsl.htm

Cable Modems

The television cable companies have been delivering television services to homes for years and they recently started delivering data transmission services for users who have cable modems and want to connect to the Internet at high speeds.

Cable modems provide high-speed access, up to 50 Mbps, to the Internet through existing cable coaxial and fiber lines. The cable modem provides upstream and downstream conversions.

Coaxial and fiber cables are used to bring hundreds of television stations to users and one or more of the channels on these lines are dedicated to carrying data. The bandwidth is shared between users in a local area; therefore, it will not always stay at a static rate. So if Mike attempts to download a program from the Internet at 5:30 P.M., he most likely will have a much slower connection than if he attempted it at 10:00 A.M. This is because many people come home from work and hit the Internet at the same time. So as more people access the Internet within his local area, Mike's Internet access performance drops.

Sharing the same media brings up a slew of security concerns because users with network sniffers can easily view their neighbors traffic and data as it travels to and from the Internet. Many cable companies are looking into encryption and other security mechanisms. The growth of cable modems has also increased the use of personal firewalls.

Always Connected

Unlike modem connections, DSL lines and cable modems are connected to the Internet all the time. No dial-up steps are required as in modem connections. This can cause a huge security issue because many hackers look for just these types of connections. Systems using these types of connections are always online and available for scanning, probing, hacking, and attacking. However, these systems are often used in distributed DoS (DDoS) attacks. Because the systems are on all the time, attackers plant Trojan horses that lay dormant until they get the command from the attacker to launch an attack against a victim. A lot of the DDoS attacks use systems with DSL and cable modems as their accomplices and usually the owner of the computer has no idea.

Reference

www.cablemodeminfo.com

VPN

Here's the secret handshake. Now you can use the secret tunnel.

A *virtual private network (VPN)* is a secure private connection through a public network, or an otherwise unsecure environment, as shown in Figure 7-49. It is a private connection because the encryption and tunneling protocols are used to ensure the

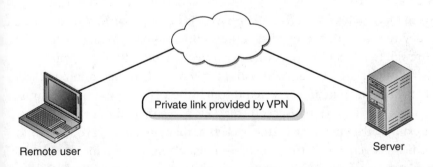

Remote user   Private link provided by VPN   Server

Figure 7-49 A VPN provides a virtual dedicated link between two entities across a public network.

confidentiality and integrity of the data in transit. The protocols that can be used for VPNs are Point-to-Point Tunneling Protocol (PPTP), IPSec, and L2TP.

The sending and receiving end must have the necessary hardware and software to set up an encrypted tunnel, which provides the private link. It is private because the tunneling encryption protocol that is used encrypts the data and protects it as it travels through the untrusted public network, usually the Internet.

Many times remote users, or road warriors, use VPNs to connect to their company network to access their e-mail, network resources, and personal files. A remote user must have the necessary software on his computer. Usually the user would first make a PPP connection to an ISP and the ISP would make a full connection for the user to the destination network. PPP encapsulates datagrams to be properly transmitted over an IP network. Once this connection has been made, the user's software initiates a VPN connection with the destination network. Because data exchanged between the two entities will be encrypted, the two entities go through a handshaking phase to agree upon the type of encryption that will be used and the key that will be employed to actually encrypt their data. So the ISP is involved with the creation of the PPP connection, which is a type of foundation for the VPN connection. Once the PPP connection is set up, the ISP is out of the picture and the VPN parameters are negotiated and decided upon by the user and the destination network. After this is complete, the user and network can then communicate securely through their newly created virtual connection.

VPN connections can be used for remote users to access a network and they can also be used to provide a connection between two routers (many times called gateway-to-gateway connection) or two users. It is very flexible, and the only requirements are that each entity has a dial-up connection, VPN software, the necessary protocols, and the same encryption mechanisms. Once the VPN connection is made, the user can access network resources in the same manner that he can access them via dial-up connections.

Up to now we have been discussing VPN that takes place over dial-up connections; a VPN can also take place between firewalls that have VPN functionality. Within a network, the VPN device sits on the outer edge of the security domain. When a company implements a firewall that has VPN functionality embedded, this allows for centralization of administration for the VPN and firewall. In this type of configuration, packets that enter the network can come in encrypted through the VPN connection and must be decrypted to allow the firewall to inspect the packets and either allow or deny them. Because there is extra work being done on the packets as they enter and leave a network, much more overhead is generated. This causes degradation in performance. However, today most of the processing that takes place is being moved to hardware and integrated circuits, which can work at much faster speeds than pure software.

Tunneling Protocols

How do we get our message through this sea of packets? Answer: Create a tunnel.

It was mentioned that VPNs use tunneling protocols, but what the heck are they anyway? Well, a tunnel is a virtual path across a network that delivers packets that are encapsulated and possibly encrypted. Encapsulation and encryption sound very much alike, but they describe two different reasons a tunnel would be used in the first place.

If there is one network that uses NetBIOS Enhanced User Interface (NetBEUI) that needs to be connected to another network that also uses NetBEUI, but they are two states apart, what is the problem? NetBEUI is nonroutable. So for these two networks to communicate, the NetBEUI packets must be encapsulated within a routable protocol, like IP. This type of encapsulation happens all the time on the Internet and between networks. When an Ethernet network is connected to an FDDI backbone, that FDDI network will not understand the Ethernet frame format; thus, the packets must be encapsulated within the FDDI protocol when they are to be sent over the FDDI network. If two networks use IPX and need to communicate across the Internet, these messages must also be encapsulated in a protocol that the Internet can understand, like IP.

The second variation to a tunnel is encapsulation *and* encryption. The encapsulation reasons stay the same and the encryption is used to protect the data's confidentiality and integrity as it travels through untrusted environments. These are both ways of tunneling through another network.

Tunneling is the main ingredient to a VPN because that is how it creates its private connection. There are three main tunneling protocols used in VPN connections: PPTP, L2TP, and IPSec. (*IPSec is described in depth in Chapter 8.*)

PPTP

Point-to-Point Tunneling Protocol (PPTP) is an encapsulation protocol based on PPP. It works at the data link layer and it enables a single point-to-point connection, usually between a client and a server.

PPTP actually encrypts and encapsulates PPP packets, which creates the virtual private connection. PPTP does provide a level of security because it authenticates and encrypts data, but there are a few weaknesses. When the negotiation takes place, PPTP cannot encrypt the negotiation information because encryption is in the process of being invoked. So data that actually goes through the tunnel is protected, but the negotiation information is done in clear text and can be easily sniffed. This might not sound like much, but there is some important information exchanged during the negotiation process that a hacker might be interested in such as the client and server IP address, username, sometimes the hashed password value, and the software being used by the client computer. So this means the authentication information is sent in clear text.

PPTP is a commonly used tunneling protocol, although L2TP is becoming more popular. PPTP is a Microsoft-developed protocol, so of course, most of the world is familiar with using it.

L2TP

Cisco had developed a tunneling protocol, Layer 2 Forwarding (L2F), which was later combined with the PPTP protocol. The result was *Layer 2 Tunneling Protocol (L2TP)*, which is another protocol that tunnels through networks. There are a few differences between it and PPTP:

- PPTP can only run on top of IP networks—it is dependent upon the IP protocol. L2TP, on the other hand, can run on top and tunnel through networks that use other protocols like IPX, SNA, and IP.

- PPTP is an encryption protocol and L2TP is not; thus, L2TP lacks the security to be called a true VPN solution. Many times L2TP is used in conjunction with IPSec to provide the necessary encryption.

- L2TP supports TACACS+ and RADIUS and PPTP does not.

If a user were going to use L2TP to form a VPN to his corporation network, he would first dial into his ISP using his modem. This sets up a PPP connection between him and the ISP. When the ISP receives this call and a request to access the corporation network, the ISP sends this request to the corporation network, most likely a RADIUS server. The RADIUS server looks up the user's information to see if he is allowed to dial in. The RADIUS server gives the ISP the message to allow the connection and will instruct the ISP to set up a L2TP connection. The L2TP tunnel is set up between the ISP and the corporation network and the user authentication is sent to the RADIUS server on the corporation network. Once authentication completes, communication begins.

So what does tunneling mean at the packet level? It means the packet has a new hairdo. Actually, it has a new header. If the client is using a dial-up connection, which means his packets are encapsulated within the PPP protocol; once the tunnel is set up, the frame that is encapsulated within PPP is then encapsulated within L2TP. This encapsulation process gives the packet a new header. This new header creates the tunnel. It's like speaking another language that no one else knows. When the ISP and the corporate network use L2TP, their packets have these special headers and they travel in a sea of packets that have regular IP headers. So a tunnel is not an extra wire or cable—instead, it has packets that have headers that no one else understands.

The following provides an outline of VPN tunneling protocols:

Point-to-Point Tunneling Protocol (PPTP)

- Designed for client/server connectivity
- Sets up a single point-to-point connection between two computers
- Works at the data link layer
- Transmits over only IP networks

Layer 2 Forwarding (L2F)

- Created before L2TP by Cisco
- Merged with PPTP, which resulted in L2TP
- Provides mutual authentication
- No encryption

Layer 2 Tunneling Protocol (L2TP)

- Hybrid of L2F and PPTP
- Sets up a single point-to-point connection between two computers
- Works at the data link layer
- Transmits over multiple types of networks, not just IP
- Combined with IPSec for security

IPSec

- Handles multiple connections at the same time
- Provides secure authentication and encryption
- Supports only IP networks
- Focuses on LAN-to-LAN communication rather than a dial-up protocol
- Works at the network layer, and provides security on top of IP
- Can work in *tunnel mode*, meaning the payload and header is encrypted, or *transport mode*, meaning that only the payload is encrypted

PPP

Point-to-Point Protocol (PPP) is used to encapsulate messages and transmit them through an IP network, like the Internet, over a serial line. PPP is used to establish dial-up Internet connections between routers, user-to-router, and user-to-user. PPP is the protocol used to establish a dial-up Internet connection between a computer and an Internet point of presence (POP). A POP is usually a bank of modems and access servers at an ISP location. The user dials into this POP over the Internet and communicates using the PPP protocol.

During the setup phase between the ISP and remote user, authentication and the assignment of an IP address take place. Different networks can use different protocols, IPX/SPX, NetBEUI, or TCP/IP. Other than TCP/IP, these protocols cannot successfully travel over the Internet, so they need to be encapsulated within a protocol that can be transmitted throughout the Internet. Another reason to use PPP is standardization. Since there are so many different types of hardware, software, protocols, and configurations for each, the service provider should not have to worry about all of these just to pass one packet from one place to another. When the datagrams are encapsulated with PPP, this protocol uses headers and control information that the service provider's equipment and software is expecting and knows how to interpret.

PPP supports different authentication methods such as Password Authentication Protocol (PAP), Challenge Handshake Authentication Protocol (CHAP), and Extensible Authentication Protocol (EAP). The authentication phase follows the link establishment phase. This enables a limited connection to be made so that the authentication server can ask for the necessary credentials to be delivered.

> **NOTE** PPP is a full-duplex protocol that provides bidirectional links over synchronous, asynchronous, ISDN, frame relay, and SONET connections. PPP supports different types of authentication methods, which are described in the next sections.

PPP has, for the most part, replaced *Serial Line Internet Protocol (SLIP)*. SLIP is an older protocol that was used for encapsulating data to be sent over IP networks via an asynchronous serial connection. PPP has several capabilities that SLIP does not have:

- PPP implements header and data compression for efficiency and better use of bandwidth.
- PPP has error correction.
- PPP supports different authentication methods.
- PPP can encapsulate protocols other than just IP.
- PPP does not require both ends to have an IP address assigned before data transfer can occur.

- PPP supports other types of connections than just asynchronous and SLIP only works over asynchronous connections.

PAP, CHAP, and EAP

Hey, how do I know you are who you say you are?

Password Authentication Protocol (PAP) is an authentication protocol used by remote users. It provides identification and authentication of the user attempting to access a network from a remote system. This protocol requires a user to enter a password before being authenticated. The password and the username are the credentials that are sent over the network to the authentication server after a connection has been established via PPP. The authentication server has a database of user credentials that are compared to the supplied credentials to authenticate users.

PAP is one of the least secure ways of authenticating because the credentials are sent in clear text. This causes them to be easily captured by network sniffers. Although it is not recommended, some systems revert to PAP if they cannot agree on any other authentication protocol. During the handshake process of a connection, the two entities negotiate how authentication is going to take place, what connection parameters to use, the speed of data flow, and so on. Both entities will try to negotiate and agree upon the most secure method of authentication; thus, they may start with EAP, and if one computer does not have EAP capability, they will try to agree on CHAP. If one of the computers does not have CHAP capabilities either, they may be forced to use PAP. If this type of authentication is unacceptable, then the administrator will configure the RAS to only accept CHAP authentication and higher, and PAP cannot be used at all.

PAP is also vulnerable to replay attacks because it uses a static username and password scheme. This means that if an attacker captured a user's credential set, he could replay or send these same credentials and get authenticated to the network as that user very easily.

Challenge Handshake Authentication Protocol (CHAP) is also an authentication protocol. It uses a challenge/response mechanism to authenticate instead of sending a username and password. When a user wants to establish a PPP connection and both ends have agreed that CHAP will be used for authentication purposes, the user's computer sends the authentication server a logon request. The server sends the user a challenge, which is a random value. This challenge is encrypted with the use of a predefined password as an encryption key and the encrypted challenge value is returned to the server. The authentication server also uses the predefined password as an encryption key and encrypts the original challenge value and compares the results to what was received from the user. If the two results are the same, the authentication server deduces

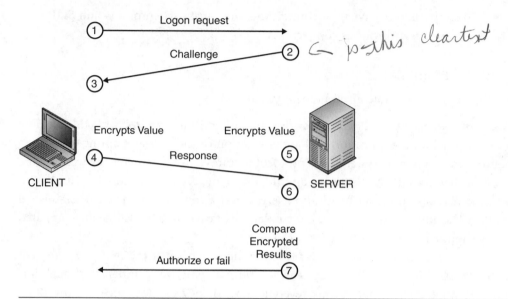

Logon request ①

Challenge ② ← *is this cleartext*

③

Encrypts Value   Encrypts Value

④   Response   ⑤

CLIENT   SERVER

⑥

Compare
Encrypted
Authorize or fail   Results
⑦

Figure 7-50 CHAP uses a challenge/response mechanism instead of having the user send the password over the wire.

that the user must have entered the correct password and authentication is granted. The steps that take place in CHAP are depicted in Figure 7-50.

PAP is vulnerable to sniffing because it sends the password in plain text, but is also vulnerable to man-in-the-middle attacks. CHAP is not vulnerable to man-in-the-middle attacks because it continues this challenge/response activity throughout the connection to ensure that the authentication server is still communicating with a user who holds the necessary credentials. CHAP is also not vulnerable to replay attacks, as PAP is, because of its challenge/response mechanism.

PAP versus CHAP

PAP Characteristics

- Provides identification and authentication automatically for remote users
- Sends credentials in clear text during transmission
- Decreases in use because it does not provide a high level of security
- Supported by most networks and network access servers
- Authentication takes place by static passwords

CHAP Characteristics

- Used the same way PAP is used but provides a higher degree of security

- Authenticates using a challenge/response method instead of static passwords

- Used by remote users, routers, and NASs to provide authentication before providing connectivity

Extensible Authentication Protocol (EAP) is also an authentication method that PPP supports. Actually, EAP is not a specific authentication mechanism like PAP and CHAP; instead, it provides a framework to enable many types of authentication techniques to be used during PPP connections. As the name states, it extends the authentication possibilities from the norm (PAP and CHAP) to other methods like one-time passwords, token cards, biometrics, and future mechanisms. So when a user dials into an authentication server and both have EAP capabilities, they can negotiate between a longer list of possible authentication methods.

PAP Reference

www.linuxdoc.org/HOWTO/PPP-HOWTO/pap.html

EAP Reference

www.ietf.org/html/charters/pppext-charter.html

www.msg.net/kadow/answers/extras/rfc/rfc2284.html

Remote Access Guidelines

Many companies do not exactly know who is accessing their network remotely or why. Remote users should be identified and their activities audited to ensure that no malicious activity is taking place and that no one is abusing their access rights. All remote users should be justified in their right to access the network and this should be reviewed on an annual basis. If Brian worked in the software development group and required remote access to work from home, and then six months later was moved into the logistics group, he might not require remote access any longer; thus, remote access should no longer be available to him.

Expected activity and behavior pertaining to remote access should be within the company's security policy or in a special purpose policy that outlines who should do what and when. This policy should be presented and available to all users. This will clear up confusion and enable the company to take steps if someone is abusing her use of remote access.

The phone lines that are used for remote access should be restricted to outbound access for dial-out services only and the modems should be set to answer after the fourth ring. Many times war dialers are configured to move onto another phone number if the number they are dialing rings past two or three times. This is because if a connection rings past three times, it is usually a telephone line and not a data line. So configuring the modem to answer on the fourth ring or higher is done in the hopes to not let attackers know that the telephone line is actually being used for remote data access.

The remote access facilities should be consolidated when at all possible. This means that all access servers and modem pools are housed in the same server room and administered by the same person or group. This helps ensure that there is consistency in how remote entry points are maintained and monitored, and when changes take place they happen to all entry points. This would also allow for centralized auditing and logging, and it makes it harder to forget all the different ways the company is allowing users into the environment.

Strong two-factor user authentication should be used via RADIUS or TACACS+ servers, which are explained in Chapter 4. If the data that users and the company will be transmitting is confidential or sensitive, users should connect via VPN. Different levels of security should be provided to different types of users entering the network. This helps ensure that each user only has the necessary access rights and permissions necessary.

Many times a company restricts access based on the address of the source computer trying to gain access. If the address is unknown or not on the access control list, then the connection should be denied. A firewall can also be implemented to ensure that remote users only access the services and ports the network administrator wants them to access.

Caller ID and/or callback settings should be configured on the RAS server. The *caller ID* functionality can see the source telephone number and make a decision on if access is to be allowed or not based on a predefined list of approved phone numbers. For an attacker to get around this, she must call from a pre-authorized telephone number or compromise the telephone company's central office equipment. The *callback* option requires the RAS to call the user requesting access back. This is when a user authenticates to the RAS and it drops the connection and calls the user back at a preconfigured telephone number. This does not protect unauthorized access from an authorized location and can be bypassed by call forwarding.

Caller ID and callback options are great, but are usually not practical because they require users to call in from a static phone number each time they access the network.

Most users are accessing the network remotely because they are on the road, and moving from place to place.

References

www.microsoft.com/windows2000/library/howitworks/communications/
  remoteaccess/default.asp

www.firstvpn.com/papers/nortel/remote.pdf

www.ietf.org/html.charters/nasreq-charter.html

www.iec.org/tutorials/index.html

Network and Resource Availability

In the triangle of security services, availability is one of the foundational components, the other two being confidentiality and integrity. Network and resource availability is not fully appreciated until it is gone. That is why administrators and engineers need to implement effective backup and redundant systems to make sure that when something happens (and something will happen), that the users' productivity will not be drastically affected.

The network needs to be properly maintained to make sure that the network and its resources will always be available when needed. The cables need to be the correct type for the environment and technology used and cable runs should not exceed the recommended lengths. Older cables should be replaced for newer ones and cable cuts and malfunctions should be tested for periodically.

A majority of networks use Ethernet technology, which is very resistant to failure. Token Ring was designed to be fault tolerant and does a good job when all the computers within this topology are configured and act correctly. If one NIC is working at a different speed than the others, then the whole ring can be affected and traffic may be disrupted. Also, if two systems have the same MAC address, the whole network can be brought down. These issues need to be considered when maintaining an existing network. If an engineer is installing an NIC on a Token Ring network, he should ensure that it is set to work at the same speed as the others and that there is no possibility for duplicate MAC addresses.

Single Points of Failure

Don't put all eggs in one basket or all electrons in one device.

A *single point of failure* can bring a lot of potential risk to a network because if the device that is the single point of failure goes down, a segment or the entire network is negatively affected. Devices that could provide single points of failure are firewalls, routers, network access servers, T1 lines, switches, bridges, hubs, and authentication servers to name a few. The best defenses against being vulnerable to these are proper maintenance, backups, and redundancy.

There should be multiple paths between routers in case one route goes down and dynamic routing protocols should be used so that each router will be informed when a change to the network takes place. For WAN connections, there should be a failover option configured, which enables an ISDN or modem connection to be available if the WAN router fails.

Uninterruptible power supply (UPS) and redundant array of inexpensive disks (RAID) should be in place and properly configured. UPS is addressed in Chapter 6, so we will just touch on it here and show how it relates to network availability.

The UPS should be able to provide a clean and steady power source to the crucial systems and resources on the network. RAID is put in place to provide fault tolerance for hard drives and can improve system performance. Redundancy and speed are provided by breaking up the data and writing it across several disks so that different disk heads can work simultaneously to retrieve the requested information. Control data is also spread across each disk, which is called *striping*, so that if one disk does fail, the other disks can work together and restore its data.

RAID

Everyone be calm—this is a raid. Answer: Wrong raid.

Redundant Array of Inexpensive Disks (RAID) is a technology used for redundancy and performance improvement. It combines several physical disks and aggregates them into logical arrays. When data is saved, it is written across all drives. A RAID appears as a single drive to applications and other devices.

When data is written across all drives, the technique of striping is used. This activity divides and writes the data over several drives. The write performance is not affected, but the read performance is increased dramatically because more than one head is retrieving data at the same time. It might take the RAID system six seconds to write a block of data to the drives and only two seconds or less to read the same data from the disks.

There are different levels of RAID, which dictate the type of activity that will take place within the RAID system. Some levels deal only with performance issues, whereas other levels deal with performance and redundancy. If redundancy is one of the services that a RAID level is providing, then parity is involved. *Parity* data is written to each disk, which works as a backup. If a drive fails, the parity data is used to rebuild a new drive and all the information is restored. Most RAID systems have hot-swapping disks (replace drives while the system is running). When a drive is swapped out, or added, the parity data that is written to each disk rebuilds the data on the new disk that was just added.

The most common RAID levels used today are levels 1, 3, and 5. Table 7-11 describes each of the possible RAID levels.

References

www.raid-advisory.com

http://members.home.com/slater/raid/index.htm

Clustering

Okay, everyone gather over here and perform the same tasks.

Clustering is a fault tolerant server technology that is similar to redundant servers except each server takes part in processing services that are requested. A server cluster is a group of servers that are viewed logically as one server to users and are managed as a single system. Clustering provides for availability and scalability. It groups physically different systems and combines them logically, which provides immunity to faults and improves performance. Clusters work as an intelligent unit to balance traffic and users who access the cluster do not know that they may be accessing different systems at different times. To the users, all servers within the cluster are seen as one unit.

If one of the systems within the cluster fails, processing continues because the rest just pick up the load, although there could be degradation in performance. This is more attractive than having a secondary server that waits in the wings in case a primary server fails because this secondary server may just sit idle for a long period of time, which is wasteful. When clustering is used, all systems are used to process requests and none sit in the background waiting for something to fail.

Clustering brings a lot to the table instead of just availability. It provides load balancing (each system takes a part of the processing load), redundancy, and failover (other systems will continue to work if one fails).

Table 7-11 RAID Options

RAID Level	Description	
Level 0	Data striped over several drives, but no redundant drive. No redundancy or parity. If one volume fails, the entire volume is unusable. It is used for performance.	Striping
Level 1	Mirroring of drives. Data is written to two drives at once. If one drive fails, the other drive has exact some data. Usually one mirrored drive is used at a time. This is an expensive option because every drive has another full drive with the exact same information.	Mirroring
Level 2	Data striping over all drives at the bit level. Parity data created with hamming code, which identifies any errors. Specifies 39 disks: 32 for storage and 7 for error recovery data. This is not used in practice.	Hamming code parity
Level 3	Data striping over all drives and parity data held on one drive. If a drive fails, it can be reconstructed from parity drive.	Byte-level parity
Level 4	Same as level 3 except data is striped in disk sector units instead of blocks of bits or bytes.	Block-level parity
Level 5	Data is written in disk sector units to all drives. Parity is written to all drives. Uses XOR algorithm to calculate parity. Because parity is written to all drives, there is not a single point of failure.	Interleave parity
Level 6	Similar to level 5 but with added fault tolerance, which is a second set of parity data written across all drives.	Second parity data
Level 10	Level 1 and level 0 with striping applied across multiple RAID 1 pairs.	1 + 0
Level 15	Level 1 and level 5 and two complete RAID 5 systems are mirrored for fault tolerance.	1 + 5

Backups

Backing up software and having backup hardware devices is a large part of network availability. (These issues are covered extensively in Chapters 6 and 9 so they are only discussed briefly here.)

It is important to be able to restore data if a hard drive fails, a disaster takes place, or there has been some type of software corruption.

A policy needs to be developed that indicates what gets backed up, how often, and how these processes should take place. If users have important information on their workstations, a method needs to be worked out that indicates that backups include certain directories on users' workstations or that users move their critical data to a server share at the end of each day to ensure that it gets backed up. Backups may occur once or twice a week, every day, or every three hours. It is up to the company to determine this routine. The more frequent the backups, the more staff time will be dedicated to it, so there needs to be a balance between backing up costs and the actual risk of potentially losing data.

A company may find that it is more economical and effective to have automatic backups done through specialized software instead of spending IT work hours towards the task. It is important to check the integrity of these backups to ensure that things are happening as expected versus finding out right after two major servers blow up that the automatic backups were only saving temporary files. Please review Chapters 6 and 9 for more information on backup issues.

Wireless Technologies

Look mom, no wires!

Wireless communication takes place much more than we think and there is a wide range of broadband wireless data transmission technologies that take place in different frequency ranges. Broadband wireless occupies the frequency bands from 2 to 24 GHz and this range is broken up between microwave, millimeter-wave, satellite, radar, and ham radio use. We use these technologies for television transmissions, cellular phones, satellite transmissions, spying, surveillance, and garage door openers.

The IEEE 802.16 pertains to wireless MANs, which are developed to deploy fixed broadband wireless access to enable many smaller LANs to communicate. However, we are going to look at the 802.11 standard that deals with wireless LANs.

Wireless Communications

When two people are talking, they are using wireless communication because their vocal cords are altering airwaves, which are signals that travel to another person with no cables attached. Wireless communication involves transmitting signals via radio waves through air and space, which also alters airwaves.

Signals are measured in frequency and amplitudes. Wireless deals with frequencies because the frequency of a signal dictates how much data it can carry and how far. The higher the frequency, the more data that the signal can carry, but the higher the frequency, the more susceptible the signal is to atmosphere interference. So a higher frequency can carry more data, but over a shorter distance. Wireless LANs (WLANs) work in the 2.4- and 5-GHz unlicensed frequency band. As of this writing, there are two IEEE standards dealing with WLANs: 802.11a and 802.11b. 802.11 was the initial standard that operated in the 2.4 GHz range at the speed of 1 to 2 Mbps. The second standard, 802.11b, operated in the same frequency but provided speeds up to 11 Mbps. The most recent standard, as of this writing, is 802.11a, which works in the 5 GHz range and provides up to 54 Mbps in data transferring speeds.

These technologies were developed to provide the same functionality as wired networks, but without the need of all those fussy cables. Networking can become much cheaper if it does not require cable implementation and maintenance. It gives users much more freedom because they can take their laptops from their office to the conference room and still stay connected to the network without having to plug into the wall socket.

The 802.11 standard uses the *Wireless Application Protocol (WAP)*, which is a set of communication protocols used to standardize the way that wireless devices interface with each other and the Internet. The WAP model contains protocols that perform similar functionalities when compared to the TCP/IP stack. Because this is a Web-based technology, there must be a way to present Web pages. Personal computers and servers use HTML or XML to present Web-based material and JavaScripts to perform the processing in the background. WAP uses Wireless Markup Language (WML) and WMLScript to perform these similar tasks. WAP has its own session and transaction protocols and transport layer security protocol called Wireless Transport Layer Security (WTLS), which is similar to TLS and SSL.

These protocols and technologies have been developed to work on small mobile phones, Personal Digital Assistants (PDAs), laptops, and other mobile devices. These devices have much less memory, hard drive space, and computing power so it is important that the protocols and applications that run on them are efficient in their use of resources. The developers of these types of protocols and applications are extremely limited in the environment they have to work in (the wireless mobile device); thus, some new programming languages had to be developed.

The vision of developing this type of technology and these devices is to provide users the functionality to be able to check their e-mail, voice messages, calendar, and more from anywhere without needing to physically plug into any network. A user can watch the stock market on her PDA while riding a bus and hit a few buttons when she wants to sell her stocks because of a dip in the market. Users can also transfer funds from one bank account to another on their mobile phones, receive the daily news, and much more. The devices could communicate with their financial institutions, or other organizations that provide them with information and wireless capabilities through the Internet. Because these devices use a different set of protocols, a gateway is required to

Figure 7-51 A WAP gateway is required to translate WAP protocols to Internet protocols.

translate between WAP and the Internet's protocols and application types, as shown in Figure 7-51. Service providers can provide this gateway much like they can provide the service for users and companies to access the Internet today.

When data comes from the wireless mobile device, it can be encrypted with WTLS, which must be translated into TLS or SSL by the gateway. Because the wireless devices use the Internet for transmission, and the Internet does not understand WTLS, it must be translated into a protocol it does understand. This translation takes place at the server provider's gateway.

A security concern is that this data will be decrypted at the service provider's site and then encrypted with SSL or TLS. That means for a second or two the data is not protected. This is referred to as the *gap in the WAP*. This has caused a lot of concern for businesses and security professionals and is still one of the issues that need to be properly dealt with.

Wireless Personal Area Network

As stated, wireless technologies are used for WAN and MAN connectivity (802.16) and LAN connectivity (802.11) and there are also wireless technologies that support an even smaller concentric circle of connectivity to devices within a short range of each other. The most popular development is Bluetooth, which enables devices to spontaneously set up small wireless networks. It is designed for telephones, mobile devices, headsets, wearable devices, keyboards, joysticks, PDAs, desktops, and more.

An example of how Bluetooth is marketed to be used is if a user has a mobile phone that contains a contact list and calendar, he only needs to set it down next to his PDA, which also has these components. The two devices will sense the presence of one another, automatically set up a network between them, and synchronize the data held within their contact lists and calendars. So if the user added a couple of meetings to his phone calendar, he does not need to update the PDA manually—he only needs to set his mobile phone close to it.

The devices have to have the necessary software installed to recognize other devices that are Bluetooth enabled so that they can properly configure themselves to commence communication.

Bluetooth devices will initiate a challenge-response with other devices and they can each be configured to have a domain of trust so that not just any device in an airport can synch up to a person's laptop and download data. These devices use short-range radio waves and have encryption and other types of authentication mechanisms. They use different technologies than what is now used by wireless mice and keyboards and other devices that use infrared connectivity methods.

Bluetooth has been around for years and has caused great interest and commotion within the computing arena, but the interface card is expensive and a lack of full acceptance has stood in the way of it being fully deployed and useable.

Summary

This chapter touched on many of the different players within a network and how they work together to provide an environment for users to be able to communicate, share resources, and be productive. Each piece of networking is important to security because almost any piece can introduce unwanted vulnerabilities and weaknesses in the infrastructure. It is important that the security professional understands how different devices, protocols, authentication mechanisms, and services work individually and how they interface and interact with other entities. This can be an overwhelming task because of all the different possible technologies involved. However, it is knowledge and hard work that will keep security professionals up to speed and hopefully in front of the hackers and attackers.

Quick Tips

- Dual-homed firewalls can be compromised if the operating system does not have packet forwarding disabled.
- A protocol is a set of rules that dictate how computers will communicate over networks.
- The application layer, layer 7, has services and protocols required by the user.
- The presentation layer, layer 6, negotiates how data is represented by different applications and deals with the syntax of the data, not the meaning.

- Routers work at the network layer, layer 3.

- The session layer, layer 5, sets up, maintains, and breaks down the dialog (session) between two computers. It controls the dialog organization and synchronization.

- The transport layer, layer 4, provides reliable, transparent data transfers between session entities.

- The transport layer deals with error detection and correction, regulates the flow of traffic, and multiplexes data. It provides end-to-end connectivity, sequencing, and virtual circuits.

- The network layer, layer 3, provides routing, segmenting, and relaying of data. This layer can determine alternate routes to avoid network congestion.

- The data link layer, layer 2, prepares data for the network wire by framing it. This is where the different LAN and WAN technologies live.

- The physical layer, layer 1, provides physical connections for transmission and performs electrical encoding of data. This layer transforms bits to electrical signals.

- TCP/IP is a suite of protocols that is a de facto standard to transmit data across the Internet. TCP is a reliable connection-oriented protocol and IP is an unreliable connectionless-oriented protocol.

- Data is encapsulated as it travels down the OSI model on the source computer and the process is reversed on the destination computer. During encapsulation, each layer adds its own information so that the corresponding layer on the destination computer knows how to process the data.

- The data link layer defines how the physical layer transmits the network layer packets. ARP and RARP are two protocols at this layer.

- Two main protocols at the transport layer are TCP and UDP.

- UDP is connectionless-oriented protocol that does not send or receive acknowledgments when a datagram is received. It does not ensure that data arrives at its destination. It provides best-effort delivery.

- TCP is a connection-oriented protocol that sends and receives acknowledgments. It ensures that data arrives at its destination.

- ARP translates the IP address into a MAC address (physical Ethernet address) and RARP translates a MAC address into an IP address.

- ICMP works at the network layer and informs hosts, routers, and devices of network or computer problems. It is the major component of the ping utility.

- DNS resolves hostnames into IP addresses and has distributed databases all over the Internet to provide name resolution.

- Altering an ARP table so that an IP address is mapped to a different MAC address is masquerading and can redirect traffic to an attacker's computer or unattended system.

- Packet filtering (screening routers) is accomplished by ACLs and is a first-generation firewall. Traffic can be filtered by addresses, ports, and services.

- Tunneling protocols move frames from one network to another by placing them inside of routable encapsulated frames.

- Packet filtering provides application independence, high performance, and scalability, but provides low security and no protection above the network layer.

- Firewalls that use proxies transfer an isolated copy of each approved packet from one network to another network.

- An application proxy requires a proxy for each approved service and can understand and make access decisions on the services used and the commands within those services. Circuit-level firewalls also use proxies, but at a lower layer. Circuit-level firewalls do not look as deep within the packet as application proxies.

- A proxy server is the middleman in communication. It does not allow anyone to directly connect to a protected host within the internal network. Proxy services are used in most second-generation application firewalls.

- Application proxy firewalls provide good security, have full application layer awareness, but have poor performance, limited application support, and poor scalability.

- Stateful inspection keeps track of each communication session and only lets packets in that are responding to an internal host's request. It must maintain a state table that contains data about each connection. It is used in third-generation application firewalls.

- VPN uses tunneling protocols to provide a secure network link between two networks. A private and secure connection can be made across an unsecure network.

- VPN can use PPTP, L2F, L2TP, or IPSec as tunneling protocols.

- PPTP works at the data link layer. IPSec works at the network layer and can handle multiple tunnels at the same time.

- Dedicated links are usually the most expensive type of connectivity because the fee is based on distance between the two destinations versus amount of bandwidth used. T1 and T3 are examples of dedicated links.

- Frame relay and X.25 are packet-switched WAN technologies, which use virtual circuits instead of dedicated ones.

- An intranet is an internal network using Web-based technology and an extranet is a private network that connects to an external network using Internet protocols. An extranet is usually set up between partners, suppliers and vendors, and with customers.

- A hub (concentrator) in star topologies serves as the central meeting place for all cables from computers and devices.

- A bridge divides networks into more controllable segments to ensure more efficient use of bandwidth. Bridges work at the data link layer and understand MAC addresses, not IP addresses.

- A switch is a device with combined repeater and bridge technology. It works at the data link layer and understands MAC addresses.

- Routers link two or more network segments where each segment can function as an independent network. A router works at the network layer, works with IP addresses, and has more network knowledge than bridges, switches, or repeaters.

- A bridge filters by MAC addresses and a router filters by IP addresses. Bridges forward broadcast traffic and routers do not.

- Layer 3 switching combines switching and routing technology.

- Attenuation is the loss of signal strength when a cable exceeds its maximum length.

- STP and UTP are twisted-pair cabling types that are the most popular, cheapest, and easiest to work with. However, they are the easiest to tap into, have crosstalk issues, and are vulnerable to electromagnetic interference (EMI).

- Coaxial cable is more expensive than UTP and STP, is more resistant to EMI, and can carry baseband and broadband technologies.

- Fiber optic carries data in light waves, is very expensive, can transmit data at high speeds, is very hard to tap into, and is resistant to EMI. If security is extremely important, then fiber cabling should be used.

- ATM transfers data in fixed cells, is a WAN technology, and transmits data at very high rates. It supports voice, data, and video applications.

- FDDI is a LAN and MAN technology, usually used for backbones, uses token-passing technology, and has redundant rings in case the primary ring goes down.

- Ethernet, 802.3, is the most used LAN implementation and can operate at 10 to 1,000 Mbps.

- Token Ring, 802.5, is an older LAN implementation that uses a token-passing technology.

- Ethernet uses CSMA/CD, which means all computers compete for the shared network cable, listen to see when they can transmit data, and are susceptible to data collisions.

- WAN circuit-switching technologies set up a circuit that will be used during a data transmission session, just like making a phone call. Packet-switching technologies do not set up circuits—instead, packets can travel along many different routes to arrive to the same destination.

- A PVC is a permanent virtual circuit that is programmed into WAN devices and SVCs are temporary. SVCs are set up and torn down quickly when they are no longer needed.

- CSU/DSU is used when a LAN device needs to communicate with WAN devices. It ensures that the necessary electrical signaling and format is used. It interfaces between a DTE and a DCE.

- ISDN has a BRI rate that uses two B channels and one D channel, and a PRI that uses up to 24 BRI channels. They support voice, data, video, and graphics.

- Frame relay is a WAN protocol that works at the data link layer and performs packet switching. It is an economical choice because the fee is based on bandwidth usage.

- PPP is an encapsulation protocol for dial-up connections. It replaced SLIP and is ideal for connecting different types of devices over serial lines.

- DSL transmits high-speed bandwidth over existing phone lines.

- Remote access servers can be configured to callback remote users, but this can be compromised by enabling call forwarding.

- PAP sends credentials in clear text and CHAP authenticates using a challenge/response mechanism, and therefore does not send credential information over the network.

- SOCKS is a proxy-based firewall solution that can also be used for VPNs. It uses circuit-based proxies, not application-based proxies.

- IPSec tunnel mode encrypts payload and header information of a packet and transport mode only encrypts the payload.

- RAID can provide increased performance and fault tolerance depending on the level used.

- A screened-host firewall is between the border router and the LAN.

- A screened-subnet is a DMZ that is sandwiched between two routers.

- NAT is used when companies do not want systems to know internal hosts' addresses and enables companies to use private, nonroutable IP addresses.

Questions

Please remember that these questions are formatted and asked in a certain way for a reason. The questions and answers may seem odd or vague, but this is what you will see on the actual CISSP test.

1. Which of the following is not considered a passive attack?
   a. Spoofing
   b. Network sniffing
   c. Wiretapping
   d. Traffic analysis

2. What does the term *phreaking* pertain to?
   a. Spamming mail servers in the hopes of bringing them down
   b. Footprinting and port scanning networks
   c. Fraudulent use of telephone services
   d. Compromising tunneling protocols

3. What does a packet sniffer do?
   a. It performs port scans and footprinting.
   b. It identifies cabling faults.
   c. It detects hanging modems not protected by the firewall.
   d. It captures traffic for data analysis.

4. What can be used to compromise and defeat callback security?
   a. Passive wiretapping
   b. Call forwarding
   c. Packet spoofing
   d. Brute force attack

5. Which is not considered a firewall technology used to protect networks?
   a. Screened host
   b. Screened subnet
   c. NAT gateway
   d. Dual-homed host

6. Packet-switching infrastructures are safer environments because _____.
   a. They are harder to sniff traffic since the computers have virtual private connections.
   b. They are just as unsafe as non-switched environments.
   c. The data link encryption does not permit wiretapping.
   d. Switches are more intelligent than bridges and implement security mechanisms.

7. What functionality hangs up on a remote caller and looks at a table of predefined phone numbers?
   a. Caller ID
   b. RAS
   c. Callback
   d. NOS

8. Which of the following protocols is considered connection oriented?
   a. IP
   b. ICMP
   c. UDP
   d. TCP

9. Which of the following best describes Ethernet transmissions over a LAN?
   a. Traffic is sent to a gateway that sends it to the destination system.
   b. Traffic is bursty in nature and broadcasts data to all hosts on the subnet.
   c. Traffic streams and does not broadcast data.
   d. Traffic is contained within collision domains but not broadcast domains.

10. Which of the following proxies cannot make access decisions on protocol commands?
    a. Application
    b. Generic
    c. Circuit
    d. Stateful

11. A security concern that is prevalent in distributed environments and systems is _____.
    a. Knowing the proper proxy and default gateway
    b. Knowing whom to trust
    c. Knowing what authentication method is most appropriate
    d. Knowing how to resolve hostnames

12. Which protocol is commonly used to authenticate users on a dial-up connection?
    a. PPTP
    b. IPSec
    c. CHAP
    d. L2F

13. Which of the following shows the sequence of layers as layer 2, 5, 1, 4, and 3?
    a. Data link, session, application, transport, and network
    b. Data link, transport, application, session, and network
    c. Network, session, application, network, and transport
    d. Network, transport, application, session, and presentation

14. What is another name for a VPN?
    a. Transport session
    b. Tunnel
    c. Data link encryption session
    d. Pipeline

15. When security is a high priority, why is fiber-optic cabling used?
    a. It has high data transfer rates and is less vulnerable to EMI.
    b. It multiplexes data, which can confuse attackers.
    c. It has a high degree of data detection and correction.
    d. Data interception is next to impossible.

16. Why are mainframes considered more secure than LAN environments?
    a. They have fewer entry points.
    b. They have stronger authentication mechanisms.
    c. They have more auditing and encryption implemented.
    d. They are actually weaker than LANs.

17. What does it mean when computers communicate logically and physically to each other?
    a. They speak physically through headers and trailers and logically through virtual connections.
    b. They speak physically through PVCs and logically through SVCs.
    c. They speak physically when connected to a backbone network and logically when they speak to each other within the same LAN.
    d. They speak physically through electrons and network cables and logically through layers in the OSI model.

18. How does data encapsulation and the protocol stack work?
    a. Each layer in the OSI model multiplexes other packets to the data as it is passed down the protocol stack.
    b. Each layer in the OSI model adds its own information to the data as it is passed down the protocol stack.
    c. The packet is encapsulated and grows as it hops from router to router.
    d. The packet is encapsulated and grows when it is passed up the protocol stack.

19. Systems that are built on the OSI framework are considered open systems. What does this mean?
    a. They do not have authentication mechanisms configured by default.
    b. They have interoperability issues.
    c. They are built with international protocols and standards so that they can easily communicate with other systems.
    d. They are built with international protocols and standards so that they can choose what types of systems they will communicate with.

20. Which of the following protocols works in the following layers: application, data link, network, and transport?
    a. FTP, ARP, TCP, and UDP
    b. FTP, ICMP, IP, and UDP
    c. TFTP, ARP, IP, and UDP
    d. TFTP, RARP, IP, and ICMP

21. What is the purpose of the presentation layer?
    a. Addressing and routing
    b. Data syntax and formatting
    c. End-to-end connection
    d. Framing

22. What is the purpose of the data link layer?
    a. End-to-end connection
    b. Dialog control
    c. Framing
    d. Data syntax

23. What takes place at the session layer?
    a. Dialog control
    b. Routing
    c. Packet sequencing
    d. Addressing

24. What layer does a bridge understand?
    a. Session
    b. Network
    c. Transport
    d. Data link

25. Which best describes the IP protocol?
    a. Connectionless protocol that deals with dialog establishment, maintenance, and destruction
    b. Connectionless protocol that deals with addressing and routing of packets
    c. Connection-oriented protocol that deals with addressing and routing of packets
    d. Connection-oriented protocol that deals with sequencing, error detection, and flow control

26. Which protocol is described as a best-effort protocol?
    a. TCP
    b. ICMP
    c. UDP
    d. ARP

27. Which of the following best describes TCP versus UDP protocols?
    a. TCP provides more services and is more reliable, but UDP provides more security services.
    b. TCP provides a best-effort delivery and UDP sets up a virtual connection with the destination.
    c. TCP is reliable and UDP deals with flow control and ACKs.
    d. TCP provides more services and is more reliable in data transmission, whereas UDP takes less resources and overhead to transmit data.

Answers

1. A.	8. D.	15. D.	22. C.
2. C.	9. B.	16. A.	23. A.
3. D.	10. C.	17. D.	24. D.
4. B.	11. B.	18. B.	25. B.
5. C.	12. C.	19. C.	26. C.
6. A.	13. A.	20. C.	27. D.
7. C.	14. B.	21. B.	

Cryptography

In this chapter, you will learn about the following items:

- History of cryptography
- Cryptography components and their relationships
- Government involvement in cryptography
- Symmetric and asymmetric key cryptosystems
- Public key infrastructure (PKI) concepts and mechanisms
- Hashing algorithms and uses
- Types of attacks on cryptosystems

Cryptography is a method of storing and transmitting data in a form that only those it is intended for can read and process. It is a science of protecting information by encoding it into an unreadable format. Cryptography is an effective way of protecting sensitive information as it is stored on media or transmitted through network communication paths.

Although the ultimate goal of cryptography, and the mechanisms that make it up, is to hide information from unauthorized individuals, most algorithms can be broken and the information can be revealed if the attacker has enough time, desire, and resources. So a more realistic goal of cryptography is to make obtaining the information too work-intensive to be worth it to the attacker.

The first encryption methods date back to 4,000 years ago and were considered more of an ancient art. As encryption evolved, it was mainly used to pass messages through hostile environments of war, crisis, and for negotiation processes between conflicting groups of people. Throughout history, individuals and governments have worked to protect communication by encrypting it. As time went on, the encryption algorithms and the devices that used them increased in complexity, new methods and algorithms were continually introduced, and it became an integrated part of the computing world.

11001010101011000011010101010110001000111110010 [101]0101011011001010 ⟶

Figure 8-1 Today, encrypted binary data passes through network cables and airwaves.

Cryptography

Cryptography has had an interesting history and has undergone many changes through the centuries. It seems that keeping secrets has been important throughout the ages of civilization for one reason or another. Keeping secrets gives individuals or groups the ability to hide true intentions, gain a competitive edge, and reduce vulnerability.

The changes that cryptograph has undergone throughout history closely follow the advances in technology. Cryptography methods began with a person carving messages into wood or stone, which were then passed to the intended individual who had the necessary means to decipher the messages. This is a long way from how cryptography is being used today. Cryptography that used to be carved into materials is now being inserted into streams of binary code that passes over network wires, Internet communication paths, and airwaves, as shown in Figure 8-1.

In the past, messengers were used as the transmission mechanism, and encryption helped protect the message in case the messenger was captured. Today, the transmission mechanism has changed from human beings to packets carrying 0's and 1's passing through network cables or open airwaves. The messages are still encrypted in case an intruder captures the transmission mechanism (the packets) as they travel along their paths.

History of Cryptography

Look, I scrambled up the message so no one can read it. Answer: Yes, but now neither can we.

Cryptography has roots that began around 2000 B.C. in Egypt when hieroglyphics were used to decorate tombs to tell the story of the life of the deceased. The practice was not as much to hide the messages themselves, but to make them seem more noble, ceremonial, and majestic. An illustration of hieroglyphics is shown in Figure 8-2.

Encryption methods evolved from being mainly for show into practical applications used to hide information from others.

Figure 8-2   Hieroglyphics are the first recorded use of cryptography.

A Hebrew cryptographic method required the alphabet to be flipped so that each letter in the original alphabet is mapped to a different letter in the flipped alphabet. The encryption method was called *atbash*. An example of an encryption key used in the atbash encryption scheme is shown in following:

```
ABCDEFGHI JK LMNOPQ R STU VW XYZ
ZYXWVUTSR QP ONMLKJ I HGF ED CBA
```

For example, the word "security" is encrypted into "hvxfirgb." What does "xrhhk" come out to be? This is a *substitution cipher*, because one character is replaced with another character. This type of substitution cipher is referred to as a *monoalphabetic substitution* because it uses only one alphabet, compared to other ciphers that use multiple alphabets at a time.

This simplistic encryption method worked for its time and for particular cultures, but eventually more complex mechanisms were required.

Around 400 B.C., the Spartans used a system of encrypting information by writing a message on a sheet of papyrus, which was wrapped around a staff. (This would look like a piece of paper wrapped around a stick or wooden rod.) The message was only readable if it was around the correct staff, which allowed the letters to properly match

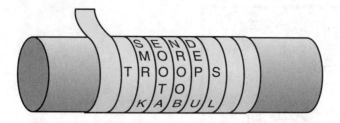

Figure 8-3　The scytale was used by the Spartans to decipher encrypted messages.

up. This is referred to as the *scytale* cipher, as shown in Figure 8-3. When the papyrus was removed from the staff, the writing appeared as just a bunch of random characters. The Greek government had carriers run these pieces of papyrus to different groups of soldiers. The soldiers would then wrap the papyrus around a staff of the right diameter and length and all the seemingly random letters would match up and form an understandable message. These could be used to instruct the soldiers on strategic moves and provide them with military directives.

In another time and place in history, Julius Caesar developed a simple method of shifting letters of the alphabet, similar to the atbash scheme. Today this technique seems too simplistic to be effective, but in that day not many people could read in the first place, so it provided a high level of protection. The evolution of cryptography continued as Europe refined its practices using new methods, tools, and practices throughout the Middle Ages, and by the late 1800s, cryptography was commonly used in the methods of communication between military factions.

During World War II, simplistic encryption devices were used for tactical communication, which drastically improved with the mechanical and electromechanical technology that provided the world with telegraphic and radio communication. The rotor cipher machine, which is a device that substitutes letters using different rotors within the machine, was a huge breakthrough in military cryptography that provided complexity that proved difficult to break. This work gave way to the most famous cipher machine in history to date: Germany's *Enigma* machine. The Enigma machine had three rotors, a plugboard, and a reflecting rotor.

The originator of the message configured the Enigma machine to its initial settings before starting the encryption process. The operator would type in the first letter of the message and the machine would substitute the letter with a different letter and present it to the operator. This encryption was done by moving the rotors a predefined number of times, which would substitute the original letter with a different letter. So if the operator typed in a *T* as the first character, the Enigma machine might present an *M* as the substitution value. The operator would write down the letter *M* on his sheet. The operator would then advance the rotors and enter the next letter. Each time a new letter was to be encrypted, the operator advanced the rotors to a new setting. This process was done until the whole message was encrypted. Then the encrypted text was transmitted over the airwaves most likely to a U-boat. The chosen substitution for each letter was dependent upon the rotor setting, so the crucial and secret part of this process (the key) was how the operators advanced the rotors when encrypting and decrypting a message. The operators at each end needed to know this sequence of increments to advance each rotor in order to enable the German military units to properly communicate.

Although the mechanisms of the Enigma were complicated for the time, a team of Polish cryptographers broke its code and gave Britain insight into Germany's attack plans and military movement. It is said that breaking this encryption mechanism shortened World War II by two years. After the war, details about the Enigma machine were published—one of the machines is exhibited at the Smithsonian Institute.

Cryptography has a deep, rich history. Mary, the Queen of Scots, lost her life in the sixteenth century when an encrypted message she sent was intercepted. During the Revolutionary War, Benedict Arnold used a codebook cipher to exchange information on troop movement and strategic military advancements. The military has always had a big part in using cryptography by encoding information and attempting to decrypt their enemy's encrypted information. William Frederick Friedman published *The Index of Coincidence and Its Applications in Cryptography*. He is referred to as the "Father of Modern Cryptography" and broke many messages that were intercepted during WWII. Encryption has been used by many governments and militaries and has allowed great victory for some because of the covert maneuvers that could be accomplished in shrouded secrecy. It has also brought great defeat to others when their cryptosystems were discovered and deciphered.

As computers came to be, the possibilities for encryption methods and devices advanced, and cryptography efforts expanded exponentially. This era brought unprecedented opportunity for cryptographic designers and encryption techniques. The most well-known and successful project was *Lucifer*, which was developed at IBM. Lucifer introduced complex mathematical equations and functions that were later adopted and modified by the U.S. National Security Agency (NSA) to come up with the U.S. Data Encryption Standard (DES). DES has been adopted as a federal government standard, is used worldwide for financial transactions, and is imbedded into numerous commercial applications. DES has had a rich history in computer-oriented encryption and has been in use for over 20 years.

Cryptography has had its days in the political limelight with governments enforcing transborder restrictions and hindering the use of cryptography in certain sectors by imposing export regulations. Law enforcement developed their own encryption chip, the *Clipper Chip*, to decipher communication that had to do with suspected criminal activity and drug movements, which has raised many questions about the public's privacy versus the government's right to eavesdrop. (These issues are addressed further in "The Government's Involvement in Cryptography" section.)

A majority of the protocols developed at the dawn of the computing age have had upgraded to include cryptography to add necessary layers of protection. Encryption is used in hardware devices and software to protect data, banking transactions, corporate extranets, e-mail, Web transactions, wireless communication, storing of confidential information, faxes, and phone calls.

The code breakers and cryptanalysis efforts and the amazing amount of number-crunching capabilities of the microprocessors hitting the market each year have quickened the evolution of cryptography. As the bad guys get smarter and more resourceful, the good guys must increase efforts and strategy. *Cryptanalysis* is a science of studying and breaking the secrecy of encryption algorithms and their necessary pieces. It is performed in academic settings and by curious and motivated hackers, either to quench their inquisitiveness or use their findings to commit fraud and destruction. Different types of cryptography have been used throughout civilization, but today it is deeply rooted in every part of our communication and computing world. Automated information systems and cryptography play a huge role in the effectiveness of militaries, functionality of governments, and economics of private businesses. As our dependency upon technology increases, so does our dependency upon cryptography, because secrets will always need to be kept.

References

www.infosecuritymag.com/articles/july01/columns_logoff.shtml

http://all.net/books/ip/Chap2-1.html

www.cs.cornell.edu/Courses/cs513/2000 SP/L23.html

www.execpc.com/~alcourt/crypt.intro.html

www.trincoll.edu/depts/cpsc/cryptography/index.html

http://dmoz.org/Science/Math/Applications/Communication_Theory/
   Cryptography/Historical/

Cryptography Definitions

Why can't I read this? Answer: It is in ciphertext.

Encryption is a method of transforming original data, called *plaintext* or *cleartext*, into a form that appears to be random and unreadable, which is called *ciphertext*. Plaintext is either in a form that can be understood by a person (a document) or by a computer (executable code). Once it is transformed into ciphertext, neither human nor machine can properly process it until it is decrypted. This enables the transmission of confidential information over insecure channels without unauthorized disclosure. When data is stored on a computer, it is usually protected by logical and physical access controls. When this same sensitive information is sent over a network, it can no longer take these controls for granted, and the information is in a much more vulnerable state.

The process of encryption transforms plaintext into ciphertext and
the process of decryption transforms ciphertext into plaintext.

A system that provides encryption and decryption is referred to as a *cryptosystem* and can be created through hardware components or program code in an application. The cryptosystem uses an encryption algorithm, which determines how simple or complex the process will be. Most algorithms are complex mathematical formulas that are applied in a specific sequence to the plaintext. Most encryption methods use a secret value called a key (usually a long string of bits), which works with the algorithm to encrypt and decrypt the text, as depicted in Figure 8-4.

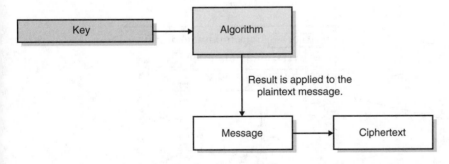

Figure 8-4   The key is inserted into the mathematical algorithm and the result is applied to the message, which ends up in ciphertext.

The *algorithm*, the set of mathematical rules, dictates how enciphering and deciphering take place. Many algorithms are publicly known and are not the secret part of the encryption process. The way that encryption algorithms work can be kept secret from the public, but many of them are publicly known and well understood. If the internal mechanisms of the algorithm are not a secret, then something must be. The secret piece of using a well-known encryption algorithm is the key. The *key* can be any value that is made up of a large sequence of random bits. Is it just any random number of bits crammed together? Not really. An algorithm contains a *keyspace*, which is a range of values that can be used to construct a key. The key is made up of random values within the keyspace range. The larger the keyspace, the more available values can be used to represent different keys, and the more random the keys are, the harder it is for intruders to figure them out.

A large keyspace allows for more possible keys. The encryption algorithm should use the entire keyspace and choose the values to make up the keys as random as possible. If a smaller keyspace were used, there would be fewer values to choose from when forming a key, as shown in Figure 8-5. This would increase an attacker's chance of figuring out the key value and deciphering the protected information.

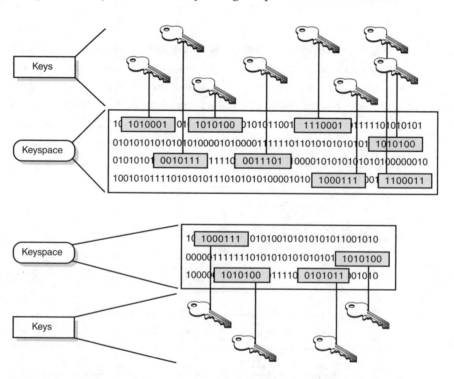

Figure 8-5   Larger keyspaces allow for more possible keys.

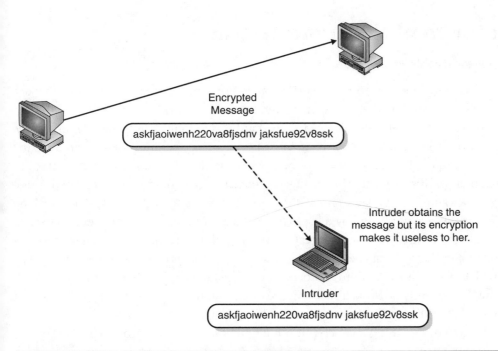

Encrypted
Message

askfjaoiwenh220va8fjsdnv jaksfue92v8ssk

Intruder obtains the
message but its encryption
makes it useless to her.

Intruder

askfjaoiwenh220va8fjsdnv jaksfue92v8ssk

Figure 8-6   Without the right key, the captured message is useless to an attacker.

If an eavesdropper captures a message as it passes between two people, she can view the message, but it appears in its encrypted form and is therefore unusable. Even if this attacker knows the algorithm that the two people are using to encrypt and decrypt their information, without the key, this information remains useless to the eavesdropper, as shown in Figure 8-6.

NOTE   Making and Breaking Encryption: Cryptography is the science of encrypting and decrypting written communication. It comes from the Greek word "kryptos," meaning hidden, and "graphia," meaning writing. Cryptography involves developing, testing, and studying the science of encryption methods. Cryptanalysis is the process of trying to decrypt encrypted data without the key. When new algorithms are tested, they go through stringent processes of cryptanalysis to ensure that the new encryption process is unbreakable or that it takes too much time and resources to break.

Strength of the Cryptosystem

You are the weakest link. Goodbye!

The *strength* of the encryption method comes from the algorithm, secrecy of the key, length of the key, initialization vectors, and how they all work together. When strength is discussed in encryption, it refers to how hard it is to figure out the algorithm or key, whichever is not made public. Breaking a key has to do with processing an amazing number of possible values in the hopes of finding the one value that can be used to decrypt a specific message. The strength correlates to the amount of necessary processing power and time it takes to break the key or figure out the value of the key. Breaking a key can be accomplished by a brute force attack, which means trying every possible key value until the resulting plaintext is meaningful. Depending on the algorithm and length of the key, this can be a very easy task or a task that is close to impossible. If a key can be broken with a Pentium II processor in three hours, the cipher is not strong at all. If the key can only be broken with the use of a thousand multiprocessing systems, and it takes 1.2 million years, then it is pretty darn strong.

The goal of designing an encryption method is to make compromise too expensive or too time consuming. Another name for cryptography strength is *work factor*, which is an estimate of the effort it would take an attacker to penetrate an encryption method.

The strength of the protection mechanism should be used in correlation to the sensitivity of the data being encrypted. It is not necessary to encrypt information about a friend's Saturday barbeque with a top secret NSA encryption algorithm, and it is not a good idea to send the intercepted KGB spy information using Pretty Good Privacy (PGP). Each type of encryption mechanism has its place and purpose.

Even if the algorithm is very complex and thorough, there are other issues within encryption that can weaken the strength of encryption methods. Because the key is usually the secret value needed to actually encrypt and decrypt messages, improper protection of the key can weaken the encryption strength. An extremely strong algorithm can be used, using a large keyspace, and a large and random key value, which are all the requirements for strong encryption, but if a user shares her key with others, these other pieces of the equation really don't matter.

An algorithm with no flaws, a large key, using all possible values within a keyspace, and protecting the actual key are important elements of encryption. If one is weak, it can prove to be the weak link that affects the whole process.

Goals of Cryptosystems

Cryptosystems can provide confidentiality, authenticity, integrity, and nonrepudiation services. It does not provide availability of data or systems. *Confidentiality* means that unauthorized parties cannot access information. *Authenticity* refers to validating the source of the message to ensure the sender is properly identified. *Integrity* provides assurance that the message was not modified during transmission, accidentally or intentionally. *Nonrepudiation* means that a sender cannot deny sending the message at a later date, and the receiver cannot deny receiving it. So if your boss sends you a message telling you that you will be receiving a raise that doubles your salary and it is encrypted, encryption methods can ensure that it really came from your boss, that someone did not alter it before it arrived to your computer, that no one else was able to read this message as it traveled over the network, and that your boss cannot deny sending the message later when he comes to his senses.

Different types of messages and transactions require a higher degree of one or all of the services that encryption methods can supply. Military and intelligence agencies are very concerned about keeping information confidential, so they would choose encryption mechanisms that provide a high degree of secrecy. Financial institutions care about confidentiality, but care more about the integrity of the data being transmitted, so the encryption mechanism they would choose may differ from the military's encryption methods. If messages were accepted that had a misplaced decimal point or zero, the ramifications could be far reaching in the financial institution world. Legal agencies may care more about the authenticity of messages that they receive. If information that was received ever needed to be presented in a court of law, its authenticity would certainly be questioned; therefore, the encryption method used should ensure authenticity, which confirms who sent the information.

Cryptography Definitions

- **Algorithm**   Set of mathematical rules used in encryption and decryption

- **Cryptography**   Science of secret writing that enables you to store and transmit data in a form that is available only to the intended individuals

- **Cryptosystem**   Hardware or software implementation of cryptography that transforms a message to ciphertext and back to plaintext

- **Cryptanalysis**   Practice of obtaining plaintext from ciphertext without a key or breaking the encryption

- **Cryptology**   The study of both cryptography and cryptanalysis
- **Ciphertext**   Data in encrypted or unreadable format
- **Encipher**   Act of transforming data into an unreadable format
- **Decipher**   Act of transforming data into a readable format
- **Key**   Secret sequence of bits and instructions that governs the act of encryption and decryption
- **Key clustering**   Instance when two different keys generate the same ciphertext from the same plaintext
- **Keyspace**   Possible values used to construct keys
- **Plaintext**   Data in readable format, also referred to as cleartext
- **Work factor**   Estimated time, effort, and resources necessary to break a cryptosystem

NOTE   Repudiation: If David sends a message and then later claims that he did not send the message, this is an act of repudiation. When an encryption mechanism provides nonrepudiation, it means that the sender cannot deny sending the message and the receiver cannot deny receiving it. It's a way of keeping everybody honest.

Types of Ciphers

There are two basic types of encryption ciphers: substitution and transposition (permutation). The *substitution cipher* replaces bits, characters, or blocks of characters with different bits, characters, or blocks. The *transposition cipher* does not replace the original text with different text, but moves the original text around. It rearranges the bits, characters, or blocks of characters to hide the original meaning.

Substitution Cipher

A substitution cipher uses a key to know how the substitution should be carried out. In the Caesar Cipher, each letter is replaced with the letter three places beyond it in the alphabet. This is referred to as a shift alphabet.

If the Caesar Cipher is used with the English alphabet, when George wants to encrypt a message of "FBI," the encrypted message would be "IEL." Substitution is used in today's algorithms, but it is extremely complex compared to this example. Many different types of substitutions take place usually with more than one alphabet. This example is only meant to show you the concept of how a substitution cipher works in its most simplistic form.

Transposition Cipher

In a *transposition cipher*, permutation is used, meaning that letters are scrambled. The key determines the positions that the characters are moved to, as illustrated in Figure 8-7.

This is a simplistic example of a transposition cipher and only shows one way of performing transposition. When introduced with complex mathematical functions, transpositions can become quite sophisticated and difficult to break. Most ciphers used today use long sequences of complicated substitutions and permutations together on messages. The key value is inputted into the algorithm and the result is the sequence of operations (substitutions and permutations) that are performed on the plaintext.

Simple substitution and transposition ciphers are vulnerable to attacks that perform *frequency analysis*. In every language, there are words and patterns that are used more often than others. For instance, in the English language, the words "the," "and," "that," and "is" are very frequent patterns of letters used in messages and conversation. The beginning of messages usually starts "Hello" or "Dear" and ends with "Sincerely" or "Goodbye." These patterns help attackers figure out the transformation between plaintext to ciphertext, which enables them to figure out the key that was used to perform the transformation. It is important for cryptosystems to not reveal these patterns.

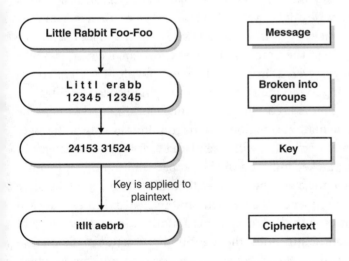

Figure 8-7 Transposition cipher

More complex algorithms usually use more than one alphabet for substitution and permutation, which reduces the vulnerability to frequency analysis. The more complicated the algorithm, the more the resulting text (ciphertext) differs from the plaintext; thus, the matching of these types of patterns becomes more difficult.

Running and Concealment Ciphers

I have my decoder ring, spyglasses, and secret handshake. Now let me figure out how I will encrypt my messages.

More of the spy-novel-type ciphers would be the running key cipher and the concealment cipher. The ***running key cipher*** could use a key that does not require an electronic algorithm and bit alterations, but clever steps in the physical world around you. For instance, a key in this type of cipher could be a book page, line number, and word count. If I get a message from my super-secret spy buddy and the message reads "14967.29937.91158," this could mean for me to look at the first book in our predetermined series of books, the 49th page, 6th line down the page, and the 7th word in that line. So I write down this word, which is "cat." The second set of numbers start with 2, so I go to the 2nd book, 99th page, 3rd line down, and write down the 7th word on that line, which is "is." The last word I get from the 9th book in our series, the 11th page, 5th row, and 8th word in that row, which is "dead." So now I have come up with my important secret message, which is "cat is dead." This means nothing to me and I need to look for a new spy buddy.

Running key ciphers can be used in different and more complex ways, but I think you get the point. Another type of spy novel cipher is the ***concealment cipher***. If my other super-secret spy buddy and I decide our key value is every third word, then when I get a message from him, I will pick out every third word and write it down. So if he sends me a message that reads, "The saying, 'The time is right' is not cow language, so is now a dead subject." Because my key is every third word, I come up with "The right cow is dead." This again means nothing to me and I am now turning in my decoder ring.

No matter which type of cipher is used, the roles of the algorithm and key are the same, even if they are not mathematical equations. In the running key cipher, the algorithm states that encryption and decryption will take place by choosing characters out of a predefined set of books. The key indicates the book, page, line, and word within that line. In substitution cipher, the algorithm dictates that substitution will take place using a predefined alphabet or sequence of characters, and the key indicates that each character will be replaced with the third character that follows it in that sequence of characters. In actual mathematical structures, the algorithm is a set of mathematical functions that will be performed on the message and the key can indicate in which order these functions take place. So even if an attacker knows the algorithm, say the predefined set of books, if he does not know the key, the message is still useless to him.

References

www-math.cudenver.edu/~wcherowi/courses/m5410/m5410cc.html

www.math.nmsu.edu/~crypto/Caesar.html

www.ssuet.edu.pk/taimoor/athar/ce-408/encryption/

http://home.ecn.ab.ca/~jsavard/crypto/pp0102.htm

Steganography

alqaeda used this to communicate

Where's the top-secret message? Answer: In this picture of my dogs.

Steganography is a method of hiding data in another message so that the very existence of the data is concealed. Steganography is mainly used by hiding messages in graphic images. The least significant bit of each byte of the image can be replaced with bits of the secret message. This practice does not affect the graphic enough to be detected.

Steganography does not use algorithms or keys to encrypt information, but this is a process to hide data within another object so no one will detect its presence. A message can be hidden in a wave file, in a graphic, or in unused spaces on a hard drive or sectors that are marked as unusable. Steganography can also be used to insert a digital watermark on digital images in the hopes of detecting illegal copies of the images.

Steganography can hide a message inside a graphic.

Secret Communist Message hidden in the picture. → Weapons hidden under the Kremlin.

References

www.jjtc.com/Steganography/

www.rit.edu/~vxr8205/crypto2/cryptopaper.html

The Government's Involvement with Cryptography

Big Brother is watching you! Um, I mean we are only watching the bad guys.

The government's cryptographic agency, the NSA, was granted the power to regulate the export of cryptographic mechanisms and equipment. This was done with the hopes of making encryption technology harder to obtain and be used by terrorists and criminals. Harry Truman created the NSA in 1952, and its main mission is to listen in on communications in the interest of national security for the United Sates. Its very existence is kept at an extremely low profile and its activities are highly secret. The NSA also conducts research in cryptology to create secure algorithms and to break other cryptosystems to enable eavesdropping and spying.

The government attempted to restrict the use of public cryptography so that enemies of the United States could not employ encryption methods that were too strong for it to break. These issues have caused tension and controversy between cryptography researchers, vendors, and the NSA pertaining to new cryptographic methods and the public use of them. The fear is that if the government controls all types of encryption and is allowed to listen in on private citizens' conversations, the obtained information may be misused in Big Brother ways. Also, if the government had the ability to listen in on everyone's conversations, there is little trust that this ability would not fall into the wrong hands for the wrong reasons.

Clipper Chip

In 1993, the government made a case that would enable them to place their own encryption chip, the *Clipper Chip*, in every American-made device that had a computer or computer components. This included telephones, TVs, personal computers, and more. The Clipper Chip was based on the SkipJack algorithm that was classified and never opened for public review or testing. A majority of the algorithms used today in cryptography have been publicly tested to ensure that the developers did not miss any important steps in building a complex and secure mechanism. Because the SkipJack algorithm was not open for public review, many people in the public do not trust its effectiveness.

The Clipper Chip was a NSA-designed tamperproof chip for encrypting data. It is one of the two chips implemented in the U.S. government's Escrowed Encryption Standard (EES). Each chip has a unit key, which is used to encrypt a copy of each user's session key, not the message itself. Each Clipper Chip has a unique serial number and a copy of the unit key is stored in the database under this serial number. The sending Clipper Chip generates and sends a Law Enforcement Access Field (LEAF) value included in the transmitted message. This field value contains the serial number of the Clipper Chip used to encrypt the message in the first place. This is how the government, or law enforcement, knows which unit key to retrieve from the database. This unit key enables them to decrypt and find out the session key, which enables them to actually decrypt the message and eavesdrop on the conversation, as shown in Figure 8-8. The unit key is split into two pieces and kept in different databases maintained by two different escrow agencies.

[handwritten margin note: how would the intended receiver decrypt the message? BW issues?]

There was quite a public outcry pertaining to the Clipper Chip and its threat on personal privacy. Eventually, the government stopped supporting the Clipper Chip and most companies turned to software-based encryption programs instead of an actual hardware chip. Several deficiencies were found in the Clipper Chip and because it was viewed as being very invasive to the public's privacy, it quickly lost support and was dropped. The Clipper Chip initiative was abandoned and replaced with policies aimed at controlling the proliferation and use of cryptography in the public. It was just too Big Brother for society.

Some Weaknesses Found in the Clipper Chip

- The SkipJack algorithm was never publicly scrutinized and tested.
- An 80-bit key is very weak.
- A 16-bit checksum can be defeated.
- The Clipper Chip ID tagged and identified every communication session.

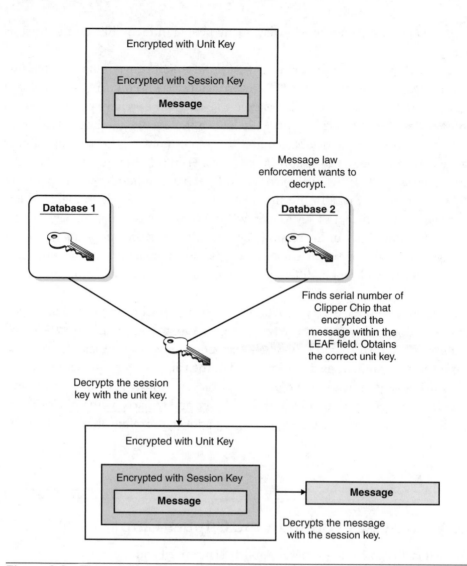

Figure 8-8   The unit key decrypts the session key.

References

www.swiss.ai.mit.edu/6095/articles/froomkin-metaphor/partIC.html#ToC27

http://cse.stanford.edu/class/cs201/current/Projects/clipper-chip/debate.html

www.rsa.com/rsalabs/faq/6-2-4.html

Key Escrow

In many cases, it is necessary for law enforcement to have access to certain conversations to try and learn about possible terrorist attacks, drug deals, or murder attempts. However, there is always a tricky balance between this activity and a citizen's right to private communication. There needs to be a proper system of checks and balances in place to ensure that abuse of this type of power is not taking place. This is where key escrow comes in. The unit keys are split into two sections and are given to two different escrow agencies to maintain. This is done so that one agency does not have the ability to abuse this technology by itself and that three entities are involved with decrypting this type of data: two agencies and a law enforcement representative.

For an officer to access data that is encrypted, he must get a court order to request the unit key in the first place. The officer submits this court order to both escrow agencies, which in turn release the key sections, as shown in Figure 8-9. The sections are combined into a full unit key, and it is used on only the specified data that is outlined in the court order. This is all outlined in the U.S. EES.

The Clipper Chip uses the concept of key escrow and key recovery. A key escrow implementation can also be used in software using public key cryptography. In these cases, the public key is available to encrypt and decrypt messages, but the private key is split up into two or more pieces and stored by different entities. When it is necessary to decrypt information, say during a wiretap, then each entity must supply its piece of the private key, which will be combined to create one useful key. This provides another layer of protection because two or more people would have to supply part of the private key to decrypt information. This is referred to as the *fair cryptosystems*, which uses software instead of hardware chips. The algorithm in fair cryptosystems does not need to be secret; thus, well-tested and well-known algorithms and protocols can be used.

References

www.itl.nist.gov/fipspubs/fip185.htm

http://security.isu.edu/isl/fips185.html

www.cs.georgetown.edu/~denning/crypto/Lathe-Gambit.txt

www.sims.berkeley.edu/courses/is224/s99/GroupC/pr2/s4.html

Methods of Encryption

Although there can be several pieces to an encryption method, the two main pieces are the algorithms and the keys. As stated earlier, algorithms are usually complex

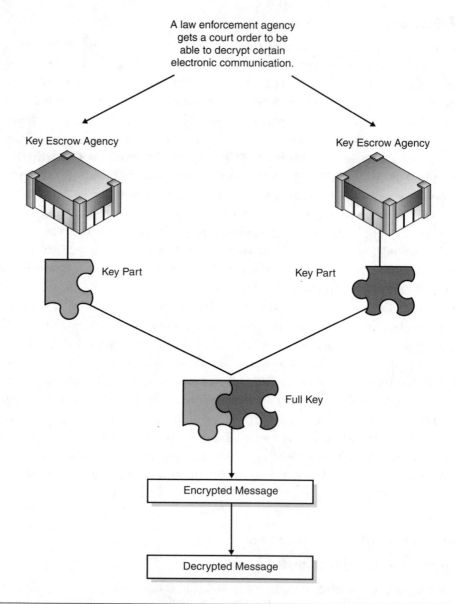

A law enforcement agency
gets a court order to be
able to decrypt certain
electronic communication.

Key Escrow Agency

Key Escrow Agency

Key Part

Key Part

Full Key

Encrypted Message

Decrypted Message

Figure 8-9 In a key escrow arrangement, the key necessary to decrypt traffic is split and kept by at least two different parties.

mathematical formulas that dictate the rules of how the plaintext will be turned into ciphertext. A key is a string of random bits that will be inserted into the algorithm. For two entities to be able to communicate via encryption, they must use the same algorithm and, many times, the same key. In some encryption methods, the receiver and the sender use the same key and in other encryption methods, they must use different keys for encryption and decryption purposes. The following sections explain the difference between these two types of encryption methods.

Symmetric versus Asymmetric Algorithms

Cryptography algorithms use either *symmetric keys*, also called secret keys, or *asymmetric keys*, also called public keys. As if encryption was not complicated enough, the titles that are used to describe the key types only make it worse. Just pay close attention and we will get through this just fine.

Symmetric Cryptography

In a cryptosystem that uses symmetric cryptography, both parties will be using the same key for encryption and decryption, as shown in Figure 8-10. This provides dual functionality. As we said, symmetric keys are also called secret keys because this type of encryption relies on each user to keep the key a secret and properly protected. If this key got into an intruder's hand, that intruder would have the ability to decrypt any intercepted message encrypted with this key.

Each pair of users who want to exchange data using symmetric key encryption must have their own set of keys. This means if Dan and Iqqi want to communicate, both need to obtain a copy of the same key. If Dan also wants to communicate using symmetric

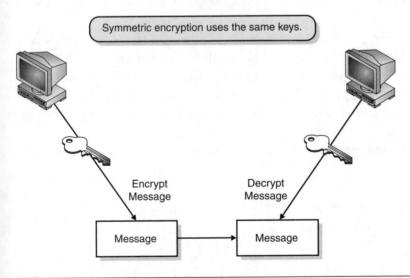

Symmetric encryption uses the same keys.

Encrypt
Message

Decrypt
Message

Message → Message

Figure 8-10 When using symmetric algorithms, the sender and receiver use the same key for encryption and decryption functions.

encryption with Norm and Dave, he now needs to have three separate keys, one for each friend. This might not sound like a big deal until Dan realizes that he may communicate with hundreds of people over a period of several months, and keeping track and using the correct key that corresponds to each specific receiver can become a very daunting task. If Dan were going to communicate with 10 other people, then he would need to keep track of 45 different keys. If Dan were going to communicate with 100 other people, then he would have to maintain and keep up with 4,950 symmetric keys. Dan is a pretty bright guy, but does not necessarily want to spend his days looking for the right key to be able to communicate with Dave.

The security of the symmetric encryption method is completely dependent on how well users protect the key. This should raise red flags to you if you have ever had to depend on a whole staff of people to keep a secret. If a key is compromised, then all messages encrypted with that key can be decrypted and read by an intruder. This is complicated further by how symmetric keys are actually shared and updated when necessary. If Dan wants to communicate to Norm for the first time, Dan has to figure out how to get Norm the right key. It is not safe to just send it in an e-mail message because the key is not protected and it can be easily intercepted and used by attackers. Dan has to get the key to Norm through an *out-of-band method*. Dan can save the key on a floppy disk and walk over to Norm's desk, send it to him via snail mail, or have a secure carrier deliver it to Norm. This is a huge hassle, and each method is very clumsy and insecure.

Because both users use the same key to encrypt and decrypt messages, symmetric cryptosystems can provide confidentiality, but they cannot provide authentication or nonrepudiation. There is no way to prove who actually sent a message if two people are using the exact same key.

Well, if symmetric cryptosystems have so many problems and flaws, why use them at all? They are very fast and can be hard to break. Compared to asymmetric systems, symmetric algorithms scream in speed. They can encrypt and decrypt large amounts of data that would take an unacceptable amount of time if an asymmetric algorithm was used instead. It is also very difficult to uncover data that is encrypted with a symmetric algorithm if a large key size was used.

The following list outlines the strengths and weakness of symmetric key systems:

- Strengths
  - Much faster than asymmetric systems
  - Hard to break if using a large key size
- Weaknesses
  - **Key distribution**   It requires a secure mechanism to deliver keys properly.

- **Scalability**   Each pair of users needs a unique pair of keys, so the number of keys grow exponentially.

- **Limited security**   It can provide confidentiality, but not authenticity or nonrepudiation.

The following are examples of symmetric key cryptography algorithms and will be explained in the "Stream and Block Ciphers" section:

- Data Encryption Standard (DES)

- Triple DES (3DES)

- Blowfish

- IDEA

- RC4, RC5, and RC6

References

http://csrc.nist.gov/publications/nistpubs/800-7/node208.html

http://developer.netscape.com/docs/manuals/security/pkin/contents.htm

www1.tepkom.ru/users/ant/Articles/Pkcstane.html

Asymmetric Cryptography

Some things you can tell the public, but some things you just want to keep private.

In symmetric key cryptography, a single secret key is used between entities, whereas in public key systems, each entity has different keys, or *asymmetric keys*. The two different asymmetric keys are mathematically related. If a message is encrypted by one key, the other key is required to decrypt the message.

In a public key system, the pair of keys is made up of one public key and one private key. The *public key* can be known to everyone, and the *private key* must only be known to the owner. Many times, public keys are listed in directories and databases of e-mail addresses so they are available to anyone who wants to use these keys to encrypt or decrypt data when communicating with a particular person. Figure 8-11 illustrates an asymmetric cryptosystem.

The public and private keys are mathematically related, but cannot be derived from each other. This means that if an evildoer gets a copy of Bob's public key, it does not mean he can now use some mathematical magic and find out Bob's private key.

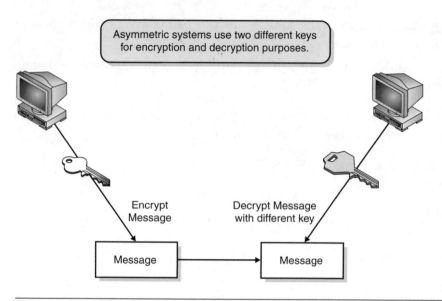

Asymmetric systems use two different keys for encryption and decryption purposes.

Encrypt Message

Decrypt Message with different key

Message

Message

Figure 8-11   Asymmetric cryptosystem

If Bob encrypts a message with his private key, the receiver must have a copy of Bob's public key to decrypt it. The receiver can decrypt Bob's message and decide to reply back to Bob in an encrypted form. All she needs to do is encrypt her reply with Bob's public key, and then Bob can decrypt the message with his private key. It is not possible to encrypt and decrypt using the exact same key when using an asymmetric key encryption technology.

Bob can encrypt a message with his private key and the receiver can then decrypt it with Bob's public key. By decrypting the message with Bob's public key, the receiver can be sure that the message really came from Bob. A message can only be decrypted with a public key if the message was encrypted with the corresponding private key. This provides authentication, because Bob is the only one who is supposed to have his private key. When the receiver wants to make sure Bob is the only one that can read her reply, she will encrypt the response with his public key. Only Bob will be able to decrypt the message because he is the only one who has the necessary private key.

Now the receiver can also encrypt her response with her private key instead of using Bob's public key. Why would she do that? She wants Bob to know that the message came from her and no one else. If she encrypted the response with Bob's public key, it does not provide authenticity because anyone can get a hold of Bob's public key. If she uses her private key to encrypt the message, then Bob can be sure that the message came from her and no one else. Symmetric keys do not provide authenticity because the same key is used on both ends. Using one of the secret keys does not ensure that the message originated from a specific entity.

If confidentiality is the most important security service to a sender, she would encrypt the file with the receiver's public key. This is called a *secure message format* because it can only be decrypted by the person who has the corresponding private key.

If authentication is the most important security service to the sender, then she would encrypt the message with her private key. This provides assurance to the receiver that the only person who could have encrypted the message is the individual who has possession of that private key. If the sender encrypted the message with the receiver's public key, authentication is not provided because this public key is available to anyone.

Encrypting a message with the sender's private key is called an *open message format* because anyone with a copy of the corresponding public key can decrypt the message; thus, confidentiality is not ensured.

For a message to be in a *secure and signed format*, the sender would encrypt the message with her private key and then encrypt it again with the receiver's public key. The receiver would then need to decrypt the message with his own private key and then decrypt it again with the sender's public key. This provides confidentiality and authentication for that delivered message. The different encryption methods are shown in Figure 8-12.

Each key type can be used to encrypt and decrypt, so do not get confused and think the public key is only for encryption and the private key is only for decryption. They both have the capability to encrypt and decrypt data. However, if data is encrypted with a private key, it cannot be decrypted with a private key. If data is encrypted with a private key, it must be decrypted with the corresponding public key. If data is encrypted with a public key, it must be decrypted with the corresponding private key. Figure 8-13 further explains the steps of a signed and secure message.

An asymmetric cryptosystem works much slower than symmetric systems, but can provide confidentiality, authentication, and nonrepudiation depending on its configuration and use. Asymmetric systems also provide for easier and more manageable key distribution than symmetric systems and do not have the scalability issues of symmetric systems. The "Public Key Cryptography" section will show how these two systems can be used together to get the best of both worlds.

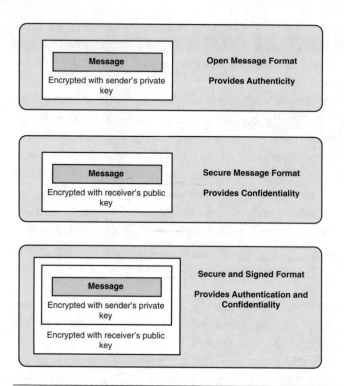

Figure 8-12 The way that the sender encrypts the message dictates the type of security service that will be provided.

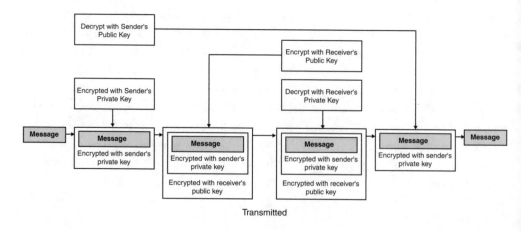

Figure 8-13 A secured and signed message is encrypted twice with the sender and the receiver's keys.

The following outlines the strengths and weaknesses of asymmetric key systems:

- Strengths
  - Better key distribution than symmetric systems
  - Better scalability than symmetric systems
  - Can provide confidentiality, authentication, and nonrepudiation
- Weaknesses
  - Works much slower than symmetric systems

The following are examples of asymmetric key algorithms:

- RSA
- Elliptic Curve Cryptosystem (ECC)
- Diffie-Hellman
- El Gamal
- Digital Signature Standard (DSS)

(These will be explained further in the sections under the "Asymmetric Encryption Algorithms" heading later in the chapter.)

References

http://csrc.nist.gov/publications/nistpubs/800-7/node210.html

www.eco.utexas.edu/~norman/BUS.FOR/course.mat/SSim/history.html

www.maths.mq.edu.au/~steffen/old/PCry/report/node8.html

www.emporia.co.za/TechnicalEncryption.asp

Stream and Block Ciphers

Which should I use, the stream or block cipher? Answer: The stream cipher because it makes you look skinnier.

There are two main types of symmetric algorithms: stream and block ciphers. Like their names sound, block ciphers work on blocks of plaintext and ciphertext, whereas stream ciphers work on streams of plaintext and ciphertext, one bit or byte at a time.

Block Cipher

When a *block cipher* algorithm is used for encryption and decryption purposes, the message is divided into blocks of bits. These blocks are then put through substitution, transposition, and other mathematical functions. The algorithm dictates all the possible functions available to be used on the message, and it is the key that will determine what order these functions will take place. Strong algorithms make reengineering, or trying to figure out all the functions that took place on the message, basically impossible.

It has been said that the properties of a cipher should contain confusion and diffusion. Different unknown key values cause confusion, because the attacker does not know these values, and diffusion is accomplished by putting the bits within the plaintext through many different functions so that they are dispersed throughout the algorithm. An analogy is an example where Dusty was given the task of finding 25 people. The 25 people start off as one group in his living room and have their own map that lays out paths to their destinations. Each person has a destination of a particular city in a different state. The 25 people disperse and reach their destinations and it is up to Dusty to find them. Because he does not have a copy of each and every person's map (or their keys), it brings confusion to the game. Because each person is in a different state throughout the United States, it brings along diffusion.

Block ciphers use diffusion and confusion in their methods. Figure 8-14 shows a simple block cipher. It has 16 inputs and each input represents a bit. This block cipher has two layers of 4-bit substitution boxes called *S-boxes*. Each S-box contains a lookup table that instructs how the bits should be permuted or moved around. The key that is used in the encryption process dictates what S-boxes are used and in what order.

Figure 8-14 shows that the key dictates what S-boxes are to be used when scrambling the original message from readable plaintext to encrypted nonreadable ciphertext. Each S-box can have different types of functions, mathematical formulas, and methods to be performed on each particular bit. The key provides the confusion because the attacker would not know which S-boxes would be used during the encryption process and all the permutations that happen on the bits is the diffusion, because they are moved between different S-boxes and put through different steps of scrambling. In this example, only two rounds are performed on the message.

This example is very simplistic—most block ciphers work with blocks of 64 bits and many more S-boxes are usually involved. Strong and efficient block cryptosystems use random key values so an attacker cannot find a pattern as to which S-boxes are chosen and used.

Stream Cipher

As stated earlier, a block cipher performs mathematical functions on blocks of data. A stream cipher does not divide a message up into blocks; instead, a stream cipher treats

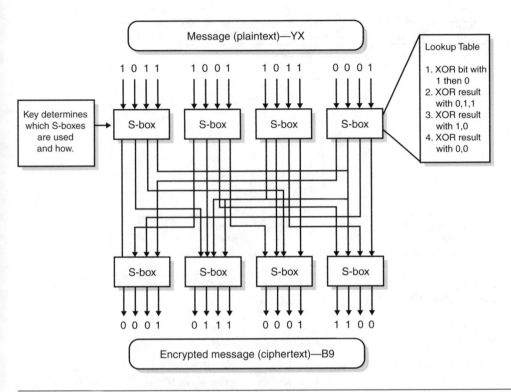

Figure 8-14 In block cipher algorithms, a message is divided into blocks of bits and mathematical functions are performed on those blocks.

the message as a stream of bits or bytes and performs mathematical functions on them individually.

When using a stream cipher, the same plaintext bit or byte will be transformed into a different ciphertext bit or byte each time it is encrypted. Some stream ciphers use a *keystream generator*, which produces a stream of bits that is XORed with the plaintext bits to produce ciphertext, as shown in Figure 8-15. (XOR stands for exclusive OR.)

NOTE Exclusive OR (XOR) Functionality: XOR is an operation that is applied to two bits. It is a function in binary mathematics. If both bits are the same, the result is zero (1 + 1 = 0). If the bits are different than each other, the result is one (1 + 0 = 1).

Example:
Message stream	1001010111
Keystream	0011101010
Ciphertext stream	1010111101

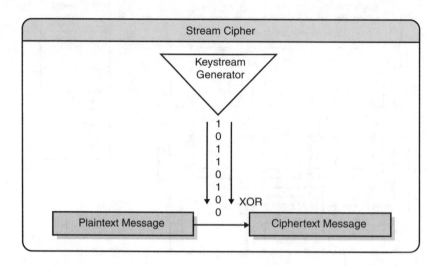

Figure 8-15 The value that is generated by the keystream generator is XORed with the bits of the plaintext message.

If the cryptosystem was only dependent upon this keystream generator, an attacker could get a copy of the plaintext and the resulting ciphertext, XOR them together, and find the keystream to use in decrypting other messages. So the smart people decided to stick a key into the mix.

In block ciphers, it is the key that determines what functions are applied to the plaintext and in what order. It is the key that provides the randomness of the encryption process. As stated earlier, most encryption algorithms are public so people know how they work. So the secret to the secret sauce is the key. In stream ciphers, the key also provides randomness, but to the keystream that is actually applied to the plaintext. The key is a random value input into the stream cipher, which it uses to ensure the randomness of the keystream data. This concept is shown in Figure 8-16.

A strong and effective stream cipher algorithm contains the following characteristics:

- Long periods of no repeating patterns within keystream values.
- Statistically unpredictable.
- The keystream is not linearly related to the key.
- Statistically unbiased keystream (as many 0's as 1's).

Because stream ciphers encrypt and decrypt one bit at a time, they are more suitable for hardware implementations. Block ciphers are easier to implement in software because they work with blocks of data that the software is used to working with, which

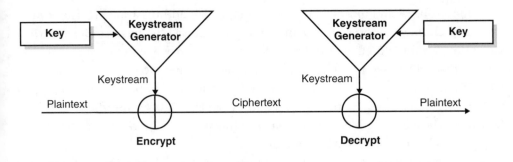

Figure 8-16   A keystream and key are needed for the encryption and the decryption process.

is usually the width of a data bus (64 bits). Stream ciphers are intensive because each bit must be manipulated, which works better at the silicon level. To make things just a little more confusing, block ciphers sometimes work in a mode that emulates a stream cipher. No one said cryptography was easy and we have not even touched any of the mathematics involved!

Types of Symmetric Systems

There are several types of symmetric algorithms used today. They have different methods of providing encryption and decryption functionality. The one thing they all have in common is that they are symmetric algorithms, meaning two identical keys are used to encrypt and decrypt the data.

Data Encryption Standard (DES)

Data Encryption Standard (DES) has had a long and rich history within the computer community. The National Institute of Standards and Technology (NIST) researched the need for the protection of computer systems during the 1960s and initiated a cryptography program in the early 1970s. NIST invited vendors to submit data encryption techniques to be used as a public cryptographic standard. IBM had been developing encryption algorithms to protect financial transactions. In 1974, IBM's 128-bit algorithm, named *Lucifer*, was submitted and accepted. There was controversy about if the NSA weakened Lucifer on purpose to give the agency the ability to decrypt messages not intended for them, but in the end, Lucifer became a national cryptographic standard in 1977 and an American National Standards Institute (ANSI) standard in 1978.

DES has been implemented in a majority of commercial products using cryptography functionality and in almost all government agencies. It was tested and approved as one of the strongest and most efficient cryptographic algorithms available. The continued overwhelming support of the algorithm is what caused the most confusion when NSA announced in 1986 that as of January 1988, the agency would no longer endorse DES and that DES-based products would no longer fall under compliance of the Federal Standard 1027. The NSA felt that because DES had been so popular for so long, it would surely be targeted for penetration and become useless as an official standard. Many researches disagreed, but DSA wanted to move on to a newer, more secure, and less popular algorithm as the new standard.

NSA's decision caused major concern and negative feedback pertaining to dropping its support for DES. At that time, it was shown that DES still provided the necessary level of protection, it would take a computer thousands of years to crack it, it was already embedded in thousands of products, and there was no equivalent substitute. NSA reconsidered its decision and NIST ended up recertifying DES for another five years.

In 1998, the Electronic Frontier Foundation built a computer system for $250,000, which broke DES in three days. It contained 1,536 microprocessors running at 40 MHz, which performed 60 million test decryptions per second per chip. Although most people do not have these types of systems to conduct such attacks, as Moore's Law holds true and microprocessors increase in processing power, this type of attack will only become more feasible for the average attacker. This brought around 3DES, which provides stronger protection. 3DES performs encryption, decryption, and then encryption on a message with independent keys.

DES was later replaced by the Rijndael algorithm as the *Advanced Encryption Standard (AES)* by NIST. This means that Rijndael is the new approved method of encrypting sensitive but unclassified information for the U.S. government and will most likely be accepted and widely used in the public arena.

How Does DES Work?

How does DES work again? Answer: Voodoo magic and a dead chicken.

DES is a block encryption algorithm. When 64-bit blocks of plaintext go in, 64-bit blocks of ciphertext come out. It is also a symmetric algorithm, meaning the same key is used for encryption and decryption. It uses a 64-bit key, 56 bits make up the true key, and 8 bits are used for parity.

When the DES algorithm is applied to data, it divides the message into blocks and operates on them one at a time. A block is made up of 64 bits and is divided in half and each character is encrypted one at a time. The characters are put through 16 rounds of transposition and substitution functions. The order and type of transposition and substitution functions depend on the value of the key that is inputted into the algorithm. The result is a 64-bit block of ciphertext.

There are several modes of operations when using block ciphers. Each mode specifies how a block cipher will operate. One mode may work better in one type of environment for specific functionality, whereas another mode may work in a different environment with totally different types of requirements. It is important that vendors who employ DES understand the different modes and which one to use for which purpose.

DES has four distinct modes of operation that are used in different situations for different types of results.

Electronic Code Book (ECB) Mode This mode is the native encryption method for DES and operates like a code book. A 64-bit data block is entered into the algorithm with a key and a block of ciphertext is produced. For a given block of plaintext and a given key, the same block of ciphertext is always produced. Not all messages end up in neat and tidy 64-bit blocks, so ECB incorporates padding to address this problem. This mode is usually used for small amounts of data like encrypting and protecting encryption keys.

Every key has a different code book. The code book provides the recipe of substitutions and permutations that will be performed on the block of plaintext. Because this mode works with blocks of data independently, data within a file does not have to be encrypted in a certain order. This is very helpful when using encryption in databases. A database has different pieces of data accessed in a random fashion. If it is encrypted in ECB mode, then any record or table can be added, encrypted, deleted, or decrypted independent of any other table or record. Other DES modes are dependent upon the text that was encrypted before them; this dependency makes it harder to encrypt and decrypt smaller amounts of text because the previous encrypted text would need to be decrypted first.

This mode is used for challenge-response operations and some key management tasks. It is also used to encrypt personal identification numbers (PINs) in ATM machines for financial institutions. It is not used to encrypt large amounts of data because patterns would eventually show themselves.

Cipher Block Chaining (CBC) Mode In ECB mode, a block of plaintext and a key will always give the same ciphertext. This means that if the word "balloon" was encrypted and the resulting ciphertext was "hwicssn" each time it was encrypted using the same key, the same ciphertext would always be given. This can show evidence of a pattern, which if an evildoer put some effort into revealing, could get him a step closer to compromising the encryption process. *Cipher Block Chaining (CBC)* does not reveal a pattern because each block of text, the key, and the value based on the previous block is processed in the algorithm and applied to the next block of text, as shown in Figure 8-17. This gives a more random resulting ciphertext. A value is extracted and used from the previous block of text. This provides dependence between the blocks and in a

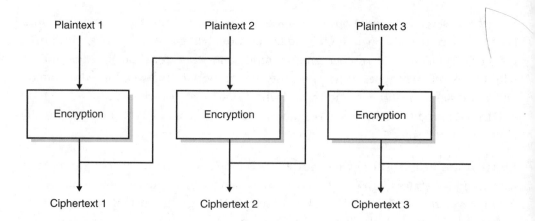

Figure 8-17 In CBC mode, ciphertext from the pervious block of data is used in encrypting the next block of data.

sense they are chained together. This is where the title of Cipher Block Chaining (CBC) comes from, and it is this chaining effect that hides any repeated patterns.

The results of one block are fed into the next block, meaning that each block is used to modify the following block. This chaining effect means that a particular ciphertext block is dependent upon all blocks before it, not just the previous block.

Cipher Feedback (CFB) Mode   In this mode, the previously generated ciphertext from the last encrypted block of data is inputted into the algorithm to generate random values. These random values are processed with the current block of plaintext to create ciphertext. This is another way of chaining blocks of text together, but instead of using a value from the last data block, CFB mode uses the previous data block in the ciphertext and runs it through a function and combines it with the next block in line. This mode is used when encrypting individual characters is required.

Output Feedback (OFB) Mode   This mode is very similar to *Cipher Feedback (CFB)* mode, but if DES is working in *Output Feedback (OFB)* mode, it is functioning like a stream cipher by generating a stream of random binary bits to be combined with the plaintext to create ciphertext. The ciphertext is fed back to the algorithm to form a portion of the next input to encrypt the next stream of bits.

As previously stated, block cipher works on blocks of data and stream ciphers work on a stream of data. Stream ciphers use a keystream method of applying randomization and encryption to the text, whereas block ciphers use an S-box-type method. In OFB mode, the DES block cipher crosses the line between block cipher and stream cipher and uses a keystream for encryption and decryption purposes.

 NOTE Do not get flustered with the complexity of these different DES modes. As of this writing, the CISSP test does not delve that deeply into the intricacies of algorithms. These modes are good to know and understand, but if all of these concepts are new to you, focus on the main components of DES.

References

www.rsa.com/rsalabs/faq/3-2.html

http://axion.physics.ubc.ca/crypt.html

www.cryptography.com/

Triple-DES (3DES)

We went from DES to Triple-DES (3DES), so it might seem that we skipped Double-DES. We did. Double-DES has a key length of 112 bits, but its work factor is about the same as DES; thus, it is no more secure than DES. So we will move on to 3DES.

Many successful attacks against DES and the realization that the useful lifetime of DES was about up brought much support for 3DES. Many financial and banking applications have incorporated 3DES.

3DES uses 48 rounds in its computation, which makes it highly resistant to differential cryptanalysis and approximately 2^{56} times stronger than DES. However, because of the extra work that 3DES performs, there is a heavy performance hit and it can take up to three times longer than DES to perform encryption and decryption.

Although NIST has selected the Rijndael algorithm to replace DES as the AES, NIST and others expect 3DES to be around and used for quite some time to come.

Advanced Encryption Standard (AES)

After DES was used as an encryption standard for over 20 years and it was able to be cracked in a relative short amount of time, NIST decided a new standard, the Advanced Encryption Standard (AES), needed to be put into place. This decision was announced in January 1997, and a request for AES candidates was made. The AES was to be a symmetric block cipher algorithm supporting keys sizes of 128-, 192-, and 256-bit keys. The following five algorithms were the finalists:

- **MARS**   Developed by the IBM team that developed Lucifer
- **RC6**   Developed by the RSA Laboratories
- **Serpent**   Developed by Ross Anderson, Eli Biham, and Lars Knudsen
- **Twofish**   Developed by Counterpane Systems
- **Rijndael**   Developed by Joan Daemon and Vincent Rijmen

Rijndael was the NIST's choice in replacing DES. It is now the algorithm that is required to protect sensitive, but unclassified, U.S. government information. Rijndael is a block cipher with a variable block length and key length.

IDEA

International Data Encryption Algorithm (IDEA) is a block cipher and operates on 64-bit blocks of data. The key is 128 bits long. The 64-bit data block is divided into 16 smaller blocks and each has eight rounds of mathematical functions performed on it.

The IDEA algorithm offers different modes similar to the modes described in the DES section, but it is much harder to break than DES. IDEA is used in the PGP encryption software. It was thought to replace DES, but it is patented, meaning that licensing fees would have to be paid to use it.

Blowfish

Blowfish is a block cipher that works on 64-bit blocks of data. The key length can be up to 448 bits and the data blocks go through 16 rounds of cryptographic functions. Bruce Schneier designed it.

RC5

RC5 is a block cipher that has a variety of parameters it can use for block size, key size, and the number of rounds used. It was created by Ron Rivest and analyzed by RSA Data Security, Inc. The block sizes used in this algorithm are usually 32, 64, or 128 bits and the key size goes up to 2,048 bits. RC5 was patented by RSA Data Security in 1997.

Asymmetric Encryption Algorithms

There are several types of asymmetric algorithms used in the computing world today. They may have different internal mechanisms and methods, but the one thing they do have in common is that they are all asymmetric. This means that a different key is used to encrypt a message than the key that is used to decrypt a message.

RSA

RSA, named after its inventors Ron Rivest, Adi Shamir, and Leonard Adleman, is a public key algorithm that is the most understood, easiest to implement, and most popular when it comes to asymmetric algorithms. RSA is a worldwide de facto standard and can be used for digital signatures and encryption. It was developed in 1978 at MIT and provides authentication as well as encryption.

The security of this algorithm comes from the difficulty of factoring large numbers. The public and private keys are functions of a pair of large prime numbers and the necessary activities required to decrypt a message from ciphertext to plaintext using a public key is comparable to factoring the product of two prime numbers. (A prime number is a positive whole number with no proper divisors, meaning the only numbers that can divide a prime number is one and the number itself.)

One advantage of using RSA is that it can be used for encryption and digital signatures. Using its one-way function, RSA provides encryption and signature verification and the inverse direction performs decryption and signature generation.

RSA is used in many Web browsers with the Secure Sockets Layer (SSL) protocol. PGP and government systems that use public key cryptosystems (encryption systems that use asymmetric algorithms) also use RSA.

El Gamal

El Gamal is a public key algorithm that can be used for digital signatures and key exchange. It is not based on the difficulty of factoring large numbers, but is based on calculating discrete logarithms in a finite field.

Elliptic Curve Cryptosystems (ECCs)

Elliptic curves are rich mathematical structures that have shown usefulness in many different types of applications. An *Elliptic Curve Cryptosystem (ECC)* provides much of the same functionality that RSA provides: digital signatures, secure key distribution, and encryption. One differing factor is ECC's efficiency. Some devices have limited processing capacity, storage, power supply, and bandwidth like the newer wireless devices and cellular telephones. With these types of devices, efficiency of resource use is very important. ECC provides encryption functionality requiring a smaller percentage of the resources required by RSA and other algorithms, so it is used in these types of devices.

In most cases, the longer the key length, the more protection that is provided, but ECC can provide the same level of protection with a key size that is smaller than what RSA requires. Because longer keys require more resources to perform mathematical tasks, the smaller keys used in ECC require fewer resources of the device.

ECC cryptosystems use the properties of elliptic curves in their public key systems. The elliptic curves provide ways of constructing groups of elements and specific rules of how the elements within these groups combine. The properties between the groups are used to build cryptographic algorithms.

References

www.cs.berkeley.edu/~daw/crypto.html

http://csrc.nist.gov/encryption/aes/

www.rsa.com/rsalabs/faq/3-6-8.html

www.sans.org/infosecFAQ/encryption/blowfish.htm

www.cryptoman.com/elliptic.htm

Hybrid Encryption Methods

Comparisons were made between symmetric and asymmetric algorithms earlier. So because symmetric has some downfalls, surely asymmetric will be our saving grace, right? Not so fast.

Asymmetric does provide more security services than the symmetric methods. It provides confidentiality by encryption. It also provides nonrepudiation when a sender encrypts a message using his private key, it provides integrity because if the message was tampered with it could not be properly decrypted, and it provides access control because only the people with the private key and corresponding public key can access the encoded data. However, asymmetric algorithms are unacceptably slow. Their algorithms are so complex and intensive that they require more system resources and take too long to encrypt and decrypt messages.

We just can't seem to win. So we turn to a hybrid system that uses symmetric and asymmetric encryption methods together and call it public key cryptography.

Public Key Cryptography

Public key cryptography uses two keys (public and private) generated by an asymmetric algorithm for protecting encryption keys and key distribution, and a secret key is generated by a symmetric algorithm and used for bulk encryption. It is a hybrid use of two different algorithms: asymmetric and symmetric. Each algorithm has its pros and cons, so using them together can bring together the best of both worlds.

How Does Public Key Cryptography Work?

We have established that symmetric cryptography provides limited security because two users use the same key, and although asymmetric cryptography enables the two users to use different keys, it is too slow when compared to symmetric methods. So some really smart people decided to use them together to accomplish a high level of security in an acceptable amount of time.

In the hybrid approach, the two different approaches are used in a complementary manner, with each performing a different function. A symmetric algorithm creates keys that are used for encrypting bulk data and an asymmetric algorithm creates keys that are used for automated key distribution.

When a secret key is used for bulk data encryption, this key is used to encrypt the message you want to send. When your friend gets the message you encrypted, you want him to be able to decrypt it. So you need to send him the necessary key to use to decrypt the message. You do not want this key to travel unprotected, because if the message was intercepted and the key was not protected, an evildoer could intercept the message that contains the necessary key to decrypt your message and read your information. If the secret key that is needed to decrypt your message is not protected, then there is no use in encrypting the message in the first place. So we use an asymmetric algorithm to encrypt the secret key, as depicted in Figure 8-18. Why do we use the symmetric algorithm on the message and the asymmetric algorithm on the key? We said earlier that the asymmetric algorithm takes longer because the math is more complex. Because your message is most likely going to be longer than the length of the key, we use the faster algorithm on the message (symmetric) and the slower algorithm on the key (asymmetric).

So how does this actually work? Let's say Bill is sending Paul a message that Bill wants only Paul to be able to read. Bill encrypts his message with a secret key, so now Bill has ciphertext and a secret key. The key needs to be protected so Bill encrypts the secret key with an asymmetric key. Remember that asymmetric algorithms use private and public keys, so Bill will encrypt the secret key Paul needs to perform decryption with Paul's public key. Now Bill has ciphertext from the message and ciphertext from the secret key. Why did Bill encrypt the secret key with Paul's public key instead of his own private key? Because if Bill encrypted it with his own private key, then anyone with

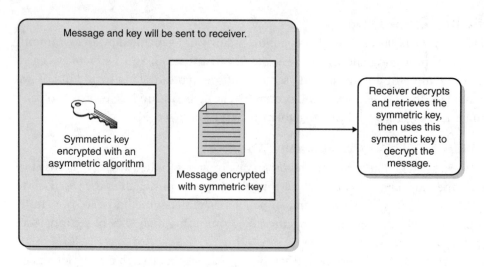

Figure 8-18 In a hybrid system, the asymmetric key is used to encrypt the secret key and the secret key is used to encrypt the message.

Bill's public key could decrypt it and retrieve the secret key. However, Bill does not want anyone who has his public key to read his message to Paul. Bill only wants Paul to be able to read it. So Bill encrypts the secret key with Paul's public key. If Paul has done a good job protecting his private key, then he will be the only one who can read Bill's message.

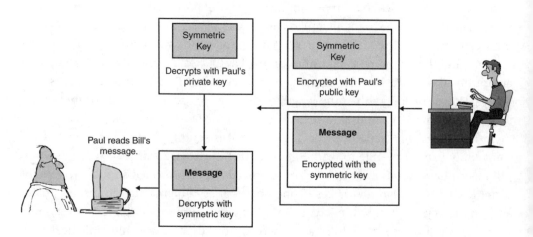

Bill uses public key cryptography to send Paul a message.

So Paul receives Bill's message and Paul uses his private key to decrypt the secret key. Paul then uses the secret key to decrypt the message. Paul then reads Bill's very important and confidential message that asks Paul how his day is.

Now when I say that Bill is using this key to encrypt and that Paul is using that key to decrypt, those two individuals do not necessarily need to go find the key on their hard drive and know how to properly apply it. We have software to do this for us — thank goodness.

If this is your first time with these issues, don't worry. I remember when I first started with these concepts and they turned my brain into a pretzel.

Just remember the following points:

- Asymmetric algorithm performs encryption and decryption by using public and private keys.

- Symmetric algorithm performs encryption and decryption by using a secret key.

- A secret key is used to encrypt the actual message.

- Public and private keys are used to encrypt the secret key.

- A secret key is synonymous to a symmetric key.

- An asymmetric key refers to a public or private key.

NOTE   Diffie-Hellman Key Exchange: In 1976, Dr. W. Diffie and Dr. M.E. Hellman performed open research in cryptography and were the first to introduce the notion of public key cryptography. This notion allowed users to handle key distribution electronically in a secure fashion. This evolved into the Diffie-Hellman key exchange.

This method of key exchange enables users to exchange secret keys over a nonsecure medium. The Diffie-Hellman algorithm is used for key distribution and it cannot be used to encrypt and decrypt messages.

This means that Dr. Diffie and Dr. Hellman came up with the whole public key/private key concept.

NOTE   Public versus Private Key Cryptography: It can get confusing when one is trying to learn the concepts of cryptography and unfortunately, the naming scheme does not always help out.

When the term "public key cryptography" is used, it is describing a system that uses an asymmetric algorithm that encrypts the secret keys. This system employs public and private keys. A sender might encrypt a message with the receiver's public key, and the receiver must decrypt it with her private key.

When the term "private key cryptography" is used, it is describing a system that is using a symmetric algorithm; thus, the sender and receiver use the same key for encryption and decryption purposes.

That is how a hybrid system works. The symmetric algorithm creates a secret key that will be used to encrypt the bulk, or the message, and the asymmetric key (either public or private key) encrypts the secret key. Table 8-1 outlines the differences between symmetric and asymmetric algorithms.

Session Keys

A *session key* is a secret key that is used to encrypt messages between two users. A session key is not any different than the secret key that was described in the previous section, but it is only good for one communication session between users.

If Tanya had a secret key she used to encrypt messages between Lance and herself all the time, then this secret key would not be regenerated or changed. They would use the exact same key each and every time they communicated using encryption. However, using the same key over and over again increases the chances of the key being captured and the secure communication being compromised. If, on the other hand, a new secret key was generated each time Lance and Tanya wanted to communicate, as shown in Figure 8-19, it would only be used during their one dialog and then destroyed. If they wanted to communicate an hour later, a new session key would be created and shared.

Table 8-1   Different Characteristics Between Symmetric and Asymmetric Systems

Attributes	Symmetric	Asymmetric
Keys	One key is shared between two or more entities.	One entity has a public key and the other entity has a private key.
Key exchange	Out-of-band.	Symmetric key is encrypted and sent with message; thus, the key is distributed by inbound means.
Speed	Algorithm is less complex and faster.	Algorithm is more complex and slower.
Key length	Fixed-key length.	Variable-key length.
Use	Bulk encryption, which means encrypting files and communication paths.	Key encryption and distributing keys.
Security service provided	Confidentiality and integrity.	Confidentiality, integrity, authentication, and nonrepudiation.

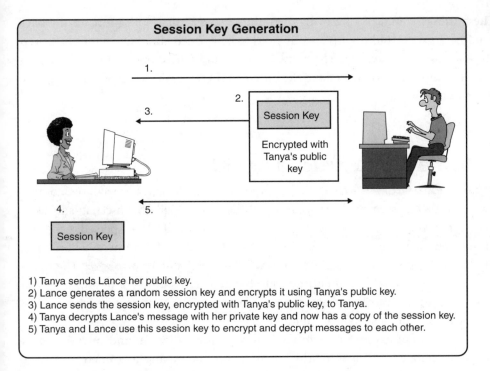

Session Key Generation

1.

2.

Session Key

Encrypted with
Tanya's public
key

3.

4.   5.

Session Key

1) Tanya sends Lance her public key.
2) Lance generates a random session key and encrypts it using Tanya's public key.
3) Lance sends the session key, encrypted with Tanya's public key, to Tanya.
4) Tanya decrypts Lance's message with her private key and now has a copy of the session key.
5) Tanya and Lance use this session key to encrypt and decrypt messages to each other.

Figure 8-19 A session key is generated so that all messages can be encrypted during one particular session between users.

A session key provides security because it is only valid for one session between two computers. If an attacker captured the session key, she would have a very small window of time to use it to try and decrypt messages being passed back and forth.

When two computers want to communicate using encryption, they must first go through a handshaking process. The two computers agree on the encryption algorithms that will be used and exchange the session key that will be used for data encryption. In a sense, the two computers set up a virtual connection between each other and are said to be in session. When this session is done, each computer tears down any data structures it built to enable this communication to take place, the resources are released, and the session key is destroyed.

So there are keys used to encrypt data and different types of keys used to encrypt keys. These keys must be kept separate from each other and neither should try to perform the other key's job. A key that has a purpose of encrypting keys should not be used to encrypt data and anything encrypted with a key used to encrypt other keys should not appear in clear text. This will reduce the vulnerability to certain brute force attacks.

These things are taken care of by operating systems and applications in the background, so a user would not necessarily need to be worried about using the wrong type of key for the wrong reason. The software will handle this, but as a security professional, it is important to understand the difference between the key types and the issues that surround them.

Public Key Infrastructure (PKI)

Public key infrastructure (PKI) consists of programs, data formats, procedures, communication protocols, security policies, and public key cryptographic mechanisms working in a comprehensive manner to enable a wide range of dispersed people to communicate in a secure and predictable fashion. PKI is an ISO authentication framework that uses public key cryptography and the X.509 standard protocols. The framework was set up to enable authentication to happen across different networks and the Internet. Specific protocols and algorithms are not specified, and that is why it is called a framework and not a specific technology.

PKI provides authentication, confidentiality, nonrepudiation, and integrity of the messages exchanged. PKI is a hybrid system of symmetric and asymmetric key algorithms and methods, which was discussed in earlier sections.

There is a difference between public key cryptography and PKI. So to be clear, public key cryptography entails the algorithms, keys, and technology required to encrypt and decrypt messages. PKI is what its name states—it is an infrastructure. The infrastructure of this technology assumes that the receiver's identity can be positively ensured through certificates and that the Diffie-Hellman exchange protocol (or another type of key exchange protocol) will automatically negotiate the process of key exchange. So the infrastructure contains the pieces that will identify users, create and distribute certificates, maintain and revoke certificates, distribute and maintain encryption keys, and enable all technologies to communicate and work together for the purpose of encrypted communication.

Public key cryptography is one piece in PKI, but there are many other pieces that are required to make up this infrastructure. An analogy is the e-mail protocol Simple Mail Transfer Protocol (SMTP). SMTP is the technology used to get e-mail messages from here to there, but many other things must be in place before this protocol can be productive. We need e-mail clients, e-mail servers, and e-mail messages, which together build a type of infrastructure, an e-mail infrastructure. PKI is made up of many different parts: certificate authorities, registration authorities, certificates, keys, and users. The following sections explain these parts and how they all work together.

[handwritten: not unique to me — signature from CA!]

Each person who wants to participate in a PKI requires a *digital certificate*, which is a credential that contains the public key of that individual along with other identifying information. The certificate is signed (digital signature) by a trusted third party or a *certificate authority (CA)*. The CA is responsible for verifying the identity of the key owner. When the CA signs the certificate, it binds the individual's identity to the public key and the CA takes liability for the authenticity of that public key. It is this trusted third party (the CA) that allows people who have never met to authenticate to each other and communicate in a secure method. If Kevin has never met David, but would like to communicate securely with him and they both trusted the same CA, then Kevin could retrieve David's public key from that CA and start the process. *[handwritten: → important]*

Certificate Authorities

How do I know I can trust you? Answer: The CA trusts me.

A CA is an organization that maintains and issues public key certificates. When a person requests a certificate, the CA verifies that individual's identity, constructs the certificate, signs it, delivers it to the requester, and maintains the certificate over its lifetime. When another person wants to communicate with this person, the CA will basically vouch for that person's identity. When David receives a message from Kevin, which contains Kevin's public key, David will go back to the CA and basically say, "Hey, is this guy really Kevin Chaisson?" The CA will look up in its database and reply, "Yep, that's him, and his certificate is valid." Then David feels more comfortable and allows Kevin to communicate with him.

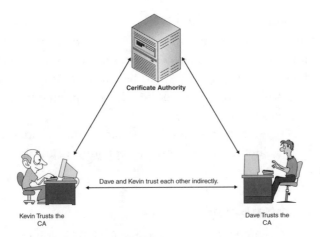

Public key cryptography is based on the users trusting the CA, which lets them trust each other indirectly.

The CA can be internal to an organization. This type of setup would enable the company to control the CA server, configure how authentication will take place, maintain the certificates, and recall certificates when necessary. Other CAs are organizations dedicated to this type of service and other individuals and companies pay them to supply this type of functionality. Some well-known CAs are Entrust and Verisign. Many browsers have several well-known CAs configured by default so the user does not need to figure out how to contact the CA and go through the processes of verifying other users' certificates. It is all taken care of in the background processing of the Web browser.

The CA is responsible for creating and handing out certificates, maintaining them, and revoking them if necessary. Revocation is handled by the *certificate revocation list (CRL)*. This is a list of every certificate that has been revoked for one reason or another. This list is maintained and updated periodically. A certificate may be revoked because the key holder's private key was compromised, the CA discovered that the certificate was issued to the wrong person, or the lifetime of the certificate had expired. An analogy of the use of a CRL is how a driver's license is used by a police officer. If an officer pulls over Sean for speeding, the officer will ask to see Sean's license. The officer will then run a check on the license to find out if Sean is wanted for any other infractions of the law and verifies that the license has not expired. The same thing happens when a person checks with a CA pertaining to another's certificate. If the certificate became invalid for some reason, the CRL is the mechanism for the CA to let others know this information.

Certificates

One of the most important pieces a PKI is its public key certificate. A *certificate* is the mechanism used to associate a public key with a collection of components sufficient to uniquely authenticate the claimed owner. Each certificate has a unique serial number within the CA, which binds that certificate to its particular owner. The most popular public key certificate is the X.509 v3 certificate. Many cryptographic protocols use this type of certificate, including SSL.

The certificate includes the serial number, version number, identity information, algorithm information, lifetime dates, and the signature of the issuing authority, as shown in Figure 8-20.

Registration Authority

As the number of entities that a CA is responsible for grows, sometimes it is logical to offload some of the work to another component. Many large PKI implementations use a *registration authority (RA)*, which performs the certification registration duties. The

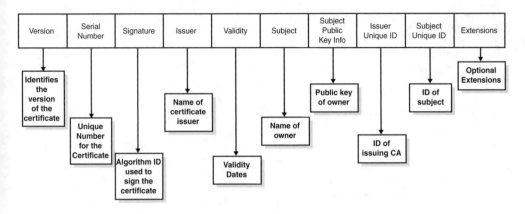

Figure 8-20 Each certificate has a structure with all the necessary identifying information in it.

RA may establish and confirm the identity of an individual, distribute shared keys to end users, initiate the certification process with a CA on behalf of an end user, and perform certificate life cycle management functions. The RA cannot issue certificates, but can act as a middleman between the user and the CA. Sometimes this is beneficial in a distributed environment. If the CA is in New York and there is an office in New Mexico that requires a lot of certificate support, it may be more efficient to have a RA in the New Mexico office, as illustrated in Figure 8-21. When new certificates are needed, users would make requests to the RA and the RA would direct these requests to the CA. This streamlines the communication between the New Mexico office and the CA in New York and lets the RA offload much of the work from the CA.

PKI Steps

Now that we know some of the main pieces of a PKI and how they actually work together, let's walk through an example.

John needs to establish a public/private key pair for himself, so he makes a request to the CA. The CA requests certain identification from John, like a copy of his driver's license, his phone number, address, and other identification information. Once the CA receives the required information from John and verifies it, the CA registers him in its database and performs a key pair generation. The CA creates a certificate with John's public key and identity information embedded. (The private key is either generated by the CA or on John's machine, which depends on the systems' configurations. If it is created at the CA, it needs to be sent to him by secure means.) Now John is registered and can participate in a PKI. John decides he wants to communicate with Diane so he

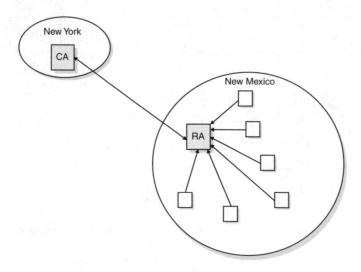

New York

CA

New Mexico

RA

Figure 8-21 An RA can remove much of the load from a CA and reduce network traffic in distributed environments.

requests Diane's public key from the same CA. The CA sends Diane's public key and John uses this to encrypt a session key that will be used to encrypt their messages. John sends the encrypted session key to Diane. John then sends his certificate, containing his public key, to Diane. When Diane receives John's certificate, her browser looks to see if it trusts the CA that digitally signed this certificate. Diane's browser trusts this CA and she makes a request to the CA to see if this certificate is still valid. The CA responds that the certificate is valid so Diane decrypts the session key with her private key. Now they can both communicate using public key cryptography. These concepts are shown in Figure 8-22.

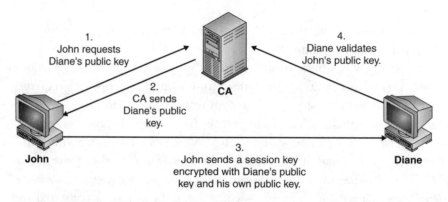

1.
John requests
Diane's public key

2.
CA sends
Diane's public
key.

CA

4.
Diane validates
John's public key.

John

3.
John sends a session key
encrypted with Diane's public
key and his own public key.

Diane

Figure 8-22 CA and user relationships

PKI is made up of the following entities and functions:

- CA
- RA
- Certificate repository
- Certificate revocation system
- Key backup and recovery system
- Automatic key update
- Management of key histories
- Cross-certification with other CAs
- Timestamping
- Client-side software

PKI supplies the following security services:

- Confidentiality
- Access control
- Integrity
- Authentication
- Nonrepudiation

> **NOTE** Separate Keys: Most implementations of public key cryptography have separate keys for digital signatures and encryption. This separation can add layers of necessary protection. Each key type can have its own expiration date, backup procedures, storage (hard drive, database, or smart card), and strength (64-bit encryption and 128-bit signature). One person may have different digital signatures with different strengths also. Joe may have a digital signature key he uses as an information warfare engineer, another as the lead of logistics, and another as the part owner of a small business. This separation provides more flexibility and the right level of security where it is needed.

→ how?

References

www.rsa.com/rsalabs/faq/4-1-3-1.html

www.pki-page.org/

www.webtools.com/story/security/TLS20010222S0001

www.nwfusion.com/research/crypto.html

One-Way Function

A *one-way function* is a mathematical function that is easier to compute in one direction than in the opposite direction. An analogy of this is when you drop a glass on the floor. Although dropping a glass on the floor is easy, putting back all the pieces to have the glass again is next to impossible. This concept is similar to how a one-way function is used in cryptography.

The easy direction of computation in a one-way function is like multiplying two large prime numbers. It is easy to multiply the two numbers and get the resulting product, but it is much harder to factor the product and recover the two initial large prime numbers. Many public key encryption algorithms are based on the difficulty of factoring large numbers that are the product of two large prime numbers. So when there are attacks on these types of cryptosystems, the attack is not necessarily trying every possible key value, but trying to factor the large number. So the easy function in a one-way function is multiplying two large prime numbers and the hard function is working backwards by figuring out the large prime numbers that were used to calculate the obtained product number.

Public key cryptography is based on *trapdoor one-way functions*. When a user encrypts a message with a public key, this message is encoded with a one-way function (breaks a glass). This function supplies a trapdoor (knowledge of how to put the glass back together), but the only way the trapdoor can be taken advantage of is if it is known about and the correct code is applied. The private key provides this service. The private key knows about the trapdoor and has the necessary programming code to take advantage of this secret trapdoor to unlock the encoded message (reassembling the broken glass). Knowing about the trapdoor and having the correct functionality to take advantage of it makes a private key a private key.

Only the corresponding Private Key will know how to open the one-way function trap door.

Because only the private key knows how to open the trapdoor, it provides a high level of protection.

One-way
Function Trap Door

The crux of this section is that public key cryptography provides security by using mathematical equations that are easy to perform one way (using the public key) and next to impossible to perform the other way (using the private key). An attacker would have to go through a lot of work to perform the mathematical equations in reverse (or figure out the private key).

Message Integrity

Cryptography can detect if a message has been modified in an unauthorized manner in a couple of different ways. The first way is that the message will usually not decrypt properly if parts of it have been changed. The same type of issue happens in compression. If a file is compressed and then some of the bits are modified, either intentionally or accidentally, many times the file cannot be uncompressed because it cannot be successfully transformed from one form to another.

Parity bits have been used in different protocols to detect modifications of streams of bits as they are passed from one computer to another, but parity bits can usually only detect unintentional modifications. Unintentional modifications can happen if there is a spike in the power supply, if there is interference or attenuation on a wire, or if some other type of physical condition occurs that causes the corruption of bits as they travel from one destination to another. Parity bits cannot identify if a message was captured by an intruder, altered, and then sent on to the intended destination because the intruder can just recalculate a new parity value that includes his changes and the receiver would never know the difference. For this type of protection, cryptography is required to successfully detect intentional and unintentional unauthorized modifications to data.

One-Way Hash

Now, how many times does the one-way hash run again? Answer: One, brainiac.

A *one-way hash* is a function (usually mathematical) that takes a variable-length string, a message, and compresses and transforms it into a fixed-length value referred to as a hash value. A hash value is also called a *message digest*. I know, more confusing names!

The reason to go through these steps is to create a fingerprint of this message. Just as fingerprints can be used to identify individuals, hash values can be used to identify a specific message. If Kevin wants to send a message to Maureen and he wants to ensure that the message does not get altered in an unauthorized fashion while it is being transmitted, he would calculate a hash value for the message and append it to the message itself. When Maureen receives the message, she performs the same hashing function Kevin used and compares her result with the hash value that was sent with the message. If the two values are the same, Maureen can be sure that the message was not altered during transmission. If the two values are different, Maureen knows that the message was altered, either intentionally or unintentionally, and she discards the message.

The hashing function, usually an algorithm, is not a secret—it is publicly known. The secrecy of the one-way hashing function is its "one-wayness." The function is only run in one direction, not the other direction. This is different than the one-way function used in public key cryptography. In public key cryptography, the security is provided because it is very hard, without knowing the key, to perform the one-way function backwards on a message and come up with readable plaintext. However, one-way hash functions are never used in reverse; they create a hash value and call it a day. The receiver does not attempt to reverse the process at the other end, but instead runs the same hashing function one way and compares the two results. (Several hashing algorithms are described in the section "Different Hashing Algorithms.")

The hashing one-way function takes place without the use of any keys. This means that anyone who receives the message can run the hash value and verify the message's integrity. However, if a sender only wants a specific person to be able to view the hash

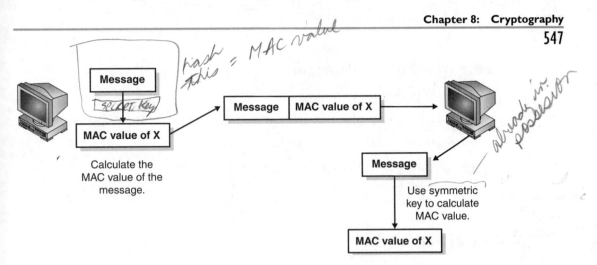

Figure 8-23 The receiver compares her calculated MAC value with the value that was sent with the message.

value sent with the message, the value would be encrypted with a key. This is referred to as the *message authentication code (MAC)*. MAC is the same thing as a one-way hashing function, except that the resulting hash value is the function of the message and the key, as shown in Figure 8-23. This ensures that only the person with the necessary key can verify the integrity of this message.

> **NOTE** A MAC is a key dependent one-way hash function. It has the same functionality as a one-way hash, but it requires a symmetric key to be used in the process and a one-way hash does not. Basically, the MAC is a one-way hash value that is encrypted with a symmetric key.

One-Way Function Used in Encryption versus One-Way Hashing

One-Way Function Used in Public Key Cryptography

- It helps the encryption algorithm to provide confidentiality and authentication, because only the private key can reverse the one-way function to result in plaintext

- The function encrypts in one direction and then decrypts in the reverse direction.

One-Way Hashing Function

- It is never performed in reverse.
- It provides integrity of a message, not confidentiality or authentication.
- The results of a one-way hash is a hashing value.
- It is used in hashing to create a fingerprint for a message.

Digital Signatures

To do a digital signature, do I sign my name on my monitor screen? Answer: Sure.

A *digital signature* is an encrypted hash value. From our previous example, if Kevin wanted to ensure that the message he sent to Maureen was not modified and he wants her to be sure that it came only from him, he can digitally sign the message. This means that a one-way hashing function would be run on the message and then Kevin would encrypt that hash value with his private key.

When Maureen receives the message, she will perform the hashing function on the message and come up with her own hash value. Then she will decrypt the sent hash value with Kevin's public key. She then compares the two values and if they are the same, she can be sure that the message was not altered during transmission. She is also sure that the message came from Kevin because the value was encrypted with his private key.

The hashing function ensures the integrity of the message and the signing of the hash value provides authentication and nonrepudiation. The act of signing just means that the value was encrypted with a private key. The steps of a digital signature are outlined in Figure 8-24.

We need to be clear on all the available choices within cryptography, because different steps and algorithms provide different types of security services:

- A message can be encrypted, which provides confidentiality.
- A message can be hashed, which provides integrity
- A message can be digitally signed, which provides authentication and integrity.
- A message can be encrypted and digitally signed, which provides confidentiality, authentication, and integrity.

Some algorithms can only perform encryption, whereas others can perform digital signatures and encryption. When hashing is involved, a hashing algorithm is used, not an encryption algorithm.

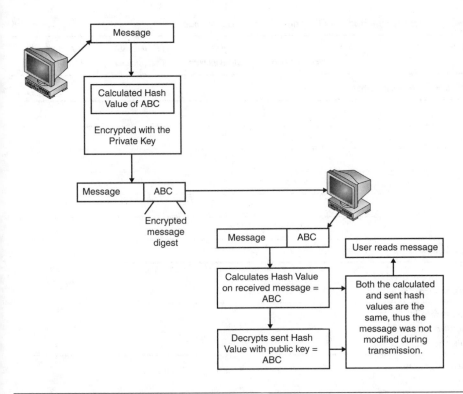

Figure 8-24   Steps of digital signature

It is important to understand that all encryption algorithms cannot necessarily provide all security services. Most of these algorithms are used in some type of combination to provide all the necessary security services required of an environment.

Table 8-2 shows the different services provided by the different algorithms.

Table 8-2   Various Functions of Different Algorithms

Algorithm Types	Encryption	Digital Signature	Hashing Function	Key Distribution
Asymmetric Key Algorithms				
RSA	×	×		×
ECC	×	×		×
Diffie-Hellman				×
El Gamal		×		×

(continued)

Table 8-2 Different Functions of Different Algorithms *(continued)*

Algorithm Types	Encryption	Digital Signature	Hashing Function	Key Distribution
Symmetric Key Algorithms				
DES	x			
3DES	x			
Blowfish	x			
IDEA	x			
RC4	x			
SAFER	x			
Hashing Algorithms				
RSA message digest used within RSA operations			x	
Ronald Rivest family of hashing functions MD2, MD4, and MD5			x	
Secure Hash Algorithm (SHA) used with Digital Signature Algorithm [DSA])		x	x	
HAVAL (variable-length hash values using a one-way function design)			x	

Digital Signature

A digital signature is the encrypted hash value of a message. The act of signing means encrypting the message's hash value with a private key, as shown in Figure 8-25.

Digital Signature Standard (DSS)

Because digital signatures can hold such importance on proving who sent what messages and when, the government decided to erect standards pertaining to its functions

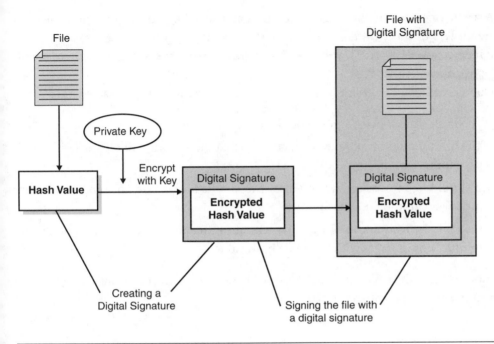

Figure 8-25   Creating a digital signature for a message

and acceptable use. In 1991, NIST proposed a federal standard called the Digital Signature Standard (DSS). It was developed for federal departments and agencies, but most vendors designed their products to meet these specifications also. The federal government requires its departments to use the Digital Signature Algorithm (DSA) and the Secure Hash Algorithm (SHA). The SHA creates a 160-bit output, which is then inputted into the DSA. The SHA is used to ensure the integrity of the message and the DSA is used to digitally sign the message. This is an example of how two different algorithms are combined to provide the right combination of security services.

RSA and DSA are the best known and most widely used digital signature algorithms. Unlike RSA, DSA can only be used for digital signatures and is part of the DSS. RSA can be used for digital signatures and message encryption.

Different Hashing Algorithms

As stated in an earlier section, the goal of using a one-way hash function is to provide a fingerprint of the message. If two different messages produced the same hash value, then it would be easier for an attacker to break that security mechanism because patterns would be revealed.

A strong one-hash function is hard to break and also does not provide the same hash value for two or more different messages. If a hashing algorithm takes steps to ensure that it does not create the same hash value for two or more messages, it is said to be *collision free*, or repetitive free.

Good cryptographic hash functions should have the following characteristics:

- The hash should be computed on the entire message.
- The hash should be a one-way function so that messages are not disclosed by their signatures.
- It should be impossible, given a message and its hash value, to compute another message with the same hash value.
- It should be resistant to birthday attacks, meaning an attacker should not be able to find two messages with the same hash value.

Table 8-3 and the following sections quickly describe some of the available hashing algorithms used in cryptography today.

MD4

MD4 is a one-way hash function designed by Ron Rivest. It produces 128-bit hash, or message digest, values. It is used for high-speed computation in software implementations and is optimized for microprocessors.

Table 8-3   The Different Hashing Algorithms Available

Message Digest 2 (MD2) algorithm	One-way function. Produces a 128-bit hash value. Much slower than MD4 and MD5.
Message Digest 4 (MD4) algorithm	One-way function. Produces a 128-bit hash value.
Message Digest 5 (MD5) algorithm	One-way function. Produces a 128-bit hash value. More complex than MD4. Processes text in 512-bit blocks.
HAVAL	One-way function. Variable-length hash value. Modification of MD5 algorithm and provides more protection against attacks that affect MD5. Processes text in 1,024-bit blocks.
SHA	One-way function. Produces a 160-bit hash value. Used with DSA.
SHA-1	Updated version of SHA.

MD5

MD5 is the newer version of MD4. It still produces a 128-bit hash, but the algorithm is a bit more complex to make it harder to break than MD4. The MD5 added a fourth round of operations to be performed during the hashing functions and makes several of its mathematical operations carry more steps or more complexity to provide a higher level of security.

MD2

MD2 is also a 128-bit one-way hash function designed by Ron Rivest. It is not necessarily any weaker than the previously mentioned hash functions, but it is much slower.

SHA

SHA was designed by NIST and NSA to be used with the DSS. The SHA was designed to be used in digital signatures and developed when a more secure digital signature algorithm was required for federal applications.

SHA produces a 160-bit hash value, or message digest. This is then inputted into the DSA, which computes the signature for a message. The message digest is signed instead of the whole message because it is a much quicker process. The sender computes a 160-bit hash value, encrypts it with his private key (signs it), appends it to the message, and sends it. The receiver decrypts the value with the sender's public key, runs the same hashing function, and compares the two values. If the values are the same, the receiver can be sure that the message has not been tampered with while in transit.

SHA is similar to MD4. It has some extra mathematical functions and produces a 160-bit hash instead of 128-bit, which makes it more resistant to brute force attacks, including birthday attacks. (Birthday attacks are described in "Attacks Against One-Way Hash Functions" section.)

HAVAL

HAVAL is a variable-length one-way hash function and is the modification of MD5. It processes message blocks twice the size of those used in MD5; thus, it processes blocks of 1,024 bits.

References

http://csrc.nist.gov/encryption/aes/

www.counterpane.com/tutorials.html

www.the-search-directory.com/cryptography/

http://theory.lcs.mit.edu/~rivest/rfc1321.txt

Attacks Against One-Way Hash Functions

A good hashing algorithm should not produce the same hash value for two different messages. If the algorithm does produce the same value for two distinctly different messages, this is referred to as a *collision*. If an attacker finds an instance of a collision, he has more information to use when trying to break the cryptographic methods used.

A complex way of attacking a one-way hash function is called the *birthday attack*. Now hold on to your hat while we go through this—it is a bit tricky.

In standard statistics, a birthday paradox exists. It goes something like this:

> How many people must be in the same room for the chance to be greater than even that another person has the same birthday as you?
>
> Answer: 253
>
> How many people must be in the same room for the chance to be greater than even that at least two people share the same birthday?
>
> Answer: 23

This seems a bit backwards, but the difference is that in the first instance, you are looking for someone with a specific birthday date, which matches yours. In the second instance, you are looking for any two people who share the same birthday. There is a higher probability of finding two people who share a birthday than you finding another person sharing your birthday—thus, the birthday paradox.

So why do we care? Well, it can apply to cryptography also. The main way that an attacker can find the corresponding hashing value that matches a specific message is through a brute force attack. If he finds a message with a specific hash value, it is equivalent to finding someone with a specific birthday. If he finds two messages with the same hash values, it is equivalent to finding two people with the exact same birthday.

The output of a hashing algorithm is n and to find a message through a brute force attack that results in a specific hash value would require hashing 2^n random messages. Then to take this one step further, finding two messages that hash to the same value would only require $2^{n/2}$.

This means that if an attacker has one hash value and wants to find a message that hashes to that same hash value, this process could take him years. However, if he just wants to find any two messages with the same hashing value, it could take him only a couple of hours.

The hash function used in digital signatures usually uses the value of n that is large enough to make it collision free. This would make $2^{n/2}$ practically impossible to guess or obtain. So the MD5 algorithm that has a 128-bit output will require 2^{64} computations to break. An algorithm that has 160-bit output, like SHA1, will require 2^{80} computations to break. This means that there is less than 1 in 2^{80} chance that someone will break an encryption system. The main point of this paradox and this section is to show how important longer hashing values truly are. A hashing algorithm that has a larger bit output is stronger and less vulnerable to brute force attacks like a birthday attack.

References

www.stack.nl/~galactus/remailers/attack-3.html

www.rsa.com/rsalabs/faq/2-4-6.html

One-Time Pad

A *one-time pad* is a perfect encryption scheme because it is unbreakable and each pad is used exactly once.

A one-time pad uses a truly nonrepeating set of random bits that are combined bitwise XOR with the message to produce ciphertext. The random key is the same size as the message and is only used once. Because the entire key is random and as long as the message, it is said to be unbreakable even with infinite resources. Each bit in the key is XORed with a bit in the message and this ensures that each bit is encrypted by a nonrepeating pattern of bits. The sender encrypts the message and then destroys the one-time pad and after the receiver decrypts the message, he destroys his copy of the one-time pad.

One-time pads are integrated in some applications. There is a pseudorandom sequence generator that feeds values to the algorithm, which in turn creates the one-time pad and then XORs it to the message. A one-time pad is unbreakable if the same pad is never used more than once and the bits used in the key are truly random. This ensures that even if an attacker intercepted a message, he would not be able to decrypt it because he would have to have the one-time pad value. If an attacker was actually successful in intercepting a copy of the one-time pad key, it would not be useful because the pad is only good for a one-time use.

Let's walk through this. Two copies of a pad containing a set of completely random numbers are created. This set contains at least as many numbers as characters in the message that is to be encrypted. The numbers within the set are produced by a secure random number generator, which can be seeded by the date, time, or other sources like radioactive decay. The seed is the starting value, which determines all subsequent values in the sequence used to generate the one-time pad.

Although this approach to encryption can provide a very high degree of security, it is impractical in most situations because it is difficult to distribute the pads of random numbers to all the necessary parties. Each possible pair of entities that might want to communicate in this fashion must receive a key that is as long, or longer, than the actual message. This type of key management can be overwhelming and require more overhead than it is worth. The distribution of the pad, or key, can be challenging and the sender and receiver must be perfectly synchronized so that each is using the same pads. The steps of encryption using a one-time pad are shown in Figure 8-26.

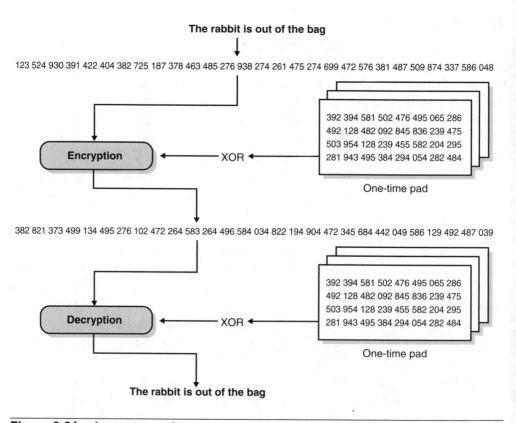

Figure 8-26   A one-time pad

Key Management

I am the manager of all keys! Answer: I am sorry.

Cryptography can be used as a security mechanism to provide confidentiality, integrity, and authentication, but not if the keys are compromised in any way. The keys can be captured, modified, corrupted, or disclosed to unauthorized individuals. Cryptography is based on a trust model. Individuals trust each other to protect their own keys, they trust the administrator that is maintaining the keys, or they trust a server that holds, maintains, and distributes the keys.

Many administrators know that key management causes one of the biggest headaches in cryptographic implementation. There is more to key maintenance than using them to encrypt messages. The keys have to be distributed to the right entities and updated continuously. The keys need to be protected as they are being transmitted and while they are being stored on each workstation and server. The keys need to be generated, destroyed, and recovered properly. Key management can be handled through manual or automatic processes.

The keys are stored before and after distribution. When a key is distributed to a user, it is not going to just hang out on the desktop; it needs a secure place within the file system to be stored and used in a control method. The key, the algorithm that will use the key, configurations, and parameters are stored in a module that also needs to be protected. If an attacker was able to obtain these components, she could masquerade as another user, and decrypt, read, and reencrypt messages that were not intended for her.

Historically, cryptographic keys were kept in secured boxes and delivered by escorted couriers. The keys could be distributed to a main server, and then the local administration would distribute them, or the courier would visit each computer individually. Some implementations distributed a master key to a site and then that key was used to generate unique secret keys to be used by individuals at that location. Today most key distributions take place by a protocol through automated means and not manually by an individual. The overhead of key management, required security level, and cost-benefit issues need to be evaluated for a company to decide on how it will conduct key management, but overall automation provides a more accurate and secure approach.

When using the Kerberos protocol (described in Chapter 4), a Key Distribution Center (KDC) is used to store, distribute, and maintain cryptographic session keys. This method provides an automated method of key distribution. The computer that wants to access a service on another computer will request access via the KDC. The KDC then calculates a session key to be used between the requesting computer and the computer providing the requested resource or service. The automation of this process reduces the possible errors that can happen through a manual process, but if the KDC gets compromised in any way, then all the computers and their services are affected and possibly compromised.

Other key exchange protocols are RSA and Diffie-Hellman, discussed earlier, and a variation of the Diffie-Hellman algorithm called the key exchange algorithm (KEA).

Unfortunately, many companies use cryptographic keys, but rarely change them out, if at all. This is because of the hassle of key management and the network administrator is already overtaxed with other tasks or does not realize the task actually needs to take place. The frequency of use of a cryptographic key can have a direct correlation to how often the key should be changed. The more a key is used, the more likely it is to be captured and compromised. If a key is used infrequently, then this risk drops dramatically. The necessary level of security and the frequency of use can dictate the frequency of key updates. A mom-and-pop diner might only change their cryptography keys every six months, whereas an information warfare military unit might change them every day. The important thing is that the keys are being changed in a secure method.

Key management is the most challenging part of cryptography. It is one thing to develop a very complicated and complex algorithm and key method, but if the keys are not securely stored and transmitted, it does not really matter how strong the algorithm is. Keeping keys secret is a challenging task.

Key Management Principles

Keys should not be in cleartext outside the cryptography device. As stated previously, many cryptography algorithms are known publicly, which puts more stress on protecting the secrecy of the key. If attackers know how the actual algorithm works, then in many cases, all they need to figure out is the key to compromise a system. This is why keys should not be available in cleartext; the key is what brings secrecy to encryption.

These steps, and all of key distribution and maintenance, should be automated and hidden from the user. These processes should be integrated into software or the operating system. It only adds complexity and opens the doors for more errors when processes are done manually and if the process depends upon end users to perform certain functions.

Keys are at risk of being lost, destroyed, or corrupted. Backup copies should be available and easily accessible when required. If data is encrypted and then the user accidentally loses the necessary key to decrypt it, this information would be lost forever if there was not a backup key to save the day. The application being used for cryptography may have key recovery options or it may require copies of the keys to be kept in a secure place. There are different scenarios that can show the need for key recovery or backup copies of keys. If Bob has possession of all the critical bid calculation, stock value information, and the corporate trend analysis needed for tomorrow's senior executive presentation, and Bob has an unfortunate confrontation with a bus, someone is going to need to access this data after the funeral. If an employee left the company and encrypted important documents on her computer before departing, the company would probably want to have a way to still have access to that data. Similarly, if the vice president did not know that running a large magnet over the diskette that holds his private key was not a good idea, he would want his key replaced immediately instead of listening to a lecture about electromagnetic fields and how they rewrite sectors on media.

Of course, having more than one key can increase the chance of disclosure, so a company needs to decide if it will have key backups and what precautions will be put into place to protect them properly. A company can choose to have multiparty control for emergency key recovery. This means that if a key needs to be recovered, more than one person is required to be involved with this process. The key recovery process could require two other individuals to present their private keys or three individuals to supply their individual PINs. These individuals should not all be members of the IT department. There should be a member from management, maybe an individual from auditing, and one individual from the IT department. All of these requirements reduce the potential for abuse and would require collusion for fraudulent activities to take place. This is an example of key escrow, which was previously explained in the "Key Escrow" section.

Rules for Keys and Key Management

- The key length should be long enough to provide the necessary level of protection.
- Keys should be stored and transmitted by secure means.
- Keys should be extremely random and use the full spectrum of the keyspace.

- The key's lifetime should correspond with the sensitivity of the data it is protecting (less secure data may allow for a longer key lifetime, whereas more sensitive data might require a shorter key lifetime).

- The more the key is used, the shorter its lifetime should be.

- Keys should be backed up or escrowed in case of emergencies.

- Keys should be properly destroyed when their lifetime comes to an end.

References

http://home.ecn.ab.ca/~jsavard/sicrypt.htm

www.rsa.com/rsalabs/faq/

www.faqs.org/faqs/cryptography-faq/part05/

www.cs.georgetown.edu/~denning/crypto/

www.ssh.fi/tech/crypto/intro.html

Link versus End-to-End Encryption

There are two communication levels at which encryption can be performed, each with different types of protection and implications. These two general modes of encryption implementation are link and end-to-end. *Link encryption* encrypts all the data along a specific communication path like a satellite link, T3 line, or telephone circuit. Not only is the user information encrypted, but the header, trailers, addresses, and routing data that are part of the packets are also encrypted. This provides extra protection against packet sniffers and eavesdroppers. In *end-to-end encryption*, the headers, addresses, routing, and trailer information are not encrypted; therefore, attackers can learn more about a captured packet and where it is headed.

Link encryption, which is sometimes called online encryption, is usually provided by service providers and is incorporated into network protocols. All of the information is encrypted and the packets have to be decrypted at each hop so the computer or router knows where to send the packet next. The computer, or router, must decrypt the packet, read the routing and address information within the header, and then reencrypt it and send it on its way.

With end-to-end encryption, the packets do not need to be decrypted and then encrypted again at each hop because the headers and trailers are not encrypted. The computers in between the origin and destination just read the necessary routing information and pass the packets on their way. Although link encryption provides extra protection as it travels though the communication path, it does expose the packets at each computer that has to decrypt it. There is always a little bad with the good, isn't there?

End-to-end encryption is usually initiated at the application layer of the originating computer. It provides more flexibility for the user to be able to determine if certain messages will get encrypted or not. It is called end-to-end because the message stays encrypted from one end of its journey to the other. Which is different than link encryption, which has to decrypt the packets at every computer between the two ends.

Encryption can happen at the highest levels of the OSI model or the lowest levels. If the encryption happens at the lower layers, then it is link encryption and at the higher levels, it is considered end-to-end encryption.

Link encryption is at the physical layer, as depicted in Figure 8-27. Hardware encryption devices interface with the physical layer, which encrypt all data that pass through them. All data, routing, and protocol information are encrypted through these devices if link encryption is in place. Because no part of the data is available to an attacker, she cannot learn basic information about how data flows through the environment. This is referred to as traffic-flow security.

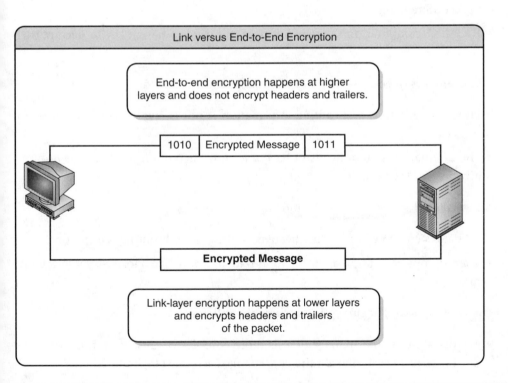

Figure 8-27   Link and end-to-end encryption happen at different OSI layers.

NOTE A hop is a computer that helps a packet get to its destination. It is usually a router that looks at the packet address to determine where the packet needs to go next. Packets usually go through many hops between the sending and receiving computers.

Encryption can take place within software or through specialized devices. If a device is going to encrypt the data, then the computer sends its data to the specialized hardware device for encryption before sending it to the lower layers of communication to prepare for transmission.

The following section outlines the advantages and disadvantages of end-to-end and link encryption methods.

Advantages of end-to-end encryption include the following:

- It protects information from start to finish throughout the network.
- It provides more flexibility to the user in choosing what gets encrypted and how.
- Higher granularity of encryption is available because each application or user can use a different key.
- Each hop computer on the network does not need to have a key to decrypt each packet.

Disadvantages of end-to-end encryption include the following:

- Headers, addresses, and routing information is not encrypted, and therefore not protected.
- The destination system needs to have the same encryption mechanisms to properly decrypt the message.

Advantages of link encryption include the following:

- All data is encrypted, including headers, addresses, and routing information.
- Users do not need to do anything to initiate it; it works at a lower layer in the OSI model.

Disadvantages of link encryption include the following:

- Key distribution and management is more complex because each hop computer must receive a key and when the keys change each must be updated.
- Messages are decrypted at each hop; thus, there are more points of vulnerability.

Reference

www.rand.org/publications/RM/RM3765/RM3765.chapter3.html

Hardware versus Software Cryptography Systems

Encryption can be done through software or hardware, and there are trade-offs with each. Generally, software is less expensive and provides a slower throughput than hardware mechanisms. Software cryptography methods can be more easily modified and disabled when compared to hardware systems, but it depends on the application and the hardware product.

If a company needs to perform high-end encryption functions at a higher speed, the company will most likely implement a hardware solution.

E-mail Standards

Just like in other types of technologies, cryptography has industry standards and de facto standards. Standards are necessary because they help ensure interoperability between vendor products. Standards usually mean that a certain technology has been under heavy scrutiny and properly tested and accepted by many similar technology communities. A company will still need to decide on what type of standard to follow and what type of technology to implement.

The goals of the technology need to be evaluated and a cost-benefit analysis needs to be performed on the competing standards and products within the chosen standards. For cryptography implementation, the company would need to decide on what needs to be protected by encryption, if digital signatures are necessary, how key management should take place, what type of resources are available to implement and maintain the technology, and what the overall cost will amount to.

If a company only needs to encrypt some e-mail messages here and there, then PGP may be the best choice. If the company wants all data encrypted as it goes throughout the network and to sister companies, then a link encryption implementation may be the best choice. If a company wants to implement a single-sign on environment where users need to authenticate to use different services and functionality throughout the network, then implementing a PKI might service them best. Each type of technology and standard should be understood to help make the most informative decision and each competing product within the chosen technology should be researched and tested before making the final purchase. Cryptography can be a complicated subject, and so is implementing and maintaining it. Doing homework versus buying into buzzwords and flashy products might help a company reduce its headaches down the road.

The following sections quickly describe some of the most used e-mail standards in use.

Privacy-Enhanced Mail

Privacy-Enhanced Mail (PEM) is an Internet standard to provide secure e-mail over the Internet. The protocols within PEM provide authentication, message integrity, encryption, and key management. This standard was developed to provide compatibility with many types of key-management processes and symmetric and public key methods of encryption.

PEM is a series of message authentication and encryption procedures developed by several governing groups. PEM can use DES for encryption and RSA for sender authentication and key management. It also provides support for nonrepudiation. The following outlines specific components that can be used in PEM:

- Messages encrypted with DES in CBC mode.
- Authentication provided by MD2 or MD5.
- Public key management provided using RSA.
- X.509 standard used for certification structure and format.

Message Security Protocol

The *Message Security Protocol (MSP)* is the military's PEM. It was developed by the NSA and is an X.400-compatible application level protocol used to secure e-mail messages. MSP can sign and encrypt messages and perform hashing functions. Like PEM, applications that incorporate MSP enable different algorithms and parameters to be used to provide greater flexibility.

References

www.cs.auckland.ac.nz/~pgut001/tutorial/

www.informweb.com/webportal/articles/tosecs.htm

Pretty Good Privacy (PGP)

Pretty Good Privacy (PGP) was designed by Phil Zimmerman as a freeware e-mail security program and released in 1991. It was the first widespread public key encryption program. PGP is a complete working system that uses cryptographic protection to protect e-mail and files. It mainly uses RSA public key encryption for key management and IDEA symmetric cipher for bulk encryption of data, although the user has the option of picking different types of algorithms to use. PGP can provide confidentiality through the IDEA encryption algorithm, integrity by using the MD5 hashing algorithm, authentication by using the public key certificates, and nonrepudiation through the use of cryptographically signed messages. (PGP enables different algorithms to be plugged in, so some implementations may use different algorithms than are listed here.)

The user's private key is generated and encrypted when the application asks the user to randomly type on her keyboard for a specific amount of time. Instead of using passwords, PGP uses passphrases. The passphrase is used to encrypt the user's private key that is stored on her hard drive.

PGP does not use a hierarchy of CAs, but relies on a "web of trust" in its key management approach. Each user generates and distributes his or her public key and users sign each other's public keys, which creates a community of users who trust each other. This is different than the CA approach where no one trusts each other; they only trust the CA.

For example, if Mark and Mike want to communicate using PGP, Mark can give his public key to Mike. Mike signs Mark's key and keeps a copy for himself. Then Mike gives a copy of his public key to Mark so they can start communicating securely. Later, Mark would like to communicate with Joe, but Joe does not know Mark, and does not know if he can trust him. Mark sends Joe his public key, which has been signed by Mike. Joe has Mike's public key, because they have communicated before, and trusts Mike. Because Mike signed Mark's public key, Joe now trusts Mark also and sends his public key and begins communicating with him.

So basically it is a system of "I don't know you, but my buddy Mike says you are an all right guy, so I will trust you on behalf of Mike's word."

Each user keeps a collection of signed public keys he has received from other users in a file referred to as a *key ring*. Each key in that ring has a parameter that indicates the level of trust assigned to that user and the validity of that particular key. If Steve has known Liz for many years and trusts her, he might have a higher level of trust indicated on her stored public key than Tom, whom he does not trust much at all. There is also a field indicating who can sign other keys within in Steve's realm of trust. If Steve receives a key from someone he doesn't know, like Kevin, and the key is signed by Liz, he can look at the field that pertains to who he trusts to sign other people's keys. If the field indicates that Steve trusts Liz enough to sign another person's key, then Steve will accept Kevin's key and communicate with him.

However, if Steve receives a key from Kevin and it is signed by untrustworthy Tom, then Steve might choose to not trust Kevin and not communicate with him.

These fields are available for updating and alteration. If one day Steve really gets to know Tom and finds out he is okay after all, he can modify these parameters within PGP and give Tom more trust when it comes to cryptography and secure communication.

Because the web of trust does not have a central leader, like a CA, certain standardized functionality is harder to accomplish. If Steve lost his private key, it means anyone else trusting his public key must be notified that it should no longer be trusted. In a PKI, Steve would only need to notify the CA and anyone attempting to verify the validity of Steve's public key will be told not to trust it when the other users contacted the CA. In the PGP world, this is not as centralized and organized. Steve can send out a key revocation certificate, but there is no guarantee that it will reach each user's key ring file.

PGP is a public domain software that uses public key cryptography. It has not been endorsed by the NSA, but because it is a great product and free for individuals to use, it has become somewhat of an encryption standard on the Internet.

References

http://web.mit.edu/network/pgp.html

www.pgpi.org/doc/pgpintro/

http://axion.physics.ubc.ca/crypt.html#PGP

www.pgpi.org/

Internet Security

The Web is not the Internet. The Web runs on top of the Internet, in a sense. The Web in the collection of Hypertext Transfer Protocol (HTTP) servers that hold and process Web sites that we see. The Internet is the collection of physical devices and communication protocols used to transverse these Web sites and interact with them. (These issues were touch upon in Chapter 2.) The Web sites look the way they look because the creator used a language that dictates the look, feel, and functionality of the page. The Web browser lets users read Web pages by enabling them to request and accept Web pages via HTTP and the user's browser converts the language (HTML, DHTML, and XML) into a format that can be viewed on the monitor. The browser is the user's window to the World Wide Web.

Browsers can understand a lot of different protocols and have the capability to process many types of commands, but they do not understand them all. For the protocols or commands they do not know how to process, the user must download a viewer or plug-in. This is a quick and easy way to expand the functionality of the browser by installing a modular component of code that integrates itself into the system or browser. This has caused serious security compromises because the payload of the module can easily carry viruses and malware that the users do not know about until it is already installed and has started its damage.

Start with the Basics

Why do we even connect to the Internet? This is a basic question at first, but as we dive deeper into the question, the complexity creeps in. We connect to download MP3s, check e-mail, order security books, look at Web sites, communicate with friends, and much more. But what are we really dong? We are using services provided by a computer's protocols and software. The services can be file transferring provided by FTP, remote connectivity provided by Telnet, Internet connectivity provided by HTTP, secure connections provided by SSL, and much, much more. Without these tools, there would be no way to even connect to the Internet.

Management needs to decide what functionality employees should have pertaining to Internet use and the administrator needs to implement these decisions by controlling services that can be used inside and outside the network. There are different ways of restricting services: allow certain services to only run on a particular system and restrict access to that system, employ a secure version of a service, filter the use of services, or block them altogether. These decisions will determine how secure the site will be and indicate what type of technology is needed to provide this type of protection.

HTTP

TCP/IP is the protocol of the Internet and HTTP is the protocol of the Web. HTTP sits on top of TCP/IP. When a user clicks her mouse on a link within a Web page, her browser uses HTTP to send a request to the Web server hosting that Web site. The Web server finds the corresponding file to that link and sends it to the user via HTTP. So where is TCP/IP in all of this? The TCP protocol controls the handshaking and maintaining the connection between the user and the server and the IP protocol makes sure that it is routed properly throughout the Internet to get from the Web server to the user. So the IP protocol finds the way to get from A to Z, TCP makes sure that the origin and destination are correct and that no packets are lost along the way, and upon arrival of the destination, HTTP presents the payload, which can be a Web page.

HTTP is a stateless protocol, which means the client and Web server make and break a connection for each operation. When a user requests to view a Web site, that Web server finds the requested Web site, presents it to the user, and then breaks the connection. If the user requests a link within the newly received Web page, a new connection has to be set up, the request goes to the Web server, and the Web server sends the requested item and breaks the connection.

S-HTTP *— like PGP ; packet at time*

Secure Hypertext Transport Protocol (S-HTTP) is HTTP with added on security features. It was developed to provide secure communication between a client and a server over the Internet. The client and server both have a list of cryptographic preferences and keying material. When a client makes a request to a server and the server deems that this type of communication should be protected, the server will query the client about the type of encryption methods it is configured to use. Once the client and server agree upon a specific encryption method, the client sends the server its public key. The server generates a session key from this public key, encrypts the session key with the client's public, and sends it back. From here on out, the client and server encrypt their messages with the newly calculated session key.

S-HTTP can also provide data integrity and sender authentication capabilities. S-HTTP computes a hash value of the message and the value can then be digitally signed. It was stated earlier that HTTP is a stateless protocol, meaning that after an operation is complete, the connection is disconnected. This is not the case with S-HTTP because it would require too much overhead if the client and server had to handshake and agree upon security parameters for each and every operation.

S-HTTP can support multiple encryption modes and types. It can use public key technology, PEM, and even symmetric key encryption. S-HTTP does not require the client to obtain a public key certificate if symmetric session key operations are allowed. This is a much less secure way of communicating, but it shows the flexibility of S-HTTP.

HTTPS

There is a difference between S-HTTP and HTTPS. S-HTTP is a technology that protects each message that is sent between two computers. *HTTPS* protects the communication channel between two computers, messages and all. HTTPS uses SSL and HTTP to provide a protected circuit between a client and server. So S-HTTP is used if an individual message needs to be encrypted, but if all information that passes between two computers needs to be encrypted, then HTTPS is used, which is SSL over HTTP.

SSL

Secure Sockets Layer (SSL) is similar to S-HTTP, but it protects a communication channel instead of individual messages. It uses public key encryption and provides data encryption, server authentication, message integrity, and optional client authentication. When a client accesses a Web site, it is possible for that Web site to have secured and public portions. The secured portion would require the user to be authenticated in some fashion. When the client goes from a public page on the Web site to a secured page, the Web server will start the necessary tasks to invoke SSL and protect this type of communication.

The server sends a message back to the client indicating that a secure session needs to be established, and the client sends its public key and security parameters. The server compares those security parameters to its own until it finds a match. This is the handshaking phase. The server authenticates to the client by sending it a digital certificate and if the client decides to trust the server, the process continues. The server can require the client to send over a digital certificate for mutual authentication, but that is rare.

The client creates a pre-master secret key for the session, encrypts it with the server's public key and sends it to the server. The client and server use this value to create the session keys that are used throughout the current session.

Just like S-HTTP, SSL keeps the communication path open until one of the parties requests to end the session. Usually the client will click on a different URL, and the session is complete.

SSL protocol requires an SSL-enabled server and browser. SSL will provide security for the connection but does not provide security for the data once it is received. This means the data is encrypted while it is being transmitted, but once it is received by a computer, it is no longer encrypted. So if a user sends bank account information to a financial institution via a connection protected by SSL, that communication path is protected but the user must trust the financial institution that receives this information because at this point, SSL's job is done.

In the protocol stack, SSL lies beneath the application layer and above the transport layer. This ensures that SSL is not limited to specific application protocols and can still use the communication transport standards of the Internet.

The user can verify a secure connection by looking at the URL to see that it states https://. The same is true for a padlock or key icon, depending on the browser type, at the bottom corner of the browser window.

Reference

http://csgrad.cs.vt.edu/~mlorch/securityprotocols/6.6.html

MIME

Multipurpose Internet Mail Extension (MIME) is a technical specification indicating how multimedia data and e-mail attachments are to be transferred. The Internet has mail standards that dictate how mail is to be formatted, encapsulated, transmitted, and opened. If a message or document contains a multimedia attachment, MIME dictates how that portion of the message should be handled.

When a user requests a file from a Web server that contains an audio clip, graphic, or some other type of multimedia component, the server will send the file with a header that describes the file type. For example, the header might indicate that the MIME type is Image and the subtype is jpeg. Although this will be in the header, many times systems also use the file's extension to identify the MIME type. So in our example, the file's name might be stuff.jpeg. The user's system will see the extension jpeg, or see that data in the header field, and look in its association list to see what program it needs to initialize to open this particular file. If the system has jpeg files associated with the Explorer application, then the Explorer will open and present the picture to the user.

Sometimes systems either do not have an association for a specific file type or do not have the necessary helper program necessary to review and use the contents of the file. When a file has an unassociated icon assigned to it, it might require the user to choose the Open With command and choose an application in the list to associate this file with that program. So when the user double-clicks on that file, the associated program will initialize and present the file. If the system does not have the necessary program, the Web site might offer the necessary helper program, like Acrobat or an audio program that plays wave files.

So MIME is a specification that dictates how certain file types should be transmitted and handled. This specification has several types and subtypes, enables different computers to exchange data in varying formats, and provides a standardized way of presenting the data. So if Sean views a funny picture that is in GIF format, he can be sure that when he sends it to Debbie, it will look exactly the same.

S/MIME

Secure MIME (S/MIME) is a standard for encrypting and digitally signing electronic mail that contains attachments and providing secure data transmissions. S/MIME extends the MIME standard by allowing for the encryption of e-mail and attachments. The encryption and hashing algorithms can be specified by the user of the mail package instead of having it dictated to them.

S/MIME provides confidentiality through the user's encryption algorithm, integrity through the user's hashing algorithm, authentication through the use of X.509 public key certificates, and nonrepudiation through cryptographically signed messages.

References

www.imc.org/smime-pgpmime.html

www.rsa.com/standards/smime/faq.html

http://nsi.org/Library/Internet/security.htm

www.ece.umn.edu/users/kjhan/security/

SET

Secure Electronic Transaction (SET) is a security technology proposed by Visa and MasterCard to allow for more secure credit card transaction possibilities than what is currently available. SET has been waiting in the wings for full implementation and acceptance as the standard for quite sometime. Although SET provides a very effective way of transmitting credit card information, businesses and users do not see it as efficient because it requires more parties to coordinate their efforts, more software installation and configuration for each entity involved, and more effort and cost than the widely used SSL method.

SET is a cryptographic protocol developed to send encrypted credit card numbers over the Internet. It is comprised of three main parts: the electric wallet, the software running on the merchant's server at its Web site, and the payment server that is located at the merchant's bank.

To use SET, a user must enter her credit card number into electronic wallet software. This information will be stored on the user's hard drive or on a smart card. The software will then create a public and private key used specifically for encrypting financial information before it is sent.

Let's say Tanya wants to buy her mother a gift from a Web site using her electric wallet. When she finds the perfect gift and decides to purchase it, her encrypted credit card information is sent to the merchant's Web server. The merchant does not decrypt this information, but instead digitally signs it and sends it on to its processing bank. At the bank, the payment server decrypts the information, verifies that Tanya has the necessary funds, and transfers the funds from Tanya's account to the merchant's account. Then the payment server sends a message to the merchant telling it to finish the transaction and a receipt is sent to Tanya and the merchant.

This is basically a very secure way of doing business over the Internet, but today everyone seems to be happy enough with the security SSL provides and they do not feel motivated enough to move to a different and more encompassing technology.

References

www.bankinfo.com/ecomm/setpart1.html

www.sans.org/infosecFAQ/covertchannels/SET.htm

www.cs.jcu.edu.au/~pei/cryptography.htm

Cookies

Hey, I found a Web site that is giving out free cookies! Answer: Great, I will bring the milk!

HTTP is a stateless protocol, meaning that each HTTP connection has no memory of any prior connections. This is one main reason to use cookies. They retain the memory between HTTP connections by saving prior connection data to the client's computer.

Cookies are text files that a browser maintains on a user's hard drive. There are different uses for cookies, but they are mainly used for demographic and advertising information. As a user travels from site to site on the Internet, the sites could be writing data to the cookies stored on the user's system. The sites can keep track of the user's browsing and spending habits and user's specific customization for certain sites. For example, if Emily goes to mainly Christian sites on the Internet, those sites will most likely be recording this information and the types of items in which she shows most interest. Then when Emily comes back to one of the same or similar sites, it will retrieve her cookies, find that she has shown interest in Christian books in the past, and present her with their line of Christian books. This increases the likelihood of Emily purchasing a book of her likening. This is a way of zeroing in on the right marketing tactics for the right person.

The servers at the Web site determine how cookies are actually used. When a user adds items to his shopping cart on a site, this data is usually added to a cookie. Then when the user is ready to check out and pay for his items, all the data in this specific cookie is extracted and the totals are added.

Cookies can also be used as timestamps to ensure that a session between a user and a server is restricted to a specific length of time. For example, if a user enters her credentials to access her banking information through her online bank account, she will need to be authenticated. Once she is authenticated, the server puts a cookie on her hard drive with a timestamp of four minutes. When she requests to go to another secure page within the site, the server will query the cookie to see if their session has timed out yet. If the session did time out, the user is asked to reenter her credentials to initiate another session.

A majority of the data within a cookie is meaningless to any entities other than the servers at specific sites, but some cookies can contain usernames and passwords for different accounts on the Internet. The cookies that contain sensitive information should be encrypted by the server on the site that distributed them, but this does not always happen and a nosey attacker can find this data on the user's hard drive and attempt to use it for mischievous activity. Some people who live on the paranoid side of life do not allow cookies to be downloaded to their systems (controlled through browser security controls). Although this provides a high level of protection against types of cookie abuse, it also reduces their functionality on the Internet. Some sites require cookies because there is specific data within the cookies that the site needs to perform correctly and to be able to provide the user with the services she requested.

There are third-party products that can limit the type of cookies downloaded, hide the user's identities as he travels from one site to the next, or mask the user's e-mail addresses and the mail servers he uses.

what types are these

SSH

Secure Shell (SSH) functions as a type of tunneling mechanism that provides terminal-like access to remote computers. SSH is a program that can be used to log into another computer over a network. The program can let Paul, who is on computer A, access computer B's files, run applications on computer B, and retrieve files from computer B without ever physically touching that computer. SSH provides authentication and secure transmission over vulnerable channels, like the Internet.

SSH should be used instead of telnet, ftp, rlogin, rexec, or rsh, which provides the same type of functionality that SSH provides but in a much less secure manner. SSH is a program and a set of protocols that work together to provide a secure tunnel between two computers. The two computers go through a handshaking process and exchange a session key that will be used during the session to encrypt and protect the data that is exchanged. The steps of an SSH connection are outlined in Figure 8-28.

what is the diff between this + VPN?

Once the handshake takes place and a secure channel is established, the two computers now have a pathway to exchange data with the assurance that the information will be encrypted and its integrity will be protected.

what layer does this operate on

SSH establishes a secure channel between two computers.

Secure Channel

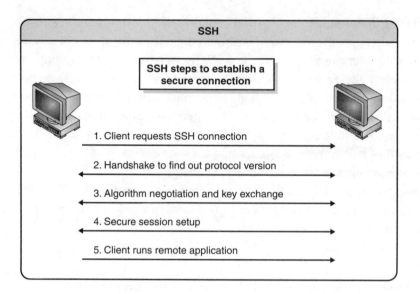

Figure 8-28 SSH is used for remote terminal-like functionality.

References

www.uni-karlsruhe.de/~ig25/ssh-faq/

www.onsight.com/faq/ssh/ssh-faq.html

http://wks.uts.ohio-state.edu/sysadm_course/html/sysadm-558.html

IPSec

The *Internet Protocol security (IPSec)* protocol is a method of setting up a secure channel for protected data exchange between two devices. The devices that share this secure channel can be two servers, two routers, a workstation and a server, or two gateways between different networks. IPSec is a widely accepted standard for secure network layer transport. It is more flexible and less expensive than application and link-layer encryption methods.

IPSec has strong encryption and authentication methods that employ public key cryptography. Although it can be used to enable communication between two computers, it is usually used to establish virtual private networks (VPNs) between networks across the Internet.

IPSec is not a strict protocol that dictates the type of algorithm, keys, and authentication method to be used, but it is an open, modular framework that provides a lot of flexibility for companies when they choose to use this type of technology. IPSec uses two basic security protocols: *Authentication Header (AH)* and the *Encapsulating Security Payload (ESP)*. AH is the authenticating protocol and ESP is an authenticating and encrypting protocol that uses cryptographic mechanisms to provide source authentication, confidentiality, and message integrity.

IPSec can work in one of two modes: *transport mode*, where the payload of the message is encrypted, and *tunnel mode*, where the payload and the routing and header information is also encrypted. The transport mode encrypts the actual message information so that it cannot be sniffed and uncovered by an unauthorized entity. The tunnel mode provides a higher level of protection by also protecting the header and trailer data that an attacker may find useful. Figure 8-29 shows the high-level view of the steps of setting up an IPSec connection.

Each device will have one *security association (SA)* for each session that it uses. The SA is critical to the IPSec architecture and is a record of the configurations the device needs to support an IPSec connection. The SA can contain the authentication and encryption keys, the agreed upon algorithms, key lifetime, and the source IP address. When a device receives a packet on the IPSec protocol, it is the SA that tells the device what to do with the packet. So if device B received a packet from device C via IPSec, device B will look to the SA to tell it how to decrypt the packet, how to properly authenticate the source of the packet, which key to use, and how to reply to the message if necessary.

A device will have one SA for each connection. It will have one SA for outbound traffic and a different SA for inbound traffic. If it is connecting to three devices, it will have six SAs, one for each inbound and outbound connection per remote device. So how can a device keep all of these SAs organized and ensure that the right SA is invoked for the right connection? Well, with the mighty *security parameter index (SPI)*, that's how. Each device has an SPI index that keeps track of the different SAs and tells the device which one is appropriate to invoke for the different packets it receives. The relationships between the SPI and the different SAs are depicted in Figure 8-30.

The AH protocol can authenticate the sender of the packet by user or source IP address. The ESP protocol can provide authenticity, integrity, and confidentiality if the devices are configured for this type of functionality. If both protocols are used, the following steps outline the process a receiving device goes through once it receives a packet:

1. Identify the appropriate SPI, SA, secret key, and algorithm (MD5 or SHA-1).

2. Calculate the hash value on packet to authenticate source and verify data integrity.

3. Authenticate the source.

4. Identify the correct cryptographic algorithm (DES or 3DES) and secret key.

5. Decrypt the message.

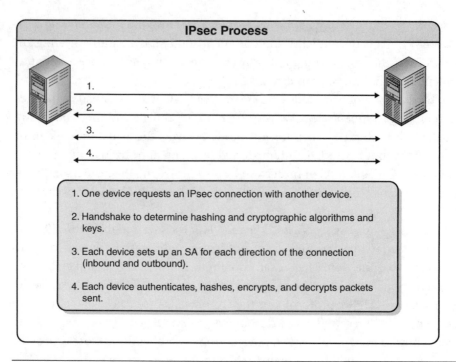

Figure 8-29   Steps that two computers follow when using IPSec

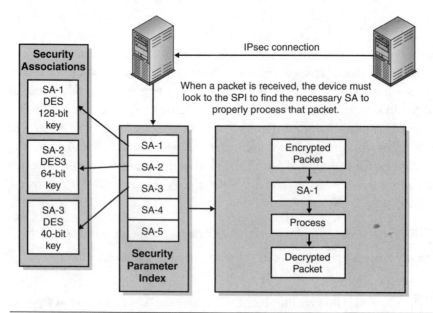

Figure 8-30   The SPI and SA help the system to encrypt and decrypt when using IPSec.

Because IPsec is a framework, it does not dictate what hashing and encryption algorithms are to be used or how keys are to be exchanged between devices. Key management can be handled through manual process or automated by a key management protocol. The *Internet Security Association and Key Management Protocol (ISAKMP)* is an authentication and key exchange architecture that is independent of the type of keying mechanisms used. Basically, the ISAKMP provides the framework and companies can choose how they will deal with key exchanges in their environments and how they will work within the ISAKMP framework.

For more in-depth information please refer to the following references.

References

www.ietf.org/html.charters/ipsec-charter.html

www.cs.arizona.edu/xkernel/www/ipsec/ipsec.html

www.cisco.com/warp/public/cc/so/neso/sqso/eqso/ipsec_wp.htm

www.counterpane.com/ipsec.html

Attacks

Eavesdropping, network sniffing, and capturing data as it passes over a network is considered passive because the attacker is not affecting the protocol, algorithm, key, message or any parts of the encryption system. *Passive attacks* are hard to detect, so methods are put in place to try and prevent them rather than detect and stop them.

Altering messages, modifying system files, and masquerading as another individual are acts that are considered *active attacks* because the attacker is actually doing something instead of sitting back gathering data. Passive attacks are usually used to gain information prior to carrying out an active attack. The following sections go over active attacks that can relate to cryptography.

Ciphertext-Only Attack

In this type of an attack, the attacker has the ciphertext of several messages. Each of the messages has been encrypted using the same encryption algorithm. The attacker's goal is to discover the plaintext of the messages by figuring out the key used in the encryption process. Once the attacker figures out the key, she can now decrypt all other messages encrypted with the same key.

Known-Plaintext Attack

In this type of attack, the attacker has the plaintext and ciphertext of one or more messages. Again, the goal is to discover the key used to encrypt the messages so that other messages can be deciphered and read.

Chosen-Plaintext Attack

In this attack, the attacker has the plaintext and ciphertext, but what makes this type of attack different is that she can choose the plaintext that gets encrypted. This gives the attacker more power and possibly a deeper understanding of the way that the encryption process works so that she can gather more information about the key that is being used. Once the key is discovered, other messages encrypted with that key can be decrypted.

Chosen-Ciphertext Attack

In this attack, the attacker can choose the ciphertext to be decrypted and has access to the resulting decrypted plaintext. Again, the goal is to figure out the key.

These are the definitions, but how do these attacks actually get carried out? An attacker may make up a message and send it to someone she knows will encrypt the message and then send it out to others. In that case, the attacker knows the plaintext and can then capture the message as it is being transmitted, which gives her the ciphertext.

Also, messages usually start with the same type of beginnings and ends. An attacker might know that each message a general sends out to his commanders always starts with certain greetings and ends with specific salutations and the general's name and contact information. In this instance, the attack has some of the plaintext (the data that is the same on each message) and can capture an encrypted message, and therefore capture the ciphertext. Once a few pieces of the puzzle are discovered, the rest is accomplished by reverse-engineering and trial-and-error attempts. Known-plaintext attacks were used by the United States against the Germans and the Japanese during World War II.

The public mainly uses algorithms that are known and understood versus the secret algorithms where the internal processes and functions are not released to the public. In general, the strongest and best engineered algorithms are the ones that are released for peer review and public scrutiny, because a thousand brains are better than five and many times some smarty-pants within the public population can find problems within an algorithm that the developers did not think of. This is why vendors and companies have competitions to see if anyone can break their code and encryption processes. If someone does break it, that means the developers must go back to the drawing board and strengthen this or that piece.

Not all algorithms are released to the public, such as the ones used by the NSA. Because the sensitivity level of what they are encrypting is so important, they want as much of the process as secret as possible. It does not mean that their algorithms are weak because they are not released for public examination and analysis. Their algorithms are developed, reviewed, and tested by many top cryptographic smarty-pants and are of very high quality.

Man-in-the-Middle Attack

If David is eavesdropping on different conversations that happen over a network and would like to know the juicy secrets that Lance and Tanya pass between each other, he can perform a *man-in-the-middle* attack. The following are the steps for this type of attack:

1. Tanya sends her public key to Lance and David intercepts this key and sends Lance his own public key. Lance thinks he has received Tanya's key, but in fact received David's.

2. Lance sends Tanya his public key. David intercepts this key and sends Tanya his own public key.

3. Tanya sends a message to Lance, encrypted in 'Lance's' public key. David intercepts the message and can decrypt it because it is encrypted with his own public key, not Lance's. David decrypts it with his private key, reads the message, and reencrypts it with Lance's real public key and sends it to Lance.

4. Lance answers Tanya by encrypting his message with 'Tanya's' public key. David intercepts it, decrypts it with his private key, reads the message, and encrypts it with Tanya's real public key and sends it on to Tanya.

Many times public keys are kept on a public server for anyone to access. David can intercept queries to the database for individual public keys or David can substitute his public key in the database itself in place of Lance and Tanya's public keys.

The SSL protocol has been known to be vulnerable to some man-in-the-middle attacks. The attacker injects herself right at the beginning of the authentication phase so that she obtains both parties' public keys. This enables her to decrypt and view messages that were not intended for her.

Using digital signatures during the session-key exchange can circumvent the man-in-the-middle attack. If using Kerberos, when Lance and Tanya obtain each other's public keys from the KDC, the public keys are signed by the KDC. Because Tanya and Lance have the public key of the KDC, they both can decrypt and verify the signature on each other's public key and be sure that it came from the KDC itself. Because David does not have the private key of the KDC, he cannot substitute his public key during this type of transmission.

When Lance and Tanya communicate, they can use digital signatures, which means they sign the message with their private keys. Because David does not have Tanya or Lance's private key, he cannot intercept the messages, read them, and encrypt them again as he would in a successful man-in-the-middle attack.

Dictionary Attacks

If Daniel steals a password file that is filled with one-way function values, how can this be helpful to him? He can take 100,000, or 1,000,000 if he is more motivated, of the most commonly used passwords and run them through the same one-way function and store them in a file. Now Daniel can compare his file results of the hashed values of the common passwords to the password file he stole from an authentication server. The ones that match will correlate to the passwords he entered as commonly used passwords.

For example, Table 8-4 represents Daniel's homemade password file that he ran through a one-way function. Table 8-5 represents the stolen password file.

Comparing the two results, Daniel now knows that STomanio is using the password Computer02, StSheperson is using Server1, and that SFoster is using the password Debbie04. Now Daniel can log on as these individuals and access the network resources using their security credentials.

Table 8-4   Daniel's Homemade Password File

Commonly Used Passwords	One-way Function Value
Password	abc
Kristy01	124
Cowboys	8yt
Computer02	83d
Administrator	dks
Server1	qwk
Lab003	39c
Elvis03	Dk7
Debbie04	3k5

Table 8-5 The Password File that Daniel Stole

User	One-way Function Value
EmGorenz	329
MitHockabout	aks
MarFairbairn	12p
STomaino	83d
SKowtko	00d
StSheperson	qwk
DKress	8sn
DFerguson	0d0
SFoster	3k5

This process is an example of how dictionary attacks take place. Most of the time the attacker does not need to come up with thousands or millions of passwords. This work is already done and is readily available at many different hacker sites on the Internet. The attacker only needs a dictionary program and he can then insert the file of common passwords, or dictionary file, into the program and run it against a captured password file.

Replay Attack

A big concern in distributed environments is replay attacks. Kerberos is especially vulnerable to this type of attack. A *replay attack* is when an attacker copies a ticket and breaks the encryption and then tries to impersonate the client and resubmit the ticket at a later time to gain unauthorized access to a resource.

Replay attacks do not only happen in Kerberos. Many authentication protocols are susceptible to these types of attacks because the goal of the attacker is usually to gain access to authentication information of an authorized person so that she can turn around and use it herself to gain access to the network. The Kerberos ticket is a form of authentication credentials, but an attacker can also capture passwords or tokens as they are transmitted over the network. Once captured she will resubmit the credentials, or replay them, in the hopes of being authorized.

Timestamps and sequence numbers are two countermeasures to the replay vulnerability. Packets can contain sequence numbers so each machine will be expecting a specific number on each receiving packet. If a packet has a sequence number that had been previously used, this is an indication of a replay attack. Packets can also be time-stamped. A threshold can be set on each computer to only accept packets within a certain time frame. If a packet is received that is past this threshold, it can help identify a replay attack.

Summary

Cryptography has been used in one form or another for over 4,000 years and the attacks on cryptography have probably been in process for 3,999 years and 364 days. As one group of people works to find new ways to hide and transmit secrets, another group of people is right on their heals finding holes in the newly developed ideas and products. This can be viewed as evil and destructive behavior, or hackers can be viewed as the thorn in the side of the computing world that requires them to build better and more secure products and environments.

Cryptographic algorithms provide the underlining tools to most security protocols used in today's infrastructures. The algorithms work off of different mathematical functions and provide different types of functionality and different levels of security. A big leap was made when encryption went from symmetric key use to public key cryptography. This evolution provided users and maintainers much more freedom and flexibility when it came to communicating with a variety of different types of users all over the world.

Encryption can be supplied at different layers of the OSI model by a range of different applications, protocols, and mechanisms. Today not much thought has to be given to cryptography and encryption because it is taken care of in the background by many operating systems, applications, and protocols. However, for administrators who maintain these environments, security professionals who consult and implement security solutions, and for those interested in obtaining a CISSP certification, knowing the ins and outs of cryptography is essential.

Quick Tips

- Cryptography is the science of protecting information by encoding it into an unreadable format.

- The most famous rotor encryption machine is the Enigma used by the Germans in WWII.

- A readable message is in a form called plaintext and once it is encrypted, it is in a form called ciphertext.

- The process of encryption turns plaintext into ciphertext and decryption transforms ciphertext back into the original plaintext.

- Cryptographic algorithms are the mathematical rules that dictate the functions of enciphering and deciphering.

- Cryptanalysis is the study of breaking cryptosystems.

- Nonrepudiation is a service that ensures that the sender cannot later falsely deny sending a message and the receiver cannot deny receiving the message.

- Key clustering is an instance when two different keys generate the same ciphertext.

- The range of possible keys is referred to as the keyspace. A larger keyspace and the full use of the keyspace allows more random keys to be created. This brings higher security.

- The two basic types of encryption ciphers are substitution and transposition. Substitution ciphers change a character (or bit) out for another and transposition ciphers scramble the characters (or bits).

- A polyalphabetic cipher uses more than one alphabet to defeat frequency analysis.

- Steganography is a method of hiding data within another form, like a graphic, wave file, or document. This method is used to hide the very existence of the data.

- The Clipper Chip was an encryption chip the U.S. government wanted to implement into many American-made devices so that they could listen to communication that contained suspected information about illegal activities.

- The Clipper Chip used the SkipJack algorithm, which was developed by the NSA to enable the government to decrypt any traffic encrypted using the Clipper Chip.

- Key escrow is a practice that splits up the necessary key required to decrypt information. Different agencies, or entitles, hold onto the different pieces and come together when decryption is necessary.

- Fair cryptosystems also separate the necessary key required for decryption, but this method takes place in software encryption processes using public key cryptography, whereas key escrow is mainly used when hardware encryption chips are used.

- A key is a random string of bits that is inserted into an encryption algorithm. The result determines what encryption functions will be carried out on a message and it what order.

- In symmetric key algorithms, the sender and receiver use the same key for encryption and decryption purposes.

- In asymmetric key algorithms, the sender and receiver use different keys for encryption and decryption purposes.

- Symmetric key processes provide barriers of key distribution, scalability, and key secrecy. However, symmetric key algorithms perform much faster than asymmetric key algorithms.

- Symmetric key algorithms can provide confidentiality, but not authentication or nonrepudiation.

- Examples of symmetric key algorithms include DES, 3DES, Blowfish, IDEA, and RC4.

- Asymmetric algorithms are used to encrypt keys and symmetric algorithms are used to encrypt data.

- If a user encrypts a secret key with his private key, it can only be decrypted by his public key.

- Public and private keys can be used for encryption and decryption processes. If a message is encrypted with a public key, it is decrypted with a private key and vice versa.

- Asymmetric key algorithms are much slower than symmetric key algorithms but can provide confidentiality, authentication, and nonrepudiation services.

- Examples of asymmetric key algorithms include RSA, ECC, Diffie-Hellman, El Gamal, and DSS.

- Two main types of symmetric algorithms are stream and block ciphers. Stream ciphers use a keystream generator and encrypt a message one bit at a time. A block cipher divides the message into groups of bits and encrypts them.

- Block ciphers are usually implemented in software and stream ciphers are usually implemented in hardware.

- Both stream and block ciphers algorithms are usually publicly known, so the secret part of the process is the key. The key provides the necessary randomization to encryption.

- Data Encryption Standard (DES) is a block cipher that divides a message into 64-bit blocks and employs S-box type functions on them.

- When DES was successfully broken Triple-DES (3DES) was developed to be used instead. 3DES uses 48 rounds of computation and up to three different keys.

- International Data Encryption Algorithm (IDEA) is a block symmetric cipher with a key of 128 bits.

- RSA is an asymmetric algorithm developed by Rivest, Shamir, and Adleman and is the de facto standard for digital signatures.

- Elliptic Curve Cryptosystems (ECC) are used as asymmetric algorithms and can provide digital signature, secure key distribution, and encryption functionality. It uses much less resources, which makes it better for wireless device and cell phone encryption use.

- When symmetric and asymmetric key algorithms are used together, this is called a hybrid system or public key cryptography. The asymmetric algorithm encrypts the symmetric secret key and the secret key encrypts the data.

- A session key is a symmetric key used by the sender and receiver of messages for encryption and decryption purposes. The session is only good while that communication session is active and then it is destroyed.

- A public key infrastructure (PKI) is a framework of programs, procedures, communication protocols, and public key cryptography that enables a diverse group of individuals to communicate securely.

- A certificate authority (CA) is a trusted third party that generates and maintains user certificates, which hold their public keys.

- The CA uses a certification revocation list to revoke certificates when they have been compromised in some fashion.

- A certificate is the mechanism the CA uses to associate a public key to a person's identity.

- A registration authority (RA) offloads some of the CA's workload by confirming individual identities, distributing shared keys, and submitting requests to the CA on behalf of the users. However, it cannot issue certificates to users.

- A one-way function is a mathematical function that is easier to compute in one direction than in the opposite direction.

- Public key encryption algorithms are based on one-way trapdoor functions. When a message is encrypted with a public key, it is encoded with a one-way function and with a trapdoor. Only the private key knows how to use this trapdoor and decrypt the message.

- Message integrity can be ensured by using hashing algorithms.

- When a hash algorithm is applied to a message, it produces a message digest, and this value is signed with a private key to produce a digital signature.

- When using hash algorithms, the sender runs the message through a hashing algorithm and sends the resulting value with the message to the receiver. The receiver runs the same algorithm and compares the two results. If the results are the same, the receiver can be sure the message was not modified in transit.

- Examples of hashing algorithms include SHA, MD2, MD4, MD5, and HAVAL.

- HAVAL produces a variable-length hash value, whereas the others produce a fixed-length value.

- SHA produces a 160-bit hash value and is used with the Digital Signature Algorithm (DSA).

- A birthday attack is an attack on hashing functions through brute force. The attacker tries to find two messages with the same hashing value.

- A one-time pad uses a pad, or key, with random values that are XORed against the message to produce ciphertext. The pad is at least as long as the message itself and is used once and then discarded.

- A digital signature is the result of a user signing a hash value with a private key. It provides authentication and nonrepudiation. The act of signing is the actual encryption of the value with the private key.

- Examples of algorithms used for digital signatures include: RSA, El Gamal, and DSA.

- Key management is one of the most challenging pieces of cryptography. It pertains to creating, maintaining, distributing, and destroying cryptographic keys.

- The Diffie-Hellman protocol is a key exchange protocol and does not provide encryption for data.

- Encryption can happen at the physical layer, which is link encryption, or at the application layer, which is end-to-end encryption.

- Link encryption encrypts the entire packet, including headers and trailers and has to be decrypted at each hop. End-to-end encryption does not encrypt the headers and trailers, and therefore does not need to be decrypted at each hop.

- Privacy-Enhanced Mail (PEM) is an Internet standard that provides secure e-mail over the Internet by using encryption, digital signatures, and key management.

- Message Security Protocol (MSP) is the military's PEM.

- Pretty Good Privacy (PGP) is a freeware e-mail security program that uses public key encryption. It uses a web of trust instead of the hierarchical structure used in public key crytography.

- S-HTTP provides protection for each message that is sent between two computers, but not the actual link. HTTPS protects the communication channel. HTTPS means HTTP is using SSL for security purposes.

- Secure Electronic Transaction (SET) is a proposed electronic commerce technology that provides a safer method for customers and merchants to perform transaction over the Internet.

Questions

Please remember that these questions are formatted and asked in a certain way for a reason. The questions and answers may seem odd or vague, but this is what you will see on the actual CISSP test.

1. What is the goal of cryptanalysis?
   a. To determine the strength of an algorithm
   b. To increase the substitution functions in a cryptographic algorithm
   c. To decrease the transposition functions in a cryptographic algorithm
   d. To determine the permutations used

2. The brute force attacks have increased because _____.
   a. Of increased use of permutations and transpositions in algorithms.
   b. As algorithms get stronger, they get less complex, and thus more susceptible to attacks.
   c. Of the increase in processor speed and power.
   d. Of the reduction in key length over time.

3. Which of the following is not a property or characteristic of a one-way hash function?
   a. It converts a message of arbitrary length into a value of fixed length.
   b. Given the digest value, it is computationally infeasible to find the corresponding message.
   c. It is computationally infeasible to derive the same digest from two different messages.
   d. It converts a message of fixed length to an arbitrary length value.

4. What would indicate that a message had been modified?
   a. The public key has been altered.
   b. The private key has been altered.
   c. The message digest has been altered.
   d. The message has been encrypted properly.

5. Which of the following is a U.S. standard developed for creating secure message digests?
   a. Data Encryption Standard
   b. Digital Signature Standard
   c. Secure Hash Algorithm
   d. Data Signature Standard

6. If an attacker stole a password file that contained one-way encrypted passwords, what type of attack would she perform to find the encrypted passwords?
   a. Man-in-the-middle attack
   b. Birthday attack
   c. Denial of service attack
   d. Dictionary attack

7. What is an advantage of RSA over the DSS?
   a. It can be provide digital signature and encryption functionality.
   b. It uses fewer resources and encrypts quicker because it uses symmetric keys.
   c. It is a block cipher versus a stream cipher.
   d. It employs a one-time encryption pad.

8. Many countries restrict the use or exportation of cryptographic systems. What is the reason given when these types of restrictions are put into place?
   a. Without standards, there would be many interoperability issues when trying to employ different algorithms into different programs.
   b. It can be used by some countries to be used against their local people.
   c. Criminals could use encryption to avoid detection and prosecution.
   d. Laws are way behind, so adding different types of encryption would confuse the laws more.

9. What is used to create a digital signature?
   a. The receiver's private key
   b. The sender's public key
   c. The sender's private key
   d. The receiver's public key

10. Which of the following best describes a digital signature?
    a. A method of transferring a handwritten signature to an electronic document
    b. A method to encrypt confidential information
    c. A method to provide an electronic signature and encryption
    d. A method to let the receiver of the message prove the source and integrity of a message

11. How many bits make up the effective DES key?
    a. 56
    b. 64
    c. 32
    d. 16

12. When would a certificate authority revoke a certificate?
    a. If the user's public key has become compromised
    b. If the user changed over to using the PEM model that uses a web of trust
    c. If the user's private key has become compromised
    d. If the user moved to a new location

13. What does DES stand for?
    a. Data Encryption System
    b. Data Encryption Standard
    c. Data Encoding Standard
    d. Data Encryption Signature

14. What is the function of a certificate authority?
    a. An organization that issues private keys and the corresponding algorithms
    b. An organization that validates encryption processes
    c. An organization that verifies encryption keys
    d. An organization that issues certificates

15. What does the acronym DEA stand for?
    a. Data Encoding Standard
    b. Data Encoding Application
    c. Data Encryption Algorithm
    d. Digital Encryption Algorithm

16. Who was involved in developing the first public key encryption system?
    a. Adi Shamir
    b. Ross Anderson
    c. Bruce Schneier
    d. Martin Hellman

17. What process takes place after creating a DES session key?
    a. Key signing
    b. Key escrow
    c. Key clustering
    d. Key exchange

18. DES performs how many rounds of permutation and substitution?
    a. 16
    b. 32
    c. 64
    d. 56

19. Which of the following is a true statement pertaining to data encryption when it is used to protect data?
    a. It verifies the integrity and acc uracy of the data.
    b. It requires careful key management.
    c. It does not require much system overhead in resources.
    d. It requires keys to be escrowed.

20. If different keys generate the same ciphertext for the same message, what is this called?
    a. Collision
    b. Secure hashing
    c. MAC
    d. Key clustering

21. What is the definition of an algorithm's work factor?
    a. Time it takes to encrypt and decrypt the same plaintext
    b. Time it takes to break the encryption
    c. Time it takes to implement 16 rounds of computation
    d. Time it takes to apply substitution functions

Answers

1. A.	7. A.	12. C.	17. D.
2. C.	8. C.	13. B.	18. A.
3. D.	9. C.	14. D.	19. B.
4. C.	10. D.	15. C.	20. D.
5. B.	11. A.	16. D.	21. B.
6. D.			

Disaster Recovery and Business Continuity

In this chapter, you will learn about the following items:

- Business impact analysis
- Operational and financial impact analysis
- Contingency planning requirements
- Selecting, developing, and implementing disaster and contingency plans
- Backup and off-site facilities

The recent earthquake in Seattle did not do as much damage as it could have, but many businesses were hit with a disaster they did not expect. Hurricane Andrew, in Miami, Florida, could hardly have caused any more damage than it did to that area; businesses were not merely affected but their buildings were destroyed and lives were lost. Kobe, Japan, was hit by an earthquake that was unexpected and its aftermath was full of damage and destruction. California had power fluctuations because of the lack of power supplies in the summer of 2001, which several businesses were clearly not ready to deal with. The World Trade Center towers coming down after terrorists crashed planes into them affected many surrounding businesses, U.S citizens, the government, and the world in a way that most people would have never dreamed. Thousands of businesses are affected by floods, fires, tornados, terrorist attacks, and vandalism that happen every single year in one area or another. The companies that survive these traumas are the ones that thought ahead, planned for the worst, estimated the possible damages that could occur, and put the necessary steps in place to protect themselves. This is a very small percentage of businesses today; most businesses affected by these types of events have to close their doors forever.

591

An organization is extremely dependent upon several resources, personnel, and tasks that are performed on a daily basis in order to stay healthy, happy, and profitable. Most organizations have tangible resources, intellectual property, employees, computers, communication links, facilities, and facility services. If any one of these is damaged or inaccessible for one reason or another, the company can be crippled. If more than one is damaged, the company may be in a darker situation and the longer one of these items is unusable, the longer it will probably take for an organization to get back on its feet. Some companies are never able to get back on their feet after certain disasters. However, the companies that thought ahead, planned for the possible disasters, and did not put all their eggs in one basket have had a better chance of coming back to business and in time thrive in the market again.

Business Continuity and Disaster Recovery

Disaster recovery has the goal of minimizing the effects of a disaster and taking the necessary steps to ensure that the resources, personnel, and business processes are able to resume operation in a timely matter. This is different than contingency planning, which deals with providing methods and procedures for dealing with longer-term outages and disasters. A disaster recovery plan has a goal of dealing with the disaster and its ramifications right after the disaster hit. A disaster recovery plan will be carried out when everything is still in emergency mode and scrambling to get critical systems back online. A contingency plan deals with a longer look of the problem: getting critical systems to another environment while repair of the original facilities is taking place, getting the right people to the right places, performing business in a different mode until regular conditions are back in place, and dealing with customers, partners, and shareholders through different channels until everything returns to normal. So disaster recovery deals with, "Oh my goodness the sky is falling," and contingency planning deals with, "Okay, the sky fell, now how to we stay in business until someone can put the sky back where it belongs?" Figure 9-1 is an example of the proverbial sky in the processes of falling.

There is a continual theme throughout many of the chapters in this book: availability, integrity, and confidentiality. Because each chapter is dealing with a different topic, it looks at these three security characteristics in slightly different ways. In Chapter 4, which discussed access control, availability meant that resources should always be available to users and subjects and not be hindered by any access control methods. The access control method should not violate the integrity or confidentiality of a resource.

Figure 9-1 Disasters are unpredictable and sometimes the best protection is good planning.

In fact, it must take many steps to ensure that the resource is kept confidential and that there is no possibility of altering its contents while they are being accessed. In this chapter, the integrity and confidentiality needs to be considered not in everyday procedures, but in the procedures that will be taking place right after a disaster. It may not be appropriate to leave a server that holds confidential information in one building while everyone else moves to another building. A company is much more vulnerable after a disaster hits, so it is important that the secret stuff still stays secret and the integrity of data and systems is ensured even when people are in dire straits. Availability is extremely important in disaster recovery and business continuity. The resources that keep the business going must be available to the people and systems that rely on them. This may mean that backups need to be done religiously, redundancy factored into the architecture, and that if communication lines are disabled, there is a quick and sure way of establishing other methods of communication.

Recovery Planning Definition

Recovery planning involves developing a plan and preparing for a disaster before it takes place in the hopes of minimizing loss and ensuring the availability of critical systems and personnel.

When looking at disaster recovery and business contingency planning, some companies focus mainly on backed up data and providing redundant hardware. Although these items are extremely important, they are just a small piece of the company's pie. Hardware and computers need people to configure and operate them and data is usually not useful unless it is accessible by other systems and possibly outside entities. Thus, a large picture of how the business works needs to be understood and planning needs to include getting the right people to the right places, documenting the necessary configurations, and making sure a redundant power supply is available. It is also important to understand how automated tasks can be carried out manually, if necessary, and how business processes can be safely altered to keep the operation of the company going. Without this type of vision and planning after a disaster hits, a company could have its backup data and redundant servers, but people would be standing around in a daze not knowing where to start or how to perform in such a different environment.

Make It Part of the Security Policy and Program

As stated in Chapter 5, each and every company has to have a security policy, procedures, standards, and guidelines. When all of these come together, they are considered a security program that should be a living entity. This means that because a company will always go through changes, the program should also go through changes to stay current, usable, and effective.

Disaster recovery and business contingency should be a part of the security policy and program and not an entity that stands off in a corner by itself. If it is properly integrated with other security issues, it has a better chance of being continually updated and improved upon and it can help ensure that security is thought of in each and every step of the disaster and contingency plan. They are both essential foundational pieces of an effective security program.

A very important question to be asked when first developing a disaster and contingency plan is why. This may seem silly and the answer obvious, but not always. One would think that the reason to have these plans is to deal with an unexpected disaster and to get people back to their tasks at hand. Why are most companies in business? To make money and be profitable. If these are usually the main goals of businesses, then the plans need to be developed to help achieve these goals also. The main reason to develop these plans in the first place is to reduce the risk of financial loss by improving the company's ability to recover and restore operations. This encompasses the goals of mitigating the effects of the disaster.

NOTE   Small companies may have their contingency plan as part of their overall security plan. Larger, more complex companies should contain a synopsis of the contingency plan within the security plan, but each should be separate documents.

The most critical piece to disaster recovery and continuity planning is management support. They must be convinced of its necessity. Therefore, a business case must be made to obtain this support. The business case can include current vulnerabilities, regulatory and legal obligations, current status of recovery plans, and recommendations. Management will be mostly concerned with cost/benefit issues, so several preliminary numbers will need to be gathered and potential losses estimated. The decision of how a company should plan to recover is purely a business decision and should be treated as such.

Business Impact Analysis

Disaster recovery and contingency planning deals with uncertainty and chance. The point of making these plans is to try and think of all the possible disasters that could take place, estimate the potential damage and loss, and develop viable alternatives in case those events do actually take place.

Risk assessment and analysis needs to be performed to evaluate all potential threats. (For a full examination of risk analysis, refer to Chapter 3.) Threats can come in the form of man-made, natural, or technical. A man-made threat may be an arsonist, terrorist, or simple mistakes that can have serious outcomes. Natural threats can be tornados, floods, hurricanes, and earthquakes, shown in Figure 9-2. Technical threats can be

Figure 9-2 A company should walk through scenarios of each and every potential threat the company faces, including earthquakes.

data corruption, loss of power, device failure, or loss of a T1 line. It is important to identify all possible threats and estimate the probability of them happening. Some issues may not come to mind when developing these plans like an employee strike, vandals, disgruntled employees, or hackers. These issues are best addressed in a group with scenario-based exercises. This ensures that if a threat became true, the plan includes the ramifications on *all* business tasks, departments, and critical operations. The more issues that are thought of, the better prepared a company can be when these issues actually take place.

The next step in risk analysis is assigning a value to the assets that could be affected by each threat. This helps in establishing economic feasibility of the overall plan. Once the team knows about the possible threats and the amount of potential loss, they can look at the top five or ten issues and document this information so that management can clearly understand the threats that the company faces.

These issues are part of a *business impact analysis (BIA)*, which is a crucial first step in disaster recovery and contingency planning. Qualitative and quantitative impact information should be gathered and then properly analyzed and interpreted. The goal is to see exactly how a business will be affected by different threats. The effects can be economical, operational, or both. This information can be gathered through standard

Figure 9-3   Continuity plans are business decisions that should be based on real numbers and facts.

survey tools or questionnaires given to the most knowledgeable people within the company. This will give a fuller understanding of all the possible business impacts.

This information should be gathered and documented in a clear and understandable format, which is presented to management, shown in Figure 9-3. It is one thing to know that if a tornado hit, it would be *really bad*, and it is another thing to know that if a tornado hit that affected 65 percent of the facility, the company could be at risk of losing computing capabilities for up to 72 hours, power supply up to 24 hours, and a full stop of operations for 76 hours, which equates to a loss of $125,000 each day. Management has a hard time dealing with *really bad* compared to real numbers.

Disaster recovery planning should be brought into normal business decision making. This ensures that it is considered and dealt with when other business changes are introduced.

NOTE   A BIA is performed at the beginning of disaster recovery and continuity planning to identify the areas that would suffer the greatest financial or operational loss in the event of a disaster or disruption. It identifies the company's critical systems needed for survival and estimates the outage time that can be tolerated by the company as a result of a disaster or disruption.

Essential business functions need to be identified and loss criteria needs to be developed. The business functions can include

- IT network support
- Data processing
- Accounting
- Software development
- Payroll
- Customer support
- Order entry
- Production scheduling
- Purchasing
- Communications

There may be interdependencies between these departments and functions that need to be identified so that they are also properly protected and put back into place during a recovery procedure.

Once threats are identified and critical business functions acknowledged, specific loss criteria must be applied. The criteria can contain

- Loss in reputation and public confidence
- Loss in profits
- Loss of competitive advantages
- Increase in operational expenses
- Violations of contract agreements
- Violations of legal and regulatory requirements
- Delayed income costs
- Loss in revenue
- Loss in productivity

Some of these costs can be direct or indirect and must be properly accounted for.

So if the disaster recovery planning team is looking at the threat of a terrorist bombing, it is important to identify which business function would be most likely targeted, how all business functions could be affected, and how each bulleted item in the loss criteria would be directly or indirectly affected. Many times the timeliness of the disruption can cause everlasting effects. If the customer support functionality was out of commission for two days, it may be acceptable, but if it is out five days, the company could be in financial ruin. So time-loss curves that show the total impact over specific time periods should be developed and analyzed, as shown in Figure 9-4.

It is necessary to try and think of all the possible events that could take place, which could turn out to be detrimental to a company. It is also necessary to understand that not all events will be thought of and protection may not be available for each and every scenario introduced. This goes back to a main reason that companies are in business— to be profitable. A disaster and contingency plan should provide the necessary level of security within the economical constraints. This requires comprehensive risk analysis to understand the possible events and estimate the potential damage, which will provide economical justification. In other words, if the company has a facility in a flood zone and they could lose up to 1.2 million dollars if a large flood hit, it would not make

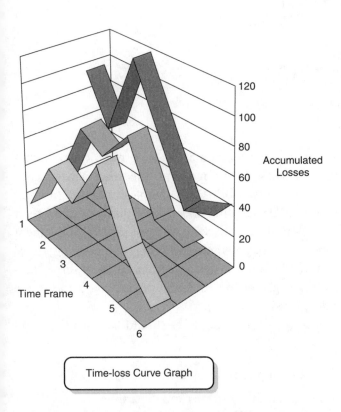

Time-loss Curve Graph

Figure 9-4 Time-loss curves should be constructed to portray the real effects a company would experience if it were out of commission for certain periods of time.

sense for the company to spend 2 million dollars in protection against a flood. If the company has a facility in a flood zone, there is a high probability that a flood would take place; therefore, this disaster should be dealt with and planned for first. It is also possible that the company could experience a massive alien abduction, but that disaster should be way down on the list because it is not as common as a flood.

True threats should get the most attention versus the more unlikely threats, like alien abduction.

Interdependencies

It is important to look at a company as a complex animal instead of a static two-dimensional entity. It is comprised of many types of equipment, people, tasks, departments, communication, and interfaces to the outer world. The complexity of true disaster recovery and continuity planning is understanding all of these intricacies and their interrelationships. A team may develop plans to back up and restore data, implement redundant data processing equipment, educate employees on how to carry out automated tasks manually, and obtain redundant power supplies, but if all of these components have no idea how to work together in a different environment to get the products out the door, it might all be a waste of time.

The following interrelation and interdependency issues should be researched and addressed in the resulting plan:

- Define essential business functions and supporting departments.
- Identify interdependencies between these functions and departments.
- Discover all possible disruptions that could affect the mechanisms necessary to allow these departments to function together.

- Identify and document potential threats that could disrupt interdepartmental communication.

- Gather quantitative and qualitative information pertaining to those threats.

- Provide alternative methods of restoring functionality and communication.

- Provide a brief statement of rationale for each threat and corresponding information.

This information, along with other data explained in previous sections, should be presented to the senior management staff. After their approval of the information, the actual development of the plan should begin.

Reference

www.disasterrecoveryworld.com/bia.htm

Contingency Planning Requirements

A major requirement for anything that has such far-reaching ramifications as business contingency planning is management support. It is very important that management understands what the real risks are to the company, the consequences of those risks, and the potential loss values for each and every risk. Without this understanding, management may only give lip service to disaster recovery and contingency planning and in some cases, this is worse than not having any plans at all because of the false sense of security. Without management support, the necessary resources, funds, and time will not be devoted to these plans, which could end up in bad plans that again can provide a false sense of security. Failure of these plans usually means a failure in management understanding, vision, and due care responsibilities.

Executives may be held responsible and liable under various legal and regulatory issues. They could be sued by stockholders and/or customers if they do not practice due diligence and fulfill all of their responsibilities when it comes to disaster recovery and business continuity items. Some business types have strict regulatory rules and laws that they have to abide by and these should be researched and integrated into the plan from the beginning. Banking and investment organizations must ensure that even if a disaster occurred, their customers' confidential information would not be made readily available to unauthorized individuals or be vulnerable in any way. Disaster recovery, continuity development, and planning work best in the top-down approach, not the bottom-up approach.

Many companies do not see the benefit in spending time and resources on disaster recovery issues because they are running so fast to try and keep up with a dynamic and changing business world. Those who *do* see the value in these efforts many times have a hard time convincing top management because management does not see a profit margin or increase in market shares as a result, but if a disaster does hit and they did put in the effort to properly prepare, the result is priceless. It is just like the story of the tortoise and the hare. The hare would selfishly want to run fast and beat the competition to the finish line, but the tortoise took his time and did things correctly and methodically. Today's business world requires a little of both; the drive to produce a great product or service and get it to the market, and the insight and wisdom to know that unexpected trouble can easily find its way to one's doorstep.

The policies and goals of the planning effort need to be established by management. The management sees the company in a much larger view than other employees. They should have an understanding of the complexity of keeping a business going and thriving and how a disruption to any of these processes can have a far-reaching effect. It is important that management set the overall goals of disaster recovery and contingency planning, and they must make the priorities of what should be dealt with first. Once management sets the goals, policies, and priorities, other staff members who are responsible for these plans can fill in the rest. However, management's support does not just stop there. They need to make sure that the plans and procedures developed are actually productive and successful, and management needs to make sure that the plans stay updated and represent the priorities of a company, which can change over time.

The main goals of a disaster recovery plan is to improve responsiveness by the employees in different situations, ease confusion by providing written procedures and participation in drills, and help make logical decisions during a crisis. If the employees know where to go when the all-hands-on-deck alarm is called and are familiar with what tasks are expected of them and how to perform these tasks, then the people in position to make decisions on how to properly deal with the event can do so in a calmer and more controlled manner. This can prove to be a crucial element in disaster recovery.

 NOTE Another requirement is performing continual data backups. This task can seem like an irritating day in and day out task, but if everything else failed and the company's information was still saved, this irritating task could be the actual event that helped the company stay afloat. This data files can be restored to enable the company to start reconstruction. Not only should crucial files be backed up, but the programs used to access these files should also be backed up. Even if no other steps are taken for disaster recovery and business continuity, backing up critical information and vital records should always be performed.

Figure 9-5   Representatives from each department and management personnel should be interviewed.

The parameters of the plan need to be established. This would happen by interviewing senior management and personnel in each department, as shown in Figure 9-5. First, the concerns and priorities of management need to be determined, which will basically dictate a majority of the scope of the project and plan. The scope may be broken down geographically, organizationally, or functionally. Representatives from each department and management personnel should be interviewed to ensure that all of the company's concerns and priorities pertaining to disaster recovery and business continuity are covered.

Developing Goals for Contingency Plans

If you do not have established goals, then how do you know that you are done and if your efforts were actually successful? Goals are established so that everyone knows the ultimate objectives. Establishing goals is important for any task, but especially for contingency plans. The definition of the goals helps direct the proper allocation of resources and tasks, develops necessary strategies, and assists in economical justification of the plans and program overall. Once the goals are set, they provide a guide to the development of the contingency plan. Anyone who has been involved in large projects that must also deal with many small, complex details, knows that at times it is easy to get off track and not actually accomplish the major goals of the project. Goals are established to keep everyone on track and ensure that the efforts pay off in the end. A simple outline of how goals are accomplished is depicted in Figure 9-6.

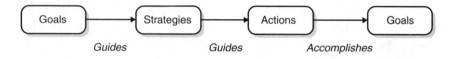

Figure 9-6 Goals, strategies, and actions have an integrated relationship.

Great, we have established that goals are important. But the goal could be, "Keep the company in business if an earthquake hits." Good goal, but not a useful goal though. To be useful, a goal must contain certain key information such as the following:

- **Responsibility**   Each individual involved with business contingency should have his responsibilities spelled out in writing to ensure a clear understanding in a chaotic situation. All tasks should be divided and assigned to the most logical individuals. However, these individuals must know what is expected of them, which is done through training, drills, communication, and documentation. So instead of just running out of the building screaming, an individual knows she is responsible for shutting down the servers before she can run out the building screaming.

- **Authority**   In times of crisis, it is important to know who is in charge. Teamwork is important in these situations and almost every team does much better with an established and trusted leader. These people must know they will be expected to step up to the plate and understand what type of direction they should be providing to the rest of the employees. Clear-cut authority will aid in reducing confusion and increasing cooperation.

- **Priorities**   It is extremely important to know what is critical versus nice to have. Different departments provide different functionality for an organization. The critical departments must be singled out versus the departments that provide functionality that the company can live without for a week or two. It is necessary to know which department must come online first, which second, and so on. This way, the efforts are used in the most useful, effective, and focused manner. Along with the priorities of departments, the priorities of systems, information, and programs must be established. It may be more necessary to ensure that the database is up and running before working to bring the file server online. The general priorities must be set by the management with the help of the different departments and IT staff.

- **Implementation and testing**   It is great to write down very profound ideas and developed plans, but unless they are actually implemented, carried out, and tested, they may not add up to a hill of beans. Once a disaster recovery plan and contingency plan is developed, it actually has to be put into action. It needs to be documented and put in places that are easily accessible in times of crisis, the people that are assigned specific tasks need to be taught and informed, and actual dry runs need to be done to walk people through different situations. The drills should take place at least once a year and the entire program should be continually updated and improved.

Studies have shown that 65 percent of businesses that lose computing capabilities for over one week are never able to recover and go out of business. Not being able to bounce back quickly or effectively by setting up shop somewhere else can make a company lose business, and more importantly, its reputation. In such a competitive world, customers can have a lot of options; if one company was not prepared to bounce back afer a disruption or disaster, they may go to another vendor and stay there.

very important (handwritten margin note)

Developing the Team

Once it is decided that a contingency plan is needed, senior management must appoint specific people to perform the necessary tasks. Knowing these tasks will help management ensure that they appoint the right people to the team.

The team must then work with the management staff to develop the ultimate goals of the plan, identify the critical parts of the business that must be dealt with first during a disaster, and the priorities of departments and tasks. Once these directives are handed down from management, the team now has goals, objectives, and priorities with which to shape the program. The team must focus on each threat and how that threat can affect the issues deemed most important by management. They develop procedures and tasks that must be performed in each situation and assign responsibility to different employees in charge of the different tasks. The more time given to this step in the process will result in a more useful, effective, and complete plan.

The team may need to contact outside vendors to establish off-site solutions, redundant communication methods, data backup services, and redundant hardware. All agreements must be documented and outlined so that there is less confusion in the time of crisis.

It is important that the team is made up of people who are either familiar with each and every department within the company, or is made up of representatives from each department. This is because each department is unique in its functionality and has unique risks and threats. The best plan is when all issues and threats are brought to the table and discussed; this cannot be done effectively with a few people who are only familiar with a couple of departments. It is important that representatives from each

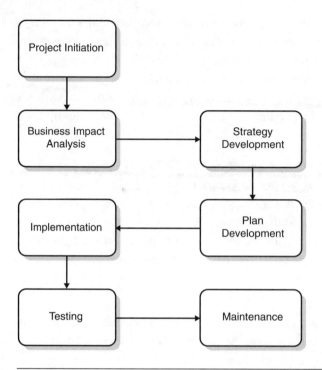

Figure 9-7 The phases of a disaster recovery and continuity plan

department are involved with not only the planning stages, but also the testing and implementation stages.

Disaster recovery and business continuity planning have different phases of development, shown in Figure 9-7. We have only addressed a few of these phases so far (the rest will be addressed throughout this chapter), however, it is important to see the phases together as one complete program.

Advanced planning for emergencies covers issues that were thought of and foreseen. Many other problems may arise that are not covered in the plan; thus flexibility in the plan is crucial. The plan is a systematic way of providing a checklist of actions that should take place right after a disaster. These actions have been thought through in advance to help the people involved be more efficient and effective in dealing with traumatic situations.

Enterprisewide

The main goal of disaster recovery and business continuity is to resume business as quickly as possible spending the least amount of money. The main plan must be enter-

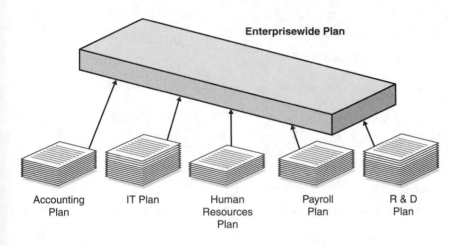

Enterprisewide Plan

Accounting Plan — IT Plan — Human Resources Plan — Payroll Plan — R & D Plan

Figure 9-8   Each department should have its own disaster recovery plan, which is integrated into the enterprise plan.

prisewide. In large corporations, individual departments should have their own disaster recovery and continuity plans because it would be hard to create one large plan that would provide enough granularity to be useful to each and every department. So each department may need to develop its own plan, which is then integrated with other department's plans into the overall recovery plan for the company, as shown in Figure 9-8.

The overall business interruption and resumption plan should cover all organizational elements, identify critical services and functions, provide alternatives for emergency operations, and integrate each departmental plan. This can be accomplished by in-house appointed employees, outside consultants, or a combination of both. A combination can bring many benefits to the company because the consultants are experts in this field and know the necessary steps, questions to ask, issues to look out for, and general reasonable advice, whereas the in-house employees know their company intimately and have a full understanding of how certain threats can affect operations. It is good to cover all the necessary ground, and many times a combination of consultants and employees provides just the right recipe.

Up until now, we have established the management's responsibilities as the following:

- Full commitment
- Policy and goal setting
- Making available the necessary funds and resources

- Taking responsibility for the outcome of the development of the disaster recovery and business continuity plan

- Appointing a team for the process

The team's responsibilities are as follows:

- Identifying regulatory and legal requirements that must be met

- Identifying all possible threats and risks

- Estimating the possibilities of these threats and the loss potential

- Performing a BIA

- Outlining which departments, systems, and processes must be up and running before any others

- Developing procedures and steps in resuming business after a disaster

- Assigning tasks to individuals that they would perform during a crisis situation

- Documenting, communicating to employees, and performing training and drills

There are several software tools developed for developing disaster recovery and contingency plans, which simplify the process. Automation of these procedures can quicken the pace of the project, and many of the necessary items are provided on the boilerplate templates.

Plan Development

The plan should address all sections described in the previous sections in detail. The actual format of the plan will depend on the environment, goals of the plan, priorities, and identified risks. After each of those items are examined and documented, the following part of the plan can be divided into four categories: end-user environment, backup alternatives, recovery, and restoration. There may be more sections depending on the company and its needs. It also will depend upon the identified disaster effects. One type of disaster could require that only the data center be relocated to a different site, another disaster could require a majority of the users to be relocated, or a disruption of communication could require an alternate communication method be implemented.

Reasons Plans Become Outdated

- Infrastructure and environment changes.
- Reorganization of company, layoffs, and merges.
- Change in hardware, software, and applications.
- After plan is constructed, people feel their job is done.
- Personnel turnover.
- Large plans can take a lot of work to maintain.
- Does not have a direct line to profitability.

Ways to Keep the Plan Updated

- Make disaster recovery and business continuity a part of every business decision.
- Insert the maintenance responsibilities into job descriptions.
- Include maintenance in personnel evaluations.
- Perform internal audits that include disaster recovery and continuity documentation and procedures.
- Perform regular drills that use the plan.

There is a general six-step approach to contingency planning described in the following sections. The goal of each is to avert potential contingencies and disasters or minimize the damage an organization may endure.

References

www.disasterrecoveryworld.com/

www.business-continuity-and-disaster-recovery-world.co.uk/

www.dri.ca/dric_pp3.html

Identifying Business Critical Functions

It is difficult to protect what is most important to a company if it is not first identified. Senior management is usually involved with this step because they have a point of view that extends beyond each function manager's focus area of responsibility. The company's business plan usually defines the company's critical mission and business function. The functions must have priorities set upon them to indicate which is most crucial to a company's survival.

Identifying the Resources and Systems That Support the Critical Functions

After identifying the critical functions, it is necessary to find out exactly what is required for these functions to take place. These are not necessarily just computer systems, but personnel, procedures, tasks, supplies, and vendor support. It needs to be understood that if one or more of these support mechanisms is not available, the critical function may be doomed. The team must determine what type of effect unavailable resources and systems will have on these critical functions.

An analysis of these resources should be done by people who understand them and how they provide functionality to the company. These are the people that would mostly understand the interdependencies between the different resources and the true effects of their absence.

Estimating Potential Disasters

This step can be challenging in identifying all possible contingencies and disasters. This is one reason why outside consultants can be beneficial: They may be able to think of issues the team cannot. Scenarios are usually used to step through specific threats to estimate all possible risks in each and every threat type.

Selecting Planning Strategies

This step includes developing plans on how to recover the critical resources and evaluate alternatives. A disaster recovery and contingency plan usually consists of emergency response, recovery, and resumption activities. Emergency response deals with protecting lives and limiting further damages. Recovery encompasses the steps necessary to get the critical functions back online and resumption is the acts taken to return the company back to original operations.

The strategy is based on logical, feasible, and cost-effective measures. Decisions need to be made pertaining to certain sacrifices that might have to be made in order to recover the critical functions.

Implementing Strategies

Once the strategies have been decided upon, they need to be documented and put into place. This moves the efforts from a purely planning stage to an actual implementation and action phase.

Testing and Revising the Plan

The disaster recovery and continuity plan should be tested periodically because an environment continually changes and each time it is tested, more improvements may be uncovered. The responsibility of periodic tests and maintaining the plan should be assigned to a specific person or persons.

The plan's maintenance can be incorporated into change management procedures so that any changes in the environment will be sure to be reflected in the plan itself.

References

www.drj.com/new2dr/model/bcmodel.htm

www.so.cc.va.us/its/models/secpl.htm

albany.bcentral.com/albany/stories/1999/05 /24/focus5.html

End-User Environment

Because the end-users are usually the worker bees of a company, it is important that they are provided a functioning environment as soon as possible after a disaster hits. This means the current functioning environment needs to be understood and critical pieces examined so they can be replicated.

The first issue pertaining to users is how they will be notified of the disaster and who will tell them where to go and when. A tree structure of managers can be developed so that once a disaster hits, the person at the top of the tree calls two managers, and they in turn call three managers, and so on until all managers are notified. Each manager would be responsible for notifying the people he is responsible for until everyone is on the same page. Then, one or two people must be in charge of coordinating the issues pertaining to users. This could mean directing them to a new facility, making sure they have the necessary resources to complete their tasks, restoring data, and being a liaison between the different groups.

The user environment must be understood, which means the planners have to know issues like if the users can work on stand-alone PCs or if they have to be connected in a network to fulfill specific tasks. For example, in a financial institution, users who work on stand-alone PCs might be able to accomplish some small tasks like filling out account forms, word processing, and accounting tasks, but would need to be connected to a host system to update customer profiles and to interact with the database.

Also, some or all data from user machines may be backed up and kept off-site. The planners must be aware of this fact and provide procedures for retrieving the data and installing it after a disruption or disaster. If the users' systems were destroyed, do they need to be replaced with the exact same hardware or similar hardware? If backups are done on images, then the exact same hardware may be required, but if the backup only contains files, then other hardware may suffice.

Backup Alternatives

Backup alternatives can come in the form of hardware, data, personnel, and off-site facilities. It is up to each company and its continuity team to decide if all of these components are necessary for its survival. The following sections explain how these backup alternatives can be initiated.

Hardware Backup

Backup for physical equipment is an important element in contingency plans because companies are so dependent upon it. The hardware backup procedures should address on-site and off-site strategies. Because most disruptions or disasters are small in nature, localized single pieces of hardware should be able to be quickly and easily replaced. A company can choose to have redundant devices so that an extra device can be quickly exchanged, but this approach is usually too expensive for most companies. The next step is to have a service agreement with a vendor so that the device would be repaired within a number or hours or days, or a replacement would be shipped in a reasonable amount of time.

There are three main categories of disruptions; they are usually classified as nondisasters, disasters, and catastrophes. A *nondisaster* is a disruption in service as a result from a device malfunction. The solution could include hardware, software, or file restoration. A *disaster* is an event that causes the entire facility to be unusable for a day or longer. This usually requires the use of an alternate processing facility and restoration of software and data from off-site copies. The alternate site must be available to the company until their main facility is repaired and usable. A *catastrophe* is a major disruption that destroys the facility altogether. This requires a short-term solution, which would be an off-site facility and a long-term solution, which may require rebuilding the original facility.

Disasters and catastrophes are rare compared to nondisasters, thank goodness. Nondisasters can usually be taken care of by replacing a device or restoring files from on-site backups. On-site backup requirements need to be thought out and decisions should be made with good judgment. It might make sense for a company to have an on-site backup of the server that processes all of their important transactions and customer purchases, but not so smart to have a backup of the file server that is hardly used. The critical equipment needs to be identified and their mean time between failure (MTBF) and mean time to repair (MTTR) should be estimated to provide the necessary statistics of when a device may be meeting its maker and a new device may be required.

For the larger disasters that negatively affect the primary facility, an off-site backup facility must be accessible. Companies can choose from three main types:

- **Hot site**   This is a facility that is fully configured and would be ready to operate within a few hours. The equipment and system software must be compatible with the data being backed up from the main site and cause no negative interoperability issues. These sites are a good choice for a company that needs to ensure that a site will be available to them as soon as possible and will be used only by them; thus, the company has exclusive rights of the facility. A hot site can support a short- or long-term outage and is flexible in its configuration and options. Most hot site facilities support annual tests that can be done by the company to ensure the site is functioning in the necessary state. This is the most expensive of the three types of off-site facilities and can have problems if a company requires proprietary or unusual hardware or software.

- **Warm site**   These facilities are usually partially configured with some equipment, but not the actual computers. Filling a facility with duplicate hardware and computers configured for immediate operation is extremely expensive, so a warm site provides the facility and some peripheral devices. This is the most widely used model. It is less expensive than a hot site; it usually has availability that is ensured for a longer period of time and can promise exclusive use. It may be a better choice for companies that depend upon proprietary and unusual hardware and software, because they will be bringing their own hardware and software with them to the site after the disaster hits. However, the annual testing available with hot site contracts are not usually available with warm site facilities and a company can not be sure that they will be back to operations within hours.

- **Cold site** These facilities do supply the basic environment, electrical wiring, air conditioning, plumbing, and flooring, but it may take weeks to get the site activated and ready for work. The cold site can receive equipment, but does not provide any. The cold site is the least expensive option, but will take the most time and effort to actually get up and functioning right after a disaster.

A company would choose a hot site only if downtime cost them a major amount of money and they needed to have operations back in place within hours. The company must also be able to afford to keep a hot site fully loaded with redundant systems and devices. Commercial companies that specialize in subscription service provide these facilities. The cost for the use of a commercial hot site usually includes a basic subscription cost, an activation cost when the site is actually used, and an hourly or daily use charge. Hot sites are usually used for short-term solutions because of the added expenses to regular operational cost.

Most companies use warm sites, which have some devices like disk drives, tape drives, and controllers, but nothing else. These companies usually cannot afford a hot site, and the extra downtime would not be detrimental. A warm site can provide a longer-term solution than a hot site. The companies that decided to go with a cold site must be able to be out of operation for a week or two. The cold site usually includes power, raised flooring climate control, and wiring.

The following provides a quick overview of the differences between the different off-site facilities:

- **Hot Site Advantages**
  - Ready within hours for operations
  - Highly available
  - Usually used for short-term solutions, but available for longer stays
  - Flexible configurations
  - Annual testing available
  - Exclusive use

- **Hot Site Disadvantages**
  - Very expensive
  - Limited on hardware and software choices

- **Warm and Cold Site Advantages**
  - Less expensive
  - Usually exclusive use

- Availability for longer timeframes because of the reduced costs

- Practical for proprietary hardware or software use

• **Warm and Cold Site Disadvantages**

- Not immediately available

- Operational testing not usually available

- Resources for operations not immediately available

If backup tapes or other media are kept at hot sites, then they should be tested periodically on the equipment kept at the hot site to make sure the media is readable by those systems. If backup tapes or media are kept at warm sites, then the tapes should be brought to the original site and tested on those systems. The reason for the difference is that when a company uses a hot site, it will be depending on the systems kept there all the time; therefore, the media needs to be readable by those systems. If a company is depending on a warm site, they will most likely be bringing their original equipment with them, so the media needs to be able to be read by the original systems.

 NOTE   When choosing a facility, it should be far enough away from the original site so that it will not be affected by a disaster that the original site was affected by. In other words, it is not logical to have the backup site only a few miles away if the company is concerned about tornado damage because the backup site could also be affected or destroyed.

Another approach to alternate off-site facilities is establishing a *reciprocal agreement* with another company. This means that Company A agrees to allow Company B to use its facilities if Company B is hit with a disaster. This is a cheaper way to go than the other off-site choices, but it is not necessarily a good choice. Most environments are maxed out pertaining to the use of facility space, resources, and computing capability. To allow another company to come in and work out of the same shop could prove to be detrimental to both companies. The stress of two companies working in the same environment could cause tremendous levels of stress, comically shown in Figure 9-9. If it did work out, it would only provide a short-term solution; configuration management could be a nightmare, and the mixing of operations could introduce many security issues.

Reciprocal agreements are at best a secondary option for disaster protection. The agreements are not enforceable, so there is no guarantee that this facility will really be available to the company in a time of need. However, many companies do opt for this solution because of the low cost and in some cases, it may be the only viable solution.

Figure 9-9 A reciprocal agreement can result in stress and conflicts not previously imagined.

There are important issues that need to be addressed before a disaster hits if a company decides to participate in a reciprocal agreement with another company:

- How long will the facility be available to the company in need?
- How much assistance will the staff supply in the means of integrating the two environments and ongoing support?
- How quickly can the company in need move into the facility?
- What are the issues pertaining to interoperability?
- How many of the resources will be available to the company in need?
- How will differences and conflicts be addressed?
- How does change control and configuration management take place?
- How often can drills and testing take place?

Some companies choose to have **redundant sites,** meaning one site is equipped and configured exactly like the primary site, which serves as a partial redundancy environment.

The other types of facility backups include *rolling hot sites*, where the back of a large truck or trailer is turned into a data processing or working area. The trailer can be brought to the company's parking lot or another location. Another solution is prefabricated buildings that can be easily and quickly put together.

It is best if a company is aware of all available options for hardware and facility backups so that they can have many options to make the best decision for themselves.

Software Backup

Hardware is usually not worth much to a company without the software required to run on it. The software that needs to be backed up can be in the form of applications, files, utilities, databases, and operating systems. The contingency plan must have provisions to back up and protect these items along with hardware and facilities.

Software usually changes more often than hardware, so backing up procedures must happen on a continual basis. It is important to have a process that backs up software for the company that makes sense. If data in the files change several times a day, then backup procedures should happen a couple times a day or nightly to ensure that all the changes are captured and kept. If data is changed once a month, backing up software every night is a waste of time and resources. It is usually desirable to back up a file and its corresponding changes instead of having multiple copies of that one file. Online files usually have the changes to a file made to a transaction log, which is separate from the original file.

Important data should be backed up to an on-site area and an off-site area. The on-site backup copies are easily accessible in the case of nondisasters and provide a quick restore process so operations can return to normal. However, on-site backup copies are not enough to provide real security. The software should also be held in an off-site facility in case of actual disasters. One choice that needs to be made is where the off-site location should be located in reference to the main facility. The closer the off-site backup storage site is, the easier it is to access, but this can put the backup copies in danger if a disaster took out the company's main facility and backup facility. It may be wiser to choose a backup facility farther away, which makes accessibility harder. Some companies choose to have more than one backup facility: one that is close and one that is farther away.

The on-site backup information should be stored in a fire-resistant safe. The procedures for backing up and restoring data should be easily accessible and comprehendible. In an emergency situation, the same guy who always does the backing up and restoring may not be around, so this information should be readily available to others.

Master files should be updated at sensible intervals and transaction files should be preserved to coincide with those master files. This enables a prior generation master file to be easily brought up-to-date to recreate the current master file that represents all of the new data. Backup strategy must take into account that failure can take place at any step of the process, so if there is a problem during the backing up or restoring process that could corrupt the data, there should be a graceful way of backing out or reconstructing the data from the beginning.

Databases require specialized backup operations and this is why backup operations are usually integrated into the database management software as a feature. Databases can be configured to use *disk-shadowing*, or data-mirroring technologies. A disk-shadowing subsystem uses two physical disks and the data is written to both at the same time for redundancy purposes. This subsystem performs data-mirroring functionality. If one disk fails, the other is readily available. This is different than *disk duplexing*, which has more than one disk controller. If one disk controller fails, the other is ready and available.

File descriptions need to be maintained along with separate data dictionaries. Each of these needs to coincide with the file version, so the backing up procedures should happen in a predictable way each time and in concert. Databases have functionality that enables them to be restored and have roll forward processes. *(Database concepts and issues are addressed in Chapter 11.)*

Different Backup Types

- **Incremental backup**   A procedure that backs up only those files that have been modified since the pervious backup of any sort. It does remove the archive attribute.

- **Differential backup**   A procedure that backs up all files that have been modified since the last full backup. It does not remove the archive attribute.

- **Full backup**   A procedure that backs up all files, modified or not, and removes the archive attribute.

Incremental backups finish more quickly than differential backups, but they take longer to restore because each incremental backup has to be restored since the last full backup.

Manually backing up systems and data can be time consuming, error prone, and costly. There are several technologies that serve as automated backup alternatives. These are usually more expensive, but are quicker and more accurate, which may be necessary for online information that changes often. *Electronic vaulting* makes an immediate copy of a changed file or transaction and sends it to a remote location where the original backup is stored. The information can be stored in an off-site facility and retrieved from that facility in a short period of time. This takes place in many financial institutions, so when a bank teller accepts a deposit or withdrawal, the change to the customer's account is made locally to that branch and to the remote site that maintains the backup copies of all customer records. Another technology used for automated backups is *hierarchical storage management* (HSM). In this situation, the HSM system dynamically manages the storage and recovery of files, which are copied to storage media devices that vary in speed and cost. The faster media holds the data that is accessed more often and the seldom-used files are stored on the slower devices, or *near-line* devices. The different storage media range from optical disks, magnetic disks, and tapes. This functionality happens in the background without the knowledge of the user or need for user intervention.

Electronic vaulting is a method of transferring bulk information to off-site facilities for backup purposes. *Remote journaling* is another method of transmitting data off-site, but this usually only includes moving the journal or transaction logs to the off-site facility, not the actual files.

It may be necessary to keep different versions of software and files, especially in a software development environment. The object and source code should be backed up along with libraries, patches, and fixes. The off-site facility should mirror the on-site facility, meaning it does not make sense to keep all of this data at the on-site facility and only the source code at the off-site facility. Each site should have a full set of the most current and updated information and files.

Choosing a Software Backup Facility

There are several issues that need to be addressed and questions that need to be asked when a company is deciding upon a storage facility for its backup materials. The following provides a list of just some of the issues that need to be thought through before committing to a specific facility:

- Can the records or redundant hardware be accessed in the necessary timeframe?
- Is the facility closed on weekends, holidays, and does it only operate during specific hours of the day?
- Are the access control mechanisms tied to an alarm or the police station?
- Is the facility fire resistant in its construction?

- What is the physical layout of the facility?
- Will the physical layout provide any obstacles in its use?
- Does the facility have the capability to properly store the media that the company's backups are stored on?
- What is the availability of a bonded transport service?
- Are there any geographical environmental hazards such as floods, earthquakes, tornados, and so on?
- Is there a fire detection and suppression system?
- Does the facility provide temperature and humidity monitoring and control?

The questions and issues that need to be addressed will vary depending on the type of company, its needs, and the requirements of a backup facility.

Documentation

Documentation seems to be a dreaded task to most people, and many people will find many other tasks to take on to ensure that they are not the ones stuck with document-ing processes and procedures. However, a company can do a great and responsible job of backing up hardware and software to an off-site facility, maintaining it, keeping everything up-to-date and current, and when a disaster hits, no one knows how to put Humpty-Dumpy back together again.

Restoration of files can be challenging, but restoring a whole environment that was swept away in a tornado can be overwhelming if not impossible. Procedures need to be documented because when they are actually needed, it will most likely be a chaotic and frantic time with a demanding time schedule. The documentation may need to include how to install images, configure operating systems and servers, and properly install util-ities and proprietary software.

Most environments have evolved over time, software has been installed on top of other software, configurations have been altered over the years to properly work in a unique environment, and service packs and patches have been installed to fix this prob-lem or that issue. To expect one person or a group of people to go through all of these steps and end up with an environment exactly like the original environment that works together seamlessly, may be a lofty dream.

So the dreaded task of documentation may be the saving grace one day. It is an essen-tial piece of business, and therefore an essential piece in disaster recovery and business continuity.

Recovery and Restoration

A restoration team should be identified and trained in their tasks. There can be one team that has the responsibility of getting the alternate site into a working and functioning environment and another team to start the recovery of the original site. Depending on the company's size and needs, this can consist of either two different teams, or one team that takes care of the alternate site and then addresses the needs of the original site.

The team must know how to do many tasks, such as how to install operating systems, configure workstations and servers, string wire and cabling, set up the network and configure networking services, and install equipment and applications. The team must also know the proper steps of restoring data from backup facilities, which can be harder than it sounds.

A company is not out of an emergency state until it is back in operations at the original primary site. There are many logistic issues to consider when a company must return from the alternate site to the original site. The least critical work should be moved back first, so if there are issues in procedures, connectivity that does not perform, or important steps not addressed, the critical operations of the company are not negatively affected.

Testing and Drills

Tests and disaster recovery drills should be performed at least once a year. A company should have no real confidence in a developed plan until it has actually been tested. The tests and drills prepare personnel for what they may be faced with and enable them to learn the tasks expected of them. These tests and drills also point out issues to the planning team and management that were not previously thought about and addressed. The tests and drills will demonstrate if a company can actually recover after a disaster.

The test should have a predetermined scenario that the company may indeed be faced with one day. Specific parameters and a scope of the test must be worked out before sounding the alarms. The team of testers must agree upon what exactly is getting tested and how to properly determine success or failure. The timing and duration of the test, who will participate in the test, who will receive which assignments, and what steps should be taken, must be agreed upon. Also, it needs to be determined if hardware, software, personnel, procedures, and communication lines are going to be tested, and whether it is some, all, or a subset combination. If the test will include moving some equipment to an alternate site, then transportation, extra equipment, and alternate site readiness must be addressed.

Most companies cannot afford for these tests to interrupt production or productivity, so the tests may need to take place in sections, which will require logistics planning. Written test plans should be developed that will test for specific weaknesses in the overall disaster recovery plan. The first test should not include all 3,500 employees, but a small group of people here and there until each learns his or her responsibilities. Then larger drills can take place so that overall operations will not be negatively affected. The people carrying out these drills should expect problems and mistakes; this is why they are having the drills in the first place. A company would want employees to make mistakes during a drill so that they can learn from them and perform more effectively during a real disaster.

There are a few different types of drills and tests that can take place, each with its own pros and cons. The following sections explain the different types of drills.

Checklist Test

In this type of test, copies of the disaster recovery and business continuity plan are distributed to the different departments and functional areas for review. This is done so that each functional manager or team can review the plan and indicate if anything has been left out or if some approaches should be modified or deleted. This is a method that ensures that some things have not been taken for granted or omitted. Once the departments have reviewed their copy and made suggestions, the planning team then integrates those changes into the master plan.

Structured Walk-Through Test

In this test, representatives from each department or functional area come together to go over the plan to ensure its accuracy. The group will go over the objectives of the plan, discuss the scope and assumptions of the plan, review the organization and reporting structure, and evaluate the testing, maintenance, and training requirements described. This gives the people who will be responsible for making sure that a disaster recovery happens effectively and efficiently a chance to review what has been decided upon and what is expected of them.

The group will walk through different scenarios of the plan from beginning to end to make sure nothing was left out and to raise the awareness of the recovery team members, as shown in 9-10.

Figure 9-10 A structured walk-through test is where representatives from different departments come together and go through the plan step by step.

Simulation Test

This type of test takes a lot more planning and people. In this situation, all employees who participate in operational and support functions, or their representatives, come together to practice executing the disaster recovery plan based on a specific scenario. The scenario is used to test the reaction of each operational and support representative. Again, this is done to ensure that specific steps were not left out, certain threats were not thought of, and will act as a catalyst to raise the awareness of the people involved.

The drill will have only those materials that will be available in an actual disaster to portray a more realistic environment. The simulation test continues up to the point of actual relocation to an on-site facility and actual shipment of replacement equipment.

Parallel Test

A parallel test is done to ensure that the critical systems can actually perform adequately at the alternate off-site facility. The systems are moved to the alternate site and processing takes place. The results are compared with the regular processing that is done at the original site. This points out any necessary tweaking, reconfiguring, or steps that need to take place.

Full-Interruption Test

This type of test is the most intrusive to regular operations and business productivity. The original site is actually shut down and processing takes place at the alternate site. The recovery team fulfills their obligations in preparing the systems and environment for the alternate site. All processing will be done only on devices at the alternate off-site facility.

This is a full-blown drill that takes a lot of planning and coordination, but can find a lot of holes in the plan that need to be fixed before an actual disaster hits.

The type of organization will dictate what type of training approach is most effective. Each organization can have a different approach and unique aspects. If detailed planning methods and processes are going to be taught, then specific training may be required, rather than general training that provides an overview. Higher quality training will result in an increase of interest and commitment.

During and after each type of test, a record of the significant events should be recorded and reported to management so that they are aware of the outcome of the test.

Other Types of Training

There are other issues employees need to be trained on besides disaster recovery drills. These include first aid and CPR, how to properly use a fire extinguisher, evacuation routes and methods, emergency communication procedures, and how to properly shut down equipment in different types of disasters.

For the more technical employees, they may need to know how to redistribute network resources and use different telecommunication lines if the main one goes down. Redundant power supply needs to be investigated and the procedures of how to move critical systems from one power supply to the next should be understood and tested.

Emergency Response

Many times how an emergency is initially responded to can affect the ultimate outcome. Emergency response procedures are the prepared actions that are developed to help people in a crisis situation better cope with the disruption. They are the first line of defense when dealing with a crisis situation.

People who are familiar and up-to-date on their knowledge pertaining to disaster recovery will perform the best and this is why training and drills are very important. Emergencies are unpredictable so no one really knows when they will be called to to perform.

Protection of life is of the utmost importance and should be dealt with first before looking to save material objects. Training and drills should show the people with the responsibility of authority how to evacuate personnel and all personnel should know their designated emergency exists and destinations. Many times one person in each designated group is responsible for making sure that all people are accounted for. One person in particular should be responsible for notifying the appropriate authorities: the police department, security guards, fire department, emergency rescue, and management. With proper training, employees will be better equipped with handling emergencies rather than just running to the exit as shown in Figure 9-11.

If the situation is not life threatening, then systems should be shut down in an orderly fashion and critical data files or resources should be removed during evacuation. The documented disaster recovery and continuity plans should be found and the necessary activities carried out.

Once things have approached a reasonable plateau of activity, one or more people will most likely be required to interface with external entities. These entities can be the press, customers, shareholders, and civic officials. One or more people should be prepped in their reaction and response to the recent disaster so that a uniform and reasonable reaction is given to explain the circumstances, how the company is dealing with the disaster, and what customers and others should now expect from the company. The company should quickly present this information instead of having others come to their own conclusions and start false rumors. At least one person should be available to the press to ensure that proper messages are being reported and sent out.

Figure 9-11 Untrained employees may forget all responsibilities and head for the door during an emergency.

Figure 9-12 In emergency situations, security needs to be strictly enforced so that others do not take advantage of the situation.

Another unfortunate issue needs to be addressed prior to an emergency and that is looting, vandalism, and fraud opportunities. After a company is hit with a large disturbance or disaster is usually when it is most vulnerable and others may take advantage of this, as shown in Figure 9-12. It needs to be thought through how these issues will be dealt with so the necessary and expected level of protection is provided at all times.

References

dmoz.org/Business/Industries/Security/Emergency_Management/

www.businesscontinuityworld.com/toolkit.htm

www.utoronto.ca/security/drp.htm

Summary

Although disaster recovery and business continuity is usually pushed to the back of the bus in most organizations today, this in no way means that it is not important and crucial. Unfortunately, many companies have to experience the pain to understand how they could have circumvented or mitigated the events that caused the pain to occur.

To develop and carry out disaster recover and business continuity efforts successfully, plenty of thought, planning, time, and effort must go into the different phases of this activity. The real threats must be identified and understood, reasonable countermeasures put into place, and detailed plans put into place for the unfortunate day that they are needed.

Quick Tips

- A recovery plan is created in advance to minimize loss and ensure availability of critical systems.

- A business continuity plan ensures continuity of critical business functions and provides rapid recovery to reduce the overall impact of a disaster or disruption.

- A disaster recovery plan provides procedures for emergency responses, extended backup operations, and postdisaster recovery.

- There should be an enterprisewide plan and each individual organizational unit should also have its own disaster recovery plans.

- The executive management should support and perform the final approval of the plan. Senior management should identify and prioritize the critical missions of the company.

- Executives may be held liable if a proper disaster recovery and business contingency plan is not developed and used.

- Threats can be natural, man-made, or technical.

- Disaster recovery planning involves identifying critical resources, identifying potential threats and possible damages, and developing plans to respond to those threats.

- The steps of recovery planning include initiating the project, performing business impact analysis, developing recovery strategy, developing a recovery plan, implementing, testing, and maintaining.

- The project initiation phase involves getting management support, developing the scope of the plan, securing funding, and identifying disaster scenario assumptions.

- The business impact analysis is one of the most important first steps in the planning development. Qualitative and quantitative data needs to be gathered, analyzed, interpreted, and presented to management.

- Executive commitment and support is the most critical element in developing the disaster recovery and business continuity plan.

- A business need must be made to gain executive support by explaining regulatory and legal requirements, vulnerabilities, accompanied with recommendations.

- Plans should be prepared by the people who will actually carry them out.

- The planning group should be made up of representatives from all departments or organizational units.

- The plan should include individuals who will interact with external entities like the press, shareholders, customers, and civic officials. Response to the disaster should be given quickly, honestly, and should be uniform with any other employee response.

- Disaster recovery planning should be brought into normal business decision-making procedures.

- The loss criteria for disasters is much more than direct dollar loss. It can be added operational costs, loss in reputation and public confidence, loss of competitive advantage, violation of regulatory or legal requirements, loss in productivity, delayed income interest costs, and loss in revenue.

- A survey should be developed and given to the most knowledgeable people within the company to obtain the most realistic information pertaining to a company's risk and recovery procedures.

- The plan's scope can be determined by geographical, organizational, or functional means.

- Many things need to be understood pertaining to the working environment so that it can be replicated at an alternate site after a disaster.

- Subscription services can supply hot, warm, or cold sites.

- A reciprocal agreement is when one company promises another company they can "move in" if they experience a disaster. These agreements are hard to enforce and rarely work out. However, they are cheap and sometimes the only choice.

- A hot site is fully configured with hardware, software, and environmental needs. It can usually be up and running in a matter of hours. It is the most expensive option, but some companies cannot be out of business longer than a day without detrimental results.

- A warm site does not have computers, but it does have some peripheral devices like disk drives, controllers, and tape drives. This is less expensive than hot sites, but takes more effort and time to get operational.

- A cold site is just the shell of a building with power, raised floors, and utilities. There are no devices available. This is the cheapest of the three options, but can take weeks to get up and operational.

- Electronic vaulting is the process of backing up bulk data immediately to an off-site facility.

- When returning to the original site, the least critical organizational units should go back first.

- An important part of the disaster recovery and contingency plan is to communicate its requirements and procedures to all employees.

- Testing and drills demonstrate the actual ability to recover and can verify compatibility of backup facilities.

- Before tests are performed, there should be a clear indication of what is being tested, how success will be determined, how written test plans should be developed, and how mistakes should be expected.

- Checklist testing is when copies of the plan are handed out to each functional area to ensure that the plan properly deals with their needs and vulnerabilities.

- A structured walk-through test is when representatives from each functional area or department get together and walk through the plan beginning to end.

- A simulation test is when a practice execution of the plan takes place. A specific scenario is established and the simulation continues up to the point of actual relocation to the alternate site.

- A parallel test is when the critical systems are actually run at the alternate site. The results from this processing are compared to the processing done at the original site.

- A full-interruption test is when regular operations are stopped and processing is moved to the alternate site.

- Remote journaling is transmitting the journal or transaction log off-site to a backup facility.

Questions

Please remember that these questions are formatted and asked in a certain way for a reason. The questions and answers may seem odd or vague, but this is what you will see on the actual CISSP test.

1. What procedures should take place to restore a system and its data files after a system failure?
   a. Restore from storage media backup.
   b. Perform a parallel test.
   c. Implement recovery procedures.
   d. Perform a walk-through test.

2. What is the first step in developing a disaster recovery plan?
   a. Identify all critical systems and functions of the company.
   b. Decide if the company needs to perform a walk-through, parallel, or simulation test.
   c. Perform a business impact analysis.
   d. Interview a representative from each department.

3. How often should a disaster recovery and business continuity plan be tested?
   a. At least every six months
   b. Only when the infrastructure or environment changes
   c. At least every two years
   d. At least every year

4. During a recover procedure, one important step is to maintain records of important events that happen during the procedure. What other step is just as important?
   a. Schedule another test to address issues that took place during that procedure.
   b. Make sure someone is prepared to talk to the media with the appropriate responses.
   c. Report the events to management and the appropriate agencies.
   d. Identify essential business functions.

5. Which of the following issues is least important when quantifying risks associated with a potential disaster?
   a. Information gathered from agencies that report the probability of certain natural disasters taking place in that area
   b. Identifying the company's key functions and business requirements
   c. Identifying critical systems that support the company's operations
   d. Estimation of the potential loss and impact the company would face based on how long the outage lasted

6. The purpose of initiating emergency actions right after a disaster takes place is to prevent loss of life, injures, and _____.
   a. Secure the area to ensure that no looting or fraud takes place.
   b. Mitigate further damage.
   c. Protect evidence and clues.
   d. Investigate the extent of the damages.

7. Which of the following is the best way to ensure that the company's backup tapes are being properly maintained at a warm site?
   a. Retrieve the tapes from the off-site facility and verify that the equipment at the original site can read them.
   b. Ask the off-site vendor to test them and label the ones that were properly read.
   c. Test them on the vendor's machine, which won't be used during an emergency.
   d. Inventory each tape kept at the vendor's site twice a month.

8. Which best describes a hot-site facility versus a warm- or cold-site facility?
   a. A site that has disk drives, controllers, and tap drives
   b. A site that has all necessary PCs, servers, and telecommunications
   c. A site that has wiring, central air, and raised flooring
   d. A site that is mobile that can be brought to the company's parking lot

9. Which is the best description of remote journaling?
   a. Backing up bulk data to an off-site facility
   b. Backing up transaction logs to an off-site facility
   c. Capturing and saving transactions to two mirror servers in house
   d. Capturing and saving transactions to different media types

10. Which of the following is something that should be required of an off-site backup facility that stores backed up media for companies?
    a. The facility should be within 10 to 15 minutes of the original facility to ensure easy access.
    b. The facility should contain all necessary PCs, servers, and raised flooring.
    c. The facility should be protected by an armed guard.
    d. The facility should protected against unauthorized access and entry.

11. Which item will a business impact analysis not identify?
    a. If the company is best suited for a parallel or full-interrupt test
    b. What areas would suffer the greatest operational and financial loss in the event of a particular disaster or disruption
    c. What systems are critical for the company and must be highly protected
    d. What amount of outage time a company can endure before it is permanently crippled

12. Which areas of a company are business plans recommended?
    a. The most important operational and financial areas
    b. The areas that house the critical systems
    c. All areas
    d. The areas that the company cannot survive without

13. What is the difference between disaster recovery and business continuity?
    a. Disaster recovery deals with the actions that need to take place right after a disaster and business continuity deals with the actions that need to take place to keep operations running over a longer period of time.
    b. Business continuity deals with the actions that need to take place right after a disaster and disaster recovery deals with the actions that need to take place to keep operations running over a longer period of time.
    c. They are one in the same.
    d. Disaster recovery deals with operations and business continuity deals with mitigating risks.

14. Who has the final approval of the disaster recovery and business continuity plan?
    a. The planning committee
    b. Each representative of each department
    c. Management
    d. External authority

15. Which are the proper steps of developing a disaster recovery and continuity plan?
    a. Project initiation, strategy development, business impact analysis, plan development, implementation, testing, and maintenance
    b. Strategy development, project initiation, business impact analysis, plan development, implementation, testing, and maintenance
    c. Implementation and testing, project initiation, strategy development, business impact analysis, and plan development
    d. Plan development, project initiation, strategy development, business impact analysis, implementation, testing, and maintenance

16. What is the most crucial piece of developing a disaster recovery plan?
    a. Business impact analysis
    b. Implementation, testing, and following through
    c. Participation from each and every department
    d. Management support

17. During development, testing, and maintenance of the disaster recovery and continuity plan, a high degree of interaction and communication is crucial to the process. Why?
    a. This is a regulatory requirement of the process.
    b. The more people that talk about it and are involved will increase awareness.
    c. This is not crucial to the plan and should not be interactive because it will most likely affect operations.
    d. Management will more likely support it.

18. To get proper management support and approval of the plan, a business case must be made. Which of the following is least important to this business case?
    a. Regulatory and legal requirements
    b. Company vulnerabilities to disasters and disruptions
    c. How other companies are dealing with these issues
    d. The impact the company can endure if a disaster hit

Answers

1. C.	6. B.	11. A.	16. D.
2. C.	7. A.	12. C.	17. B.
3. D.	8. B.	13. A.	18. C.
4. C.	9. B.	14. C.	
5. A.	10. D.	15. A.	

Law, Investigation, and Ethics

10

In this chapter, you will learn about the following items:

- Ethics, pertaining to security professionals and best practices
- Computer crimes and computer laws
- Motivations and profiles of attackers
- Computer crime investigation process and evidence collection
- Incident-handling procedures
- Different types of evidence
- Laws and acts put into effect to fight computer crime

Computer and information crimes can be looked at as the result of the growing trend of society depending upon and improving its use of technology. However, crime has always taken place, with or without a computer. A computer is just another tool and like other tools in the past, it can be used for good or evil.

Fraud, theft, and embezzlement have always been a fact of life, but the computer age has brought on new opportunities for thieves and crooks. A new degree of complexity has been added to accounting, record keeping, communication, funds transfer, and other parts of life. This degree of complexity brings along its own set of vulnerabilities, which many crooks are all too eager to take advantage of.

Companies are being blackmailed by cybercriminals who discover vulnerabilities in their networks. Company trade secrets and confidential information are being stolen when security breaches take place. Online banks are seeing a rise in fraud, and retailers' databases are being attacked and credit card information is being stolen. More and more companies are losing money in profits and productivity because of the rise in denial of service (DoS) attacks.

As e-commerce and online business become a part of today's business world, these types of issues become more important and more dangerous. Hacking and attacks are continually on the rise and companies are well aware of it. The legal system and law enforcement is way behind in their efforts in trying to track down cybercriminals and successfully prosecuting them. New technologies to fight many types of attacks are on their way, but there needs to be proper laws, policies, and methods of actually catching the bad guys and making them pay for the damage they cause. This chapter looks at some of these issues.

Laws, Investigation, and Ethics

Legal issues are very important to companies because a violation in legal commitments can be damaging. A company has many liable, ethical, and legal responsibilities to live up to pertaining to computer fraud. The more knowledge one has about these responsibilities, the easier it is to stay within the proper boundaries.

These issues can fall under laws and regulations, incident handling, privacy protection, computer abuse, control of evidence, and the ethical conduct expected of companies, their management, and employees. This is an interesting time for law and technology because technology is changing at an exponential rate. Laws, the courts, judges, law enforcement, and prosecutors are behind the eight ball because of their lack of skill in the computing world and the complexity of the issues involved. Law enforcement needs to know how to capture a cybercriminal, properly seize and control evidence, and hand it over to the prosecutor and defense teams. Both of these teams must understand what actually took place in a computer crime, how it was carried out, and what legal precedents to use to prove their points. Many times judges and juries are confused by the terms and concepts used in these types of trials, and laws are not written fast enough to properly punish the guilty cybercriminals. Law enforcement, the court system, and the legal community are definitely experiencing growth pains as they are being pulled into the technology of the twenty-first century.

Many companies are doing business across state lines and in different countries. This brings even more challenges when it comes to who has to follow what laws. Different states can interpret the same law differently and some countries do not consider some issues against the law, whereas another country has determined that the same issue demands five years in prison. One of the complexities in these issues is jurisdiction. If Ravi in India steals a bunch of credit cards from an American financial institution and he is caught, a court in America would want to prosecute him—however, his homeland may not see this issue as illegal at all. Although the attackers are not restricted or hampered by country boarders, the laws are in many cases.

Despite all this confusion, there are some clear-cut responsibilities that companies have pertaining to computer security issues and specifics on how companies are expected to prevent, detect, and report crimes.

Ethics

Just because something is not illegal does not make it right.

Ethics are based on many different issues and foundations. They can be relative to different situations and interpreted differently from individual to individual—therefore, they are often a topic of debate. However, some ethics are less controversial than others, and these types of ethics are easier to expect of all people.

(ISC)² requires all certified system security specialists to commit to fully supporting its Code of Ethics. If a CISSP intentionally or knowingly violates this Code of Ethics, he or she can be subject to a peer review panel who will decide if the certification should be relinquished.

The full set of (ISC)² Code of Ethics is listed on their Web site at **www.isc2.org**. The following list is an overview, but each CISSP candidate should read the full version and understand the Code of Ethics before attempting this exam.

Code of Ethics Summary

- Act honestly, justly, responsibly, and legally, and protect society.

- Work diligently and provide competent services and advance the security profession.

- Encourage the growth of research—teach, mentor, and value the certification.

- Discourage unnecessary fear or doubt, and do not consent to bad practices.

- Discourage unsafe practices, and preserve and strengthen the integrity of public infrastructures.

- Observe and abide by all contracts, expressed or implied, and give prudent advice.

- Avoid any conflict of interest, respect the trust that others put in you, and take on only those jobs you are fully qualified to perform.

- Stay current on skills and do not become involved with activities that could injure the reputation of other security professionals.

There is an interesting relationship between law and ethics. Most often, laws are based on ethics and are put in place to ensure that others act in an ethical way.

However, sometimes laws do not apply to everything—that is when ethics should kick in. Some things may not be illegal, but it does not mean they are ethical.

Corporations should have a guide developed on computer and business ethics. They can be part of an employee handbook, used in orientation, posted, and part of training sessions.

There are some common ethical fallacies that are used by many in the computing world. They exist because some people look at issues differently and interpret, or mis-interpret, specific rules and laws that have been put into place. The following shows some examples of these ethical fallacies:

- Hackers only want to learn and improve their skills. Many of them are not making a profit off of their deeds—thus, it should not be illegal or unethical.

- The First Amendment protects and provides the right of U.S. citizens to write viruses.

- Information should be shared freely and openly—thus, sharing confidential information and trade secrets should be legal and ethical.

- Hacking does not actually hurt anyone.

Computer Ethics Institute

The Computer Ethics Institute is a nonprofit organization that works to help advance technology by ethical means. This is "a public-interest alliance of computer scientists and others who are concerned about the impact of computer technology on society," as stated on their Web site at **www.cpsr.org**.

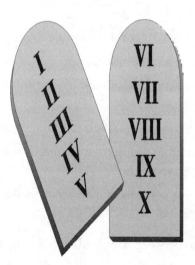

The Computer Ethics Institute has developed its own Computer Ethics.

This institute has developed its own Ten Commandments of Computer Ethics:

1. Thou shall not use a computer to harm people.

2. Thou shall not interfere with other people's computer work.

3. Thou shall not snoop around in other people's computer files.

4. Thou shall not use a computer to steal.

5. Thou shall not use a computer to bear false witness.

6. Thou shall not copy or use proprietary software for which you have not paid.

7. Thou shall not use other people's computer resources without authorization or proper compensation.

8. Thou shall not appropriate other people's intellectual output.

9. Thou shall think about the social consequences of the program you are writing or the system you are designing.

10. Thou shall use a computer in ways that ensure consideration and respect for your fellow humans.

Internet Activities Board

The Internet Activities Board (IAB) is the coordinating committee for Internet design, engineering, and management. It is an independent committee of researchers and professionals with a technical interest in the health and evolution of the Internet. The IAB has two principal subsidiary task forces: the Internet Engineering Task Force (IETF) and the Internet Research Task Force (IRFT).

The IAB considers the Internet as a resource that depends upon the availability and accessibility to be useful to a wide range of people. It is mainly concerned with irresponsible acts on the Internet that could threaten its existence or negatively affect others. It sees the Internet as a great gift and works hard to protect it for all that depend upon it. IAB sees the use of the Internet as a privilege, which should be treated as such and used with respect.

The IAB considers the following acts as unethical and unacceptable behavior:

- Purposely seeking to gain unauthorized access to Internet resources
- Disrupting the intended use of the Internet
- Wasting resources (people, capacity, and computers) through purposeful actions
- Destroying the integrity of computer-based information
- Compromising the privacy of others
- Involving negligence in the conduct of Internet-wide experiments

The IAB vows to work with federal agencies to take whatever actions necessary to protect the Internet. This could be through new technologies, methods, or procedures that are intended to make the Internet more resistant to disruption. There is a balance between protection and reducing functionality. One of the Internet's main purposes is to enable information to flow freely and not be prohibited—thus, the IAB must be logical and flexible in its approaches and the restrictions it attempts to implement. The Internet is everyone's tool—therefore, everyone should work together to protect it.

Generally Accepted System Security Principles (GASSP)

international level

The Generally Accepted System Security Principles (GASSP) Committee seeks to develop and maintain GASSP with guidance from security professionals, IT product developers, information owners, and other organizations having extensive experience in defining and stating the principles of information security.

The committee creates, maintains, and monitors the adherence to the GASSP for information security on an international level. The following lists the committee's objectives:

- Identify and develop pervasive, broadly functional, and detailed GASSP and protection profiles in a comprehensive framework of emergent principles, standards, conventions, and mechanisms that will preserve the availability, confidentiality, and integrity of information.

- Be an authoritative source for opinions, practices, and principles for information owners, information security practitioners, information technology products, and information systems.

- Define, implement, and subsequently operate under the governing GASSP infrastructure.

- Define and establish linkage to the Common Criteria Project.

- Maintain close liaison and coordination with other international authoritative bodies that have developed related works to establish and maintain GASSP based on these efforts.

- Define and establish liaison with bodies responsible for certifying professionals to encourage convergence.

- Promote broad awareness of information security and GASSP.

- Address management, user, and other interested parties' concerns at all levels to gain the broadest acceptance.

It would be great if everyone played by all of the rules that different organizations have laid out. However, we know they do not and in fact, security would not be such an important subject in the computing world if everyone did play by the rules.

Many times when figuring out a computer crime, or any type of crime, one has to understand why crimes are committed and how. To be a good detective, one would need to know how a criminal thinks, what motivates him to do the things he does, what his goals and demons are, and how these are reflected in the crimes the criminal commits. The reason this is important is because this is how the detective gets inside the criminal's mind so that he might be able to predict his next move and understand what circumstances and environments are more prone to fraud and illegal acts. This is true with cybercrime. To properly stop, reduce, or prohibit cybercrime, it is best to know why people do what they do in the first place.

References

www.isc2.org

http://all.net/books/gassp2/

www.iab.org/iab/

http://web.mit.edu/security/www/GASSP/gassp021.html

www.cpsr.org/

Motivations, Opportunities, and Means

MOM did it.

To understand the whys in crime, many times it is necessary to understand the motivations, opportunities, and means—or MOM.

Motivations are the who and why of a crime. These motivations can either be induced by internal or external conditions. A person may be driven by the excitement, challenge, and the adrenaline of committing a crime, which would be an internal condition, or, the person may be in financial trouble, has a sick family member, or is in dire straits. Figuring out the motivation for a crime is an important piece of figuring out who would engage in such an activity. For example, many hackers attack big name sites because when the sites go down, it is splashed in the news. However, once technology advances to where attacks cannot bring down these sites, the individuals will eventually stop initiating these types of attacks because their motivation would have been diminished.

Opportunities are the where and when of a crime. Opportunities usually arise when certain vulnerabilities or weaknesses are present. If a company does not have a firewall, then hackers and attackers have all types of opportunities within that network. If a company does not perform access control, auditing, and supervision, employees can have many opportunities to embezzle funds and fraud the company. Once a crime fighter finds out why a person would want to commit a crime (motivation), he will look at what could allow the criminal to be successful (opportunity).

Means pertains to the capabilities a criminal would need to be successful. Say a crime fighter was asked to investigate a complex embezzlement that took place within a financial institution. If the suspects were three people who knew how to use the mouse, keyboard, and a word processing application, and the other person was a programmer and a system analyst, the crime fighter would see that the last person may have the means to commit this crime much more successfully than the other three individuals.

Hackers and Crackers

A majority of the hackers, sometimes called crackers, are usually curious young males who are interested to see how far their skill will take them, or they are interested in seeing what type of destruction a new tool can cause. They see hacking as a type of intellectual game where only the smartest people actually win. However, it is the definition of winning that can get disturbing. People who write viruses usually do so to see how far the virus can spread and how much damage one small program they wrote can cause, as shown in Figure 10-1. It usually is not an act of vengeance against a particular target, although that does happen.

Some hackers may get a thrill about being able to break into a corporation's network and snoop around. This was Kevin Mitnick's drive. He did not intend to hurt anyone or any company per se—he just wanted to see what he could get away with. It is the thrill of the challenge. Other hackers like to see their acts in headlines and will work to bring down large Web sites like Microsoft, Yahoo!, eBay, and Excite. This gives them self-satisfaction and bragging rights to other hackers.

There is another breed of hackers who are usually more serious in nature, as depicted in Figure 10-2. These hackers usually work in small groups and have goals of stealing funds, credit card information, confidential information, and military secrets. These groups are usually much more organized and driven than the other types of hackers, and are therefore more dangerous. An example of this type of hacker is the group of Ukrainian hackers who stole credit card information from financial institutions in the United States, which affected several thousands of people. This group then threatened

Figure 10-1 A majority of hackers are interested in seeing how far their computer skills will take them in the hacking world.

Figure 10-2 Another type of hacker knows the extent of the damage he can cause and hacks with malicious intent.

the institutions with publishing the credit cards on a public Web site if they were not paid hundreds of thousands of dollars, which was extortion. (This case is discussed further in Chapter 2.) It is similar to the evolution of the bank robber, who enters a bank through the front door with a gun—hackers enter the bank through telephone lines with a set of potentially dangerous tools. Why do people rob banks? That is where the money is.

Therefore, the people who want to be successful in fighting crime over computer wires and airwaves must understand the mentality of the enemy, just like the cops on the street who must understand their type of criminal.

Operations Security

There are several categories of computer crimes that can be committed and different methods of committing those crimes. The following sections go over the more popular types of computer fraud and abuses.

Salami

Salami involves subtracting a small amount of funds from an account with the hope that such an insignificant amount would be unnoticed. An example would be if an employee altered a banking software program to subtract 5 cents from each of its customers' accounts once a month and moved this amount to the employee's bank account. If this happened to all of the bank's 50,000 customer accounts, the intruder could make up to $30,000 a year.

Salami usually takes place in the accounting departments of companies.

Restaurateurs in Quebec used a program called *zapper* that deleted sales records in the point-of-sale terminals, which reduced their reported tax liabilities. This ended up saving them an estimated $940,000, but they were caught and prosecuted.

Data Diddling   — *Very similar to Adams* (handwritten annotation)

Can I just diddle the data a little? Answer: Nope, it's illegal.

Data diddling refers to the alteration of existing data and many times this modification happens before it is entered into an application or as soon as it completes processing and is outputted from an application. For instance, if a loan processor was entering information for a customer's loan of $100,000, but instead entered $150,000 and then moved the extra approved money somewhere else, this would be a case of data diddling. Another example is if a cashier entered an amount of $40 into the cash register, but really charged the customer $60 and kept the extra $20.

There are many reasons to enter false information into a system or application, but the usual reason is to overstate revenue and assets and understate expenses and liabilities. Sometimes managers do this to deceive shareholders, creditors, superiors, and partners.

There was an account in 1997, in Maryland, where a Taco Bell employee was sentenced to ten years in jail because he reprogrammed the drive-up window cash register to ring up every $2.99 order as one penny and he pocketed the other $2.98. He made $3,600 before his arrest.

This type of crime is extremely common and one of the crimes easiest to prevent by using access and accounting controls, supervision, auditing, separation of duties, and authorization limits. This is just one example of how insiders can be more dangerous than outsiders.

Excessive Privileges

This is a common security issue that is extremely hard to control in vast, complex environments. It occurs when a user has more computer rights, permissions, and privileges than what is required for the tasks she needs to fulfill. If a user only needs to be able to read and print materials on the file server, then she should not be granted full control. A common example of this is when a person, let's say, is a manager in accounting and is granted Full Control of all files on a specific server, including payroll information. Now when this person is moved from accounting to the development department, his rights should be revoked or at least reduced, but most companies do not have strict procedures to make sure this happens. Now he has full control over the account records and the development records—thus, he has *excessive privileges*. If he ever became disgruntled for one reason or another, the company could have much more damage to deal with than if they had properly restricted his access.

Password Sniffing

I think I smell a password!

Password sniffing is just what it sounds like—sniffing network traffic in the hopes of capturing passwords being sent between computers. There are several tools available on the Internet that provide this functionality. It is tricky to capture a password because it is a piece of data that is usually only used when a user wants to authenticate into a domain or access a resource. Once the password is caught, it is also tricky to decipher because it is usually encrypted or only the hash value of the password is sent. Some systems and applications do send passwords over the network in clear text, but a majority of them do not anymore. Instead, the user's workstation performs a one-way hashing function on the password and sends only the resulting value to the authenticating system or service. The authenticating system has a file containing all users' password hash values, not the passwords themselves, and when the authenticating system is asked to verify a user's password, it compares the hashing value sent to what it has in its file.

Many of the tools that are used to capture passwords also have the functionality of breaking the encryption of the password. They have several dictionaries of words that are commonly used as passwords and these tools run all of these possibilities against the captured password until a match is found. Some tools are devised to do this against a captured password file also, so after a *dictionary attack* is run on the captured password file, the attacker has many users' passwords on the network.

IP Spoofing

Networks and the Internet are based on IP addresses. Each computer is assigned an IP address so that packets know where they came from and where they are going. However, many attackers do not want anyone to know their real location so they either manually change the IP address within a packet to point to another address, or more likely, they use a tool that is programmed to provide this functionality, which is referred to as *IP spoofing*. Almost all attacks that take place use spoofed IP addresses, which gives the victim little hope of finding the real system and individual who initiated the attack.

One reason that IP spoofing is so easily accomplished is because the protocol of the Internet, IP, was developed in a time when security was rarely considered. At that point in time, the developers were much more focused on functionality and probably could not imagine all the types of attacks that would be carried out using the protocols they developed.

IPv6 and IPv4 using IPSec, described in Chapter 8, can be used to help fight IP spoofing, but for this to be successful, everyone would need to use this technology. Change is hard when it means that thousands or millions of people would need to modify the way they do things.

Denial of Service

Denial of service (DoS) is a general term for many different types of attacks. However, each attack has one thing in common, which is denying others the service that the victim system usually provides.

Most DoS attacks occur over the Internet and are pointed at a company's Web servers, routers, or firewalls. Each of these devices has a finite set of resources and the attacks that are waged on them have the goal of using up these resources so that no resources are left. Once a system has no resources available, they cannot fulfill requests from legitimate systems. An analogy is a bank. If a bank's main purpose is to lend others money and a bank robber takes all the money, then when people request a loan from the bank, the bank no longer has the necessary resources to fulfill its main purpose. (Simplistic example, I know, but I think you get the point.)

Some attackers like to target well-known Web sites like Yahoo!, Microsoft, eBay, and others with DoS attacks because when these sites are brought down, the event will be on the news and in the headlines. This type of attention usually stokes and strokes certain attackers' egos. At the time of this writing, it is estimated that 4,000 DoS attacks happen each and every week.

There are several types of tools available to perform DoS attacks, which makes DoS attacks extremely easy to carry out. Most systems are vulnerable to SYN attacks, Ping of Death, fragment attacks, and distributed denial of service (DDoS) attacks. This is because these attacks are mainly aimed at the use of the protocols within the TCP/IP stack, which almost all computers have to use.

There are not many successful methods of fighting DoS attacks because they come in so many different forms, originate from all over the Internet, and are using fake, or spoofed, addresses. Only recently have service providers and ISPs started looking at new technology and products that will help them stop DoS attacks so that they do not pass through their networks and onto their customers' networks.

Dumpster Diving

Dumpster diving refers to someone rummaging through another person's garbage for discarded documents, information, and other precious items that could then be used against that person or company. The intruder would have to gain physical access to the premises, but the area where the garbage is kept is usually not highly guarded. Dumpster diving is legal, but unethical.

Industrial spies can raid corporate dumpsters to find proprietary and confidential information and credit card thieves can go through dumpsters to retrieve credit card information from thrown away receipts. Phreakers have been known to dumpster dive at telephone companies hoping to find manuals on how the internals of the telephone systems worked. (Phreakers are described in the "Well-Known Computer Crimes" section.)

Most companies do not think about the confidential information that others could be extracting from their garbage.

Emanations Capturing

Emanations and the way that attackers eavesdrop on them is described in Chapter 4 in the "TEMPEST" section. Basically, every electrical device emits electrical waves into the surrounding environment. These waves contain information comparable to how wireless technology works. These waves can be carried over a distance, depending on the strength of the waves and the material and objects in the surrounding area. Attackers have used devices to capture these waves and port them to their own computer systems so that they can have access to information not intended for them.

Attackers need to have specialized tools that tune into the frequency that these waves are carried over. They also have to be within a close proximity of the building that is emitting the waves. Companies having such sensitive information that would cause attackers to go through so much trouble, usually have special computer systems with covering that permits only a small amount of electrical waves to be emitted—one example is TEMPEST. The companies can also use material within the walls of the building to stop these types of electrical waves from bypassing them.

These types of attacks are usually what spy novels are made of, which have three guys parked in a service van in the parking lot of a company that is full of high-grade technological devices. However, a recent trend has caused this type of eavesdropping to happen without such spy-like activities: wireless networks. When a company installs a wireless network, there are certain configurations that can be set to prevent outsiders from being able to eavesdrop on their employees' network traffic. Unfortunately, most companies do not employ these configurations for one reason or another. This enables anyone with a laptop and a wireless network interface card to drive into a company's parking lot and be able to eavesdrop on network traffic. (Wireless technology and its security ramifications are covered in Chapter 7.)

Wiretapping

Most communication signals are vulnerable to some type of *wiretapping* or eavesdropping. It can usually be done undetected and is referred to as a *passive* attack versus an *active* attack. Tools used to intercept communication can be cellular scanners, radio receivers, microphone receivers, tape recorders, network sniffers, and telephone-tapping devices.

It is illegal to intentionally eavesdrop on another person's conversation under the U.S. Federal Wiretap Law. This action is only acceptable if the person consents or there is a court order allowing law enforcement to perform these types of activities. Under these circumstances, the law enforcement officers must have probable cause of criminal activity and can only listen to relevant conversations. These regulations are in place to protect an individual's privacy and Fourth Amendment rights.

Social Engineering

Hi, I am someone else. Now, tell me all your secrets!

Social engineering provides a very important piece in many different types of attacks. It is the art of tricking people and using the information they unknowingly supply in a malicious way. For example, if a technical help-desk employee gets a frantic call from someone who claims to be the vice president of the company claiming that he forgot his password and needs it right now or heads are going to roll, the help-desk employee may quickly hand over this information. If this person was not the vice president, the employee was just a victim of social engineering. If the person was a vice president, he should understand that he is not above the rules of security and should not put the employee in such a tough position.

Social engineering can come in many different forms. Sometimes employees are called by someone claiming to be the network administrator who explains to the employee that there has been some technical difficulties pertaining to many different accounts and to please change her current password to "password". If the employee believes this person and does what was asked of her, an attacker could now know that employee's password and use it for malicious purposes.

Social engineering can be in the form of an e-mail with a source address of someone the victim knows or someone showing up in person spinning a tale for others to believe in the hopes of accessing information not intended for him. One example is a person who shows up to a company in a uniform that indicates he was there to work on a broken device or network problem. If he convinces the person at the greeting desk, he can then go to some place in the network and attempt to sniff the network, break into computers and servers, or plant Trojan horses, viruses, or backdoors. The possibilities are overwhelming.

Masquerading

Masquerading can be considered a type of social engineering. It is a method that an attacker can use to fool others of her real identity. Many times e-mails coming from a malicious source are configured with a familiar sending address. This is how many viruses are successful in spreading through e-mail clients. When Kevin receives an e-mail that says it is from his friend Dave, he does not think much about it when he opens it and double-clicks on the attachment. If this e-mail was actually sent via a program written to spread a virus, then Kevin's system would now be used to spread the same virus to everyone in his e-mail address book. This is how the Melissa, ILOVEYOU, Life Stages, and Naked Wife viruses got populated around the world so quickly.

References

www.cccure.org/Documents/HISM/522-525.html

http://cui.unige.ch/OSG/courses/infrcom/lectures/security/security.html

www.uwsg.iu.edu/usail/tasks/security/security.html

http://courses.cs.vt.edu/~cs3604/lib/Crime/notes.html

http://netsecurity.about.com/cs/socialengineering/

www.sans.org/infosecFAQ/securitybasics/awareness.htmhttp://www.sans.org/infosecFAQ/social/social_list.htm

Well-Known Computer Crimes

Most computer crimes do not hit the news and headlines because companies choose to keep them quiet. This is done mainly for two reasons: to avoid the embarrassment of everyone finding out their dirty laundry and the fact that they have vulnerabilities, and also to avoid pointing out the vulnerabilities to other opportunistic hackers.

However, there are some computer crimes that have gone down in the history book of hacking and this section takes a quick look at some of them.

The 2600 group publishes the *2600: The Hacker Quarterly* magazine, which is full of ways to hack into computers and telephone systems. The name 2600 stands for the tone that phreakers used to be able to send down a telephone line and get free long distance in return. This 2600 tone tricked the system at the other end into thinking that the person making the call was authorized to receive long distance access so it opened up a line and let the person make that type of a call. The 2600 group is made up of basically *phreakers*, depicted in Figure 10-3, which are hackers who specialize in telephone and private branch exchange (PBX) systems.

One of the earliest actual hacking clubs called itself the *414 Club* because they all lived in that area code. This group of hackers was suspected of breaking into over 60 businesses and government systems in the United States and Canada in the early 1980s. Today a group of hackers breaking into 60 businesses would not cause the stir that it

Figure 10-3 A phone phreaker is a hacker who specializes in defrauding the telephone companies.

did in 1983. *Newsweek* magazine even ran a story of this group in the mid-1980s with a picture of one of the group members and his TRS-80 computer.

Cuckoo's Egg

The *Cuckoo's Egg* is actually a book describing how Cliff Stoll, an astronomy student at Berkeley, was assigned to track down a 75-cent accounting error in the late 1980s. This small error started him on an investigation only to find that someone was on the school's network who was not supposed to be. He tracked this intruder, back in the days when few sophisticated software tools were available to do this, and found out that the intruder had been breaking into U.S. military systems and stealing sensitive information. He set up one of the first known honeypots and lured the hacker into one of the university's servers claiming to be holding confidential information. Cliff then worked with people and companies all over the United States and other countries to track this intruder while the connection was still active. This mainly had to be done by workers at the phone company—at the time, the ability to perform these types of tasks was far from automated as they are today. After many attempts, he finally got the U.S. counter-intelligence agents involved, and it ended up being a small group of hackers in the former Soviet Union working for the KGB.

This is an amazing and true story of someone who stumbled onto an intruder, did not have any sophisticated tracking tools (because they did not exist yet), and was incredibly creative, intelligent, and motivated enough to make many people all over the world help him track down this individual, who happened to be working for the KGB.

Kevin Mitnick

Kevin Mitnick is one of the most well-known hackers and at one time was one of the FBI's most wanted criminals. He was in jail for almost five years for wire fraud and illegally stealing files from Sun Microsystems, Nokia, Motorola, and others.

Mitnick violated his previous probation terms in 1992, three years before his arrest and five-year jail term, and went into hiding for two years. During that time, he stole corporate secrets, hacked into computers, broke into the national defense warning system, and scrambled telephone networks. He was finally caught, charged, and pled guilty to five felony charges.

The main reason that he is so popular is because he is a martyr to many hackers. He claims he did not do any damage and that he could have done massive damage if his intentions were malicious. Mitnick, like many others, views hacking as an intellectual challenge and said he did it mainly to learn how different systems worked and were integrated.

Chaos Computer Club

This club is a group of German hackers committed to freedom of information across borders. It was formed in 1981 and has tested many corporations and technologies in their security strength and has made demonstrations of the ones they found lacking. They demonstrated how easy it was to clone information from European ATM cards and fraud different financial institutions. They also demonstrated how a Web-based Trojan horse could siphon money from a bank account. This ActiveX application scanned users' computers to see which had Quicken installed and extracted bank account information from that program. The Trojan then made a bogus transaction to one of their own bank accounts.

The hackers who make up these different groups are quite talented and computer-savvy individuals.

Cult of the Dead Cow

This is a group of hackers who have come up with many different hacking tools. The best known tool that they developed was Back Orifice, which was designed to remotely take over Windows 95 and Windows 98 systems. It can record keystrokes, record logins and passwords, take screen shots, delete files, and run programs.

Phone Phreakers

You're a phreak. Answer: I know, now give me the phone.

This is not necessarily a specific group, but a classification of hackers who specialize in telephone fraud. The first known case of toll fraud was committed in 1961 when Bell

Telephone Company uncovered a method, called **Blue Boxing**, that enabled people to make free long-distance phone calls. At that time, all long-distance trunks were sensitive to signals at the 2,600-Hz frequency. The Blue Box device simulated this tone and other tones to trick telephone systems and gain free, unauthorized long-distance access.

Later came **Red Boxes**, which simulated the tones of coins being deposited into a payphone. This enabled phreakers to also get free local and long-distance calls. Then came **Black Boxes**, which manipulated line voltage to enable people to call toll-free. As the telephone companies advanced their systems and went digital, most of the phreaker phone tricks were no longer effective.

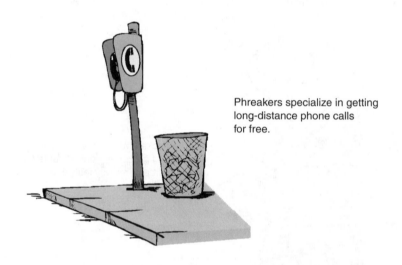

Phreakers specialize in getting long-distance phone calls for free.

In 1972, a blind phreaker called Cap'n Crunch made it known that a toy whistle in Cap'n Crunch® cereal could generate the 2,600-Hz tone used to fool the telephone company systems and give anyone free long-distance phone calls.

Although these types of crimes are no longer effective, there is still a lot of fraud that takes place at different PBXs. Today, phreakers still steal phone services from PBXs and other systems, and charge the long-distance charges to the owners of those systems. This crime is very hard to trace, but it is mainly successful because large companies do not audit their phone bills.

As stated earlier, many attacks are carried out by curious semitalented or very talented individuals who want to see how far they can go. Although the individuals may not be out to cause massive damage or actually harm others directly, their efforts can cost companies thousands or millions of dollars—therefore, companies and authorities take these acts very seriously.

Some attackers have specific goals in sight, instead of trying to bring down a system they come across here or there. One company can perform espionage on their competitors by breaking into networks and servers and stealing trade secrets and copyright information. Countries can also do this to other countries, which is referred to as *international economic espionage*, or *information warfare*. (In Chapter 2, information warfare is described at some length.) Information warfare and international espionage will most likely only increase because society is becoming more and more dependent upon technology. Governments are looking at these issues much more seriously and are putting the funds and resources towards training their own soldiers to be able to participate in this type of warfare. You can be sure that many of these activities will not be in the news or headlines like we see when a Microsoft site is brought down. These activities are much more covert in nature.

References

http://dmoz.org/Computers/Hacking/Groups/

http://anticode.antionline.com/text-archive.php

www.qub.ac.uk/mgt/itsoc/security.html

http://www3.cnn.com/SPECIALS/1999/mitnick.background/

www.soci.niu.edu/~cudigest/

Identification, Protection, and Prosecution

Hacking, cracking, and attacking have only increased over the years and will not stop anytime soon. There are several issues that deal with why these activities have not been properly stopped or even curbed, which are the proper identification of the attackers, the necessary level of protection for networks, and the effective prosecution once an attacker is captured.

Most attackers are never caught because they spoof their addresses and use methods to cover their footsteps. Many attackers break into networks, take whatever resources they were after, and clean the logs that tracked their movements and activities. Because of this, many companies do not even know that they have been violated. Even if an attacker's activities trigger an intrusion detection system (IDS), it does not usually find the true identity of the individual, but it does alert the company that a specific vulnerability was exploited.

The FBI and Secret Service work together on the larger computer crimes and international crimes.

Law enforcement, FBI, and the Secret Service are called in on some of the larger crimes, and although each of these entities works to train their people on how to identify and track computer crimes, they are very far behind the times in their skill and tools —they are outnumbered by the amount of hackers actively attacking networks. Because the attackers use tools that are automated, they can perform several serious attacks in a short time frame. When law enforcement is called in, their efforts are usually purely manual in checking logs, interviewing people, scanning for vulnerabilities, and setting up traps in case the attacker comes back. So because each agency can only spare a small amount of people for computer crimes, and their steps are manual, they are behind in their expertise compared to many hackers. Most attackers are never found, much less prosecuted.

As mentioned earlier, there are not many laws that deal specifically with computer crimes so it is more challenging to successfully prosecute the attackers who are caught. Many companies that are victims of an attack usually just want to ensure that the vulnerability the attacker exploited is patched and removed instead of spending the time and money towards going after and prosecuting the attacker.

NOTE The author of the **ILOVEYOU** virus was caught, but could not be prosecuted because there was not a specific law indicating that his actions were wrong. This virus cost companies millions of dollars and the responsible person did not get fined a dollar or spend any time in jail.

These trends will most likely change, but changes will probably happen a lot slower than most would like. As companies lose more and more money to these types of attacks, there will be more and more pressure on the law enforcement agencies to stop this type of crime. Each agency will put more money and resources into this problem, and the courts will devise useful laws to hold individuals who are doing these types of acts accountable. Down the road, people will most likely think twice about letting loose a crippling e-mail virus after 20 other people have been jailed for the same actions.

Another thing that is changing everyday is how companies are protecting themselves from these types of attacks. Five to ten years ago, most companies had never heard of a firewall, but today it is a known essential. Five to ten years ago, someone would only have a full-time position in computer security if he worked for a government, but today most organizations are screaming for help when it comes to their network and information security. Security is not only part of the IT staff's vocabulary, but it is an issue that has forced itself into board meetings, shareholders' concerns, and has cost executives their jobs if they did not make sure computer security took place correctly within their organization. As the attackers and hackers evolve in their skills and numbers, many business-oriented individuals who would rather deal with other issues have been forced to make security a priority.

Because an attacker must have access to the systems holding the wanted resources, it is usually easier for insiders, or employees, than outsiders to access resources that companies fight to protect. In this sense, employees can present a greater potential for computer crimes than outsiders trying to get in. Many statistics and security professionals have indeed indicated that employees cause more security breaches and computer fraud than outside attackers, but the media usually touts the stories about hackers and crackers—therefore, more attention and effort is put towards fighting off that group of people rather than the threat of employees taking advantage of their position and access.

Liability and Its Ramifications

As the courts, law enforcement, laws, and legal methods evolve in their approaches towards computer crimes, so must corporations. They should evolve not only their preventive, detective, and mitigative approaches, but also their liability and responsibility approaches. As these crimes increase in frequency and sophistication, so will their destruction and lasting effects. In most cases, the attackers are not caught, but there is enough blame to be passed around, so corporations will need to take many steps to ensure that the blame and liability do not land clearly at their doorstep.

The same is true for other types of threats that corporations have to deal with today. If a company has a facility that burns down to the ground, the arsonist is only one small piece of this tragedy. The company is responsible for providing fire detection and suppression systems, fire-resistant construction material in certain areas, alarms, exits, fire extinguishers, and backups of all the important information that could be affected by a fire. If a building burns to the ground and takes all the records (information, customer data, inventory records, and the like that is necessary to rebuild), then this company did not perform its *due diligence* in ensuring that it is protected from such disasters. In this case, the employees, shareholders, customers, and everyone affected could successfully sue the company. However, if the company did everything expected of it in the previously listed respects, it could not be successfully sued for negligence and not practicing due diligence.

Due care means that a company did all that it could have reasonably done to try and prevent security breaches, and also took the necessary steps to ensure that if a security breach did take place, that the damages were much more reduced compared to not practicing due care. Due care means that a company practiced common sense and prudent management practices with responsible actions. Due diligence means that the company kept up with these practices in a disciplined way rather than doing them once and letting them fall out of date and become useless.

The same type of responsibility is starting to be expected of corporations pertaining to computer crime and resource protection. Computer security is developed and erected to protect an organization's valuable resources—thus, appropriate safeguards need to be in place to protect the company's mission by protecting its tangible and intangible resources, reputation, employees, and legal position. Computer and information security is one piece of this that works as a means to an end and not an end within itself. Security is not practiced just for the sake of doing it. Security should be practiced in a way to accomplish fully understood, planned, and attainable goals.

 NOTE In 1997, the Federal Sentencing Guidelines were extended to cover computer crimes and specified that senior corporate officers could be personally responsible to pay up to $290 million in fines if their company did not comply with the laws set out for them.

Senior management has an obligation to protect the company from a long list of activities that can negatively affect the company, including protection from malicious code, natural disasters, individual privacy, violation of the law, and more.

It is dictated that management must follow the *prudent man rule*, which requires them to perform duties that prudent people would exercise in similar circumstances. They are to perform these duties with diligence and care when carrying out their responsibilities.

The costs and benefits of security should be evaluated in monetary and nonmonetary terms to ensure that the cost of security does not outweigh the expected benefits. Security should be proportional to the value of and degree of reliance required by the company pertaining to the severity, likelihood, and extent of potential damage.

Security mechanisms should be employed to reduce the frequency and severity of security-related losses. A sound security program is a smart business practice.

The senior management needs to decide upon the amount of risk they are willing to take on, pertaining to computer and information security, and implement security in a cost benefit manner. (These issues are discussed in great detail in Chapter 3.) These risks do not always stop at the boundaries of the organization. Many companies have extranets set up with other companies, value-added networks (VAN), telecommunication lines, and more to enable them to work quickly and efficiently with other organizations. However, these relationships can get more complicated when it comes to liability and responsibilities.

When companies come together to work in an integrated manner such as extranets and VANs, special care must be taken to ensure that each party promises to provide the necessary level of protection, liability, and responsibility needed, which should be clearly defined in the contracts that each party signs. (These topics are sometimes referred to as *downstream liabilities*.) Auditing and testing should be performed to ensure that each party is indeed holding up its side of the bargain and that its technology integrates properly with all the other parties. Interoperability can become a large, frustrating, and expensive issue in these types of arrangements.

NOTE Accountability versus Responsibility: Responsibility generally refers to the obligations and expected actions and behaviors of a particular party. An obligation can have a defined set of specific actions required or a more general and open approach, which enables the party to decide how it will fulfill the particular obligation. Accountability refers to the ability to hold a party responsible for certain actions or nonactions.

Computer security usually has some interesting interdependencies with other factions of the company like management functions, legal issues, employee privacy, disaster recovery and business continuity plans, and daily operations. The company that can clearly understand these types of issues and the interrelations between them can better plan, implement, and maintain their computer security program.

The following list describes some of the actions required to show that due care is being properly practiced in a corporation:

- Physical and logical access controls
- Telecommunication security, which could require encryption
- Information, application, and hardware backups
- Disaster recovery and business continuity plans
- Periodic review, drills, tests, and improvement to disaster recovery and business continuity plans
- Properly informing employees of expected behavior and ramifications of not following these expectations
- Developing a security policy, standards, procedures, and guidelines
- Performing security awareness training
- Running updated antivirus software
- Periodically performing penetration tests from outside and inside the network
- Implementing dial-back or preset dialing features on remote access applications
- Abiding by and updating external service level agreements (SLAs)
- Ensuring that downstream security responsibilities are being met
- Implementing measures that ensure that software piracy is not taking place
- Ensuring that proper auditing and reviewing of those audit logs are taking place
- Conducting background checks on potential employees

Each company will have different requirements when it comes to this list of due care responsibilities. If these steps are not taken, the company can be charged with negligence. For negligence to be proven in court, there usually needs to be a *legally recognized obligation*, which means there is a standard of conduct expected of the company to protect others from unreasonable risks. The company must fail to conform to this standard, which results in injury or damage to another. There must also be *proximate causation*, meaning someone can prove that the damage that was caused was the company's fault.

The following are some scenarios that show how a company can be proved negligent in its action and responsibilities.

Personal Information

A company, Medical Information Inc., which holds patient medical information, does not have strict procedures on how patient information is disseminated or shared.

A person pretends to be a physician and calls into Medical Information Inc. and requests medical information on the patient Don Ho. The receptionist does not question the caller and explains that Don Ho has AIDS and a brain tumor. A week later, Don Ho does not receive the job he interviewed for and finds out that the employer called Medical Information Inc. for his medical information.

1. Legally recognized obligation

    a. The Medical Information Inc. company does not have policies and procedures in place to protect patient information.

    b. The employer does not have the right to make this kind of call and is not able to use medical information against potential employees.

2. Failure to conform to the required standard

    a. Sensitive information was released to an unauthorized person by a Medical Information Inc. employee.

    b. The employer requested information it did not have a right to.

3. Proximate causation and resulting in injury or damage

    a. The information leaked by Medical Information Inc. caused Don Ho great embarrassment and prevented him from obtaining a specific job.

    b. The employer made his decision based on information he did not have a right to inquire about in the first place.

The outcome was a long legal battle, but Don Ho ended up successfully suing both companies, recovered from AIDS and his brain tumor, bought an island, and has never had to work again.

Hacker Intrusion

A financial institution, Cheapo Inc., buys the necessary middleware to enable them to offer online bank account transactions for its customers, but does not add any of necessary security safeguards required for this type of communication and transactions to take place over the Internet.

Within the first two weeks, 22 customers had their checking and savings accounts hacked into with a combined loss of $439,344.09.

1. Legally recognized obligation

   a. Cheapo Inc. did not implement a firewall or IDS, harden the database holding the customer account information, or use encryption for customer transactions.

   b. Cheapo Inc. did not effectively protect its customers' assets.

2. Failure to conform to the required standard

   a. By not erecting the proper security policy and program and implementing the necessary security controls, Cheapo broke 12 federal regulations used to govern financial institutions.

3. Proximate causation and resulting injury or damage

   a. The fact that 22 individuals lost $439,344.09 was directly related to the financial institution's lack of implementing the basic requirements of online banking and not practicing due care.

Eventually, a majority of the accounts were attacked and drained, a class action suit was brought against Cheapo Inc., a majority of the people got most of their money back, and the facility Cheapo Inc. was using as a financial institution is now used to sell tacos.

These scenarios are simplistic and described in jest, but failure to implement computer and information security properly can expose a company and its board of directors to litigation and legal punishment. Many times people cannot hide behind the corporation, but will be held accountable individually and personally. The board of directors can compromise its responsibilities to the stockholders, customers, and employees by not ensuring that due care is practiced and that the company was not being negligent in any way.

Types of Laws

There has always been different types of laws and computer crime is no different. The three main categories of laws are civil, criminal, and administrative.

Civil law, also called *tort*, deals with wrongs against individuals or companies that result in damages or loss. A civil lawsuit would result in financial restitution instead of jail sentences. If someone took another person to court over a civil law issue, the jury

would decide upon innocence or guilt, and if guilt was chosen, then the jury would decide upon the punitive damages of the case.

Criminal law is used when an individual's conduct violates the government laws, which have been developed to protect the public. Jail sentences are commonly the punishment for criminal law cases versus civil law cases where the punishment is usually an amount of money that the guilty individual owes the victim. In the O.J. Simpson case, he was first tried and found innocent in the criminal law case and then found guilty in the civil law case.

Administrative law deals with regulatory standards that regulate performance and conduct. Government agencies create these standards, which are usually applied to companies and individuals within those companies. Some examples of administrative law standards could be that every building used for business must have a fire detection and suppression system, they must have easily seen exist signs, and the doors cannot be blocked in case of a fire. Companies that produce and package food and drug products are exposed to many types of standards that they must live up to so that the public is protected and aware of its actions. If a case was made that specific standards were not abided by, high officials in the companies usually would be held accountable, like in a company that makes tires that shred after a couple years of use. The people who were in high positions of this company were most likely aware of these conditions but chose to ignore them to keep profits up. Under administrative, criminal, and civil law, they will most likely pay dearly for these decisions.

Not every country uses each category of these laws, and many countries interpret or use them differently for different reasons. This is one challenge of fighting cybercrime. If someone from Germany broke into a financial institution in Russia, but each country had different laws with different meanings applied to this type of action, which law is used to punish the criminal? Is it the German version because the criminal committed the crime from Germany or is the Russian version used because the actual crime took place there? These types of issues and more are being debated, but clear-cut resolutions are much farther down the road.

Intellectual Property Laws

Intellectual property laws are different than the three main categories of law. These laws are not necessarily looking at who is right or wrong, but how a company can protect what is rightfully theirs and what can be done if these laws are violated.

A major issue in many intellectual property cases is what the company did to protect the resources it claims had been violated in one fashion or another. A company must go through many steps to protect resources that it claims to be intellectual property and must show due diligence in its efforts to protect those resources. If an employee sent a file to a friend and the company charged that employee with illegally sharing intellectual property, it must show the court and jury why this file is so important to the company, what type of damage it could cause if it was indeed shared, and most importantly, what the company had done to protect that file. If the company did not secure the file and tell the employees that they were not allowed to copy and share that file, then the company will most likely lose the case. However, if the company went through many steps to protect that file, explained to the employees that it was wrong to copy and share the information within the file, and that the punishment could be termination, then the company could not be charged with falsely terminating an employee.

Intellectual property can be protected by several different laws, depending upon the type of resource it is.

Trade Secret

The trade secret law protects certain types of information or resources from unauthorized use or disclosure. For a company to have this resource qualify as a trade secret, it must provide the company with some type of competitive value or advantage. A resource can be protected by law if it is not generally known and if it requires special skill, ingenuity, and/or expenditure of money and effort to develop it. This means that a company cannot say that the sky is blue and call it a trade secret.

A trade secret is something that is proprietary to that company and important for its survival and profitability. The resource that is claimed to be a trade secret must be confidential and protected with certain security precautions and actions. A trade secret could be the recipe of a soft drink, source code of a program, method of making the perfect jellybean, algorithm used in a technology, or ingredients in a barbeque sauce.

Many companies require their employees to sign a nondisclosure agreement contract indicating that they understand and promise not to share the company's trade secrets with competitors. Companies do this to inform the employees of the importance of keeping certain information secret, deter the act of sharing this information, and have the ability to fire the employee or bring charges if the employee does not uphold his part of the contract.

Copyright

In the United States, the copyright law protects the right of an author to control the public distribution, reproduction, display, and adaptation of his original work. The law covers many categories of work: pictorial, graphic, musical, dramatic, literary, pantomimes, motion picture, sculptural, sound recording, and architectural. A copyright law does not cover the specific resource like the trade secret law does—instead, it protects the expression of the idea of the resource instead of the resource itself. A copyright law is usually used to protect an author's writings, song lyrics, an artist's drawings, a programmer's source code, or specific rhythms and structures of a musician's creation. Names of products can be protected under copyright laws. Computer programs and manuals are just two examples of items protected under the Federal Copyright Act. The item is covered under the copyright law once the program or manual has been written. Although it is not required to include a warning and the copyright symbol, © it is encouraged so that others cannot claim innocence after copying another's work.

The protection does not extend to any method of operations, process, concept, or procedure, but it does protect from unauthorized copying and distribution of a work. It protects the form of expression rather than the subject matter. A patent deals more with the subject matter of an invention—copyright deals with how that invention is reproduced and distributed.

NOTE A copyright protects the expression of ideas rather than the ideas themselves. A trade secret protects the idea itself.

Computer programs can be protected under the copyright law as literary works. The law protects both the source and object code, which can be an operating system, application, or database. In some instances, the law can protect not only the code, but also the structure, sequence, and organization. The user interface is part of the definition of a software application structure—therefore, one vendor could not copy the exact composition of another vendor's user interface.

Trademark

My trademark is my stupidity. Answer: Good for you!

A trademark is slightly different than a copyright in that it is used to protect a word, name, symbol, sound, shape, color, device, or combination of these. The reason a company would trademark one of these, or a combination, is because it represents their company to a group of people or to the world. Companies have marketing departments that work very hard in coming up with something new that will make them be noticed and stand out in a crowd of competitors, and trademarking the result of this work is a way of properly protecting it and ensuring that others cannot copy and use it.

Patent

Patents are given to individuals or companies to grant the owner legal ownership and enable the owner to exclude others from using or copying the invention covered by the patent. The invention must be novel, useful, and nonobvious, which means, for example, that a company could not patent air. Thank goodness. If a company figured out how to patent air, we would have to pay for each and every breath we took!

After the inventor completes an application for a patent and it is approved, the patent grants a limited property right to exclude others from making, using, or selling the invention for 17 years. This has been used by pharmaceutical companies where one company develops a specific drug and acquires a patent for it. This company is the only one that can manufacture and sell this drug until the seventeenth year is up. After that, all companies are allowed to manufacture and sell this product.

This also takes place with algorithms. If an inventor of an algorithm acquires a patent, she has full control over who can use it in their products. If the inventor lets a vendor incorporate the algorithm, then she will most likely get a fee and possibly a royalty fee on each instance of the product sold.

Internal Protection of Intellectual Property

Ensuring that specific resources are protected by the previously mentioned laws is very important, but there are other measures that must be taken internally to make sure the resources that are confidential in nature are properly identified and protected.

The resources protected by one of the previously mentioned laws, need to be identified and integrated into the company's data classification scheme. This should be directed by management and carried out by the IT staff. The identified resources should have the necessary level of access control protection, auditing enabled, and proper storage environment. If it is deemed secret, then not everyone in the company should be able to access it. Once the individuals who are allowed to have access are identified, their level of access and interaction with the resource should be defined in a granular method. The attempts of access and manipulation should be properly audited, and the resource should be stored on a protected server with the necessary security mechanisms.

Employees must be informed of the level of secrecy or confidentiality of the resource, and their expected behavior, pertaining to that resource, must be explained.

If a company fails in one or all of these steps, they may not be covered by the laws described previously because they are not practicing due care and properly protecting the resource they have vowed to be so important to the survival and competitiveness of their company.

References

www.loc.gov/copyright/

www.eff.org/Intellectual_property/

www.caltech.edu/ott/security/OIPC_Home.htm

www.ksu.edu/uauc/intprop/tutorial.htm

Software Piracy

Software piracy indicates that the intellectual or creative work of an author has been used or duplicated without permission or compensation to the author. It is an act of infringement on ownership rights and if someone is caught, the person could be sued civilly for damages, be criminally prosecuted, or both. Duplicate software is everywhere and software piracy is everywhere. Up until now, there have not been efficient mechanisms put into place to ensure that software could not be copied and illegally used. Companies are testing out new features, and within time, it will most likely not be as easy to illegally copy and use software as it is now.

When a vendor develops an application, the program is usually licensed and not sold outright. The license agreement contains provisions relating the use and security of the software and the corresponding manuals. If an individual or company fails to observe and abide by those requirements, the license may be terminated, and depending on the actions, criminal charges may be implemented. The risk to the vendor developing and selling the software is the loss of profits that it would have earned. Many companies and their employees do not abide by their software licenses and the employees use the company's software for their home use, as depicted in Figure 10-4.

Some software vendors sell bulk licenses, which enable several users to use the product simultaneously. The vendor could have incorporated a monitoring system that keeps track of the usability to ensure that the customer does not go over her limit. The network administrator or security officer should be aware of all these types of contractual commitments required by software companies. This person needs to be educated on the restrictions the company is under and make sure proper enforcement mechanisms are in place. If a company is found guilty of illegally copying software or using more copies than their license permits, the network administrator or security officer who was put in charge of this task will be the first called to the carpet.

Figure 10-4   Software privacy is one of the most common computer crimes committed.

The Software Protection Association (SPA) has been formed by major companies to enforce proprietary rights of software. The association was formed to protect its own software developments, but it also helps others to ensure that their software is properly licensed. These are huge issues for companies that develop and produce software because a majority of their revenue comes from licensing fees.

Other international groups have been formed to protect against software pirates and stealing. These include the Federation Against Software Theft (FAST), headquartered in London, and the Business Software Alliance (BSA), based in Washington, D.C. They provide similar functionality as the SPA and make efforts to protect software around the world.

One of the offenses an individual or company can commit is decompiling vendor object code. This is usually done to figure out how the application works, which is confidential, and perhaps to reverse engineer it in the hopes of understanding the intricate details of its functionality. Another purpose of reverse engineering products is to be able to detect security flaws within the code that can later be exploited. This is how some buffer overflows are discovered.

Many times the object code is decompiled into source code and the individual either finds security holes to take advantage of or alters the source code to produce some type of functionality that the original vendor did not want to exist. One example is an individual who decompiled a program that displays e-books and publications. The vendor did not want anyone to be able to copy the e-publications its product displayed and inserted an encoder that enforced this limitation within the object code of their product. The individual decompiled the object code and figured out how to create a decoder that would overcome this restriction and enable users to make copies of the e-publications, which infringed upon those authors' and publishers' copyrights.

The individual was arrested and prosecuted under the new Digital Millennium Copyright Act (DMCA), which makes it illegal to create products that circumvent copyright protection mechanisms. As of this writing, this new act and how it will be enforced has caused many debates and controversy because of its possible negative effects on free speech.

Interestingly enough, many computer-oriented individuals protested this individual's arrest, several marches took place, and the company that was pressing charges (Adobe) quickly decided to drop all charges.

Discarding Equipment and Software Issues

When equipment is being discarded, sold, or moved to a different department, all previous information and files should be completely erased. This is logical. However, there could be some not so obvious and logical requirements pertaining to the hardware and the software that is loaded on it. Depending on the vendor of the system, it may be illegal to sell a computer with an operating system without proper licensing, or it may be illegal to sell the system without an operating system at all.

In one example, a company wanted to sell 2,000 of its older 486 and lower-end Pentium systems. The network administrator instructed the network engineers to format and fdisk each and every system. After this task was complete, the network administrator found out that through its agreement with the vendor of the computers, it would be illegal to sell even one of those computers without a functioning operating system. It is vendor and license dependent and the network administrator or security officer should investigate the proper procedures to protect the company. In this instance, the network engineers had to go back and reinstall the necessary operating system on each of the 2,000 computers.

 NOTE Illegal Use of Software: Most reporting of illegal use of software comes from disgruntled employees.

Trade secret, copyright, patent, and trademark laws can differ from country to country. Any vendor that is interested in selling its product should be aware of these differences and should take the necessary steps to properly protect its product.

Computer Crime Investigations

As mentioned earlier in the chapter, law enforcement has many challenges and barriers when it comes to fighting cybercrime. They only have a small faction that is properly trained, the rules of jurisdiction can get fuzzy, and determining exactly what laws have been broken in this quickly evolving computing age can be overwhelming at best. Another issue that law enforcement has to deal with is properly gathering evidence from a computer or media, which is much different than collecting evidence from a regular crime scene. This section will go over some of these barriers and many of the issues that have been addressed, and guidelines that have been developed to help with future investigations.

A Different Approach

Many computer crimes go unreported because the victim is not aware of the incident or wants to just patch the hole the hacker came in through and keep the details quiet to escape embarrassment or the risk of hurting its reputation. This makes it harder to know the real statistics of how many attacks happen each day, what degree of damage that is caused, and what types of attack and methods are being used.

This lack of reporting crimes does not make fighting this type of crime any easier. A law enforcement agent who investigates a computer crime has to deal with a shift from physical damage and thefts to an intangible electronic environment that requires a different type of skill to get around in, identify clues, and be able to obtain usable evidence. The ease of committing a cybercrime, the relative anonymity available to the attacker, and the difficulty in tracking down the attacker usually gives the criminal more advantages than the cybercop. The Internet and interconnection of computers are making targets much more accessible than ever before and the criminals have much lower risk of getting caught.

Law enforcement agents who fight cybercrime must be very talented.

Many of the existing theft, damage, and extortion laws are written to protect physical property, not necessarily the type of damage that can be done by bytes over a phone line or network wire.

When a company endures a computer crime, they should leave the environment and evidence unaltered and contact the authorities. Someone who is unfamiliar with the proper process of collecting data and evidence from a crime scene could destroy evidence, and all hope of prosecuting and achieving a conviction would be lost. Companies should have procedures for many issues in computer security such as enforcement procedures, disaster recovery and continuity procedures, and backup procedures. It would be best if they also had a procedure for dealing with a cybercrime. Most companies do not have a clue who to call or what to do right after they have been the victim of a cybercrime. This means the company should have an incident response policy and procedures set up just for this type of event before it actually takes place.

The incident response policy should indicate if systems can be taken offline to try and save evidence or if systems have to continue functioning with the risk of destroying evidence. Each system and functionality should have a priority assigned to it. For instance, if the file server is hit, it should be removed from the network, but not shut down. However, if the mail server is hit, it should not be removed from the network or shut down because of the priority the company attributes to the mail server over the file server. Trade-offs and decisions will have to be made, but it is better to think through these issues before the situation occurs because better logic is usually possible before a crisis with less emotion and chaos.

If the company would like to handle these types of issues in-house, then an *incident response team* should be developed who is responsible for responding to major security incidents. The team should have someone from senior management, the network administrator, security officer, possibly a network engineer and/or programmer, and a liaison for public affairs. The purpose of having an incident response team is to ensure that there is a group of people who are properly skilled, who follow a standard set of procedures, and who are singled out and called upon when this type of event takes place.

The team should have proper reporting procedures established, the ability to provide prompt reaction, have coordination with law enforcement, and be an important element of the overall security program.

The incident response team should have the following basic items:

- List of outside agencies and resources to contact or report to
- List of computer or forensics experts to contact
- Steps on how to secure and preserve evidence
- Steps on how to search for evidence
- List of items that should be included on the report
- A list that indicates how the different systems should be treated in this type of situation (removed from the Internet, removed from the network, and powered down)

When a suspected crime is reported, there are some steps that should be followed that ensure uniformity in approach and help to make sure steps have not been skipped. First, the report should be investigated and it should be determined that an actual crime has been committed. Senior management should be informed immediately. The sooner the documenting of events, the better, so if the starting time of the crime could be documented along with the company employees and resources involved, it would provide a good start. At this point, the company must decide if it wants to conduct its own forensics investigation or call in the big guns. If experts are going to be called in, the system that was attacked should be left alone to try and preserve as much evidence of the attack as possible. If the company decides to conduct its own forensics, there are many issues to deal with and tricky elements to address.

Computer Forensics and Proper Collection of Evidence

I just spilled coffee on our only evidence. Answer: Case closed, let's all go home.

It is very important that the person, or people, conducting the forensics investigation is skilled in this trade and knows what to look out for. If a person reboots the attacked system or goes around looking at different files, it could corrupt viable evidence, change timestamps on key files, and erase footprints the criminal may have left. One very good first step is to make a sound image of the attacked system and perform forensic analysis on this copy. This will ensure that the evidence stays unharmed on the original system in case some steps in the investigation actually corrupt or destroy data. Also the memory of the system should be dumped to a file before doing any work on the system or powering it down. This is another method of capturing fragile information.

The response team will need specialized forensics tools, an evidence collection notebook, containers, a camera, and evidence identification tags. It is important that the notebook is not a spiral notebook, but a notebook that is bound in a way that one can tell if pages have been removed.

NOTE An investigator's notebook cannot be used as evidence in court. It can only be used by the investigator to refresh his memory during a proceeding, but it cannot be submitted as evidence in any form.

The next crucial piece is to keep a proper *chain of custody* of the evidence. Because evidence from these types of crimes can be very volatile and easily dismissed from court because of improper handling, it is important to follow very strict and organized procedures when collecting and tagging evidence.

When copies of data need to be made, this process must meet certain standards to ensure quality and reliability. Specialized software for this purpose can be used. The copies must be able to be independently verified and tamperproof.

Each piece of evidence should be marked in some way with the date, time, initials of the collector, and a case number if one has been assigned. Magnetic disk surfaces should not be marked on and diskettes should only be marked with a felt tip pen. Reel-to-reel magnetic tape can be marked on the nonshiny side of the tape within the first 10 to 15 feet, also known as the *leader* part. The piece of evidence should then be sealed in a container and the container should be marked with the same information. The container should be sealed with evidence tape and if possible, the writing should be on the tape so a broken seal can be detected.

NOTE The chain of custody dictates that all evidence be labeled with information indicating who secured and validated it.

Wires and cables should be labeled and a photograph of the labeled system should be taken before it is actually dissembled. Media should be write-protected and storage should be dust free, kept at room temperature without much humidity, and, of course, not close to any strong magnets.

If possible, the crime scene should be photographed, including behind the computer if the crime involved some type of physical break in. Documents, papers, and devices should be handled with cloth gloves and placed into containers and sealed. All storage media should be contained, even if it has been erased because data still may be obtainable.

Because this type of evidence can be easily erased or destroyed and is complex in nature, identification, recording, collection, preservation, transportation, and interpretation are all important. After everything is properly labeled, a chain of custody log should be made of each container and an overall log should be made capturing all events.

For a crime to be successfully prosecuted, solid evidence is required. Computer forensics is the art of retrieving this evidence and preserving it in the proper ways to make it admissible in court. Without proper computer forensics, hardly any computer crimes could ever be properly and successfully presented in court.

The most common reasons for improper evidence collection are no established incident response team, no established incident response procedures, poorly written policy, and a broken chain of custody.

 NOTE Chain of Custody: A chain of custody is a history that shows how evidence was collected, analyzed, transported, and preserved in order to be presented as evidence in court. Because electronic evidence can be easily modified, a clearly defined chain of custody demonstrates that the evidence is trustworthy.

There are other issues to think through when a company is developing incident response procedures such as how the issue will be explained to the press, customers, and shareholders. This could require the collaboration of the public relations department, management, human resources (if employees are involved), IT department, and the legal department. There can be several different types of legal ramifications in a cybercrime that does not seem apparent right from the beginning and must be handled delicately. The company should decide how it will report the matter to outsiders, because if they do not present it the way they want it to be viewed, it could be presented in a totally different light.

Incident Handling

In the previous sections, incident handling was addressed in an indirect manner, but a clear definition of incident handling and its place within a company is important.

There are many types of threats a computer and network can face, each requiring a specialized way to properly recover. However, a basic outline of how all incidents are to be handled should be drafted and enforced. This is a much better approach than the way that most companies deal with these threats, which is usually in an ad hoc and confusing manner. A clearly defined incident-handling process can be more cost effective, enables recovery to happen more quickly, and provides a uniform approach with certain expectation of its results.

Incident handling should be closely related to disaster recovery planning and should be part of the company's disaster recovery plan. Both are reacting to some type of incident that can require a quick reaction so that the company can return to normal operations. Incident handling can be the portion of a recovery plan that responds to malicious technical threats.

The primary goal of incident handling is to contain and repair any damage caused by an event and to prevent any further damage. It can also improve internal communications and a company's ability to be prepared for threats and disasters.

Without an effective incident-handling program, individuals who have the best intentions can sometimes make the situation worse by damaging evidence, systems, or spreading malicious code. Many times the attacker booby-traps the compromised system to erase specific critical files if a user does something as simple as lists the files in a directory. A compromised system can no longer be trusted because the internal commands listed in the path could be altered to perform unexpected activities, the system could now have a back door for the attacker to enter when he wants, and there could be Trojan horses silently waiting for a user to start snooping around only to destroy any and all evidence.

Incident handling should be closely linked to the company's security training and awareness program to ensure that these types of mishaps do not take place. The past issues that the incident recovery team encountered can be used in future training sessions to help others learn about what the company is faced with.

It is important that employees know how to report an incident to the incident-handling team. The process must be centralized, easy to accomplish (or they won't bother), convenient, and welcomed. Some employees feel reluctant to report incidents because they are afraid they will get pulled into something they do not want to be involved with or accused of something they did not do. There is nothing like trying to do the right thing and getting hit with a big stick. Employees should feel comfortable about the process, which means suggestions on improving the process should be looked at seriously.

A sound incident-handling program works with outside agencies and counterparts. The members of the team should be on the mailing list of the Computer Emergency Response Team (CERT) so that they can be aware of new issues and can spot malicious events, hopefully, before they get out of hand. CERT is a group that is responsible for monitoring and advising users and companies about security preparation and security breaches on the Internet. The team tracks and reports security issues and develops recommendations with clearly written steps to be taken if faced with specific threats.

References

www.cert.org/

www.sans.org/newlook/publications/incident_handling.htm

www.uga.edu/compsec/

www.cert.dfn.de/eng/pre99papers/certbib.html

http://csrc.nist.gov/topics/inchand.html

What Is Admissible in Court?

He is guilty because I say so. Answer: Um, I need more than that.

Computer logs are important in many aspects of the IT world and are usually used to troubleshoot an issue or used as a tool to try to understand the events that took place at a specific moment in time. When computer logs are to be used as evidence in court, they must be collected in the regular course of business. Most of the time, computer-related documents are considered *hearsay*, meaning the evidence is secondhand evidence. Hearsay evidence is not normally admissible in court unless it has firsthand evidence that can be used to prove the evidence's accuracy, trustworthiness, and reliability like a businessperson who generated the computer logs and collected them. It is important that this person generates and collects logs as a normal part of his business and not just this one time for court. The value of evidence depends upon the genuineness and competence of the source.

It is important to show that the logs, and all evidence, have not been tampered with in any way, which is the reason for the chain of custody of evidence.

When evidence is being collected, one issue that can come up is the user's expectation of privacy. If an employee is suspected and being charged of a computer crime, he might claim that his files on the computer he uses is personal and not available to law enforcement and the courts. This is why it is important for companies to conduct security awareness training, have employees sign contracts pertaining to the acceptable use of the company's computers and equipment, and to have legal banners pop up on each and every employees' computer when they log on. These items are key elements to establish that a user has no right to privacy when he is using company equipment. The following banner is suggested by CERT Advisory:

"This system is for the use of authorized users only. Individuals using this computer system without authority, or in excess of their authority, are subject to having all of their activities on this system monitored and recorded by system personnel.

In the course of monitoring an individual improperly using this system, or in the course of system maintenance, the activities of authorized users may also be monitored.

Anyone using this system expressly consents to such monitoring and is advised that if such monitoring reveals possible evidence of criminal activity, system personnel may provide the evidence of such monitoring to law enforcement officials."

This explicit warning strengthens a legal case that can be brought against an employee or intruder because the continued use of the system after viewing this type of warning implies that the person acknowledges the security policy and gives permission to be monitored.

Evidence has its own life cycle and it is important that the individuals involved with the investigation understand these different phases of the life cycle and properly follow them.

The life cycle of evidence includes

- Collection and identification
- Storage, preservation, and transportation
- Presentation in court
- Being returned to victim or owner

There are several types of evidence that can be used in a trial: written, oral, computer generated, and visual or audio. Written documents have to be the original documents and not copies. Oral evidence is a testimony of a witness—visual or audio is usually a captured event during the crime or right after it.

Not all evidence is equal in the eyes of the law and some types of evidence have more clout than other types. The following items quickly describe the different ways evidence can be categorized and valued.

Best Evidence

Best evidence is the primary evidence used in a trial because it provides the most reliability. This category is used for documentary evidence such as contracts. Oral evidence is not considered best evidence, and therefore does not have as good of a standing as legal documents. Oral evidence cannot be used to dispute a legal document, but it can be used to interpret the document.

Secondary Evidence

Secondary evidence is not viewed as reliable and strong in proving innocence or guilt when compared to best evidence. Oral evidence, such as a witness testimony, and copies of original documents are placed in the secondary evidence category.

Direct Evidence

Direct evidence can prove a fact all by itself instead of needing backup information to refer to. When using direct evidence, presumptions are not required. One example of direct evidence is the testimony of a witness who saw a crime take place. Although this oral evidence would be secondary in nature, meaning a case could not rest on just it alone, it is also direct evidence, meaning the lawyer does not necessarily need to provide other evidence to back it up. Many times direct evidence is based on information gathered from a witness's five senses.

Conclusive Evidence

Conclusive evidence is irrefutable and cannot be contradicted. Conclusive evidence is very strong all by itself and does not require corroboration.

Circumstantial Evidence

Circumstantial evidence can prove an intermediate fact that can then be used to deduce or assume the existence of another fact. This type of fact is used so that the judge or jury will logically assume the existence of a primary fact. For example, if a suspect told a friend he was going to bring down eBay's Web site, a case could not rest on that piece of evidence alone because it is circumstantial. However, this evidence can cause the jury to assume that because the suspect said he was going to do it and hours later it happened, may be he was the one who did the crime.

Corroborative Evidence

Corroborative evidence is supporting evidence used to help prove an idea or point. It cannot stand on its own, but is used as a supplementary tool to help prove a primary piece of evidence.

Opinion Evidence

When a witness testifies, the *opinion rule* dictates that she must testify to only the facts of the issue and not her opinion of the facts. This is slightly different than when an expert witness is used because he is used primarily for his educated opinion. Most lawyers will call in expert witnesses to testify and help the defending or prosecuting sides to better understand the subject matter so that they can help the judge and jury to better understand the matters of the case.

Hearsay Evidence

Hearsay evidence pertains to oral or written evidence that is presented in court that is secondhand and that has no firsthand proof of accuracy or reliability. If a witness testifies about something he heard someone else say, it is too far removed from fact and has too many variables that can cloud the truth. If business documents were made during regular business routines, they can be admissible. However, if these records were made just to be presented in court, they could be categorized as hearsay evidence.

It is important that evidence be sufficient, reliable, and relevant to the case at hand. These characteristics of evidence provide a foundation for a case and help ensure that the evidence is legally permissible.

For the evidence to be *sufficient*, it must be persuasive enough to convince a reasonable person of the validity of the findings. This means that the evidence cannot be wishy-washy in that one person interprets it to mean one thing and another person interprets to mean something else. Sufficient evidence also means that it cannot be easily doubted.

For evidence to be *reliable*, or competent, it must be consistent with fact. Evidence cannot be reliable if it is based on someone's opinion or copies of an original document, because there is too much room for error. Reliable evidence means that it is factual and not circumstantial.

For evidence to be *relevant*, it must have a reasonable and sensible relationship to the findings. If a judge rules that a person's past traffic tickets cannot be brought up in a murder trial, this means that the judge has ruled that the traffic tickets are not relevant to the case at hand. Thus, the prosecuting lawyer cannot even mention them in court.

If a piece of evidence is found to be sufficient, reliable, and relevant to the case, it must also be legally permissible, meaning that it was obtained in a legal way. The evidence must not have been obtained through an unlawful search and seizure, recorded illegally, or through a coerced confession. All of these steps must be taken to ensure that the evidence will not be thrown out once it gets to court.

Surveillance, Search, and Seizure

There are two main types of surveillance when it comes to identifying computer crimes: physical and via the computer. Physical surveillance pertains to security cameras, security guards, and closed-circuit TV (CCTV) (shown in Figure 10-5), which may capture evidence. Physical surveillance can also be used by an undercover agent who learns about the suspect's spending activities, family and friends, and personal habits in the hopes of gathering more clues for the case.

Figure 10-5 Surveillance can happen through CCTVs, cameras, keyboard monitoring, network sniffers, or line monitors.

Computer surveillance pertains to auditing events, which passively or actively monitors events by using network sniffers, keyboard monitors, wiretaps, and line monitoring. Active monitoring may require a search warrant. To legally monitor an individual, the person had to have been warned ahead of time that her activities may be subject to this type of monitoring.

must be in security policy or not legal

Keyboard monitoring captures all the characters an individual types.

Search and seizure activities can get tricky depending on what is being searched for and where. American citizens are protected by the Fourth Amendment against unlawful search and seizure. So law enforcement agencies must have probable cause and request a search warrant from a judge or court. The actual search can only take place in the areas outlined by the warrant. Private citizens are not subjected to protecting these Fourth Amendment rules of others unless they are acting as police agents. So if Kristy's boss warned all employees that the management could remove files from their computers at anytime, and her boss was not a cop or acting as a police agent, she could not successfully claim that her Fourth Amendment rights were violated. There are exceptions to requiring a search warrant for a search and seizure such as if the suspect tries to destroy the evidence. This is referred to as *exigent circumstances*, and a judge will later decide if this was carried out properly and legally so that the evidence can be admitted. For example, if a police officer had a search warrant that allowed him to search a suspect's living room but no other rooms and then he saw the suspect dumping cocaine down the toilet, the police officer could obtain the cocaine even though it was in a room not covered under his search warrant.

After evidence is gathered, the chain of custody needs to be enacted and enforced to make sure the evidence's integrity is not compromised.

Enticement and Entrapment

There can be a thin line between enticement and entrapment when it comes to capturing a suspect's actions. *Enticement* is legal and ethical—*entrapment* is neither legal nor ethical. In the world of computer crimes, a honeypot is always a good example to show the difference between enticement and entrapment. Companies put systems in their demilitarized zone (DMZ) that either emulate services attackers usually like to take advantage of or actually have the services enabled on those systems. The hope is that if an attacker breaks into the company's network, she will go right to the honeypot instead of the systems that are actual production machines. The attacker will be enticed to go to the honeypot system because it has many open ports and services running and exhibits vulnerabilities that the attacker would want to exploit. The company can log the attacker's actions and later attempt to prosecute. This example is legal unless the company crosses the line to entrapment. For example, if there is a link on one computer Web page that indicates that if the attacker would click on it, she could then download thousands of MP3 files for free. However, when the attacker clicks on that link, she is taken to the honeypot system instead and the company records all of her actions and attempts to prosecute. Entrapment does not prove that the suspect had the intent of committing a crime—it only proves that she was successfully tricked.

Interviewing and Interrogating

Once surveillance and search and seizure activities have been performed, it is very likely that suspects must be interviewed and interrogated. When this is needed, there should be one person in charge of the interview or interrogation, with one or two others present. The topics of discussion and questions should be prepared beforehand and asked in a calm fashion. The purpose of an interrogation is to obtain evidence for a trial—therefore, it should be properly planned and carried out.

Interrogating employees requires specific guidelines and procedures to make it successful.

The employee interrogator should be senior to the employee suspect. A vice president is not going to be very intimidated or willing to spill his guts to the mailroom clerk. The interrogation should be held in a private place, and the suspect should be relatively comfortable and at ease. If exhibits are going to be shown to the suspect, they should be shown one at a time, and otherwise kept in a folder. It is not necessary to read a person their rights before questioning unless law enforcement officers do the interview.

What the interrogators do not want to happen during an interrogation is to be deceived by the suspect, to relinquish important information pertaining to the investigation, or to have the suspect flee before a trial date is set.

Import and Export Laws

As stated earlier, different countries have different laws pertaining to copyright, trade secrets, trademarks, and such, and countries also have different import and export restrictions.

The main technology that countries restrict in transborder issues is encryption. Some countries restrict the type or strength of encryption that can be used between countries or that can be bought and sold between different countries. This is because governments want to be able to break the encryption and listen in on communications if they are suspected of being about illegal activities.

NOTE   There are no restrictions on domestic use in the United States pertaining to encryption products.

If a vendor wants to sell encryption technologies to another country or include encryption within its product, it must thoroughly research the restrictions of the source and destination countries and seek legal advice to ensure that no laws or regulations are being broken accidentally.

In the United States, the Bureau of Export Administration (BXA), in the U.S. Department of Commerce, governs exportation of encryption mechanisms. In the past, exportation of these types of technologies had been extremely strict. In October 2000, the BXA published a rule creating a "free-trade zone," approved by the president and the vice president, which enables U.S exporters to export most encryption products to 15 European Union member states and 8 additional trading partners. This included PCs, laptops, hand-held devices, wireless technologies, software, and network devices.

This greatly reduced the processes vendors had to go through to get their products approved to be able to be sold in other countries.

There are still strict exportation regulations on the countries considered terrorist-supporting states. For further information on these issues, please refer to the references provided.

References

www.bxa.doc.gov/

www.ntis.gov/product/export-regulations.htm

http://chaos.fedworld.gov/bxa/faq.html

Privacy

There is a sense that privacy is becoming more threatened as the world relies more and more on technology.

There have been privacy laws enacted and enforced, such as the Federal Privacy Act of 1974, and new laws, such as the Gramm Leach Bliley Act of 1999 and Health Insurance Portability and Accountability Act (HIPAA), which show an increase in the need to protect personal privacy issues. Basically, the privacy laws state that any data collected must be done in a fair and lawful manner. The data is only to be used for the purposes it was collected for and only for a reasonable amount of time. If an agency collects data on a person, that person has the right to receive a report outlining data collected about him if it is requested.

The laws also state that the information must be accurate, kept up-to-date, and cannot be disclosed to a third party unless authorized by statute or consent of that individual. People also have the right to make a correction to their personal information. If data is to be transmitted to a location where the equivalent security protection cannot be ensured, then transmission is prohibited.

Within a corporation, there are several employee privacy issues that must be thought through and addressed if the company wants to be properly protected. An understanding that each state can have different privacy regulations should prompt the company to investigate exactly what they can and cannot monitor before doing so.

If a company has learned that the state the facility is located in permits keyboard, e-mail, and surveillance monitoring, they must take the proper steps in ensuring that the employees know that these types of monitoring may be put into place. This is the best way for a company to protect itself, make sure it has a legal leg to stand on if necessary, and not present the employees with any surprises.

The monitoring has to be work related, meaning that a manager may have the right to listen on his employees' conversations with customers, but he does not have the right to listen in on personal conversations that are not work related. Monitoring also must happen in a consistent way where all employees are subjected to monitoring instead of picking out one or two people.

If a company feels that it may be necessary to monitor e-mail messages and usage, this needs to be explained to the employees through a banner or training. It is best to have an employee read a document describing what type of monitoring they could be encountered with, what is considered acceptable behavior, and what the consequences of not meeting those expectations are. The employees should sign this document, which can later be treated as a legal document if necessary.

A company that wants to be able to monitor e-mail should have a specialized security policy devised just for this purpose. It should outline who can and cannot read employee messages, describe the circumstance where e-mail monitoring may be acceptable, and where the e-mail can be assessed. Some companies indicate that they will only monitor e-mail that lives on the mail server, whereas other companies declare the right to read employee messages if they reside on the mail server or the employee's computer. It is important that the company does not promise privacy to employees, because that could initiate a suit.

Because many IT and security professionals have access to many parts of computer systems and the network, this does not mean it is ethical and right to overstep the bounds that could possibly threaten a user's privacy. Only the tasks necessary to enforce the security policy should take place and nothing further that could compromise another's privacy.

Prescreening Personnel

Chapter 3 described why it is important to properly screen individuals before hiring them into a corporation. These steps are necessary to help the company protect itself and to ensure that it is getting the type of employee that is required for the job. This chapter will look at some of the issues on the other side of the table, which deals with that individual's privacy rights.

There are limitations on the type and amount of information an organization can obtain on a potential employee. The limitations and regulations for background checks vary from state to state, so the hiring manager would want to consult the legal department with any of these questions. Usually human resources will develop an outline for hiring managers to follow when it comes to interviews and background checks.

There are also potential problems when an employee leaves the company. If the employee is fired, laid off, moves on to a competitor company, or has any unresolved issues with the company, there may be instances of fraud, destruction, or sharing of confidential information. An exit interview should be performed that requires the employee to sign a document indicating he does not have any confidential papers and promises not to violate the trade secret and confidential information rules that he agreed to when he was hired.

Laws, Directives, and Regulations

Regulation in computer and information security can cover many areas for many different reasons. Some issues that require regulation are data privacy, computer misuse, software copyright, data protection, and controls on cryptography. These regulations can be implemented in different arenas like the government and private sectors for reasons dealing with environmental protection, intellectual property, national security, personal privacy, public order, health and safety, and prevention of cruelty and corruption. Regulations have had to provide an interesting, and many times debated, balance between the individual and the corporation.

Security professionals need to keep up-to-date on computer laws and regulations.

Security professionals have so much to keep up with these days from understanding how the new worm works and how to properly protect against it, grasping how three new versions of DoS attacks take place and what tools are used to accomplish them, what new security products are released and how they compare to the existing products, new technologies, service patches, hotfixes, encryption methods, access control mechanisms, telecommunication security issues, social engineering, and physical security. There is a lot to learn and keep up with, and laws and regulations are not usually at the top of security professionals' list of interest or things to know. However, they are important for many different reasons and especially if you are asked to be involved with identifying and investigating a computer crime or asked to provide your professional opinion or work as an expert witness. Laws and regulations can be another item on the large heap of information a security professional is expected to keep current on, but in many situations it is just as important as any other security issues.

 NOTE Legislative Strategy: To deal more effectively with computer crime, legislative bodies have broadened the definition of property to include data.

Laws, regulations, and directives developed by the government, or appointed agencies, do not usually provide detailed instructions to follow to properly protect computers and company assets. Each environment is too diverse in topology, technology, infrastructure, requirements, functionality, and personnel. Because technology changes at such a fast pace, these laws and regulations could never successfully represent reality. Instead, they specify requirements expected from different business types. It works as a framework of rules, and it is up to each company to fill in that framework, but properly stay within the bounds.

Health Insurance Portability and Accountability Act (HIPAA)

The Health Insurance Portability and Accountability Act (HIPAA), a new federal regulation, has been mandated to provide national standards and procedures for the electronic storage, use, and transmission of personal medical information and healthcare data. This regulation provides a framework and guidelines to ensure security, integrity, and privacy when handling confidential medical information. HIPAA outlines how security should be managed for any facility that creates, accesses, shares, or destroys medical information.

People's health records can be used and misused in different scenarios for many different reasons. As health records migrate from a paper-based system to an electronic system, they become easier to maintain, access, and transfer, but they also become easier to manipulate and access in an unauthorized manner. Traditionally, healthcare facilities have lagged behind other businesses in their information and network security mechanisms, architecture, and security enforcement because there was no real business need to expend the energy and money to put these items in place. Now there is.

HIPAA brings steep federal penalties for noncompliance. If medical information is used in a way that violates the privacy standards dictated by HIPAA, even by mistake, there are monetary penalties of $100 per violation up to $25,000 per year, per standard. If protected health information is obtained or disclosed knowingly, the fines can be as much as $50,000 and one year in prison. If the information is obtained or disclosed under false pretenses, the cost can go up to $250,000 and ten years in prison if there is intent to sell or use the information for commercial advantage, personal gain, or malicious harm. This is serious business. (Please review Appendix C for more in-depth information on HIPAA including a compliancy matrix.)

Gramm Leach Bliley Act of 1999

This act requires financial institutions to develop privacy notices and give their customers the option to prohibit the banks from sharing their information with nonaffiliated third parties. The act dictates that the board of directors are responsible for many of the security issues within a financial institution, indicates that risk management must be implemented, all employees need to be trained on information security issues, and that implemented security measures must be fully tested. It also requires these facilities to have a written security policy to be in place by July 1, 2001. (Please review Appendix F for further information pertaining to this act.)

Computer Fraud and Abuse Act

This act was written in 1986 and amended in 1996 and is the primary federal anti-hacking statute. It categorizes seven forms of activity as federal crimes:

- Prohibits the knowing access of computers of the federal government to obtain classified information without authorization or access through the use of excess of authorization

- Prohibits the intentional access of a computer to obtain information from a financial institution, the federal government, or any protected computer involved in interstate or foreign communications without authorization or through the use of excess of authorization

- Prohibits the intentional and unauthorized access of computers of the federal government, or computers used by or for the government when the access affects the government's use of that computer

- Prohibits the knowing access of a protected computer without authorization or in excess of authorization with the intent to defraud

- Prohibits anyone from knowingly causing the transmission of a program, information, code, or command, and as a result of such conduct, intentionally causing damage without authorization to a protected computer

- Prohibits the knowing trafficking of computer passwords with the intent to defraud

- Prohibits the transmission of communications containing threats to cause damage to a protected computer

These acts range from felonies to misdemeanors with a range of large to small fines and jail sentences if any of these listed activities are committed.

Federal Privacy Act of 1974

In the mid-1960s, there was a proposal that the U.S. government would collectively hold each individual's information, pertaining to Social Security, Census, Internal Revenue Service, Bureau of Labor Statistics, and other limbs of the government, which would be compiled and held in a main federal data bank. The committee that proposed it saw it as an efficient way of gathering and centralizing data—others saw it as a dangerous move against individual privacy. The federal data bank never came to pass because of strong opposition.

To keep the government in check on gathering information on U.S. citizens and other matters, a majority of its files are considered open to the public. Government files are open to the public unless there are specific issues enacted by legislature deeming specific files unavailable. This is what is explained in the Freedom of Information Act. This is different than what the Privacy Act outlines and protects. The Privacy Act applies to records and documents developed and maintained by specific branches of the federal government such as executive departments, government corporations, independent regulatory agencies, and government-controlled corporations. It does not apply to congressional, judiciary, or territorial subdivisions.

An actual *record* is information about an individual's education, medial history, financial history, criminal, employment, and other similar types of information. Agencies can only maintain this type of information if it is necessary and relevant to accomplishing the agency's purpose. The Privacy Act dictates that an agency cannot disclose this information without written permission from the individual. However, like most government acts, legislation, and creeds, there is a list of exceptions.

So what does all of this dry legal mumbo-jumbo mean? Basically, agencies can gather information about individuals, but it must be relevant and necessary for its approved cause. In addition, that agency cannot go around town sharing other people's private information. If they do, private citizens have the right to sue in order to protect their privacy.

This leaks into the computer world because this information is usually held by one type of computer or another. If an agency's computer is holding an individual's confidential information, it must provide the necessary security mechanisms to ensure it cannot be compromised or copied in an unauthorized way.

The Privacy Act of 1974

This act requires the following stipulations:

- Disclosure of personal information is limited to only authorized persons.
- The records must be accurate, relevant, timely, and complete.
- Safeguards are required to ensure security and confidentiality of records.

Computer Security Act of 1987

This act requires federal agencies to identify computer systems that will contain sensitive information. The agency must develop a security policy and plan for each of these systems and conduct periodic training for individuals who operate, manage, or use these systems. Federal agency employees must be provided with security awareness training and be informed of how the agency defines acceptable computer use and practices.

Because the federal government deals with a lot of important, confidential, and secret information, it wants to make sure that all individuals and systems within all federal government agencies meet a certain level of awareness and protection.

Security and Freedom Through Encryption Act

This was approved in 1997 and guarantees the right of all U.S. citizens and residents to be able to use and sell encryption products and technology. This act was developed to relax encryption export controls and to make it legal for people to own and use encryption software no matter what algorithm it employs or key length it uses. It also prohibits state and federal governments from requiring anyone to relinquish his encryption key so that these agencies can snoop on conversations or decrypt information. This means that the governments cannot require key escrow.

Federal Sentencing Guidelines

In 1991, U.S. Federal Sentencing Guidelines were developed and passed down to provide judges with courses of action to take when overseeing white collar crimes that take place within organizations. These guidelines deal with antitrust, federal securities, mail and wire fraud, bribery, contracts, and money laundering.

These guidelines provided ways that companies and law enforcement should prevent, detect, and report computer crimes. It outlined how senior executives are responsible for the computer and information security decisions that they make and what actually took place within their organizations and set a maximum fine of $290 million dollars.

The actual punishments and fines could be reduced if the company in question exercised due diligence and showed steps of responsible behavior. It required companies to develop security policies, standards, and procedures, and to properly inform the employees of these issues.

Economic Espionage Act of 1996

Industry and corporate espionage was taking place with no real guidelines of who could properly investigate the events. This act provided the necessary structure when dealing with these types of cases and further defined trade secrets to be technical, business, engineering, scientific, or financial. This meant that an asset did not necessarily need to be tangible to be protected or to be stolen. This act enables the FBI to investigate industrial and corporate espionage cases.

International Cooperation Efforts

Governments all over the world have realized that they must cooperate with each other if they hope to properly deal with computer crimes. This means different channels of communication had to be opened, agreements on the meaning and definitions of specific crimes had to be made, and barriers that usually stood in the way of effective investigative work that crossed geographical boundaries had to be lessened or erased. The following sections quickly describe some of the organizations that are involved with this type of work.

G8

The G8 group represents the world's leading industrialized countries and Russia. In May 2000, they agreed to cooperate to fight cybercrime during their Paris meeting. This was prompted by the global concern over the growing threat of cybercrime, and the recent success of the viruses like ILOVEYOU, which cost companies all over the world thousands to millions of dollars. It vowed to extend the powers of the European law enforcement agency, Europol, to fight illegal acts committed with technology.

This was done so that countries would work together to develop similar laws and open doors to help each other enforce laws and regulations pertaining to computer and information crimes.

Interpol

The international police organization, Interpol, collects and distributes information about cross-border crimes. It works to keep companies, law enforcement agencies, and governments informed about cybercrimes and who is becoming targets of malicious hackers.

European Union

In January 2000, the European Commission revealed its proposals on fighting cyber-crime. The Commission presented its paper to the Council of Ministers of the European Union and Parliament, which outlined a policy that describes the methods necessary to fight computer crimes without hindering e-commerce. The proposal suggests harmonizing the member states' laws to deal with criminal law on high-tech crimes including hacking and DoS attacks.

References

www.interpol.int/Public/TechnologyCrime/CrimePrev/ITSecurity.asp

www.interpol.com/Public/TechnologyCrime/default.asp

www.cnn.com/2000/TECH/computing/05/18/global.security.idg/

www.cbsnews.com/now/story/0,1597,195452-412,00.shtml

Summary

Law, ethics, and investigations are very important pieces to computer and information security. They are elements not usually brought to mind when one speaks of computer security, but they are a must if a society is serious about controlling this type of crime and punishing the guilty.

In many ways, the laws and courts are in their infancy stages when attempting to deal with computer crimes. They are faced with not having many precedents to fall back on when interpreting what is legal and illegal and what the proper punishments are for each type of computer crime. However, the legal system is quickly developing laws and providing ways for proper interpretation of these laws to help all arms of the law enforcement agencies and the victims. Over the last few years hacking and attacking have been performed for fun, mainly by curious computer individuals, but as the punishments increase, the fun may quickly come to an end.

Security professionals should be aware and versed on computer security laws and regulations so that they properly inform their customers of expected responsibilities and so the security professionals themselves know what boundaries they are expected to work within.

Quick Tips

- Dumpster diving is going through someone's trash to find confidential or useful information. It is legal, but unethical.
- Wiretapping is a passive attack that eavesdrops on communication. It is only legal with prior consent or a warrant.
- Social engineering is the act of tricking a person into giving confidential or sensitive information that could then be used against him or his company.
- Data diddling is the act of modifying information, programs, or documentation in the efforts to commit fraud.
- Excessive privileges means that an employee has more computer rights than necessary to complete her tasks.
- Criminal law deals with an individual's conduct that violates the government laws, which were developed to protect the public.
- Civil law deals with wrongs committed against individuals or companies that result in injury or damages. Civil law does not use prison time as a punishment, but usually financial restitution.
- Administrative, or regulatory law, are standards of performance or conduct expected by government agencies from companies, industries, and certain officials.
- A patent grants ownership and enables that owner to legally enforce his rights to exclude others from practicing the invention covered by the patent.
- Copyright covers the expression of ideas rather than the ideas themselves.

- Trademarks cover words, names, product shape, symbol, color, or a combination of these used to identify products. These items are used to distinguish products from the competitors' products.

- Trade secrets are deemed proprietary to a company and can be information that provides a competitive edge. The information is protected as long as the owner takes the necessary security actions.

- Crime over the Internet has brought about jurisdiction problems for law enforcement and the courts.

- Privacy laws dictate that data collected by agencies must be collected fairly and lawfully, must be used only for the purpose it was collected, must be used for a reasonable amount of time, and must be accurate and timely.

- If companies are going to use any type of monitoring, they need to make sure it is legal in their area and inform all employees that they may be subjected to monitoring.

- Employees need to be informed regarding what is expected behavior pertaining to computer systems, network use, e-mail, and phone use. They need to also know what the ramifications are for not meeting those expectations.

- Logon banners should be used to inform users of what could happen if they do not follow the rules pertaining to using company devices. This provides legal protection for the company.

- Countries differ in their view of the seriousness of computer crime or have different penalties for certain crimes. This makes enforcing laws much harder across country borders.

- The three main types of harm addressed in computer crime laws pertain to unauthorized intrusion, unauthorized alteration or destruction, and using malicious code.

- The Federal Sentencing Guidelines gave judges and courts procedures of how prevention, detection, and reporting of crimes should happen along with penalty ranges. This also made senior executives responsible for their company's actions.

- Law enforcement and the courts have a hard time with computer crimes because of the newness of the types of crimes, the complexity involved, jurisdiction issues, and evidence collection. New laws are being written to properly deal with cybercrime.

- If a company does not practice due care in its efforts to protect itself from computer crime, it can be found to be negligent and legally liable for damages.

- Elements of negligence include not fulfilling a legally recognized obligation, failure to conform to a standard, and proximate causation, which result in injury or damage.

- Most computer crimes are not reported because the victims are not aware of the crime or are too embarrassed to let anyone know.

- Theft is no longer restricted to physical constraints. Assets are now viewed as intangible objects that can also be stolen or disclosed via technology means.

- The primary reason for the chain of custody for evidence is to ensure that it will be admissible in court.

- Companies should develop their own incident response team, which is made up of people from management, IT, legal, human resources, public relations, and security.

- Hearsay evidence is secondhand and usually not admissible in court.

- To be admissible in court, business records have to be made and collected in the normal methods of business, not specially generated for a case in court. Business records can easily be hearsay if there is no firsthand proof of their accuracy and reliability.

- To make computer-generated material admissible, a witness needs to testify about what it is, what it means, and how reliable it is.

- The life cycle of evidence includes identification and collection of the evidence, storage, preservation, transportation, and presentation in court—the evidence is then returned to the owner.

- Collection of computer evidence is a very complex and detail-oriented task. Only skilled people should attempt it—otherwise, evidence can be ruined forever.

- When looking for suspects, it is important to consider the means, opportunity, and motives (MOM).

- For evidence to be admissible in court, it needs to be relevant, sufficient, and reliable.

- Evidence must be legally permissible, meaning that it was seized legally and the chain of custody was not broken.

- All evidence should be marked and stored in a container, which is also marked.

- Law enforcement agencies must get a warrant to search and seize an individual's property, as stated in the Fourth Amendment. Private citizens are not subject to protecting the Fourth Amendment of others unless acting as a police agent.

- Enticement is luring an intruder and is legal. Entrapment induces a crime, tricks a person, and is illegal.

- Know what issues the Internet Activities Board (IAB) considers unethical.

- Salami is an act of skimming off a small amount of money in the hopes that no one will notice.

- Phreakers are hackers who specialize in committing crimes against the phone companies.

- Blue Boxing simulates a tone that tricks the telephone company's system into thinking the user is authorized for long distance service, which enables him to make the call.

- Red Boxing simulates the sound of coins being dropped into a payphone.

- Black Boxing manipulates the line voltage to receive a toll-free call.

- After a computer system is seized, the investigators should make a copy of the storage media before doing anything else.

Questions

Please remember that these questions are formatted and asked in a certain way for a reason. The questions and answers may seem odd or vague, but this is what you will see on the actual CISSP test.

1. Which of the following does the IAB consider a violation of the "Ethics and the Internet"?
    a. Creating a computer virus
    b. Entering information into a Web page
    c. Performing a penetration test on a host on the Internet
    d. Disrupting Internet communications

2. What is the study of computer and surrounding technologies and how they relate to crime?
    a. Computer forensics
    b. Computer criminology
    c. Incident handling
    d. Computer information criteria

3. Which of the following does IAB consider unethical behavior?
    a. Internet users who conceal unauthorized accesses
    b. Internet users who waste computer resources

    c. Internet users who write viruses

    d. Internet users who monitor traffic

4. After a forensics investigator seizes a computer during a crime investigation, what is the next step?

    a. Label and put it into a container, and label the container.

    b. Dust the evidence for fingerprints.

    c. Make an image copy of the disks.

    d. Lock the evidence in the safe.

5. A CISSP candidate signs a nondisclosure statement prior to taking the CISSP examination. Which of the following would be a violation of the Code of Ethics that could cause the candidate to lose his certification?

    a. E-mailing information or comments about the exam or information taught in the class to other CISSP candidates

    b. Submitting comments on the questions of the exam to $(ISC)^2$

    c. Submitting comments to the board of directors regarding the test and content of the class

    d. Conducting a presentation about the CISSP certification and what the certification means

6. If your company gives you a new PC and you find residual information about confidential company issues, what should you do based on the $(ISC)^2$ Code of Ethics?

    a. Contact the owner of the file and inform him about it. Copy it to a disk, give it to him, and delete your copy.

    b. Delete the document because it was not meant for you.

    c. Inform management of your findings so they can make sure this type of thing does not happen again.

    d. E-mail it to the author and to management so that everyone is aware of what is going on.

7. Why is computer crime difficult to investigate and track down the criminal?

    a. Privacy laws are written to protect people from being investigated for these types of crimes.

    b. Special equipment and tools are necessary to detect these types of criminals.

    c. Criminals can spoof their address and hop from one network to the next.

    d. The police have no jurisdiction over the Internet.

8. Protecting evidence and providing accountability for who handled it at different steps during the investigation is referred to as what?

   a. Rule of best evidence

   b. Hearsay

   c. Evidence safety

   d. Chain of custody

9. If an investigator needs to communicate to another investigator, but does not want the hacker to find this traffic, what type of communication should be used?

   a. Digitally signed messages

   b. Out-of-band messages

   c. Forensics frequency

   d. Authentication and access control

10. Why is it challenging to collect and identify evidence to be used in a court of law?

    a. The evidence is mostly intangible.

    b. The evidence is mostly corrupted.

    c. The evidence is mostly encrypted.

    d. The evidence is mostly tangible.

11. The chain of custody of evidence describes who obtained the evidence and _____.

    a. Who secured it and controlled it

    b. Who controlled it and transcribed it

    c. Who secured it and validated it

    d. Who controlled it and duplicated it

12. Before shutting down a system suspected of an attack, the investigator should do what?

    a. Remove and back up the hard drive.

    b. Dump memory contents to disk.

    c. Remove it from the network.

    d. Save data in spooler queue and temporary files.

13. Why is computer-generated documentation usually considered nonreliable evidence?

    a. It is primary evidence.

    b. It is too difficult to detect prior modifications.

    c. It is corroborative evidence.

    d. It is not covered under criminal law, but it is covered under civil law.

14. Which of the following is a necessary characteristic of evidence to be admissible?
    a. It must be real.
    b. It must be noteworthy.
    c. It must be reliable.
    d. It must be important.

15. What agency usually works with the FBI when investigating computer crimes?
    a. (ISC)^2
    b. Secret Service
    c. CIA
    d. State police

16. If a company deliberately planted a flaw in one of their systems in the hopes of detecting an attempted penetration and exploitation of this flaw, what would this be called?
    a. Incident recovery response
    b. Entrapment
    c. Illegal
    d. Enticement

17. If an employee is suspected of wrong doing in a computer crime, what department must be involved?
    a. Human resources
    b. Legal
    c. Auditors
    d. Payroll

18. When would an investigator's notebook be admissible in court?
    a. When he uses it to refresh memory
    b. When he cannot be present for testimony
    c. When requested by the judge to learn the original issues of the investigations
    d. When no other physical evidence is available

19. Disks and other media that are copies of the original evidence are considered what?
    a. Primary evidence
    b. Reliable and sufficient evidence
    c. Hearsay evidence
    d. Conclusive evidence

20. If a company does not inform employees that they may be monitored and does not have a policy stating how monitoring should take place, what should a company do?
    a. Don't monitor employees in any fashion.
    b. Monitor during off-hours and slow times.
    c. Obtain a search warrant before monitoring an employee.
    d. Monitor anyway—they are covered by two laws allowing them to do this.

21. What is one reason why successfully prosecuting computer crimes is so challenging?
    a. There are no ways to capture electrical data reliably.
    b. The evidence in computer cases does not follow best evidence directives.
    c. These crimes do not fall into the traditional criminal activity.
    d. Wiretapping is hard to do legally.

22. When can executives be charged with negligence?
    a. If they do not follow the transborder laws
    b. If they do not properly report and prosecute attackers
    c. If they do not properly inform users that they may be monitored
    d. If they do not practice due care when protecting resources

23. To better deal with computer crime, several legislative bodies have taken what steps in their strategy?
    a. Expanded several privacy laws
    b. Broadened the definition of property to include data
    c. Required corporations to have computer crime insurance
    d. Redefined transboarder issues

24. Some privacy laws dictate which of the following rules?
    a. Individuals have a right to remove any data they do not want others to know.
    b. Agencies do not need to ensure that the data is accurate.
    c. Agencies need to allow all government agencies access to the data.
    d. Agencies cannot use the data for a purpose different than what it was collected for.

25. Which of the following is not true about dumpster diving?
    a. It is legal.
    b. It is illegal.
    c. It is a breach of physical security.
    d. It is gathering data from places people would not expect to be raided.

26. If an employee alters a program to take a few pennies from every customer's bank account each month, what is this called?
    a. Salami
    b. Social engineering
    c. Spoofing
    d. Dumpster diving

Answers

1. D.	8. D.	15. B.	21. C.
2. A.	9. B.	16. D.	22. D.
3. B.	10. A.	17. A.	23. B.
4. C.	11. C.	18. A.	24. D.
5. A.	12. B.	19. C.	25. B.
6. C.	13. B.	20. A.	26. A.
7. C.	14. C.		

Application and System Development

In this chapter, you will learn about the following items:

- Different types of software controls and implementation
- Database concepts and security issues
- Data warehousing and data mining
- Software life cycle development processes
- Change control concepts
- Object-oriented programming components
- Expert systems and artificial intelligence

Applications and computer systems are usually developed for functionality first, not security first. To get the best of both worlds, security and functionality would have to be developed at the same time. Security should be interwoven into the core of a product and provide protection at different layers; this is a better approach than trying to develop a front end or wrapper that may reduce the overall functionality and leave security holes when this product has to be integrated with other applications.

Applications and System Development

Application system controls come in many different flavors with many different goals. They can control input, processing, number-crunching methods, interprocessing communication, interfacing to the system and other programs, access control, and output. They should be developed with the potential risks in mind, and many types of threat

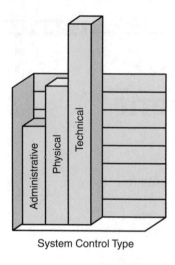

System Control Type

Figure 11-1 Applications and operating systems have different types of controls, but most of them are technical in nature.

models and risk analyses should be invoked at different stages of development. The goal is to prevent security compromises and reduce the probability of attacks and data corruption. The controls can be preventive, detective, or corrective. They can come in the form of administrative and physical, but are usually more technical (see Figure 11-1).

The specific application controls depend upon the application itself, its objectives, the security goals of the developers, and the environment the application will be placed in. If an application is purely proprietary and will only run in closed trusted environments, fewer security controls may be needed than those required for applications that will connect businesses over the Internet and provide financial transactions. The trick is understanding the security needs of an application, implementing the right controls and mechanisms, thoroughly testing the mechanisms and how they integrate into the application, following structured development methodologies, and providing secure and reliable distribution methods. This can be harder than it sounds.

Device versus Software Security

Today, many security efforts look to devices to solve security problems. These devices are firewalls, intrusion detection systems (IDSs), sensors, and vulnerability scanners. This occurs because networks, and how they are thought of, work on a basic outside and inside notion. The bad people and potential threats are on the outside, and what needs to be protected is on the inside. This notion has worked, to an extent, because networks were closed environments, which usually meant controlled environments. However, our environments then incorporated electronic data interchange (EDI), remote dial-in capabilities, Internet sites, and virtual private networks (VPNs). Now environments are incorporating wireless communication, value added networks (VANs), and business-to-business (B2B) capabilities, which add complexity to the concept of us and them and inside and outside.

The division between software security and device security deals with providing security at the beginning stages of software development versus providing devices that protect the perimeters of networks. The perimeter devices try to prevent attackers from exploiting the security holes that reside in the software. Firewalls and IDSs are studied and talked about within circles of security much more than inadvertent flaws in design and poorly written software. In reality, the flaws within the software cause a majority of the vulnerabilities in the first place. Figure 11-2 illustrates two distinct approaches to security. Perimeter devices are considered for security versus software development for several reasons:

- In the past, it was not crucial to implement security during the software development stages, thus many programmers do not practice these procedures.

- Many security professionals are not software developers.

- Software vendors are trying to rush to market with their eyes set on functionality, not security.

- The computing society is used to receiving software with bugs and applying patches.

- A combination of all the above.

Finger-pointing and quick judgments are not useful or necessarily fair at this stage of our computing evolution. Twenty years ago mainframes had tight security because a handful of people knew how to run them, users worked on computers (dumb terminals) that could not introduce malicious code to the mainframe, and environments were closed. The core protocols and framework were developed in a time when threats and attacks were not prevalent; therefore, there was not a need for such security. Then computer and software evolution took off and the possibilities splintered into a thousand different directions. The high demand for computer technology and different types of software increased the demand for programmers, system designers, administrators, and engineers. This high demand brought in a wave of people who had little experience. The lack of experience, the high change rate of technology, and the race to market add problems to security, which are not always clearly understood. Although it

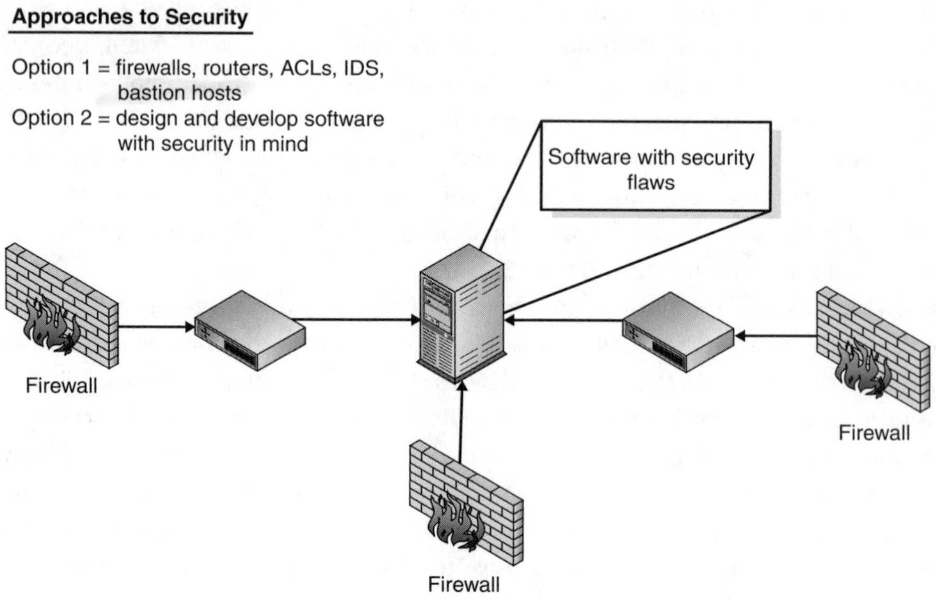

Approaches to Security

Option 1 = firewalls, routers, ACLs, IDS,
bastion hosts
Option 2 = design and develop software
with security in mind

Software with security
flaws

Firewall

Firewall

Firewall

Figure 11-2   There are two main ways to approach security.

is easy to point to the big software vendors in the sky for producing flawed or buggy software, this is driven by the customer demand. Understanding how security works within programs, how programs integrate into environments, and how compromises take place will cause consumers to demand more security-oriented software and better programming and development practices.

This chapter is an attempt to show how to address security at its source, which is at the software and development level. This requires a shift from *reactive* actions towards security matters to *proactive* actions in order to try to make sure they do not happen in the first place or at least happen to a smaller extent. Figure 11-3 illustrates our current way of dealing with security issues.

Different Environments Demand Different Security

Today a network administrator is in an overwhelming position of integrating different applications and computer systems to keep up with his company's demand on expandable functionality and the new gee-wiz components that executives buy off on and

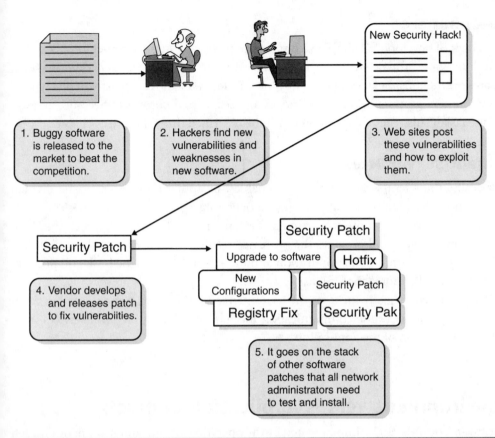

1. Buggy software is released to the market to beat the competition.

2. Hackers find new vulnerabilities and weaknesses in new software.

3. Web sites post these vulnerabilities and how to exploit them.

New Security Hack!

Security Patch

4. Vendor develops and releases patch to fix vulnerabiities.

Security Patch

Upgrade to software

Hotfix

New Configurations

Security Patch

Registry Fix

Security Pak

5. It goes on the stack of other software patches that all network administrators need to test and install.

Figure 11-3 The usual trend of software being released to the market and how security is dealt with

demand quick implementation. This is further frustrated by the company's race to provide a well-known presence on the Internet by implementing Web sites with the capabilities of taking online orders, storing credit card information, and setting up extranets with partners. This can quickly turn into a confusing ball of protocols, devices, interfaces, incompatibility issues, routing and switching techniques, telecommunication routines, and management procedures. It could make an administrator choose to buy some land in Montana and raise goats instead.

On top of this, security is expected, required, and depended upon. When security compromises creep in, the finger-pointing starts, liability issues are tossed like hot potatoes, and heads might even roll. This requires an understanding of the environment, what is currently in it, and how it works, so the new technologies can be implemented in a more controlled and comprehendible fashion.

7

E-Commerce

The days of developing a simple Web page and posting it on the Internet to sell candles are long gone. Today, customer front-end, complex middleware, and third-tier data warehousing must be developed and work seamlessly. As the complexity of this type of environment grows, tracking down errors and security compromises becomes an awesome task. (This type of environment will be described throughout this chapter.)

Client/Server Model

Basically, the client/server architecture enables an application system to be divided across multiple platforms that can range in operating systems and hardware. The client requests services and the server fulfills these requests. The server handles the data-processing services and provides the processed result to the client. The client performs the front-end portion of an application and the server performs the back-end portion, which is usually more labor intensive.

The front end usually includes the user interface and local data manipulation capabilities, and provides the communication mechanisms that can request services from the server portion of the application.

Environment versus Application Controls

Software controls can be implemented by the operating system, application, or through database management controls, and usually a combination of all three. Each has its strengths and weaknesses, but if they are all understood and programmed to work in a concerted effort, then many different scenarios and types of compromises can be thwarted. One downside to relying mainly on operating system controls is that they can control a subject's access to different objects and restrict the actions of that subject within the system, but not necessarily within an application. If an application has a security compromise that is created by the programming code, it is hard for the operating system to predict that this type of compromise could take place or audit it once it does happen. A file system is a broad environment for many applications to work within. It is unfair to expect the operating system to understand all the nuances of different programs and their internal mechanisms.

On the other hand, application controls and database management controls are very specific to their needs and the security compromises they understand. Although an application might be able to protect data by allowing only certain types of input and not allowing certain users to view data kept in sensitive database fields, it cannot prevent the user from deleting msdos.sys or inserting bogus data into the Address Resolu- *why not?* tion Protocol (ARP) table. Operating system and application controls have their place and limitations. The trick is to find out where one type of control stops so the next type of control can kick into action.

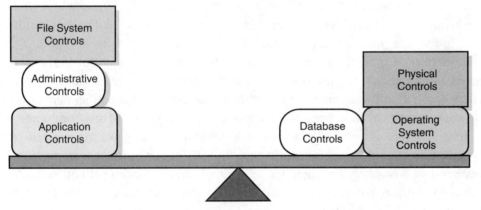

The different types of controls need to be understood
and utilized to provide a balanced and useful security level.

Security has been mainly provided by environmental devices rather than controls built into applications. Environmental devices can be supplied across a wide range of applications, they can be controlled by a centralized management, and are further away from application control. However, this approach does not always provide the necessary level of granularity, and it does not approach compromises that can take place because of problematic coding and programming routines. Firewalls and access control mechanisms can provide a level of protection by preventing attackers from exploiting buffer overflows, but the real protection happens at the core of the problem—proper software development and coding practices must be in place.

Complexity of Functionality

Programming is a complex trade—the code itself, routine interaction, global and local variables, input received from other programs, output fed to different applications, attempts to envision future user inputs, calculations, and restrictions for a laundry list of possible consequences. Many times trying to account for all the what-ifs and programming on the side of caution can reduce the overall functionality of the application.

As one limits the functionality and scope of an application, the market share and potential profitability of that program can reduce. There is always a balance between functionality and security, and in the development world, functionality is usually deemed the most important.

So this means programmers and application architects need to find a happy medium between the necessary functionality of the program, the security requirements, and the mechanisms that should be implemented to provide this security. This can add more complexity to an already complex task.

There may be more than one road that leads to enlightenment, but as these roads increase in number, it is hard to know if a path will eventually bring you to bliss or to a fiery doom of unpleasantness. Many programs accept data from different parts of the program, other programs, the system itself, and user input. Each of these paths needs to be followed in a methodical way and each possible scenario and input needs to be thought through and tested to provide a deep level of assurance. It is important that each module is capable of being tested individually and in concert with other modules. This level of understanding and testing will make the product more secure by catching flaws that could be exploited.

Data Types, Format, and Length

We have all heard about the recent uproar pertaining to buffer overflows, as if they were new to the programming world. They are not necessarily new, but are now being exploited on a reoccurring basis.

Buffer overflows were discussed in Chapter 5 and it was explained that attacks are carried out when the application does not check the length of input that is actually being accepted. Extra data could be executed in a privileged mode that would enable an attacker to take control of the system. If a programmer wrote a program that expected the input length to be 5KB, then this needs to be part of the code so that the right amount of buffer space is available to hold this data when it actually comes in. However, if that program does not make sure the 5KB is accepted, and only 5KB is accepted, an evildoer can input the first 5KB for the expected data to process and then another 50KB that contains malicious instructions can also be processed by the CPU.

Length is not the only thing programmers need to be worried about when it comes to accepting input data. Data also needs to be in the right format and data type. If the program is expecting alpha ASCII characters, it should not accept hexadecimal or binary values.

The accepted value also needs to be reasonable. This means that if an application asks Stacy to enter the amount she would like to transfer from her checking account to her savings account, she should not be able to enter "Bob." This can fall under data format and data type (numbers versus alphabet characters), but parameters also need to be in place to watch for bogus entries so errors can stop at the place of origin instead of being passed to calculations and logic procedures.

These examples are extremely simplistic compared to what programmers have to face in the real programming world. However, they are presented to show that software needs to be developed to accept the correct data types, format, and length of inputted data for security and functionality purposes.

Implementation and Default Issues

As many people in the computer field are aware of, out-of-the-box implementations are usually far from secure. Most security has to be configured and turned on after installation; not understanding this fact can be dangerous for the inexperienced IT person. Windows NT has been through its share of criticism for lack of security for one reason or another, but in many ways the platform can be secured; it just comes out of the box in an insecure state. This is done because settings will have to be configured to properly integrate into different environments and this is a friendlier way of installing the product for users. If Mike installed a new software package that continually threw messages of "Access Denied" when he was attempting to configure it to interoperate with other applications and systems, his patience might wear thin and he might decide to hate that vendor for years to come because of the stress and confusion put upon him.

Yet again we are at a hard place for developers and architects. When a security application or device is installed, it should default to "No Access." This means that when Lance installs a packet-filter firewall, it should not allow any packets to pass into the network that were not specifically granted access. However, this requires Lance to know how to configure the firewall for it to ever be useful. There is a fine line between security, functionality, and user-friendliness. If an application is extremely user-friendly, it is probably not as secure. For an application to be user-friendly, it usually requires a lot of extra coding for errors, dialog boxes, wizards, and step-by-step instructions. Sadly, this extra coding can allow for bloated code that can create unforeseeable compromises. So vendors have a hard time winning, but they usually keep making money as they keep trying.

Implementation

Implementation errors and misconfigurations are common issues that cause a majority of the security issues in networked environments. Many people do not realize that many services are enabled when a system is installed. These services can provide evil-doers with information that can be used during an attack and many services provide an actual way into the environment itself. NetBIOS services can be enabled to permit sharing resources in Windows environments and remote procedure call (RPC) services, which let remote users run command shells and other programs can be enabled with no restrictions. These are just two examples of services that can open a system up to the whole world.

Many systems have File Transfer Protocol (FTP), Telnet, and Internet Relay Chat (IRC) services enabled that are not being used and have no real safety measures. Some of these services are enabled by default so when an administrator installs an operating system and does not check these services to properly restrict or disable them, they are available for attackers to uncover and use.

Because vendors have user friendliness and user functionality in mind, the product will usually be installed with defaults that provide no or very low security protection. It would be very hard for vendors to know the different security levels required in all the different environments that the product will be installed in, so they usually do not attempt it. It is up to the person installing the product to learn how to properly configure the settings to achieve the necessary level of protection.

Another problem in implementation and security is the number of unpatched systems. Once security issues are identified, vendors develop patches to address and fix these security holes. However, many times they do not get installed on the systems that are vulnerable. The reasons for this vary from an administrator not keeping up-to-date on the recent security vulnerabilities and patches, not fully understanding the importance of these patches, or being afraid that the patches will cause other problems. All of these reasons are quite common, but they all end in the same result—insecure systems. Many vulnerabilities that are being exploited have had patches developed and released months or years ago.

It is unfortunate that adding security (or service) patches can adversely affect other mechanisms within the system. The patches should be tested for these types of activities before they are applied to production servers and workstations to help prevent service disruptions that can affect network and employee productivity.

Failure States

Many circumstances are unpredictable, and are therefore hard to plan for. However, unpredictable situations can be planned for in a general sense rather than trying to plan and code for each and every situation. If an application fails for any reason, it should resume to a safe state. This could require the application to shut down or present the user with a logon screen to start the application from its initialization state. This is why some systems blue screen and/or restart. When this occurs, something is going on within the system that is unrecognized or unsafe, so the system dumps its memory contents and starts all over.

Different system states were discussed in Chapter 5, which described how processes can be executed in a privileged or user state. If an application fails and is executing in a privileged state, these processes should be shut down properly and released to ensure that disrupting a system could not provide compromises that could be exploited. If a privileged process does not shut down properly and it stays active, an attacker can figure out how to access the system, using this process, in a privileged state. This means that the attacker could have administrative or root access to a system, which opens the door for more severe destruction.

Database Management

Databases have a long history of storing important intellectual property and items that are considered valuable and proprietary to companies. Because of this, they usually live in an environment of mystery to all but the database and network administrators. The less anyone knows about the databases, the better. Users usually access databases indirectly through a client interface and their actions are restricted to ensure the confidentiality and integrity of the data held within the database and the structure of the database itself.

NOTE Database Management System (DBMS): A database management system (DBMS) is usually a suite of programs used to manage large sets of structured data with ad hoc query capabilities for many types of users.

This norm is changing as companies run to connect their networks to the Internet, which usually includes indirect access to a back-end database. In the past, employees accessed customer information held in databases instead of customers accessing it themselves. Today, many companies allow their customers to access data in their databases through a browser. The browser makes a connection to the company's middleware, which then connects them to the backend database. This adds levels of complexity and the database will be accessed in new and unprecedented ways.

One example is in the banking world where online banking is all the rage. Many financial institutions want to keep up with the times and add the services they think their customers will want. But online banking is not just another service like being able to order checks. Most banks work in closed (or semiclosed) environments and opening their environments to the Internet is a huge undertaking. The perimeter network needs to be secured, middleware software has to be developed or purchased, and the database should be behind one, preferably two, firewalls. Many times components in the business application tier are used to extract data from the databases and process the customer requests.

Database access control can be restricted by only allowing roles. The database administrator can define specific roles that are allowed to access the database. Each role will have assigned rights and permissions, and customer and employees are then ported into these roles. Any user that is not within one of these roles is denied access. This means that if an attacker was able to compromise the firewall and other perimeter network protection mechanisms and was then able to make requests to the database, since he is not in one of the predefined roles, the database is still safe. This process streamlines access control and ensures that no users or evildoers can access the database directly but must access it indirectly through a role account. Figure 11-4 illustrates these concepts.

Database Management Software

A *database* is a collection of data stored in a meaningful way that enables multiple users and applications to access, view, and modify data as needed. Databases are managed with software that provide these type of activities; it also enforces access control restrictions, provides data integrity and redundancy, and sets up different procedures for data manipulation. This software is referred to as the *database management system (DBMS)* and is usually controlled by a database administrator. Databases not only store data, but they also process data and represent it in more usable and logical form. Database management systems interface with programs, users, and data within the database. They help us store, organize, and retrieve information effectively and efficiently.

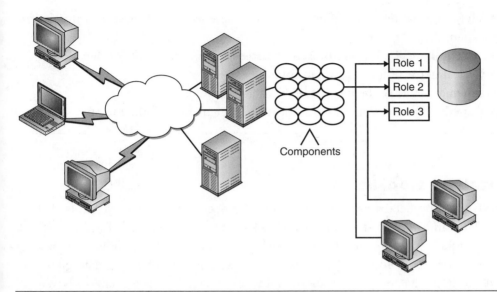

Figure 11-4 One type of database security is employing roles.

A database is the mechanism that provides structure for data that is collected. The actual specifications of the structure can be different per database implementation because different organizations or departments work with different types of data and need to perform diverse functions upon that information. There may be different workloads, relationships between the data, hardware platforms, performance requirements, and varying security goals.

Because the needs and requirements for databases vary, different data models can be implemented that align with different business and organizational needs.

Database Jargon

- **Record**   Collection of related data items
- **File**   Collection of records of the same type
- **Database**   Cross-referenced collection of files
- **DBMS**   Manages and controls the database
- **Base relation**   A table stored in a database
- **Tuple**   A row in a database
- **Attribute**   A column in a database
- **Primary key**   Columns that make each row unique (A table must include a primary key for every row.)

- **View**   Virtual relation defined by the database to control subjects from viewing certain data
- **Foreign key**   Attribute of one table that is the primary key of another table
- **Cell**   Intersection of a row and column
- **Schema**   Holds data that describes a database
- **Data dictionary**   Central repository of data elements and their relationships

Database Models

The database model defines the relationships between different data elements, dictates how data can be accessed, defines acceptable operations, the type of integrity offered, and how the data is organized. This model provides a formal method of representing data in a conceptual form and provides the necessary means of manipulating the data held within the database. There are several types of data models for databases; we will only touch on three of them.

A *relational data model* uses attributes (columns) and tuples (rows) to contain and organize information (see Figure 11-5). The relational model is the most widely used method of organizing databases today. It presents information in the form of tables. A relational database is composed of two-dimensional tables and each table contains unique rows, columns, and cells (the intersection of a row and a column). A primary key is a field that links all the data within a record to a corresponding value. For example, in the following table, the primary keys are Product G345 and G978. When an application or another record refers to this primary key, it is actually referring to all the data within this one row.

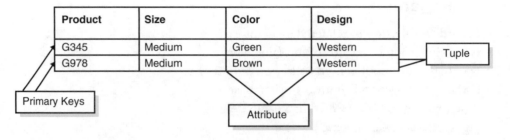

Figure 11-5   Relational databases hold data in table structures.

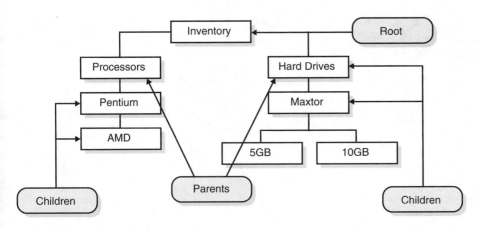

Figure 11-6   Hierarchical databases use a tree structure and a parent/child relationship.

A *hierarchical data model* is another commonly used database model (see Figure 11-6). The structure and relationship between the data elements are different than those in a relational database. A hierarchical model combines records and fields that are related in a logical tree structure.

The parents can have one child, many children, or no children. The tree structure contains branches and each branch has a number of leaves, or data fields. These databases have well-defined, prespecified access paths, but they are not as flexible in relating information as a relational database. Hierarchical databases are useful for mapping one-to-many relationships.

A *distributed data model* has data stored in more than one database, but it is logically connected (see Figure 11-7). It uses hierarchy, but each lower-level data element may be related to more than one parent. These relationships provide many-to-many relationships.

Different databases may live at different places on a network or reside in totally different networks. Because they are logically connected, the users see the database as one full entity, instead of several entities. When users access data, they do not need to know which database they are accessing; one database may transfer a user to another database, which is transparent to the user.

This model enables different databases to be managed by different administrators, although one person or group must manage the entire logical database. This may be useful if each database contains information that is specialized, but the complexity of load balancing, fault tolerance, and shifting of users is quite high.

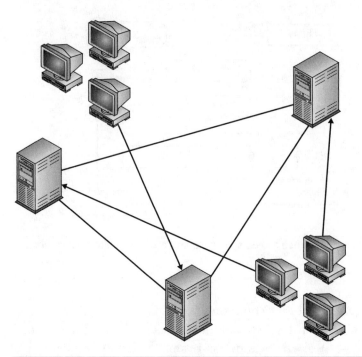

Figure 11-7 A distributed database may contain databases in different areas, which are logically connected and viewed as one database.

Relational Database Components

Like all software, databases are built with programming languages. Some database languages include a *data definition language (DDL)*, which defines the schema, a *data manipulation language (DML)*, which examines and manipulates the data within the database, a *data control language (DCL)*, which defines the internal organization of the database, and an ad hoc *query language (QL)* for users to make queries and access the data within the database.

Each type of database can be different in its model with many other differences, which vary from vendor to vendor. Most, however, contain the following basic core functionalities:

- Data definition language (DDL)
- Data manipulation language (DML)

- Query language (QL)

- Report generator

DDL defines the structure and schema of the database. The structure could mean the table size, key placement, views, and data element relationship. The *schema* describes the type of data that will be held and manipulated and their properties. It defines the structure of the database, access operations, and integrity procedures.

DML contains all the commands that enable a user to view, manipulate, and use the database (view, add, modify, sort, and delete commands). QL enables users to make requests of the database and the report generator produces printouts of data in a user-defined manner.

Data Dictionary

A *data dictionary* is a central repository of data elements and their relationships. It stores critical information about data usage, data relationships, data sources, and data formats. It is a tool used to centrally manage parts of a database by controlling data about the data within the database. It provides a cross-reference between groups of data elements and the databases.

A data dictionary is a central collection of data element definitions, schema objects, and reference keys. The schema objects can contain tables, views, indexes, procedures, functions, and triggers. A data dictionary can contain the default values for columns, integrity information, the names of users, the privileges and roles for users, and auditing information.

The database management software reads the data dictionary to ascertain that schema objects exist and checks to see if specific users have the process access rights to view them (see Figure 11-8). When users look at the database, they can be restricted by specific views. The different view settings for each user are held within the data dictionary. Users can read data within the data dictionary to find out information about the database itself. When new tables, new rows, or new schema are added, the data dictionary is updated to reflect this.

Primary versus Foreign Key

The primary key is an identifier of a table, this must be unique. Each table must have a primary key. When a user requests to view a record, the database tracks this record by

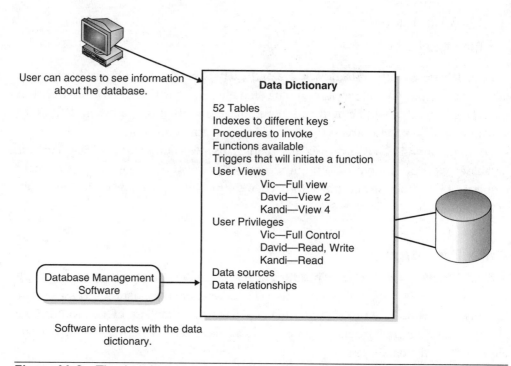

Figure 11-8 The data dictionary is a centralized program that contains information about a database.

its unique primary key. If the primary key was not unique, the database would not know which record to present to the user. In the following illustration, the primary keys for Table A are the dogs' names.

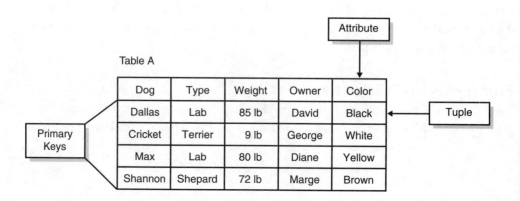

A primary key is different than a foreign key, although they are closely related. If an attribute in one table has a value matching the primary key in another table, this attribute is considered a foreign key. This foreign key is not necessarily the primary key in its current table; it only has to contain the same information that is held in another table's primary key. In the following illustration, a primary key for Table A is Dallas. Because Table B has an attribute that contains the same data as this primary key, it is referred to as a foreign key. This is another way for the database to track relationships between data that it houses.

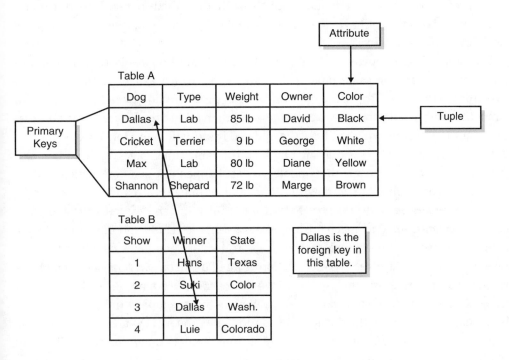

Integrity

Like other resources within a network, a database can run into *concurrency* problems. Concurrency has to do with making sure that different subjects receive the most up-to-date information. If a group uses one price sheet to know how many supplies to order for the next week and also to calculate the expected profit, this is an important file. If Dan and Elizabeth copy this price sheet from the file server to their workstations, they each have a copy of the original file. Dan changes the stock level of computer books from 120 to 5, because they sold that many in the last three days. He also uses the current prices listed in the price sheet to estimate his expected profits for next week. Elizabeth reduces the price on several software packages and sees that the stock level of computer books is still over 100, so she chooses to not order any more for next week. Dan and Elizabeth do not communicate this different information to each other, but place it on this price sheet for everyone to view and use.

Dan copies his changes back to the file server and then 30 seconds later Elizabeth copies her changes over Dan's changes. So the file only reflects Elizabeth's changes. Because they did not synchronize their changes, they are both now using incorrect data. Dan's profits are off because he does not know that Elizabeth reduced the prices and next week Elizabeth will have no computer books because she did not know that the stock level dropped to five.

The same thing happens in databases. If controls are not in place, two users can access and modify the same data at the same time, which can be detrimental to a dynamic environment. To ensure that concurrency problems do not exist, processes can *lock* tables within a database, make changes, and then release the lock. The next process that accesses the table will then have the updated information and locking ensures that two processes do not access the same table at the same time. Pages, tables, rows, and fields can be locked to ensure that updates to data happen one at a time, which enables each process and subject to work with correct and accurate information.

Database software performs two main types of integrity services: semantic and referential. A *semantic integrity* mechanism makes sure that structural and semantic rules are enforced. These rules pertain to data types, logical values, uniqueness constraints, and operations that could adversely affect the structure of the database. A *referential integrity* mechanism would ensure that no record would contain a reference to a primary key of a nonexisting record, or a null value. This guarantees that the tuple is uniquely identified by primary key values. In the previous illustration, the primary keys are the names of the dogs. For the sake of table integrity, every tuple must contain one primary key. If it does not have a primary key, it cannot be referenced by the database.

Also, the database must not contain unmatched foreign key values. Every foreign key refers to an existing primary key. In the previous illustration, if the foreign key in Table B is Dallas, then the primary key that it is related to in Table A must have the same value, which is Dallas. If these values do not match, then their relationships can be broken and again the database cannot reference the information properly.

Other configurable operations are available to help protect the integrity of the data within a database. These operations are rollbacks, commits, and checkpoints.

The *rollback* is a statement that ends a current transaction and cancels all other changes to the database. These changes could have taken place with the data itself or with schema changes that were typed in. When a rollback statement is executed, the changes are cancelled and the database returns to its previous state. A rollback can take place if the database has some type of unexpected glitch or if outside entities disrupt its processing sequence. Instead of transmitting and posting partial or corrupt information, the database will roll back to its original state and log these errors and actions so that they can be reviewed at a later time.

The *commit* statement terminates a transaction and executes all changes that were just made by the user. Just like its name indicates, once the commit command is executed, the changes are committed and reflected in the database. These changes can be made to data or schema information, and by committing these changes, they are then available to all other applications and users. If a user attempted to commit a change and it could not complete correctly, a rollback is performed. This ensures that partial changes do not take place and that data is not corrupted.

Checkpoints are used to make sure that if a system failure occurs, or if an error is detected, the user can always return to a point in time before the system crashed. For a conceptual example, say Dave typed, "Jeremiah was a bullfrog. He was <checkpoint> a good friend of mine." (The system inserted a checkpoint.) Then a freak storm came through and rebooted the system. When Dave got back into the database application, he would see "Jeremiah was a bullfrog. He was," but the rest was lost. Therefore, the checkpoint saved some of his work.

Checkpoints are easy to implement within databases, but a balance has to be drawn between too many and not enough. Too many checkpoints can degrade the performance of the database, whereas not enough checkpoints bring the risk of losing data and decreasing user productivity because the data would have to be reentered. Checkpoints can be initiated by a time interval, a specific action by the user, or the number of transactions or changes made to the database. A database can set a checkpoint every 15 minutes, every 20 transactions completed, each time a user gets to the end of a record, or every 12 changes made to the databases.

So a checkpoint restores data by providing the user the ability to go back in time before the system crashed or hiccuped. This can lower frustration levels and help us all live in harmony.

Database Security Issues

The two main security issues we are going to address are aggregation and inference. *Aggregation* happens when a user does not have the clearance or permission to access specific information, but she does have the permission to access components of this information; she can then figure out the rest and obtain restricted information. She can learn of information from different sources and combine them to learn something that she does not have the clearance to know.

 NOTE Aggregation is the act of combining information from separate sources. The combination of the information forms new information, which the subject does not have the necessary rights to access. The combined information has a sensitivity that is greater than the individual parts.

The following is a silly conceptual example. Let's say a database administrator does not want anyone in the Users group to be able to figure out a specific sentence so he segregates the sentence into components and restricts the User group from accessing it, as represented in Figure 11-9. However, Emily can access components A, C, and F. Because she is a particularly bright girl, she figures out the sentence and now knows the restricted secret.

To prevent aggregation, the subject, and any application or process acting on the subject's behalf, needs to be prevented from gaining access to the whole collection, including the independent components. The objects can be placed into containers, which are classified at a higher level to prevent access from subjects with lower-level permissions or

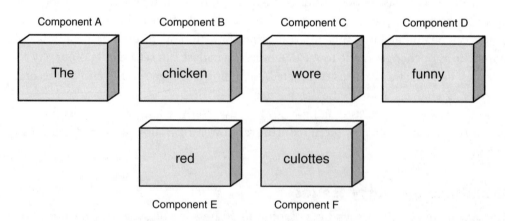

Figure 11-9 Because Emily has access to components A, C, and F, she can figure out the secret sentence through aggregation.

clearances. A subject's queries can also be tracked and context-dependent classification can be enforced. This would keep a history of the objects a subject has accessed and restrict an access attempt if there was an indication that an aggregation attack is underway.

The other security issue is *inference*, which is very similar to aggregation. The inference problem happens when a subject deduces information that is restricted from data he has access to. This is seen when data at a lower security level indirectly portrays data at a higher level.

NOTE Inference is the ability to derive information that is not explicitly available.

For example, if a clerk was restricted from knowing the planned movements of troops based in Saudi Arabia, but did have access to food shipment requirements forms and tent allocation documents, he could figure out that the troops were moving to a place outside of Dubia because that is where the food and tents are being shipped. The food shipment and tent allocation documents were classified as confidential and the troop movement was classified as top secret. Because of the varying classifications, the clerk could access and ascertain information he was not supposed to know.

The trick is to prevent the subject, or any application or process acting on the behalf of that subject, from indirectly gaining access to the inferable information. This problem is usually dealt with in the development of the database by implementing content- and context-dependent classification rules; this tracks the subject's query requests and restricts patterns that represent inference.

Database security takes a different approach than operating system security. In an operating system, the identity and authentication of the subject controls access. This is done through access control lists (ACLs), capability tables, roles, and security labels. The operating system only makes decisions about whether a subject can access a file; it does not make this decision on the contents of the file itself. If Mitch can access file A, it does not matter if that file contains information about a cookie recipe or secret information from the Cold War. On the other hand, database security does look at the contents of a file when it makes an access control decision, which is referred to as *content-dependent access control*. This type of access control increases processing overhead, but it provides higher granular control.

Countermeasures for inference

couldn't this be used in aggregation also

Common attempts to prevent inference attacks are cell suppression, partitioning the database, and noise and perturbation. *Cell suppression* is a technique used to hide or not show specific cells that contain information that could be used in inference attacks. *Partitioning* a database involves dividing the database into different parts, which makes it much harder for an unauthorized individual to find connecting pieces of data that can be brought together and other information that can be deduced or uncovered. *Noise and perturbation* is a technique of inserting bogus information in the hopes of misdirecting an attacker or confusing the matter enough that the actual attack will not be fruitful.

Many times security is not integrated into the planning and development of a database. Security is an afterthought and a trusted front end is developed to be used with the database instead. This approach is limited in the granularity of security and the types of security functions that can take place.

A common theme in security is a balance between effective security and functionality. In many cases, the more you secure something, the less functionality you have. Although this could be the desired result, it is important to not impede user productivity when security is being introduced.

Database Views

Don't show your information to everybody, only a select few.

Databases can permit one group, or a specific user, to see certain information, while restricting another group from viewing it altogether. This functionality happens through the use of *database views*. If a database administrator wants to allow middle management to see their departments' profits and expenses, but not show them the whole company's profits, she can implement views. Senior management would be given all views, which contain all the departments' and the company's profit and expense values, whereas each individual manager would only be able to view his or her department values.

Like operating systems, databases can employ discretionary access control (DAC) and mandatory access control (MAC) (explained in Chapter 4). So views can be displayed according to group membership, user rights, or security labels. If DACs were being employed, then groups and users could be granted access through views based on their identity, authentication, and authorization. If MACs were in place, then groups and users would be granted access based on their security level and the data's sensitivity level.

Polyinstantiation

There are times when a company does not want users at one level to access and modify data at a higher level. There are different ways of handling this type of situation. One approach is when a lower-level user attempts to access a higher-level object, access is denied. However, this gives away information indirectly by telling the lower-level entity that something sensitive lives inside that object at that level.

Another way of dealing with this issue is *polyinstantiation*. This enables a relation to contain multiple tuples with the same primary keys with each instance distinguished by a security level. When this information is inserted into a database, lower-level subjects need to be restricted from this information. Instead of just restricting access, another set of data is created to fool the lower-level subjects into thinking that the information actually means something else. For example, if a naval base has a cargo shipment going from Delaware to the Ukraine that contains weapons via the Oklahoma ship, this type of information could be classified as top secret. Only the subjects with the security clearance of top secret and above should know this information, so a dummy file is created that states that the Oklahoma is carrying a shipment going from Delaware to Africa containing food and it is given a security clearance of unclassified, as shown in Table 11-1. It will be obvious that the Oklahoma ship is gone, but individuals at lower security levels will think that the ship is on its way to Africa, instead of to the Ukraine. This will also make sure that no one at a lower level will try to commit the Oklahoma for any other missions. The lower-level subjects know that the Oklahoma ship is not available and they will look at other ships to use for cargo shipments.

 NOTE Polyinstantiation is a process of interactively producing more detailed versions of objects by populating variables with values or other variables.

Table 11-1 An Example of Polyinstantiation by Providing a Cover Story to Subjects at a Lower Level

Level	Ship	Cargo	Origin	Destination
Top Secret	Oklahoma	Weapons	Delaware	Ukraine
Unclassified	Oklahoma	Food	Delaware	Africa

Polyinstantiation creates two versions of the same object so the lower-level subjects will not know the true information and it stops them from attempting to use or change that data in any way. It is a way of providing a cover story for the entities that do not have the necessary security level to know the truth.

Online Transaction Processing (OLTP)

Online transaction processing (OLTP) is usually used when databases are clustered to provide fault tolerance and higher performance. OLTP provides mechanisms that watch for problems and deal with them appropriately when they do occur. For example, if a process stops functioning for one reason or another, the monitor mechanisms within OLTP can detect this and attempt to restart the process. If the process cannot be restarted, then the transaction that was taking place will be rolled back to ensure that no data is corrupted or that only part of a transaction happens. Any erroneous or invalid transactions that are detected should be written to a transaction log and to a report log to be reviewed at a later time.

OLTP will load balance incoming requests if it is necessary. This means that if requests to update databases increase and one system reduces in performance because of the large volume, OLTP can move some of these requests to other systems. This makes sure that all requests are handled and that the user, or whoever is making the requests, does not have to wait a long period of time for the transaction to complete.

When there is more than one database, it is important that they all contain the same information. If database A has a value for Katie's checking account of $3,500 and database B has the value of $10,000, this could cause some problems, as illustrated in Figure 11-10. The reason the difference would occur is that Katie withdrew several

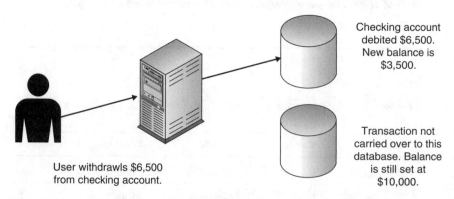

Checking account debited $6,500. New balance is $3,500.

Transaction not carried over to this database. Balance is still set at $10,000.

User withdrawls $6,500 from checking account.

Figure 11-10 If each database is not updated with the correct information, many types of problems can take place.

thousand dollars and only one database received that request. If the real value is $3,500 and Katie makes a request to check her checking account amount, this request may go to the database that still has the old value of $10,000. Although this information might make Katie surprised and happy, it is incorrect information. OLTP will make sure that a transaction is not complete until all databases receive and reflect this change. This is a *two-phase commit* service.

Data Warehousing and Data Mining

Data warehousing combines data from multiple databases into a large database with the purpose of a fuller extent of information retrieval and data analysis. Data from different databases is extracted and transferred to a central data stored called a warehouse. This enables users to query one entity rather than accessing and querying different databases.

This is not a process of just mirroring data from different databases and presenting the data in one place. It is a method of selecting useful information that is then processed and presented in a more useful and understandable way. Related data is summarized and correlated before it is presented to the user. Instead of having each and every piece of data presented, the user is given data in a more abridged form that best fits her needs.

Although this provides easier access and control, because the data warehouse is in one place, it also requires more stringent security. If an intruder were to get into the data warehouse, he can access all of the company's information at once.

Data mining is the process of massaging the data held in the data warehouse into more useful information. Data mining tools are used to find an association and correlation in data to produce *metadata.* Metadata can produce previously unseen relationships between individual subsets of information. It can find abnormal patterns that were not previously apparent. A simplistic example could be detecting insurance fraud. If millions of customers, their information, claims, and specific habits were kept in a database, or warehouse, and a mining tool looked for certain patterns in claims, it could be found that each time John Smith moved, he had an insurance claim two to three months following the move. If he moved in 1967 and two months later had a suspicious fire, then moved in 1973 and had a motorcycle stolen three months after that, and then moved again in 1984 and had a burglary break-in two months afterwards, a pattern arises. This may be hard for people to manually catch because he had different insurance agents over the years, the files were just updated and not reviewed, or the files were not kept in a centralized place for agents to review.

Data mining can look at complex data and simplify it by using Fuzzy logic, set theory, and neural networks to perform the mathematical functions and look for patterns in data that are not so apparent. In some ways, the metadata is more valuable than the data it was derived from; thus, it must be highly protected. (Fuzzy logic and neural networks are discussed later in the "Artificial Neural Networks"section).

NOTE Data mining: The process of analyzing a database using tools that look for trends or anomalies without having the knowledge of the meaning of the data.

Metadata: Data goes into a database and metadata comes out of the database. Metadata is the result of storing data within a database and mining the data with tools (see Figure 11-11).

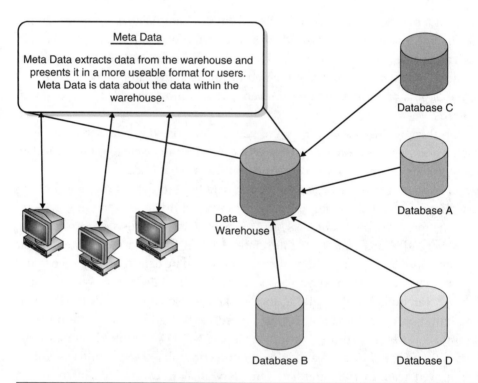

Figure 11-11 Mining tools are used to extract data from a data warehouse, identify patterns, and present it in useful formats for users.

System Development

Security is most effective if it is planned and managed throughout the life cycle of a system or application rather than applying a third-party package as a front end at the end of development. There are many security risks, analyses, and events that occur during its lifetime and these issues should be dealt with from the initial planning stage and continue through the design, coding, implementation, and operational stages. If security is added at the end of a project development versus being involved with each and every step of the life cycle, the cost and time of adding security increases dramatically. Security should not be looked at as a short sprint, but should be seen as a long run with many hills and obstacles.

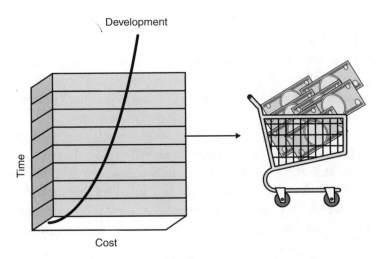

Security should be implemented at each developmental phase.
Adding a security at the end costs a lot more money.

Many developers, programmers, and architects know that security is much more expensive and complicated when it is added at a later phase of the system's life cycle instead of integrating it into the planning and designing phase. Different security components can affect many different aspects of a system, and if it is thrown in at the last moment, it will surely affect other mechanisms negatively, restrict some already developed functionality, and cause the system to perform in unusual and unexpected ways. This approach costs more money because of the amount of times the developers have to go back to the drawing board, recode completed work, and rethink different aspects of the system's architect.

Management of Development

Many developers know that good project management keeps the project moving in the right direction, allocates the necessary resources, provides the necessary information, and plans for the worst and hopes for the best. Project management is an important part of product development and security management is an important part of project management.

A security plan should be drawn up at the beginning of a development project and integrated into the functional plan to ensure that security is not overlooked. The first plan is broad, covers a wide base, and refers to documented references for more detailed information. The references could include computer standards (RFCs, IEEE standards, and best practices), documents developed in previous projects, security policies, accreditation statements, incident-handling plans, and national or international guidelines (Orange Book, Red Book, and Common Criteria). This makes the plan easier to read and more usable.

The security plan should have a lifetime of its own. It will need to be added to, subtracted from, and explained in more detail as the project continues. It is important to keep it up-to-date for future reference. It is always easy to lose track of actions, activities, and decisions once a large and complex project gets underway.

The security plan and project management activities will most likely be audited so that security-related decisions can be understood. When assurance in the system needs to be guaranteed, indicating that security was fully considered in each phase of the life cycle, the procedures, development, decisions, and activities that took place during the project will be reviewed. It is important that the documentation accurately reflects how the system or product was built and how it operates once implemented into an environment.

Life Cycle Phases

There are several types of models used for system or application development, which includes varying life cycles. This section outlines one model. Each model basically accomplishes the same thing; the main difference is how the development and lifetime of a system is broken into sections.

A project can start with a good idea and then the programmers and engineers just wing it, or the project can be carefully thought out and structured to follow the necessary life cycles. The first option may seem more fun in the beginning because stuffy requirements and steps can be skipped, documentation can be blown off, and the product can get out the door in a shorter time and under budget. However, more fun would actually be had by the team that took its time to think through all of the scenarios of each phase of the life cycle because its product would be more sound, become more trustworthy by the market, the team would make more money in the long run, and it would not need to chaotically develop several service and security patches to fix problems missed the first time around.

A system or product usually adheres to the following life cycle phases:

- Project initiation
- Functional design analysis and planning
- System design specifications
- Software development
- Installation/implementation
- Operational/maintenance
- Disposal

You may notice that security is not a bullet point, indicating it is dealt with in one phase or another. This is because security should be embedded throughout all phases. It costs a lot more money to address security issues after the product is released compared to addressing it during the development of the product. Functionality is the main driving force of developing products and there are several considerations that need to take place within that realm, but we will be addressing the *security* issues that also need to take place at each phase of the product's life cycle.

Project Initiation

This is the phase when everyone involved attempts to understand why the project is needed and what the scope of the project entails. Either a specific customer needs a new system or application or there is a demand for the product in the market. At this point, the characteristics of the system and proposed functionality are discussed, brainstorming sessions take place, and obvious restrictions are reviewed.

A conceptual definition of the project needs to be initiated and developed to ensure that everyone is on the right page and that this is a proper product to develop that will be, hopefully, profitable. This phase could include evaluating products that were currently on the market and identify any demands that are not being met by current vendors. It could also be a direct request for a specific product from a current or future customer.

In either case, because this is for a specific client or market, an initial study of the product needs to be started and a high-level proposal should be drafted that outlines the necessary resources for the project and the predicted timeline of development. The estimated profit expected from the product also needs to be conducted. This information is submitted to senior management who will determine if the next phase should begin or if further information is required.

In this phase, the user needs are identified and basic security objectives of the product are acknowledged. It must be determined if the product will be processing sensitive data and if so, the levels of sensitivity involved should also be defined. An initial risk analysis can be initiated that evaluates threats and vulnerabilities to estimate the cost/benefit ratios of the different security countermeasures. Issues pertaining to security integrity, confidentiality, and availability need to be addressed. The level of each security attribute should be focused upon so that a clear direction of security controls can begin to take shape.

A basic security framework is designed for the project to follow and risk management processes are established. Risk management will continue throughout the lifetime of the project. Some of the following risk information may start to be gathered and evaluated in the project initiation phase, but it will become more granular in nature as the phases graduate into the functional design and design specification phase.

Risk Management

Okay, question one. How bad can we screw up?

One of the most important pieces of risk management is to know the right questions to ask.

Risk management was discussed in Chapter 3, but it dealt with identifying and mitigating risks that directly affect the business as a whole. Risk management must also be performed when developing and implementing software. Although the two functions are close in concepts, goals, and objectives, they have different specific tasks.

Software development usually has a focus on rich functionality and getting it out the door and on the shelves for customers to buy as soon as possible. Most of the time security is not part of the process or quickly falls to the wayside when a deadline seems to be just around the corner. It is not just the programmer that should be thinking about coding in a secure manner, but the design of the product should have security integrated and layered throughout the project, and software engineering should address security threat scenarios and solutions during their tasks. It is not just one faction of a development team that falls down when it comes to security. It just has never really been treated as an important function of the process—that is until the product is bought by several customers who undergo attacks and compromises that tie directly to how the product was developed and programmed. Then security is quite a big deal, but it is too late to integrate security into the project; instead, a patch is developed and released.

The first step in risk management is to identify the threats and vulnerabilities and calculate the level of risk involved. When all the risks are evaluated, management will decide upon the acceptable level of risk they are willing to take on and accept. Of course, it would be nice for management to not accept any risks and for the product to be designed and tested until it was foolproof; however, this would cause the product to be in development for a long time and be too expensive to purchase, so compromises and intelligent business decisions need to be made to provide a balance between risks and economic feasibility.

Risk Analysis

A risk analysis is performed to identify the relative risks and the potential consequences. This process usually involves asking many, many questions to find out the laundry list of threats, the probability of these threats being exploited, and the outcome if one of these threats actually becomes real and a compromise takes place. The questions vary from product to product, its intended purpose, the expected environment it will be implemented into, the personnel involved, and the types of businesses that would purchase and use this type of product. The following is a small list of the types of questions that should be asked during a software risk analysis:

- What is the possibility of buffer overflows and what type of outcome would they bring?
- Are threat agents on the outside of the environment and the inside? What are those threat agents?
- What type of businesses would depend on this product and what type of business loss would it cause if the product went offline for a specific period of time?
- Are there covert channel issues that need to be dealt with?
- What type of fault tolerance is integrated into the product and when would it be initiated?

- Is encryption needed? Which type? What strength?

- Are contingency plans needed for emergency issues?

- Would another party (ISP or hosting agency) be maintaining this product for the customer?

- Is mobile code necessary? How and why?

- Is this product going to be in an environment that is connected to the Internet? What effects could this have on the product?

- Does this product need to interface to vulnerable systems?

- How could this product be vulnerable to denial of service (DoS) attacks?

- How could this product be vulnerable to viruses?

- Are intrusion alert mechanisms necessary?

- Would there be motivation for insiders or outsiders to sabotage this product? How and why?

- Would competitor companies of the purchaser want to commit fraud via this product? How and why?

- What other systems would be affected if this product failed?

This is a short list and each question can branch off into other questions to ensure that all possible threats and risks are identified and thought through.

Once all the risks are identified, the probability of them actually taking place needs to be quantified and the consequences of these risks need to be properly evaluated to ensure that the right countermeasures are implemented within the development phase and the product itself. If a product will only be used to produce word documents, a lower level of security countermeasures and tests would be needed compared to a product that maintains credit card data.

Many of the same risk analysis steps outlined in Chapter 3 can be applied in the risk analysis that needs to be performed when developing a product. Once the risks are identified, the probability of these risks actually taking place is estimated, and the consequences of these risks are calculated, the risks can be listed in order of importance. If the possibility of a DoS taking place is high and could devastate a customer, then this is at the high end of importance. If the possibility of fraud is low, then this is pushed to the back of the bus. The most probable and potentially devastating risks are approached first, and the less likely and less damaging are dealt with after the more important risks.

These risks need to be addressed in the design and architecture of the product as well as the functionality the product provides, the implementation procedures, and the required maintenance. A banking software product may need to be designed to have Web server farms within a demilitarized zone (DMZ) of the branch, but have the components and databases behind another set of firewalls to provide another layer of protection. This would mean that the architecture of the product would include splitting it up among different systems and developing communication methods between the different parts. If the product is going to provide secure e-mail functionality, then all the risks involved with just this service need to be analyzed and properly accounted for. Implementation procedures need to be thought through and addressed. How will the customer set this product up? What are the system and environment requirements? Does this product need to be supplied with a public key infrastructure (PKI)? The level of maintenance required after installation is important to many products. Will the vendor need to keep the customer abreast of certain security issues? Should any logging and auditing take place? The more these things are thought through in the beginning, the less scrambling will be involved at the end of the process.

It is important to understand the difference between project risk analysis and security risk analysis. Many times they are confused or combined. The project team may do a risk analysis pertaining to the risk of the project failing. This is much different than the security risk analysis, which has different threats and issues. The two should be understood and used, but in a distinctively different manner.

Functional Design Analysis and Planning

In this phase, a project plan is developed to define the security activities and develop security checkpoints to ensure that quality assurance for security controls takes place and that the configuration and change control process is identified. This is the point of the project where resources are identified, test schedules start to form, and evaluation criteria is developed to be able to properly test the security controls. A formal functional baseline is formed, meaning the expectations of the product are outlined in a formal manner, usually through documentation. A test plan is developed, which will be updated through each phase to ensure that all issues are properly tested.

Determining security requirements can be derived from several different sources:

- Functional needs of the system or application

- National, international, or organizational standards and guidelines

- Export restrictions

- Sensitivity level of data being processed (military strategic data versus private sector data)

- Relevant security policies

- Cost/benefit analysis results

- Required level of assurance to achieve the targeted security level rating

The initial risk assessment will most likely be updated throughout the project as more information is uncovered and learned. In some projects, more than one risk analysis needs to be performed at different stages of the life cycle. For example, if the project team knows that the product will need to identify and authenticate users in a domain setting requiring a medium level of security, an initial risk analysis is performed. Later in the life cycle, if it is determined that this product should work with biometric devices and have the capability to integrate with systems that require high security levels, a whole new risk analysis will need to be performed because new morsels have been added to the mix.

This phase addresses the functionality required out of the product and is captured in a design document. If the product is being developed for a customer, the design document is used as a tool to explain to the customer what the developing team understands of the requirements of the product. A design document is usually drawn up by analysts, with the guidance of engineers and architects, and presented to the customer. The customer can then decide if more functionality needs to be added or subtracted and dialogs between the customer and development team begin hammering out exactly what is expected from the product.

In security issues, this is where high-level questions are asked. Examples of these questions include the following: Is authentication and authorization necessary? Is encryption needed? Will the product need to interface with other systems? Will the product be directly accessed via the Internet?

Many companies skip the functional design phase and jump right into developing specifications for the product. Or a design document is not shared with the customer. This can cause major time delays and rework efforts because a broad vision of the product needs to be developed before looking strictly at the details. If the customer is not involved at this stage, the customer most likely thinks the developers will be developing a product that accomplishes X, while the development team thinks that the customer wants Y. A lot of wasted time can go into developing a product that is not what is actually wanted by the customer so clear direction and goals need to be drawn out before the beginning of coding. This is usually an important function of the project management team.

System Design Specifications

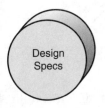

Software requirements come from informational, functional, and behavioral models. The informational model dictates the type of information to be processed and how it will be processed. The functional model outlines the tasks and functions that the application needs to carry out. The behavioral model explains the states that the application will be in during and after specific transitions take place. For example, an antivirus software application may have an informational model that dictates what information is to be processed by the program, such as virus signatures, modified system files, checksums on critical files, and virus activity. It would also have a functional model that dictates that the application should be able to scan a hard drive, check e-mail for known virus signatures, monitor critical system files, and update itself. The behavioral model would indicate that when the system starts up, the antivirus software application will scan the hard drive. The computer coming online would be the event that changes the state of the application. If a virus was found, the application would change state and deal with the virus appropriately. The occurrence of the virus is the event that would change the state. Each state has to be accounted for to ensure that the product does not go into an insecure state and act in an unpredictable way.

So the informational, functional, and behavioral model information goes into the software design as requirements. What comes out of the design is the data, architectural, and procedural design, as shown in Figure 11-12.

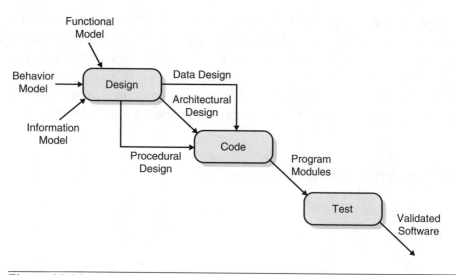

Figure 11-12 Information from three models can go into the design, which can result.

The data design takes the informational model information and transforms it into data structures that will be required to implement the software. The architectural design defines the relationships between the major structures and components of the application. The procedural design transforms structural components into descriptive procedures.

This is the point where access control mechanisms are chosen, subject rights and permissions are defined, the encryption method and algorithm are chosen, the handling of sensitive data is ironed out, the necessary objects and components are identified, the interprocessing communication is evaluated, the integrity mechanism is identified, and any other security specifications are appraised and solutions are determined.

The work breakdown structure (WBS) for future phases needs to be confirmed, which includes the development and implementation stages. This includes a timeline and detailed activities for testing, development, staging, integration testing, and product delivery.

The system design is a tool used to describe the user requirements and the internal behavior of a system. It then maps the two elements to show how the internal behavior actually accomplishes the user requirements.

This phase starts to look at more details of the product and the environment that it will be implemented within. The required functionality was determined in the last phase. This phase addresses what mechanisms are needed to provide this functionality and determine how it will be coded, tested, and implemented.

The modularity and reusability of the product, or the components of the product, need to be addressed. Code that provides security-critical functions should be simple in design in order to catch errors in a less confusing fashion, and be small enough to be fully tested in different situations. Components can be called and used by different parts of the product or by other applications. This attribute, reusability, can help streamline the product and provide for a more efficient and more structured coding environment.

The product could have portability issues that need to be dealt with and handled at the early stages of the product development. If the product needs to work on Unix and NT systems, then different coding requirements are needed compared to a product that will only be installed on mainframes. Also, the environment that will implement this product needs to be considered. Is this product going to be used by individual users or are all the users within the network going to access this product in one fashion or another? Being a single-user product rather than a multiuser product has large ramifications on the development of the necessary specifications.

The testability of the product and components need to be thought about at this early phase instead of at later phases. Programmers can code in *hooks* that show the testers the state of the product at different stages of data processing. Just because the product appears to act correctly and produces the right answers at the end of the processing phases, it does not mean that internal errors are not taking place. This is why testing should happen in modular ways, the flow of data through the product needs to be followed, and each step should be analyzed.

This phase should look closer at all the questions asked at the project initiation and ensure that specifications are developed for each issue addressed. For example, if authentication is required, this phase will lay out all the details necessary for this process to take place. If fraud is a large risk, then all the necessary countermeasures should be identified and shown how they integrate into the product. If covert channels are a risk, then these issues should be addressed and psuedocode should be developed to show how they will be reduced or eliminated.

If the product is being developed for a customer, the specifications of the product should be shared with them to again ensure that everyone is still on the same page and headed in the right direction. This is the stage to hammer out any confusion or misunderstanding before the actual coding begins.

The decisions made during the design phase are pivotal steps to the development phase. The design is the only way that the customer requirements are translated into software; thus, software design serves as the foundation. Software quality and maintenance are greatly affected by the design of the software, as indicated in Figure 11-13.

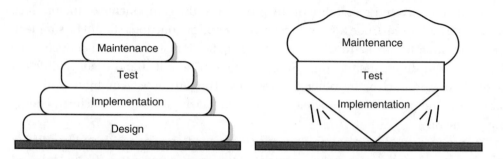

Figure 11-13   If a good product design is not put into place in the beginning, the following phases will be much more challenging.

Software Development

This is the phase where the programmers and developers become deeply involved. They are usually involved up to this point for their direction and advice, but at this phase, it is basically put into their laps. Let the programming and testing begin!

This is the stage where the programmers should code in a way that does not permit software compromises. Checking input lengths so buffer overflows cannot take place, coding to prevent the presence of covert channels, checking for proper data types, making sure checkpoints cannot be bypassed by users, syntax verification, and performing checksums are just some of the issues to be addressed. Different attack scenarios should be played out to see how the code could be attacked or modified in an unauthorized fashion. Debugging and code reviews should be carried out by peer developers and everything should be clearly documented.

Most programmers do not like to document and will find a way to get out of the task. Then 6 to 12 months down the road no one can remember specific issues that were addressed, how they were handled, the solutions to problems that have already been encountered, or the programmer who knew all the specific details went to work for a competitor or won the lottery and moved to an island. This is another cause of rework and wasting of man-hours. Documentation is extremely important for many different reasons and can save a company a lot of money in the long run.

Formal and informal testing should begin as soon as possible. Unit testing can start very early in development. After a programmer develops a component, or unit of code, it is tested with several different input values and in many different situations. Unit testing usually continues throughout the development phase. A totally different group of people should carry out the formal testing. This is an example of *separation of duties*. A programmer should not develop, test, and release software. The more eyes upon the code and the more fingers punching keys, the greater the chance that bugs will be found before the product is released.

Separation of Duties

Different environmental types (development, testing, and production) should be properly separated and functionality and operations should not overlap. Developers should not have access to code used in production. The code should be tested, submitted to the library, and then sent to the production environment.

Of course, any software hooks inserted for testing or modification purposes need to be removed prior to being released to production because these can easily provide attackers back doors into the product.

There is no cookie-cutter recipe for security testing because the applications and products can be so diverse in functionality and security objectives. It is important to map security risks to test cases and code. Linear lines of thinking can be followed by identifying a risk, providing the necessary test scenario, performing the test, and reviewing the code for how it deals with such a risk, as illustration in Figure 11-14. At this

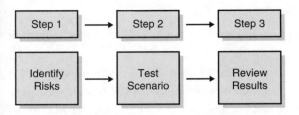

Figure II-I4   After risks are identified, test scenarios need to be developed and used to verify that those risks are addressed.

phase, tests are conducted in an integrated system, which should mirror the production environment to ensure the code does not only work in the labs.

Security attacks and penetrations usually take place during this phase to identify any missed vulnerabilities. Functionality, performance, and penetration resistance is evaluated. All the necessary functionality required of the product should be in a checklist to ensure that each and everyone is accounted for.

Security tests should be run to test against the risks identified earlier within the project. Buffer overflows should be attempted, the product should be hacked and attacked, interfaces should be hit with unexpected inputs, DoS situations should be tested, unusual user activity should take place, and if a system crashes, the product should react by reverting back to a more secure state. The product should be tested in different environments with different applications, configurations, and hardware platforms. A product may respond fine when installed on a clean Windows 2000 installation on a stand-alone PC, but it may throw unexpected errors when installed on a laptop that is remotely connected to a network and that has a SMS client installed.

At this stage, there are usually things found in unit and formal testing that are told to the development team in problem reports. The problems are fixed and testing happens again. This is a continual process until everyone is satisfied that the product is ready for production. If there is a specific customer, he would run through a range of tests before formally accepting the product. Then the product is formally released to the market or customer.

Installation/Implementation

The implementation stage focuses on how to use and operate the developed system or application.

At this phase, the customer has purchased the developed product and installed it into his environment. The product would then be configured for the right level of protection. Functionality and performance tests can be performed and the results can be analyzed and compared to the company's security requirements.

The configurations should be documented. User guides and operation and maintenance manuals are developed so users know how to properly use the systems and members of the technical staff know how to properly configure the product if there is ever a need. Monitoring security activities needs to be performed to ensure that the system or application performs in the manner promised by the service level agreement.

Accreditation should occur between development and the beginning of operational use of the system or application. This process follows the certification process, which formally or informally tests all the security features to determine if they accomplish the required security needs. Certification is the process of reviewing and evaluating security controls and is usually a task assigned to an outside, independent reviewer. (Certification and accreditation were covered in detail in Chapter 5.)

The accreditation is the formal acceptance of the system by management and an explicit acceptance of risk. The accreditation looks at the whole system, not just at an application or a newly upgraded feature. This is because security is not a compartmentalized attribute, but it is a service that takes place at different layers of the system and can be manifested in many different manners. The accreditation process forces the management and technical staff to work together to ensure quality and a level of protection provided by purchased and implemented technologies. The technical staff understands operational and mechanical issues and the management staff understands mission, financial, and liability issues. Together, they can cover a lot of ground during the accreditation process.

Once they are sure of the security provided by the new system and understand and accept the residual risk, management should issue a formal accreditation statement.

Auditing needs to be enabled and monitored and contingency recovery plans and procedures should be developed and tested to make sure the system and product reacts as planned in the event of a system failure or emergency situation.

Operational and Maintenance

This is not a phase where you can think that security is done and in control, and that all you have to do now is sit back and eat donuts. On the contrary, security is just as, or more, important during the operational phase than during earlier phases.

The initial part of this phase includes the configuration of the new system and inserting it properly into the network and environment. Many times security controls are not enabled or properly configured for the environment, so even if they were correctly coded from the beginning, it does not really matter if they are not actually used or used in an unattended method.

Operational assurance is carried out by continually conducting vulnerabilities tests, monitoring activities, and auditing events. It is through operational assurance activities that an administrator learns of new vulnerabilities or security compromises, so the proper actions can take place.

If major changes happen to the system, product, or environment, a new risk analysis may need to be performed along with a new certification and accreditation process. These major changes could include new systems and/or new applications added, a relocation of the facility, or changes in data sensitivity or criticality.

Disposal

All good things must come to an end.

When it is time for out with the old and in with the new, certain steps may need to take place to make sure this transition happens in a secure manner. Depending on the sensitivity level of the data held on a system, different disposal activities may need to take place. Information may need to be archived, backed up to another system, discarded, or destroyed. If the data is sensitive and needs to be destroyed, it may need to be purged by overwriting, degaussing, or physically destroying the media. It depends on the data and the company's policy in destroying sensitive information.

Postmortem Review

It is important that a team gather after the completion of a project to exhale, talk about the overall project, and discuss things that should be improved for the next time. If this phase is taken seriously and handled properly, the company can save money and time on different projects because lessons will have been learned, mistakes will not be

System Life Cycle Phases

- **Project initiation**
  - Conception of project definition
  - Proposal and initial study
- **Functional design analysis and planning**
  - Requirements uncovered and defined
  - System environment specifications determined
- **System design specifications**
  - Functional design review
  - Functionality broken down
  - Detailed planning put into place
  - Code design
- **Software development**
  - Developing and programming software
- **Installation**
  - Product installation and implementation
  - Testing and auditing
- **Maintenance support**
  - Product changes, fixes, and minor modifications
- **Revision and replacement**
  - Modifying the product with revisions or replacing it altogether

repeated, and the process will be streamlined. All of these activities will help the next project run more smoothly with fewer mistakes and in a less amount of time.

This should be a structured event where someone is leading the meeting(s) and notes are being taken, but it should be a relaxed atmosphere for each team member to feel comfortable in expressing opinions and ideas. It is important that the review does not come down to a finger-pointing session or become a cesspool of complaining. It is

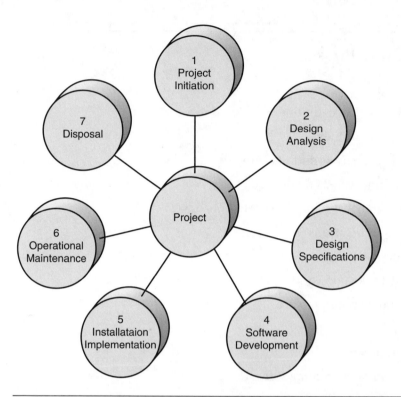

Figure 11-15 This chapter explains a life cycle containing seven different phases. Other models can use different cycles and a different number of phases, but they accomplish the same thing.

a method of looking at the project from an objective view and identifying issues that could be improved upon the next time around.

Some companies do not see the value in this exercise and just race off to start the next project, which will most likely be cursed with the problems of the prior project. Projects are learning processes and business is about making the best product in the least amount of time for the least amount of money. It is beneficial for management to understand how the two go together and make sure that a postmortem review is part of each and every project. The most successful businesses streamline the processes of projects and project management and hone them to become a repeatable procedure that produces the expected level of quality. These businesses continually take the time to look at how processes can be improved and built upon.

Change Control

Changes during development or production can cause a lot of havoc if not done properly. There are several reasons for changes to take place. During the development phases, a customer may alter requirements and ask that certain functionality be added, removed, or modified. In production, changes may need to happen because of other changes in the environment, new requirements of a product or system, or newly released patches or upgrades. These changes should be controlled to make sure they are approved, incorporated properly, and that no original functionality was affected in an adverse way. Configuration management is the process of controlling the life cycle of an application and documenting the necessary change control activities.

A system of dealing with changes needs to be in place at the beginning of a project, so everyone knows how changes are dealt with and what is expected of each entity when a change request is made. Some projects have been doomed from the start because proper change control was not put into place and enforced. Many times in development, the customer and vendor agree on the design of the product, requirements, and specifications. The customer is then required to sign a contract saying that this is the agreement and if they want any further modifications, they will need to pay the vendor for that extra work. If this is not put into place, then the customer can continually request changes, the development team puts in the extra hours to provide these changes, the vendor loses money, and the product does not meet its completion deadline.

Change Control

Changes must be authorized, tested, and recorded. Changed systems may require certification and accreditation.

There are other reasons to have change control in place. These reasons deal with organization, standard procedures, and expected results. If a product is in the last phase of development and a change request comes in, the team should know how to deal with this. Usually the team leader must tell the project manager how much extra time will be required to complete the project if this change is incorporated and what steps need to be taken to ensure that this change does not affect other components within the product. In addition, security cannot be compromised, and management must approve the change. If these processes are not controlled, one part of a development team could implement the change, while another part of the team is unaware of the change. This could actually break some of their pieces. When the pieces of the product are integrated and it is found that some pieces are incompatible, heads might roll because management never approved the change in the first place.

The change must be approved, documented, and tested. Some tests may need to be rerun to ensure that the change does not affect the product's capabilities. When a programmer makes a change to source code, it should be done on the test version of the code. Under no conditions should a programmer make changes to the code that is already in production. The changes to the code should be made, and then the new code should go to the librarian. Production code should come only from the librarian and not from a programmer or directly from a test environment.

Change control should be evaluated during system audits. It is possible to overlook a problem that a change has caused in testing, so the procedures of how change control is implemented and enforced should be examined during a system audit.

The following are some necessary steps for a change control process:

1. Make a formal request of change.
2. Analyze the request.
   - Develop the implementation strategy.
   - Calculate the costs of this implementation.
   - Review any security implications.
3. Record the change request.
4. Submit the change request for approval.
5. Develop the change.
   - Recode segments of the product, and add or subtract functionality.
   - Link these changes in the code to the formal change control request.
   - Submit software for testing and quality approval.
   - Repeat until quality is adequate.
   - Make version changes.

Change Control and Security

Change control needs to ensure that the security policy can still be implemented and that the security mechanisms have not been negatively affected.

The changes to systems may require another round of certification and accreditation. If the changes to a system are significant, then the functionality and level of protection may need to be reevaluated (certified) and management would have to approve the overall system including the new changes (accreditation).

Application Development Methodology

Applications are written in programming code and it is this code that tells the operating system and hardware what needs to happen to accomplish the user's requirements when operating a specific application. Programming languages have gone through several generations, each generation building on the next, providing richer functionality and providing the computing society with more options as they evolve.

There are different types of languages: machine language, assembly language, and high-level languages. *Machine language* is in a form that the computer and processor can understand and work with directly. *Assembly* and *high-level languages* cannot be understood directly by the system and must be processed, which results into machine language. The process is typically done by a compiler, whose function is to turn human-understandable programming language into machine-understandable language, or object code.

When a customer purchases a program, it is in machine language form. The program has already been compiled and it is ready to be executed and set up on the system. The compiler will put it into a form that specific processors can understand. This is why a program that works on a computer with an Alpha processor may not work on a computer with a Pentium processor. They use different processors and require a different form of machine language.

If the program was actually sold in the form of original source code, it would have to be complied on the customer's computer; thus, the customer must have the correct complier. Also, original source code would enable competing vendors to view each other's original ideas and techniques.

There are a few different types of programs that are used to turn high-level programming code (or source code) into machine code (or object code). They are compliers, assemblers, and interpreters. They work as translators. *Interpreters* translate one command at a time during execution and *compilers* translate large sections of code at a time. *Assemblers* translate assembly language into machine language. Most applications are compiled, whereas many scripting languages are interpreted. The relationship between these entities is shown in Figure 11-16.

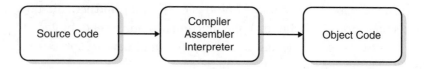

Figure 11-16 Different types of programs are used to translate source code to object code.

Compiled or Interpreted

Interpreted programs have instructions that are read and interpreted by a program one instruction at a time. This program, the interpreter, converts high-level instructions into machine-readable format in real time.

Compiled programs are written in a high-level language and turned into machine-readable format by a program called a compiler.

Object-Oriented Concepts

Software development used to be done by classic input-processing-output methods. This used an information flow model from hierarchical information structures. Data was inputted into a program and the program passed the data from the beginning to end, performed logical procedures, and returned a result, as illustrated in Figure 11-17.

Object-oriented programming (OOP) methods perform the same functionality with different techniques that work in a more efficient manner. First, the basic concepts of OOP need to be understood.

OOP works with classes and objects within those classes. A real-world object, such as a table, is a member (or instance) of a larger class of objects called "furniture." The class can have a set of attributes associated with every object in the class furniture. The attributes can be color, dimensions, weight, style, and cost. These attributes apply if a chair, table, or loveseat is being examined. Because the table is a member of the class furniture, the table inherits all attributes defined for the class (see Figure 11-18).

Once the class is defined, the attributes can be reused for each new member, or instance, of the class that is created. The attributes can be modified and this happens when the object has an operation, or method, applied to it. If the object chair is painted

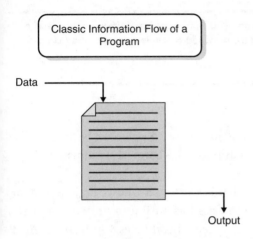

Classic Information Flow of a Program

Data

Output

Figure 11-17 The nonobject-oriented approach to programming usually inputs data into the beginning of the program, which results in the output.

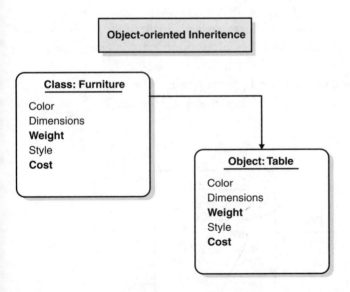

Object-oriented Inheritence

Class: Furniture

Color
Dimensions
Weight
Style
Cost

Object: Table

Color
Dimensions
Weight
Style
Cost

Figure 11-18 Each object belongs to a class and takes on the attributes of that class. This provides for a more module and organized program and design.

NOTE In object-oriented programming (OOP), objects are unique instances of a data structure defined by the template provided by their corresponding classes.

purple, the method is the act of painting and the new color value is purple. The methods are the ways that the objects are manipulated. Figure 11-19 illustrated this example).

Another example would be a customer of a bank. Customer Cheryl Craig is a member of the customer class. Each member of the class has attributes of name, address, phone number, and checking account balance. When Cheryl takes $40 from an ATM, she is reducing her checking account balance by $40. This action is the method that affects the attribute checking account balance. These methods are predefined as acceptable actions and are inherited from the class. Figure 11-20 illustrates this example.

The objects encapsulate the attribute values, which means that this information is packaged under one name and can be reused as one entity by other objects. Objects need to be able to communicate to each other and this happens by using messages. If Object A needs to tell Object B that Cheryl's checking account needs to be reduced by $40, it will send the object a message. The message is made up of the destination, the method that needs to be performed, and the corresponding arguments. Figure 11-21 shows this example.

An object can have a shared portion and a private portion. The shared portion is the interface that enables it to interact with other components. Messages enter through the

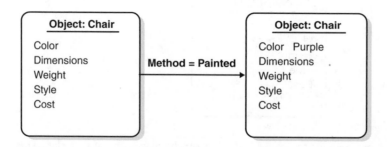

Figure 11-19 Attributes of objects are modified by methods.

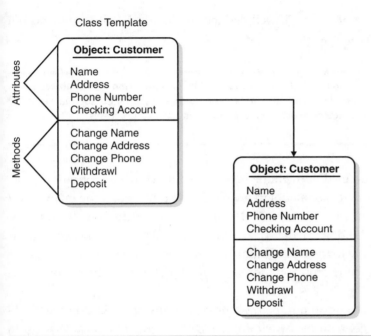

Figure 11-20 The object inherits the attributes and methods, which are acceptable actions that can be taken on the object's data.

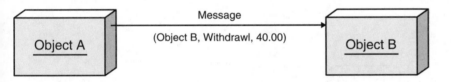

Figure 11-21 Objects communicate via messages. The message format is destination, operation that needs to be performed, arguments.

interface to specify the requested operation or method to be performed. The private part of an object can be how it actually works and performs the requested operations. There is no need for other components to know how each object works internally— only that it does the job requested of it. This is how *information hiding* is possible. The details of the processing are hidden from all other program elements outside the object. Objects communicate through well-defined interfaces; therefore, they do not need to know how each other work.

> **NOTE** Encapsulation: Data hiding is provided by encapsulation, which protects an object's private data from outside access. No object should be allowed or have the need to access another object's internal data or processes.

Once the objects are defined, it might be necessary to develop a classification structure. This means that instances of an object are defined and named. If the main object is named Dog, then the three objects under and related to this object could be Labrador, Terrier, and Bulldog. Figure 11-22 shows the relationship between these objects. This gives structure to the classification and defines the necessary relationships between the objects. Structure representation is a way of partitioning the requirements of the model.

These objects can grow to great numbers, so the complexity of understanding, tracking, and analyzing can get a bit overwhelming. Many times the objects are shown in connection to a reference or pointer in documentation. Figure 11-23 shows how related objects are represented as a specific piece, or reference, in an ATM system. This enables analysts and developers to look at a higher level of operation and procedures without having to look at each individual object. This modularity provides for a more easily understood model.

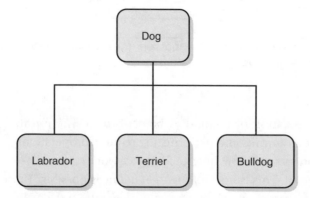

Figure 11-22 A classification structure can be developed to provide better organization of the relationships between the objects.

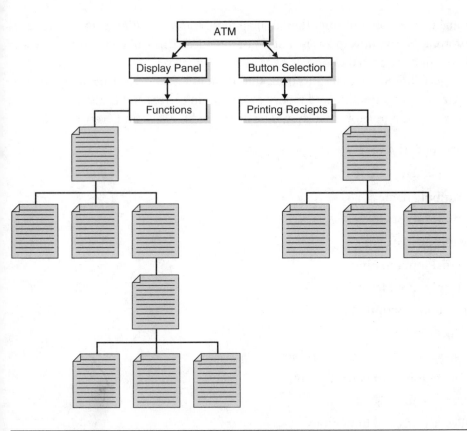

Figure 11-23   Programs can get very complicated with many different objects. They are usually represented by references, which point to several objects, to show the main functionality of the application itself.

Abstraction is the capability to suppress unnecessary details so that the important, inherent properties can be examined and reviewed. It enables the separation of conceptual aspects of a system. For example, if a software architect needed to understand how data flows through the program, she would want to understand the big pieces of the program and trace the steps that data takes from first being inputted into the program all the way until it exits the program as output. It would be difficult to understand this concept if the small details of how each and every piece of the program were presented. Instead, through abstraction, all the details are suppressed so that she can understand a crucial part of the product.

Messaging can happen in several different ways. Two objects can have a single connection (one to one), a multiple connection (one to many), and a mandatory connection or an optional connection. It is important to map these communication paths out to identify if information can flow in a way that is not intended. This will help ensure that sensitive data cannot be passed to objects of a lower security level.

Each object should have specifications that it should adhere to. This discipline will provide cleaner programming and reduce programming errors and omissions. The following list is an example of what should be developed for each and every object:

- Object name
- Attribute descriptions
  - Attribute name
  - Attribute content
  - Attribute data type
- External input to object
- External output from object
- Operation descriptions
  - Operation name
  - Operation interface description
  - Operation processing description
  - Performance issues
  - Restrictions and limitations
- Instance connections
- Message connections

Each object can be reused, which is the beauty of OOP. This enables more efficient use of resources and the programmer's time. Different applications can use the same objects so that there is a reduction in redundant work, and as an application grows in functionality, objects can be easily added and integrated into the original structure.

The objects can be catalogued in a library, which provides an economical way for more than one application to call upon the objects (see Figure 11-24). The library provides an index and pointers to where the objects actually live within the system or on another system.

When applications are developed in a modular approach, like object-oriented methods, components can be reused, complexity is reduced, and parallel development can be done. These characteristics allow for fewer mistakes, easier modification, resource efficiency, and more timely coding than the classic information flow models. OOP also

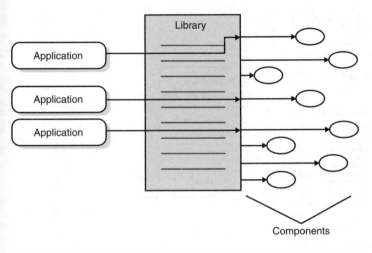

Figure 11-24   Applications can access and reuse components by using indexes within the component library.

provides functional independence, which means that each module addresses a specific subfunction of requirements and has an interface that is easily understood by other parts of the application.

An object is encapsulated, meaning that the data structure, the operation's functionality, and the acceptable ways of accessing are grouped into one entity. Other objects, subjects, and applications can use this object and its functionality by accessing it through controlled and standardized interfaces and sending it messages (see Figure 11-25).

Object-oriented design (OOD) creates a representation of a real-world problem and maps it to a software solution. The result of an OOD is a design that modularizes data and procedures. The design interconnects data objects and processing operations. This programming approach is different than others because it allows for abstraction, modularity, and information hiding. (Information hiding was explained in the "Object-Oriented Concepts" section.) Modularity is accomplished by using objects, applets, and agents.

NOTE   Object-oriented design (OOD) is a design method where a system is modeled as a collection of cooperating objects. Each individual object is treated as an instance of a class within a class hierarchy.

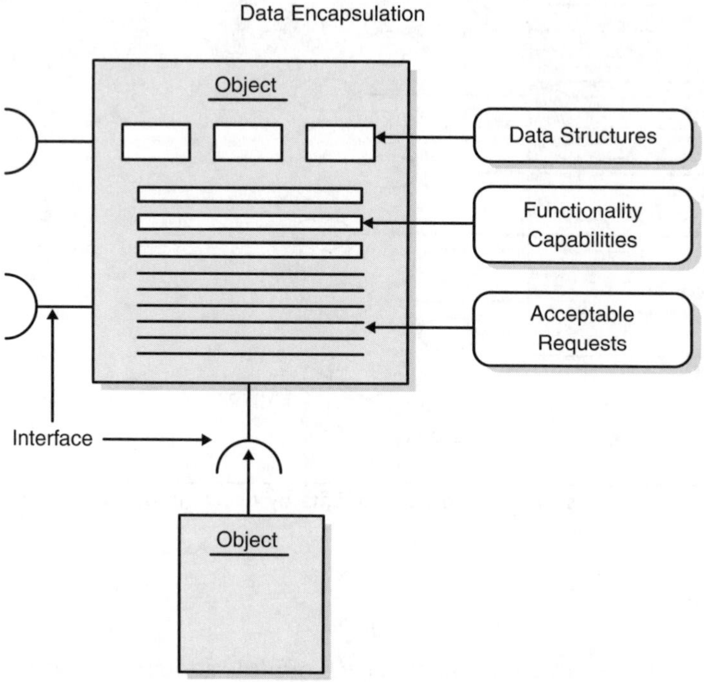

Data Encapsulation

Figure 11-25 The different components of an object and the way that it works are hidden from other objects. As long as there are interfaces that provide clear communication, the objects do not need to know how other objects work.

Polymorphism

Polymorphism adds another dimension to an object's behavior and aids in providing a better description for the object. *Polymorphism* means that an object's response to a message is determined by the class to which the object belongs. Different objects that belong to different classes can be addressed in a uniform manner, but they exhibit different behaviors.

A simplistic example of polymorphism would be three different objects that receive the input "Bob." Object A would process this input and produce the output "43-year-old white male." Object B would receive the input "Bob" and produce the output "Husband of Sally." Object C would produce the output of "Member of User group." Each object received the exact same input, but responded with a different output.

NOTE Polymorphism is when different objects respond to the same command, input or message, in different ways.

Object-oriented analysis (OOA) is the process of classifying objects that will be appropriate for a solution. A problem is analyzed to determine the classes of objects to be used in the application.

OOD enables an engineer, or developer, to indicate the objects that will derive from each class and how these objects will work together. So the problem needs to be analyzed and a solution should be decided upon. Then the details of that solution are attacked and hammered out.

OOP is a class of programming languages and techniques that are based on the concepts of objects and a set of routines and methods, which operate on the data. The following lists the features of OOP:

- **Encapsulation**   Hides internal data and operations
- **Polymorphism**   Makes copies of objects and makes changes to those copies
- **Polyinstantiation**   Multiple distinct differences between data within objects to discourage lower-level subjects from learning information at a higher-level of security
- **Inheritance**   Shares properties and attributes

Data Modeling

The previous paragraphs have provided a simple look at a *structured analysis approach*. A full structured analysis approach looks at all objects and subjects of an application, and maps the interrelationships, communication paths, and inheritance properties. This is different than *data modeling*. Data modeling considers data independently of the way that the data is processed and the components that process the data. A data model will follow an input value from beginning to end and verify that the output is correct. OOA is an example of a structure analysis model approach. If an analyst is reviewing the OOA of an application, she will make sure that all relationships are set up correctly, that the inheritance flows in a predictable and useable manner, that the instances of objects are practical and provide the necessary functionality, and that the attributes of each class cover all the necessary values used by the application. When another analyst does a data model review of the same application, he will follow the data and the returned values after processing takes place. An application can have a perfect OOA structure, but when 1 + 1 is entered and it returns −3, something is wrong. This is what the data modeling looks at.

 NOTE Inheritance means that objects derive functionality and data automatically from another object.

Another example of data modeling deals with databases. Data modeling can be used to provide insight into the data and the relationships that govern it. A data item in one file structure, or data store, might be a pointer to another file structure, or a different data store. It is important that these pointers are actually pointing to the right place. Data modeling would verify this, not OOA structure analysis.

Software Architecture

Software architecture relates the components that make up a software solution to the parts of a real-world problem. It is a higher point of view than the programmers who are focused on data structures, coding rules, variables, and communication paths between objects. An architectural view looks at how the application actually meets and fulfills the requirements recognized and agreed upon in the design phase.

Software architecture involves the process of partitioning requirements into individual problems that can be solved by individual software solutions. This process is the transition phase between the software requirement analysis and the design of the actual components that make up the resulting application, as shown in Figure 11-26.

If the requirements are that the application will scan hard drives and e-mail messages for viruses, the software architecture will break these requirements into individual units that need to be achieved by functionality within that application. These units can include

- Virus signature storage
- An agent that compares software strings on hard drives to virus signatures
- A process of parsing an e-mail message before the user can view it
- Procedures necessary if data on hard drive is compressed

- Actions taken if a virus is found

- Actions taken if e-mail attachment is encrypted

This way of developing a product provides more control and modularity of issues and solutions. If a group of programmers is told to develop an antivirus software package, the group may sit there like deer caught in headlights. However, if one developer is told to write a piece of the program that holds and updates signature files, another developer is told to determine how software on the hard drive will be compared to the signatures within the signature files, and another developer is instructed to program a way to read compressed files, then the programmers will have set goals and start pounding at the keyboards.

Software architects need to provide this type of direction: a high level view of the application's objectives and a vision of the overall goals of the project.

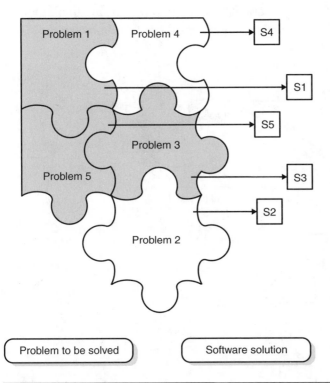

Figure 11-26 Software architects look at real-world problems and break them down into pieces that can be solved by software components.

Data Structures

A *data structure* is a representation of the logical relationship between elements of data. It dictates the degree of association between elements, methods of access, processing alternatives, and the organization of data elements.

The structure can be simple in nature, like the scalar item, which represents a single element that can be addressed by an identifier and accessed by a single address in storage. The scalar items can be grouped in arrays, which provide access by indexes. Other data structures include hierarchical structures by using multilinked lists that contain scalar items, vectors, and possibly arrays. The hierarchical structure provides categorization and association. If a user can make a request of an application to find all computer books written on security and that application returns a list, then this application is using a hierarchical data structure of some kind. Figure 11-27 shows simple and complex data structures.

Cohesion and Coupling

A *cohesive* module can perform a single task with little or no help from other modules. A cohesive module does just one function, and it does it will little interaction from

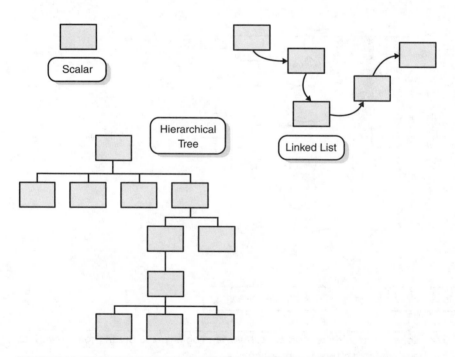

Figure 11-27 Data structures can be very simple to very complex in nature.

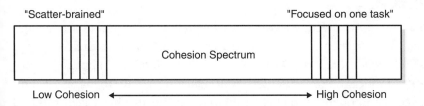

Figure 11-28 A cohesion spectrum shows the different levels of cohesion that a module can obtain.

other modules. The more a module can do on its own, the better, because requiring a lot of interaction between modules makes it harder to modify one module down the road without affecting other modules. Similarly, the more interactions, the more complexity, which makes it harder to track down problems. The best programming uses the most cohesive modules possible, but because different modules need to pass data and communicate, they usually cannot be totally cohesive. Figure 11-28 shows a linear approach of looking at cohesion.

Coupling is a measure of interconnection among modules in an application. The level of coupling involved between modules depends on the interface's complexity, the data being passed between modules, and the point of entry or reference made to the module itself. The lower the coupling, the better the software design, because it promotes module independence. The more independent a component is, the less complex the application is, and the easier it is to modify and troubleshoot.

An example of low coupling would be one module passing a variable value to another module. An example of a high coupling situation is when Module A passes a value to Module B, which performs calculations on the data and passes it to Module C. Module C then performs a lookup in a database to make sure this value is within a range and then passes the resulting value back to Module A. This high level of interconnection and interdependence is referred to as high coupling.

 NOTE Modular Code: Modules should be self-contained and perform a single logical function, which is high cohesion. Modules should not drastically affect each other, which is low coupling.

ORBs and CORBAs

The Object Management Architecture (OMA) provides a high-level overview of a complete distributed environment. It contains two main parts: system-oriented components (*object request brokers [ORBs]* and object services) and application-oriented components (application objects and common facilities). ORB manages all communication between components and enables them to interact in a heterogeneous and distributed environment, as shown in Figure 11-29. ORB works independently from the platforms where the objects reside, which provides greater interoperability.

ORB relies on object services to provide access control, track relocated objects, and create objects. The application objects and common facilities are farther from the system and closer to the end user. When they need services from the system, they invoke services from ORB and object services.

Common Object Request Broker Architecture (CORBA) provides interoperability among the vast array of different software, platforms, and hardware in environments today. CORBA enables applications to communicate with one another no matter where the application is located or who developed it.

The Object Management Group (OMG) developed a model for the use of these different services in an environment. The model defines object semantics so that the external visible characteristics are standard and viewed the same to all other objects in the environment. This standardization enables many different developers to write hundreds or thousands of components that can interact with other components in an

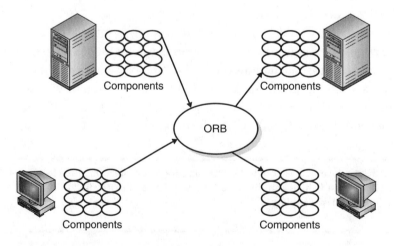

Components   Components

ORB

Components   Components

Figure 11-29 The ORB enables different components throughout a network to communicate and work with each other.

environment without having to know how the component actually works. The developers know how to communicate with the components because the interfaces are uniform and follow the rules of the model.

In the model, clients request services from objects. The client passes the object a message that contains the name of the object, the requested operation, and any necessary parameters.

ORB is the middleware that establishes the client/server relationship between objects. When a client needs to access an object on a server for that object to perform an operation, or method, the ORB intercepts the request and is responsible for finding the object. Once the object is found, ORB invokes a method (or operation), passes the parameters, and returns the result back to the client. The client software does not need to know where the object resides and go through the trouble of finding it. That is the ORB's job. The objects can be written in different languages and reside on different operating systems and platforms, but the client does not need to worry about any of this (see Figure 11-30).

When objects communicate to each other, they use pipes, which are intercomponent communication services. There are different types of pipes like RPCs and ORBs. ORBs

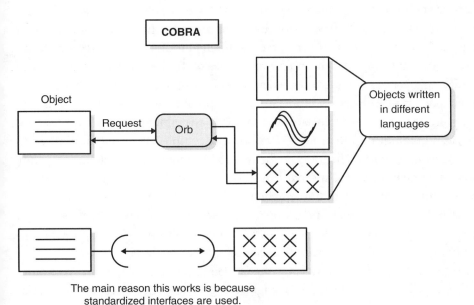

Figure 11-30 CORBA provides standard interface definitions between OMG-compliant objects, which provides greater interoperability and communication methods in heterogeneous environments.

provide communication between distributed objects. If an object on a workstation needs to have an object that is on a server process data, it can make a request through ORB, which will track down the needed object and facilitate the communication path between these two objects until the process is complete. This is the client/server communication pipe used in many networking environments.

ORBs are mechanisms that enable objects to communicate locally or remotely. They enable objects to make requests to objects and receive responses. This happens transparently to the client and provides a type of pipeline between all corresponding objects. CORBA specifies specific interface definitions and APIs that interface to the ORB. Using CORBA enables an application to be usable on many different types of ORBs. It provides portability for applications and tackles many of the interoperability issues that many vendors and developers run into when their product is implemented into different environments.

Computer-Aided Software Engineering (CASE)

Computer-aided software engineering (CASE) tools are broad and far reaching in functionality and uses. CASE tools is a general term for many types of tools used by programmers, developers, project managers, and analysts that help them make program applications quicker and with fewer errors in an automated fashion and run the project in a controlled and organized manner. There are different tools that provide managerial, administrative, and technical help in software projects. They provide several layers of organization that is not available when a developer is just programming by hand, notes are written in word processors, and timetables are inputted into static spreadsheets.

The first CASE tools were translators, compilers, assemblers, linkers, and loaders. However, as programming and projects became more complex, the need for more complex tools grew in demand. The tools graduated into program editors, debuggers, code analyzers, and version control mechanisms. The tools aid in keeping more detailed records of requirements, design, implementation, and testing the program and project overall. A CASE tool is aimed at supporting one or more software engineering tasks and activities in the process of developing software. They apply engineering principles to the development and analysis of specifications using specific tools.

Many vendors can get their products to the market faster because they are "computer aided." The CASE tools enable software engineering to be done correct and fast, relatively speaking.

When the automation covers the complete life-cycle process of a product, the tools are referred to as integrated computer-aided software engineering (I-CASE), and if tools are used for one specific part of the life cycle, then the tools are referred to as CASE tools.

Many CASE tools utilize *rapid prototyping* technologies that enable applications to be developed faster with higher quality and lower cost. A prototype can be made so that testing can begin earlier in the development process. The more testing that is done, the more errors that can be caught. Because it costs more to find and fix problems at the end of a project compared to the beginning of a project, prototyping can save a lot of time and money.

As previously stated, there is a wide range of tools that fall under the general term of CASE tools. The tools can provide and support the data flow, aid for a structured development, produce documentation, provide design method support, and generate application code for a specific goal within the project. They also help when a project is large with many developers working on specific pieces of the product. It is easy to get disjointed when everyone has his own little piece he is responsible for, and when the different pieces come together, they may not integrate properly. The different tools can work together with a shared database and a conceptual notion like a shared philosophy on architecture and common semantics about the objects and the tools that manipulate them.

Prototyping

Many times it is necessary to build a model of the gathered requirements of a software product to be used for a customer and the developers. This model, called a *prototype*, can show the customer where the development team is headed and its interpretation of the customer's stated requirements. This enables the customer to agree on the direction the team is headed and get an idea of what the product will look like, or enables the customer to make changes and further explain any requirements that were gray or confusing. The prototype also enables testing to begin earlier in the development process so that errors or problems can be uncovered and addressed.

Some projects are very large and may require that partitioning the product is necessary so that each part has its own prototype to be reviewed and built upon. In either case, partitioning or prototyping the full product, an analyst will develop an abbreviated representation of the requirements for the prototype. The software can be created using prototyping tools, which speed up the process. This enables the design to be translated into executable form.

Security testing can begin at an earlier stage if a prototype is developed. Penetration, vulnerability, and data format tests can be performed at each stage of development and with each prototype developed.

If a software prototype is impractical for one reason or another, paper prototypes can be developed where interaction, queries, displays, and logic are shown on paper for the customer to see and the developers to walk through. A series of storyboard sheets can be used to represent each screen shot and the actions that take place behind the screen.

COM and DCOM

Component Object Model (COM) defines how components interact and provides an architecture for simple interprocess communication (IPC). *Distributed Component Object Model (DCOM)* supports the same model for component interaction, but supports distributed IPC. COM enables applications to use components on the same systems, and DCOM enables applications to access objects that reside in different parts of a network.

Without DCOM, programmers would have to write much more complicated code to find necessary objects, set up network sockets to allow communication, and incorporate the services necessary to allow communication. DCOM takes care of these issues and more and enables the programmer to focus on his tasks at hand. DCOM has a library that takes care of session handling, synchronization, buffering, fault identification and handling, and data format translation.

DCOM works as the middleware that enables distributed processing and provides developers with services that support process-to-process communication across networks (see Figure 11-31).

There are other types of middleware that provide similar functionality: ORB, message-oriented middleware (MOM), RPC, open database connectivity (ODBC), and so on. DCOM provides ORB services, data connectivity services, distributed messaging

[handwritten margin note: How is DCOM different from ORB]

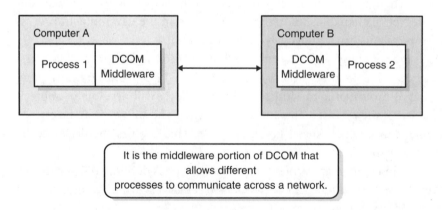

It is the middleware portion of DCOM that allows different processes to communicate across a network.

Figure 11-31 Although DCOM provides communication mechanisms in a distributed environment, it still works off of the COM architect.

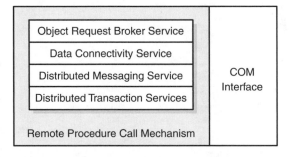

Figure 11-32 DCOM provides several services over its RPC mechanism and a COM interface.

services, and distributed transaction services layered over its RPC mechanism. DCOM integrates all of these functionalities into one technology that uses the same interface as COM (see Figure 11-32).

relational?

Open Database Connectivity (ODBC)

Open database connectivity (ODBC) is a de facto standard that provides a standard SQL dialect that can be used to access many types of rational databases. ODBC is the middleman between applications and databases. An application makes a request to the ODBC driver manager. The ODBC driver manager decides which driver needs to be used for communication purposes. (The driver is a piece of software that will provide communication between a system and a database. Different databases require different drivers.) The request is passed through the ODBC manager, through the driver, and to the database, as shown in Figure 11-33. The database answers the request, which goes back through the driver, through ODBC, and to the application.

Object Linking and Embedding (OLE)

Object linking and embedding (OLE) provides a way for objects to be shared on a local personal computer and use COM as its foundation base. OLE enables objects to be embedded into documents, like graphics, pictures, and spreadsheets. In this book, there are many graphics placed throughout the text. The OLE technology puts those graphics into the text documents that make up this book.

OLE also allows for linking different objects and documents. When Chrissy creates a document that contains a Uniform Resource Locator (URL), that URL turns blue and is underlined indicating that a user can just double-click on it and he will be taken to the appropriate Web site. This is an example of linking capabilities. If Chrissy adds a

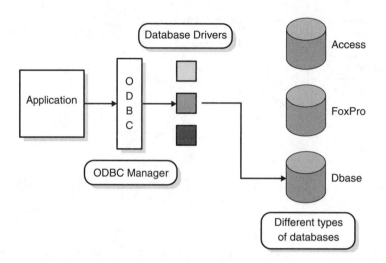

Figure 11-33 ODBC provides a standardized interface for many different applications to be able to communicate with many different types of databases.

spreadsheet to her document, this is an example of embedding. If she needs to edit the spreadsheet, she can double-click on the spreadsheet and the operating system will open the correct environment (which might be Excel) to let her make her changes.

OLE

The capability for one program to call another program is *linking*. The capability to put a piece of data inside a foreign program or document is *embedding*.

This technology was evolved to work on the World Wide Web (WWW) and is called an ActiveX. The components are like other components but are meant to be portable. ActiveX components can run on any platform supporting DCOM, using the COM model, or communicating using DCOM services.

Dynamic Data Exchange

Dynamic Data Exchange (DDE) enables different applications to share data by providing IPC. It is based on the client/server model and enables two programs to send commands to each other directly. DDE is a communication mechanism that enables direct conversation between two applications. The source of the data is called the *server* and the receiver of the data is the *client*.

A spreadsheet can use a DDE link to another program that keeps track of stock prices. The spreadsheet can display the current trading information because updates are being received from the server via a DDE communication link.

Distributed Computing Environment

Distributed Computing Environment (DCE) is a standard that was developed by the Open Software Foundation (OSF), also called Open Group. It is basically middleware that is available to many vendors to use within their products. It is middleware that has the capability to support many types of applications across an enterprise. DCE provides a RPC service, security service, directory service, time service, and distributed file support.

DCE is a set of management services with a communication layer based on RPC. It is a layer of software that sits on the top of the network layer and provides services to the applications above it. DCE and DCOM provide a lot of the same functionality. DCOM was developed by Microsoft and is more proprietary in nature.

DCE's time service provides host clock synchronization and enables applications to determine sequencing and scheduling events based on clock synchronization. This time synchronization is for applications. Users cannot access this functionality directly. The directory service enables users, servers, and resources to be contacted anywhere on the network. When the directory service is given the name, it returns the network address of the resource along with other necessary information. DCOM uses a *globally unique identifier (GUID)* and DCE uses a *universal unique identifier (UUID)*. They are both used to uniquely identify users, resources, and components within an environment. DCE is illustrated in Figure 11-34.

The (RCP) function collects the arguments and commands from the sending program and prepares them for transmission over the network. (RCP) determines the network transport protocol that is to be used and finds the receiving host's address in the directory service. The threads service provides real-time priority scheduling in a multi-threading environment. The security services support authentication and authorization services. The distributed file service (DFS) provides a single integrated file system that all DCE users can use to share files. This is important because many environments have different operating systems that cannot understand other file systems. However, if DCE is being used, a DCE local file system exists alongside the native file system.

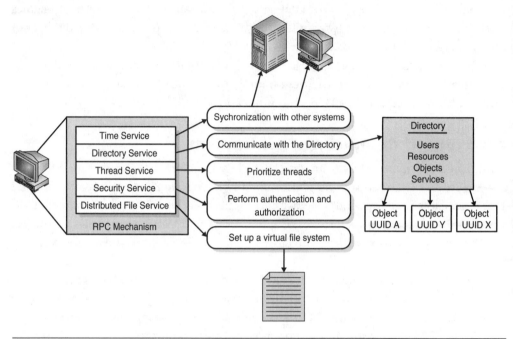

Figure 11-34 DCE provides many services wrapped into one technology.

Expert Systems and Knowledge-Based Systems

Expert systems, also called *knowledge-based systems*, use artificial intelligence (AI) to solve problems.

AI software uses nonnumerical algorithms to solve complex problems, recognize hidden patterns, prove theorems, play games, mine data, and help in forecasting and diagnosing a range of different issues. The type of computation done by AI software cannot be accomplished by straightforward analyses and regular programming logic techniques.

Expert systems emulate human knowledge to solve problems that would usually require human intelligence and intuition. These systems represent expert knowledge as data or rules within the software of a system and this data and these rules are called upon when it is necessary to solve a problem. Knowledge-based systems collect data of human know-how and hold it in some type of database. These fragments of data are used to reason through a problem.

Expert System

An expert system is a computer program containing a knowledge base and set of algorithms and rules used to infer new facts from knowledge and incoming data.

A regular program can only deal with inputs and parameters the way that it has been designed and programmed to. Although a regular program can calculate the mortgage payments of a house over 20 years at an 8-percent interest rate, it cannot necessarily forecast the placement of stars in 100 million years because of all the unknowns and possible variables that come into play. Although both programs, a regular program and an expert system, have a finite set of information available to them, the expert system will attempt to think like a person, reason through different scenarios, and provide an answer even without all the necessary pieces in place. Conventional programming deals with procedural manipulation of data, whereas humans attempt to solve complex problems using abstract and symbolic approaches.

A book may contain a lot of useful information, but a person has to read that book, interpret its meaning, and then attempt to use those interpretations within the real world. This is what an expert system, also called a knowledge-based system, attempts to do.

AI is the development of techniques that provide the modeling of information at higher levels of abstraction. The techniques are part of the languages and tools used, which enable programs to be developed that closely resemble human logic. The programs that can emulate human expertise in specific domains are called expert systems.

Rule-based programming is a common way of developing expert systems. The rules are based on if-then logic units. This specifies a set of actions to be performed for a given situation. This is one way that expert systems are used to find patterns, which is called *pattern matching*. A mechanism, called the *inference engine*, automatically matches facts against patterns and determines which rules are applicable. The actions of the corresponding rules are executed when the inference engine is instructed to begin execution.

Huh? Okay, let say Dr. Gorenz is puzzled by a patient's symptoms and is unable to match the problems the patient is having to a specific ailment and find the right cure. So he uses an expert system to help him in his diagnosis. Dr. Gorenz can initiate the expert system, which will then take him through question-and-answer situations. The expert system will use the information gathered through this interaction and it will go step by step through the different facts looking for patterns that can be tied to known diseases, ailments, and medical issues. Although Dr. Gorenz is very smart and one of the top doctors in his field, he cannot necessarily recall all possible diseases and ailments. The expert system can know this information because it is working off of a database that has been stuffed full of medical information that can fill up several libraries.

As the expert system goes through the medical information, it may see that the patient had a case of severe hives six months ago, a case of ringing in the ears and blurred vision three months ago, and a history of diabetes. The system will look at the patient's recent complaints of joint aches and tiredness. With each finding, the expert system will dig deeper looking for further information, and then use all information obtained and compare it to the knowledge base that is available to it. In the end, the expert system returns a diagnosis to Dr. Gorenz that says that the patient is suffering from a rare disease found only in Brazil that is caused by a specific mold that grows on bananas. Because the patient has diabetes, his sensitivity is much higher to this contaminant. The system spits out the necessary treatment. Then Dr. Gorenz marches back into the room where the patient is waiting and explains the problem and protects his reputation of being a really smart doctor.

The system not only uses a database of facts, but it also collects a wealth of knowledge from experts in a specific field. This knowledge is captured by using interactive tools that have been engineered specifically to capture human knowledge. This knowledge base is then transferred to automated systems that help in human decisions by offering advice, free up experts from repetitive routine decisions, ensure that decisions are made in a consistent manner in a quicker fashion, and help a company retain its organization's expertise even as employees come and go.

An expert system usually consists of two parts: an inference engine and a knowledge base. The inference engine handles the user interface, external files, scheduling, and program-accessing capabilities. The knowledge base contains data pertaining to a specific problem or domain. Expert systems use the inference engine to decide how to execute a program or how the rules should be initiated and followed. The inference piece of a knowledge-based system provides the necessary rules for the system to take the original facts and combine them to form new facts. It is a process of learning.

The systems employ AI programming languages to allow for real-world decision making. The system is built by a knowledge system builder (programmer), a knowledge engineer (analyst), and subject matter expert(s), as shown in Figure 11-35. The system is built on facts, rules of thumb, and the expert's advice. The information gathered from the expert(s) during the development of the system is kept in a knowledge base and is used during the question-and-answer session with the end user. The system works as a consultant to the end user and can recommend several alternative solutions by considering competing hypotheses at the same time.

Expert systems are commonly used to automate a security log review for an IDS.

NOTE Expert systems use automatic logical processing, inference engine processing, and general methods of searching for problem solutions, as shown in Figure 11-35.

Artificial Neural Networks

An *artificial neural network (ANN)* is an electronic model based on the neural structure of the brain. Computers perform activities like computing large numbers, keeping large ledgers, and performing complex mathematical functions, but they cannot recognize patterns or learn from experience as the brain can. ANNs contain many simple units or neurons each with a small amount of memory. The units work on data that is inputted through their many connections. Through training rules, the systems are able to learn from examples and have the capability to generalize.

The brain stores information in forms of patterns. People have the ability to recognize another person's face from several different angles. Each angle of that person's face is made up of a complex set of patterns. Even if only half the face is seen or the face is viewed in a shadow or dark lighting, the human brain can insert the missing pieces and people can recognize their friends and acquaintances. A computer that uses conventional programming and logic would have to have each piece of the pattern and the full face in one particular angle to be able to match or recognize it.

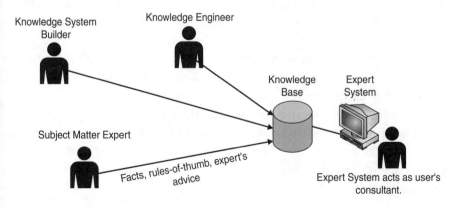

Figure 11-35 This graphic shows what goes into developing an expert system and how it is used once developed.

The brain uses neurons to remember, think, apply previous experiences, perform logic, and recognize patterns. The capacity of the brain comes from the large number of neurons and the multiple connections between them. The power of the brain comes from genetic programming and learning.

ANNs try to replicate the basic functions of neurons and their circuitry to solve problems in a new way. They consist of many simple computational neural units connected to each other. An input value is presented to one, some, or all the units, which will in turn perform functions on the data.

The brain has clusters of neurons that process in an interactive and dynamic way. Biologically, neurons have no restrictions of interconnections between themselves; therefore a neuron can have thousands of connections. In addition, the neurons in the brain work in a three-dimensional world, whereas the electronic units in ANN have a physical limitation on the possible number of connections and operate in a two-dimensional world.

Like the brain, the ANN's real power comes from its capability to learn. Within the brain, when something is learned and used often, the connection path to where that information is stored is strengthened to provide quicker access. This is why sometimes you know something but 'can't put your finger on it.' This means that there is not a pronounced pathway to the information that is stored somewhere in the brain. If a person is asked her phone number, she can rattle it off without any real energy. But if you ask her who her third-grade teacher was, it might take more time and energy. Both facts are held within her brain, but the phone number has a more pronounced connection path and comes to mind quicker and easier. In ANN, a connection between two units that is often activated might be strengthened, which is a form of learning.

It is known that when something happens to someone and they are in a highly emotional state, that person is more likely to remember specifics about a situation or incident. If Joyce had a surprise party on her 35th birthday, which was filled with fun and emotion, she will most likely remember that birthday more than her 36th birthday when her husband only bought her a card. But she and her husband will probably remember her 45th birthday when her husband forgot her birthday because the fight that occurred was full of emotion and activity. The reason that some memories are more vivid than others is because more emotion is tied to them, or more weight is assigned to them. In ANN, some inputs have higher weights assigned to them than other inputs, which amplifies the meaning or importance of the inputs just like emotion does with human beings.

NOTE Neural Networks: Decisions by neural networks are only as good as the experiences they are given.

Intuition is a hard issue to replicate in electrical circuits and logic gates. Fuzzy logic and other mathematical disciplines are used for intuition, forecasting, and intelligent guessing. These approaches work with types of probability within mathematics and memberships of different sets. One simple example of the use of Fuzzy logic is the use of a washing machine. When a person puts a load of clothes in the washing machine and the tank fills with water, the machine sends a beam from one part of the tank to the other. Depending on how much light actually was received at the receiving end, it can determine how dirty the clothes are because of the density of the dirt in the water. Then there are other tests to see if the dirt is oily or dry and other relevant attributes. The washing machine will take in all of this information and guess at the right temperature and the right amount of laundry soap to use. This will provide a more efficient way of washing by saving on water and soap and washing the clothes in the right temperature for the right amount of time. The washing machine does not necessary know all the facts or know that the information that it gathered is 100-percent correct, but it can make guesses that will be pretty close to reality.

Neural networks are programmed with the capability to decide and learn to improve its deciding functionality through massive trial-and-error decision making.

Fuzzy logic is necessary because a regular computer system does not see the world in shades of gray. It cannot differentiate between good, bad, few, and many. Fuzzy logic is an approach to enable the computer to use these vague values that mean something to humans but nothing to computers.

Insurance and financial risk assessments are examples of where Fuzzy logic can be used and is most beneficial. They both require a large number of variables and decision-making information from experts in those particular domains. The system can indicate which insurance or financial risks are good or bad without the user having to input a stack of conditions, if-then statements, and variable values.

Conventional systems see the world in black and white and work in a sea of precision and decimal points. Fuzzy logic enables the computer to incorporate imprecision into the programming language, which opens up a whole new world for computing and attacking complex issues. Neural network researchers attempt to understand more of how the brain works and of nature's capabilities so that more complex problems can be solved by newly engineered ANN solutions versus the traditional computing means.

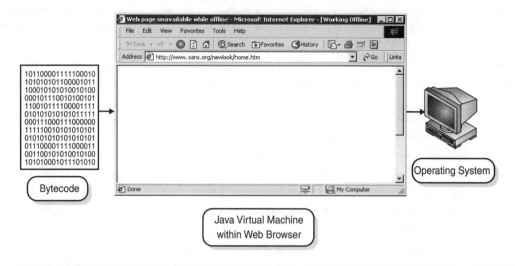

```
101100001111100010
101010101100001011
100010101010010100
000101110010100101
110010111100001111
010101010101011111
000111000111000000
111110010101010101
010101010101010101
011100001111000011
001100101010010100
101010001011101010
```
Bytecode

Address http://www.sans.org/newlook/home.htm

Operating System

Java Virtual Machine
within Web Browser

Figure 11-36 Java is platform independent because it is not compiled to processor-specific machine code. The Java Virtual Machine compiles bytecode to machine code for that specific computer system.

Java

Java is an object-oriented, platform-independent programming language. It is used as a full-fledged programming language and used to write short programs, *applets*, which run on a user's browser.

Other languages are compiled to machine code (ones and zeros), but each processor type understands a different machine code. This is why an application may run on Windows and Unix, but not run on Macintosh. An Intel processor does not necessarily understand machine code compiled for an Alpha processor and vice versa. Java is platform independent because it creates intermediate code, bytecode, which is not processor specific. The Java Virtual Machine then converts the bytecode to the machine code that the processor on that particular system can understand (see Figure 11-36). Let's quickly walk through these steps:

1. The user downloads the Java applet.

2. If the user's browser is Java-enabled and has the Java Virtual Machine installed, the browser knows what to do.

3. The Java compiler converts the high-level code into bytecode (nonprocessor specific).

4. The Java Virtual Machine converts the bytecode into machine level code (processor specific).

5. The applet runs.

Java Security

Java applets use a security scheme that employs a *sandbox* to limit the applet's access to certain specific areas within the user's system and protects the system from malicious or poorly written applets. The applet is supposed to run only within the sandbox. The sandbox restricts the applet's environment by restricting access to a user's hard drives and system resources. If the applet does not go outside the sandbox, it is considered safe.

Browser Settings

Java applets and the actions that they perform can be prevented and controlled by specific browser settings. These settings do not affect full-fledged Java applications running outside of the browser.

However, as with many other things in the computing world, the bad guys have figured out how to escape their confines and restrictions. Programmers have figured out how to write applets that enable the code to access hard drives and resources that are supposed to be protected by the Java security scheme. This code can be malicious in nature and cause destruction and mayhem to the user and her system.

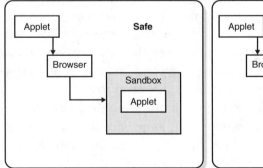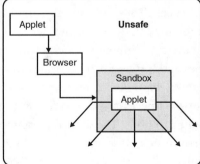

Java employs a sandbox in its security scheme, but if an applet can escape the confines of the sandbox, the system can be easily compromised.

There is a different type of Java applet, which is deemed *trusted* because it provides a digital signature. This type of applet has access to all system resources and is not confined to a sandbox. This type of applet is usually not a component on the Internet for users to download and install, but is developed by in-house programmers and distributed within an intranet to provide some type of business-oriented functionality. The browser will check the digital signature presented by the Java applet and make a decision on if it comes from a known, trusted source before allowing it to execute.

ActiveX

ActiveX is a Microsoft technology that is used to write controls that Internet users can download to increase their functionality and Internet experience. Instead of trying to keep ActiveX components in a safe area for its computations and activities, this language practices security by informing the user where the program came from. The user can decide whether it trusts this origin or not.

ActiveX technology provides security levels and authentication for users to be able to control the security of the ActiveX components they download. Unlike Java applets, ActiveX components are downloaded to a user's hard drive when he chooses to add the functionality that the component provides. This means the ActiveX has far greater access to the user's system.

The security level setting of the user's browser dictates if an ActiveX component is downloaded automatically or if the user is first prompted with a warning. The security level is configurable by the user via his browser controls. As the security level increases, it increases the browser's sensitivity level to signed and unsigned components and controls, the initialization of ActiveX scripts, and other cookie restrictions.

So the main difference between Java and ActiveX security is that Java sets up a sandbox for the code to execute in and this restricts the code's access to resources within the user's computer. ActiveX uses Authenticode technology that relies on digital certificates and trusting certificate authorities. (Signing, digital certificates, and certificate authorities are explained in detail in Chapter 8.) Although both are good and interesting technologies, there are inherent flaws. Java has not been able to ensure that all code stays within the sandbox, which has caused several types of security compromises; these instances are examples of malware. (*Malware* is a general term for malicious code.) ActiveX doesn't necessarily provide security, but it provides annoying dialog boxes that are presented to users. The users do not necessarily know what they are viewing and can become confused and scared or continually click OK because they don't understand the risks involved.

Malicious Code

There are several types of malicious code: viruses, worms, Trojan horses, and logic bombs. They usually are dormant until activated by an event the user or system initiates. They can be spread through using e-mail, sharing media (floppy disks), sharing documents and programs, downloading things from the Internet, or they can be purposely inserted by an attacker.

The usual rule of not opening an e-mail attachment that comes from an unknown source is one of the best ways of combating malicious code. However, recent viruses and worms have infected personal e-mail address books, so this precaution is not a sure thing to protect systems from malicious code. If an address book is infected and used during an attack, the victim gets an e-mail message that seems to have come from a person he knows. Because he knows this person, he will proceed to open the e-mail message, double-click on the attachment, and bam, his address book is now infected and his system just spread the virus to all his friends and acquaintances.

Antivirus software should be installed to watch for known virus signatures and host intrusion detection software can watch for suspicious activity, file access, and changes to help detect evildoers and their malicious activity.

Malicious code can be detected by the following ways:

- File size increase
- Many unexpected disk accesses
- Change in update or modified timestamp

- Sudden decrease of hard drive space

- Unexpected and strange activity by applications

The following section gives a quick look at a few types of malicious code.

Virus

A *virus* is a small application, or string of code, that infects applications. The main function of a virus is to reproduce, and it requires a host application to be able to do this. In other words, viruses cannot replicate on their own. A virus infects files by inserting or attaching a copy of itself to the file. The virus may also cause destruction by deleting system files, displaying graphics, reconfiguring systems, or overwhelming mail servers.

Several viruses have been released that achieved self-perpetuation by mailing themselves to every entry in a victim's personal address book. The virus masqueraded itself as coming from a trusted source. The ILOVEYOU, Melissa, and Naked Wife viruses used the programs Outlook and Outlook Express as their host applications and were replicated when the victim chose to open the message.

Virus

A virus is a program that searches out other programs and infects them by embedding a copy of itself. When the infected program executes, the embedded virus is executed, which propagates the infection.

Macros are programs written in Word Basic, Visual Basic, or VBScript and are usually used with Microsoft Office products. Macros automate different tasks that users would otherwise have to carry out themselves. Users can define a series of activities and common tasks for the application to perform when a button is pushed instead of doing each of those tasks individually. A *macro virus* is a virus written in one of these programming languages and is platform independent. They infect and replicate in templates and within documents. Macro viruses are common because they are extremely easy to write and Office products are in wide use.

Macro Languages

Macro languages enable programmers to edit, delete, and copy files. Because these languages are so easy to use, many more types of macro viruses are possible.

Some viruses infect the boot sector (*boot sector viruses*) of a computer and either move data within the boot sector or overwrite the sector with new information. Some boot sector viruses have part of their code in the boot sector, which can initiate the virus, and have the rest of the virus code in sectors on the hard drive it has marked off as bad. Because the sectors are marked as bad, the operating system and applications will not attempt to use those sectors; thus, they will not get overwritten.

Other types of viruses append themselves to executables on the system and compress them using the user's permissions (*compression viruses*). When the user chooses to use that executable, the system automatically decompresses it and the malicious code, which usually causes the malicious code to initialize and perform its dirty deeds.

A *stealth virus* hides the modifications that it has made to files or boot records. This can be accomplished by monitoring system functions used to read files or sectors and forging the results. This means that when applications or users attempt to read an infected file, or sector, the original, uninfected form will be presented instead of the actual infected form.

So a stealth virus is a virus that hides its tracks after infecting a system. Once infected, the virus can make modifications to make the computer appear the same as before. The virus can show the original file size of a file it infected instead of the new larger size to try trick antivirus software into thinking that no changes have been made.

A *polymorphic virus* produces varied but operational copies of itself. This is done in the hopes of outwitting a virus scanner. Even if one or two copies are found and disabled, other copies may still remain active within the system.

The polymorphic virus can use different encryption schemes requiring different decryption routines. This would require an antivirus scan to have to exploit several scan strings, one for each possible decryption method, in order to identify all copies of this type of virus.

These viruses can also vary the sequence of their instructions by including *noise*, or bogus instructions, with other useful instructions. They can also use a mutation-engine and a random-number generator to change the sequence of their instructions in the hopes of not being detected. A polymorphic virus has the capability of changing its own code, enabling the virus to have hundreds or thousands of different variants. These activities are done so that the virus scanner will not properly recognize the virus and will leave it alone.

A *multipart virus* infects both the boot sector of a hard drive and executable files. The virus first becomes resident in memory and then infects the boot sector. Once it is in memory, it can infect the entire system.

A *self-garbling virus* attempts to hide from antivirus software by garbling its own code. As the virus spreads, it changes the way its code is encoded. A small portion of the virus code decodes the garbled code when activated.

Worm

Worms are different than viruses in that they can reproduce on their own with no need for a host application and that they are self-contained programs. A worm can propagate itself by using e-mail, TCP/IP, and disk drives. The definitions of a worm and virus are continually merging and the distinction is becoming more gray rather than black and white. The ILOVEYOU program was a worm. When the user executed an e-mail attachment, several processes were spawned automatically. The worm was copied and sent to all addresses within the victim's address book. Some files on the hard drive were deleted and replaced. If these were opened, the worm self-propagation started again. ILOVEYOU acts as a virus by requiring the use of an e-mail client, like Outlook, and works as a worm by reproducing itself when the user opens infected files that reside on his hard drive.

Logic Bomb

A *logic bomb* will execute a program, or string of code, when a certain event happens. For example, if a user accesses her bank account software, a logic bomb may be initiated and a program may be kicked off to copy the user's account number and transaction codes. Another example is when a user accesses the Internet through his modem, as shown in Figure 11-37. This action can initiate a planted bomb that will send a message to an attacker over the Internet to let him know that the user is online and in position for an attack.

Trojan Horse

A *Trojan horse* is a program that is disguised as another program. For example, a Trojan horse can be named Notepad.exe and have the same icon as the regular Notepad program. However, when a user executes Notepad.exe, the program can delete system files. Some Trojan horses will perform the useful functionality in addition to the malicious functionality in the background. So the Trojan horse named Notepad.exe may still run the Notepad program for the user and in the background manipulate files or cause some other malicious acts. A host IDS can be configured to watch certain files and

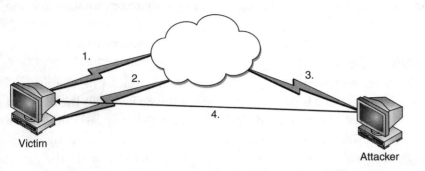

1. Victim connects to the Internet, which is the event that kicks off a logic bomb.
2. The logic bomb "calls" the attacker to indicate that the victim is on the Internet.
3. The attacker receives the message.
4. The attacker attacks the victim.

Figure 11-37   A logic bomb is initiated by specific events. This graphic explains what could happen if the event was the user logging on to the Internet.

detect when they grow in size, which is often a sign of a Trojan horse. If the original Notepad.exe was 50KB in size and then grew to 2MB, it may indicate that a Trojan horse has infected that program.

Trojan Horse

A Trojan horse is a useful program that contains hidden code exploiting the authorization of process to violate security.

So a Trojan horse appears to serve one purpose, but in reality, it performs different and often malicious tasks. This malware was named after the Trojan horse of Greek mythology that Greek soldiers snuck into the city of Troy. The horse looked like a gift, but it was filled with Greek soldiers ready for battle.

Attacks

This section will attempt to show how software weaknesses and bugs are used to provide determinable methods of bringing down systems and/or networks. The weaknesses can reside in the applications, the operating system, or protocols and the network stack.

Denial of Service (DoS)

The network stack is the portion of the operating system that enables devices to communicate over the network. This is where packets are built and sent over the wire and where packets are received and processed. Different operating systems and vendors interpret the Request for Comments (RFCs) for networking protocols differently, which end up in slightly different network stacks. These differences can contain their own flaws that can be taken advantage of to produce a *denial of service (DoS)* attack. These attacks can be performed by sending malformed packets to a system, and because the system does not recognize the format, it does not know how to properly process it. This can cause the system to crash or stop processing other packets (denial of service).

DoS costs businesses millions of dollars each year because of system downtime, lost revenue and productivity, and the man-hours involved in tracking down the problem and fixing it. DoS can interrupt service or complete deny legitimate users of needed system resources.

DoS attacks can consume a victim's bandwidth by flooding the network connection either from an attacker with more bandwidth than the victim, or several attackers working together to saturate the victim's network and bringing it to its knees. If more than one attack is involved, each attacker amplifies the effects of the other attackers by combining their bandwidth capabilities and overwhelming the victim's network segment, as Figure 11-38 illustrates.

Another type of DoS attack can use up all the victim's resources instead of consuming the system's bandwidth. The resources can be processes, file system quotas, memory allocation, and CPU utilization. The following sections discuss some of the possible DoS attacks available.

Smurf

The Internet Control Message Protocol (ICMP) is the minimessenger of Transmission Control Protocol/Internet Protocol (TCP/IP) and is used to find out what systems are up and running (or alive), it reports routing issues, and transmits reply messages from the alive systems. When a user pings another computer, it actually sends an ECHO message and if the system is up and running, it will answer back with a REPLY message. Which basically says, "Hello computer 10.10.10.1, are you up and running?" and that computer answers back, "Yep."

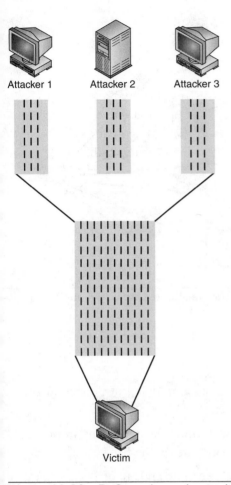

Attacker 1 Attacker 2 Attacker 3

Victim

Figure 11-38 DoS attacks can be amplified by several attackers combining their bandwidth and attacks at once.

The *smurf* attack requires three players: the attacker, the victim, and the amplifying network, as shown in Figure 11-39. The attacker spoofs, or changes the source IP address in a packet header, to make an ICMP ECHO packet seem as though it originated at the victim's system. This ICMP ECHO message is broadcasted to the amplifying network, which will reply to the message in full force. The victim system and victim's network is overwhelmed. The ECHO and REPLY functions of ICMP are there for basic functionality of determining if a computer is up and running and accepting requests. However, this attack takes advantage of the protocol not having certain safety measures built in to protect computers from being overwhelmed with REPLY messages.

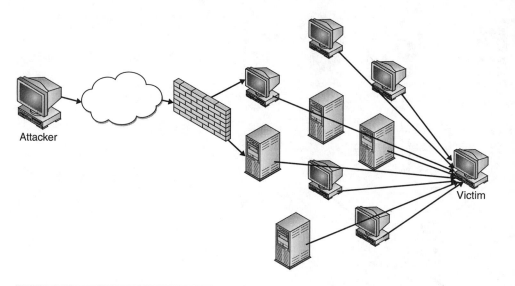

Figure 11-39   The smurf attack takes three players: the attacker, the victim, and the amplifying network.

Countermeasures

- To make sure a certain network is not used as an amplifying site, direct broadcast functionality can be disabled at border routers.

- Packets that contain IP addresses that originate within the internal network should not be accepted by border routers. These packets are spoofed.

- Only the necessary ICMP traffic should be allowed into and out of an environment.

- A network IDS should be employed to watch for suspicious activity.

- The Internet service provider (ISP) should be contacted to see if they are properly protecting the network from these types of attacks.

- Some systems are more sensitive to certain types of DoS and patches have already been released. The appropriate patches should be applied.

Fraggle

Fraggle is an attack similar to smurf, but instead of using ICMP, it uses User Datagram Protocol (UDP) as its weapon of choice. The attacker broadcasts a spoofed UDP packet to the amplifying network, which in turn replies to the victim's system. The larger the amplifying network, the larger the amount of traffic that is pointed at the victim's network.

Different ICMP and UDP packets should be restricted from entering a network for many reasons. Many times an attacker uses this protocol to learn the topology of a network, locate routers, and learn about the type of systems within the network. Because we want to limit the amount of information available to attackers, these restrictions should take place at the ISP, prior to even reaching the network's boarder routers.

- To make sure a certain network is not used as an amplifying site, direct broadcast *How?* functionality can be disabled at border routers.

- Packets that contain IP addresses that originate within the internal network should not be accepted by border routers. These packets are spoofed.

- The ISP should be contacted to see if they are properly protecting the network from these types of attacks.

- Only the necessary UDP should be allowed into and out of an environment.

- Network IDS should be employed to watch for suspicious activity.

- Some systems are more sensitive to certain types of DoS and patches have already been released. The appropriate patches should be applied.

SYN Flood

Because TCP is a connection-oriented protocol, it must set up a virtual connection between two computers. This virtual connection requires handshaking and when using the TCP protocol, this requires a three-way process (see Figure 11-40). If computer Blah would like to communicate with computer Yuck, Blah will send a synchronous (SYN) packet to a specific port on Yuck that is in a LISTEN state. If Yuck is up, running, and accepting calls, it will reply to Blah with an SYN/ACK acknowledgment message. After receiving that message, Blah will send an ACK message to Yuck and the connection will be established.

Systems, and their network stack, are expected to only have to deal with a certain number of these types of connections, so they have allocated only a certain number of resources necessary for these types of functions. A quick analogy is in order. If Katie is only expecting three to five friends to show up at her house for a get together on Friday night, she will most likely only buy a couple of six packs of beer and munchies. When Friday night comes around and over 100 people show up, the party comes to a stand still when there is no more beer and only a bag of pretzels to go around. The same sort of thing is true within the network stack. Once 10 to 12 SYN requests are received, the system runs out of resources to process any more requests to set up communication paths.

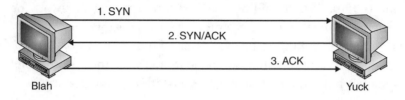

Figure 11-40 When using TCP/IP, a three-way handshake must take place to establish a connection.

Attackers can take advantage of this design flaw by continually sending the victim SYN messages with spoofed packets. The victim will commit the necessary resources to set up this communication socket, and it will send its SYN/ACK message waiting for the ACK message in return. However, the victim will never receive the ACK message because the packet is spoofed and the victim system sent the SYN/ACK message to a computer that does not exist. So the victim system receives an SYN message and it dutifully commits the necessary resources to set up a connection with another computer. This connection is queued waiting for the ACK message, and the attacker sends another SYN message. The victim system does what it is supposed to and commits more resources, sends the SYN/ACK message, and queues this connection. This may only need to happen a dozen times and the victim system no longer has the necessary resources to open up another connection. This makes the victim computer unreachable from legitimate computers, denying other systems service from the victim computer.

The SYN message does not take a lot of bandwidth and this type of attack can leave the victim computer in this state from about a minute and a half up to 23 minutes, depending on the TCP/IP stack. Because the SYN packet is spoofed, it makes it more difficult to track down the evildoer. Vendors have released patches that will increase the connection queue and/or decrease the connection establishment timeout period, which will enable the system to flush its connection queue.

Countermeasures

- Decrease the connection-established timeout period. (This will only lessen the effects of an SYN attack.)

- Increase the size of the connection queue in the IP stack.

- Different vendors have different ways of dealing with SYN attacks, and many patches have been developed to address them. The proper patches should be installed.

- A network IDS can watch of this type of activity to alert the responsible parties when this type of attack is underway.

Teardrop

When packets travel through different networks, they may need to be fragmented or recombined depending on the network technology of each specific network. Each network technology has a maximum transmission unit (MTU), which indicates the largest packet size it can process. Some systems make sure that packets are not too large, but do not check to see if a packet is too small. Attackers can take advantage of this design flaw and send very small packets that would cause a system to freeze or reboot.

Operating systems that fell prey to these types of attacks have provided necessary service packs or implemented the fixes in their newer version and upgrades.

Countermeasures

- Install necessary patch or upgrade operating system.
- Disallow fragments of packets to enter environment.
- Use a router that will combine all fragments into a full packet prior to routing it to the destination system.

Distributed Denial of Service (DDoS)

A *distributed denial of service (DDoS)* attack is a logical extension of the DoS, which gets more computers in the act. DoS attacks overwhelm computers by one computer sending bad packets or continually requesting services until the system's resources are all tied up and cannot honor any further requests. The DDoS does a similar process by using hundreds or thousands of computers to request services from a server or server farm until the system or Web site is no longer functional.

The more recent victims of this type of attack have been Yahoo!, CNN.com, ZDNet, and E*Trade. These sites are developed to handle many hits to their sites and have the capability to process a large number or service requests each hour. However, a DDoS implements a volume of service requests that could overload any site to date. The attack can use other computers that knowingly participate, but most likely are unknowingly used as slaves in the process. The attacker creates master controllers that can in turn control *slaves*, or *zombie* machines. The master controllers are systems that an attacker is able to achieve administrative rights to so that programs can be loaded that will wait and listen for further instructions. The components of the third tier of computers are referred to as zombies because they do not necessarily know that they are involved in an attack. Scripts that have been put on their hard drives execute, and together all the

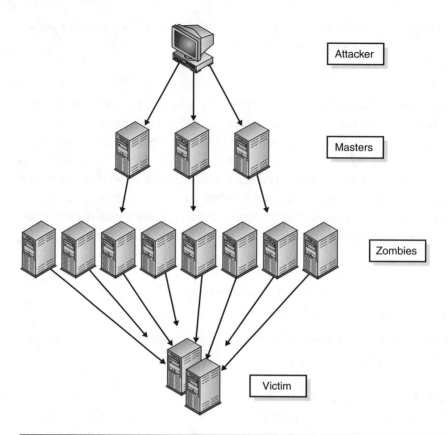

Figure 11-41 In a DDoS attack, the attacker uses masters to control zombies to overwhelm the victim with requests.

zombie slaves work in concert to overwhelm other computers and Web sites. An example of a DDoS attack is shown in Figure 11-41.

Countermeasures

- Border routers restrict unnecessary ICMP and UDP traffic.

- Context-based access control can be implemented.

- A network IDS can be employed to watch for this type of suspicious activity.

- Disable unused subsystems on computers.

- Rename administrator account and implement strict password management so systems cannot be used unknowingly.

- Packets with IP addresses that indicate that the packet came from within the internal network should not be allowed past border routers.

DNS DoS Attacks

Domain Name System (DNS) servers are used to map hostnames to IP addresses. It is a service used on almost every network and all over the Internet. People understand hostnames (**www.isc2.org**) and the network layer of the network stack understands IP addresses. So when a user types in a URL, it is a DNS server that transforms this addresses into something understandable by computers and network devices. Once the system and network devices know the right IP address, they know how to route the packets properly. It is like stopping at a gas station for directions. If you tell the guy behind the counter that you are looking for the post office, he would tell you that the post office is on Main street and proceed to tell you the streets and turns to get to this destination. Thank goodness for gas stations and DNS servers!

Each DNS server is responsible for certain hosts, which are collectively referred to as a *zone*. Each host has its own record within the DNS server that contains its IP addresses, and this is how the DNS translates the hostname to the IP address. If a record that indicates that **www.isc2.org** is mapped to 10.10.10.1 is replaced with a record that says that **www.isc2.org** is mapped to 0.0.0.2 instead, the real Web site would not be able to receive hits. Users would not be able to get to this site; therefore, there would be a DoS.

This is how DNS DoS attacks can occur. If the actual DNS records are unattainable to the attacker for him to alter in this fashion, which they should be, the attacker can insert this data into the cache of the server instead of replacing the actual records, which is referred to as *cache poisoning*. Many times DNS servers will cache previously resolved requests to make the next request for that hostname quicker. If the attacker replaces real data with bogus information in the server's cache, the DNS server and user would not necessarily know about this violation.

Because DNS servers are responsible only for a finite number of clients, many times one DNS server will have to ask another DNS server for help in finding out the requested information for the user. The DNS server can ask a root server for the address of the DNS server that is authoritative for the destination domain. This recursively resolves DNS names and the original DNS server acts as a middleman by sending the user the address of the DNS responsible for the host the user is asking about. An attacker can send a bogus response to the requesting DNS server and the DNS server will in turn send this bogus information to the requesting user. This will point the user to a different site than what was planned and DoS has been committed because the user cannot get the service he requested.

Countermeasures

- DNS servers should have public and internal records. The public records serve Internet requests and contain no sensitive information pertaining to the internal network. The internal records should be unreachable from the Internet and are used to resolve queries from internal users.

- DNS servers should also be redundant by using a primary and secondary per zone.

- Different DNS BIND versions have different vulnerabilities. The BIND version should be updated.

- Employ secure DNS, which is explained in the next section.

Secure DNS

DNS servers contain records that enable the mapping between hostnames and IP addresses, as stated earlier. There are primary DNS servers that make all the necessary changes to the records when host and/or IP addresses change, and these records are then distributed to the secondary DNS servers. If a secondary server received bogus records from an attacker instead of the primary DNS server, it would not know the difference and update its records accordingly. Then when a user's computer contacted this secondary DNS server to translate hostnames to IP addresses, the records could contain incorrect information. Attacks like this have taken place mainly to embarrass businesses because users were redirected to indecent sites or competitors' sites. However, this also causes DoS because the users cannot get where they need to go.

When secure DNS is implemented, the secondary DNS servers must authenticate the systems that are updating their records. Integrity checks are also performed to ensure that records were not modified or corrupted during transmission. Secure DNS protects DNS servers from having their records updated by unauthorized sources.

Summary

Although functionality is the number one driver when developing software, it would be beneficial if security was brought into the mix before the project started and integrated into each and every step of the development process. Although many companies do not view this as the most beneficial approach to software development, they are learning it over time as more security patches and fixes have to be developed and released.

Software development is a very complex task, especially as technology changes at the speed of light, environments evolve, and more and more expectations are brought to vendors wishing to be the 'king of the mountain' within the software market. This complexity also makes implementing effective security more challenging. For years programmers and developers did not need to consider security issues within their code, but this trend is changing. Education, experience, awareness, enforcement, and the demand of the consumers are all necessary pieces to bring more secure practices and technologies to the program code we all use.

Quick Tips

- Security controls can be preventive, detective, or corrective, and come in the form of administrative, physical, or technical.
- Buffer overflows happen when an application does not check the length of data that is inputted and can cause the elevation of privilege for malicious code.
- If an application fails for any reason, it should go directly to a safe state.
- A database management system (DBMS) is the software that controls the access restrictions, data integrity, redundancy, and the different types of manipulation available for a database
- A database row is called a tuple.
- A database primary key is how a specific key is located from other parts of the database.
- A view is an access control mechanism used in databases to ensure that only authorized subjects can access sensitive information.
- A relational database uses two-dimensional tables with rows (tuples) and columns (attributes).
- A hierarchical database uses a treelike structure to define relationships between data elements, using a parent/child relationship.
- A distributed database, or network database, has databases that are physically in different areas but logically connected to represent one main database.
- Most databases have data definition language (DDL), data manipulation language (DML), query language (QL), and a report generator.
- A data dictionary is a central repository that describes the data elements within a database and their relationship. A data dictionary contains data about a database.
- Database integrity is provided by concurrency mechanisms. One concurrency control is locking, which prevents users from accessing and modifying data that is in use by another user.

- Referential integrity makes sure that a row, or tuple, is uniquely identified by a primary key and that every foreign key refers to an existing primary key.

- A rollback cancels changes and returns the database to its previous state. This takes place if there was a problem during a transaction.

- A commit statement terminates a transaction and executes all changes to the database.

- A checkpoint is used if there is a system failure or problem during a transaction. The user is returned to the state of the last checkpoint.

- Aggregation can happen if a user does not have access to a group of elements, but has access to some of the individual elements within the group. Aggregation happens if the user combines the information of these individual elements and figures out the information of the group of data elements, which is at a higher sensitivity level.

- Inference is the capability to derive information that is not explicitly available.

- Common attempts to prevent inference attacks are partitioning the database, cell suppression, and adding noise to the database.

- Polyinstantiation is the process of creating two versions of the same object so that the subjects at the lower level of security cannot access information at a higher level of sensitivity.

- Polymorphism is when different objects are given the same input and react differently.

- Data warehousing combines data from multiple databases.

- Data mining is the process of massaging data held within a data warehouse to provide more useful information to users.

- Data mining tools produce metadata, which can contain previously unseen relationships and patterns.

- Security should be addressed in each phase of system development. Security should not be addressed at the end of development because of the added cost, time, effort, and lack of functionality.

- Systems and applications can use different models that use different life cycles, but one group of life cycles is project initiation, functional design analysis and planning, system design specifications, software development, installation, operations and maintenance, and disposal.

- Risk management and assessments should start at the beginning of a project and continue throughout the lifetime of the product.

- If proper design for a product is not put into place in the beginning, more effort will have to take place in the implementation, testing, and maintenance phases.

- Separation of duties should be practiced in roles, environments, and functionality pertaining to development of a product.

- A programmer should not have direct access to code in production. This is an example of separation of duties.

- Certification deals with testing and assessing the security mechanism in a system and accreditation pertains to the management formally accepting the system and its security level.

- Systems that contain sensitive information must be disposed of in a controlled and secure way. This may mean physical destruction of the media.

- Change control needs to be put in place at the beginning of a project and must be enforced through each phase.

- Changes must be authorized, tested, and recorded. The changes must not affect the security level of the system or its capability to enforce the security policy.

- High-level programming languages are translated into machine languages for the system and its processors to understand.

- Source code is translated into machine code, or object code, by compilers, assemblers, and interpreters.

- Object-oriented programming provides modularity, reusability, and more granular control within the programs themselves.

- Objects are members, or instances, of classes. The classes dictate the objects data types, structure, and acceptable actions.

- Objects communicate with each other through messages.

- When an action takes place on an object, it is referred to as a method. Each object has only specific acceptable methods that it can react to.

- Data and operations internal to objects are hidden from other objects, which is referred to as data hiding. Each object encapsulates its data and processes.

- Objects can communicate properly because they are using standard interfaces.

- Object-oriented design represents a real-world problem and modularizes the problem into cooperating objects that work together to solve the problem.

- Object-oriented programming uses programming languages that work with objects and methods.

- If an object can perform a function without the help of others, it has high cohesion.

- If an object does not require much interaction with other modules, it has low coupling.

- The best programming design enables objects to be as independent and modular as possible; therefore, the higher the cohesion and the lower the coupling, the better.

- Object request broker (ORB) manages communication between components and enables them to interact in a heterogeneous and distributed environment.

- Common Object Request Broker Architecture (CORBA) provides a standardized way for objects within different applications, platforms, and environments to communicate. It accomplishes this by providing standards for interfaces between objects.

- Component Object Model (COM) provides an architect for components to interact on a local system. Distributed COM (DCOM) uses the same interfaces as COM, but enables components to interact over a distributed, or networked, environment.

- Open database connectivity (ODBC) enables several different applications to communicate with several different types of databases by calling the required driver and passing data through that driver.

- Object linking and embedding (OLE) enables a program to call another program (linking) and enables a piece of data to be inserted inside another program or document (embedding).

- Dynamic Data Exchange (DDE) enables applications to work in a client/server model by providing the interprocess communication (IPC) mechanism.

- Distributed Computing Environment (DCE) provides much of the same functionality as DCOM, which enables different objects to communicate in a networked environment.

- DCE uses universal unique identifiers (UUIDs) to keep track of different subjects, objects, and resources.

- An expert system uses a knowledge base full of facts, rules of thumb, and expert advice. It also has an inference machine that matches facts against patterns and determines which rules are to be applied.

- Expert systems are used to mimic human reasoning and replace human experts.

- Artificial neural networks (ANNs) attempt to mimic a brain by using units that react like neurons.

- ANNs can learn from experiences and match patterns that regular programs and systems cannot.

- Java security employs a sandbox so that the applet is restricted from access the user's hard drive or system resources. Programmers have figured out how to write applets that escape the sandbox.

- ActiveX uses a security scheme that includes digital signatures. The browser security settings determine how ActiveX controls are dealt with.

- A virus is an application that requires a host application of replication.

- Macro viruses are common because the languages used to develop macros are easy to use and they infect Office products, which are everywhere.

- A boot sector virus overwrites data in the boot sector and can contain the rest of the virus in a sector it marked bad.

- A stealth virus hides its tracks and its actions by presenting the user with original data.

- A polymorphic virus tries to escape detection by changing parts of itself.

- Multipart viruses have one part in the boot sector and another part of the virus in on the hard drive.

- A self-garbling virus tries to escape detection by changing, or garbling, its own code.

- A worm does not require a host application to replicate.

- A logic bomb executes a program when a predefined event takes place.

- A Trojan horse is a program that performs useful functionality and malicious functionally without the user knowing.

- Smurf and Fraggle are two examples of DoS attacks that take advantage of protocol flaws.

- Expert systems use inference engine processing, automatic logical processing, and general methods of searching for problem solutions.

Questions

Please remember that these questions are formatted and asked in a certain way for a reason. The questions and answers may seem odd or vague, but this is what you will see on the actual CISSP test.

1. What is the final stage in the change control management process?
   a. Configure the hardware properly.
   b. Update documentation and manuals.
   c. Inform users of the change.
   d. Report the change to management.

2. Which best describes a logic bomb?
   a. Used to move assets from one computer to another
   b. Action triggered by a specified condition
   c. Self-replicating
   d. Performs a useful action and a malicious action

3. An application is downloaded from the Internet to perform disk cleanup and delete unnecessary temporary files. The application is also recording network login data and sending it to another party. This application is best described as which of the following?
   a. Virus
   b. Trojan horse
   c. Worm
   d. Logic bomb

4. Why are macro viruses so prevalent?
   a. They replicate quickly.
   b. They infect every platform in production.
   c. The languages used to write macros are very easy to use.
   d. They are activated by events that happen commonly on each system.

5. Which action is not part of change management?
   a. Logical configuration
   b. Operating system configuration and settings
   c. Hardware configuration
   d. Application settings and configuration

6. Expert systems are used to automate security log review for what purpose?
    a. Develop user behavioral models.
    b. Ensure best access methods.
    c. Detect intrusion.
    d. Provide statistics that will be used for baselines.

7. Which form of malware has a purpose of reproducing itself utilizing system resources?
    a. Worm
    b. Virus
    c. Trojan horse
    d. Multipart virus

8. Expert systems use each of the following items except for _____.
    a. Automatic logical processing
    b. General methods of searching for problem solutions
    c. Inference engine
    d. Cycle-based reasoning

9. Which of the following replicates itself by attaching to other programs?
    a. Worm
    b. Virus
    c. Trojan horse
    d. Malware

10. What is the importance of inference in a knowledge-based system?
    a. The knowledge base contains facts, but must also be able to combine facts to drive new facts.
    b. The inference machine is important to create metadata.
    c. The knowledge base must work in units to mimic neurons in the brain.
    d. The access must be controlled to prevent unauthorized access.

11. A system has been patched many times and has recently become infected with a dangerous virus. If antivirus software indicates that disinfecting a file may damage it, what is the correct action?
    a. Disinfect the file and contact the vendor.
    b. Back up the data and disinfect the file.
    c. Replace the file with the file saved the day before.
    d. Restore an uninfected version of the patched file from backup media.

12. Which of the following centrally controls data and manages different aspects of the data?
    a. Data storage
    b. Database
    c. Data dictionary
    d. Access control

13. What is the purpose of polyinstantiation?
    a. To restrict lower-level subjects from accessing low-level information
    b. To restrict lower-level subjects from inferring the existence of data at a higher level
    c. To create different objects that will react the different ways to the same input
    d. To create different objects that will take on inheritance attributes from their class

14. When a database detects an error, what enables it to start processing at a designated place?
    a. Checkpoint
    b. Data dictionary
    c. Metadata
    d. Data mining tool

15. Database views provide what type of security control?
    a. Detective
    b. Corrective
    c. Preventative
    d. Administrative

16. If one department can view employees' work history and another group cannot view their work history, what is this an example of?
    a. Context-dependent access control
    b. Content-dependent access control
    c. Separation of duties
    d. Mandatory access control

17. Which of the following is used to deter database inference attacks?
    a. Partitioning, cell suppression, and noise and perturbation
    b. Controlling access to the data dictionary
    c. Partitioning, cell suppression, and small query sets
    d. Partitioning, noise and perturbation, and small query sets

18. What is a disadvantage of content-dependent access control when it comes to databases?
    a. It can access other memory addresses.
    b. It can cause concurrency problems.
    c. It increases processing and resource overhead.
    d. It can cause deadlock situations.

19. If security was not part of the development of a database, how is it usually handled?
    a. Cell suppression
    b. Trusted back end
    c. Trusted front end
    d. Views

20. What is an advantage of content-dependent access control in databases?
    a. Processing overhead
    b. Ensures concurrency
    c. Disallows data locking
    d. Granular control

21. Which of the following is used in the Distributed Computing Environment technology?
    a. Global unique identifier (GUID)
    b. Universal unique identifier (UUID)
    c. Universal global identifier (UGID)
    d. Global universal identifier (GUID)

22. When should security first be addressed in a project?
    a. During requirements development
    b. During integration testing
    c. During design specifications
    d. During implementation

23. Online application systems that detect an invalid transaction should do which of the following?
    a. Roll back and rewrite over original data.
    b. Terminate all transactions until properly addressed.
    c. Write a report to be reviewed.
    d. Checkpoint each data entry.

24. What is the final phase of the system development life cycle?
    a. Certification
    b. Unit testing
    c. Maintenance
    d. Accreditation

Answers

1. D.	7. A.	13. B.	19. C.
2. B.	8. D.	14. A.	20. D.
3. B.	9. B.	15. C.	21. B.
4. C.	10. A.	16. B.	22. A.
5. A.	11. D.	17. A.	23. C.
6. C.	12. C.	18. C.	24. D.

Operations Security

In this chapter, you will learn about the following items:

- Administrative management responsibilities
- Product evaluation and operational assurance
- Change configuration management
- Trusted recovery states
- E-mail security
- Threats to operational security

Operation security pertains to everything that takes place to keep a network, computer system, and environment up and running in a secure and protected manner. Operations take place after the network is developed and implemented. This includes the continual maintenance of an environment and the activities that should take place on a day-to-day or week-to-week basis. These activities are routine in nature and enable the network and individual computer systems to continue to run correctly and securely.

Networks and environments are evolving entities; just because they are secure one week does not mean that they are still secure three weeks later. Many companies have paid security consultants who come in and advise them on how to improve their infrastructure, policies, and procedures. A company can then spend thousands of dollars to implement the consultant's suggestions and install properly configured firewalls, intrusion detection systems (IDSs), antivirus software, and patch vulnerable systems. However, if the IDSs and antivirus software do not continually have updated signatures, if the systems are not continually patched, and if firewalls and devices are not tested for vulnerabilities, then the company can easily slip back into an insecure and dangerous place. This would happen because it did not keep up on its operational security tasks.

Most of the necessary operational security issues have been addressed in earlier chapters. They were integrated with different related topics and not necessarily pointed out as actual operational security issues. So instead of repeating what has already been previously stated, this chapter will review and point out the operational security topics that are important for organizations and CISSP candidates.

Operational Security

The continual effort of making sure that the correct policies, procedures, and standards are in place and being followed is an important piece of the *due care* and *due diligence* that companies need to perform. Due care and due diligence is comparable to the "prudent man" concept. A prudent man is seen as responsible, careful, cautious, and practical, and a company practicing due care and due diligence is seen in the same light. If a company installs antivirus software on all of its computers, this can be an example of due care, but if the company does not keep the antivirus signatures updated, the company is not practicing due diligence.

The right steps need to be taken to achieve the necessary level of security, but it takes continued effort and discipline to retain this level of security. This is what operational security is all about.

Although operational security is the practice of continual maintenance to keep an environment running at a necessary security level, there can also be liable and legal responsibilities when it comes to performing these tasks. Companies, and senior executives at those companies, many times have legal obligations to ensure that resources are protected, that safety measures are in place, and that security mechanisms are tested to guarantee that they are still providing the necessary level of protection. If these operational security responsibilities are not fulfilled, the company may have more than antivirus signatures to be concerned about. (Please refer to Chapter 10 to learn more about the legal, regulatory, and ethical responsibilities of companies when it comes to information security.)

Administrative Management

Administrative management is a very important piece of operational security. One aspect of administrative management is dealing with personnel issues. This includes separation of duties and job rotation. The objective of *separation of duties* is to ensure that one person acting alone cannot compromise the company's security in any way.

High-risk activities should be broken up into different parts and distributed to different individuals. This way the company does not need to put a dangerously high level of trust on certain individuals and if fraud were to take place, collusion would need to be committed, meaning more than one person would have to be involved in the fraudulent activity.

Separation of duties also helps to prevent many different types of mistakes that can take place if one person is performing a task from the beginning to the end. For instance, a programmer should not be the one to test her own code. A different person with a different job and agenda should perform functionality and integrity testing on the programmer's code because the programmer may have a focused view of what the program is supposed to accomplish and only test certain functions, input values, and in certain environments.

Another example of separation of duties is the difference between the functions of a computer operator versus the functions of a system administrator. There must be clear-cut lines drawn between system administrator duties and computer operator duties. This will vary from environment to environment and will depend on the level of security required within the environment. The system administrators usually have the responsibility of performing backups and recovery procedures, setting permissions, adding and removing users, setting user clearance, and developing user profiles. The computer operator, on the other hand, may be allowed to install software, set an initial password, alter desktop configurations, and modify certain system parameters. The computer operator should not be able to modify her own security profile, add and remove users globally, or set user security clearance. This would breach the concept of separation of duties.

Job rotation means that more than one person fulfills the tasks of one position within the company. This enables the company to have more than one person who understands tasks and responsibilities of a specific job title, which provides backup and redundancy if a person leaves the company or is absent. Job rotation also helps to identify fraudulent activities. If Keith has performed David's position, he knows the regular tasks and routines that are to be completed to fulfill the responsibilities of that job. This would allow Keith to better identify if David does something out of the ordinary and suspicious. (Please refer to Chapters 4 and 6 for further examples pertaining to job rotation.)

Rotation of Duties Definition

"Interrupt opportunity to create collusion to subvert operation for fraudulent purposes." This is ISC[(2)]'s definition, which is confusing to say the least. It means that if employees rotated jobs, it would make it harder for one employee to commit fraudulent activities without other employees finding out.

Least privilege and need-to-know are also administrative-type controls that should be implemented. *Least privilege* means that an individual should have just enough permissions and rights to fulfill his role in the company and no more. If an individual has excessive permissions and rights, it could open the door to abuse of access and put the company in more risk than is necessary. If Dusty is a technical writer for a company, he does not necessarily need to have access to the company's source code. So the mechanisms that control Dusty's access to resources should not let him access source code. This would be properly fulfilling operational security controls that are in place to protect resources.

Least privilege and *need-to-know* have a symbiotic relationship. Each user should have a need-to-know of the resources that he is allowed to access. If Mike does not have a need-to-know of how much the company paid last year in taxes, then his system rights should not include access to these files, which would be an example of exercising least privilege.

A user's access rights can be a combination of the least privilege attribute, the user's security clearance, the need-to-know, the sensitivity level of the resource, and the mode at which the computer operates. A system can operate at different types of modes depending on the sensitivity of the data being processed, the clearance level of the users, and what those users are authorized to do. The mode of operation describes the conditions under which the system actually functions. These are clearly defined in Chapter 5. (Please refer to Chapters 3, 4, and 5 for further discussion on these topics.)

Mandatory vacations are another type of administrative control that may sound a bit odd at first. Chapter 3 touches on reasons to make sure that employees take their vacations; this has to do with being able to identify fraudulent activities and enable job rotation to take place. If an accounting employee has been performing data diddling by shaving off pennies from multiple accounts and putting the money into his own account, a company would have a better chance of figuring this out if that employee was required to take a vacation for a week or longer. When the employee is on vacation, another employee has to fill in and she might uncover questionable documents and clues of previous activities or the company may see a change in certain patterns once the employee who is frauding them is gone for a week or two.

A company could be unaware that any illegal activities were taking place until a new person had to fill someone else's position and then uncovered suspicious evidence. Many people who perform fraudulent activities at their jobs do not take the vacation they earn so that they will not be caught; this is why it is called a mandatory vacation.

Accountability

User access to resources must be limited and properly controlled to ensure that excessive privileges do not provide the opportunity to cause damage to a company and its resources. Users' access attempts and activities while using a resource, or information, need to be properly monitored, audited, and logged. The individual user ID needs to be included in the audit logs to enforce individual responsibility. Each user should understand his responsibility when using company resources and be accountable for his actions.

Capturing and monitoring audit logs helps to determine if a violation has actually occurred or if system and software reconfiguration is needed to better capture only the activities that fall outside of established boundaries. If user activities were not captured and reviewed, it would be very hard to determine if users have excessive privileges or if there has been unauthorized access.

Auditing needs to take place in a routine manner. There is also really no reason to audit and log events if no one looks at the output. Many times audit and function logs contain too much cryptic information to be interpreted manually. This is why there are products that parse logs for companies and report important findings. Logs should be monitored and reviewed either through manual or automatic methods to uncover suspicious activity or if an environment is shifting away from its original baselines. This is how administrators can be warned of many different types of problems before they become too big and out of control. (Please look at Chapters 3, 6, and 10 for auditing, logging, and monitoring issues.)

Certain questions need to be asked when monitoring audit information and user activities, which pertain to the users, their actions, and the current level of security.

- *Are users accessing information and performing tasks that are not necessary for their job description?*
  - This would indicate that users' rights and permissions need to be reevaluated and possibly modified.
- *Are repetitive mistakes being made?*
  - This would indicate that users need to have further training.

• *Do too many users have rights and privileges to sensitive or restricted data or resources?*

  • This would indicate that access rights to the data and resources need to be reevaluated, the number of individuals accessing them needs to be reduced, and/or the extent of their access rights should be modified.

Security Operations and Product Evaluation

When products are evaluated for the level of trust and security they provide, many times *operational assurance* and *life cycle assurance* are part of the evaluation. Operational assurance concentrates on the architecture of the product and the embedded features and functionality that enable a customer to continually obtain the necessary level of security when using the product. Examples of operational assurances examined in the evaluation process are access control mechanisms, the separation of privileged and user program code, auditing and monitoring capabilities, covert channel analysis, and trusted recovery when the product experiences unexpected circumstances.

Life cycle assurance pertains to the product's architecture and how it was developed and maintained. Each stage of the product's life cycle has standards and expectations it must fulfill before it can be deemed as a highly trusted product. Examples of life cycle assurance standards are design specifications, clipping level configurations, unit and integration testing, configuration management, and trusted distribution. The products that are looking to achieve one of the higher security ratings will have each of these issues evaluated and tested.

The following sections address several of these types of operational assurance and life cycle assurance issues as they pertain to evaluation, but also as they pertain to a company's responsibilities once the product is implemented. A product is just a tool for a company to use for functionality and security; it is up to the company to ensure that this functionality and security is continually available through responsible and proactive steps.

Clipping Levels

Companies set certain thresholds for certain types of errors or mistakes allowed and the amount of these mistakes that can take place before it is considered suspicious. The threshold is a baseline for violation activities that may be normal for a user to commit before alarms are raised. This baseline is referred to as a *clipping level*. Once this clipping level has been exceeded, further violations are recorded for review. Most of the time IDS software is used to track these activities and behavior patterns because it would be too overwhelming for an individual to continually monitor stacks of audit logs and properly identify certain activity patterns. Once the clipping level is exceeded, the IDS can e-mail a message to the network administrator, send a message to his pager, or just add this information to the logs. It depends upon how the IDS software is configured.

Clipping levels, auditing, and monitoring are done with the hopes of discovering problems before major damage occurs and, at times, be alerted if a possible attacker is at work within the network.

NOTE It is important that the security controls and mechanisms that are in place have a degree of transparency. This enables the user to perform tasks and duties without having to go through extra steps because of the presence of the security controls. Transparency also does not let the user know too much about the controls, which helps prevent him from figuring out how to circumvent them. Also, if the controls are too obvious, an attacker can figure out how to compromise them more easily.

Resource Access

It is important to give users the level of access required to fulfill their role within the company and no more. When analyzing user access, the security professional must distinguish between the user's access to discretionary information resources and nondiscretionary resources. Discretionary access is regulated by which users have access to the resources and to what degree. The information that is written to audit logs under discretionary access models is what data was accessed, the user ID, and the level of authority the user had when accessing the resource. It does not usually log what the user did with this information after he accessed it.

Nondiscretionary access usually works under a more strictly regulated methodology. A centralized authority makes the decisions on which users can access what resources and the functions that those users can carry out. The auditing and logging capabilities of nondiscretionary access can be more detailed in nature and show more granularity to what a user did once he accessed a particular resource. (Please review Chapter 4 for a more in-depth understanding of these types of access controls.)

Change Management Control

Every company should have a policy indicating how changes take place within a facility, who can make the changes, how they are approved, and how these changes are documented and communicated to other employees. Without these policies in place, different people can make changes that others do not know about and have not been approved, which can result in a confusing mess. This is usually when vulnerabilities are introduced into an environment and tracking down and reversing the changes can be a complicated task.

The changes can happen to network configuration, system parameters, and settings by adding new technologies, application configurations, devices, or modifying the facility's environmental devices. Change control is important for an environment, but also for a product during its development and life cycle. It is important that changes be effective and orderly because it is easy to waste time and money by continually making changes that do not meet an ultimate goal.

NOTE Change control is the management of security features and a level of assurance provided through the control of the changes made to the system's hardware, software, and firmware configurations throughout the development and operational life cycle.

Some changes can cause a serious disruption to a network and affect the system's availability. This means that changes must be thought through, approved, and carried out in a structured fashion. Backup plans may be necessary in case the change causes unforeseen negative effects. For example, if a facility is changing its power supply, there should be backup generators on hand in case the transition does not take place as smoothly as planned. Or if a server is going to be replaced with a different server type, there could be interoperability issues that could prevent users from accessing specific resources, so a backup or redundant server should be in place to ensure availability and continued productivity.

A well-structured change management process should be put into place to aid staff members through many different types of changes to the environment. This process would be laid out in the change control policy. Although the types of changes vary, a standard list of procedures can help to keep the process under control and to be carried out in a predictable manner. The following steps are examples of the types of procedures that should be part of any change control policy:

1. **Request for a change to take place** Requests should be presented to an individual or group that is responsible for approving changes and overseeing the activities of changes that take place within an environment.

2. **Approval of the change** The individual requesting the change must justify the reasons and clearly show the benefits and possible pitfalls of the change. Some-

times the requester is asked to conduct more research and provide more information before the change is approved.

3. **Documentation of the change**   Once the change is approved, it should be entered into a change log and the log should be updated as the process continues toward completion.

4. **Tested and presented**   The change must be fully tested to uncover any unforeseen results. Depending on the severity of the change and the company's organization, the change and implementation may need to be presented to a change control committee. This helps show different sides to the purpose and outcome of the change and the possible ramifications.

5. **Implementation**   Once the change is fully tested and improved, a schedule should be developed that outlines the projected phases of the change being implemented and the necessary milestones. These steps should be fully documented and progress should be monitored.

6. **Report changes to management**   A full report should be submitted to management summarizing the change. This report can be submitted on a periodic basis to keep management up-to-date and ensure continual support.

These steps, of course, usually apply to large changes that take place within a facility. These types of changes are usually expensive and can have lasting effects on a company. However, smaller changes should also go through some type of change control process. If a server needs to have a patch applied, it is not good practice to have an engineer just apply it without properly testing it on a nonproduction server, without having the approval of the manager of the IT department or network administrator, and without having backup plans in place in case the patch causes some negative effect on the production server. Of course, these changes need to be documented. (Please refer to Chapter 7 for a further look at change control procedures.)

Change Control Documentation

Documentation should be done on a regular basis so that changes are identified and written down and available for future use. There are numerous changes that can take place in a company:

- New computers installed
- New applications installed
- Different configurations implemented

- Patches and updates installed
- New technologies integrated
- Updated policies, procedures, and standards
- New regulations and requirements
- Identified and implemented fixes for network or system problems
- Different network configuration
- New networking devices integrated into the network

The list can go on and on and can be general or detailed. Many companies have experienced some major problem that affects the network and employee productivity. The IT department may run around trying to figure out the issue and go through hours or days of trial-and-error exercises of finding and applying the necessary fix. If no one properly documents the incident and what was done to fix the issue, the company can be doomed to replay the same dance in a year or two down the road.

Media Controls

Media and devices require a variety of controls to ensure that they are properly preserved and that the integrity, confidentiality, and availability of the data that is held on them is not compromised.

The operational controls that pertain to these issues come in many flavors. The first are controls that prevent unauthorized access, which can require physical, administrative, and technical controls to be put into place. If the company's backup tapes are to be properly protected, then they need to be in a place where only the necessary people have access, which could be in a locked server room or off-site facility. If the tapes need to be protected from environmental issues like humidity, heat, cold, fire, and natural disasters, then they should be kept in a fireproof safe in a regulated environment or in an off-site facility that controls the environment to be hospitable to data processing components. These issues are covered in detail in Chapter 6.

Many times companies have a media library with a librarian in charge of protecting its resources. Users may be required to check out specific types of media and resources instead of having the resources readily available for anyone and everyone to access them. If the library controls media-holding data, each should be labeled with the following information:

- The date of creation
- The individual who created it

- The retention period (how long the media is good for)

- The classification

- The volume name and version

Media should be clearly marked and logged, its integrity should be verified, and it should be destroyed properly when necessary. When media is cleared of its contents, it is said to be *sanitized*. There are different methods for sanitation: overwriting, degaussing, and destruction. As stated in earlier chapters, deleting files on a piece of media does not actually make the data disappear; it only deletes the pointers to where those files still live on the disk. This is how companies that specialize in restoration can recover the deleted files intact after they had been apparently destroyed.

NOTE A device that performs degaussing generates a coercive magnetic force that reduces the magnetic flux density of the storage media to zero. This magnetic force is what properly erases data from media.

Data remanence is the residual physical representation of information that was saved and then erased in some fashion. This remanence may be enough to enable the data to be reconstructed and restored back into a readable form. This can cause a security threat to a company who thought that they properly erased confidential data from their media.

If the media does not hold confidential or sensitive information, then overwriting or deleting the files may be the appropriate steps to take. If the data is sensitive, then degaussing may be required. If the data is highly confidential or the media cannot be properly degaussed, then the appropriate action would be to physically destroy it. (Please refer to Chapters 3 and 4 for further discussion on these issues.)

System Controls

System controls are also part of operational security. Within the operating system itself, certain controls must be in place to ensure that instructions are being executed in the correct security context. The system has mechanisms that restrict the execution of certain types of instructions, which can only take place when the operating system is in a privileged or supervisor state. This protects the overall security and state of the system and helps to ensure that it runs in a stable and predictable manner.

An operating system does not provide direct access to hardware by processes of lower privilege, which are usually processes used by user applications. If a program needs to send instructions to hardware devices, the request is passed off to a process of higher privilege. To execute privileged hardware instructions, a process must be running in a restrictive and protective state. This is an integral part of the operating system's architecture and the determination of what processes can submit what type of instructions is made based on the operating system's control tables.

Many I/O instructions are defined as privileged and can only be executed by the operating system kernel processes. When a user program needs to send I/O information, it must notify the system's core, privileged processes that work at the inner rings of the system. These processes either authorize the user program processes to perform these actions and temporarily increase their privileged state or the system's processes complete the request on behalf of the user program. (Please review Chapter 5 for a more in-depth understanding of these types of system controls.)

Trusted Recovery

When an operating system or product crashes or freezes, it should not put the system in any type of insecure state. The usual reason for a system crash in the first place is because it encountered something that it perceived as insecure or did not understand and decided that it was safer to freeze, shut down, or reboot than perform the current activity.

An operating system's response to a type of failure can be classified as one of the following:

- System reboot
- Emergency system restart
- System cold start

A *system reboot* takes place after shutting down the system in a controlled manner in response to a trusted computer base (TCB) failure. If the system finds inconsistent object data structures or if there is not enough space in some critical tables, a system reboot is performed. This releases resources and returns the system to a more stable and safe state.

An *emergency system restart* takes place after a system failure happens in an uncontrolled manner. This can be a TCB or media failure that could be caused by lower-privileged user processes attempting to access memory segments that are restricted. The system sees this as an insecure activity that it cannot properly recover from without rebooting. The system goes into a maintenance mode and recovers from the actions taken. The system is brought back up in a consistent and stable state.

A *system cold start* takes place when an unexpected TCB or media failure happens and the regular recovery procedure cannot recover the system to a more consistent state.

The system, TCB, and user objects may remain in an inconsistent state while the system attempts to recover itself, and intervention may be required by the computer operator or administrator to restore the system.

It is important that the system does not enter an insecure state when it is affected by any of these types of problems and that it shuts down and recovers properly in a secure and stable state. (Please refer to Chapter 5 for more information on TCB components and activities.)

Input and Output Controls

What is inputted into an application has a direct correlation to what that application outputs; thus, it needs to be monitored for errors and suspicious activity. If a checker at a grocery store continually puts in the amount of $1.20 for each prime rib steak that customers buy, the store could eventually lose a good amount of money. This activity could be done by accident, which would require proper training, or done on purpose, which would require disciplinary actions.

Because so many companies are extremely dependent upon computers and applications to process their data, input and output controls are very important. Chapter 10 addresses illegal activities that take place when users alter the data going into a program or the output generated by a program, usually for financial gain.

The applications themselves also need to be programmed to only accept certain types of values inputted into them and to do some type of logic checking about the received input values. If an application requests the user to input a mortgage value of a property and the user enters 25 cents, the application should re-ask the user for the value so that wasted time and processing is not done on an erroneous inputted value. Also, if an application has a field that is to be used for holding monetary values, a user should not be able to enter "bob" in the field without the application barking. These and many more input and output controls are discussed in Chapter 11.

It is important that all of the controls mentioned in the previous sections are in place and continue to function in a predictable and secure fashion so that the systems, applications, and the environment as a whole continue to be operational.

Electronic Mail Security

The Internet was first developed mainly for military and universities to communicate and share information, but today businesses depend upon it as market share, productivity, and profitability. Millions of individuals depend upon it for their window to a larger world and as a quick and efficient communication tool.

E-mail has become an important and integrated part of people's lives. It is used to communicate with family and friends, business partners and customers, coworkers and management, and online merchants and government offices. Generally, the security, authenticity, and integrity of an e-mail message are not considered in day-to-day use. Users are more aware that attachments can carry viruses than aware of the fact that an e-mail can be easily spoofed and its contents can be changed while in transmission.

It is very easy to spoof e-mail messages, meaning altering the name in the FROM field. All a user needs to do is modify information within the preferences section of his mail client and restart the application. An attacker could send a message to the CEO's secretary telling her that the IT department is having problems with some servers and if she could change her network logon to "password," it would really help them out. If she receives this e-mail and the FROM field has the network administrator's name in it, she will probably fulfill this request without thinking twice.

This type of activity is rare in the world today, but will probably become more used as a social engineering tactic. (This type of activity is used in information warfare.) The problem requires proper authentication to ensure that the message actually came from the source indicated. Companies that regard security as one of their top priorities would implement an e-mail protection application like Pretty Good Privacy (PGP) or use a public key infrastructure (PKI) and use digital signatures. These companies may also consider using an encryption protocol that works at the data link layer to help fight against network sniffing and the unauthorized interception of messages, but that will only protect the network segments the company can control. Encryption at the data link layer does not protect the message as it travels throughout the Internet.

An e-mail message that travels from Arizona to Maine has many hops in between the source and destination. There are several potential interception points that can enable an attacker to intercept, view, modify, or delete the message during its journey, as shown in Figure 12-1.

If a user is going to use a security scheme to protect his messages from eavesdropping, modification, and forgery, then he and the recipient must use the same encryption scheme. If public key cryptography is going to be used, then both users must have a way to exchange encryption keys. This is true for PGP, digital signatures, and S/MIME, which are discussed in detail in Chapter 8. This type of protection happens at the application layer of the Open System Interconnect (OSI) model. If an administrator, or security professional, wants to ensure that all messages are encrypted between two points and does not want to have to depend on the users to properly encrypt their messages, she can implement Secure Sockets Layer (SSL) (also discussed in chapter 8). However, this will only work for the paths that the company can control. When e-mail goes from one company to another, it is processed by many routers, bridges, switches, and mail

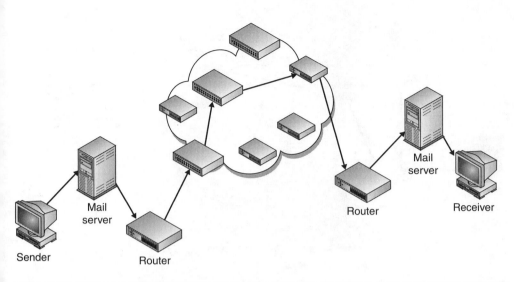

Figure 12-1 There are several possible points where an e-mail message can be intercepted.

servers throughout the Internet, which one company does not control. So, if a message needs to be protected as it travels throughout the Internet, the message itself needs to be encrypted at the application layer. *end to end encryption*

How E-mail Works

A user has a mail client that is used to create, modify, address, send, receive, and forward messages. This client can provide other functionality like using a personal address book, adding attachments, setting flags, recalling messages, and storing messages within different folders.

Great, the user has created a lovely message through his e-mail client, but the message is of no use unless it is actually sent somewhere. This is where *Simple Mail Transfer Protocol (SMTP)* comes in. SMTP works as a message transfer agent, as shown in Figure 12-2, and moves the message from the user's computer to the mail server when the user hits the Send button. SMTP is also a message-exchange standard and most people are used to seeing its familiar addressing scheme: **something@somewhere.com**.

Many times a message will need to travel throughout the Internet and through different mail servers before arriving at its destination mail server. SMTP is the protocol that will carry this message and it works on top of the Transport Control Protocol (TCP). TCP is used as the transport protocol because it is a reliable protocol and will provide sequencing and acknowledgements to ensure that the e-mail message arrived successfully at its destination.

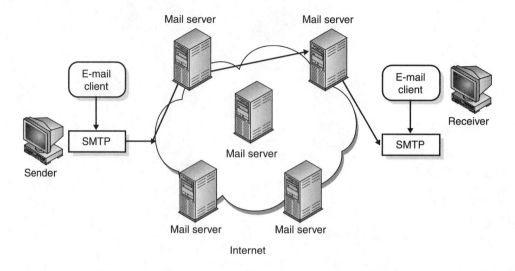

Figure 12-2 SMTP works as a transfer agent for e-mail messages.

The user's e-mail client must be SMTP compliant to be properly configured to use this protocol. The client provides an interface to the user so that he can create and modify messages as needed, and then the client passes the message off to SMTP. So if the analogy of a post office was used, the e-mail client could be the typewriter a person uses to write the message, SMTP could be the mail courier who picks up the mail and delivers it to the post office, and the post office could be the mail server. The mail server has the responsibility of understanding where the message is heading and properly routing the message to that destination. The mail server is often referred to as an SMTP server.

The most common SMTP server within the Unix world is Sendmail. This means that Unix uses Sendmail software to store, maintain, and route e-mail messages. Within the Microsoft world, Microsoft Exchange is mostly used and in Novell, Groupwise is the common SMTP server. SMTP works closely with two mail server protocols, POP and IMAP, which are explained in the following sections.

POP

Post Office Protocol (POP) is an Internet mail server protocol that supports incoming and outgoing messages. The mail server using POP stores and forwards e-mail messages and works with SMTP to move messages between mail servers.

A company may consist of one POP server that holds employee mailboxes and larger companies may have several POP servers, one for each department within the organization. There are also Internet POP servers that enable people all over the world to exchange messages.

This system is useful because the messages will be held on the mail server until users are ready to download their messages instead of trying to push messages right to a person's computer, which may be down or offline. The e-mail server can implement different authentication schemes to ensure that an individual is authorized to access a particular mailbox, but it is usually handled through usernames and passwords.

IMAP

Internet Message Access Protocol (IMAP) is also an Internet protocol that enables users to access mail on a mail server. IMAP provides the same types of functionality as the POP, but has more capabilities and functionality. If a user is using POP when he accesses his mail server to see if he has received any new messages, all messages are automatically downloaded to his computer. Once the messages are downloaded from the POP server, they are usually deleted from that server. POP can cause frustration for mobile users because the messages are automatically pushed down to their computer or device and they may not have the necessary space to hold all these messages. This is especially true for mobile devices that can be used to access e-mail servers. This is also inconvenient for people checking their mail on other people's computers. If Christina checks her e-mail on Jessica's computer, all of Christina's new mail could be downloaded to Jessica's computer.

If a user uses IMAP instead of POP, she can download all the messages or can leave them on the mail server within her remote message folder, referred to as a mailbox. The user can also manipulate the messages within this mailbox on the mail server in the same way she can as if the messages resided on her local computer. She can create, delete, or rename mailboxes, delete messages, search for specific messages, and set and clear flags. This gives the user much more freedom and keeps the messages in a central repository until the user specifically chooses to download all messages from the mail server.

IMAP is a store-and-forward mail server protocol that is considered POP's successor. IMAP enables a user to have a mailbox on the mail server instead of having all messages automatically downloaded to his system. This is helpful for remote users and users who are using Personal Digital Assistants (PDAs) or other devices that do not have the storage area to be able to hold mail messages. IMAP also gives the administrators more capabilities when it comes to administering and maintaining the users' messages.

E-mail Relaying

E-mail has changed drastically from the purely mainframe days. In those days, mail used simple Systems Network Architecture (SNA) protocols and ASCII format. Today there are several types of mail systems that run on different operating systems offering a wide range of functionality. Sometimes companies need to implement different types of mail servers and services within the same network, which can become a bit overwhelming and a challenge to secure.

Most companies have their mail servers in their demilitarized zone (DMZ) and may have one or more mail servers within their local area networks (LANs). The mail servers in the DMZ are in this protected space because they are directly connected to the Internet. These servers should be tightly locked down and their relaying mechanisms should be correctly configured. Mail servers use a *relay agent* to send a message from one mail server to another. This needs to be properly configured so that a company's mail server is not used by another for spamming activity. Many times spamming is actually illegal, so the people doing the spamming do not want the traffic to seem as though it originated from their equipment. They will find mail servers on the Internet, or within company DMZs, that have loosely configured relaying mechanisms and use these computers to send their spam. If relays are configured on a mail server, it can be used to receive *any* mail message and send it onto the intended recipient, as shown in Figure 12-3. This means that if a company accidentally enables mail relaying, their server can be used to distribute advertisements for other companies, spam messages, and pornographic material. It is important that mail servers have proper antispam features enabled, which are actually antirelaying features. A company's mail server should only accept mail destined for its domain and not forward messages onto other mail servers and domains.

Many companies employ antivirus and content-filtering applications on their mail servers to try to stop the spread of malicious code and not allow unacceptable messages through the e-mail gateway. It is important to filter both incoming and outgoing messages. This helps ensure that inside employees are not spreading viruses or sending out messages that are against company policy.

References

www.ietf.org/html.charters/smime-charter.html

www.imc.org

www.emailman.com

http://idm.internet.com/foundation/imap4.shtml

www.rad.com/networks/tutorial.htm

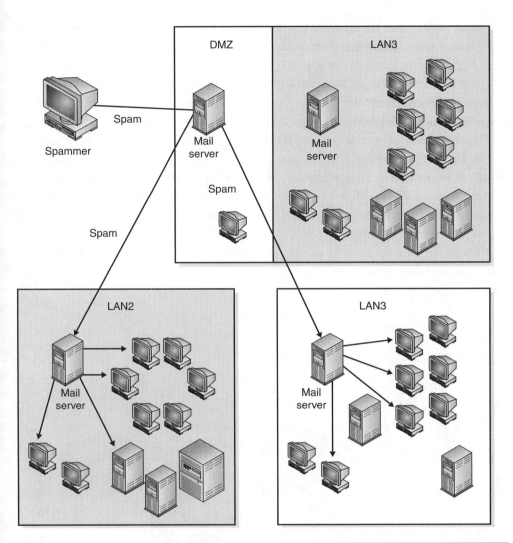

Figure 12-3 Mail servers can be used for spam if relay functionality is enabled.

Facsimile Security

Faxing information is a very popular way of delivering information today and like other types of communication channels, it must be incorporated into the security policy and program of companies.

Fax machines can present some security issues if they are being used to transmit sensitive or confidential information. The information has to be scanned into the device, which is then transmitted over a phone line and printed out on the destination fax machine. Many times the received fax just sits in a bin until the recipient walks over to retrieve it. If it contains confidential information, it might not be a good idea to have it just lying around for anyone to see it.

Some companies use *fax servers*, which are systems that manage incoming and outgoing faxed documents. When a fax is received by the fax server, it properly routes it to the individual it is addressed to so that it is not actually printed, but held in an electronic form. Many times the received fax is routed to the recipient's electronic mailbox.

The fax server lets many users transmit documents from their computers to the fax server, as illustrated in Figure 12-4, without having to pass the document through a scanner of a fax device. This reduces on the amount of sensitive documentation that needs to be properly destroyed and can save money on printing and thermal paper required by stand-alone fax machines.

A fax server usually has the capability of enabling someone to print the received faxes, but this can present the same security breaches of a stand-alone fax device. In

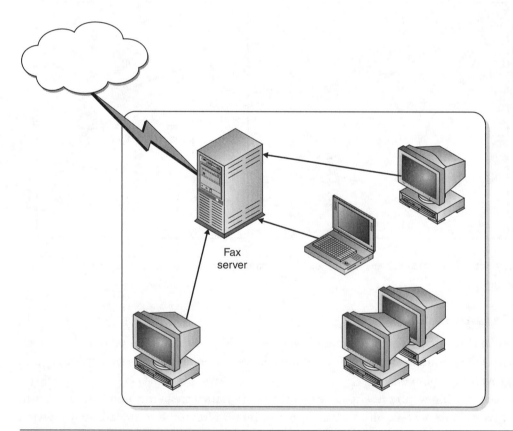

Fax
server

Figure 12-4   A fax server can be used instead of stand-alone fax devices.

environments that demand high security levels, the print feature can be disabled so that sensitive documents can be stored and viewed by authorized individuals only and never printed.

Extensive logging and auditing is available for faxing servers and should be implemented and monitored in companies that require this level of security. Because data will be traveling to and from the fax server in a clear text form, some companies may want to implement encryption for faxed materials. *Fax encryptor*, a bulk data link encryption mechanism, may be put into place. The fax encryptor encrypts any and all fax data that hits the network cable or telephone wire. This would be put into place if a company did not want to depend on each individual user to encrypt documents that are faxed; instead, the company is sure that all data leaving that system is properly encrypted.

References

www.faximum.com/faqs/fax

www.faxserver.com

Hack and Attack Methods

Several different types of attacks have been explained in the chapters throughout this book. This section is presented to bring these types of attack methods, and others that have not be presented, together to show how they are related, how they can be detected, and how they can be countermeasured.

A majority of the tools used by hackers have dual capabilities in that they can be used for good or evil. An attacker could use tool "ABC" to find a vulnerability to exploit and a security professional could use the same tool to identify a vulnerability so that she could fix it. When this tool is used by black hats (attackers), it is referred to as *hacking*; when a white hat (security professional) uses this tool, it is considered *ethical hacking* or *vulnerability testing*.

The evolution of the tools used to perform attacks on networks and systems has allowed a moderately skilled individual (sometimes called a *script kiddie*) to perform damaging attacks. This is because the tools are simple to use and many times come with a graphical user interface (GUI) that walks the person through the steps of resource identification, network mapping, and the actual attack. The person no longer needs to understand protocol stacks, know what protocols fields are used by different systems, understand how operating systems process program and assembly code, or know how to write program code at all. The user just needs to insert an IP range within a GUI and press Go.

Hacking tools are easily and widely available to anyone who wants them. At one time, these types of tools were only available to a small group of highly skilled people, but today there are hundreds of Web sites devoted to telling people how to perform exploits and providing the tools for a small fee or for free. The ease of use of these types of tools, the increased interested in hacking, and the deep dependence that companies and people have upon technology have provided the ingredients to a recipe that can cause continuous, destructive damage.

Any network administrator that maintains a firewall, or any person who runs a personal firewall on a computer, knows how active the Internet is with probes and port scanners. These front-end protection devices are continually getting hit with packets requesting information from them. Some probes are looking for specific types of computers like Unix systems, web servers, or databases because the attacker has specific types of attacks she wants to carry out and these attacks target specific types of operating systems or applications. These probes could also be looking to plant Trojan horses or viruses onto computers in the hopes of causing destruction or compromising the systems so that they can be used in future distributed denial of service (DDoS) attacks. These types of probes scan thousands of networks and computers with no one target in mind. They just look for any and all vulnerabilities, and the attacker does not necessarily care where the vulnerable system happens to be located.

Sometimes the attacker has a specific target in mind and thus does not send out a wide sweeping probe. When an attacker identifies her target, she will do network mapping and port scanning. Network-mapping tools send out seemingly benign packets to many different systems on a network. These systems will respond to these packets and the mapping tool interrogates the returned packets to find out what systems are up and running, the types of systems that responded, and possibly their place within the network. This might seem like a lot of information from just some packets being sent out, but these tools are highly calibrated to dig as much data from the returned packet as possible. Different operating systems vary in their protocol stacks, meaning they use different fields within protocol frames or populate those fields differently than other operating systems. So, if the tool sent a message to two different computers running different operating systems, they may respond with two slightly different answers. They may both respond with the same basic answer using the same protocol, but because the two operating systems use varied protocol stacks, one computer may use a certain field within the response and the other system may use a different field within its response, as shown in Figure 12-5. When the tool receives these two slightly different responses, it can determine what type of operating system just replied. The tool and the attacker start to put together the topology of the victim's network.

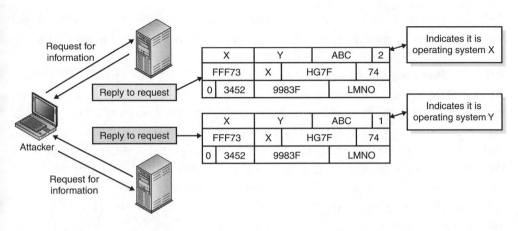

Figure 12-5 A tool can be used to determine the type of operating system with which an attacker is communicating.

The network-mapping tool has a database that maps operating systems, applications, and versions to the type of responses and message field they use. So if the networking tool received a reply from its ICMP ping sweep, which sends out ICMP packets to targets within a configured IP address range, and one reply has the ICMP Don't fragment bit enabled, the tool may determine that the target is a Unix host. Or if the tool sent out a TCP SYN packet and the response received was a FIN/ACK, the tool may determine that the target is a Windows NT system. This activity is referred to as *operating system fingerprinting*.

It is important to the attacker to know what systems are alive on the network. When the tool first sends out packets, it is looking to see what computers respond, which indicates they are powered on and alive. Normally, when a computer sends a SYN packet, it is requesting to set up a conversation channel with the destination computer and is the first step in the TCP/IP handshaking procedure. However, hacking tools that use the SYN packet have no intention of setting up a real conversation channel, but hope to trick the target system into replying. The normal response to a SYN packet is SYN/ACK, but the network administrator may have blocked this type of traffic at the firewall or router or disabled the port on the computer. The attacker may receive no response or receive a message saying "Port Unreachable." This response tells the network-mapping tool that the company's firewall allows this type of traffic to enter the network, but that specific port is closed on the target machine. These are all clues used by the attacker to learn more and more about an environment. This knowledge enables her to figure out the most successful ways of attacking.

So, the first step for the attacker is to find out what systems are alive, attempt to find out what type of operating systems the targets are running, and start to build the network's topology. The next step for an attacker is to do a port scanning on the target machines. *Port scanning* identifies open ports on a computer. Ports provide doors into the operating system for other computers, processes, protocols, and attackers. If an attacker can find out what ports are open, then she can have a pretty good idea of what services are running on the systems. Knowing what services are available can further clarify the type of system the target is; for example, if a target computer responds to an SMTP packet sent to its port 25, the attacker could think that this computer may be an e-mail server. However, more work would need to be done to ensure this.

The attacker wants to know what operating systems, applications, and services are running so that she knows what type of attacks to run. If she finds a Unix server running Apache, she must run totally different types of attacks on it than if she found a Windows 2000 server running Exchange. Each operating system, application, and service has its own vulnerabilities and properly identifying these enables the attacker to be more successful in her attack.

There are 65,535 TCP and 65,535 UDP ports on every computer system. The first 1,024 are said to be well-known ports. These means that a specific port number under 1,025 is usually mapped to a well-known and used protocol. For instance, port 80 is almost always mapped to the Hypertext Transfer Protocol (HTTP) protocol, port 21 is mapped to File Transfer Protocol (FTP), and port 25 is mapped to SMTP. These ports can be reconfigured so that port 21 is mapped to HTTP, let's say, but that is very uncommon.

A port scanning utility is used to find out what ports are open on a system so the attacker knows what doors are available to her. This tool will send packets to each and every port on a system and listen for its response. If there is no response or a message indicating "Port Unreachable," this usually indicates that the port and its corresponding service is disabled. If a predictable response comes from the port, then the attacker knows that the port is open and available for attack.

Sometimes a port needs to be open for functionality. For example, most networks require the use of SMTP, port 25, for e-mail activity. The administrator needs to put a barrier between the potential attackers and this vulnerable port and its service. Of course, the first step is to implement a perimeter network with firewalls, proxy servers, and routers that only permit acceptable connections to the internal hosts. However, if an administrator or security professional wanted to add another layer of protection, he could implement *TCP Wrappers*. These wrappers monitor incoming network traffic and controls that can and cannot access the services mapped to specific ports. When a request comes to a computer at a specific port, the target operating system will check to see if this port is enabled. If it is enabled and the operating system sees that the corresponding service is wrapped, it knows to look at an access control list, which spells out who can access this service. If the person or computer attempting to access this service is allowed within the access control list, then the operating system allows the connection to be made. If this person or computer is not allowed, the packet is dropped or a message is sent back to the initiator of the request indicating that the request is refused.

Countermeasures to Port Scanning and Network Mapping

- Disable unnecessary ports and services.
- Block access at the perimeter network using firewalls, routers, and proxy servers.
- Use an IDS to identify this type of activity.
- Use TCP Wrappers on vulnerable services that have to be available.
- Remove as many banners as possible within operating systems and applications.
- Upgrade or update to more security operating systems, applications, and protocols.

read more on TCP Wrappers

At this point, the attacker has an idea of what systems are alive, what ports are open, and what services are listening and available for attack. Although the search for exploitable vulnerabilities is becoming more focused, there is still an incredible amount of possible vulnerabilities one network can have. Sometimes attackers specialize in a few specific attacks that they know well enough to carry out manually or have scripts that carry out specific attacks for them, but many attackers want a large range of possible attacks available to them so they use *vulnerability scanning tools*.

Vulnerability scanning tools have a large database of vulnerabilities and have the capability to exploit many of the vulnerabilities they identify. New vulnerabilities are found each week with operating systems, Web servers, database software, and applications. It can be overwhelming to try to keep up-to-date on each of these and the proper steps to carry them out. The vulnerability scanners can do this for the security professional and unfortunately for the attacker. The tool has an engine that can connect to the target machine and run through its database of vulnerabilities to see which apply to the target machine. Some tools can even go a step further and attempt the exploit to determine the actual degree of vulnerability.

There are several types of vulnerability scanners available. Security Administrator Tool for Analyzing Network (SATAN) and Nessus are two popular ones.

As stated earlier, these tools are dual in nature. Network administrators and security professionals should be using these types of tools on their environments to see what vulnerabilities are present and available to potential attackers. This way when a vulnerability or weakness is uncovered, the security professional can fix it before an attacker finds it.

Superzapping

Computer systems sometimes malfunction, freeze, or enter a state that cannot be fixed by normal recovery procedures. This is the reason that superzapping programs were written. A *superzapping* program is a utility used in IBM mainframe centers and has the capability to bypass access controls within operating systems. An administrator would use this tool in the rare cases when nothing else seems to work and the operating system, or program, needs specific attention and possibly reconfiguration.

These types of programs can be very useful to administrators, but are dangerous if they are not properly protected and end up in an attacker's hands. The tool can enable changes to take place to operating systems and system files that cannot be easily detected, because this type of activity is not usually logged. In many cases, the only way of properly detecting the improper use of a superzapping utility is by comparing the sizes of the files to the original or parent files. This is a functionality that intrusion detection systems carry out.

Browsing

Browsing is a general term used by intruders to obtain information that they are not authorized to access. Browsing can be accomplished by looking through another person's files kept on a server or workstation, rummaging through garbage looking for information that was carelessly thrown away, or reviewing information that has been saved on diskettes. A more advanced and sophisticated example of browsing is when an intruder accesses residual information on storage media. The original user may have deleted the files from a diskette, but as stated earlier, this only removes the pointers to the files within the file system on that disk. The talented intruder can access this data (residual information) and access information that he is unauthorized to obtain.

Another type of browsing attack is called *shoulder surfing*, where a user looks over another's shoulder to see items on that person's monitor or what is being typed in at the keyboard.

Sniffers

A *network sniffer* is a tool that monitors traffic as it passes by. Many times administrators and network engineers use sniffers to diagnose network problems. Sniffers are also referred to as network analyzers or protocol analyzers. When used as a diagnostic tool, a sniffer enables the administrator to see what type of traffic is being generated in the hopes of getting closer to the root of the network problem. When it is used as a tool for an attacker, username, passwords, and confidential information can be captured as it travels over the network.

The tool is either a piece of hardware or software that runs on a computer with its network interface card (NIC) in promiscuous mode. NICs usually only pay attention to traffic addressed to them, but if they are in promiscuous mode, they see all traffic that is going past them on the network wire. Many times once a computer has been compromised by an attacker, she will install a sniffer on that system to look for interesting traffic. Some sniffers only look for passwords that are being transmitted and ignores the rest. One example is John the Ripper (**www.openwall.com/john**).

Sniffers have been very successful because a majority of LANs use Ethernet, which is a broadcast technology. Because so much data is continually broadcasted, it is easily available for an attacker who has planted a sniffer on a network segment. However, sniffers are becoming less successful because of the move to switched environments. Switched environments separate network segments by broadcast and collision domains. If the attacker is not within the broadcast and collision domain of the environment she is interested in sniffing, she will not receive the information she is looking for. This is because a switch is usually configured so that the required source and destination ports on the switch carry the traffic; thus, it is not blasted for everyone in the vicinity to hear. Switched traffic travels from point A to point B through the switch and it does not spill over to every computer on the network like purely Ethernet networks do. (Broadcast and collision domains are discussed in detail in Chapter 7.)

To combat sniffers within an environment, secure versions of services and protocols should be used whenever possible. Many services and protocols were developed to provide functionality and not security, but once it was figured out that security is also required in many environments, the protocols and services were improved upon to provide the same functionality and security. Several protocols have a secure version. This means the regular protocol operates in a way that has vulnerabilities that can be exploited and a more secure version has been developed to countermeasure those vulnerabilities. One example is *Secure RPC (S-RPC)*, which uses Diffie-Hellman public key cryptography to determine the shared secret key for encryption with the DES algorithm. The maximum key length is 192 bits, which provides a high degree of security. If

S-RPC is used in an environment, a sniffer can capture this data, but not necessarily decrypt it.

Most protocols are vulnerable because they do not require strong authentication if it is required at all. For example, the *r-utilities* used in UNIX are known to have several weaknesses (rexec, rsh, rlogin, and rcp). Authentication is usually provided through a .rhosts file that looks at IP addresses instead of individual usernames and passwords. These utilities should be replaced with ones that require stronger authentication like S-RPC and Secure Shell (SSH).

Session Hijacking

Many attackers spoof their addresses, meaning that the address within the frame that is used to commit the attack has an IP address that is not theirs. This makes it much harder to track down the attacker, which is the attacker's purpose of spoofing in the first place. This also enables an attacker to hijack sessions between two users without being noticed.

If an attacker wanted to take over a session between two computers, she would need to put herself in the middle of their conversation without being detected. Two tools used for this are Juggernaut (**www.packetfactory.net**) and Hunt (**www.cri.cz/kra/index.html**). These tools enable the attacker to spy on the TCP connection and then hijack it if the attacker decides that is what she wants to do.

If Kristy and David were communicating over a TCP session and the attacker wanted to bump David off and trick Kristy into thinking she is still communicating with David and not an attacker, the attacker would use a tool to spoof her address to be the same as David's and temporarily take David off the network with a type of DoS attack. Once this is in place, when Kristy sends a message to David, it actually goes to the attacker and the attacker can respond to Kristy. Kristy thinks she is getting a reply from David. The attacker may also choose to leave David on the network and intercept each of the users' messages, read them, and repackage them with headers that indicate that no session hijacking took place, as shown in Figure 12-6.

If session hijacking is a concern on a network, the administrator can implement a protocol that requires mutual authentication between users like IPSec. Because the attacker will not have the necessary credentials to authenticate to a user she cannot act as an imposter and hijack sessions.

Password Cracking

Chapter 4 discussed access control and authentication methods in depth. Although there are many different possible ways of authenticating a user, most of the time a static password is the method of choice for many companies. This is because the comput-

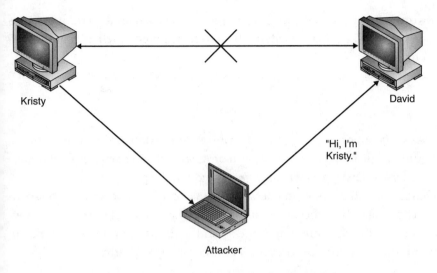

Figure 12-6 Session hijacking between Kristy and David

ing society is used to using static passwords; this is how many systems and applications have coded their authentication processes, and it is an easier technique to maintain and cheaper than other options like smart cards or biometrics.

However, this static password method is easily cracked when a determined attacker has the right tools. John the Ripper is a sniffer that listens for authentication data being passed over the network cables. Once captured, the attacker can initiate a dictionary attack using the same tool to try and reveal the captured password. The tools Crack and L0phtcrack are two powerful tools that are used to perform dictionary and brute force attacks on the capture password or password file.

Dictionary versus Brute Force Attack

A *dictionary attack* is when a large list of words is fed into a hacking tool. This tool runs a one-way hash on the captured password and on each word in the list. The tool compares the hashing results to see if they match. If they do match, the tool has discovered the password; if not, it moves to the next word in the list.

In a *brute force attack,* a tool will try many different variations of characters, run a hash value on each variation, and compare it to the hash value of the captured password. Many times a dictionary attack and a brute force attack are used together. If a tool first runs a dictionary attack and figures out that the first seven characters of the --

captured password is Jeffery, then the brute force piece will kick in and try different variations of this password like Jeffery1, Jeffery001, Jeffery01, Jeffery2, JefferyL, and so on until it finds a match.

A strong password policy is a major countermeasure to password-cracking efforts. The policy should dictate that passwords should be at least eight characters with upper- and lowercase letters and two special characters (* .,$@). If the passwords are long, contain special characters, and are hard to guess, it will take cracking tools much longer to uncover them. The longer this process takes, the higher the chance of the attacker moving onto an easier victim. Software applications and add-ons are available to ensure that the password that each user chooses meets the company's security policy.

Backdoors

In Chapter 5, backdoors and some of the potential damage that can be caused by them are discussed. However, in Chapter 5, we looked at how backdoors are inserted into the code so a developer can access the software at a later time, bypassing the usual security authentication and authorization steps. Now we will look at how and why attackers install backdoors onto victims' computers.

A backdoor is a program that is installed by an attacker to enable her to come back into the computer at a later date without having to supply login credentials or go through any type of authorization process, as shown in Figure 12-7. Access control is

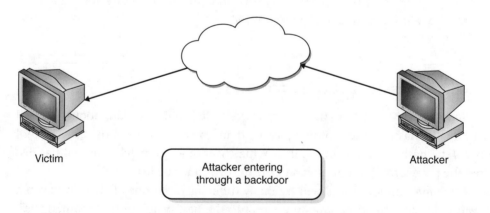

Victim

Attacker entering through a backdoor

Attacker

Figure 12-7 Attackers plant backdoors so they can enter the victim's computer at a later date.

thwarted by the attacker because she can later gain access to the compromised computer. The backdoor program actually listens on specific ports for the attacker, and once the attacker accesses those ports, the backdoor program lets her come right in.

An attacker can compromise a computer and install the backdoor program or hide the code within a virus or Trojan horse that will install the backdoor when a predefined event takes place. Many times these backdoors are installed so that the attacker can later control the computer remotely to perform the tasks she is interested in. The tools used for backdoor remote control actions are Back Orifice (**www.bo2k.com**), NetBus, and SubSeven (**http://subseven.slak.org/main.html**). A comprehensive list of backdoors and Trojans can be found at **www.tlsecurity.net/tlfaq.htm**.

Today many antivirus software applications and IDSs look for signatures of these tools and scan for the known behavior patterns that they commit. Host-based IDS can be one of the best attempts of detecting a backdoor or attempts to install one. Because the backdoor will be listening on specific ports, the host IDS can be configured to detect suspicious port activity. The administrator can also scan for known executables used by backdoor programs, view the startup files and registry entries for suspicious executables, and run checksums on system files to see if any have been altered. These types of activities are not usually done manually because of the time involved, but are done automatically through the use of antivirus and IDS software. But because attackers are smart and tricky, new tools are continually developed and old tools are morphed so that they will not be detected by these detection tools. The inevitable cat-and-mouse game continues between the hackers and the security community.

This section only talked about some of the possible attacks and many other types of attacks have been addressed in earlier chapters. One of the most beneficial things a company, network administrator, network engineer, or security professional can do is to develop some good habits that deal with the previously mentioned items. Although it is great that an administrator installs a security patch after he reads about a dangerous attack that has recently become popular, it is more important that he continues to stay on top of all potential risks and vulnerabilities, scans his network regularly, and is aware of some symptomatic effects of particular attacks, viruses, Trojan horses, and backdoors. It can be a tall order to follow, but these good habits, once developed, will keep a network healthy and the administrator's life less chaotic.

Penetration Testing

Penetration testing is a set of procedures designed to test and possibly bypass security controls of a system. Its goal is to measure an organization's resistance to an attack and to uncover any weaknesses within the environment. Organizations need to determine the effectiveness of their security measures and not just trust the promises of the security vendors. Good computer security is based on reality, not on some lofty goals of how things are supposed to work.

A penetration test will emulate the same methods that attackers would use. Attackers can be clever, creative, and resourceful in their techniques, so penetration attacks should align with the newest hacking techniques along with strong foundational testing methods. The test should look at each and every computer in the environment, as shown in Figure 12-8, because an attacker will not necessarily scan one or two computers only and call it a day.

The type of penetration test depends on the organization, its security objectives, and the management's goals. Some corporations perform periodic penetration tests on themselves using different types of tools or they may use scanning devices that continually examine the environment for new vulnerabilities in an automated fashion. Other corporations ask a third party to perform the vulnerability and penetration tests to provide a more objective view.

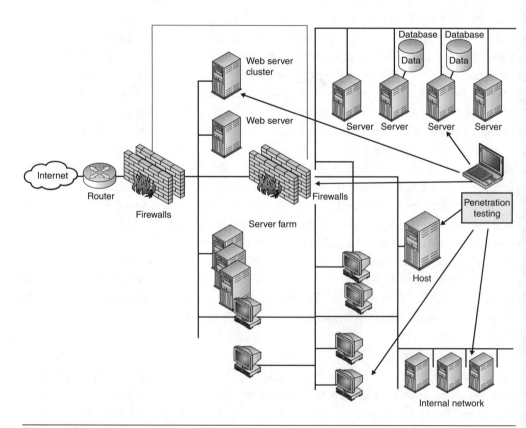

Figure 12-8   Penetration tests should be run against all systems periodically.

Penetration tests can evaluate Web servers, Domain Name Servers (DNSs), router configurations, workstation vulnerabilities, access to sensitive information, remote dial-in access, open ports, and available services properties that a real attacker might use to compromise the company's overall security. Some tests can be quite intrusive and disruptive. The time frame for the tests should be agreed upon so that productivity is not affected and personnel can bring systems back online if necessary.

The result of a penetration test is a report given to management describing the list of vulnerabilities that were identified and the severity of those vulnerabilities. From here, it is up to management to determine how the vulnerabilities are dealt with and what countermeasures are implemented.

Operations Department

Operations security encompasses safeguards and countermeasures to protect resources, information, and the hardware that they reside on. The goal is to reduce the possibility of damage that could result from unauthorized access or disclosure by limiting the opportunities of misuse.

Some organizations may have an actual operations department that is responsible for certain types of activities and procedures that are required to run smoothly to keep productivity at a certain level. Other organizations may have individuals that are responsible for these things, but there is not a structured department dedicated just to operations. Either way there are certain things that people who hold these types of responsibilities are accountable for and specific issues that must be monitored and controlled.

Operations within a computing environment pertain to software, personnel, and hardware, but many times an operations department focuses on the hardware piece. Management is responsible for employees, their behaviors, and responsibilities, and the IT department or developers are responsible for software configurations and modifications, and the people within the operations department are responsible for ensuring that hardware is protected and that it continues to run in a predictable way.

The operations department usually has the objectives of preventing reoccurring hardware problems, reducing hardware failures to an acceptable level, and reducing the impact of hardware failure or disruption. This group should investigate any unusual or unexplained occurrences, unscheduled initial program loads, deviations from standards, or other odd or abnormal conditions.

Unusual or Unexplained Occurrences

Networks and the hardware that are within them can be complex and dynamic. At times, conditions take place that are at first confusing and possibly unexplainable. It is up to the operations department to investigate these issues, understand the problem, and come up with a logical solution.

One example could be a network that has hosts that are continually kicked off the network for no apparent reason. Controlled troubleshooting should take place to make sure no possibilities are overlooked and that different types of problems are investigated. The team may look at connectivity issues between the hosts and the wiring closet, the hubs and switches that control their connectivity, and any possible cabling defects. The team could work methodically until it finds that one of the NICs on this Token Ring network is malfunctioning and sending out bogus traffic that affects other hosts connection to the network.

Deviations from Standards

In this instance, standards pertain to computing service levels and how they are measured. Each device can have certain standards applied to it, the hours of time to be online, the amount of requests that can be processed within a defined period of time, bandwidth usage, performance counters, and more. These standards provide a baseline that is used to determine if there is a problem with the device or not. For example, if a device usually accepts approximately 300 requests per minute, but suddenly it was only able to accept 3 per minute, the operations team would need to investigate the deviation of the standard that is usually provided by this device. The device may be failing or under a DoS attack.

Sometimes the standard needs to be recalibrated so that it portrays a realistic view of the service level it can provide. If a server was upgraded from a Pentium II to a Pentium III, the memory was quadrupled, the swap file was increased, and three extra hard drives were added, the service level of this server should be reevaluated.

Unscheduled Initial Program Loads (IPLs)

Initial program load (IPL) is a mainframe term for loading the operating system's kernel into the computer's main memory. On a personal computer, booting or rebooting into the operating system is the equivalent to IPLing. This activity takes place to prepare the computer for user operation.

So, the operations team would need to investigate computers that reboot for no reason, which could indicate that the operating system is experiencing major problems.

Summary

Operational security has to do with keeping up with implemented solutions, keeping track of changes, properly maintaining systems, continually enforcing necessary standards, and following through with security practices and tasks. It does not do much good for a company to develop a strong password policy if after a few months enforcement gets lax and users can use whatever passwords they want. It is similar to working out and staying physically fit. Just because someone lifts weights and jogs for a week does not mean he can spend the rest of the year eating jelly donuts and expect to stay physically fit. It requires discipline day in and day out, sticking to a regime, and practicing due diligence.

Quick Tips

- Facilities that house systems that process sensitive information should have physical access controls to limit access to authorized personnel.

- Data should be classified and the necessary technical controls should be put into place to protect its integrity, confidentiality, and availability.

- System and audit logs should be monitored and protected from unauthorized modification.

- Sensitive data should not be printed and left at stand-alone printers.

- Users should have the necessary security level to access data and resources, but must also have a need-to-know.

- Clipping levels should be implemented, which establishes a baseline of user activity.

- Separation of responsibilities and duties should be in place so that if fraud takes place it requires collusion.

- Sensitive information should contain the correct markings and labels to indicate the corresponding sensitivity level.

- Contract and temporary staff members should have more restrictive controls put upon their accounts.

- Access should be restricted to printed output storage areas.

- Change control should be put into place so that changes are approved, documented, tested, and implemented.

- Systems should not allow their bootup sequences to be altered in a way that could bypass operating system security mechanisms.

- Potential employees should have background investigations, references, experience, and education claims checked out.

- Proper fault tolerant mechanisms should be put into place to countermeasure equipment failure.

- Antivirus and IDS signatures should be updated on a continual basis.

- System, network, policy, and procedure changes should be documented and communicated.

- When objects are reused, they should contain no residual data.

- Media holding data must be properly purged, which could be overwriting, degaussing, or media destruction.

- Penetration testing should be done on a regular basis to identify new vulnerabilities.

Questions

Please remember that these questions are formatted and asked in a certain way for a reason. The questions and answers may seem odd or vague, but this is what you will see on the actual CISSP test.

1. Which of the following best describes operation security?
   a. Continual vigilance to hacker activity and possible vulnerabilities
   b. Enforcing access control and physical security
   c. Taking steps to make sure an environment, and the things with in it, stay at a certain level of protection
   d. Doing strategy planning to develop a secure environment and then implementing it properly

2. Which of the following describes why operation security is important?
   a. An environment continually changes and has the potential of lowering its level of protection.
   b. It helps an environment be functionally sound and productive.
   c. It ensures there will be no unauthorized access to the facility or its resources.
   d. It continually raises a company's level of protection.

3. What is the difference between due care and due diligence?
   a. Due care is the continual effort of ensuring that the right thing takes place, and due diligence is the continual effort to stay compliant to regulations.
   b. Due care and due diligence is in contrast with the "prudent man" concept.

c. They mean the same thing.

d. Due care is doing the right thing, and due diligence is the continual effort of making sure right things take place.

4. Why should employers make sure employees take their vacations?

a. They have a legal obligation.

b. It is part of due diligence.

c. It is a way that fraud can be uncovered.

d. To ensure the employee does not get burnt out.

5. Which of the following best describes separation of duties and job rotation?

a. Separation of duties ensures that more than one employee knows how to perform the tasks of a position, and job rotation ensures that one person cannot perform a high-risk task alone.

b. Separation of duties ensures that one person cannot perform a high-risk task alone, and job rotation can uncover fraud and ensure that more than one person knows the tasks of a position.

c. They are the same thing with different titles.

d. They are administrative controls that enforce access control and protect the company's resources.

6. If a programmer is restricted from updating and modifying production code, what is this an example of?

a. Rotation of duties

b. Due diligence

c. Separation of duties

d. Controlling input values

7. Why is it important to control input and output values?

a. Incorrect values can cause mistakes in data processing and can be evidence of fraud.

b. Incorrect values can be the fault of the programmer and not comply with the due care clause.

c. Incorrect values can be caused by brute force attacks.

d. Incorrect values are not security issues.

8. What is the difference between least privilege and need-to-know?
   a. A user should have least privileges that restrict her need-to-know.
   b. A user should have a security clearance to access resources, a need-to-know about those resources, and least privilege to give her full control of all resources.
   c. A user should have a need-to-know to access particular resources and the user should have the least privilege implemented to ensure she only accesses the resources she has a need-to-know.
   d. They are two words for the same issue.

9. Which of the following would not require updated documentation?
   a. Antivirus signature update
   b. Reconfiguration of a server
   c. Change in security policy
   d. Installing a patch to a production server

10. If sensitive data is stored on a CD-ROM and it is no longer needed, which would be the proper way of disposing of the data?
    a. Degaussing
    b. Erasing
    c. Purging
    d. Physical destruction

11. If SSL is being used to encrypt messages that are transmitted over the network, what is a major concern of the security professional?
    a. The network segments that have systems that use different versions of SSL.
    b. If the user encrypted the message with an application layer product, it will be incompatible with SSL.
    c. Network tapping and wire tapping.
    d. The network segments that the message will travel on that the company does not control.

12. What is the purpose of SMTP?
    a. To enable users to extract mail messages from a server
    b. To enable users to view and modify mail messages from a server
    c. To transmit mail messages from the client to the mail server
    d. To encrypt mail messages before being transmitted

13. What is the difference between POP and IMAP?
    a. POP downloads e-mail to the user, and IMAP gives the user the choice of downloading or keeping it on the mail server.
    b. POP gives the user the choice of downloading mail messages or keeping them on the server, and IMAP automatically downloads the messages to the user's computer.
    c. POP is used when the messages need to be transmitted over the Internet, and IMAP is used when the messages are exchanged in-house.
    d. IMAP is used when the messages need to be transmitted over the Internet, and POP is used when the messages are exchanged in-house.

14. If a company has been contacted because its mail server has been used to spread spam, what is most likely the problem?
    a. The internal mail server has been compromised by an internal hacker.
    b. The mail server in the DMZ has private and public resource records.
    c. The mail server has e-mail relaying enabled.
    d. The mail server has SMTP enabled.

15. Which of the following is not a reason that fax servers are used in many companies?
    a. They save money on having individual fax devices and paper.
    b. They provide a secure way of faxing instead of having faxed papers sitting in bins waiting to be picked up.
    c. Faxes can be routed to employee electronic mailboxes.
    d. They reduce the need for any other communication security mechanisms.

16. If a company wants to protect fax data while it is in transmission, which of the following are valid mechanisms?
    a. PGP and MIME
    b. PEM and TSL
    c. Data link encryption or fax encryptor
    d. Data link encryption and PKI

17. What is the purpose of TCP Wrappers?
    a. Monitor requests for certain ports and control access to sensitive files.
    b. Monitor requests for certain services and control access to password files.
    c. Monitor requests for certain services and control access to those services.
    d. Monitor requests to system files and ensure they are not modified.

18. How do network sniffers work?
    a. They probe systems on a network segment.
    b. They listen for ARP requests and ICMP packets.
    c. They require an extra NIC to be installed and configured.
    d. They put the NIC into promiscuous mode.

Answers

1. C.	6. C.	11. D.	16. C.
2. A.	7. A.	12. C.	17. C.
3. D.	8. C.	13. A.	18. D.
4. C.	9. A.	14. C.	
5. B.	10. D.	15. D.	

Security Policies

Security policies provide the foundation for an organization's security infrastructure. A security policy is a document or set of documents that convey the management's decision on how security will play a role within the organization. They are high level and not technical in nature. They are put into place to protect the organization's assets, ensure that mechanisms are in place to protect the assets' confidentiality, availability, and integrity. Policies can also reduce legal liability by following the due care concept.

The security policy should identify critical and important business resources, activities, and operations. Roles within the organization need to be defined, and the type of access each role, or group, requires for these critical pieces of the organization should be outlined. Then management should decide what degree of access each role, or group, is allowed and the type of security controls that should be put into place to ensure that these directives are followed and enforced.

Types of Security Policies

In smaller organizations, it may be possible to have one security policy that covers all necessary subjects, but most organizations are diverse enough to require one general policy and then smaller policies that are more specific in nature and support the more general policy. The reason to have specialized policies is because there are specific issues the management feels need to be addressed so that there is no confusion on the management's requirements when it comes to security. These specialized policies also provide the company with a stronger legal standing if the policies ever come into question.

Some of the other types of policies can include e-mail usage, remote access, Internet usage, information protection, and extranet and partnership relationships.

There are specific questions that need to be asked and answered when it comes to writing issue-oriented or functionality-oriented policies. The following sections cover some of the questions that should be asked and answered.

Information Protection Policy

This policy is drafted, implemented, and enforced to identify critical business information and to indicate how it should be properly protected. The policy should provide high-level guidelines for mid-management, the IT staff, and all employees that outline how to access and handle different types of information.

The following questions should be asked when developing the policy and answered within the policy:

- What information is critical to business operations?
- What classifications will be used to properly identify the sensitivity level of each type of information?
- How will this information be marked, labeled, and properly destroyed at the end of its life?
- Who requires access to this information and to what extent?
- How will this information be stored and transmitted?
- What type of authorization is required?
- What type of protection should be in place to ensure that the previous issues are enforced?
- What needs to take place for noncompliance activities?
- Who is responsible for enforcing all the issues decided upon within this policy?

Remote Access Policy

This policy outlines and defines what type of remote access will be used within the organization and what is and what is not acceptable when it comes to remote access.

The following questions should be asked when developing the policy and answered within the policy:

- Why is remote access required?
- How many and what type of users require remote access?

- What type of remote access should be used in the organization (dial-up, frame relay, Telnet, ATM, and so on)?

- What type of resources and information should remote users have access to?

- What protection mechanisms should be in place to ensure that authorized users can only access the resources authorized?

- What protection mechanisms should be in place to ensure that unauthorized users cannot gain access to the network?

- What type of authorization is required?

- What needs to take place for noncompliance activities?

- Who is responsible for enforcing all the issues decided upon within this policy?

Extranet and Business Partner Policy

If the organization has a connection to another organization's network via an extranet, direct channel, virtual private network (VPN), or any other method, each aspect of this connection should be reviewed and properly planned out prior to implementing it.

The following questions should be asked when developing the policy and answered within the policy:

- What other companies does the organization need to have access to and why?

- How should this connection take place (VPN, extranet, dedicated link, and so on)?

- What resources and information should the other organization(s) have access to?

- What mechanisms should be in place to ensure that these resources are available to them?

- What type of authorization is required?

- Should each organization involved have a security policy for this type of business interaction?

- What measures should be in place to protect the infrastructure from malicious activity pertaining to this type of connection?

- How should the reporting of problems take place?

- What needs to take place for noncompliance activities?

- Who is responsible for enforcing all the issues decided upon within this policy?

Policy Samples

Once the questions have been asked and answered, an actual policy should be drafted. The type of policy, structure, language, and formality may be different for different types of organizations.

Information Protection Policy

The following document outlines guidelines for the acceptance, storage, processing, and transmission of information by ABC, Inc. employees. The purpose of this policy is to ensure that information is protected, handled, and transmitted in a secure and appropriate manner. Information should not be modified or disclosed to unauthorized individuals.

In the following text, "users" refers to ABC, Inc. employees and contractors using ABC, Inc., computer systems, resources, and facilities. "Third party" refers to any individual or company not employed by ABC, Inc.

1. Unauthorized modification, transmitting, or other dissemination of proprietary information, sensitive, or confidential information of the company is strictly prohibited. Unauthorized dissemination of this information may result in suspension, termination, or result in a substantial civil liability as well as severe criminal penalties under the Economic Espionage Act of 1996.

2. Sensitive and proprietary information should be safely stored and protected while on file servers, workstations, and during any type of transmission. The information should be encrypted and authorized access enforced.

3. Any third party must sign a nondisclosure agreement document before entering or touring a facility and before receiving or discussing confidential or proprietary information.

4. Sensitive and proprietary information must be encrypted and digitally signed before it is transmitted across public networks.

5. Any documents, files, attachments, or applications received from outside of ABC, Inc. must be scanned for viruses to protect currently held information.

6. Sensitive and proprietary information should only be accessible to authorized individuals and strict access control, auditing, and monitoring should be in place.

7. The security officer is responsible for ensuring that this policy is properly enforced.

Remote Access Policy

The following document outlines guidelines for individuals to access ABC, Inc.'s computing systems and facility remotely from outside the facility. This includes, but is not limited to, any computer workstation, computer server, device, resources, and network provided by ABC, Inc. The purpose of this document is to ensure that all employees and outside individuals access ABC, Inc. in a secure, predictable, and controlled manner.

In the following text, "users" refers to ABC, Inc. employees and contractors using ABC, Inc. computer systems, resources, and facilities. "Third party" refers to any individual or company not employed by ABC, Inc.

1. Users requiring remote access to ABC, Inc.'s network or resources must be explicitly approved by a department manager and security officer.

2. Any third party that requires access to ABC, Inc.'s network or resources must obtain written approval by management and the security officer. This connection type should be temporary in nature, require strict authentication, and be closely monitored.

3. Users requiring remote access to ABC, Inc.'s network or resources must be adequately authorized via control measures, and a callback method should be implemented for each and every requested connection into the facility.

4. Users requiring remote access to ABC, Inc.'s network or resources can access the network via dial-up Internet service provider (ISP) accounts, Integrated Services Digital Network (ISDN), and cable modems.

5. Users connecting to ABC, Inc.'s facility using always-on broadband Internet connections, as in cable modems, must install antivirus scanning software on their home and mobile computers.

6. Remote access into ABC, Inc.'s facility should be properly audited and monitored for suspicious activity and unauthorized actions.

7. Unauthorized use of remote access privileges by third parties or users may result in the denial of future remote access permissions, suspension, termination, or criminal prosecution.

8. The security officer is responsible for ensuring that this policy is properly enforced.

Writing Security Policies

This section showed only two sample security policies, but there are several types that an organization may require. Developing general and specific policies is important for an organization to cover all of its bases and to ensure there is no confusion on the management or employees position when it comes to knowing what is expected.

How the policy is written will be determined on the type of policy, type of organization, and the culture of the organization. If the policy is inconsistent with the culture of the company and with other business policies, there is a greater chance of widespread noncompliance activity taking place. The policy should be realistic and express explicit support by the management. The policy should also be developed in conjunction with compliance-monitoring procedures and disciplinary actions for noncompliance activities to ensure congruency and a synergistic relationship between the different pieces of the security program.

When developing any policy, the following questions should be asked and answered to make sure that no issue was missed and that the policy is as far reaching as necessary:

- What exactly is being protected?
- Does the policy fit the organization's business needs?
- Does it relate to the activities that actually take place within the organization?
- Does the policy fit the organization's culture?
- Does the policy state what must be done and what happens if these things are not carried out?
- Is the policy enforceable?
- Who is responsible for enforcement of the policy?
- Who developed, approved, and authorized the policy and the items within the policy?
- What deviations to the policy are allowed and how are they handled?
- Who is responsible for updating and maintaining the policy?
- To whom does the policy apply and are there any limitations within the policy?
- What are the ramifications of noncompliance and who is responsible for monitoring and reporting these activities?
- When does the policy take effect?
- How is the policy communicated to each employee?

- How often should the policy be reviewed and updated?
- Is the policy properly supported by all appropriate senior management?

References

www.information-security-policies-and-standards.com

www.sans.org/newlook/resources/policies/policies.htm

British Standard 7799

The British Standard 7799 is an internationally recognized set of recommendations for developing security policies and conducting auditing. Many organizations use British Standard 7799 as a baseline to start from when developing their policies.

The standards are broken down into ten different sections that cover each aspect of an organization's security program. Each section deals with how a specific topic should be incorporated into a security policy and how activities should be properly audited to ensure compliance.

The following list gives a quick overview of each section within the standard:

- **Business Continuity Planning**   Identify critical business resources and develop plans and activities to countermeasure any significant disruption or interruption to them. These disruptions can be small in nature or large natural disasters.

- **System Access Control**   Identify resources that require access control and implement access control mechanisms. These mechanisms should prevent unauthorized access to information and computer systems. Unauthorized access and activity should be detected and dealt with properly. Access control is also an important part of remote access to an organization's assets.

- **System Development and Maintenance**   Confidentiality, integrity, and authenticity of information should be protected. Prevention of modification, misuse, corruption, or destruction of user data should be put into place. IT activities and procedures should be carried out in a secure manner. The security of application software and data should also be maintained.

- **Physical and Environmental Security** Unauthorized access to a business facility and premises should be prevented to reduce the potential damage and compromise of information and assets, as well as prevent an interruption to business activities.

- **Compliance** Compliance of outlined directives in the organization's security policy and standards should be ensured. Breaches of any criminal or civil law (statutory, regulatory, contractual obligations, and so on) should be avoided.

- **Personnel Security** Users should be aware of potential threats and know how to properly support the organization's security policy. Possible risks to personnel, resources, and the facility should be reduced. Plans should be in place to reduce damage from security incidents.

- **Security Organization** Information security should be maintained within the organization. If the responsibility of managing information processing has been outsourced to another organization, the actual information should still be protected by the organization that is responsible for it.

- **Computer and Network Management** The information processing and communication resources should be protected and their integrity and availability maintained. The infrastructure should be protected and safeguarded against possible threats. Damage to assets and business activities should be prevented. The risk of system failures should also be minimized.

- **Asset Classification and Control** Information and resources should be assigned proper classifications, and each classification should have appropriate protection components in place and maintained.

- **Security Policy** Management direction should be supplied through the security policy, which will be the foundation for the organization's security program.

Reference

www.securityauditor.net

http:/csrc.nist.gov/publications/secpubs/otherpubs/reviso-faq.pdf

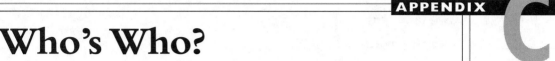
Who's Who?

NSA

The *National Security Agency* (NSA) is the agency officially responsible for security within the U.S. government. The agency was created in 1952 by President Harry Truman under the Department of Defense (DoD). Only recently has NSA been publicly discussed; for a majority of its life, most U.S. citizens did not know what the NSA was.

The NSA deals with signal intelligence, meaning that it listens to foreign communications that are deemed important and pertinent to U.S. security. The agency has extremely sophisticated and complex hardware, devices, and software to capture signals, decrypt them, and decode their meaning. NSA also conducts in-depth research in cryptology to increase their ability to decrypt other encrypted communication and to develop secure algorithms to protect U.S. military and government communication mechanisms.

NSA is also usually behind restricting any type of encryption products that may be sold outside of the United States. NSA does not want potentially threatening countries to acquire encryption mechanisms that would make its job of cracking encryption any harder. So many of the export laws that prohibit certain types of encryption software being sold outside of the United States have a direct correlation to the NSA's directives and requirements.

James Bamford wrote two books about the NSA: *The Puzzle Palace* and *Body of Secrets*.

References

www.fas.org/irp/nsa

www.cia.gov/ic/nsa.html

www.nsa.gov

NIST

The *National Institute of Standards and Technology* (NIST) is a division of the U.S. Department of Commerce. This organization was called the National Bureau of Standards (NBS) until 1988. It issues standards and guidelines to be adopted by U.S. computer system developers and vendors. NIST's core purpose is to promote open standards and interoperability with the hopes of spurring more developments within computer-based industries. The official standards that NIST produces and publishes are called *Federal Information Processing Standards* (FIPS).

In 1987 Congress passed the Computer Security Act, which authorized NIST to be responsible for defining standards to protect and ensure the security of information that is sensitive but unclassified within government agencies. NIST is responsible for sensitive but unclassified information, and NSA is responsible for classified information.

NIST's *Computer Systems Laboratory* (CSL) is responsible for developing technical, management, physical, and administrative standards and guidelines for cost-effective security used to keep the government agencies' sensitive information protected. It is required to work with other government agencies, including the NSA, to ensure the necessary level of protection for government agencies' computer systems and the programs, materials, testing, and reports pertaining to those systems. The NSA is required to provide NIST with technical guidelines dealing with personal identification, telecommunication security, and trusted technologies.

NIST's CSL provides the following:

- Develops computer security standards and works closely with accredited standards committees such as IEEE, ANSI, and ISO to develop and support these standards. The published standards are called FIPS PUBs. (Rainbow Series is an example.)

- Conducts research and publishes results on many security problems and solutions.

- Works with the NSA to ensure that solutions meet DoD security standards for protecting classified and intelligence information.

- Develops test methods to properly test security mechanisms.

U.S. government agencies that employ cryptography must use software that follows NIST standards. Many of the encryption standards mandated by NIST were developed by NSA. The public has been a bit suspicious of this relationship when it comes to developing and approving specific encryption algorithms, especially when they are not up for public review. The fear of the government inserting backdoors into algorithms unknown to the public raises many Big Brother issues and has caused outcries of these issues in the past.

References

www.nist.gov

www.csrc.ncsl.nist.gov

NCSC

The *National Computer Security Center* (NCSC) was established in 1981 within NSA to help support and drive NSA's DoD computer security responsibilities. The NCSC's responsibility was to provide a centralized agency that dealt with the evaluation process of computer security systems and products, provide technical support for government and industry groups doing computer security research and development, conduct and sponsor research in the computer and network security technology sector, develop and provide verification and analysis tools, provide computer security training, and disseminate information to other federal government agencies and to the computing industry. It also published the Rainbow Series of computing security standards.

The lines dividing NIST, NSA, and NCSC have not always been clear because they have overlapping responsibilities and throughout their histories, their responsibilities and missions expanded further into each other's territories. Basically, NSA protects classified military and intelligence information using computer security mechanisms and techniques, and NIST develops standards and computer security training programs. Evaluations of security systems were performed by NCSC through the Trusted Product Evaluation Program (TPEP), which is a part of NSA.

Vendors would request that their products go through the TPEP of an evaluation targeting a particular level of trust rating. These evaluations used the Trusted Computer System Evaluation Criteria (TCSEC) criteria to assess the product and determine if it met the necessary requirements for the requested rating. The results were published in the Evaluated Products List (EPL) in Information Systems Security Products and Services Catalogs.

After the realization that TCSEC did not meet the requirements of all organizations and their security needs, the Common Criteria was developed and accepted. The TPEP was replaced by the *Trusted Technology Assessment Program* (TTAP). TTAP is a program developed and supported by NSA and NIST that performs trusted product evaluations. The evaluations are based against the Common Criteria instead of the TCSEC.

Reference

www.radium.ncsc.mil/tpep

ISO

The *International Standards Organization* (ISO) was established in 1947 and is an international organization made up of many national standards organizations. ISO's *Open System Interconnection* (OSI) model provides a conceptual model for explaining how data communication takes place. The OSI model promotes open networking environments that enable multivendor computer systems that follow this model to communicate using internationally accepted protocols.

The ISO is a worldwide federation with representatives from over 100 countries. It is a nongovernmental organization with a mission to develop worldwide standards and promote a further international exchange of services and goods and to further develop cooperation of intellectual, technological, and scientific concepts between countries all over the world.

Reference

www.iso.ch

ANSI

The *American National Standards Institute* (ANSI) is an organization that defines coding standards and signaling schemes in the United States and represents the United States in the ISO and the International Telecommunication Union (ITU). The organization does not develop standards, but facilitates their development by bringing qualified groups together and providing them with guiding principles.

ANSI had a large part in the development of the ISO and has an active role in governing it today. ANSI promotes and advocates U.S. policies internationally within different regional standards organizations. The ANSI promotes U.S. standards by presenting them to ISOs. The organizations can choose to adopt the standards fully or extract specific parts of the standards to adopt for their regions.

Some of the well-known ANSI standards include C++, SQL, EDI, SONET, FDDI, and ANSI x9 security standards.

Reference

www.ansi.org

IEEE

The *Institute of Electrical and Electronic Engineers* (IEEE) is a nonprofit organization that develops standards, submits them for ANSI approval, and forwards drafts to the ISO. This technical association is based in the United States and develops different types of standards, including security standards. The IEEE is made up of a number of committees, or working groups, that work in specific technical areas like communications, nuclear engineering, aerospace electronics, telecommunications, security, and much more. Their local area network/metropolitan area network (LAN/MAN) standards are known as the IEEE 802 standards. IEEE has a technical committee that works strictly with security and privacy issues.

References

www.ieee.org

http://standards.ieee.org/catalog/contents.html

www.ieee-security.org/index.html

HIPAA

Are You HIPAA Compliant?

Many organizations are slowly, and sometimes painfully, learning the business needs of information and network security within their environment. This realization can be driven by the risk of attackers stealing customer credit card numbers, accessing bank account information, defacing Web sites, and/or stealing trade secrets or intellectual property. The wasted time by the IT staff tracking down inside and outside attackers and patching the holes within the infrastructure is also a consideration. However, medical organizations now have additional urgent drivers forcing them to take a hard look at the security levels within their business environment. These drivers include increased fines and possible jail time.

The *Health Insurance Portability and Accountability Act* (HIPAA), a new federal regulation, has been mandated to provide national standards and procedures for the electronic storage, use, and transmission of personal medical information and healthcare data. This regulation provides a framework to ensure security, integrity, and privacy when handling confidential medical information. HIPAA outlines how security should be managed for any facility that creates, accesses, shares, or destroys medical information.

HIPAA also mandates specific Electronic Data Interchange (EDI) standards for transactions such as health plan enrollment, eligibility, premium and claims payments, coordination of benefits, and referrals. This will enforce standardization for how different medical entities communicate with each other by ensuring that the same format is used and understood by everyone involved. Reporting identifiers (IDs) are also mandated. These include provider IDs, payer IDs, patient IDs, and employer IDs. These IDs will be used for all electronic transactions of medical information and provide an organized method for the proper tracking and auditing of medical information activities. This paper does not focus on the EDI standards, but on the security standards within the HIPAA regulations.

People's health records can be used and misused in different scenarios for many different reasons. As health records migrate from a paper-based system to an electronic system, they become easier to maintain, access, and transfer, but they also become easier to manipulate. Traditionally, healthcare facilities have lagged behind other businesses in their information and network security mechanisms, architecture, and security enforcement because there was no real business need to expend the energy and money to put these items in place. Now there is.

HIPAA brings steep federal penalties for noncompliance. If medical information is used in a way that violates the privacy standards dictated by HIPAA, even by mistake, there are monetary penalties of $100 per violation up to $25,000 per year, per standard. If protected health information is obtained or disclosed knowingly, the fines can be as much as $50,000 and one year in prison. If the information is obtained or disclosed under false pretenses, the cost can go up to $250,000 and a person could incur up to ten years in prison if there is intent to sell or use the information for commercial advantage, personal gain, or malicious harm. This is serious business.

Oh, How It's Changed

In the past, medical information was transcribed onto papers bound in a folder. That was the patient's medical record. This information was stored in file cabinets and moved or updated manually. Today medical information is stored in databases. It is not only reviewed by the nurse and doctor, but is also reviewed by insurance companies, insurance clearinghouses, group practices, Medicaid agencies, and health practitioners. In addition, this data can be accessed by many types of hospital staff from most computers throughout the hospital, and even physicians from their portable or home computers. This information usually travels unprotected across the Internet, or other open vulnerable networks, with no real restrictions on who accesses it and what they do with the information once they have accessed it. As the healthcare industry has consolidated medical information electronically, integrated delivery systems have emerged. This means that clinical information can now be shared among multiple hospitals, clinics, insurance companies, and homecare agencies all over the world.

These issues spurred the government to act and implement new standards that protected private health information from nonconsensual use. These standards give patients the right to access their medical records and the ability to know who else has accessed them. The standards restrict disclosure of this confidential information to the minimum needed for the intended purpose. They also establish new criminal and civil penalties and sanctions for not following the new standards.

What Do I Have To Do?

HIPAA does not spell out specific technology that should be used to provide the necessary security levels, but it provides a broad overview of the necessary architecture and framework it expects to see implemented. The regulation is based on already known and practiced security standards and procedures. So, if an organization has a good security baseline to start from, these mechanisms may only need to be reviewed, improved, documented, and monitored. If an organization has never considered security, and thus does not have the necessary policies, procedures, or baseline infrastructure in place, a major overhaul of the technology and methods used within the environment may need to take place.

HIPAA looks at four major factors affecting an organization's security:

- Administrative procedures
- Physical safeguards
- Technical security services
- Technical security mechanisms

Administrative Procedures

- Have formal protocols for controlling access to data.

- Certify data systems to evaluate compliance with security standards.

- Develop and maintain a chain of trust of agreements among regulated entities that will exchange and share health information.

- Use contingency plans to preserve data in the event of an emergency.

- Have formal data processing protocols.

- Have internal security audit procedures.

- Perform authentication and authorization for accessing data, ongoing training, and monitoring of activity by personnel who access medical information.

- Have security configuration management for hardware and software including the supporting documentation.

- Appoint a security information officer.

- Use formal methods of reporting and responding to security breaches.

- Develop a security management structure that maintains security policy and procedures and provides continual risk assessment capabilities.

- Have proper personnel termination activities.

- Implement training and security awareness programs.

Physical Safeguards

- Formally assign the security responsibility to a person or entity.

- Develop access controls to hardware and peripherals.

- Develop disaster and intrusion response and recovery plans.

- Restrict and control physical access to data sites with personal identification verification.

- Maintain maintenance records.

- Enforce a need-to-know basis for access to information and sites.

- Develop and document allowed activities and security configurations at the workstation level.

Technical Security Services

- Use necessary software controls to provide data integrity, confidentiality, and availability.

- Regulate access to data with a hierarchal system of rights and permissions for personnel.

- Provide data authentication and data integrity.

- Ensure user authentication and access control.

Technical Security Mechanisms

- Implement necessary security software controls to ensure proper electronic storage and transmission of data.

- Use integrity controls to ensure transmitted or stored data is valid.

- Perform message authentication to ensure that messages were not altered during transmission.

- Use access controls for transmission mechanisms or encryption.

- Use alarms and alerts to signal abnormal communication conditions.

- Maintain audit and log trail information.

Buying a firewall and configuring it is not the first step. A medical organization must understand the drivers behind their security challenges. In addition to meeting HIPAA's standards, basic business requirements, objectives, and goals should be fully explored and understood. Real planning needs to happen to give all management, departments, IT staff, and employees direction and guidelines to understanding what security means to them and their department.

Establish Security Policies, Procedures, Standards, and Guidelines

Establishing security policies, procedures, standards, and guidelines should be the first task. This provides direction for everyone in the company. A security policy is the overall expression of management's intention on how security should be implemented, maintained, and enforced.

Assess the Security Architecture

Next, the security architecture should be fully examined from a logical and physical point of view. This architecture should be fortified at every front — from the access points through the firewalls, callback restrictions via modems, virus activity, server configuration, access control mechanisms, to virtual private networks (VPNs), encryption, and application security. These processes need to be properly monitored with alerts, alarms, logs, and audit trails of suspicious activity.

Develop a Security Awareness Program

A security awareness program should be developed for the different levels of expertise within the organization. Business contingency plans should also be current with proper recovery plans in place.

This seems like a lot to review, improve, and monitor. It is, but there's more. In addition to the facility's physical network structure, how people react with the components within this facility, how data travels throughout this network, management's attitude and activities concerning securing this infrastructure, and the legal and liability issues when one piece falls to the wayside must be considered. This is a lot to take on. These things need to be accomplished by October 2002 by most facilities, or let the fines begin!

Cultural Issues

In many ways, implementing the essential security technology mechanisms is easier than making support personnel use them correctly. In many organizations, security innovations are almost always met with resistance and opposition. Change is usually hard for people, but when a change restricts actions they currently took for granted, ways of bypassing the changes usually creep in.

For security to be successful, it must be rigorously supported by the highest ranks of management. It must be considered in almost all business decisions. The proper funding must be in place to support it. Different security responsibilities must be assigned to individuals and groups. All employees must understand the meaning of security within their particular organization, the expectations of the organization, and the consequences of noncompliance.

Because a majority of medical facilities have not had restrictions concerning what files can and cannot be accessed, what can be done to the files once they are accessed, who files can be sent to, and all the necessary overhead that accompanies good security, culture adjustment may be one of the larger roadblocks to a successful security rollout.

What Are My Fist Steps?

This paper only provides a very basic overview of what is to come. Each section could easily be a detailed book by itself.

Depending on your expertise and the available time and resources, the most effective first step may be to contact a consultant agency that specializes in information and network security practices. Outside consultants can provide an objective viewpoint and knowledgeable ideas and solutions that are not tied to the old way of doing things that have political hot buttons. Without this type of perspective, these tasks can be overwhelming.

The next step is to understand the environment because you can't secure something you don't understand. The network schematic diagram that has been ignored for years needs to be brought out and properly updated. You need to understand how information comes in and out of your network, how these entry points provide authentication and authorization, where sensitive information lives, who accesses it, and why. The computers or servers that hold medical information need rigorous scrutiny. What operating system is on these computers? How updated are the patches and hot fixes? What access control lists are on these computers and what users have the right to access the information on these computers? How are these computers physically protected? Who can access these computers remotely and why?

Then you need to review remote users and their abilities. Supporting remote users creates compromising situations for organizations. How are remote users being properly authenticated? How is their activity being tracked? How do you know this isn't an easy doorway for attackers? Do you really need so many remote users? Do they really need all the rights and permissions they currently have? How do you properly provide all the necessary security mechanisms to protect your remote users and your network?

Networks are not islands anymore. What type of access do your employees have to the Internet? How do you know this is not opening your environment up to attacks and security compromises? Are there any backdoors to your network? How do you communicate with other businesses? Is this done securely? Is this monitored and audited properly?

Questions like this can go on and on. It is just as important to ask the right questions as it is to find the right answers. Organizations often don't even know where to begin, much less how to lay out a proper roadmap to accomplish and achieve all the necessary security goals and objectives. This is why the first step can be the most important step.

Summary

The HIPAA regulation accomplishes several important goals. First, patients have more control over their medical information. They can control whom it is released to; they have the right to see a copy of their health records and the ability to request a correction to their records; and they can give advanced consent for most disclosures of health information, and receive an explanation of their privacy rights and how their confidential information will be used.

Second, it ensures that medical information will be used, for health purposes only with a few exceptions, and not for nonhealth purposes like job promotions or underwriting life insurance products. Medical organizations are now accountable to protect health information against misuse or disclosure. Steep fines and possible jail time back up this accountability.

To comply with the regulations and provide all of these services and this protection, facilities must take a hard look at their current infrastructures and implemented security mechanisms. Most organizations will need to spend a lot of time and money to develop proper plans, security policies, and procedures; implement the necessary security components; and add staff to update, monitor, and audit these new activities.

These steps unquestionably have to take place. The only question is, Are you prepared? If not, do you know how to prepare yourself?

HIPAA Regulation Expectations

Administrative Procedures to Guard Data Integrity, Confidentiality, and Availability

1. **Certification** Each organization is required to evaluate and certify its computers systems and network designs to verify that the appropriate security has been implemented. This evaluation can be performed internally or by an external accrediting agency.

2. **Chain of trust partner agreement** If medical data is processed through a third party, all parties involved are required to enter into a chain of trust partner agreement. This means that all parties are bound to a contract promising to protect electronically transmitted data. It is important to have the same level of security for each link of the electronic communication path. The sender and receiver must maintain the integrity and confidentiality of the information while it is in their possession.

3. **Contingency plan** Organizations must have contingency plans in place to be able to properly respond and recover from disasters and system emergencies. Periodic backups of data are required. Critical facilities must be available for continuing operations in the event of an emergency. The contingency plan must contain the following:

   - **Applications and data criticality analysis** Formal assessment of vulnerabilities, risks, sensitivity, and security of its programs and information it receives, stores, transmits, manipulates, and accesses.

   - **A data backup plan** A documented and routinely updated plan to create and maintain data for a specific period of time. Exact copies of backup data must be retrievable.

- **A disaster recovery plan**   Necessary processes that enable an organization to restore any loss of data in the event of a natural disaster, system emergency, or vandalism.

- **An emergency mode operation plan**   Part of an overall contingency plan that enables an organization to operate in the event of a natural disaster, system emergency, or vandalism.

- **Testing and revision procedures**   A documented process of periodic testing of contingency plans to provide training, discover weaknesses, and allow for a revision of the plan as needed.

4. **Formal mechanism for processing records**   Documented policies and procedures for the routine and nonroutine receipt, manipulation, storage, dissemination, transmission, and/or disposal of health information.

5. **Information access control**   Formal, documented policies and procedures for granting different levels of access to healthcare information that includes all of the following implementation features:

   - **Access authorization**

   - **Information**   Use policies and procedures that establish the rules for granting access.

   - **Access establishment**

   - **Access modification**   Security policies and rules that determine the various types and reasons for modification to an entity's established right of access to a terminal, transaction, program, process, or some other use.

6. **Internal audit**   In-house review of the records of system activity (such as logins, file accesses, and security incidents) maintained by an organization.

7. **Personnel security**   All personnel who have access to any sensitive information have the required authorities as well as all appropriate clearances. This includes all of the following implementation features:

   - **Ensuring supervision of maintenance personnel by an authorized, knowledgeable person**   These procedures are documented formal procedures and instructions for the oversight of maintenance personnel when the personnel are near health information pertaining to an individual.

   - **Maintaining a record of access authorizations**   Ongoing documentation and review of the levels of access granted to a user, program, or procedure accessing health information.

- **Ensuring that operating and maintenance personnel have proper access authorization**   Formal documented policies and procedures for determining the access level to be granted to individuals working on, or near, health information.

- **Establishing personnel clearance procedures**   A protective measure applied to determine that an individual's access to sensitive unclassified automated information is admissible.

- **Establishing and maintaining personnel security policies and procedures**   Formal documentation of procedures to ensure that all personnel who have access to sensitive information have the required authority as well as appropriate clearances.

- **Ensuring that system users, including maintenance personnel, receive security awareness training**

8. **Security configuration management**   Measures, practices, and develops procedures for the security of information systems that must be coordinated and integrated with each other and other measures, practices, and procedures of the organization established in order to create a coherent system of security. This includes all of the following implementation features:

- **Documentation**   Written security plans, rules, procedures, and instructions concerning all components of an entity's security.

- **Hardware and software installation and maintenance review and testing for security features**   Formal, documented procedures for connecting and loading new equipment and programs, a periodic review of the maintenance occurring on the equipment and programs, and a periodic security testing of the security attributes of that hardware/software.

- **Inventory**   The formal, documented identification of hardware and software assets.

- **Security testing**   The process is used to determine that the security features of a system are implemented as designed and that they are adequate for a proposed applications environment; this process includes hands-on functional testing, penetration testing, and verification.

- **Virus checking**   The act of running a computer program that identifies and disables the following:

  - Another virus computer program, typically hidden, that attaches itself to other programs and has the capability to replicate

- A code fragment (not an independent program) that reproduces by attaching to another program

- A code embedded within a program that causes a copy of itself to be inserted in one or more other programs

9. **Security incident procedures**   Formal, documented instructions for reporting security breaches that include all of the following implementation features:

  - **Report procedures**   Documented, formal mechanism employed to document security incidents.

  - **Response procedures**   Documented, formal rules or instructions for actions to be taken as a result of the receipt of a security incident report

10. **Security management process**   Creation, administration, and oversight of policies to ensure the prevention, detection, containment, and correction of security breaches involving risk analysis and risk management. This includes the establishment of accountability, management controls (policies and education), electronic controls, physical security, and penalties for the abuse and misuse of its assets (both physical and electronic), which includes all of the following implementation features:

  - **Risk analysis**   A process whereby cost-effective security/control measures may be selected by balancing the costs of various security/control measures against the losses that would be expected if these measures were not in place.

  - **Risk management**   Process of assessing risk, taking steps to reduce risk to an acceptable level, and maintaining that level of risk.

  - **Sanction policies and procedures**   Statements regarding disciplinary actions that are communicated to all employees, agents, and contractors: for example, a verbal warning, notice of disciplinary action placed in personnel files, removal of system privileges, termination of employment, and contract penalties. They must include employee, agent, and contractor notice of civil or criminal penalties for misuse or misappropriation of health information and must make employees, agents, and contractors aware that violations may result in notification to law enforcement officials and regulatory, accreditation, and licensure organizations.

  - **Security policy**   Statement(s) of information values, protection responsibilities, and organization commitment for a system. This is the framework within which an entity establishes the necessary levels of information security to achieve the desired confidentiality goals.

11. **Termination procedures** Formal, documented instructions, which include appropriate security measures for the ending of an employee's employment or an internal/external user's access. This includes procedures for all of the following implementation features:

- **Changing locks** A documented procedure for changing combinations of locking mechanisms, both on a recurring basis and when personnel knowledgeable of combinations no longer need-to-know or require access to the protected facility or system.

- **Removal from access lists** Physical eradication of an entity's access privileges and the removal of a user account(s).

- **Termination or deletion of an individual's access privileges to the information, services, and resources for which they currently have clearance, authorization, and need-to-know when such clearance, authorization, and need-to-know no longer exist**

- **Turning in keys, tokens, or cards that provide access** Formal, documented procedure to ensure that all physical items that give a terminated employee access to a property, building, or equipment are retrieved from that employee, preferably before termination.

12. **Training** Education concerning the vulnerabilities of the health information in an entity's possession and ways to ensure the protection of that information. This includes all of the following implementation features:

- **Awareness training for all personnel, including management personnel** In security awareness, including, but not limited to, password maintenance, incident reporting, viruses, and other forms of malicious software.

- **Periodic security reminders** Employees, agents, and contractors are made aware of security concerns on an ongoing basis.

- **User education concerning virus protection** Training relative to user awareness of the potential harm that can be caused by a virus, how to prevent the introduction of a virus to a computer system, and what to do if a virus is detected.

- **User education concerning the importance of monitoring login success or failure and how to report discrepancies** Training in the user's responsibility to ensure the security of healthcare information.

- **User education about password management** Type of user training and the rules to be followed in creating and changing passwords, and the need to keep them confidential.

Physical Safeguards to Guard Data Integrity, Confidentiality, and Availability

1. **Assigned security responsibility**   Practices established by management to manage and supervise the execution and use of security measures to protect data and to manage and supervise the conduct of personnel in relation to the protection of data.

2. **Media controls**   Formal, documented policies and procedures that govern the receipt and removal of hardware/software (such as diskettes and tapes) into and out of a facility. This includes all of the following implementation features:

   - **Access control**

   - **Accountability**   The property that ensures that the actions of an entity can be traced uniquely to that entity

   - **Data backup**   A retrievable, exact copy of information

   - **Data storage**   The retention of healthcare information pertaining to an individual in an electronic format

   - **Disposal**   Final disposition of electronic data and/or the hardware on which electronic data is stored

3. **Physical access controls**   Formal, documented policies and procedures to be followed to limit physical access to an entity while ensuring that properly authorized access is allowed. This includes all of the following implementation features:

   - **Disaster recovery**   The process enabling an entity to restore any loss of data in the event of fire, vandalism, natural disaster, or system failure.

   - **An emergency mode operation**   Access controls in place that enable an entity to continue to operate in the event of a fire, vandalism, natural disaster, or system failure.

   - **Equipment control (into and out of site)**   Documented security procedures for bringing hardware and software into and out of a facility and for maintaining a record of that equipment. This includes, but is not limited to, the marking, handling, and disposal of hardware and storage media.

   - **A facility security plan**   A plan to safeguard the premises and building (exterior and interior) from unauthorized physical access and to safeguard the equipment therein from unauthorized physical access, tampering, and theft.

   - **Procedures for verifying access authorizations before granting physical access**   Formal, documented policies and instructions for validating the access privileges of an entity before granting those privileges.

- **Maintenance records** Documentation of repairs and modifications to the physical components of a facility, such as the hardware, software, walls, doors, and locks

- **Need-to-know procedures for personnel access** A security principle stating that a user should have access only to the data he or she needs to perform a particular function

- **Procedures to sign in visitors and provide escorts, if appropriate** Formal, documented procedure governing the reception and hosting of visitors

- **Testing and revision** The restriction of program testing and the revision to formally authorized personnel

4. **Policy and guidelines on workstation use** Documented instructions/procedures delineating the proper functions to be performed, the manner in which those functions are to be performed, and the physical attributes of the surroundings of a specific computer terminal site or type of site, dependent upon the sensitivity of the information accessed from that site.

    - **A secure workstation location** Physical safeguards to eliminate or minimize the possibility of unauthorized access to information: for example, locating a terminal used to access sensitive information in a locked room and restricting access to that room to authorized personnel, and not placing a terminal used to access patient information in any area of a doctor's office where the screen contents can be viewed from the reception area.

    - **Security awareness training** Information security awareness training programs in which all employees, agents, and contractors must participate, including (based on job responsibilities) customized education programs that focus on issues regarding use of health information and responsibilities regarding confidentiality and security.

Technical Security Services to Guard Data Integrity, Confidentiality, and Availability

1. **Access control that includes a procedure for emergency access and the optional use of encryption** Documented instructions for obtaining necessary information during a crisis. This includes at least one of the following implementation features:

    - **Context-based access** An access control procedure based on the context of a transaction (as opposed to being based on attributes of the initiator or target).

- Role-based access

- User-based access

2. **Audit controls**   Mechanisms employed to record and examine system activity.

3. **Authorization control**   The mechanism for obtaining consent for the use and disclosure of health information. This includes at least one of the following implementation features:

   - Role-based access

   - User-based access

4. **Data authentication**   The corroboration that data has not been altered or destroyed in an unauthorized manner. Examples of how data corroboration may be ensured include the use of a checksum, double keying, a message authentication code, or a digital signature.

5. **Entity authentication**   The corroboration that an entity is the one claimed. This includes

   - **Automatic logoff**   A security procedure that causes an electronic session to terminate after a predetermined time of inactivity, such as 15 minutes.

   - **Unique user identifier**   A combination name/number assigned and maintained in security procedures for identifying and tracking individual user identity. This includes at least one of the following implementation features:

      - **Biometric identification**   An identification system that identifies a human from a measurement of a physical feature or repeatable action of the individual (for example, hand geometry, retinal scan, iris scan, fingerprint patterns, facial characteristics, DNA sequence characteristics, voiceprints, and handwritten signature).

      - **Password**

      - **Personal identification number (PIN)**   A number or code assigned to an individual and used to provide verification of identity.

      - **A telephone callback procedure**   A method of authenticating the identity of the receiver and sender of information through a series of questions and answers sent back and forth establishing the identity of each.

      - **Token**

Technical Security Mechanisms to Guard Against Unauthorized Access to Data That Is Transmitted over a Communications Network

If an entity uses communications or network controls, its security standards for technical security mechanisms must include the following:

- **Integrity controls** A security mechanism employed to ensure the validity of the information being electronically transmitted or stored

- **Message authentication** Ensuring, typically with a message authentication code, that a received message (usually via a network) matches the message sent

These mechanisms use one of the following implementation features:

1. **Access controls** Protection of sensitive communications transmissions over open or private networks so that they cannot be easily intercepted and interpreted by parties other than the intended recipient.

2. **Encryption**

3. **Alarm** In communication systems, any device that can sense an abnormal condition within the system and provide, either locally or remotely, a signal indicating the presence of the abnormality. The signal may be in any desired form ranging from a simple contact closure (or opening) to a time-phased automatic shutdown and restart cycle.

4. **Audit trail** The data collected and potentially used to facilitate a security audit.

5. **Entity authentication** A communications or network mechanism to irrefutably identify authorized users, programs, and processes and to deny access to unauthorized users, programs, and processes.

6. **Event reporting** A network message indicating operational irregularities in physical elements of a network or a response to the occurrence of a significant task, typically the completion of a request for information.

HIPAA Security Requirements Matrix

Table C-1 Administrative Procedures to Guard Data Integrity, Confidentiality, and Availability

HIPAA Requirement	Description	Applicable IEEE Standard(s)	Implementation Method	Identification Steps
Certification	Each organization is required to evaluate and certify its computer systems and network designs to verify that the appropriate security has been implemented. This evaluation can be performed internally or by an external accrediting agency.	47	Internal or external testing and certification	Check previous and current certifications. Schedule routine certifications. Document procedures. What does the certification cover? What types of tests are carried out? What type of documentation is used to show outcomes of each test? Are there written procedures? Who is responsible for these activities?
Chain of trust partner agreement	If medical data is processed through a third party, all parties involved are required to enter into a chain of trust partner agreement. This means all parties are bound to a contract promising to protect electronically transmitted data. It is important to have the same level of security for each link of the electronic communication path. The sender and receiver must maintain the integrity and confidentiality of the information while it is in their possession.	12 and 47	Signed legal contracts	Identify electronic partner and evaluate data transfer procedures and technology. Review procedural documentation and current contracts. Review the level of security each partner is providing. Who shares medical information? What type of security is used at each partner site? What types of encryption mechanisms are used? Are there any interoperability issues? Are there written procedures? Who is responsible for these activities?

(continued)

Table C-1 Administrative Procedures to Guard Data Integrity, Confidentiality, and Availability *(continued)*

HIPAA Requirement	Description	Applicable IEEE Standard(s)	Implementation Method	Identification Steps
Contingency	Organizations must have contingency plans in place to be able to properly respond and recover from disasters and system emergencies. Periodic backups of data are required. Critical facilities must be available for continuing operations in the event of an emergency plan.	17, 47, and 53	Application and data criticality analysis	Review and evaluate current contingency plans, procedures, and documentation. Review critical application and data recoverability procedures. If a disaster happens, how will the data still be available? What steps are taken to ensure continued operations? Has the critical data been identified and mirrored? Are there cold or hot sites available? Are there written procedures? Who is responsible for these activities?
	Documented and routinely updated plan to create and maintain data for a specific period of time. Exact copies of backup data must be retrievable.	12, 17, and 47	Data backup	Review and evaluate data backup procedures, schedule timelines, and document procedures. What data is backed up? Where is it backed up to? How often is it backed up? Are there off-site facilities that hold copies? Is there a fireproof safe? Are there written procedures? Who is responsible for these activities?
	Documented process of periodic testing of contingency plans to provide training, discover weaknesses, and allow for revision of plan as needed.	12, 17, and 47	Testing and revision	Review previous contingency testing plans and procedures for updating the plans. Review training activities and supporting documentation. How often is the plan tested? What is done during the test? How is the plan revised? Are there written procedures? Who is responsible for these activities?

HIPAA Requirement	Description	Applicable IEEE Standard(s)	Implementation Method	Identification Steps
	Necessary processes that enable an organization to restore any loss of data in the event of a natural disaster, system emergency, or vandalism.	12, 17, 47, and 53	Disaster recovery plan	Review and evaluate current disaster recovery plans, procedures, and documentation. What steps will be taken to recover from a disaster? When was this plan last updated? Is it tested? Are there written procedures? Who is responsible for these activities?
	Part of an overall contingency plan that enables an organization to operate in the event of a natural disaster, system emergency, or vandalism.	47 and 53	Emergency mode operations plan	Review and evaluate emergency mode procedures and reaction plans. What happens right after a disaster? What critical functions have to be operational? What is put in place to verify that these functions are operational? Are there written procedures? Who is responsible for these activities?
Formal mechanism for processing records	Documented policies and procedures for the routine and nonroutine receipt, manipulation, storage, dissemination, transmission, and/or disposal of health information.	12 and 17	Documentation of data policy and procedures	Evaluate current data handling procedures and supporting documentation. How is medical information handled, stored, received, transmitted, and destroyed? Are there written procedures? Who is responsible for these activities?
	The security policies, and the rules established therein, that determine an entity's initial right to access a terminal, transaction, program, or process.	17, 47, and 53	Access establishment	Evaluate current authorization levels and rules implemented to control access to data. Who can access what data? How is this enforced? Are there written procedures? Who is responsible for these activities?

(continued)

Table C-1 Administrative Procedures to Guard Data Integrity, Confidentiality, and Availability (*continued*)

HIPAA Requirement	Description	Applicable IEEE Standard(s)	Implementation Method	Identification Steps
Formal mechanism for processing records (*cont.*)	Security policies and rules that determine the types of and reasons for modification to an entity's established right to access a terminal, transaction, program, process, or some other user.	12, 17, 47, and 53	Access modification	Review the procedures and standards for altering user access levels. Why are access levels changed for users? How is this carried out? Are there written procedures? Who is responsible for these activities?
Internal audit	In-house review of the records of system activity (such as logins, file accesses, and security incidents) maintained by an organization.	12, 17, 43, 44, and 47	Internal audits	Review the previous and current audit documentation and procedures. Are in-house audits carried out? If so, by whom? What is audited? Are there procedures and supporting documentation? How long are the audits kept? Where are they kept and protected? Are there written procedures? Who is responsible for these activities?
Personnel security	All personnel who have access to any sensitive information have the required authorities as well as all appropriate clearances.	17 and 47	Ensure supervision of maintenance personnel by authorized, knowledgeable person	Evaluate authorization and clearance procedures pertaining to accessing information. Who has what access to medical information and why? How is this type of accessed tracked and enforced? Are there written procedures? Who is responsible for these activities?

HIPAA Requirement	Description	Applicable IEEE Standard(s)	Implementation Method	Identification Steps
	Ongoing documentation and review of the levels of access granted to a user, program, or procedure accessing health information.	12, 17, and 47	Maintenance of record of access authorizations	Review documentation pertaining to access level evaluation procedures. Is the documentation that explains access authorization updated and maintained? If so, by whom and how often? How does this type of maintenance happen? Are there written procedures? Who is responsible for these activities
	Formal documented policies and procedures for determining the access level to be granted to individuals working on, or near, health information.	17 and 47	Operating, and in some cases, maintenance personnel who have proper access authorization	Review the access level requirements and updating procedures. Who can have access to medical information? How is this tracked, monitored, and enforced? Are there written procedures? Who is responsible for these activities?
	A protective measure applied to determine that an individual's access to sensitive unclassified automated information is admissible.	17, 47, and 53	Personnel clearance procedure	Review and evaluate current clearance level assignments and procedural activities. Who has what permissions to access and modify medical information? What are the procedures to dictate which users can access different types of information? Are there written procedures? Who is responsible for these activities?

(continued)

Table C-1 Administrative Procedures to Guard Data Integrity, Confidentiality, and Availability (*continued*)

HIPAA Requirement	Description	Applicable IEEE Standard(s)	Implementation Method	Identification Steps
Personal security (*cont.*)	Ensuring that system users, including maintenance personnel, receive security awareness training.	12, 17, 47, and 53	System users, including maintenance personnel trained in security	Review previous security awareness activities, scheduled events, literature, and documentation. Do all employees receive security awareness training? How often? What is taught in this training? Are there written procedures? Who is responsible for these activities?

Table C-2 Administrative Procedures to Guard Data Integrity, Confidentiality, and Availability

Requirement	Description	Mapped Standard(s)	Implementation	Identification Steps
Security configuration management	Measures, practices, and procedures for the security of information systems that must be coordinated and integrated with each other and other measures, practices, and procedures of the organization established in order to create a coherent system of security.	12, 17, 47, and 53	Documentation	Review and evaluate current security configuration management and documentation. When changes are made, how are they implemented? How are they tested? Is this a standard practice? Are there written procedures? Who is responsible for these activities?
	Formal, documented procedures for connecting and loading new equipment and programs, the periodic review of the maintenance occurring on that equipment and programs, and the periodic security testing of the security attributes of that hardware/software.	12, 17, and 47	Hardware/software installation and maintenance review and testing for security features	How is new hardware and software integrated into the environment? Are there specific written procedures? How is it tested? Are security issues readdressed after this type of implementation? Are there written procedures? Who is responsible for these activities?
	The formal, documented identification of hardware and software assets.	12 and 17	Inventory	Is there a list of current hardware and software resources? If so, who maintains it? How often is it updated? Are there written procedures? Who is responsible for these activities?

(continued)

Table C-2 Administrative Procedures to Guard Data Integrity, Confidentiality, and Availability *(continued)*

Requirement	Description	Mapped Standard(s)	Implementation	Identification Steps
Security configuration management *(cont.)*	Process used to determine that the security features of a system are implemented as designed and that they are adequate for a proposed applications environment; this process includes hands-on functional testing, penetration testing, and verification.	12, 17, and 47	Security testing	Are regular security vulnerability scans performed? Are security features tested? What type of testing is done? How are security mechanism functionalities verified? Are there written procedures? Who is responsible for these activities?
	The act of running a computer program that identifies and disables viruses.	12, 17, 47, and 53	Virus checking	Is there antivirus software on each computer? What are the configurations? How often are computers scanned? What happens in case of an infection? How often are the signatures updated? Are there written procedures? Who is responsible for these activities?
Security incident procedures	Documented formal mechanism employed to document security incidents.	12, 17, and 47	Report procedures	Are there written procedures dictating how incidents should be reported? Who is responsible for these reports? Where are they kept? Are there written procedures? Who is responsible for these activities?
	Documented formal rules or instructions for actions to be taken as a result of the receipt of a security incident report.	17 and 47	Response procedures	What happens if there is a security incident? Who is involved? What actions are taken? Are there written procedures? Who is responsible for these activities?

Requirement	Description	Mapped Standard(s)	Implementation	Identification Steps
Security process management	Creation, administration, and oversight of policies to ensure the prevention, detection, containment, and correction of security breaches involving risk analysis and risk management. It includes the establishment of accountability, management controls (policies and education), electronic controls, physical security, and penalties for the abuse and misuse of its assets (both physical and electronic).	12, 17, 47, and 53	Risk analysis	Are security risk analyses performed? If so, what is taken into account? How often are they done? Who performs these analyses? Are there written procedures? Who is responsible for these activities?
	Process of assessing risk, taking steps to reduce risk to an acceptable level, and maintaining that level of risk.	17 and 47	Risk management	If a risk analysis is done, what is done with the resulting information? What steps are taken to ensure an acceptable risk level? Who is responsible for risk management? How often is this approached? Are there supporting documents and procedures?

(continued)

Table C-2 Administrative Procedures to Guard Data Integrity, Confidentiality, and Availability (continued)

Requirement	Description	Mapped Standard(s)	Implementation	Identification Steps
Security process management (cont.)	Statements regarding disciplinary actions that are communicated to all employees, agents, and contractors: for example, verbal warning, notice of disciplinary action placed in personnel files, removal of system privileges, termination of employment, and contract penalties. They must include employee, agent, and contractor notice of civil or criminal penalties for misuse or misappropriation of health information and must make employees, agents, and contractors aware that violations may result in notification to law enforcement officials and regulatory, accreditation, and licensure organizations.	12, 17, 47, and 53	Sanction policy	Do all employees know what actions are expected of them and the consequences of noncompliance? How is this information disseminated? Who is responsible for this policy? Do the employees sign any contracts? What level of protection does this provide? Are there written procedures? Who is responsible for these activities?
	Statement(s) of information values, protection responsibilities, and organization commitment for a system. This is the framework within which an entity establishes the necessary levels of information security to achieve the desired confidentiality goals.	17, 47, and 53	Security policy	Does the organization have an overall security policy? If so, what does it cover? How often is it updated? Are there supporting security policies? Are there written procedures? Who is responsible for these activities?

Requirement	Description	Mapped Standard(s)	Implementation	Identification Steps
Termination procedures	Formal documented instructions, which include appropriate security measures, for the ending of an employee's employment or an internal/external user's access.	12 and 17	Combination locks changed	What steps are taken when an employee is terminated? Are these procedures documented and enforced? Who is responsible for these activities?
	Physical eradication of an entity's access privileges and removal of user account(s).	12, 17, 47, and 53	Removal from access lists	When an employee is terminated, is her access removed from all network resources? Are the accounts deleted? Who is responsible for these activities?
	Termination or deletion of an individual's access privileges to the information, services, and resources for which he currently has clearance, authorization, and the need-to-know when such clearance, authorization, and need-to-know no longer exist.	12, 17, and 47	Removal of user account(s)	When an employee is terminated, are the corresponding accounts disabled or deleted? Are all privileges and permissions ended properly? Who is responsible for this?
	Formal, documented procedure to ensure all physical items that enable a terminated employee to access a property, building, or equipment are retrieved from that employee, preferably before termination.	12, 17, and 47	Turn in of keys, token, or cards that provide access	When an employee is terminated, are his keys, swipe cards, and physical access mechanisms returned? Are there procedures for these activities? Who is responsible for this?

(continued)

Table C-2 Administrative Procedures to Guard Data Integrity, Confidentiality, and Availability *(continued)*

Requirement	Description	Mapped Standard(s)	Implementation	Identification Steps
Training	Education concerning the vulnerabilities of the health information in an entity's possession and ways to ensure the protection of that information.	12, 17, 18, 47, and 53	Awareness training for all personnel (including management)	Is informational handling training performed? If so, how often? What is covered? Who is responsible for these training sessions?
	Employees, agents, and contractors are made aware of security concerns on an ongoing basis.	12 and 18	Periodic security reminders	How are employees reminded of security awareness issues? Are there written procedures? Who is responsible for these activities?
	Training in the user's responsibility to ensure the security of healthcare information.	12, 17, and 18	User education about the importance of monitoring login success/failure and how to report discrepancies	How would an employee report identify discrepancies in medical information and how it is handled? Are the procedures for these processes?
	Type of user training in the rules to be followed in creating and changing passwords and the need to keep them confidential.	12, 18, and 47	User education in password management	Do the employees know the password management policy? How is this enforced? Are there written procedures? Who is responsible for these activities?

Table C-3 Physical Safeguards to Guard Data Integrity, Confidentiality, and Availability

Requirement	Description	Mapped Standard(s)	Implementation	Identification Steps
Assigned security responsibility	Practices established by management to manage and supervise the execution and use of security measures to protect data and to manage and supervise the conduct of personnel in relation to the protection of data.	47	Security management and enforcement	How is security monitored? How is it enforced? How are security practices monitored? Who is responsible for these activities?
Media controls	Formal, documented policies and procedures that govern the receipt and removal of hardware/software (such as diskettes and tapes) into and out of a facility.	17, 47, and 53	Access control	Is hardware and software monitored as it enters and leaves the building? Are there procedures for this? Who is responsible for these activities?
	The property that ensures that the actions of an entity can be traced uniquely to that entity.	17, 18, and 47	Accountability (tracking mechanism)	How are individuals held accountable for their actions? How are users identified? How are actions monitored? How is accountability enforced?
	A retrievable, exact copy of information.	12, 17, 47, and 53	Data backup	Review and evaluate the data backup procedures, schedule time lines, and document procedures. What data is backed up? Where is it backed up to? How often is it backed up? Are there off-site facilities that hold copies? Is there a fireproof safe? Are there written procedures? Who is responsible for these activities?

(continued)

Table C-3 Physical Safeguards to Guard Data Integrity, Confidentiality, and Availability *(continued)*

Requirement	Description	Mapped Standard(s)	Implementation	Identification Steps
Media controls *(cont.)*	The retention of healthcare information pertaining to an individual in an electronic format.	12, 17, and 47	Data storage	How is medical information stored? How it is protected? Is it mirrored and/or backed up? Are there written procedures? Who is responsible for these activities?
	Final disposition of electronic data, and/or the hardware on which electronic data is stored.	17, 47, and 53	Disposal	How is data disposed of? Is the information properly destroyed? What are the procedures? Who is responsible for these activities?
Physical access controls (limited access)	Formal, documented policies and procedures to be followed to limit physical access to an entity while ensuring that properly authorized access is allowed.	17	Disaster recovery	What is the process enabling an entity to restore any loss of data in the event of fire, vandalism, natural disaster, or system failure? Are there written procedures? Who is responsible for these activities?
	Access controls in place that enable an entity to continue to operate in the event of fire, vandalism, natural disaster, or system failure.	17	Emergency mode operation	Review and evaluate emergency mode procedures and reaction plans. What happens right after a disaster? Who can access what information right after a disaster? What is put in place to verify that these functions are operational? Are there written procedures? Who is responsible for these activities?

Requirement	Description	Mapped Standard(s)	Implementation	Identification Steps
	Documented security procedures for bringing hardware and software into and out of a facility and for maintaining a record of that equipment. This includes, but is not limited to, the marking, handling, and disposal of hardware and storage media.	17 and 47	Equipment control (into and out of site)	Is hardware and software monitored as it enters and leaves the building? Are there procedures for this? Who is responsible for these activities?
	A plan to safeguard the premises and building (exterior and interior) from unauthorized physical access and to safeguard the equipment therein from unauthorized physical access, tampering, and theft.	12, 17, and 47	Facility security plan	What are the security mechanisms in place to protect the facility from undesirable activities? How is the equipment protected? How are these activities monitored? Who is responsible for these activities?
	Formal, documented policies and instructions for validating the access privileges of an entity before granting those privileges.	17, 18, and 47	Procedures for verifying access authorizations prior to physical access	What are the facts verified before allowing an entity into the facility? How is this enforced? Are there written procedures? Who is responsible for these activities?
	Documentation of repairs and modifications to the physical components of a facility, such as hardware, software, walls, doors, and locks.	17	Maintenance records	When equipment is repaired, are these activities documented and maintained? Are any modifications to hardware, software, or to the facility tracked? Are there written procedures? Who is responsible for these activities?

(continued)

Table C-3 Physical Safeguards to Guard Data Integrity, Confidentiality, and Availability *(continued)*

Requirement	Description	Mapped Standard(s)	Implementation	Identification Steps
Physical access controls *(cont.)*	A security principle stating that a user should have access only to the data he or she needs to perform a particular function.	12, 17, 47, and 53	Need-to-know procedures for personnel access	How is it determined who has what access to information? What are the levels of access and how do the levels correlate their job functionality? How is this enforced? Are there written procedures? Who is responsible for these activities?
	Formal documented procedure governing the reception and hosting of visitors.	17	Sign-in for visitors and escort, if appropriate	Do visitors have to sign in prior to entering the facility? Are they escorted through any areas? Are there written procedures? Who is responsible for these activities?
	The restriction of program testing and revision to formally authorized personnel.	17 and 47	Testing and revision	When application or hardware testing and revisions need to happen, how is it ensured that the proper people are doing this? Are there written procedures? Who is responsible for these activities?
Policy/guideline on workstation use	Documented instructions/procedures delineating the proper functions to be performed, the manner in which those functions are to be performed, and the physical attributes of the surroundings of a specific computer terminal site or type of site, dependent upon the sensitivity of the information accessed from that site.	18	Sensitive information procedures	How are different areas within the environment delineated pertaining to the different information it holds? How are the sensitivity levels determined and enforced? Are there written procedures? Who is responsible for these activities?

Requirement	Description	Mapped Standard(s)	Implementation	Identification Steps
Secure workstation location	Physical safeguards to eliminate or minimize the possibility of unauthorized access to information: for example, locating a terminal used to access sensitive information in a locked room and restricting access to that room to authorized personnel and not placing a terminal used to access patient information in any area of a doctor's office where the screen contents can be viewed from the reception area.	17 and 53	Computer placement	Are computers that hold medical information physically protected from unauthorized access? How are they protected? Are there different levels of sensitivity pertaining to information content? Are there written procedures? Who is responsible for these activities?
Security awareness training	Information security awareness training programs in which all employees, agents, and contractors must participate, including, based on job responsibilities, customized education programs that focus on issues regarding use of health information and responsibilities regarding confidentiality and security.	12, 17, and 47		Review previous security awareness activities, scheduled events, literature, and documentation. Do all employees receive security awareness training? How often? What is taught in this training? Are there written procedures? Who is responsible for these activities?

Table C-4 Technical Security Services to Guard Data Integrity, Confidentiality, and Availability

Requirement	Description	Mapped Standard(s)	Implementation	Identification Steps
Access control	An access control procedure based on the context of a transaction (as opposed to being based on attributes of the initiator or target).	5, 12, 14, 16, 17, 40, and 47	Context-based access	What security mechanisms are in place to provide software access control? How are these monitored and audited? Are there written procedures? Who is responsible for these activities?
	Transforming confidential plaintext into ciphertext to protect it. Also called encipherment. An encryption algorithm combines plaintext with other values called keys, or ciphers, so the data becomes unintelligible. Once encrypted, data can be stored or transmitted over unsecured lines.	1, 6, 12, 14, 17, 21, 22, 23, 24, 26, 36, 28, 29, 30, 31, 47, 49, 53, 54, and 55	Encryption	What encryption mechanisms are in place? Where are they implemented? What data is being encrypted? Are there written procedures? Who is responsible for these activities?
	A procedure for emergency access. Documented instructions for obtaining necessary information during a crisis.	14, 17, and 53	Procedure for emergency access	How is it ensured that necessary entities can access specific information in a crisis? How is this tested? Are there written procedures? Who is responsible for these activities?

Requirement	Description	Mapped Standard (s)	Implementation	Identification Steps
	Role-based access control (RBAC) is an alternative to traditional access control models (for example, discretionary or nondiscretionary access control policies) that permits the specification and enforcement of enterprise-specific security policies in a way that maps more naturally to an organization's structure and business activities. With RBAC, rather than attempting to map an organization's security policy to a relatively low-level set of technical controls (typically access control lists), each user is assigned to one or more predefined roles, each of which has been assigned the various privileges needed to perform that role.	14, 16, 17, 40, 41, 47, and 53	Role-based access	Is role-based access control implemented? How is it implemented? What are the definitions of the roles? Are there written procedures? Who is responsible for these activities?
	A security mechanism used to grant users of a system access based upon the identity of the user.	11, 12, 14, 16, 17, 40, 41, 47, and 53	User-based access	Is user-based access control implemented? How is it implemented? How are users identified? Are there written procedures? Who is responsible for these activities?
Audit controls	The mechanisms employed to record and examine system activity.	12, 14, 18, 47, and 53	Audit logs	What activities are audited? How are they audited? Are these audit logs monitored? If so, how often? How long are the audit logs kept? How are they protected? Are there written procedures? Who is responsible for these activities?

(continued)

895

Table C-4 Technical Security Services to Guard Data Integrity, Confidentiality, and Availability *(continued)*

Requirement	Description	Mapped Standard (s)	Implementation	Identification Steps
Data authentication	The corroboration that data has not been altered or destroyed in an unauthorized manner. Examples of how data corroboration may be ensured include the use of a checksum, double keying, a message authentication code, or digital signature.	14, 16, 17, 18, 40, and 53	Automatic log off	Is there a security procedure that causes an electronic session to terminate after a predetermined time of inactivity, such as 15 minutes? Are there written procedures? Who is responsible for these activities?
	An identification system that identifies a human from a measurement of a physical feature or repeatable action of the individual (for example, hand geometry, retinal scan, iris scan, fingerprint patterns, facial characteristics, DNA sequence characteristics, voiceprints, and handwritten signature).	14, 16, 18, 40, 47, and 53	Biometrics	Is there any type of biometric access controls in place? If so, what type? What is it checking for? How is the biometric system used? Are there written procedures? Who is responsible for these activities?
	Confidential authentication information composed of a string of characters.	14, 16, 17, 18, 19, 40, 47, and 53	Password	Are passwords used? Is there password management in place? What are the password requirements? How is it enforced? Are there written procedures? Who is responsible for these activities?
	A number or code assigned to an individual and used to provide verification of identity.	14, 16, 18, 19, 40, and 47	PIN	Are PINs used? Is there PIN management in place? What are the PIN requirements? How is it enforced? Are there written procedures? Who is responsible for these activities?

Requirement	Description	Mapped Standard (s)	Implementation	Identification Steps
	Method of authenticating the identity of the receiver and sender of information through a series of questions and answers sent back and forth establishing the identity of each.	14, 17, 18, 47, and 53	Telephone callback	Is a callback function used? Is there callback management in place? What are the callback requirements? How is it enforced? Are there written procedures? Who is responsible for these activities?
	A physical item that's used to provide identity. Typically, this is an electronic device that can be inserted in a door or a computer system to obtain access.	14, 17, 47, 50, and 53	Token	Are tokens used? Is there token management in place? What are the token requirements? How is this enforced? Are there written procedures? Who is responsible for these activities?
Authorization control	Role-based access control (RBAC) is an alternative to traditional access control models (for example, discretionary or nondiscretionary access control policies) that permits the specification and enforcement of enterprise-specific security policies in a way that maps more naturally to an organization's structure and business activities. With RBAC, rather than attempting to map an organization's security policy to a relatively low-level set of technical controls (typically, access control lists), each user is assigned to one or more predefined roles, each of which has been assigned the various privileges needed to perform that role.	5, 14, 16, 17, 47, and 53	Role-based access	Is role-based access control implemented? How is it implemented? What are the definitions of the roles? Are there written procedures? Who is responsible for these activities?

(continued)

Table C-4   Technical Security Services to Guard Data Integrity, Confidentiality, and Availability (*continued*)

Requirement	Description	Mapped Standard (s)	Implementation	Identification Steps
Authorization control (*cont.*)	A security mechanism used to grant users of a system access based upon the identity of the user.	14, 16, 47, and 53	User-based access	Is user-based access control implemented? How is it implemented? How are users identified? Are there written procedures? Who is responsible for these activities?

Table C-5 Technical Security Services to Guard Data Integrity, Confidentiality, and Availability

Mapped Requirement	Description	Identification Standard (s)	Implementation	Steps
Communications/ network controls		14, 17, 22, 23, 39, 47, 48, and 53	Access controls	What type of access control mechanisms are used for network communication? Are there written procedures? Who is responsible for these activities?
	In communication systems, any device that can sense an abnormal condition within the system and provide, either locally or remotely, a signal indicating the presence of the abnormality. The signal may be in any desired form ranging from a simple contact closure (or opening) to a time-phased automatic shutdown and restart cycle.	14, 17, 18, 35, 36, 37, 38, and 44	Alarm, event reporting, and audit trail	Is data collected and potentially used to facilitate a security audit? What types of alarms are configured? What types of audits are performed? How are events reported? Are there written procedures? Who is responsible for these activities?
	Transforming confidential plaintext into ciphertext to protect it. Also called encipherment. An encryption algorithm combines plaintext with other values called keys, or ciphers, so the data becomes unintelligible. Once encrypted, data can be stored or transmitted over unsecured lines.	1, 6, 12, 14, 17, 21, 22, 23, 24, 26, 27, 28, 29, 30, 31, 47, 49, 52, and 53	Encryption	What encryption mechanisms are in place? Where are they implemented? What data is being encrypted? Are there written procedures? Who is responsible for these activities?
	A communications or network mechanism to irrefutably identify authorized users, programs, and processes and to deny access to unauthorized users, programs, and processes.	12, 14, 17, 18, 20, 22, 23, 31, 32, 34, 33, 51, and 53	Entity authentication	How are users authenticated for network communication? Are there written procedures? Who is responsible for these activities?

(continued)

Table C-5 Technical Security Services to Guard Data Integrity, Confidentiality, and Availability *(continued)*

Requirement	Description	Mapped Standard(s)	Implementation	Identification Steps
Communications/ network controls (cont.)	A security mechanism employed to ensure the validity of the information being electronically transmitted or stored.	14, 15, 17, 18, 22, 23, 45, and 46	Integrity controls	How is data integrity ensured? What technology is in place to monitor data integrity? What data is monitored for integrity? Are there written procedures? Who is responsible for these activities?
	Ensuring, typically with a message authentication code, that a message received (usually via a network) matches the message sent.	14, 15, 17, 18, 22, 23, 25, 45, 46, and 52	Message authentication	Are there message authentication mechanisms in place? Where are they placed? What technology is used? Are there written procedures? Who is responsible for these activities?

Table C-6 Electronic Signature

Requirement	Description	Mapped Standard(s)	Implementation	Identification Steps
Digital signature (If digital signature computed by using a following three implementation features must be implemented: • Message integrity • Nonrepudiation • User authentication Other implementation features are optional.)	An electronic signature based upon cryptographic methods of originator are they used for? What security set of rules and a set of parameters such that the identity of the signer and the integrity of the data can be verified (FDA electronic record; electronic signatures; final rule).	3, 4, 10, 11, 13, and 20	Ability to add attributes	Are digital signatures used? What is employed, the authentication, services do they provide? Attributes are possible capabilities of a digital signature technology: for example, the capability to add a timestamp as part of a digital signature. What attributes are used with these digital signatures? Are there written procedures? Who is responsible for these activities?
	The attribute that is affixed to an electronic document to bind it to a particular entity. An electronic signature process secures the user authentication (proof of claimed identity, such as by biometrics such as fingerprints, retinal scans, handwritten signature verification, and so on, tokens or passwords) at the time the signature is generated. It creates the logical manifestation of signature (including the possibility for multiple parties to sign a document and have the order of application recognized and proven) and supplies additional information such as a timestamp and signature purpose specific to that user. It also ensures the integrity of the signed document to enable transportability, interoperability, independent verifiability, and continuity of signature capability. Verifying a signature on a document verifies the integrity of the document and associated attributes and verifies the identity of the signer.	3, 4, 11, 13, 14, and 18	Continuity of signature capability	The public verification of a signature will not compromise the signer's ability to apply additional secure signatures at a later date. Can a signer apply a secure signature at a later date? How is this configured? Are there written procedures? Who is responsible for these activities?

901

(continued)

Table C-6 Electronic Signature (continued)

Requirement	Description	Mapped Standard(s)	Implementation	Identification Steps
Digital signature (cont.)	It will be possible to prove the order of application of signatures. This is analogous to the normal business practice of countersignatures, where one party signs a document that has already been signed by another party.	3, 4, 10, 11, 13, 14, and 18	Countersignature	Are countersignatures allowed? How are the different signatures differentiated? How is this configured? Are there written procedures? Who is responsible for these activities?
	The capability to verify the signature without the cooperation of the signer. Technically, it is accomplished using the public key of the signatory, and it is a property of all digital signatures performed with asymmetric key encryption.	3, 4, 11, 13, and 20	Independent verifiability	How is independent verifiability ensured? What mechanism provides this functionality? How is it configured? Are there written procedures? Who is responsible for these activities?
	The applications used on either side of a communication, between trading partners and/or between internal components of an entity and being able to read and correctly interpret the information communicated from one to the other.	3, 4, 7, 8, 9, 13, 14, and 48	Interoperability	What interoperability issues exist between different applications? What interoperability issues exist between different partners? How are these issues dealt with? Are there written procedures? Who is responsible for these activities?
	The assurance of unaltered transmission and the receipt of a message from the sender to the intended recipient.	3, 4, 10, 11, 13, 14, and 18	Message integrity	How is message integrity ensured? What technology and mechanisms are used? How is this configured? Are there written procedures? Who is respon-

902

Requirement	Description	Mapped Standard(s)	Implementation	Identification Steps
	It will be possible for multiple parties to sign a document. Multiple signatures are conceptually and simply appended to the document.	3, 4, 10, 11, 13, and 20	Multiple signatures	Is multiple signature functionality available? What technology and mechanism is used for this? How is it configured? Are there written procedures? Who is responsible for these activities?
	Strong and substantial evidence of the identity of the signer of a message and of message integrity, sufficient to prevent a party from successfully denying the origin, submission, or delivery of the message and the integrity of its contents.	2, 3, 4, 10, 11, 13, 14, and 42,	Nonrepudiation	Is nonrepudiation functionality available? What technology and mechanism is used for this? How is it configured? Are there written procedures? Who is responsible for these activities?
	A signed document can be transported (over an insecure network) to another system, while maintaining the integrity of the document.	3, 4, 11, 13, 14, and 18	Transportability	How are messages transmitted over an insecure network? How is the message integrity ensured? What technology and mechanism is used for this? How is it configured? Are there written procedures? Who is responsible for these activities?
	The provision of assurance of the claimed identity of an entity.	3, 4, 10, 11, 13, and 20	User authentication	How are users authenticated when using electronic signatures? What technology and mechanism is used for this? How is it configured? Are there written procedures? Who is responsible for these activities?

IEEE Standards

1. ANSI X3.92 Data Encryption Standard

2. ANSI X9.30 Part 1: Public Key Cryptography Using Irreversible Algorithms: Digital Signature Algorithm

3. ANSI X9.30 Part 2: Public Key Cryptography Using Irreversible Algorithms: Secure Hash Algorithm (SHA-1)

4. ANSI X9.31 Reversible Digital Signature Algorithms

5. ANSI X9.45 Enhanced Management Controls Using Digital Signatures and Attribute Certificates

6. ANSI X9.52 Triple DES Modes of Operation

7. ANSI X9.55 Extensions to Public Key Certificates and CRLs

8. ANSI X9.57 Certificate Management

9. ANSI X9.62 Elliptic Curve Digital Signature Algorithm (draft)

10. ANSI X12.58 Security Structures (version 2)

11. ASTM E 1762 Standard Guide for Authentication of Healthcare Information

12. ASTM E 1869 Draft Standard for Confidentiality, Privacy, Access, and Data Security Principles

13. ASTM PS 100-97 Standard Specification for Authentication of Healthcare Information Using Digital Signatures

14. ASTM PS 101-97 Security Framework for Healthcare Information

15. ASTM PS 102-97 Standard Guide for Internet and Intranet Security

16. ASTM PS 103-97 Authentication and Authorization Guideline

17. CEN European Prestandard

18. FDA Electronic Records—Electronic Signatures—Final Rule

19. FIPS PUB 112 Password Usage

20. FIPS PUB 196 Entity Authentication Using Public Key Cryptography

21. FIPS PUB 46-2 Data Encryption Standard

22. IEEE 802.10: Interoperable LAN/MAN Security (SILS), 1992–1996 (multiple parts)

23. IEEE 802.10c LAN/WAN Security-Key Management

24. IETF ID Combined SSL/PCT Transport Layer Security Protocol

25. IETF ID FTP Authentication Using DSA

26. IETF ID Secure Hypertext Transfer Protocol (S-HTTP)

27. IETF ID SMIME Cert Handling

28. IETF ID SMIME Message Specification

29. IETF RFC 1422 Privacy Enhanced Mail: Part 1: Message Encryption and Authentication Procedures

30. IETF RFC 1424 Privacy Enhanced Mail: Part 2: Certificate-Based Key Management

31. IETF RFC 1423 Privacy Enhanced Mail: Part 3: Algorithms, Modes, and Identifiers

32. ISO/IEC 9798-1: Information Technology—Security Techniques—Entity Authentication Mechanisms—Part 1: General Model

33. ISO/IEC 9798-2: Information Technology—Security Techniques—Entity Authentication Mechanisms—Part 2: Entity Authentication Using Asymmetric Techniques

34. ISO/IEC 9798-2: Information Technology—Security Techniques—Entity Authentication Mechanisms—Part 2: Entity Authentication Using Symmetric Techniques

35. ISO/IEC 10164-4 Information Technology—Open Systems Connection—System Management: Alarm Reporting Function

36. ISO/IEC 10164-5 Information Technology—Open Systems Connection—System Management: Event Report Management Function

37. ISO/IEC 10164-7 Information Technology—Open Systems Connection—System Management: Security Alarm Reporting Function

38. ISO/IEC 10164-8 Information Technology—Open Systems Connection—System Management: Security Audit Trail Function

39. ISO/IEC 10164-9 Information Technology—Open Systems Connection—System Management: Objects and Attributes for Access Control

40. ISO/IEC 10181-2 Information Technology—Security Frameworks in Open Systems—Authentication Framework

41. ISO/IEC 10181-3 Information Technology—Security Frameworks in Open Systems—Access Control Framework

42. ISO/IEC 10181-4 Information Technology—Security Frameworks in Open Systems—Nonrepudiation Framework

43. ISO/IEC 10181-5 Information Technology—Security Frameworks in Open Systems—Confidentiality Framework

44. ISO/IEC 10181-7 Information Technology—Security Frameworks in Open Systems—Security Audit Framework

45. ISO/IEC 10736 Information Technology—Telecommunications and Information Exchange Between Systems—Transport Layer Security Protocol (TLSP)

46. ISO/IEC 11577 Information Technology—Telecommunications and Information Exchange Between Systems—Network Layer Security Protocol (NLSP)

47. NIST Generally Accepted Principles and Practices for Secure Information Technology Systems

48. NIST MISPC Minimum Interoperability Specification for PKI Components Version 1

49. PKCS #7 Cryptographic Message Syntax Standard Version 1.5 or later

50. PKCS #11 Cryptoki B A Cryptographic Token Interface

51. RFC 1510 Kerberos Authentication Service

52. RFC 2104 HMAC: Keyed-Hashing for Message Authentication

53. For the Record—Protecting Electronic Health Information

54. ANSI X9.42 Management of Symmetric Keys Using Diffie-Hellman

55. ANSI X9.44 Key Transport Using RSA

References

www.aspe.os.dhhs.gov/admnsimp/nprm/pvclist.htm

www.hcfa.gov/hipaa/hipaahm.htm

www.ahima.org/journal/features/feature.9910.1.html

www.wedi.org/public/articles/HSSGuidelines.doc

www.hipaadvisory.com/views/Patient/myths.htm

Gramm Leach Bliley Act

The Gramm Leach Bliley act was signed into law by President Clinton on November 12, 1999. The act applies to all national banks and federal branches of foreign banks that are subject to the supervision of the Federal Reserve System, Office of Thrift Supervision (OTS), Comptroller of the Currency (OCC), or Federal Deposit Insurance Corporation (FDIC). The act's main goal is to protect individual private information. Subsidiaries need to implement their own security program or be part of a program that covers the main financial institution and its subsidiaries.

It requires a financial institution to develop privacy notices that must be given to each of its customers. The privacy notice gives the customer the option of prohibiting the bank from sharing his information with any nonaffiliated third-party organization. It also requires each financial institution to have a comprehensive information security program in place by July 1, 2001.

The act has several pieces to it and the one that is directly related to information security is Title V, section 502, referred to as "Obligations with Respect to Disclosures of Personal Information." This section mandates financial institutions to implement "administrative, technical, and physical safeguards" for their customers' personal information. The safeguards have three main objectives:

- Provide the necessary level of protection to ensure confidentiality of customer records and information.

- Protect information from threats.

- Protect against unauthorized access that would result in substantial harm or inconvenience to the customer.

The act basically forces financial institutions to have security programs that they really should have had in the first place. A good security program only helps the institution and its customers, but now that it is federally mandated. Developing and maintaining the security program will have a new benefit—keeping out of trouble with the Fed.

Security Program Components

The act states that customer "nonpublic personally identifiable information" needs to be protected, which is financial information that is not available publicly. Public information would be the customer's name, address, and phone number and nonpublic information would be the customer's bank account information, balances, loan data, and overdraft information.

Responsibility

The board of directors is responsible for approving the security policy and the security program that the financial institution develops. They must also oversee its implementation and maintenance to ensure that it is kept up-to-date and accurate. Many times the board of directors will assign some of this responsibility to the appropriate committee. Management must provide a written report of the information security program to the board of directors and appropriate appointed committees.

Risk Management

The risks and threats that can affect the confidentiality of customers' information must be assessed by each financial institution. Potential threats have to be identified and countermeasures should be put into place to ensure that customer information cannot be accessed in an unauthorized method. This includes access control, safeguards to protect the data while it is being transmitted, and physically protecting it within the facility. The monitoring of activities involved with the use of customer information, auditing, incident handling, and disaster recovery all have to be addressed, and proper procedures should be developed to ensure that customers' information is protected under all perceivable situations.

Training

The act requires all employees to be properly trained in security training by attending a security awareness class. This helps to protect customer information and also strengthens the security within the organization overall.

Test Security Measures

Financial institutions must test their security procedures and controls regularly to ensure their effectiveness. The institution has some flexibility on how often to test these measures, mainly because some environments are more complex than others and therefore require more regular testing.

Service Provider

The financial institutions are responsible for their customer information even if it is held at a service provider's facility. It is the responsibility of the financial institution to determine and ensure that their service provider has the necessary security controls implemented. This requires due diligence on the institution's part because they will need to properly select and monitor the service provider they employ.

Disclosing Procedures

Financial institutions must disclose their security policies and practices, which indicates how they protect their customers' data.

Responding to Incidents

The act requires that all intrusions be reported on the interagency Suspicious Activity Report, which is the form used to report credit card fraud, counterfeit money, money laundering, and other suspicious activities.

Summary

The Gramm Leach Bliley act provides general requirements for how customer information should be protected and emphasizes the importance of privacy. There are not many specifics, however, and the act does not delve as much into the security of the institution as a whole. Although this is an important and useful first step in protecting consumers' private information, many security professionals see this as only a first step. There are many security issues that pertain to a financial institution and how it protects bank accounts, transfers funds, deals with internal and external threats, and how it audits, logs, and monitors activity. These issues only get more complex when financial institutions offer their customers online banking services and eventually allow their customers to access accounts via wireless mobile devices.

References

www.fdic.gov/news/financial/2001/fil0103a.html

www.senate.gov/~banking/conf

www.ftc.gov/privacy/glbact

www.privacyheadquarters.com/glb/a_safeguard.html

Various Networking Components

Ethernet

Ethernet is defined by the following characteristics:

- Shared media—all devices must take turns using the same media and detect collisions.
- Uses broadcast and collision domains.
- Uses carrier sense multiple access collision detection access (CSMA/CD) method.
- Supports full-duplex on twisted-pair implementations.
- Can use coaxial or twisted-pair media.

There are a number of Ethernet IEEE 802.3 adaptations.

Ethernet 10 Mbps

- 10Base-2—ThinNet
  - Coaxial cable—RG-58 A/U
  - Maximum cable segment of 185 meters
  - Baseband transmission
- 10Base-5—ThickNet
  - Coaxial cable

- Maximum cable segment of 500 meters

- Baseband transmission

- 10Base-T

  - Twisted-pair cable, Category 3, 4, or 5

  - Maximum cable segment of 100 meters

  - RJ-45 jacks

- 10Base-FL

  - Fiber-optic cable backbones

  - Up to four kilometers of transmission

  - Approved for cross-connects between campus buildings

Fast Ethernet 100 Mbps—IEEE 802.3u

- 100Base-T4

  - Fast Ethernet over four pairs of Category 3, 4, or 5 unshielded twisted-pair (UTP) wires

  - Maximum distance of 100 meters between hub and computer

- 100Base-TX

  - Fast Ethernet over two pairs of Category 5 UTP or Category 1 STP

  - Maximum distance of 100 meters between hub and computer

- 100Base-FX

  - Fast Ethernet over fiber-optic cable

  - Cable runs of up to two kilometers

Gigabit Ethernet 1000 Mbps

- 1000Base-LX

  - Fiber-optic cable

  - Long-wavelength laser transmissions

  - Up to 550 meters over multimode fiber-optic cable

  - Up to 3,000 meters over single-mode fiber-optic cable

- 1000Base-SX

  - Fiber-optic cable

- Short-wavelength laser transmission
- Works over multimode fiber-optic cable
- <u>1000Base-CX</u>
  - High-data-rate twisted-pair cable
  - Used to connect devices over a short distance
  - Maximum distance of 25 meters
- <u>1000Base-T</u>
  - Four-pair Category 5 cable
  - Maximum distance of 100 meters per station to switch or 205 meters end to end

Fast Ethernet does use CSMA/CD and earlier Ethernet frame formats. Many implementations have subnets that work at 10 and 100 Mbps. The connecting hub must be autosensing to be able to properly negotiate between these different speeds.

Because Fast Ethernet provides much higher transmission speeds, the collision domains must be smaller to ensure an acceptable level of contention and collisions.

Table A-1 outlines the characteristics of different cables and Table A-2 indicates where different twisted-pair cables can be used.

Table A-1 Cable Characteristics

Type	Max Length	Bandwidth	Install	Interference	Cost
UTP	100 meters	10–100 Mbps	Easy	High	Cheapest
STP	100 meters	16–100 Mbps	Moderate	Moderate	Moderate
10Base2	185 meters	10 Mbps	Easy	Moderate	Cheap
10Base5	500 meters	10 Mbps	Hard	Low	Expensive
Fiber	2–100 km	100 Mbps–10 Gbps	Very Hard	None	Most expensive

Table A-2 Cable Types

Type	Standard Rating	Description
Type 1	STP	Two-pair 22 AWG wires with outer braided shield; connects computers and MAUs.
Type 2	Voice/data grade	Shielded cable; two-pair 22 AWG wires or data and four pair 26 WG for voice.

(continued)

Table A-2 Cable Types *(continued)*

Type	Standard Rating	Description
Type 3	Voice grade	Four UTP 22 or 24 AWG wires.
Type 4	Undefined	
Type 5	Fiber-optic	Two multimode optical fibers.
Type 6	Data patch	Two 26 AWG wires with dual foil and braided shield.
Type 7	Undefined	
Type 8	Carpet cable	Two STP 26 AWG; used to string wire under carpets because of its flat jacket.
Type 9	Plenum	Teflon-coated two STP AWG 22 pair with foil and braided shielding.

Ethernet Frames

Frame formats dictate the type of fields in a frame and the sequence of these fields. This controls how data is packaged into a frame and transmitted over a network.

- *Preamble*   This field contains the bit pattern 10101010, which indicates the beginning of a frame.

- *Start frame delimiter (SFD)*   This frame contains the bit pattern 10101011, which indicates the actual start of the frame itself.

- *Length of data field (LEN)*   This frame indicates how long the data portion is within the frame.

- *Cyclic redundancy check (CRC)*   The sender and receiver perform an algorithm that results in a CRC value. If the receiver calculates a different value than what was in the CRC value, the frame is considered corrupt.

Why Many Security Implementations Die in Motivation and End Up Half Baked

Many times system administrators start their security crusade with great intentions for the well being of their company's network. They have exceptional motivation, and a stack of new computer and infrastructure security books. Although this may be the necessary first step to get the network under control and running as tight and secure as a U.S. nuclear submarine, there are many unforeseen missteps and pitfalls waiting for the unexpected administrator.

Knowing about these missteps and pitfalls is the first line of defense to thwart them off and execute a healthy and successful security implementation.

Knowledge of All the Goblins and Ghouls Under the Bed

Before you can lock something down, you have to know what it is. You may successfully lock down the parts of the network you know intimately, but the less famous parts will be ignored and provide evildoers an inviting yellow brick road directly to the heart of your network.

So the first step is to update the dusty network diagram you made the last intern work on during his three-month stint in your group. This diagram should be a living document that reflects the current state of your network infrastructure. This blueprint will make your security implementation much smoother and will provide with you a guide when you are in the throws of the implementation process.

For security purposes, you want to emphasize every way into your network, every way out of your network, and how this information travels. Most administrators put 80 to 90 percent of their focus pertaining to the entrance into their network on their firewalls. Although firewalls are extremely important, need to be monitored and reconfigured at times, and can reduce a network's vulnerability by leaps and bounds, the four remote access server (RAS) modem connections and three modems your users have to access the Internet can give hackers an open door with a sign that says, "Goodies, this way."

You also want to identify the critical and most vulnerable systems in your environment. There is a twofold reason for this; you need to know which systems are most open to attack because of their importance and known vulnerabilities (DNS systems, Web servers, NT servers, and so on) and which systems are critical to your business' functionality (databases, data warehouses, and domain controllers) so they can be properly backed up in case your security rollout has undesirable backfires and effects.

There are several network discovery tools that can be used to find out this type of information. Be sure to identify any leased lines, analog lines, ISDN connections, RAS connections, lone modems, and Web servers within your perimeter and internal networks. Your company's phone bill should provide you a detailed list of used connections by location and type. To ferret out any modems and connections you still could not detect, run a wardialer against the network to point out any more modem, private branch exchange (PBX), and fax connections. This information can be used to fill in your network infrastructure diagram.

Kid in a Candy Store

Before you decide to throw every security product and implementation into your environment, take a step back and look at what it is you are trying to accomplish.

If you have a few servers, a couple of dial-up connections, and your business sells beads on the Internet, you do not need the same protection mechanisms that an organization that has the responsibility of monitoring the movement of Russian spy satellites.

Evaluate the needs and functionality of your organization, research the types of protection you can implement, and plan your rollout to be as transparent to the users and environment as possible.

Just like when cooking Italian food, you can always add more garlic and oregano later. Don't try to over do it by implementing too many things at once. If you are going to implement Secure Sockets Layer (SSL) in certain parts of your network, plan it, implement it, and let the network run for a couple of months before you decide to throw IPSec into the mix.

Step Lightly, But Don't Carry a Big Stick

At times, network administrators get stereotyped as computer-nazis and god-figures in their own mind. Little do users know that this is many times necessary when the administrators are continually asked and begged to extend compromising services that could hurt the environment and put their jobs at risk. In many organizations, the network administrator is looked to as an authoritative entity because she has the capabilities that other employees do not have and the power to enforce her decisions.

Although a computer-nazi stance is necessary at times, try to rethink this approach when you are planning and implementing your security policy. Security, by nature, restricts users' abilities and lays down rules and laws that are foreign to the previously unsecured environment. This change will not come with open arms and there will be a lack in willingness to make this change any easier on you to implement.

So the more people (management through basic users) you get to buy off on your ideas, the easier this already daunting task will be.

Do research into the current security industry, investigate and document your network's vulnerabilities, throw some pretty graphs together, and present this information to your management. Management is your most needed ally, because they provide you with the power to enforce necessary security standards and they will be the ones writing the checks for your necessary security purchases.

Have some demonstrations of the current vulnerabilities in the users' environment. Explain to them how their personal data is at risk, how the spreadsheets that hold all of their customer information can be deleted or modified, and how the company would be more effective and efficient if there were mechanisms in place to fight against hackers and evildoers.

If users buy into your story, they will be less willing to try and go around the controls you put in place. They will not feel like children being told what to do, but feel like adults that are part of the team and have the understanding that these steps are being done to help the company as a whole.

Sometimes We All Need a Little Help

Now that you have a better idea of your infrastructure, you have calmly assessed what needs to be protected and to what extent. And since you have won the admiration and respect of your coworkers and bosses pertaining to this subject, where do you begin your journey?

This could be an overwhelming question. Unfortunately, or fortunately, security is a complex subject. You need to know the types and degrees of access control, authorization, authentication, confidentiality, integrity, nonrepudiation, auditing, countermeasures, disaster recovery, legal liability, and current industry standards you now want to implement and enforce.

The next question would be how you want to implement the standards you have decided upon. Do you want to use SSL, TLS, IPSec, Kerebos, public key authentication, smart token cards, hardy password requirements, challenge-response authentication, firewalls, demilitarized zone (DMZ), secure routing, intrusion detection, telecommunication security mechanisms, and layered antiviral protection?

How do all of these play together nicely and not bring your network down to a grinding halt?

Daunting, yes. Doable, absolutely.

You may have an IT staff that can handle most or all of these issues. You may have the time and money to get individuals specialized training in different areas (Joe can be the firewall expert and Cindy can go to class on public key infrastructure [PKI] issues and public key implementations). Or you might want to call in individuals who live and breathe these issues so you can continue to keep up with all the daily printing problems, user password issues, backups and recoveries, and updating operating systems and service pack levels.

Summing It Up

You have a lot of choices on how you want to protect your environment. Before getting overwhelmed, do the necessary research, determine exactly what needs to be accomplished, bring others into your way of thinking, determine if you have the necessary skills in your staff, and decide if an outside security consultant can help you with specialized issues.

Many times network administrators just start implementing security without asking themselves all these important questions. This usually leads to partially implemented security, network disruption, unhappy management and users, and an administrator who worked a lot of hours with all the good intensions but was frowned upon in the end. In the long run, you could get very little security for a big price tag and a lot of frustration.

Do yourself and your company a favor by thinking through each step that needs to be taken. Security is not a 50-yard dash, but an ever-changing marathon that will last the life of your network. So make each step count.

Your Company's Rights versus Your Employees' Rights

Many computer trade and business magazines have stated several times that disgruntled employees and employee mistakes are the greatest threats when it comes to computer fraud, misuse, and destruction. However, it does not seem to raise enough red flags to individuals who hold top management positions, until they experience the same pain.

Misuse of computers and their connected resources does not necessarily need to be carried out with a malicious intent. Sometimes employees have the feeling that their work computers, e-mail accounts, and network resources are there to fulfill their business and personal needs. When this type of misuse causes business interruptions or turmoil, many times the company has not taken the proper steps to educate their employees on what is acceptable and not acceptable in the management's eyes, what each individual's responsibility is pertaining to computer use, and what the consequences are for certain actions. These items may seem like a waste of time and resources, but studies have shown that educated employees are less likely to abuse the equipment they use, and in the cases where abuse still continues, the company has a strong legal leg to stand on.

Many of these issues are new to organizations, so many companies look to consulting services to ensure that the proper steps are taken to protect the company legally from computer fraud and misuse, the laws and liability issues pertaining to the specific type of business and regional location are understood, the proper steps to educate employees are taken, and a balance exists between protecting the company and employee privacy rights.

Laws and Liability Issues

What applies to us and what do we need to be worried about?

If you are suspicious that an employee's intentions are malicious, if someone is improperly revealing confidential information, or if your company's proprietary trade secrets are being passed to the competition, can you read employees' e-mail messages that reside on your e-mail server to investigate?

The law has a hard time keeping up with technology and all the issues technology touches. This is understandable because it is hard to keep up with all the changes and advances in technology, not to mention governing and regulating how these changes are used and interact with society. So just because there is not a law written at this date stating that you can read your employee's e-mail while it sits on your mail server, you should properly position yourself for protection in case this type of monitoring is needed. The law can be gray and it is continually evolving.

The Computer Security Act of 1987 was a reaction to the continuous misuse of government resources by employees. The government takes such abuse seriously because of the potential impact on the security of the nation. Although one of your employees planting viruses or downloading inappropriate materials will probably not tip off the Soviet Union as to where the United States keeps its nuclear warheads, it could cause disruption to your network infrastructure, costing you time and resources to chase down the problem and fix it.

The Organization for Economic Cooperation and Development (OECD) consists of 29 member countries. Their purpose has to do with the market economy, pluralist democracy, and respect for human rights. This organization developed the Fair Information Practices, which are practices meant to encourage the fair handling of personal information and to provide a framework for privacy legislation throughout the world. This may seem too lofty and nonapplicable to your company, which does not fight for world democracy, does not drive the market economy, and is not striving for world peace for one and all, but don't be too sure.

There are several cases brought to the judicial courts that may surprise you with their outcomes and the legal precedents they have now set. A Canadian financial institution fired an employee because her password was used to wrongfully gain access to a bank account. The court ruled that the financial institution had no set password policy and because the computers were located close to each other, anyone could have used the employee's password. If this company had a security policy that outlined password requirements and employee education pertaining to their responsibility for their usernames and passwords, this ruling may of gone the other way. The employee was awarded punitive damages.

Companies have lost trade secrets to competitors because of employees. However, because the companies did not have a stated and known stance on what a trade secret was and how it should be protected, the companies ended up losing more than just their trade secrets.

In addition, some companies have found out that because they did not take the correct security precautions, their insurance companies charged them with contributing to injury and/or destruction of confidential data. So when one company had a natural disaster and looked to its insurance company for help in rebuilding, the insurance company showed in court how the company did not take the correct measures to protect itself. Thus, the insurance company was under no obligation to pay for damages.

What's the Answer?

Contacting consultant agencies that deal strictly with computer security and the laws that bound it would be a good first step. There are a lot of gray areas in these issues, and without all the proper facts and information, your organization could have a false sense of security pertaining to the coverage it has provided for itself when it comes to your employees' personal information.

When considering a consultant agency for this type of service, the following questions should be asked:

- What is your background in legal and liability issues pertaining to computer security?
- What is your service level of agreement pertaining to the correctness of the advice given?
- What type of experience do you have with writing company security policies, procedures, and standards?
- Have you ever had to prepare court documents, been involved with fraudulent investigations, or been called as a security expert witness in a trial?
- How exactly will the advice given protect my company and its employees?
- How often should my company look at reevaluating our legal and liability issues because this arena seems to be evolving at such a fast rate?
- Are you familiar with our specific type of business and region (because laws and liability expectations are different)?

- How do we inform management and our employees once this has been put into place?

- How do we properly handle security incidents and prosecute properly, if necessary?

- How will these issues affect our public relations and reputation?

- What is the cost of different types of security incidents?

Educate Your Employees

Who needs to know what?

Training is one of the last items on most managers' minds. It does not always show a direct link to profitability and therefore falls to the wayside a lot of the time. The training needs to be efficient and effective, and provide the level of security awareness and the necessary protection for the company and its employees.

Pertaining to computer fraud and misuse, training can help your company in several different ways. The consulting agency should provide you with detailed answers to the following questions:

- *How are the 'rights' and 'wrongs' presented?* Some employees do not realize it is wrong to spend hours at a time surfing the Web, exchanging inappropriate materials, bypassing security mechanisms, or altering certain preset configurations. Many times loss of information, data corruption, and wasted employee hours are done more out of ignorance than spite. Training needs to spell out all of these issues out to every employee.

- *How will consequences of noncompliance be explained and understood?* Once employees know what can happen to them if they participate in fraud or misuse, the likelihood of such actions is reduced drastically.

- *What is the legal protection for management and the company as a whole?* What specific actions need to take place to ensure management is abiding by all laws and regulations?

This training does not have to be extravagant and costly, and it does not need to happen every month. This training can be part of employee orientation and can be held once a year after the initial period. A good approach is to show them how their personal data could be vulnerable if everyone did not follow the same procedures. Explain how their work could be detrimentally affected if another person releases a virus, reduces network bandwidth, or brings a server down for a day or two. It is best to make these types of actions as personal as possible.

At the end of training, each employee should have to sign a document that lists all the ways computer fraud and misuse could take place. This document would also explicitly list the consequences for such actions, and provide a statement stating that the employee fully understands and promises to abide by the rules.

Although you might not be able to plug this type of training into a spreadsheet that reflects profitability peaks and falls, it is more of an intuitive benefit that will save you and your company in Information Technology (IT) staff time, company resources, litigation costs, and frustration.

Stop computer fraud, misuse, and abuse before they start.

Protect Your Company and Employees' Rights

These two concepts can easily compete against each other (company and employees' rights) if they are not thought out prior to implementation.

The time may come when you will need to read an employee's e-mail that is stored on your company's e-mail server because of suspicion of misdoings. Or an employee's hard drive might need to be scanned for downloaded pornographic material. If your company has not taken the proper steps to inform the employee that these actions fall under the rights of the company, your company can be charged with violating an individual's privacy rights. That would be a lose-lose situation for the company.

The most important element in computer security, which is really the issue we are discussing, is a clear and definitive security policy. A security policy is a document that states the management's intent pertaining to the use and abuse of the company's computer systems, and what should be done to protect them. This is a high-level overview that gets everyone (management members, IT staff, and employees) all on the same page. Without an explicit security policy, there can easily be confusion about what is or is not expected, who and how these expectations are to be carried out, and what the penalty is when these expectations are not met.

Once the well thought out security policy is drafted and put into place, standards, guidelines, and procedures are developed and derived directly from this policy. They have a hierarchical relationship. The policy is the general synopsis of the management's vision of what type of role security should play in the organization. Standards are mandatory activities and rules to give the policy support, structure, and meaning. Guidelines are general statements that provide the IT staff a framework to work from when unforeseen circumstances arise. Procedures are detailed steps used to spell out how the policy, standards, and guidelines will actually be implemented in an operating environment.

A consulting agency that deals with company protection and personal information relies on putting all of these tools into place. The agency should be expected to interview a representative from the IT, human resource, legal, and management departments to properly understand the unique needs and culture of your company. Current policies, procedures, standards, security incidents, and suspicious activity should be reviewed in detail to ensure that the proper protection mechanisms are implemented for your specific company and its needs.

Summary

Having the most current and relative information pertaining to laws that protect individuals' privacy and the laws that protect businesses from this type of litigation is key to finding your company's vulnerabilities. Finding out where your company's liability issues begin and end pertaining to personnel, privacy, and information and resource abuse is a specialized skill and you may very well need help with these tasks. The agency you choose to work with should provide you with all the answers to your questions, promise an acceptable level of risk, and be readily available even after the check has been cut and signed.

The agency should aid in educating all parties that are involved. Management, IT staff, and each and every employee should understand the company's position on security and the repercussions of noncompliance. This knowledge will battle ignorance, and many times ignorance is a bigger adversary than hackers and evildoers.

Protect your company by posting this information, making it easily accessible, and providing a paper trail in case of litigation proceedings. When a user logs onto his workstation, a legal banner should pop up on the screen prior to logging into the domain warning of consequences of network abuse and misuse. Employees should sign a document indicating that they understand the contents of the security policy and standards expected of them.

With these items taken care of, your company's environment will prove to be less prone to data corruption, resource misuse, and malicious activities. If these actions do take place, you are protected and so is your company.

GLOSSARY

A

access   A subject's ability to view, modify, or communicate with an object. Access enables the flow of information between the subject and the object.

access control   Mechanisms, controls, and methods of limiting access to resources only to authorized subjects.

access control list (ACL)   A list of subjects that are authorized to access a particular object. Typically, the types of access are read, write, execute, append, modify, delete, and create.

access control mechanism   Administrative, physical, and technical controls that are designed to detect and prevent unauthorized access to a resource or environment.

access level   The security level dictates the access level, which is determined by the clearance of the subject and the classification or sensitivity of the data.

accountability   A security principle indicating that individuals must be able to be identified and are to be held responsible for their actions.

accreditation   A computer system or network that has received official authorization and approval to process sensitive data in a specific operational environment. There must be a security evaluation of the system's hardware, software, configurations, and controls by technical personnel.

add-on security   Security protection mechanisms that are hardware or software retrofitted to a system to increase that system's protection level.

administrative controls   These controls include the development and publication of policies, standards, procedures, and guidelines, the screening of personnel, security awareness training, the monitoring of system activity, and change control procedures.

annualized loss expectancy (ALE)   A dollar amount that estimates the loss potential from a risk in a span of a year.

single loss expectancy (SLE) × annualized rate of occurrence (ARO) = ALE

annualized rate of occurrence (ARO)   The value that represents the estimated possibility of a specific threat taking place within a one-year time frame.

assurance   A measurement of confidence in the level of protection a specific security control delivers and the degree to which it enforces the security policy.

attack   An attempt to bypass security controls in a system with the mission of using that system or compromising it. A passive attack will listen to data, but not capture and modify it. An active attack modifies data. An attack is usually accomplished by exploiting a current vulnerability.

audit trail   A chronological set of logs and records used to provide evidence of a system's performance or activity that took place on the system. These logs and records can be used to attempt to reconstruct past events and track the activities that took place and possibly detect and identify intruders.

authenticate   To verify the identity of a subject requesting the use of a system and/or access to network resource. The steps to giving a subject access to an object should be identifying, authenticating, and authorizing.

authorization   Granting access to a subject to an object after the object has been properly identified and authenticated.

automated information system (AIS)   A computer system that is used to process and transmit data. It is a collection of hardware, software, and firmware that work together to accept, compute, communicate, store, process, transmit, and control data-processing functions.

availability   The reliability and timely access to data and resources by authorized individuals.

B

backdoor   Synonymous with trapdoor.

backup   Copying and moving data to a medium so that it may be restored if the original data is corrupted or destroyed. A full backup copies all the data from the system to the backup medium. An incremental backup copies only the files that have been modified since the previous backup. A differential backup backs up all files since the last full backup. Backup copies should be kept at an off-site facility. Backups also deal with having redundant hardware to replace failing or failed hardware.

baseline   The minimum level of security necessary throughout an organization.

Bell-LaPadula model   The computer security policy model that the Orange Book used to form and derive its security requirements. When a subject requests to access an object in a system based on the Bell-LaPadula model, the subject's clearance level is compared to the object's classification level to make the determination if the access requested is allowed. The model uses a formal state transition model that describes its access controls and how they should perform. When the system must transition from one state to another, the security of the system should never be lowered or compromised. *See* multilevel security, *-property, and simple security rule.

Biba model   A security model that conforms to a security policy that is more concerned with integrity than confidentiality. The Biba model addresses the integrity of data being threatened when subjects at lower security levels are able to write to objects at higher security levels. If implemented and enforced properly, the Biba model prevents data from any integrity level from flowing to a higher integrity level.

biometrics   When used within computer security, biometrics is used to identify individuals by physiological characteristics. This can be a fingerprint, hand geometry, or pattern in the iris.

brute force attack   An attack that continually tries different inputs to achieve at a predefined goal, which can be used to obtain login authentication credentials.

browsing   Searching through storage media looking for specific information without necessarily knowing what format the information is in. A browsing attack is one where the attacker looks around a computer system to see what looks interesting or for specific information.

C

callback A procedure for identifying a system that accessed an environment remotely. In a callback, the host system disconnects the caller and then dials the authorized telephone number of the remote terminal in order to reestablish the connection. This is synonymous with dial back.

capability When a subject has the right to access an object, that subject will have an identifier indicating this right in a system that uses capability-based authorization. A capability indicates the access rights for a specific subject; many times the capability is in the form of a ticket.

category When mandatory access control (MAC) is implemented, security labels are assigned to every subject and every object. The subject's label is made up of a classification (top secret, secret, and so on) and a category listing what information this subject can actually access. The classification defines the subject's security clearance and the category defines the subject's need-to-know. The classification piece is hierarchical, whereas the category piece is not.

certification Certification is the technical evaluation of the security components and their compliance for the purpose of accreditation. A certification process can use safeguard evaluation, risk analysis, verification, testing, and auditing techniques to assess the appropriateness of a specific system processing a certain level of information within a particular environment. The certification is the testing of the security component or system, and the accreditation is the approval from management of the security component or system.

challenge-response method A method used to ensure the identity of a subject, by authenticating a subject by sending the subject an unpredictable or random value. If the subject responds with the expected value in return, the subject is authenticated.

channel A path used to transmit information from one place to another. Many times a channel is referred to as a communication path within a computer system.

CIA triad The three security principles: confidentiality, integrity, and availability.

ciphertext Data that has been encrypted and is usually unreadable until it has been converted into plaintext. The unreadable data is also referred to as cipher, cryptotext, and codetext.

Clark-Wilson model The Clark-Wilson model is an integrity model that addresses all three integrity goals: prevent unauthorized users from making modifications, prevent authorized users from making improper modifications, and maintain internal and external consistency through auditing.

classification When mandatory access control (MAC) is implemented, security labels are assigned to every subject and object. The subject's label is made up of a classification (top secret, secret, and so on) and a category listing what information this subject can actually access. The classification level defines the subject's security clearance and the category defines the subject's need-to-know. The classification piece is hierarchical, whereas the category piece is not.

closed security environment An environment in which both of the following conditions hold true: 1) application developers (including maintainers) have sufficient clearances and authorizations to provide an acceptable presumption that they have not introduced malicious logic, and 2) configuration control provides sufficient assurance that applications and the equipment are protected against the introduction of malicious logic prior to and during the operation of system applications.

clear text See plaintext.

closed shop An environment that uses physical controls to protect a facility or department to prevent unauthorized access or entry.

collusion   More than one person would need to work together to cause some type of destruction or fraud; this drastically reduces its probability.

communications security   Controls in place to protect information as it is being transmitted, especially by telecommunication mechanisms.

COMSEC   A government program that deals with communication security techniques to prevent data from being intercepted and/or modified as it is being transmitted.

compartment   A class of information that has need-to-know access controls beyond those normally provided for access to confidential, secret, or top secret information. A compartment is the same thing as a category within a security label. Just because a subject has the proper classification, it does not mean it has a need-to-know. The category, or compartment, of the security label enforces the subject's need-to-know.

compartmentalization   Isolating the operating system, user programs, and data files from one another within a system to ensure that they do not access each other in an unauthorized and unsecured manner. Breaking down sensitive information into smaller blocks that are isolated to reduce the risk of others figuring out this information and reduce the risk of unauthorized access.

compartmented mode workstation (CMW)   A workstation that contains the necessary controls to be able to operate as a trusted computer. The system is trusted to keep data from different classification levels and categories in separate compartments.

compensating controls   Controls that are used in place of other controls. For instance, if an environment does not require a high level of security and does not have the necessary access and auditing controls, it can depend on the supervision of employees as a compensating control to the access and auditing controls.

compromise   A violation of the security policy of a system such that unauthorized disclosure or modification of sensitive information occurred.

computer fraud   Computer-related crimes involving deliberate misrepresentation, modification, or disclosure of data in order to compromise a system or obtain something of value.

confidentiality   A security principle that works to ensure that information is not disclosed to unauthorized subjects.

configuration management   The identification, control, accounting, and documentation of all changes that take place to system hardware, software, firmware, supporting documentation, and test results throughout the life span of the system.

confinement   Controlling information in a way so that it is prevented from leaking sensitive data from a program to another program, subject, or object in an unauthorized manner.

contamination   Improperly mixing information at different sensitivity and need-to-know levels.

contingency plan   A plan put in place before any potential emergencies with the mission of dealing with possible future emergencies. It pertains to training personnel, performing backups, preparing critical facilities, and recovering from an emergency or disaster so that business operations can continue.

control zone   The space within a facility that is used to protect sensitive processing equipment. Controls are in place to protect from physical or technical unauthorized entry or compromise. The zone can also be used to prevent electrical waves carrying sensitive data from leaving the area.

cost/benefit analysis   An assessment that is performed to ensure that the cost of a safeguard does not outweigh the benefit of the safeguard. It does not make good business sense to spend more protecting an asset than the asset is actually worth. All possible safeguards must be evaluated to ensure that the most security-effective and cost-effective choice is made.

ALE before implementing safeguard) − (ALE after implementing safeguard) − (annual cost of safeguard) = value of safeguard to the company

countermeasure   A control, method, technique, or procedure that is put into place to prevent a threat agent from exploiting a vulnerability. A countermeasure is put into place to mitigate risk. It is also referred to as a safeguard.

covert channel   A communication path that enables a process to transmit information in a way that violates the system's security policy.

covert storage channel   A covert channel that involves direct or indirect writing to a storage location by one process and the direct or indirect reading of the storage location by another process. Covert storage channels typically involve a finite resource (for example, sectors on a disk) that is shared by two subjects at different security levels.

covert timing channel   A covert channel in which one process signals information to another by modulating its own use of system resources (for example, CPU time) in such a way that this manipulation affects the real response time observed by the second process.

cryptoalgorithm   A mathematical set of rules that are used to produce a key stream that is combined with plaintext to result in ciphertext or vice versa.

cryptanalysis   The practice of breaking cryptosystems and algorithms used in encryption and decryption processes.

cryptography   The science of secret writing that enables you to store and transmit data in a form that is available only to the intended individuals.

cryptology   The study of cryptography and cryptanalysis.

cryptosystem   The hardware or software implementation of cryptography.

D

data classification   Assignments to data that indicate the level of confidentiality, integrity, and availability that is required for each type of information.

data custodian   An individual with the responsibility of the maintenance and protection of the data. This role is usually filled by the IT department (usually the network administrator). The duties include performing regular backups of the data, implementing security mechanisms, periodically validating the integrity of the data, restoring data from backup media, and fulfilling the requirements specified in the company's security policy, standards, and guidelines that pertain to information security and data protection.

Data Encryption Standard (DES)   A private key, or symmetric key, encryption algorithm that was adopted by the government as a federal standard for protecting sensitive unclassified information.

data flow control   Synonymous with information flow control.

database shadowing   A redundancy mechanism that uses remote journaling and duplicates database sets to multiple servers.

declassification   An administrative decision or procedure to remove or reduce the security classification information.

dedicated security mode   A system that operates in this mode if all users have the clearance or authorization and need-to-know to all data processed within the system. All users have been given formal access approval for all information on the system and have signed nondisclosure agreements pertaining to this information.

degauss This demagnetizes magnetic media so that a very low residue of magnetic induction is left on the media. It is a process used to effectively erase data from media.

Delphi technique A group decision method and is used to ensure that each member of a group gives an honest opinion of what he or she thinks the result to a particular risk will be.

denial of service (DoS) Any action, or series of actions, that prevents any part of a system, or its resources, from functioning in accordance with its intended purpose.

dial back Synonymous with callback.

dial-up The service whereby a computer terminal can use telephone lines, usually via a modem, to initiate and continue communication with another computer system.

dictionary attack Types of programs that are fed lists (dictionaries) of commonly used words or combinations of characters and apply these values to a logon prompt with the mission of discovering a user's credentials to obtain unauthorized access to a system.

digital signature A tool used to provide the authentication of the sender of a message. It can verify the origin of the message along with the identity of the sender. It is unique for every transaction and created with a private key.

disaster recovery plan A plan developed to help a company recover from a disaster. It is a procedure for emergency response, extended backup operations, and postdisaster recovery when an organization suffers a loss of computer processing capability or resources and physical facilities.

discretionary access control (DAC) An access control model and policy that restricts access to objects based on the identity of the subjects and the groups to which those subjects belong. The data owner has the discretion of allowing or denying other access to the resources it owns.

domain The set of objects that a subject is allowed to access. Within this domain, all subjects and objects share a common security policy, procedures, and rules and they are managed by the same management system.

dominate Within the mandatory access control (MAC) model, a subject is said to dominate another subject if the first subject's classification is greater than the second's. The first subject must also include at least all the categories of the second subject's categories.

due care Due care are steps that are taken to show that a company has taken responsibility for the activities that take place within the corporation and has taken the necessary steps to help protect the company, its resources, and employees.

due diligence Continual activities that make sure the protection mechanisms are continually maintained and operational.

E

electronic vaulting Electronic vaulting refers to the transfer of backup data to an off-site location. This process is primarily a batch process of transmitting data through communications lines to a server at an alternate location.

emanations Electrical and electromagnetic signals emitted from electrical equipment that can transmit through the airwaves. These signals carry information that can be captured and deciphered, which can cause a security breach. These are also called emissions.

embedded system A system that performs or controls a function, either in whole or in part, as an integral element of a larger system or subsystem.

encryption   The transformation of plaintext into unreadable ciphertext.

end-to-end encryption   A technology that encrypts data at its origin, is transmitted encrypted, and then is decrypted at its destination, versus being decrypted at each and every hop during its travels. Contrast this with link encryption.

enticement   Enticement is luring an intruder to a system that seems to be vulnerable. Enticement is legal.

entrapment   The deliberate planting of apparent flaws to induce a crime and trick a person into trespassing or performing acts that are deemed illegal. Entrapment is illegal. It is different than enticement.

Evaluated Products List (EPL)   A list of equipment, hardware, software, and/or firmware that have been evaluated and found to meet the necessary requirements of a specific trust level of the Trusted Computer System Evaluation Criteria (TCSEC) by the National Computer Security Center (NCSC).

executive state   One of several states in which a system can operate, and the only one in which certain privileged instructions can be executed. Such instructions cannot be executed when the system is operating in other (for example, user) states. This is synonymous with supervisor state.

exposure   An instance of being exposed to losses from a threat. A weakness or vulnerability can cause an organization to be exposed to possible damages.

exposure factor   The percentage of loss a realized threat could have on a certain asset.

F

failover   A backup operation that automatically switches to a standby system if the primary system fails or is taken offline. It is an important fault tolerant function that provides system availability.

fail safe   A functionality that ensures that when software or a system fails for any reason, it does not end up in a vulnerable state. After a failure, software might default to no access instead of allowing full control, which would be an example of a fail-safe measure.

firmware   Software instructions that have been written into read-only memory (ROM) or programmable ROM.

formal security policy model   A mathematically precise statement of a security policy. When an operating system is built, it is built upon a predeveloped model that lays out how all activities will take place in each and every situation. This model is expressed mathematically, which is then translated into a programming language. For the model to be secure, it must ensure that the system will not enter an insecure state under any circumstances. This and other requirements are necessary for it to be a secure system and to be acceptable as a basis for trusted computing base (TCB).

formal verification   Using automated tools to aid in the designing and testing of highly trusted systems. The tests are designed to show design verification, consistency between the formal specifications and the formal security policy model, implementation verification, consistency between the formal specifications, and the actual implementation of it.

functional testing   Security testing in which the advertised security mechanisms of the system are tested for their functionality.

G

gateway   A system or device that connects two unlike environments or systems. The gateway is usually required to translate between different types of applications or protocols. The gateway can also filter out unwanted packets.

guidelines   Recommendation actions and operational guides to users, IT staff, operations staff, and others when a specific standard does not apply.

H

handshaking procedure   A dialogue between two entities for the purpose of identifying and authenticating the entities to one another. The dialogue can take place between a user and a computer, a computer and a server, or between two computers. It is an activity that usually takes place within a protocol.

honeypot   A computer set up as a sacrificial lamb on the network in the hopes that attackers will attack this system instead of actual production systems.

I

identification   The process that enables one subject to recognize another subject or object. Identification is the first step in the authentication process.

incomplete parameter checking   A system design flaw that results when software does not properly check how data is inputted. The result of this flaw can result in incorrect data-processing results or buffer overflows.

information flow control   A procedure to ensure that information transfers within a system are not made from a higher security level object to an object of a lower security level. *See* covert channel, simple security property, and star property (*-property).

information owner   This person is usually a senior executive within the management group of the company. The information owner has final corporate responsibility of data protection and would be the one held liable for any negligence when it comes to protecting the company's information assets. The person who holds this role is responsible for assigning a classification to the information and dictating how the information should be protected.

Information System Security Officer (ISSO)   The person who is responsible for ensuring that security is provided for and implemented throughout the life cycle of a computer system and network from the beginning of the concept development plan through its design, development, operation, maintenance, and secure disposal.

integrity   A security principle that makes sure that information and systems are not modified maliciously or accidentally.

intrusion detection system (IDS)   Software employed to monitor and detect possible attacks and behaviors that vary from the normal and expected activity. The IDS can be network-based, which monitors network traffic, or host-based, which monitors activities of a specific system and protects system files and control mechanisms.

isolation   The containment of subjects and objects in a system in such a way that they are separated from one another as well as from the protection controls of the operating system.

K

kernel   See security kernel.

key   When used in the context of cryptography, it is a secret value, a sequence of characters, that is used to encrypt and decrypt messages.

keystroke monitoring   A type of auditing that can review or record keystrokes entered by a user during an active session.

L

lattice-based access control   An access control that provides an upper bound and lower bound of access capabilities when sensitivity labels are used.

least privilege   The security principle that requires each subject to be granted the most restrictive set of privileges needed for the performance of authorized tasks. The application of this principle limits the damage that can result from accident, error, or unauthorized use.

life cycle assurance   Confidence that a trusted system is designed, developed, and maintained with formal designs and controls. This includes design specification and verification, implementation, testing, configuration management, and distribution.

link encryption   A type of encryption where the data is encrypted at its origin and decrypted and reencrypted at each hop during its travel to its destination. Each network communication node, or hop, must decrypt it to read its address and routing information. This is different than end-to-end encryption.

logic bomb   A malicious program that is triggered by a specific event or condition.

loss potential   The potential losses that can be accrued if a threat agent actually exploits a vulnerability.

M

magnetic remanence   A measure of the magnetic flux density remaining after removal of the applied magnetic force, which is used to erase data. Refers to any data remaining on magnetic storage media.

maintenance hook   Instructions within a program's code that enable the developer or maintainer to enter the program without having to go through the usual access control and authentication processes. They should be removed from the code before being released for production; otherwise, they can cause serious security risks. They are also referred to as trapdoors.

malware   Malicious software. Code written to perform activities that circumvent the security policy of a system. Examples are viruses, malicious applets, Trojan horses, and worms.

mandatory access control (MAC)   An access policy that restricts subjects' access to objects based on the security level of the subject and the classification of the object. The system enforces the security policy and users cannot share their files with other users.

masquerading   Impersonating another user usually with the intentions of gaining unauthorized access to a system.

message authentication   Making sure that the message sent contains the same information as when it was sent. It ensures that a message was not altered during transmission.

message authentication code (MAC)   A value that is calculated during an encryption process and appended to a message. The receiving system receives the message and performs the same calculations and compares its results to the results appended to the message. If the values are the same, the receiver can be sure that the message was not altered during transmission.

multilevel device   A device that is used in a manner that permits it to simultaneously process data of two or more security levels without the risk of compromise. To accomplish this, sensitivity labels are normally stored on the same physical medium and in the same form (for example, machine-readable or human-readable) as the data being processed.

multilevel secure   A class of systems containing information with different sensitivities that simultaneously permits access by users with different security clearances and needs-to-know, but that prevents users from obtaining access to information for which they lack authorization.

multiuser mode of operation   A mode of operation designed for systems that process sensitive, unclassified information in which users might not have a need-to-know for all information processed in the system. This mode is also for microcomputers that are processing sensitive, unclassified information that cannot meet the requirements of the stand-alone mode of operation.

N

need-to-know   A security principle stating that users should only have access to the information and resources necessary to complete their tasks that fulfill their roles within an organization.

node   A system that is connected to a network.

O

object   A passive entity that contains or receives information. Access to an object potentially implies access to the information that it contains. Examples of objects include the following: records, blocks, pages, segments, files, directories, directory trees, and programs, as well as bits, bytes, words, fields, processors, video displays, keyboards, clocks, printers, and network nodes.

object reuse   The reassignment to a subject of a medium that previously contained information. It can be a security concern because the measures that were taken to erase the information may not have done a thorough job and the information may still be retainable; therefore, information could be disclosed to unauthorized personnel.

one-time pad   A one-time pad is a perfect encryption scheme, because it is unbreakable and each pad is used exactly once. A one-time pad uses a nonrepeating set of random bits that are combined bitwise XOR with the message to produce ciphertext.

open security environment   An environment that includes those systems in which at least one of the following conditions holds true: 1) application developers (including maintainers) do not have sufficient clearance or authorization to provide an acceptable presumption that they have not introduced malicious logic, and 2) configuration control does not provide sufficient assurance that applications are protected against the introduction of malicious logic prior to and during the operation of system applications.

operational goals   Daily goals to be accomplished to ensure the proper operation of an environment.

operator An individual who supports the operations of computer systems. The individual may monitor the execution of the system, control the flow of jobs, and develop and schedule batch jobs.

operational assurance A level of confidence of a trusted system's architecture and implementation that enforces the system's security policy. This can include system architecture, covert channel analysis, system integrity, and trusted recovery.

Orange Book The common name for the Trusted Computer Security Evaluation Criteria (TCSEC).

overt channel A path within a computer system or network that is designed for the authorized transfer of data.

P

password A sequence of characters used to prove one's identity. It is used during a login process and should be highly protected.

penetration A successful attempt at circumventing security controls and gaining access to a system.

penetration testing Testing that attempts to circumvent security controls within an environment so that vulnerabilities and weaknesses can be uncovered.

partitioned security mode A mode of operation wherein all personnel have the clearance, but not necessarily the formal access approval and need-to-know for all information contained in the system. This should not be confused with compartmented security mode.

permissions Description of the type of authorized interactions that a subject can have with an object. Examples include read, write, execute, add, modify, and delete.

personnel security The procedures that are established to ensure that all personnel who have access to sensitive information have the required authority as well as appropriate clearances. Procedures to ensure a person's background—it provides assurance of necessary trustworthiness.

physical controls These controls pertain to controlling individual access into the facility and different departments, locking systems and removing unnecessary floppy or CD-ROM drives, protecting the perimeter of the facility, monitoring for intrusion, and checking environmental controls.

physical security Controls and procedures put into place to prevent intruders from physically accessing a system or facility. The controls enforce access control and authorized access.

piggyback Pertaining unauthorized access to a system via another user's legitimate connection.

plaintext Pertaining to cryptography, it is the original text before it is encrypted.

playback Capturing and recording a message and resending the message at a later time in the hopes of tricking the receiving system.

privacy A security principle that protects an individual's information and employs controls to ensure that this information is not disseminated or accessed in an unauthorized method.

privileged instructions Instructions that are executed by the process of a higher security level within a system. The instructions are usually sent to control mechanisms within the system and can only be executed when the system is operating in an executive state.

procedure Detailed step-by-step actions to achieve a certain task, which are used by users, IT staff, operations staff, security members, and others who may need to install or configure a computer component.

protection ring   Supports the integrity and confidentiality requirements of multitasking operating systems and enables the operating system to protect itself from user programs and rogue processes.

protocols   A set of rules and formats that enable the proper exchange of information between different systems.

pseudo-flaw   An apparent loophole deliberately implanted in an operating system program as a trap for intruders.

public key encryption   A type of encryption that uses two mathematically-related keys to encrypt and decrypt messages. The private key is only known to the owner and the public key is available to anyone.

purge   The removal of sensitive data from a system, storage device, or peripheral device with storage capacity at the end of a processing period. This action is performed in such a way that there is assurance proportional to the sensitivity of the data that the data cannot be reconstructed.

Q

qualitative risk analysis   An analysis that judges an organization's risks to threats, which is based on judgment, intuition, and the experience versus assigning real numbers to this possible risks and their potential loss margins.

quantitative risk analysis   A process that attempts to assign real numbers to the costs of countermeasures and the amount of damage that can take place.

R

RADIUS   Remote Authentication Dial-in User Service (RADIUS) is a security service that authenticates and authorizes dial-up users and is a centralized access control mechanism.

read   An operation that results in the flow of information from an object to a subject and does not give the subject the ability to modify the object or the data within the object.

recovery planning   The advance planning and preparations that are necessary to minimize loss and to ensure the availability of the critical information systems of an organization after a disruption in service or a disaster.

reference monitor concept   An access-control concept that refers to an abstract machine that mediates all accesses to objects by subjects.

reference-validation mechanism   An implementation of the reference monitor concept. A security kernel is a type of reference-validation mechanism.

reliability   The assurance of a given system performing its mission adequately for a specified period of time under the expected operating conditions.

remote journaling   A method of transmitting data off-site. This takes place as parallel processing of transactions and takes place in real time to provide redundancy and fault tolerance.

repudiation   When a sender of a message denies sending the message in the first place or when a receiver denies that the received message was actually received.

residual risk   The remaining risk after the security controls have been applied.

threats $\times$ vulnerability $\times$ asset value = total risk

(threats $\times$ vulnerability $\times$ asset value) $\times$ controls gap = residual risk

risk   The likelihood of a threat agent taking advantage of a vulnerability. A risk is the loss potential, or probability, that a threat will exploit a vulnerability.

risk analysis   A method of identifying risks and assessing the possible damage that could be caused in order to justify security safeguards.

risk management   The process of identifying, assessing, and reducing the risk to an acceptable level and implementing the right mechanisms to maintain that level of risk.

role-based access control (RBAC)   This type of model provides access to resources based on the role the user holds within the company or the tasks that user has been assigned.

S

safeguards   These mitigate the potential risk. A countermeasure is a software configuration, hardware, or procedure that eliminates a vulnerability or reduces the risk of a threat agent from being able to exploit a vulnerability.

secure configuration management   The set of procedures that are appropriate for the process of controlling the life cycle of an application and documenting the necessary change control activities and ensuring that the changes will not violate the security policy.

secure state   A condition in which no subject can access any object in an unauthorized manner.

security evaluation   An evaluation that is done in order to assess the degree of trust that can be placed in systems for the secure handling of sensitive information.

security kernel   The hardware, firmware, and software elements of a trusted computing base (TCB) that implement the reference monitor concept. It must mediate all accesses between subjects and objects, be protected from modification, and be verifiable as correct.

security label   An identifier that represents the security level of an object.

security level   The combination of the classification and the categories listed within a sensitivity label.

security perimeter   An imaginary boundary between the trusted computing base (TCB) and other system mechanisms and functions. It is the distinction between trusted and untrusted processes.

security policy   The set of laws, rules, and practices that regulates how an organization manages, protects, and distributes sensitive information.

security requirements baseline   A description of minimum requirements necessary for a system to maintain an acceptable level of security.

security testing   A process that is used to test all security mechanisms and features within a system to determine the level of protection they provide. Security testing can include penetration testing, formal design and implementation verification, or functional testing.

sensitive information   Information that would cause a negative effect on the data owner if it were lost or compromised.

sensitivity label   A piece of information that represents the security level of an object. Sensitivity labels are used by the TCB as the basis for mandatory access control (MAC) decisions.

separation of duties   A security principle that splits up a task between more than one individual to ensure that one individual cannot complete a risky task by himself.

shoulder surfing   When a person looks over another person's shoulder and watches keystrokes or data as they appear on the screen in order to uncover information in an unauthorized manner.

simple security property   A Bell-LaPadula security model rule that enables a subject to read data within an object if the subject's security level dominates the security level of the object.

single-level security   Pertains to a system that gives access only to users of the same sensitivity level. A single-level device only processes data of a single security level at a time rather than a multilevel device, which can process data at different security levels at one time.

single loss expectancy (SLE)   A dollar amount that is assigned to a single event that represents the company's potential loss amount if a specific threat took place.

asset value $\times$ exposure factor $=$ SLE

social engineering   The act of tricking another person into telling confidential information by posing as an authorized individual to that information.

spoofing   Presenting false information, usually within packets, to trick other systems and hiding the origin of the message. This is usually done by hackers and attackers so that they cannot be successfully uncovered.

standards   Rules indicating how hardware and software should be implemented, used, and maintained. They provide a means to ensure that specific technologies, applications, parameters, and procedures are carried out in a uniform way across the organization. They are compulsory.

star property   A Bell-LaPadula security model rule that provides a subject write access to an object if the security level of the subject dominates the security level of the object.

strategic goals   Long-term goals that look far into the future. Operational and tactical goals support strategic goals.

subject   An active entity, generally in the form of a person, process, or device, that causes information to flow among objects or that changes the system state.

supervisor state   Synonymous with executive state.

system low   The lowest security level supported by a system at a particular time or in a particular environment.

system high   The highest security level supported by a system at a particular time or in a particular environment.

T

TACACS   Terminal Access Controller Access Control System (TACACS) is a client-server protocol that provides the same type of functionality as RADIUS and is used as a central access control mechanism mainly for remote users.

technical controls   These controls include logical access control mechanisms, password and resource management, identification and authentication methods, security devices, and the configuration of the network.

tactical goals   Midterm goals to accomplish. These may be milestones to accomplish within a project or specific projects to accomplish in the time span of a year.

TEMPEST   The study and control of spurious electronic signals emitted by electrical equipment. TEMPEST equipment is implemented to prevent intruders from picking up information through the airwaves with listening devices.

threat   Any potential danger to information or systems.

top-down approach   A project that has the initiation, support, and direction come from top management and work its way through middle management and then to staff members.

topology   The physical construction of how nodes are connected to form a network.

total risk   When a safeguard is not implemented, an organization is faced with the total risk of that particular vulnerability.

trapdoor   A hidden entry point into a system or application that is usually triggered by a certain command or keyboard sequence. Software developers and maintainers usually insert them into programming code for easy entry at a later time. This is synonymous with backdoor.

Trojan horse   A computer program that has an apparently or actually useful function that contains additional hidden, malicious capability that can exploit a vulnerability and/or provide unauthorized access into a system. A user usually accidentally initializes the Trojan horse.

trusted computer system   A system that has the necessary controls to ensure that the security policy will not be compromised and that can process a range of sensitive or classified information simultaneously.

trusted computing base (TCB)   All of the protection mechanisms within a computer system (software, hardware, and firmware) that are responsible for enforcing a security policy is referred to as the TCB. The TCB is dependent upon its mechanisms and the correct input of the system administrative personnel to properly enforce the security policy.

trusted path   A mechanism within the system that enables the user to communicate directly with the TCB. This mechanism can only be activated by the user or the TCB and not by an untrusted mechanism or process.

trusted recovery   A set of procedures that restores a system and its data in a trusted manner after the system was disrupted or a system failure occurred.

U

user   A person or process that is accessing a computer system.

user ID   A unique set of characters or code that is used to identify a specific user to a system.

V

validation   The act of performing tests and evaluations to test a system's security level to see if it complies with security specifications and requirements.

virus   A small application, or string of code, that infects applications. The main function of a virus is to reproduce, and it requires a host application to be able to do this. It can damage data directly or degrade system performance.

vulnerability   A vulnerability characterizes the absence or weakness of a safeguard that could be exploited.

wardialing   A long list of phone numbers are inserted into a wardialing program in the hopes of finding a modem that can be exploited to gain unauthorized access.

work factor   The estimated time and effort required for an attacker to overcome a security control.

worm   An independent program that can reproduce by copying itself from one system to another. It may damage data directly or degrade system performance by tying up resources.

write   An operation that results in the flow of information from a subject to an object.

INDEX

Symbols

*-property rule, 242
2600: The Hackers Quarterly, 651
3DES, 526, 529
414 Club, 651
802.11a standard, 482
802.11b standard, 482

A

abstraction, 238, 760
access controls, 121–122, 180
  accountability, 182, 185
  administrative controls,
    162–168, 171
    auditing, 179
    cable eavesdropping, 176
    computer controls, 175
    control zone, 179
    data backups, 175
    encryption, 178
    network access, 178
    network architecture, 177
    network segmentation, 174

    perimeter security, 175
    personnel controls, 172
    physical controls, 173
    security awareness training, 173
    security policies, 171
    supervisory structures, 172
    technical controls, 176
    work area separation, 175
  best practices, 189–190
  brute force attacks, 199
  dictionary attacks, 198
  layers, 170
  matrices, 160
  methods, 169
  models, 152–159
  monitoring, 193
  personnel, 322
  preventive—administrative,
    180–182
  spoofing, 200
  wardialing, 199
access criteria for security
  ACLs, 143
  groups, 142

941

M

INTERNATIONAL CONTACT INFORMATION

AUSTRALIA
McGraw-Hill Book Company Australia Pty. Ltd.
TEL +61-2-9417-9899
FAX +61-2-9417-5687
http://www.mcgraw-hill.com.au
books-it_sydney@mcgraw-hill.com

CANADA
McGraw-Hill Ryerson Ltd.
TEL +905-430-5000
FAX +905-430-5020
http://www.mcgrawhill.ca

GREECE, MIDDLE EAST,
NORTHERN AFRICA
McGraw-Hill Hellas
TEL +30-1-656-0990-3-4
FAX +30-1-654-5525

MEXICO (Also serving Latin America)
McGraw-Hill Interamericana Editores S.A. de C.V.
TEL +525-117-1583
FAX +525-117-1589
http://www.mcgraw-hill.com.mx
fernando_castellanos@mcgraw-hill.com

SINGAPORE (Serving Asia)
McGraw-Hill Book Company
TEL +65-863-1580
FAX +65-862-3354
http://www.mcgraw-hill.com.sg
mghasia@mcgraw-hill.com

SOUTH AFRICA
McGraw-Hill South Africa
TEL +27-11-622-7512
FAX +27-11-622-9045
robyn_swanepoel@mcgraw-hill.com

UNITED KINGDOM & EUROPE
(Excluding Southern Europe)
McGraw-Hill Education Europe
TEL +44-1-628-502500
FAX +44-1-628-770224
http://www.mcgraw-hill.co.uk
computing_neurope@mcgraw-hill.com

ALL OTHER INQUIRIES Contact:
Osborne/McGraw-Hill
TEL +1-510-549-6600
FAX +1-510-883-7600
http://www.osborne.com
omg_international@mcgraw-hill.com

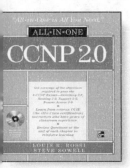

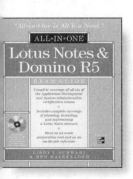
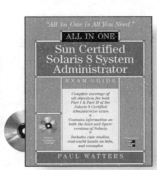

ABOUT THE CD

The CD included with this book has 255 questions from all 10 domains of the CISSP Body of Knowledge. Each domain has 15 to 30 questions that are very similar to what you will see on the actual CISSP exam. You can take as many practice exams as you would like and then set up the testing tool to allow you to take a final exam. The questions at the end of each chapter and the questions on this CD will prepare you for the intensive CISSP exam.

LICENSE AGREEMENT

THIS PRODUCT (THE "PRODUCT") CONTAINS PROPRIETARY SOFTWARE, DATA AND INFORMATION (INCLUDING DOCUMENTATION) OWNED BY THE McGRAW-HILL COMPANIES, INC. ("McGRAW-HILL") AND ITS LICENSORS. YOUR RIGHT TO USE THE PRODUCT IS GOVERNED BY THE TERMS AND CONDITIONS OF THIS AGREEMENT.

LICENSE: Throughout this License Agreement, "you" shall mean either the individual or the entity whose agent opens this package. You are granted a non-exclusive and non-transferable license to use the Product subject to the following terms:
(i) If you have licensed a single user version of the Product, the Product may only be used on a single computer (i.e., a single CPU). If you licensed and paid the fee applicable to a local area network or wide area network version of the Product, you are subject to the terms of the following subparagraph (ii).
(ii) If you have licensed a local area network version, you may use the Product on unlimited workstations located in one single building selected by you that is served by such local area network. If you have licensed a wide area network version, you may use the Product on unlimited workstations located in multiple buildings on the same site selected by you that is served by such wide area network; provided, however, that any building will not be considered located in the same site if it is more than five (5) miles away from any building included in such site. In addition, you may only use a local area or wide area network version of the Product on one single server. If you wish to use the Product on more than one server, you must obtain written authorization from McGraw-Hill and pay additional fees.
(iii) You may make one copy of the Product for back-up purposes only and you must maintain an accurate record as to the location of the back-up at all times.

COPYRIGHT; RESTRICTIONS ON USE AND TRANSFER: All rights (including copyright) in and to the Product are owned by McGraw-Hill and its licensors. You are the owner of the enclosed disc on which the Product is recorded. You may not use, copy, decompile, disassemble, reverse engineer, modify, reproduce, create derivative works, transmit, distribute, sublicense, store in a database or retrieval system of any kind, rent or transfer the Product, or any portion thereof, in any form or by any means (including electronically or otherwise) except as expressly provided for in this License Agreement. You must reproduce the copyright notices, trademark notices, legends and logos of McGraw-Hill and its licensors that appear on the Product on the back-up copy of the Product which you are permitted to make hereunder. All rights in the Product not expressly granted herein are reserved by McGraw-Hill and its licensors.

TERM: This License Agreement is effective until terminated. It will terminate if you fail to comply with any term or condition of this License Agreement. Upon termination, you are obligated to return to McGraw-Hill the Product together with all copies thereof and to purge all copies of the Product included in any and all servers and computer facilities.

DISCLAIMER OF WARRANTY: THE PRODUCT AND THE BACK-UP COPY ARE LICENSED "AS IS." McGRAW-HILL, ITS LICENSORS AND THE AUTHORS MAKE NO WARRANTIES, EXPRESS OR IMPLIED, AS TO THE RESULTS TO BE OBTAINED BY ANY PERSON OR ENTITY FROM USE OF THE PRODUCT, ANY INFORMATION OR DATA INCLUDED THEREIN AND/OR ANY TECHNICAL SUPPORT SERVICES PROVIDED HEREUNDER, IF ANY ("TECHNICAL SUPPORT SERVICES"). McGRAW-HILL, ITS LICENSORS AND THE AUTHORS MAKE NO EXPRESS OR IMPLIED WARRANTIES OF MERCHANTABILITY OR FITNESS FOR A PARTICULAR PURPOSE OR USE WITH RESPECT TO THE PRODUCT. McGRAW-HILL, ITS LICENSORS, AND THE AUTHORS MAKE NO GUARANTEE THAT YOU WILL PASS ANY CERTIFICATION EXAM WHATSOEVER BY USING THIS PRODUCT. NEITHER McGRAW-HILL, ANY OF ITS LICENSORS NOR THE AUTHORS WARRANT THAT THE FUNCTIONS CONTAINED IN THE PRODUCT WILL MEET YOUR REQUIREMENTS OR THAT THE OPERATION OF THE PRODUCT WILL BE UNINTERRUPTED OR ERROR FREE. YOU ASSUME THE ENTIRE RISK WITH RESPECT TO THE QUALITY AND PERFORMANCE OF THE PRODUCT.

LIMITED WARRANTY FOR DISC: To the original licensee only, McGraw-Hill warrants that the enclosed disc on which the Product is recorded is free from defects in materials and workmanship under normal use and service for a period of ninety (90) days from the date of purchase. In the event of a defect in the disc covered by the foregoing warranty, McGraw-Hill will replace the disc.

LIMITATION OF LIABILITY: NEITHER McGRAW-HILL, ITS LICENSORS NOR THE AUTHORS SHALL BE LIABLE FOR ANY INDIRECT, SPECIAL OR CONSEQUENTIAL DAMAGES, SUCH AS BUT NOT LIMITED TO, LOSS OF ANTICIPATED PROFITS OR BENEFITS, RESULTING FROM THE USE OR INABILITY TO USE THE PRODUCT EVEN IF ANY OF THEM HAS BEEN ADVISED OF THE POSSIBILITY OF SUCH DAMAGES. THIS LIMITATION OF LIABILITY SHALL APPLY TO ANY CLAIM OR CAUSE WHATSOEVER WHETHER SUCH CLAIM OR CAUSE ARISES IN CONTRACT, TORT, OR OTHERWISE. Some states do not allow the exclusion or limitation of indirect, special or consequential damages, so the above limitation may not apply to you.

U.S. GOVERNMENT RESTRICTED RIGHTS: Any software included in the Product is provided with restricted rights subject to subparagraphs (c), (1) and (2) of the Commercial Computer Software-Restricted Rights clause at 48 C.F.R. 52.227-19. The terms of this Agreement applicable to the use of the data in the Product are those under which the data are generally made available to the general public by McGraw-Hill. Except as provided herein, no reproduction, use, or disclosure rights are granted with respect to the data included in the Product and no right to modify or create derivative works from any such data is hereby granted.

GENERAL: This License Agreement constitutes the entire agreement between the parties relating to the Product. The terms of any Purchase Order shall have no effect on the terms of this License Agreement. Failure of McGraw-Hill to insist at any time on strict compliance with this License Agreement shall not constitute a waiver of any rights under this License Agreement. This License Agreement shall be construed and governed in accordance with the laws of the State of New York. If any provision of this License Agreement is held to be contrary to law, that provision will be enforced to the maximum extent permissible and the remaining provisions will remain in full force and effect.